ISBN 978-1-330-06800-7
PIBN 10017617

1 MONTH OF
FREE
READING

at

www.ForgottenBooks.com

By purchasing this book you are eligible for one month membership to ForgottenBooks.com, giving you unlimited access to our entire collection of over 700,000 titles via our web site and mobile apps.

To claim your free month visit: www.forgottenbooks.com/free17617

English
Français
Deutsche
Italiano
Español
Português

www.forgottenbooks.com

Mythology Photography **Fiction**
Fishing Christianity **Art** Cooking
Essays Buddhism Freemasonry
Medicine **Biology** Music **Ancient**
Egypt Evolution Carpentry Physics
Dance Geology **Mathematics** Fitness
Shakespeare **Folklore** Yoga Marketing
Confidence Immortality Biographies
Poetry **Psychology** Witchcraft
Electronics Chemistry History **Law**
Accounting **Philosophy** Anthropology
Alchemy Drama Quantum Mechanics
Atheism Sexual Health **Ancient History**
Entrepreneurship Languages Sport
Paleontology Needlework Islam
Metaphysics Investment Archaeology
Parenting Statistics Criminology
Motivational

THE

HISTORY OF ENGLAND,

FROM

THE REVOLUTION

TO THE

DEATH OF GEORGE THE SECOND.

DESIGNED AS

A CONTINUATION OF MR. HUME'S HISTORY.

BY

T. SMOLLETT, M.D.

A NEW EDITION,

WITH THE AUTHOR'S LAST CORRECTIONS AND IMPROVEMENTS.

IN FOUR VOLUMES.
VOL. II.

LONDON:

LONGMAN, BROWN, GREEN, AND LONGMANS; J. M. RICHARDSON; HATCHARD AND SON; S. BAGSTER AND SON; F. AND J. RIVINGTON; HAMILTON AND CO.; SIMPKIN, MARSHALL, AND CO.; W. H. ALLEN AND CO.; WHITTAKER AND CO ; E HODGSON; BIGG AND SON; T. BUMPUS; J. DOWDING; J. BAIN, SMITH, ELDER, AND CO ; J. CAPES AND SON; R. MACKIE, H. WASHBOURNE; J. HEARNE, W PICKERING; H. G. BOHN; W. MORRISON; T. AND W. BOONE; BICKERS AND BUSH; SOTHERAN AND CO, J. SNOW; L. BOOTH; W. WHITE; G. WILLIS; WALLER AND SON; M. COOMES; TEGG AND CO.: AND G. AND J. ROBINSON, LIVERPOOL: J. AND J. J. DEIGHTON; AND MACMILLAN AND CO., CAMBRIDGE: AND J. PARKER, OXFORD.

1848.

CONTENTS

OF

VOL II.

CHAPTER X.

ANNE.

CHAPTER XI.

CHAPTER XII.

GEORGE I.

CHAPTER XIII.

CHAPTER XIV.

CHAPTER XV.

GEORGE II.

CHAPTER XVI.

CHAPTER XVII.

CHAPTER XVIII.

CHAPTER XIX.

CHAPTER XX.

THE

HISTORY

OF

ENGLAND.

CHAPTER X.

THE French king was by this time reduced to such a
state of humiliation by the losses of the last campaign,

CHAP.
X.
1709.

CHAP.
X.

1709.
Negotia-
tion for
peace in-
effectual.

and a severe winter, which completed the misery of his subjects, that he resolved to sacrifice all the considerations of pride and ambition, as well as the interest of his grandson, to his desire of peace, which was now become so necessary and indispensable. He despatched the President Rouillé privately to Holland, with general proposals of peace, and the offer of a good barrier to the States-General, still entertaining hopes of being able to detach them from the confederacy. This minister conferred in secret with Buys and Vanderdussen, the Pensionaries of Amsterdam and Gouda, at Moerdyke, from whence he was permitted to proceed to Woerden, between Leyden and Utrecht. The states immediately communicated his proposals to the courts of Vienna and Great Britain. Prince Eugene and the Duke of Marlborough arrived at the Hague in April, and conferred with the Grand Pensionary Heinsius, Buys, and Vanderdussen, on the subject of the French proposals, which were deemed unsatisfactory. Rouillé immediately despatched a courier to Paris for farther instructions; and the Duke of Marlborough returned to England, to make the queen acquainted with the progress of the negotiation. Louis, in order to convince the states of his sincerity, sent the Marquis de Torcy, his secretary for foreign affairs, to the Hague, with fresh offers, to which the deputies would make no answer until they knew the sentiments of the Queen of Great Britain. The Duke of Marlborough crossed the seas a second time, accompanied by the Lord Viscount Townshend, as ambassador-extraordinary, and joint-plenipotentiary: Prince Eugene being likewise at the Hague, the conferences were begun. The French minister declared, that his master would consent to the demolition of Dunkirk: that he would abandon the pretender, and dismiss him from his dominions: that he would acknowledge the queen's title and the Protestant succession: that he would renounce all pretensions to the Spanish monarchy, and cede the places in the Netherlands which the States-General demanded for their barrier: that he would treat with the emperor on the footing of the treaty concluded at Ryswick, and even demolish the fortifications of Strasburg. The ministers of the allies, rendered proud and wanton by success, and seeing their own private interest

in the continuation of the war, insisted upon the restitution of the Upper and Lower Alsace to the empire ; upon
the French monarch's restoring Strasburg in its present
condition ; upon his ceding the town and castellany of
Lisle, demolishing Dunkirk, New Brisac, Fort Louis, and
Hunningen.   In a word, their demands were so insolent,
that Louis would not have suffered them to be mentioned in his hearing, had not he been reduced to the
last degree of distress.   One can hardly read them without feeling a sentiment of compassion for that monarch,
who had once given law to Europe, and been so long
accustomed to victory and conquest.   Notwithstanding
the discouraging despatches he had received from the
President Rouillé, after his first conferences with the
deputies, he could not believe that the Dutch would be
so blind to their own interest as to reject the advantages
in commerce, and the barrier which he had offered.   He
could not conceive that they would choose to bear the
burden of excessive taxes in prosecuting a war, the events
of which would always be uncertain, rather than enjoy
the blessings of peace, security, and advantageous commerce : he flattered himself that the allies would not so
far deviate from their purposed aim of establishing a
balance of power, as to throw such an enormous weight
into the scale of the house of Austria, which cherished
all the dangerous ambition and arbitrary principles, without the liberality of sentiment peculiar to the house of
Bourbon.   In proportion as they rose in their demands,
Louis fell in his condescension.   His secretary of state,
the Marquis de Torcy, posted in disguise to Holland, on
the faith of a common blank passport.   He solicited, he
soothed, he supplicated, and made concessions in the
name of his sovereign.   He found the States were wholly
guided by the influence of Prince Eugene and the Duke
of Marlborough. He found these generals elated, haughty,
overbearing, and implacable.   He in private attacked the
Duke of Marlborough on his weakest side : he offered to
that nobleman a large sum of money, provided he would
effect a peace on certain conditions.   The proposal was
rejected.   The duke found his enemies in England increasing, and his credit at court in the wane ; and he
knew that nothing but a continuation of the war, and

new victories, could support his influence in England. Torcy was sensible that his country was utterly exhausted; that Louis dreaded nothing so much as the opening of the campaign; and he agreed to those articles upon which they insisted as preliminaries. The French king was confounded at these proposals: he felt the complicated pangs of grief, shame, and indignation. He rejected the preliminaries with disdain. He even deigned to submit his conduct to the judgment of his subjects. His offers were published, together with the demands of the allies. His people interested themselves in the glory of their monarch. They exclaimed against the cruelty and arrogance of his enemies. Though impoverished and half-starved by the war, they resolved to expend their whole substance in his support; and rather to fight his battles without pay, than leave him in the dire necessity of complying with such dishonourable terms. Animated by these sentiments, they made such efforts as amazed the whole world. The preliminaries being rejected by the French king, Rouillé was ordered to quit Holland in four-and-twenty hours; and the generals of the confederates resolved to open the campaign without farther hesitation.

The allied army besieges and takes Tournay.
Prince Eugene and the Duke of Marlborough proceeded to Flanders, and towards the end of June the allied army encamped in the plain of Lisle, to the number of one hundred and ten thousand fighting men. At the same time, the Mareschal Villars, accounted the most fortunate general in France, assembled the French forces in the plain of Lens, where he began to throw up intrenchments. The confederate generals having observed his situation, and perceiving he could not be attacked with any probability of success, resolved to undertake the siege of Tournay, the garrison of which Villars had imprudently weakened. Accordingly, they made a feint upon Ypres, in order to deceive the enemy, and convert all their attention to that side, while they suddenly invested Tournay on the twenty-seventh day of June. Though the garrison did not exceed twelve weakened battalions and four squadrons of dragoons, the place was so strong, both by art and nature, and Lieutenant de Surville, the governor, possessed such admirable talents,

that the siege was protracted, contrary to the expectation of the allies, and cost them a great number of men, not-withstanding all the precautions that could be taken for the safety of the troops. As the besiegers proceeded by the method of sap, their miners frequently met with those of the enemy underground, and fought with bayonet and pistol. The volunteers on both sides presented themselves to these subterraneous combats, in the midst of mines and countermines ready primed for explosion. Sometimes they were kindled by accident, and sometimes sprung by design; so that great numbers of those brave men were stifled below, and whole battalions blown into the air, or buried in the rubbish. On the twenty-eighth day of July, the besiegers having effected a practicable breach, and made the necessary dispositions for a general assault, the enemy offered to capitulate : the town was surrendered upon conditions, and the garrison retired to the citadel. Surville likewise entered into a treaty about giving up the citadel: the articles being sent to the court of Versailles, Louis would not ratify them, except upon condition that there should be a general cessation in the Netherlands till the fifth day of September. Hostilities were renewed on the eighth day of August, and prosecuted with uncommon ardour and animosity. On the thirtieth, Surville desired to capitulate on certain articles, which were rejected by the Duke of Marlborough, who gave him to understand that he had no terms to expect, but must surrender at discretion. At length his provision being quite exhausted, he was obliged to surrender himself and his garrison prisoners of war, though they were permitted to return to France, on giving their parole that they would not act in the field until a like number of the allies should be released.

The next object that attracted the eyes of the con- The French federates was the city of Mons, which they resolved to are defeat-besiege with all possible expedition. They passed the ed at Mal-plaquet. Scheldt on the third day of September, and detached the Prince of Hesse to attack the French lines from the Haisne to the Sombre, which were abandoned at his approach. On the seventh day of September, Mareschal de Boufflers arrived in the French camp at Quievrain, content to act in an inferior capacity to Villars, although

his superior in point of seniority. The Duke of Marlborough having received advice that the French were
on their march to attack the advanced body under the
Prince of Hesse, decamped from Havre, in order to support that detachment. On the ninth the allies made a
motion to the left, by which the two armies were brought
so near each other that a mutual cannonading ensued.
The French army, amounting to one hundred and twenty
thousand men, were posted behind the woods of La
Merte and Tanieres, in the neighbourhood of Malpla-
quet. The confederates, nearly of the same number,
encamped with the right near Sart and Bleron, and the
left on the edge of the wood of Lagniere; the head-
quarters being at Blaregnies. The enemy, instead of
attacking the allies, began to fortify their camp, which
was naturally strong, with triple intrenchments. In a
word, they were so covered with lines, hedges, intrenchments, cannon, and trees laid across, that they seemed
to be quite inaccessible. Had the confederates attacked
them on the ninth, the battle would not have been so
bloody, and the victory would have proved more decisive,
for they had not then begun to secure the camp; but
Marlborough postponed the engagement until they should
be reinforced by eighteen battalions which had been employed in the siege of Tournay; and in the mean time
the French fortified themselves with incredible diligence
and despatch. On the eleventh day of September, early
in the morning, the confederates, favoured by a thick
fog, erected batteries on each wing, and in the centre;
and about eight o'clock, the weather clearing up, the
attack began. Eighty-six battalions on the right, commanded by General Schuylemburgh, the Duke of Argyle,
and other generals, and supported by two-and-twenty
battalions under Count Lottum, attacked the left of
the enemy with such vigour, that, notwithstanding their
lines and barricadoes, they were in less than an hour
driven from their intrenchments into the woods of Sart
and Tanieres. The Prince of Orange and Baron Fagel,
with six-and-thirty Dutch battalions, advanced against
the right of the enemy posted in the wood of La Merte,
and covered with three intrenchments. Here the battle
was maintained with the most desperate courage on

both sides. The Dutch obliged the French to quit the first intrenchment; but were repulsed from the second with great slaughter. The Prince of Orange persisted in his efforts with incredible perseverance and intrepidity, even after two horses had been killed under him, and the greater part of his officers either slain or disabled. The French fought with an obstinacy of courage that bordered on despair, till seeing their lines forced, their left wing and centre giving way, and their general, Villars, dangerously wounded, they made an excellent retreat towards Bavay, under the conduct of Boufflers, and took post between Quesnoy and Valenciennes. The field of battle they abandoned to the confederates, with about forty colours and standards, sixteen pieces of artillery, and a good number of prisoners: but this was the dearest victory the allies had ever purchased. About twenty thousand of their best troops were killed in the engagement; whereas the enemy did not lose half that number, and retired at leisure, perfectly recovered of that apprehension with which they had been for some years inspired and overawed by the successes of their adversaries. On the side of the allies, Count Lottum, General Tettau, Count Oxienstern, and the Marquis of Tullibardine, were killed, with many other officers of distinction. Prince Eugene was slightly wounded on the head: Lieutenant General Webb received a shot in the groin. The Duke of Argyle, who distinguished himself by extraordinary feats of valour, escaped unhurt; but several musket-balls penetrated through his clothes, his hat, and periwig. In the French army the Chevalier de St. George charged twelve times with the household troops, and in the last was wounded with a sword in the arm. The Mareschal de Villars confidently asserted, that if he himself had not been disabled, the confederates would certainly have been defeated.

Considering the situation of the French, the number of their troops, and the manner in which they were fortified, nothing could be more rash and imprudent than the attack, which cost the lives of so many gallant men, and was attended with so little advantage to the conquerors. Perhaps the Duke of Marlborough thought a victory was absolutely necessary to support his sinking

Mons surrendered.

interest at the court of Great Britain. His intention
was to have given battle before the enemy had intrenched
themselves; but Prince Eugene insisted upon delaying
the action until the reinforcement should arrive from
Tournay. The extraordinary carnage is imputed to the
impetuosity of the Prince of Orange, whose aim through
this whole war was to raise himself into consideration
with the States-General, by signal acts of military
prowess. The French having retired to Valenciennes,
the allies were left at liberty to besiege Mons, which
capitulated about the end of October; and both armies
were distributed in winter quarters. The campaign on
the Rhine produced nothing but one sharp action, between a detachment of the French army commanded
by the Count de Borgh, and a body of troops under Count
Merci, who had passed the Rhine, in order to penetrate
into Franche-Comté. The imperial officer was worsted
in this encounter, with the loss of two thousand men;
obliged to repass the river, and retire to Fribourg. In
Piedmont, Veldt-Mareschal Thaun commanded the confederates, in the room of the Duke of Savoy, who refused to take the field, until some differences which had
arisen between the emperor and him should be adjusted.
Thaun's design was to besiege Briançon; but the Duke
of Berwick had taken such precautions as frustrated his
intention, though part of the troops under the French
general were employed in suppressing an insurrection of
the Camisars, and other malecontents in the Vivarez.
They were entirely defeated in a pitched battle; and
Abraham, one of their leaders, being taken, was broken
alive upon the wheel; three-and-twenty were hanged,
and the other prisoners sent to the galleys. The pope
delayed acknowledging King Charles, under various pretences, in hopes that the campaign would prove favourable to the House of Bourbon; till at length the emperor giving him to understand that his army should
take up their winter quarters in the ecclesiastical states,
his holiness solemnly owned Charles as King of Spain,
Naples, and Sicily.

Campaign
in Spain.

The military operations in Spain and Portugal were
unfavourable to the allies. On the seventh of May, the
Portuguese and English were defeated at Caya by the

Spaniards, under the command of the Mareschal de Bay. The castle of Alicant, guarded by two English regiments, had been besieged, and held out during the whole winter. At length the Chevalier d'Asfeldt ordered the rock to be undermined, and having lodged two hundred barrels of gunpowder, gave Syburg, the governor, to understand, that two of his officers might come out and see the condition of the works. This offer being accepted, Asfeldt in person accompanied them to the mine; he told them he could not bear the thoughts of seeing so many brave men perish in the ruins of a place they had so gallantly defended; and allowed them four-and-twenty hours to consider on the resolution they should take. Syburg continued deaf to his remonstrances; and, with an obstinacy that savoured more of stupidity than of valour, determined to stand the explosion. When the sentinels that were posted on the side of the hill gave notice, by a preconcerted signal, that fire was set to the mine, the governor ordered the guard to retire, and walked out to the parade accompanied by several officers. The mine being sprung, the rock opened under their feet, and they falling into the chasm, it instantly closed and crushed them to death. Notwithstanding this dreadful incident, Colonel d'Albon, who succeeded to the command, resolved to defend the place to the last extremity. Sir Edward Whitaker sailed from Barcelona to the relief of the place; but the enemy had erected such works as effectually hindered the troops from landing. Then general Stanhope, who commanded them, capitulated with the Spanish general for the garrison, which marched out with all the honours of war, and was transported to Minorca, where the men were put into quarters of refreshment. On the frontiers of Catalonia, General Staremberg maintained his ground, and even annoyed the enemy. He passed the Segra, and reduced Balaguer : having left a strong garrison in the place, he repassed the river, and sent his forces into winter quarters. The most remarkable event of this summer was the battle of Pultowa, in which the King of Sweden was entirely defeated by the Czar of Muscovy, and obliged to take refuge at Bender, a town of Moldavia, in the Turkish dominions. Augustus immediately marched into Poland against Stanislaus, and renounced his own

CHAP.
X.

1709.

resignation, as if it had been the effect of compulsion. He formed a project with the Kings of Denmark and Prussia to attack the Swedish territories in three different places: but the emperor and maritime powers prevented the execution of this scheme, by entering into a guarantee for preserving the peace of the empire.   Nevertheless, the King of Denmark declared war against Sweden, and transported an army over the Sound of Schonen; but they were attacked and defeated by the Swedes, and obliged to re-embark with the utmost precipitation.   The war still continued to rage in Hungary, where, however, the revolters were routed in many petty engagements.

The French king's Proposals of treating rejected by the States-General.

Though the events of the summer had been less unfavourable to France than Louis had reason to expect, he saw that peace was as necessary as ever to his kingdom; but he thought he might now treat with some freedom and dignity.   His minister, Torcy, maintained a correspondence with Mr. Petkum, resident of the Duke of Holstein at the Hague: he proposed to this minister that the negotiation should be renewed; and demanded passes by virtue of which the French plenipotentiaries might repair in safety to Holland.   In the mean time, the French king withdrew his troops from Spain, on pretence of demonstrating his readiness to oblige the allies in that particular; though this measure was the effect of necessity, which obliged him to recall those troops for the defence of his own dominions.   The States-General refused to grant passes to the French ministers; but they allowed Petkum to make a journey to Versailles.   In the interim King Philip published a manifesto, protesting against all that should be transacted at the Hague to his prejudice.   Far from yielding Spain and the Indies to his competitor, he declared his intention of driving Charles from those places that were now in his possession.   He named the Duke of Alba and Count Bergheyck for his plenipotentiaries, and ordered them to notify their credentials to the maritime powers; but no regard was paid to their intimation.   Philip tampered likewise with the Duke of Marlborough; and the Marquis de Torcy renewed his attempts upon that general; but all his application and address proved ineffectual. Petkum brought back from Versailles a kind of memorial, .

importing, that those motives which influenced the French before the campaign was opened no longer subsisted: that the winter season naturally produced a cessation of arms, during which he would treat of a general and reasonable peace, without restricting himself to the form of the preliminaries which the allies had pretended to impose: that, nevertheless, he would still treat on the foundation of those conditions to which he had consented, and send plenipotentiaries to begin the conferences with those of the allies on the first day of January. The States-General inveighed against this memorial, as a proof of the French king's insincerity ; though he certainly had a right to retract those offers they had formerly rejected. They came to a resolution, that it was absolutely necessary to prosecute the war with vigour ; and they wrote pressing letters on the subject to all their allies.

The Parliament of Great Britain being assembled on the fifteenth day of November, the queen in her speech told both Houses, that the enemy had endeavoured, by false appearances and deceitful insinuations of a desire after peace, to create jealousies among the allies: that God Almighty had been pleased to bless the arms of the confederates with a most remarkable victory, and other successes, which had laid France open to the impression of the allied arms, and consequently rendered peace more necessary to that kingdom than it was at the beginning of the campaign. She insisted upon the expediency of prosecuting the advantages she had gained, by reducing that exorbitant and oppressive power, which had so long threatened the liberties of Europe. The Parliament were as eager and compliant as ever. They presented congratulatory addresses: they thanked the Duke of Marlborough for his signal services; while great part of the nation reproached him with having wantonly sacrificed so many thousand lives to his own private interest and reputation. In less than a month, the Commons granted upwards of six millions for the service of the ensuing year; and established a lottery, with other funds, to answer this enormous supply. On the thirteenth day of December, Mr. Dolben, son to the late Archbishop of York, complained to the House of two sermons preached and published by Dr. Henry Sacheverel,

rector of St. Saviour's in Southwark, as containing positions contrary to revolution principles, to the present
government, and the Protestant succession. Sacheverel
was a clergyman of narrow intellects, and an over-heated
imagination. He had acquired some popularity among
those who distinguished themselves by the name of high
churchmen; and took all occasions to vent his animosity
against the dissenters. At the summer assizes at Derby,
he had held forth in that strain before the judges; on
the fifth day of November, in St. Paul's church, he, in
a violent declamation, defended the doctrine of non-resistance; inveighed against the toleration and dissenters;
declared the church was dangerously attacked by her
enemies, and slightly defended by her false friends: he
sounded the trumpet for the church, and exhorted the
people to put on the whole armour of God. Sir Samuel
Garrard, the lord mayor, countenanced this harangue,
which was published under his protection, extolled by
the tories, and circulated all over the nation. The complaint of Mr. Dolben against Sacheverel was seconded
in the House of Commons by Sir Peter King and other
members. The most violent paragraphs were read : the
sermons were voted scandalous and seditious libels. Sacheverel being brought to the bar of the House, acknowledged himself the author of both, and mentioned the
encouragement he had received from the lord mayor to
print that which was entitled "The Perils of False Brethren." Sir Samuel, who was a member, denied he had
ever given him such encouragement. The doctor being
ordered to withdraw, the House resolved he should be impeached of high crimes and misdemeanours; and Mr. Dolben was ordered to impeach him at the bar of the House
of Lords, in the name of all the Commons of England.
A committee was appointed to draw up articles, and Sacheverel was taken into custody. At the same time, in
order to demonstrate their own principles, they resolved,
that the Reverend Mr. Benjamin Hoadly, rector of St.
Peter-le-Poor, for having often justified the principles on
which her majesty and the nation proceeded in the late
happy Revolution, had justly merited the favour and re-
commendation of the House; and they presented an address to the queen, beseeching her to bestow some dignity

in the church on Mr. Hoadly, for his eminent services both to the church and state. The queen returned a civil answer, though she paid no regard to their recommenda- tion. Hoadly was a clergyman of sound understanding, unblemished character, and uncommon moderation, who, in a sermon preached before the lord mayor of London, had demonstrated the lawfulness of resisting wicked and cruel governors; and vindicated the late Revolution. By avowing such doctrines, he incurred the resentment of the high churchmen, who accused him of having preached up rebellion. Many books were written against the maxims he professed. These he answered; and in the course of the controversy acquitted himself with superior temper, judgment, and solidity of argument. He, as well as Bishop Burnet, and several other prelates, had been treated with great virulence in Sacheverel's sermon; and the lord treasurer was scurrilously abused under the name of Volpone.

The doctor being impeached at the bar of the Upper He is im-
House, petitioned that he might be admitted to bail; but peached by
the Com-
this indulgence was refused, and the Commons seemed mons.
bent upon prosecuting him with such severity as gave disgust to men of moderate principles. Meanwhile the tories were not idle. They boldly affirmed that the whigs had formed a design to pull down the church; and that this prosecution was intended to try their strength, before they would proceed openly to the execution of their project. These assertions were supported, and even credited by great part of the clergy, who did not fail to alarm and inflame their hearers; while emissaries were employed to raise a ferment among the populace, already prepared with discontent arising from a scarcity which prevailed in almost every country of Europe. The ministers magnified the dangers to which the church was exposed from dissenters, whigs, and lukewarm prelates. These they represented as the authors of a ruinous war, which, in a little time, would produce universal famine; and as the immediate encouragers of those Palatine refugees who had been brought over, to the number of six thousand, and maintained by voluntary contributions until they could be conveniently transported into Ireland, and the plantations in America.

The charity bestowed upon those unhappy strangers exasperated the poor of England, who felt severely the effects of the dearth, and helped to fill up the measure of popular discontent. The articles against Dr. Sacheverel being exhibited, his person was committed to the deputy-usher of the black rod; but afterwards the Lords admitted him to bail. Then he drew up an answer to the charge, in which he denied some articles, and others he endeavoured to justify or extenuate. The Commons having sent up a replication, declaring they were ready to prove the charge, the Lords appointed the twenty-seventh day of February for the trial, in Westminster-hall.

His trial. The eyes of the whole kingdom were turned upon this extraordinary trial. It lasted three weeks, during which all other business was suspended; and the queen herself was every day present, though in quality of a private spectator. The managers for the Commons were Sir Joseph Jekyl, Mr. Eyre, solicitor-general, Sir Peter King, recorder of the city of London, Lieutenant-General Stanhope, Sir Thomas Parker, and Mr. Robert Walpole, treasurer of the navy. The doctor was defended by Sir Simon Harcourt and Mr. Phipps, and assisted by Dr. Atterbury, Dr. Smallridge, and Dr. Friend. A vast multitude attended him every day to and from Westminster-hall, striving to kiss his hand, and praying for his deliverance, as if he had been a martyr and confessor. The queen's sedan was beset by the populace, exclaiming " God bless your majesty and the church. We hope your majesty is for Dr. Sacheverel." They compelled all persons to lift their hats to the doctor, as he passed in his coach to the Temple, where he lodged; and among these some members of Parliament, who were abused and insulted. They destroyed several meeting-houses; plundered the dwelling-houses of eminent dissenters; and threatened to pull down those of the lord-chancellor, the Earl of Wharton, and the Bishop of Sarum. They even proposed to attack the bank; so that the directors were obliged to send to Whitehall for assistance. The horse and foot guards were immediately sent to disperse the rioters, who fled at their approach. Next day the guards were doubled at Whitehall, and the train-bands of Westminster continued in arms during the whole trial. The Commons entreated the queen, in an address, to take effectual measures for suppressing the present tumults, set on foot and fomented by Papists, nonjurors, and other enemies to her title and government. She expressed a deep sense of their care and concern, as well as a just resentment at these tumultuous and violent proceedings. She published a proclamation for suppressing the tumults; and several persons being apprehended, were afterwards tried for high treason. Two of them were convicted, and sentenced to die; but neither suffered. The Commons presented another address of thanks to her majesty, for her gracious answer to their first remonstrance. They took this occasion to declare that the prosecution of the Commons against Dr. Henry Sacheverel proceeded only from the indispensable obligation they lay under to vindicate the late happy Revolution, the glory of their royal deliverer, her own title and administration, the present established and Protestant succession, together with the toleration and the quiet of the government. When the doctor's counsel had finished his defence, he himself recited a speech, wherein he solemnly justified his intentions towards the queen and her government; and spoke in the most respectful terms of the Revolution and the Protestant succession. He maintained the doctrine of non-resistance in all cases whatsoever, as a maxim of the church in which he was educated; and, by many pathetical expressions, endeavoured to excite the compassion of the audience. He was surrounded by the queen's chaplains, who encouraged and extolled him as the champion of the church; and he was privately favoured by the queen herself, who could not but relish a doctrine so well calculated for the support of regal authority.

On the tenth day of March, the Lords being adjourned to their own house, the Earl of Nottingham proposed the following question, "Whether, in prosecutions by impeachments for high crimes and misdemeanors, by writing or speaking, the particular words supposed to be criminal are necessary to be expressly specified in such impeachments?" The judges being consulted, were unanimously of opinion that, according to law, the grounds of an indictment or impeachment ought to be expressly

Debates upon it in the House of Lords.

CHAP.
X.

1709.

mentioned in both.　One of the lords having suggested that the judges had delivered their opinions according to the rules of Westminster-hall, and not according to the usage of Parliament, the House resolved, that in impeachments they should proceed according to the laws of the land, and the law and usage of Parliament.　On the sixteenth day of the month, the queen being in the House incognito, they proceeded to consider whether or not the Commons had made good the articles exhibited against Dr. Sacheverel.　The Earl of Wharton observed, that the doctor's speech was a full confutation and condemnation of his sermon: that all he had advanced about non-resistance and unlimited obedience was false and ridiculous: that the doctrine of passive obedience, as urged by the doctor, was not reconcilable to the practice of churchmen: that if the Revolution was not lawful, many in that House, and vast numbers without, were guilty of blood, murder, rapine, and injustice; and that the queen herself was no lawful sovereign, since the best title she had to the crown, was her parliamentary title, founded upon the Revolution.　He was answered by the Lord Haversham in a long speech.　Lord Ferrars said, if the doctor was guilty of some foolish unguarded expressions, he ought to have been tried at common law.　The Earl of Scarborough observed, the Revolution was a nice point, and above the law: he moved that they should adjourn the debate, and take time to consider before they gave judgment.　Dr. Hooper, Bishop of Bath and Wells, allowed the necessity and legality of resistance in some extraordinary cases; but was of opinion that this maxim ought to be concealed from the knowledge of the people, who are naturally too apt to resist: that the Revolution was not to be boasted of or made a precedent; but that a mantle ought to be thrown over it, and it should be called a vacancy or abdication.　He said the original compact were dangerous words, not to be mentioned without great caution: that those who examined the Revolution too nicely were no friends to it; and that there seemed to be a necessity for preaching up non-resistance and passive obedience at that time, when resistance was justified. The Duke of Argyle affirmed, that the clergy in all ages had delivered up the rights and privileges of the people, preaching up the king's power, in order to govern him the more easily; and therefore they ought not to be suffered to meddle with politics. The Earl of Anglesey owned the doctor had preached nonsense, but said that was no crime. The Duke of Leeds distinguished between resistance and revolution ; for had not the last succeeded, it would have certainly been rebellion, since he knew of no other but hereditary right. The Bishop of Salisbury justified resistance from the Book of Maccabees : he mentioned the conduct of Queen Elizabeth, who assisted the Scots, the French, and the States-General, in resisting their different sovereigns, and was supported in this practice both by her Parliaments and her Convocations. He observed, that King Charles I. had assisted the citizens of Rochelle in their rebellion ; that Mainwaring incurred a severe censure from the Parliament for having broached the doctrine of the divine right of kings ; and that though this became a favourite maxim after the Restoration, yet its warmest asserters were the first who pleaded for resistance when they thought themselves oppressed. The Archbishop of York, the Duke of Buckingham, and other leaders of the tory interest, declared that they never read such a piece of madness and nonsense as Sacheverel's sermon; but they did not think him guilty of a misdemeanour. Next day, Dr. Wake, Bishop of Lincoln, accused Sacheverel of having made a strange and false representation of the design for a comprehension, which had been set on foot by Archbishop Sancroft, and promoted by the most eminent divines of the church of England. He was of opinion that some step should be taken for putting a stop to such preaching as, if not timely corrected, might kindle heats and animosities that would endanger both church and state. Dr. Trimnel, Bishop of Norwich, expatiated on the insolence of Sacheverel, who had arraigned Archbishop Grindal, one of the eminent reformers, as a perfidious prelate, for having favoured and tolerated the discipline of Geneva. He enlarged upon the good effects of the toleration. He took notice of Sacheverel's presumption in publishing inflammatory prayers, declaring himself under persecution, while he was prosecuted for offending against the law, by those who in common justice ought to be thought the fairest accusers, and before their lordships, who were justly acknowledged to be the most impartial judges. In discussing the fourth article, the Bishop of Salisbury spoke with great vehemence against Sacheverel, who, by inveighing against the Revolution, toleration, and union, seemed to arraign and attack the queen herself; since her majesty had so great a share in the first; had often declared she would maintain the second; and that she looked upon the third as the most glorious event of her reign. He affirmed that nothing could be more plain than the doctor's reflecting upon her majesty's ministers; and that he had so well marked out a noble peer there present, by an ugly and scurrilous epithet which he would not repeat, that it was not possible to mistake his meaning. Some of the younger peers could not help laughing at this undesigned sarcasm upon the lord treasurer, whom Sacheverel had reviled under the name of Volpone: they exclaimed, "Name him, name him;" and, in all probability, the zealous bishop, who was remarkable for absence of mind and unguarded expressions, would have gratified their request, had not the chancellor, interposing, declared that no peer was obliged to say more than he should think proper.

After obstinate disputes, and much virulent altercation, Sacheverel was found guilty by a majority of seventeen voices; and four-and-thirty peers entered a protest against this decision. He was prohibited from preaching for the term of three years; his two sermons were ordered to be burnt by the hands of the common hangman, in presence of the lord mayor and the two sheriffs of London and Middlesex. The Lords likewise voted, that the executioner should commit to the same fire the famous decree passed in the Convocation of the University of Oxford, asserting the absolute authority and indefeasible right of princes. A like sentence was denounced by the Commons upon a book entitled "Collections of Passages referred to by Dr. Sacheverel, in his Answer to the Articles of Impeachment." These he had selected from impious books lately published, and they were read by his counsel as proofs that the church was in danger. The lenity of the sentence passed upon Sacheverel, which was in a great measure owing to the dread of popular resentment, his friends considered as a victory obtained over a whig faction, and they celebrated their triumph with bonfires and illuminations. On the fifth day of April, the queen ordered the Parliament to be prorogued, after having, in her speech to both Houses, expressed her concern for the necessary occasion which had taken up great part of their time towards the latter end of the session. She declared that no prince could have a more true and tender concern for the welfare and prosperity of the church than she had, and should always have; and she said it was very injurious to take a pretence from wicked and malicious libels, to insinuate that the church was in danger by her administration.

The French king, seeing the misery of his people daily increase, and all his resources fail, humbled himself again before the allies, and by the means of Petkum, who still corresponded with his ministers, implored the States-General that the negotiation might be resumed. In order to facilitate their consent, he despatched a new project of pacification, in which he promised to renounce his grandson, and to comply with all their other demands, provided the electors of Cologn and Bavaria should be re-established in their estates and dignities. These overtures being rejected, another plan was offered, and communicated to the plenipotentiaries of the emperor and Queen of Great Britain. Then Petkum wrote a letter to the Marquis de Torcy intimating, that the allies required his most Christian majesty should declare, in plain and expressive terms, that he consented to all the preliminaries, except the thirty-seventh article, which stipulated a cessation of arms, in case the Spanish monarchy should be delivered to King Charles in the space of two months. He said, the allies would send passports to the French ministers, to treat of an equivalent for that article. Louis was even forced to swallow this bitter draught. He signified his consent, and appointed the Mareschal D'Uxelles and the Abbé Polignac his plenipotentiaries. They were not suffered, however, to enter Holland, but were met by the Deputies Buys and Vanderdussen, at Gertruydenburgh. Meanwhile the states desired the Queen of England to send over the Duke of Marlborough, to assist them with his advice in

c 2

these conferences. The two Houses of Parliament seconded their request in a joint address to her majesty, who told them she had already given directions for his departure; and said she was glad to find they concurred with her in a just sense of the duke's eminent services. Both the letter and the address were procured by the interest of Marlborough, to let the queen see how much that nobleman was considered both at home and abroad. But she was already wholly alienated from him in her heart, and these expedients served only to increase her disgust.

Pride and obstinacy of the Dutch.

The French ministers were subjected to every species of mortification. They were in a manner confined to a small fortified town, and all their conduct narrowly watched. Their accommodation was mean; their letters were opened; and they were daily insulted by injurious libels. The Dutch deputies would hear of no relaxation, and no expedient for removing the difficulties that retarded the negotiation. In vain the plenipotentiaries declared, that the French king could not with decency, or the least regard to his honour, wage war against his own grandson: the deputies insisted upon his effecting the cession of Spain and the Indies to the house of Austria; and submitting to every other article specified in the preliminaries. Nay, they even reserved to themselves a power of making ulterior demands after the preliminaries should be adjusted. Louis proposed that some small provision should be made for the Duke of Anjou, which might induce him to relinquish Spain the more easily. He mentioned the kingdom of Arragon; and this hint being disagreeable to the allies, he demanded Naples and Sicily. When they urged that Naples was already in possession of the house of Austria, he restricted the provision to Sicily and Sardinia. He offered to deliver up four cautionary towns in Flanders, as a security for Philip's evacuating Spain; and even promised to supply the confederates with a monthly sum of money, to defray the expense of expelling that prince from his dominions, should he refuse to resign them with a good grace. The substance of all the conferences was communicated to Lord Townshend and Count Zinzendorf, the imperial plenipotentiary; but the conduct of the deputies was regulated by the Pen-

sionary Heinsius, who was firmly attached to Prince
Eugene and the Duke of Marlborough, more averse than
ever to a pacification. The negotiation lasted from the
nineteenth day of March to the twenty-fifth of July,
during which term the conferences were several times
interrupted, and a great many despatches and new proposals arrived from Versailles. At length the plenipotentiaries returned to France, after having sent a letter to
the pensionary, in which they declared that the proposals
made by the deputies were unjust and impracticable; and
complained of the unworthy treatment to which they had
been exposed. Louis resolved to hazard another campaign, not without hope that there might be some lucky
incident in the events of war, and that the approaching
revolution in the English ministry, of which he was well
apprised, would be productive of a more reasonable
pacification. The States-General resolved, that the enemy
had departed from the foundation on which the negotiation had begun, and studied pretences to evade the execution of the capital points, the restitution of Spain and the
Indies; and, in short, that France had no other view than
to sow and create jealousy and disunion among the allies.
Lord Townshend, in a memorial, assured them, that the
queen entirely approved their resolution, and all the steps
they had taken in the course of the negotiation; and that
she was firmly resolved to prosecute the war with all possible vigour, until the enemy should accept such terms
of peace as might secure the tranquillity of the Christian
world.

The conferences did not retard the operations of the _{Douay be-}
campaign. Prince Eugene and the Duke of Marlborough _{sieged and taken by}
set out from the Hague on the fifteenth day of March for _{the confe-}
Tournay, in order to assemble the forces which were quar- _{derates, as well as}
tered on the Maese, in Flanders, and Brabant. On the 20th _{Bethune,}
of April, they suddenly advanced to Pont-a-Vendin, in _{Aire, and St. Venant.}
order to attack the lines upon which the French had been
at work all the winter, hoping by these to cover Douay
and other frontier towns, which were threatened by the
confederates. The troops left for the defence of the
lines retired without opposition. The allies having laid
bridges over the Scarpe, the Duke of Marlborough with
his division passed that river, and encamped at Vitri.

Prince Eugene remained on the other side, and invested Douay, the enemy retiring towards Cambray. Mareschal Villars still commanded the French army, which was extremely numerous and well appointed, considering the distress of that kingdom. Indeed, the number was augmented by this distress; for many thousands saved themselves from dying of hunger, by carrying arms in the service. The mareschal having assembled all his forces, passed the Scheldt, and encamped at Bouchain, declaring that he would give battle to the confederates: an alteration was immediately made in the disposition of the allies, and proper precautions taken for his reception. He advanced in order of battle; but having viewed the situation of the confederates, he marched back to the heights of St. Lawrence, where he fixed his camp. His aim was, by continual alarms, to interrupt the siege of Douay, which was vigorously defended by a numerous garrison, under the command of Monsieur Albergotti, who made a number of successful sallies, in which the besiegers lost a great number of men. They were likewise repulsed in several assaults; but still proceeded with unremitted vigour, until the besieged, being reduced to the last extremity, were obliged to capitulate on the twenty-sixth of June, fifty days after the trenches had been opened. The generals finding it impracticable to attack the enemy, who were posted within strong lines from Arras towards Miramont, resolved to besiege Bethune, which was invested on the fifteenth day of July, and surrendered on the twenty-ninth of August. Villars marched out of his intrenchments with a view to raise the siege; but he did not think proper to hazard an engagement; some warm skirmishes, however, happened between the foragers of the two armies. After the reduction of Bethune, the allies besieged at one time the towns of Aire and St. Venant, which were taken without much difficulty. Then the armies broke up, and marched into winter quarters.

King
Charles
obtains a
victory
over Philip
at Sara-
gossa, and
enters
drid.

The campaign on the Rhine was productive of no military event; nor was any thing of consequence transacted in Piedmont. The Duke of Savoy being indisposed and out of humour, the command of the forces still continued vested in Count Thaun, who endeavoured to pass the Alps, and penetrate into Dauphiné; but the Duke of Berwick had cast up intrenchments in the mountains, and taken such precautions to guard them, as baffled all the attempts of the imperial general. Spain was much more fruitful of military incidents. The horse and dragoons in the army of King Charles, headed by General Stanhope, attacked the whole cavalry of the enemy at Almennara. Stanhope charged in person, and with his own hand slew General Amessaga, who commanded the guards of Philip. The Spanish horse were entirely routed, together with nine battalions that escaped by favour of the darkness; and the main body of the army retired with precipitation to Lerida. General Staremberg pursued them to Saragossa, where he found them drawn up in order of battle; and an engagement ensuing on the ninth day of August, the enemy were totally defeated; five thousand of their men were killed, seven thousand taken, together with all their artillery, and a great number of colours and standards. King Charles entered Saragossa in triumph, while Philip with the wreck of his army retreated to Madrid. Having sent his queen and son to Victoria, he retired to Valladolid, in order to collect his scattered forces, so as to form another army. The good fortune of Charles was of short duration. Stanhope proposed that he should immediately secure Pampeluna, the only pass by which the French king could send troops to Spain; but this salutary scheme was rejected. King Charles proceeded to Madrid, which was deserted by all the grandees; and he had the mortification to see that the Castilians were universally attached to his competitor.

While his forces continued cantoned in the neigh- Battle bourhood of Toledo, the King of France, at the request of Villa-viciosa. of Philip, sent the Duke de Vendome to take the command of the Spanish army, which was at the same time reinforced by detachments of French troops. Vendome's reputation was so high, and his person so beloved by the soldiery, that his presence was almost equivalent to an army. A great number of volunteers immediately assembled to signalize themselves under the eye of this renowned general. The Castilians were inspired with fresh courage, and made surprising efforts in favour of their sovereign: so that in less than three months after his defeat at Saragossa he was in a condition to go in quest of his rival. Charles, on the other hand, was totally neglected by the courts of Vienna and Great Britain, which took no steps to supply his wants, or enable him to prosecute the advantages he had gained. In the beginning of November his army marched back to Saragossa, and was cantoned in the neighbourhood of Cifuentes, where Staremberg established his head-quarters. General Stanhope, with the British forces, was quartered in the little town of Brihuega, where, on the twenty-seventh day of the month, he found himself suddenly surrounded by the whole Spanish army. As the place was not tenable, and he had very little ammu-nition, he was obliged, after a short but vigorous resist-ance, to capitulate, and surrender himself and all his forces prisoners of war, to the amount of two thousand men, including three lieutenant-generals, one major-general, one brigadier, with all the colonels and officers of the respective regiments. He was greatly censured for having allowed himself to be surprised; for if he had placed a guard upon the neighbouring hills, according to the advice of General Carpenter, he might have re-ceived notice of the enemy's approach time enough to retire to Cifuentes. Thither he had detached his aide-du-camp with an account of his situation, on the appear-ance of the Spanish army; and Staremberg immediately assembled his forces. About eleven in the forenoon they began to march towards Brihuega; but the roads were so bad, that night overtook them before they reached the heights in the neighbourhood of that place. Staremberg is said to have loitered away his time un-necessarily from motives of envy to the English general, who had surrendered before his arrival. The troops lay all night on their arms near Villaviciosa, and on the twenty-ninth were attacked by the enemy, who doubled their number. Staremberg's left wing was utterly de-feated, all the infantry that composed it having been either cut in pieces or taken; but the victors, instead of following the blow, began to plunder the baggage; and Staremberg with his right wing fought their left with surprising valour and perseverance till night. Then they retired in disorder, leaving him master of the field of battle and of all their artillery. Six thousand of the enemy were killed on the spot; but the allies had suffered so severely that the general could not maintain his ground. He ordered the cannon to be nailed up, and marched to Saragossa, from whence he retired to Catalonia. Thither he was pursued by the Duke de Vendome, who reduced Balaguer, in which he had left a garrison, and compelled him to take shelter under the walls of Barcelona. At this period the Duke de Noailles invested Gironne, which he reduced, notwithstanding the severity of the weather; so that Philip, from a fugitive, became in three months absolute master of the whole Spanish monarchy, except the province of Catalonia, and even that lay open to his incursions. Nothing of consequence was achieved on the side of Portugal, from whence the Earl of Galway returned to England by the queen's permission. The operations of the British fleet, during this summer, were so inconsiderable as scarcely to deserve notice. Sir John Norris commanded in the Mediterranean, and with a view to support the Camisars, who were in arms in the Cevennes, sailed to Port Cette, within a league of Marseilles, and at the distance of fifteen from the insurgents. The place surrendered, without opposition, to about seven hundred men that landed under the command of Major-General Saissan, a native of Languedoc. He likewise made himself master of the town and castle of Ayde; but the Duke de Noailles advancing with a body of forces to join the Duke de Roquelaire, who commanded in those parts, the English abandoned their conquests, and re-embarked with precipitation. After the battle of Pultowa the Czar of Muscovy reduced all Livonia; but he and King Augustus agreed to a neutrality for Pomerania. The King of Sweden continued at Bender, and the grand signor interested himself so much in favour of that prince as to declare war against the Emperor of Russia. Hostilities were carried on between the Swedish and Danish fleets, with various success. The malecontents in Hungary sustained repeated losses during the summer; but they were encouraged to maintain the war by the rupture between the Ottoman Porte and Russia. They were

CHAP.
X.
1710.
The whig
ministry
disgraced.

flattered with hopes of auxiliaries from the Turks; and expected engineers and money from the French monarch.

In England, the effects of those intrigues which had been formed against the whig ministers began to appear. The trial of Sacheverel had excited a popular spirit of aversion to those who favoured the dissenters. From all parts of the kingdom addresses were presented to the queen, censuring all resistance as a rebellious doctrine, founded upon anti-monarchical and republican principles. At the same time counter-addresses were procured by the whigs, extolling the Revolution, and magnifying the conduct of the present Parliament. The queen began to express her attachment to the tories, by mortifying the Duke of Marlborough. Upon the death of the Earl of Essex she wrote to the general, desiring that the regiment which had been commanded by that nobleman should be given to Mr. Hill, brother to Mrs. Masham, who had supplanted the Duchess of Marlborough in the queen's friendship, and was, in effect, the source of this political revolution. The duke represented to her majesty, in person, the prejudice that would redound to the service from the promotion of such a young officer over the heads of a great many brave men, who had exhibited repeated proofs of valour and capacity. He expostulated with his sovereign on this extraordinary mark of partial regard to the brother of Mrs. Masham, which he could not help considering as a declaration against himself and his family, who had so much cause to complain of that lady's malice and ingratitude. To this remonstrance the queen made no other reply but that he would do well to consult his friends. The Earl of Godolphin enforced his friend's arguments, though without effect; and the duke retired in disgust to Windsor. The queen appeared at council without taking the least notice of his absence, which did not fail to alarm the whole whig faction. Several noblemen ventured to speak to her majesty on the subject, and explain the bad consequences of disobliging a man who had done such eminent services to the nation. She told them his services were still fresh in her memory, and that she retained all her former kindness for his person. Hearing, however, that a popular clamour was raised, and that the House

of Commons intended to pass some votes that would be
disagreeable to her and her new counsellors, she ordered
the Earl of Godolphin to write to the duke to dispose
of the regiment as he should think proper, and return
to town immediately. Before he received this intimation he had sent a letter to the queen, desiring she
would permit him to retire from business. In answer
to this petition, she assured him his suspicions were
groundless, and insisted upon his coming to council.
The duchess demanded an audience of her majesty, on
pretence of vindicating her own character from some as-
persions. She hoped to work upon the queen's tenderness, and retrieve the influence she had lost. She protested, argued, wept, and supplicated; but the queen
was too well pleased with her own deliverance from the
tyranny of the other's friendship, to incur such slavery
for the future. All the humiliation of the duchess
served only to render herself the more contemptible.
The queen heard her without exhibiting the least sign
of emotion, and all she would vouchsafe was a repetition
of these words, " You desired no answer, and you shall
have none," alluding to an expression in a letter she had
received from the duchess. As an additional mortification to the ministry, the office of lord chamberlain was
transferred from the Duke of Kent to the Duke of
Shrewsbury, who had lately voted with the tories, and
maintained an intimacy of correspondence with Mr.
Harley. The interest of the Duke of Marlborough was
not even sufficient to prevent the dismission of his own
son-in-law, the Earl of Sunderland, from the post of
secretary of state, in which he was succeeded by Lord
Dartmouth.

The queen was generally applauded for thus asserting
her just prerogative, and setting herself free from an
arbitrary cabal, by which she had been so long kept in
dependence. The Duke of Beaufort went to court on
this occasion, and told her majesty he was extremely
glad that he could now salute her queen in reality. The
whole whig party were justly alarmed at these alterations.
The directors of the bank represented to her majesty
the prejudice that would undoubtedly accrue to public
credit from a change of the ministry. The emperor and

The Parlia-
ment is
dissolved.

the States-General interposed in this domestic revolution. Their ministers at London presented memorials,
explaining in what manner foreign affairs would be influenced by an alteration in the British ministry. The
queen assured them that, whatever changes might be
made, the Duke of Marlborough should be continued in
his employments. In the month of August the Earl of
Godolphin was divested of his office, and the treasury
put in commission, subjected to the direction of Harley,
appointed chancellor of the exchequer and under-treasurer. The Earl of Rochester was declared president
of the council, in the room of Lord Somers: the staff
of lord steward being taken from the Duke of Devonshire, was given to the Duke of Buckingham; and Mr.
Boyle was removed from the secretary's office, to make
way for Mr. Henry St. John. The lord chancellor
having resigned the great seal, it was first put in commission, and afterwards given to Sir Simon Harcourt.
The Earl of Wharton surrendered his commission of
lord lieutenant of Ireland, which the queen conferred on
the Duke of Ormond. The Earl of Orford withdrew
himself from the board of Admiralty; and Mr. George
Granville was appointed secretary of war, in the room
of Mr. Robert Walpole. The command of the forces
in Portugal was bestowed upon the Earl of Portmore:
the Duke of Hamilton was appointed lord lieutenant of
the county-palatine of Lancaster. In a word, there was
not one whig left in any office of state, except the Duke of
Marlborough, who would have renounced his command,
had he not been earnestly dissuaded by his particular
friends from taking such a step as might have been prejudicial to the interest of the nation. That the triumph
of the tories might be complete, the queen dissolved the
whig Parliament, after such precautions were taken as
could not fail to influence the new election in favour of
the other party.

To this end nothing so effectually contributed as did
the trial of Sacheverel, who was used as an instrument
and tool to wind and turn the passions of the vulgar.
Having been presented to a benefice in North Wales, he
went in procession to that country, with all the pomp and
magnificence of a sovereign prince. He was sumptuously

entertained by the university of Oxford, and different noblemen, who, while they worshipped him as the idol of their faction, could not help despising the object of their adoration. He was received in several towns by the magistrates of the corporation in their formalities, and often attended by a body of a thousand horse. At Bridge-north he was met by Mr. Creswell, at the head of four thousand horse, and the like number of persons on foot, wearing white knots edged with gold, and three leaves of gilt laurel in their hats. The hedges were for two miles dressed with garlands of flowers, and lined with people; and the steeples covered with streamers, flags, and colours. Nothing was heard but the cry of " The Church and Dr. Sacheverel." The clergy were actuated by a spirit of enthusiasm, which seemed to spread like a contagion through all ranks and degrees of people, and had such effect upon the elections for a new Parliament, that very few were returned as members but such as had distinguished themselves by their zeal against the whig administration. Now the queen had the pleasure to see all the offices of state, the lieutenancy of London, the management of corporations, and the direction of both Houses of Parliament, in the hands of the tories. When these met on the twenty-fifth day of November, Mr. Bromley was chosen speaker without opposition. The queen, in her speech, recommended the prosecution of the war with vigour, especially in Spain. She declared herself resolved to support the church of England; to preserve the British constitution according to the union; to maintain the indulgence by law allowed to scrupulous consciences; and to employ none but such as were heartily attached to the Protestant succession in the house of Hanover. The Lords in their address promised to concur in all reasonable measures towards procuring an honourable peace. The Commons were more warm and hearty in their assurances, exhorting her majesty to discountenance all such principles and measures as had lately threatened her royal crown and dignity; measures which, whenever they might prevail, would prove fatal to the whole constitution, both in church and state. After this declaration they proceeded to consider the estimates, and cheerfully granted the supplies for the ensuing year, part of which was raised by two lotteries. In the House of Peers, the Earl of Scarborough moved that the thanks of the House should be returned to the Duke of Marlborough; but the Duke of Argyle made some objections to the motion, and the general's friends, dreading the consequence of putting the question, postponed the consideration of this proposal until the duke should return from the continent. The Earl of Peterborough was appointed ambassador-extraordinary to the imperial court: the Earl of Rivers was sent in the same quality to Hanover: Mr. Richard Hill was nominated envoy-extraordinary to the United Provinces, as well as to the council of state appointed for the government of the Spanish Netherlands, in the room of Lieutenant-General Cadogan. Meredith, Macartney, and Honeywood, were deprived of their regiments, because in their cups they had drunk confusion to the enemies of the Duke of Marlborough.

e Duke
Marl-
rough in-
lted and
viled.
This nobleman arrived in England towards the latter end of December. He conferred about half an hour in private with the queen, and next morning assisted at a committee of the privy council. Her majesty gave him to understand that he needed not to expect the thanks of the Parliament as formerly; and told him she hoped˙ he would live well with her ministers. He expressed no resentment at the alterations which had been made; but resolved to acquiesce in the queen's pleasure, and retain the command of the army on her own terms. On the second day of January, the queen sent a message to both Houses, intimating that there had been an action in Spain to the disadvantage of King Charles; that the damage having fallen particularly on the English forces, she had given directions for sending and procuring troops to repair the loss, and hoped the Parliament would approve her conduct. Both Houses seized this opportunity of venting their spleen against the old ministry. The history of England is disgraced by the violent conduct of two turbulent factions, which, in their turn, engrossed the administration and legislative power. The parliamentary strain was quite altered. One can hardly conceive how resolutions so widely different could be taken on the same subject, with any shadow of reason and decorum. Marlborough, who but a few months before

had been so highly extolled and caressed by the representatives of the people, was now become the object of
parliamentary hatred and censure, though no sensible
alteration had happened in his conduct or success. That
hero, who had retrieved the glory of the British arms,
won so many battles, subdued such a number of towns
and districts, humbled the pride and checked the ambition of France, secured the liberty of Europe, and, as it
were, chained victory to his chariot-wheels, was in a few
weeks dwindled into an object of contempt and derision.
He was ridiculed in public libels, and reviled in private
conversation. Instances were everywhere repeated of his
fraud, avarice, and extortion; his insolence, cruelty, ambition, and misconduct: even his courage was called in
question; and this consummate general was represented
as the lowest of mankind. So unstable is the popularity
of every character that fluctuates between two opposite
tides of faction.

The Lords, in their answer to the queen's message,
declared, that as the misfortune in Spain might have
been occasioned by some preceding mismanagement, they
would use their utmost endeavour to discover it, so as to
prevent the like for the future. They set on foot an inquiry concerning the affairs of Spain; and the Earl of
Peterborough being examined before the committee, imputed all the miscarriages in the course of that war to
the Earl of Galway and General Stanhope. Notwithstanding the defence of Galway, which was clear and
convincing, the House resolved, that the Earl of Peterborough had given a faithful and an honourable account
of the councils of war in Valencia; that the Earl of
Galway, Lord Tyrawley, and General Stanhope, in advising an offensive war, had been the unhappy occasion
of the battle of Almanza, the source of our misfortunes
in Spain, and one great cause of the disappointment of
the expedition to Toulon, concerted with her majesty.
They voted that the prosecution of an offensive war in
Spain was approved and directed by the ministers, who
were therefore justly blamable, as having contributed
to all our misfortunes in Spain, and to the disappointment of the expedition against Toulon; that the Earl of
Peterborough, during his command in Spain, had per-

formed many great and eminent services; and, if his
opinion had been followed, it might have prevented the
misfortunes that ensued. Then the Duke of Buckingham moved, that the thanks of the House should be
given to the earl for his remarkable and eminent services; and these he actually received from the mouth of
the Lord-keeper Harcourt, who took this opportunity
to drop some oblique reflections upon the mercenary disposition of the Duke of Marlborough. The House proceeding in the inquiry, passed another vote, importing,
that the late ministry had been negligent in managing
the Spanish war, to the great prejudice of the nation.
Finding that the Portuguese troops were posted on the
right of the English at the battle of Almanza, they resolved that the Earl of Galway, in yielding this point,
had acted contrary to the honour of the imperial crown
of Great Britain. These resolutions they included in an
address to the queen, who had been present during the
debates, which were extremely violent: and to every
separate vote was attached a severe protest. These were
not the proceedings of candour and national justice, but
the ebullitions of party zeal and rancorous animosity.

Severe
votes in the
House of
Commons
against
those who
invited
over the
poor Pala-
tines.
While the Lords were employed in this inquiry, the
Commons examined certain abuses which had crept into
the management of the navy; and some censures were
passed upon certain persons concerned in contracts for
victualling the seamen. The inhabitants of St. Olave's
and other parishes presented a petition, complaining that
a great number of Palatines inhabiting one house might
produce among them a contagious distemper, and in
time become a charge to the public, as they were destitute of all visible means of subsistence. This petition
had been procured by the tories, that the House of Commons might have another handle for attacking the late
ministry. A committee was appointed to inquire upon
what invitation or encouragement those Palatines had
come to England. The papers relating to this affair
being laid before them by the queen's order, and perused,
the House resolved, that the inviting and bringing over
the poor Palatines of all religions, at the public expense,
was an extravagant and unreasonable charge to the kingdom, and a scandalous misapplication of the public

money, tending to the increase and oppression of the
poor, and of dangerous consequence to the constitution
in church and state; and that whoever advised their
being brought over was an enemy to the queen and
kingdom. Animated by the heat of this inquiry, they
passed the bill to repeal the act for a general naturalization of all Protestants; but this was rejected in the
House of Lords. Another bill was enacted into a law,
importing that no person should be deemed qualified for
representing a county in Parliament, unless he possessed
an estate of six hundred pounds a year; and restricting
the qualification of burgess to half that sum. The design of this bill was to exclude trading people from the
House of Commons, and to lodge the legislative power
with the landholders. A third act passed, permitting the
importation of French wine in neutral bottoms; a bill
against which the whigs loudly exclaimed as a national
evil, and a scandalous compliment to the enemy.

A violent party in the House of Commons began to Harley
look upon Harley as a lukewarm tory, because he would stabbed at
the council-
not enter precipitately into all their factious measures: board by
they even began to suspect his principles, when his credit Guiscard;
and created
was re-established by a very singular accident. Guis- Earl of
card, the French partisan, of whom mention hath already Oxford.
been made, thought himself very ill-rewarded for his
services, with a precarious pension of four hundred
pounds, which he enjoyed from the queen's bounty. He
had been renounced by St. John, the former companion
of his pleasures: he had in vain endeavoured to obtain
an audience of the queen, with a view to demand more
considerable appointments. Harley was his enemy, and
all access to her majesty was denied. Enraged at these
disappointments, he attempted to make his peace with
the court of France, and offered his services in a letter
to one Moreau, a banker in Paris. This packet, which
he endeavoured to transmit by the way of Portugal, was
intercepted, and a warrant issued out to apprehend him
for high treason. When the messenger disarmed him
in St. James's Park, he exhibited marks of guilty confusion and despair, and begged that he would kill him
directly. Being conveyed to the Cockpit, in a sort of
frenzy, he perceived a penknife lying upon a table, and

took it up without being perceived by the attendants. A committee of council was immediately summoned, and Guiscard brought before them to be examined. Finding that his correspondence with Moreau was discovered, he desired to speak in private with Secretary St. John, whom, in all probability, he had resolved to assassinate. His request being refused, he said, "That's hard! not one word!" St. John being out of his reach, he stepped up to Mr. Harley, and exclaimed "Have at thee, then!" stabbed him in the breast with the penknife which he had concealed. The instrument broke upon the bone, without penetrating into the cavity: nevertheless, he repeated the blow with such force that the chancellor of the exchequer fell to the ground. Secretary St. John, seeing him fall, cried out, "The villain has killed Mr. Harley;" and drew his sword. Several other members followed his example, and wounded Guiscard in several places. Yet he made a desperate defence, until he was overpowered by the messengers and servants, and conveyed from the council-chamber, which he had filled with terror, tumult, and confusion. His wounds, though dangerous, were not mortal; but he died of a gangrene occasioned by the bruises he had sustained. This attempt upon the life of Harley by a person who wanted to establish a traitorous correspondence with France, extinguished the suspicions of those who began to doubt that minister's integrity. The two Houses of Parliament, in an address to the queen, declared their belief that Mr. Harley's fidelity to her majesty and zeal for her service had drawn upon him the hatred of all the abettors of popery and faction. They besought her majesty to take all possible care of her sacred person; and, for that purpose, to give directions for causing Papists to be removed from the cities of London and Westminster. A proclamation was published, ordering the laws to be strictly put in execution against Papists. When Harley appeared in the House of Commons after his recovery, he was congratulated upon it by the speaker, in a florid and fulsome premeditated speech. An act was passed, decreeing, that an attempt upon the life of a privy councillor should be felony without benefit of clergy. The Earl of Rochester dying, Harley became sole minister, was

Burnet.
Quincy.
Feuquie-
res. Torcy.
Burchet.
History of
the Duke
of Marl-
borough.
Mil. Hist.
Conduct
of the
Duchess
of Marl-
borough.
Tindal.
Lives of the
Admirals.
Voltaire.

created Baron of Wigmore, and raised to the rank of earl, by the noble and ancient titles of Oxford and Mortimer: to crown his prosperity, he was appointed lord treasurer, and vested with the supreme administration of affairs.

The Commons empowered certain persons to examine all the grants made by King William, and to report the value of them, as well as the considerations upon which they were made. Upon their report a bill was formed and passed that House; but the Lords rejected it at the first reading. Their next step was to examine the public accounts, with a view to fix an imputation on the Earl of Godolphin. They voted, that above five-and-thirty millions of the money granted by Parliament remained unaccounted for. This sum, however, included some accounts in the reigns of King Charles and King William. One-half of the whole was charged to Mr. Bridges, the paymaster, who had actually accounted for all the money he had received, except about three millions, though these accounts had not passed through the auditor's office. The Commons afterwards proceeded to inquire into the debts of the navy, that exceeded five millions, which, with many other debts, were thrown into one stock, amounting to nine millions four hundred and seventy-one thousand three hundred and twenty-five pounds. A fund was formed for paying an interest or annuity of six per cent. until the principal should be discharged; and with this was granted a monopoly of a projected trade to the South Sea, vested in the proprietors of navy bills, debentures, and other public securities, which were incorporated for this purpose. Such was the origin of the South Sea Company, founded upon a chimerical supposition that the English would be permitted to trade upon the coast of Peru in the Pacific. Perhaps the new ministry hoped to obtain this permission, as an equivalent for their abandoning the interest of King Charles, with respect to his pretensions upon Spain. By this time the Emperor Joseph had died of the small-pox, without male issue; so that his brother's immediate aim was to succeed him on the imperial throne. This event was, on the twentieth day of April, communicated by a message from the queen to both

Houses. She told them that the States-General had
concurred with her in a resolution to support the House
of Austria; and that they had already taken such measures as would secure the election of Charles as head of
the empire.

Represen-
tation by
the Com-
mons to
the queen.

The House of Commons, in order to demonstrate their
attachment to the church, in consequence of an address
from the Lower House of Convocation, and a quickening
message from the queen, passed a bill for building fifty
new churches in the suburbs of London and Westminster, and appropriated for this purpose the duty upon
coals, which had been granted for the building of St.
Paul's, now finished. This imposition was continued
until it should raise the sum of three hundred and fifty
thousand pounds. At the close of the session, the Commons presented a remonstrance or representation to the
queen, in which they told her, that they had not only
raised the necessary supplies, but also discharged the
heavy debts of which the nation had so long and justly
complained. They said that, in tracing the causes of
this debt, they had discovered fraud, embezzlement, and
misapplication of the public money: that they who of
late years had the management of the treasury were
guilty of notorious breach of trust and injustice to the
nation, in allowing above thirty millions to remain unaccounted for; a purposed omission that looked like a
design to conceal embezzlements. They begged her
majesty would give immediate directions for compelling
the several impressed accountants speedily to pass their
accounts. They expressed their hope that such of the
accountants as had neglected their duty in prosecuting
their accounts ought no longer to be entrusted with the
public money. They affirmed, that from all these evil
practices and worse designs of some persons, who had, by
false professions of love to their country, insinuated themselves into her royal favour, irreparable mischief would
have accrued to the public, had not her majesty, in her
great wisdom, seasonably discovered the fatal tendency
of such measures, and removed from the administration
those who had so ill answered her majesty's favourable
opinion, and in so many instances grossly abused the
trust reposed in them. They observed that her people

could with greater patience have suffered the manifold injuries done to themselves, by the frauds and depredations of such evil ministers, had not the same men proceeded to treat her sacred person with undutifulness and disregard. This representation being circulated through the kingdom, produced the desired effect of inflaming the minds of the people against the late ministry. Such expedients were become necessary for the execution of Oxford's project, which was to put a speedy end to a war that had already subjected the people to grievous oppression, and even accumulated heavy burdens to be transmitted to their posterity. The nation was inspired by extravagant ideas of glory and conquest, even to a rage of war-making; so that the new ministers, in order to dispel those dangerous chimeras, were obliged to take measures for exciting their indignation and contempt against those persons whom they had formerly idolized as their heroes and patriots. On the twelfth day of June, the queen, having given the royal assent to several public and private bills, made an affectionate speech to both Houses. She thanked the Commons, in the warmest expressions, for having complied with all her desires; for having baffled the expectations of her enemies in finding supplies for the service of the ensuing year; in having granted greater sums than were ever given to any prince in one session; and in having settled funds for the payment of the public debts, so that the credit of the nation was restored. She expressed her earnest concern for the succession of the House of Hanover; and her fixed resolution to support and encourage the church of England as by law established. Then the Parliament was prorogued.

Of the Convocation which was assembled with the new Parliament, the Lower House chose Dr. Atterbury their prolocutor. He was an enterprising ecclesiastic, of extensive learning, acute talents, violently attached to tory principles, and intimately connected with the prime minister, Oxford; so that he directed all the proceedings in the Lower House of Convocation in concert with that minister. The queen, in a letter to the archbishop, signified her hope that the consultations of the clergy might be of use to repress the attempts of loose and pro-

Proceedings in the Convocation.

fane persons. She sent a licence under the broad seal, empowering them to sit and do business in as ample a manner as ever had been granted since the Reformation. They were ordered to lay before the queen an account of the extensive growth of infidelity and heresy, as well as of other abuses, that necessary measures might be taken for a reformation. The bishops were purposely slighted and overlooked, because they had lived in harmony with the late ministers. A committee being appointed to draw up a representation of the present state of the church and religion, Atterbury undertook the task, and composed a remonstrance that contained the most keen and severe strictures upon the administration, as it had been exercised since the time of the Revolution. Another was penned by the bishops in more moderate terms; and several regulations were made, but in none of these did the two Houses agree. They concurred, however, in censuring some tenets favouring Arianism, broached and supported by Mr. Whiston, mathematical professor in Cambridge. He had been expelled the university, and wrote a vindication of himself, dedicated to the Convocation. The archbishop doubted whether this assembly could proceed against a man for heresy: the judges were consulted, and the majority of them gave in their opinion that the Convocation had a jurisdiction. Four of them professed the contrary sentiment, which they maintained from the statutes made at the reformation. The queen, in a letter to the bishops, said, that as there was now no doubt of their jurisdiction, she expected they would proceed in the matter before them. Fresh scruples arising, they determined to examine the book, without proceeding against the author, and this was censured accordingly. An extract of the sentence was sent to the queen; but she did not signify her pleasure on the subject, and the affair remained in suspense. Whiston published a work in four volumes, justifying his doctrine, and maintaining that the apostolical constitutions were not only canonical, but also preferable in point of authority to the epistles and the gospels.

The new ministry had not yet determined to supersede the Duke of Marlborough in the command of the army. This was a step which could not be taken with-

The Duke
of Marl-
borough
continues
to com-

out giving umbrage to the Dutch and other allies. He
therefore set out for Holland in the month of February,
after the queen had assured him that he might depend
upon the punctual payment of the forces. Having conferred with the deputies of the states about the operations of the campaign, he, about the middle of April,
assembled the army at Orchies, between Lisle and
Douay; while Mareschal de Villars drew together the
French troops in the neighbourhood of Cambray and
Arras. Louis had by this time depopulated as well as
impoverished his kingdom; yet his subjects still flocked
to his standard with surprising spirit and attachment.
Under the pressure of extreme misery, they uttered not
one complaint of their sovereign, but imputed all their
calamities to the pride and obstinacy of the allies. Exclusive of all the other impositions that were laid upon
that people, they consented to pay the tenth penny of
their whole substance; but all their efforts of loyalty
and affection to their prince would have been ineffectual,
had not the merchants of the kingdom, by the permission of Philip, undertaken repeated voyages to the South
Sea, from whence they brought home immense treasures;
while the allies took no steps for intercepting these supplies, though nothing could have been more easy for the
English than to deprive the enemy of this great resource,
and convert it to their own advantage. Had a squadron
of ships been annually employed for this purpose, the
subjects of France and Spain must have been literally
starved, and Louis obliged to submit to such terms as
the confederates might have thought proper to impose.
Villars had found means to assemble a very numerous
army, with which he encamped behind the river Sanset,
in such an advantageous post as could not be attacked
with any prospect of success. Meanwhile the Duke of
Marlborough passed the Scarpe, and formed his camp
between Douay and Bouchain, where he was joined by
Prince Eugene on the twenty-third day of May. This
general, however, did not long remain in the Netherlands. Understanding that detachments had been made
from the army of Villars to the Rhine, and that the
Elector of Bavaria intended to act in the empire, the
prince, by order from the court of Vienna, marched to-

wards the Upper Rhine with the imperial and Palatine troops, to secure Germany. The Duke óf Marlborough repassing the Scarpe, encamped in the plains of Lens, from whence he advanced towards Aire, as if he had intended to attack the French lines in that quarter. These lines, beginning at Bouchain on the Schelde, were continued along the Sanset and the Scarpe to Arras, and thence along the Upper Scarpe to Canché. They were defended by redoubts and other works in such a manner that Villars judged they were impregnable, and called them the *Ne plus ultrà* of Marlborough.

He surprises the French lines.

This nobleman, advancing within two leagues of the French lines, ordered a great number of fascines to be made, declaring he would attack them the next morning; so that Villars drew all his forces on that side, in full expectation of an engagement. The duke, on the supposition that the passages of the Sanset by Arleux would be left unguarded, had ordered the Generals Cadogan and Hompesch to assemble twenty battalions and seventeen squadrons from Douay and the neighbouring garrisons, to march to Arleux, where they should endeavour to pass the Sanset. Brigadier Sutton was detached with the artillery and pontoons, to lay bridges over the canal near Goulezen, and over the Scarpe at Vitry, while the duke, with the whole confederate army, began his march for the same place about nine in the evening. He proceeded with such expedition, that by five in the morning he passed the river at Vitry. There he received intelligence that Hompesch had taken possession of the passes on the Sanset and Schelde without opposition, the enemy having withdrawn their detachments from that side, just as he had imagined. He himself, with his vanguard of fifty squadrons, hastened his march towards Arleux, and before eight of the clock arrived at Bacá-Bachuel, where in two hours he was joined by the heads of the columns into which he had divided his infantry. Villars being certified of his intention, about two in the morning decamped with his whole army, and putting himself at the head of the king's household troops, marched all night with such expedition, that about eleven in the forenoon he was in sight of the Duke of Marlborough, who had by this time joined Count Hompesch. The French general immediately retreated to the main body of his army, which had advanced to the high road between Arras and Cambray, while the allies encamped upon the Schelde, between Oisy and Estrun, after a march of ten leagues without halting, scarcely to be paralleled in history. By this plan, so happily executed, the Duke of Marlborough fairly outwitted Villars, and, without the loss of one man, entered the lines which he had pronounced impregnable. This stroke of the English general was extolled as a master-piece of military skill, while Villars was exposed to the ridicule even of his own officers. The field deputies of the States-General proposed that he should give battle to the enemy, who passed the Schelde at Crevecœur, in order to cover Bouchain: but the duke would not hazard an engagement, considering how much the army was fatigued by the long march; and that any misfortune, while they continued within the French lines, might be fatal. His intention was to besiege Bouchain; an enterprise that was deemed impracticable, inasmuch as the place was situated in a morass, strongly fortified, and defended by a numerous garrison, in the neighbourhood of an army superior in number to that of the allies. Notwithstanding these disadvantages, and the dissuasions of his own friends, he resolved to undertake the siege; and, in the mean time, despatched Brigadier Sutton to England, with an account of his having passed the French lines; which was not at all agreeable to his enemies. They had prognosticated that nothing would be done during this campaign, and began to insinuate that the duke could strike no stroke of importance without the assistance of Prince Eugene. They now endeavoured to lessen the glory of his success; and even taxed him with having removed his camp from a convenient situation to a place where the troops were in danger of starving. Nothing could be more provoking than this scandalous malevolence to a great man who had done so much honour to his country, and was then actually exposing his life in her service.

On the tenth day of August Bouchain was invested, Reduces and the Duke of Marlborough exerted himself to the Bouchain.

utmost extent of his vigilance and capacity, well knowing the difficulties of the undertaking, and how much
his reputation would depend upon his success. Villars
had taken every precaution that his skill and experience
could suggest, to baffle the endeavours of the English
general. He had reinforced the garrison to the number
of six thousand chosen men, commanded by officers of
known courage and ability. He made some efforts to
raise the siege; but they were rendered ineffectual by
the consummate prudence and activity of the Duke of
Marlborough. Then he laid a scheme for surprising
Douay, which likewise miscarried. If we consider that
the English general, in the execution of his plan, was
obliged to form lines, erect regular forts, raise batteries,
throw bridges over a river, make a causeway through a
deep morass, provide for the security of convoys against
a numerous army on one side, and the garrisons of Condé
and Valenciennes on the other, we must allow this was
the boldest enterprise of the whole war: that it required
all the fortitude, skill, and resolution of a great general,
and all the valour and intrepidity of the confederate
troops, who had scarcely ever exhibited such amazing
proofs of courage upon any other occasion as they now
displayed at the siege of Bouchain. In twenty days
after the trenches were opened, the garrison were obliged to surrender themselves prisoners of war; and this
conquest was the last military exploit performed by the
Duke of Marlborough: the breaches of Bouchain were
no sooner repaired than the opposite armies began to
separate, and the allied forces were quartered in the
frontier towns, that they might be at hand to take the
field early in the spring. They were now in possession
of the Maese, almost as far as the Sambre; of the
Schelde from Tournay; and of the Lys as far as it is
navigable. They had reduced Spanish Guelderland,
Limburg, Brabant, Flanders, and the greatest part of
Hainault: they were masters of the Scarpe; and, by
the conquest of Bouchain, they had opened to themselves a way into the very bowels of France. All these
acquisitions were owing to the valour and conduct of the
Duke of Marlborough, who now returned to the Hague,
and arrived in England about the middle of November.

The queen had conferred the command of her forces in Spain upon the Duke of Argyle, who was recalled from the service in Flanders for that purpose. He had long been at variance with the Duke of Marlborough; a circumstance which recommended him the more strongly to the ministry. He landed at Barcelona on the twenty-ninth of May, and found the British troops in the utmost distress for want of subsistence. The treasurer had promised to supply him liberally; the Commons had granted one million five hundred thousand pounds for that service. All their hopes of success were fixed on the campaign in that kingdom; and indeed the army commanded by the Duke de Vendome was in such a wretched condition, that if Staremberg had been properly supported by the allies, he might have obtained signal advantages. The Duke of Argyle, having waited in vain for the promised remittances, was obliged to borrow money on his own credit before the British troops could take the field. At length Staremberg advanced towards the enemy, who attacked him at the Pass of Prato del Rey, where they were repulsed with considerable damage. After this action the Duke of Argyle was seized with a violent fever, and conveyed back to Barcelona. Vendome invested the castle of Cardona, which was vigorously defended till the end of December, when a detachment being sent to the relief of the place, defeated the besiegers, killed two thousand on the spot, and took all their artillery, ammunition, and baggage. Staremberg was unable to follow the blow: the Duke of Argyle wrote pressing letters to the ministry, and loudly complained that he was altogether unsupported: but all his remonstrances were ineffectual: no remittances arrived; and he returned to England without having been able to attempt any thing of importance. In September, King Charles, leaving his queen at Barcelona, set sail for Italy, and at Milan had an interview with the Duke of Savoy, where all disputes were compromised. That prince had forced his way into Savoy, and penetrated as far as the Rhine; but he suddenly halted in the middle of his career, and after a short campaign repassed the mountains. Prince Eugene, at the head of the German forces, protected the electors

CHAP.
X.

1711.
King
Charles
elected
emperor.

at Frankfort from the designs of the enemy, and Charles was unanimously chosen emperor; the Electors of Cologn and Bavaria having been excluded from voting, because they lay under the ban of the empire. The war between the Ottoman Porte and the Muscovites was of short duration. The czar advanced so far into Moldavia that he was cut off from all supplies, and altogether in the power of his enemy. In this emergency he found means to corrupt the grand vizir in private, while in public he proposed articles of peace that were accepted. The King of Sweden, who was in the Turkish army, charged the vizir with treachery, and that minister was actually disgraced. The grand signor threatened to renew the war; but he was appeased by the czar's surrendering Asoph.

Expedition
to Canada.

The English ministry had conceived great expectations from an expedition against Quebec and Placentia, in North America, planned by Colonel Nicholson, who had taken possession of Nova Scotia, and garrisoned Port Royal, to which he gave the name of Annapolis. He had brought four Indian chiefs to England, and represented the advantages that would redound to the nation in point of commerce, should the French be expelled from North America. The ministers relished the proposal. A body of five thousand men was embarked in transports, under the command of Brigadier Hill, brother to Mrs. Masham; and they sailed from Plymouth in the beginning of May, with a strong squadron of ships, commanded by Sir Hovenden Walker. At Boston, in New England, they were joined by two regiments of provincials; and about four thousand men, consisting of American planters, Palatines, and Indians, rendezvoused at Albany, in order to march by land into Canada, while the fleet sailed up the river of that name. On the twenty-first day of August, they were exposed to a violent storm, and driven among rocks, where eight transports perished, with about eight hundred men. The admiral immediately sailed back to Spanish-river bay, where it was determined in a council of war, that as the fleet and forces were victualled for ten weeks only, and they could not depend upon a supply of provisions from New England, they should return home, without making

any further attempt. Such was the issue of this paltry
expedition, entrusted to the direction of an officer without talents and experience.

In the Irish Parliament held during the summer, the
Duke of Ormond and the majority of the peers supported
the tory interest, while the Commons expressed the
warmest attachment to revolution principles. The two
Houses made strenuous representations, and passed severe
resolutions against each other. After the session, Sir
Constantine Phipps, the chancellor, and General Ingolds-
by, were appointed justices in the absence of the Duke
of Ormond, who returned to England in the month of
November. In Scotland the Jacobites made no scruple
of professing their principles and attachment to the pretender. The Duchess of Gordon presented the faculty
of advocates with a silver medal, representing the Chevalier de St. George; and on the reverse the British
islands, with the motto " *Reddite*." After some debate,
it was voted by a majority of sixty-three voices against
twelve, that the duchess should be thanked for this token
of her regard. This task was performed by Dundas of
Arnistoun, who thanked her grace for having presented
them with a medal of their sovereign lord the king;
hoping, and being confident, that her grace would very
soon have an opportunity to compliment the faculty
with a second medal, struck upon the restoration of the
king and royal family, upon the finishing rebellion, usurp-
ing tyranny, and whiggery. An account of this transaction being laid before the queen, the lord advocate was
ordered to inquire into the particulars. Then the faculty
were so intimidated that they disowned Dundas, and
Horne his accomplice. They pretended that the affair
of the medal had been transacted by a party at an occasional meeting, and not by general consent; and by a
solemn act they declared their attachment to the queen
and the Protestant succession. The court was satisfied
with this atonement: but the resident from Hanover
having presented a memorial to the queen, desiring that
Dundas and his associates might be prosecuted, the
government removed Sir David Dalrymple from his office
of lord advocate, on pretence of his having been too

remiss in prosecuting those delinquents; and no farther inquiry was made into the affair.

1711.
A nego̅ti̅a-
tion set on
foot be-
tween the
courts of
France and
England. For some time a negotiation for peace had been carried on between the court of France and the new ministers, who had a double aim in this measure: namely, to mortify the whigs and the Dutch, whom they detested, and to free their country from a ruinous war, which had all the appearance of becoming habitual to the constitution. They foresaw the risk they would run by entering into such measures, should ever the opposite faction regain the ascendancy: they knew the whigs would employ all their art and influence, which was very powerful, in obstructing the peace, and in raising a popular clamour against the treaty. But their motives for treating were such as prompted them to undervalue all those difficulties and dangers. They hoped to obtain such advantages in point of commerce for the subjects of Great Britain as would silence all detraction. They did not doubt of being able to maintain the superiority which they had acquired in Parliament; and perhaps some of them cherished views in favour of the pretender, whose succession to the crown would have effectually established their dominion over the opposite party. The Earl of Jersey, who acted in concert with Oxford, sent a private message to the court of France, importing the queen's earnest desire of peace, representing the impossibility of a private negotiation, as the ministry was obliged to act with the utmost circumspection, and desiring that Louis would propose to the Dutch a renewal of the conferences, in which case the English plenipotentiaries should have such instructions that it would be impossible for the States-General to prevent the conclusion of the treaty. This intimation was delivered by one Gualtier, an obscure priest, who acted as chaplain to Count Gallas, the imperial ambassador, and had been employed as a spy by the French ministry, since the commencement of hostilities. His connexion with Lord Jersey was by means of that nobleman's lady, who professed the Roman Catholic religion. His message was extremely agreeable to the court of Versailles. He returned to London, with a letter of compliment from the Marquis

de Torcy to the Earl of Jersey, in which that minister
assured him of his master's sincere inclination for peace,
though he was averse to a renewal of the conferences
with the States-General. Gualtier wrote a letter to Versailles, desiring, in the name of the English ministry,
that his most Christian majesty would communicate to
them his proposals for a general peace, which they would
communicate to the States-General, that they might
negotiate in concert with their allies. A general answer
being made to this intimation, Gualtier made a second
journey to Versailles, and brought over a memorial,
which was immediately transmitted to Holland. In the
mean time the pensionary endeavoured to renew the
conferences in Holland. Petkum wrote to the French ministry, that if his majesty would resume the negotiation,
in concert with the Queen of Great Britain, he should
certainly have reason to be satisfied with the conduct of
the Dutch deputies. This proposal Louis declined, at
the desire of the English ministers.

The States-General having perused the memorial,
assured Queen Anne that they were ready to join with
her in contributing to the conclusion of a durable peace;
but they expressed a desire that the French king would
communicate a more particular plan for securing the interests of the allied powers, and for settling the repose of
Europe. Gualtier was once more sent to Versailles,
accompanied by Mr. Prior, who had resided in France as
secretary to the embassies of the Earls of Portland and
Jersey. This gentleman had acquired some reputation
by his poetical talents; was a man of uncommon ability,
insinuating address, and perfectly devoted to the tory
interest. He was empowered to communicate the preliminary demands of the English; to receive the answer
of the French king; and demand whether or not King
Philip had transmitted a power of treating to his grandfather. He arrived incognito at Fontainebleau, and presented the queen's memorial, in which she demanded a
barrier for the Dutch in the Netherlands, and another
on the Rhine for the empire; a security for the Dutch
commerce, and a general satisfaction to all her allies.
She required that the strong places taken from the Duke
of Savoy should be restored; and that he should possess

such towns and districts in Italy as had been ceded to
him in treaties between him and his allies: that Louis
should acknowledge Queen Anne and the Protestant
succession ; demolish the fortifications of Dunkirk; and
agree to a new treaty of commerce; that Gibraltar and
Port Mahon should be yielded to the crown of England:
that the negro trade in America, at that time carried on
by the French, should be ceded to the English, together
with some towns on that continent, where the slaves might
be refreshed. She expected security that her subjects
trading to Spain should enjoy all advantages granted by
that crown to the most favoured nation ; that she should
be put in possession of Newfoundland and Hudson's Bay,
either by way of restitution or cession ; and that both
nations should continue to enjoy whatever territories they
might be possessed of in North America at the ratification of the treaties. She likewise insisted upon a security
that the crowns of France and Spain should never be
united on the same head. Her majesty no longer insisted
upon Philip's being expelled from the throne of Spain by
the arms of his own grandfather. She now perceived
that the exorbitant power of the house of Austria would
be as dangerous to the liberty of Europe, as ever that of
the family of Bourbon had been in the zenith of its glory.
She might have remembered the excessive power, the
insolence, the ambition of Charles V. and Philip II., who
had enslaved so many countries, and embroiled all Europe.
She was sincerely desirous of peace, from motives of
humanity and compassion to her subjects and fellow-
creatures : she was eagerly bent upon procuring such
advantages to her people as would enable them to discharge the heavy load of debt under which they laboured,
and recompense them in some measure for the blood and
treasure they had so lavishly expended in the prosecution
of the war. These were the sentiments of a Christian
princess; of an amiable and pious sovereign, who bore a
share in the grievances of her subjects, and looked upon
them with the eyes of maternal affection. She thought
she had the better title to insist upon those advantages, as
they had been already granted to her subjects in a private
treaty with King Charles.

As Prior's powers were limited in such a manner that he

could not negotiate, Mr. Menager, deputy from the city of Rouen to the board of trade, accompanied the English minister to London, with full power to settle the pre- liminaries of the treaty. On his arrival in London, the queen immediately commissioned the Duke of Shrews-bury, the Earls of Jersey, Dartmouth, Oxford, and Mr. St. John, to treat with him; and the conferences were immediately begun. After long and various disputes, they agreed upon certain preliminary articles, which, on the eighth day of October, were signed by the French minister, and by the two secretaries of state, in consequence of a written order from her majesty. Then Menager was privately introduced to the queen at Windsor. She told him she was averse to war; that she would exert all her power to conclude a speedy peace; that she should be glad to live upon good terms with the King of France, to whom she was so nearly allied in blood : she expressed her hope that there would be a closer union after the peace between them, and between their subjects, cemented by a perfect correspondence and friendship. The Earl of Strafford, who had been lately recalled from the Hague, where he resided as ambassador, was now sent back to Holland, with orders to communicate to the pensionary the proposals of peace which France had made ; to sig-nify the queen's approbation of them, and propose a place where the plenipotentiaries should assemble. The English ministers now engaged in an intimate correspondence with the court of Versailles; and Mareschal Tallard being released from his confinement at Nottingham, was allowed to return to his own country on his parole. After the departure of Menager, the preliminaries were com-municated to Count Gallas, the emperor's minister, who, in order to inflame the minds of the people, caused them to be translated, and inserted in one of the daily papers. This step was so much resented by the queen, that she sent a message, desiring he would come no more to court; but that he might leave the kingdom as soon as he should think proper. He took the hint, and retired accordingly; but the queen gave the emperor to understand that any other minister he should appoint would be admitted by her without hesitation.

The states of Holland, alarmed at the preliminaries,

CHAP.
X.

1711.
The
French
king's pro-
posals dis-
agreeable
to the
allies.

sent over Buys, as envoy-extraordinary, to intercede with the queen that she would alter her resolutions; but she continued steady to her purpose; and the Earl of Strafford demanded the immediate concurrence of the states, declaring in the queen's name that she would look upon any delay, on their part, as a refusal to comply with her propositions. Intimidated by this declaration, they agreed to open the general conferences at Utrecht on the first day of January. They granted passports to the French ministers; while the queen appointed Robinson, Bishop of Bristol, and the Earl of Strafford, her plenipotentiaries at the congress. Charles, the new emperor, being at Milan when he received a copy of the preliminaries, wrote circular letters to the electors and the princes of the empire, exhorting them to persist in their engagements to the grand alliance. He likewise desired the States-General to join counsels with him in persuading the Queen of England to reject the proposals of France, and prosecute the war; or at least to negotiate on the foundation of the first preliminaries, which had been signed by the Marquis de Torcy. He wrote a letter to the same purpose to the Queen of Great Britain, who received it with the most mortifying indifference. No wonder that he should zealously contend for the continuance of a war, the expense of which she and the Dutch had hitherto almost wholly defrayed. The new preliminaries were severely attacked by the whigs, who ridiculed and reviled the ministry in word and writing. Pamphlets, libels, and lampoons were to-day published by one faction, and to-morrow answered by the other. They contained all the insinuations of malice and contempt, all the bitterness of reproach, and all the rancour of recrimination. In the midst of this contention the queen despatched the Earl of Rivers to Hanover, with an assurance to the elector that his succession to the crown should be effectually ascertained in the treaty. The Earl brought back an answer in writing; but, at the same time, his electoral highness ordered Baron de Bothmar, his envoy in England, to present a memorial to the queen, representing the pernicious consequences of Philip's remaining in possession of Spain and the West Indies. This remonstrance the baron published,

by way of appeal to the people, and the whigs extolled
it with the highest encomiums; but the queen and her ministers resented this step as an officious and inflammatory interposition.

The proposals of peace made by the French king were disagreeable even to some individuals of the tory party; and certain peers, who had hitherto adhered to that interest, agreed with the whigs to make a remonstrance against the preliminary articles. The court being apprised of their intention, prorogued the Parliament till the seventh day of December, in expectation of the Scottish peers, who would cast the balance in favour of the ministry. In her speech at the opening of the session, she told them that, notwithstanding the arts of those who delighted in war, the place and time were appointed for a congress; and that the States-General had expressed their entire confidence in her conduct. She declared her chief concern should be to secure the succession of the crown in the house of Hanover; to procure all the advantages to the nation which a tender and affectionate sovereign could procure for a dutiful and loyal people; and to obtain satisfaction for all her allies. She observed, that the most effectual way to procure an advantageous peace would be to make preparations for carrying on the war with vigour. She recommended unanimity, and prayed God would direct their consultations. In the House of Lords, the Earl of Nottingham, who had now associated himself with the whigs, inveighed against the preliminaries as captious and insufficient, and offered a clause to be inserted in the address of thanks, representing to her majesty that, in the opinion of the House, no peace could be safe or honourable to Great Britain or Europe, if Spain and the West Indies should be allotted to any branch of the house of Bourbon. A violent debate ensued, in the course of which the Earl of Anglesey represented the necessity of easing the nation of the burdens incurred by an expensive war. He affirmed that a good peace might have been procured immediately after the battle of Ramillies, if it had not been prevented by some persons who prolonged the war for their own private interest. This insinuation was levelled at the Duke of Marlborough, who made a long

speech in his own vindication. He bowed to the place
where the queen sat incognito; and appealed to her,
whether, while he had the honour to serve her majesty
as general and plenipotentiary, he had not constantly
informed her and her council of all the proposals of
peace which had been made; and had not desired instructions for his conduct on that subject. He declared,
upon his conscience, and in the presence of the Supreme
Being, before whom he expected soon to appear, that he
was ever desirous of a safe, honourable, and lasting
peace; and that he was always very far from entertaining any design of prolonging the war for his own private
advantage, as his enemies had most falsely insinuated.
At last the question being put, whether the Earl of
Nottingham's advice should be part of the address, it
was carried in the affirmative by a small majority. The
address was accordingly presented, and the queen, in
her answer, said, she should be very sorry any one could
think she would not do her utmost to recover Spain and
the West Indies from the house of Bourbon. Against
this advice, however, several peers protested, because
there was no precedent for inserting a clause of advice
in an address of thanks; and because they looked upon
it as an invasion of the royal prerogative. In the address
of the Commons there was no such article; and therefore
the answer they received was warm and cordial.

The Duke
of Hamil-
ton's title
of Duke of
Brandon
disallowed.
Bill against
occasional
conformity
passes.

The Duke of Hamilton claiming a seat in the House
of Peers as Duke of Brandon, a title he had lately received, was opposed by the anti-courtiers, who pretended
to foresee great danger to the constitution from admitting into the House a greater number of Scottish peers
than the act of union allowed. Counsel was heard upon
the validity of his patent. They observed that no objection could be made to the queen's prerogative in con-
ferring honours; and that all the subjects of the united
kingdom were equally capable of receiving honour. The
House of Lords had already decided the matter, in admitting the Duke of Queensberry upon his being created
Duke of Dover. The debate was managed with great
ability on both sides: the Scottish peers united in defence
of the duke's claim; and the court exerted its whole
strength to support the patent. Nevertheless, the ques-

tion being put, whether Scottish peers, created peers of Great Britain since the union, had a right to sit in that House, it was carried in the negative by a majority of five voices, though not without a protest signed by the lords in the opposition. The Scottish peers were so incensed at this decision that they drew up a representation to the queen, complaining of it as an infringement of the union, and a mark of disgrace put upon the whole peerage of Scotland. The bill against occasional conformity was revived by the Earl of Nottingham, in more moderate terms than those that had been formerly rejected; and it passed both Houses by the connivance of the whigs, upon the earl's promise, that if they would consent to this measure, he would bring over many friends to join them in matters of greater consequence. On the twenty-second day of December, the queen being indisposed, granted a commission to the lord keeper, and some other peers, to give the royal assent to this bill, and another for the land-tax. The Duke of Devonshire obtained leave to bring in a bill for giving precedence of all peers to the Electoral Prince of Hanover, as the Duke of Cambridge. An address was presented to the queen, desiring she would give instructions to her plenipotentiaries to consult with the ministers of the allies in Holland before the opening of the congress, that they might concert the necessary measures for proceeding with unanimity, the better to obtain the great ends proposed by her majesty.

The commissioners for examining the public accounts having discovered that the Duke of Marlborough had received an annual present of five or six thousand pounds from the contractors of bread to the army, the queen declared in council that she thought fit to dismiss him from all his employments, that the matter might be impartially examined. This declaration was imparted to him in a letter under her own hand, in which she took occasion to complain of the treatment she had received. She probably alluded to the insolence of his duchess; the subjection in which she had been kept by the late ministry; and the pains lately taken by the whigs to depreciate her conduct, and thwart her measures with respect to the peace. The duke wrote an answer to her *Duke of Marlborough dismissed from all his employments.*

CHAP.
  X.

1711.

majesty, vindicating himself from the charge which had been brought against his character; and his two daughters, the Countess of Sunderland and the Lady Railton, resigned their places of ladies in the bedchamber. The ministry, in order to ascertain a majority in the House of Lords, persuaded the queen to take a measure which nothing but necessity could justify. She created twelve peers at once [a], and on the second of January they were introduced into the Upper House without opposition. The lord keeper delivered to the House a message from the queen, desiring they would adjourn to the fourteenth day of the month. The anti-courtiers alleged that the queen could not send a message to any one House to adjourn, but ought to have directed it to both Houses. This objection produced a debate, which was terminated in favour of the court by the weight of the twelve new peers.

Prince Eugene of Savoy arrives in England.

At this period Prince Eugene arrived in England, with a letter to the queen from the emperor, and instructions to propose a new scheme for prosecuting the war. His errand was far from being agreeable to the ministry; and they suspected that his real aim was to manage intrigues among the discontented party, who opposed the peace. Nevertheless, he was treated with that respect which was due to his quality and eminent talents. The ministers, the nobility, and officers of distinction, visited him at his arrival. He was admitted to an audience of the queen, who received him with great complacency. Having perused the letter which he delivered, she expressed her concern that her health did not permit her to speak with his highness as often as she could wish; but that she had

---

[a] Lord Compton and Lord Bruce, sons of the Earls of Northampton and Aylesbury, were called up by writ to the House of Peers. The other ten were these: Lord Duplin, of the kingdom of Scotland, created Baron Hay of Bedwardin, in the county of Hereford; Lord Viscount Windsor, of Ireland, made Baron Mountjoy, in the Isle of Wight; Henry Paget, son of Lord Paget, created Baron Burton, in the county of Stafford; Sir Thomas Mansel, Baron Mansel, of Margam, in the county of Glamorgan; Sir Thomas Willoughby, Baron Middleton, of Middleton, in the county of Warwick; Sir Thomas Trevor, Baron Trevor, of Bromham, in the county of Bedford; George Granville, Baron Lansdown, of Biddeford, in the county of Devon; Samuel Masham, Baron Masham, of Oats, in the county of Essex; Thomas Foley, Baron Foley, of Kidderminster, in the county of Worcester; and Allen Bathurst, Baron Bathurst, of Bathelsden, in the county of Bedford.—On the first day of their being introduced, when the question was put about adjourning, the Earl of Wharton asked one of them, "Whether they voted by their foreman?"

ordered the treasurer and secretary St. John to receive his proposals, and confer with him as frequently as he should think proper. He expressed extraordinary respect for the Duke of Marlborough, notwithstanding his disgrace. The lord treasurer, while he entertained him at dinner, declared that he looked upon that day as the happiest in the whole course of his life, since he had the honour to see in his house the greatest captain of the age. The prince is said to have replied, "If I am, it is owing to your lordship:" alluding to the disgrace of Marlborough, whom the earl's intrigues had deprived of all military command. When Bishop Burnet conversed with him about the scandalous libels that were every day published against the duke, and in particular mentioned one paragraph, in which the author allowed he had been once fortunate, the prince observed it was the greatest commendation that could be bestowed upon him, as it implied that all his other successes were owing to his courage and conduct. While the nobility of both parties vied with each other in demonstrations of respect for this noble stranger; while he was adored by the whigs, and admired by the people, who gazed at him in crowds when he appeared in public; even in the midst of all these caresses, party riots were excited to insult his person, and some scandalous reflections upon his mother were inserted in one of the public papers. The queen treated him with distinguished marks of regard; and on her birthday presented him with a sword worth five thousand pounds. Nevertheless, she looked upon him as a patron and friend of that turbulent faction to which she owed so much disquiet. She knew he had been pressed to come over by the whig noblemen, who hoped his presence would inflame the people to some desperate attempt upon the new ministry: she was not ignorant that he held private conferences with the Duke of Marlborough, the Earl of Sunderland, the Lords Somers, Halifax, and all the chiefs of that party; and that he entered into a close connexion with the Baron de Bothmar, the Hanoverian envoy, who had been very active in fomenting the disturbances of the people.

Her majesty, who had been for some time afflicted with the gout, sent a message to both Houses, on the seven- Walpole expelled teenth day of January, signifying that the plenipotentiaries were arrived at Utrecht, and that she was employed in making preparations for an early campaign: she hoped, therefore, that the Commons would proceed in giving the necessary despatch to the supplies. The lord-treasurer, in order to demonstrate his attachment to the Protestant succession, brought in a bill which had been proposed by the Duke of Devonshire, giving precedence to the whole electoral family, as children and nephews to the crown; and when it was passed into an act, he sent it over to Hanover by Mr. Thomas Harley. The sixteen peers for Scotland were prevailed upon, by promise of satisfaction, to resume their seats in the Upper House, from which they had absented themselves since the decision against the patent of the Duke of Hamilton; but whatever pecuniary recompense they might have obtained from the court, on which they were meanly dependent, they received no satisfaction from the Parliament. The Commons, finding Mr. Walpole very troublesome in their House, by his talents, activity, and zealous attachment to the whig interest, found means to discover some clandestine practices in which he was concerned as secretary at war, with regard to the forage-contract in Scotland. The contractors, rather than admit into their partnership a person whom he had recommended for that purpose, chose to present his friend with five hundred pounds. Their bill was addressed to Mr. Walpole, who indorsed it, and his friend touched the money [b]. This transaction was interpreted into a bribe. Mr. Walpole was

---

[b] The commissioners appointed for taking, stating, and examining the public accounts, having made their report, touching the conduct of Mr. Walpole, the House, after a long debate, came to the following resolutions: 1. That Robert Walpole, Esq., a member of this House, in receiving the sum of five hundred guineas, and in taking a note for five hundred more, on account of two contracts for forage of her majesty's troops quartered in North Britain, made by him when secretary at war, pursuant to a power granted to him by the late lord treasurer, is guilty of a high breach of trust and notorious corruption. 2. That the said Robert Walpole, Esq., be for the said offence committed prisoner to the Tower of London, during the pleasure of this House, and that Mr. Speaker do issue his warrant accordingly. 3. That the said Robert Walpole, Esq., be for the said offence also expelled the House, and that the report of the commissioners of public accounts be taken into further consideration this day se'nnight. It appeared from the depositions of witnesses, that the public had been defrauded considerably by these contracts: a very severe speech was made in the House, and next day published, reflecting upon Mr. Walpole, as guilty of the worst kind of corruption; and Sir Peter King declared in the House, that he deserved hanging, as well as he deserved imprisonment and expulsion.

voted guilty of corruption, imprisoned in the Tower, and expelled the House. Being afterwards re-chosen by the same borough of Lynn-Regis, which he had before re- presented, a petition was lodged against him, and the Commons voted him incapable of being elected a member to serve in the present Parliament.

Their next attack was upon the Duke of Marlborough, Votes who was found to have received a yearly sum from Sir against Solomon Medina, a Jew, concerned in the contract for of Marl- furnishing the army with bread; to have been gratified borough. by the queen with ten thousand pounds a year to defray the expense of intelligence; and to have pocketed a deduction of two and a half per cent. from the pay of the foreign troops maintained by England. It was alleged, in his justification, that the present from the Jews was a customary perquisite, which had always been enjoyed by the general of the Dutch army: that the deduction of two and a half per cent. was granted to him by an express warrant from her majesty: that all the articles of the charge joined together did not exceed thirty thousand pounds, a sum much inferior to that which had been allowed to King William for contingencies: that the money was expended in procuring intelligence, which was so exact, that the duke was never surprised; that none of his parties were ever intercepted or cut off; and all the designs were by these means so well concerted, that he never once miscarried. Notwithstanding these representations, the majority voted that his practices had been unwarrantable and illegal; and that the deduction was to be accounted for as public money. These resolutions were communicated to the queen, who ordered the attorney-general to prosecute the duke for the money he had deducted by virtue of her own warrant. Such practices were certainly mean and mercenary, and greatly tarnished the glory which the duke had acquired by his military talents, and other shining qualities.

The Commons now directed the stream of their re- Resolutions sentment against the Dutch, who had certainly exerted against the all their endeavours to overwhelm the new ministry, and treaty and retard the negotiations for peace. They maintained an the Dutch. intimate correspondence with the whigs of England. They diffused the most invidious reports against Oxford and Secretary St. John. Buys, their envoy at London, acted the part of an incendiary, in suggesting violent measures to the malecontents, and caballing against the government. The ministers, by way of reprisal, influenced the House of Commons to pass some acrimonious resolutions against the States-General. They alleged that the states had been deficient in their proportion of troops, both in Spain and in the Netherlands, during the whole course of the war; and that the queen had paid above three millions of crowns in subsidies, above what she was obliged to advance by her engagements. They attacked the barrier-treaty, which had been concluded with the states by Lord Townshend, after the conferences at Gertruydenberg. By this agreement, England guaranteed a barrier in the Netherlands to the Dutch, and the states bound themselves to maintain, with their whole force, the queen's title and the Protestant succession. The tories affirmed that England was disgraced by engaging any other state to defend a succession which the nation might see cause to alter: that, by this treaty, the states were authorized to interpose in British counsels: that, being possessed of all those strong towns, they might exclude the English from trading to them, and interfere with the manufactures of Great Britain. The House of Commons voted, that in the barrier-treaty there were several articles destructive to the trade and interest of Great Britain, and therefore highly dishonourable to her majesty: that the Lord Viscount Townshend was not authorized to conclude several articles in that treaty: that he and all those who had advised its being ratified were enemies to the queen and kingdom. All their votes were digested into a long representation presented to the queen, in which they averred that England, during the war, had been overcharged nineteen millions; a circumstance that implied mismanagement or fraud in the old ministry. The states, alarmed at these resolutions, wrote a respectful letter to the queen, representing the necessity of a barrier, for the mutual security of England and the United Provinces. They afterwards drew up a large memorial in vindication of their proceedings during the war; and it was published in one of the English papers.

The Commons immediately voted it a false, scandalous, and malicious libel, reflecting upon the resolutions of the House; and the printer and publisher were taken into custody, as guilty of a breach of privilege.

They now repealed the naturalization act. They passed a bill granting a toleration to the episcopal clergy in Scotland, without paying the least regard to a representation from the General Assembly to the queen, declaring that the act for securing the presbyterian government was an essential and fundamental condition of the treaty of union. The House, notwithstanding this remonstrance, proceeded with the bill, and inserted a clause prohibiting civil magistrates from executing the sentences of the kirk judicatories. The episcopal, as well as the presbyterian clergy, were required to take the oaths of abjuration, that they might be upon an equal footing in case of disobedience; for the Commons well knew that this condition would be rejected by both from very different motives. In order to exasperate the presbyterians with further provocations, another act was passed for discontinuing the courts of judicature during the Christmas holidays, which had never been kept by persons of that persuasion. When this bill was read for the third time, Sir David Dalrymple said, "Since the House is resolved to make no toleration on the body of this bill, I acquiesce; and only desire it may be entitled, A bill for establishing Jacobitism and Immorality." The chagrin of the Scottish presbyterians was completed by a third bill, restoring the right of patronage, which had been taken away when the discipline of the kirk was last established. Prince Eugene having presented a memorial to the queen, touching the conduct of the emperor during the war, and containing a proposal with relation to the affairs of Spain, the queen communicated the scheme to the House of Commons, who treated it with the most contemptuous neglect. The prince, finding all his efforts ineffectual, retired to the continent, as much displeased with the ministry as he had reason to be satisfied with the people of England. The commons having settled the funds for the supplies of the year, amounting to six millions, the treasurer formed the plan of a bill appointing commissioners to examine

CHAP.
X.
1711.

Acts unfavourable to the presbyterian discipline in Scotland.

Burnet.
Boyer.
Lamberty.
Quincy.
Rousset.
Torcy.
Tindal.
History of the Duke of Marlborough.
Mil. Hist.
Voltaire.

the value and consideration of all the grants made since the Revolution. His design was to make a general resumption; but as the interest of so many noblemen was concerned, the bill met with a very warm opposition; notwithstanding which it would have certainly passed, had not the Duke of Buckingham and the Earl of Strafford absented themselves from the House during the debate.

CHAPTER XI.

In the month of January the conferences for peace began at Utrecht. The Earl of Jersey would have been appointed the plenipotentiary for England, but he dying after the correspondence with the court of France was

CHAP.
XI.

1712.

CHAP.
XI.

1712.
The con-
ferences
opened at
Utrecht.

established, the queen conferred that charge upon Robinson, Bishop of Bristol, lord privy seal, and the Earl
of Strafford. The chief of the Dutch deputies named
for the congress were Buys and Vanderdussen; the
French king granted his powers to the Mareschal
D'Uxelles, the Abbot (afterwards Cardinal) de Polignac,
and Menager, who had been in England. The ministers of the emperor and Savoy likewise assisted at the
conferences, to which the empire and the other allies
likewise sent their plenipotentiaries, though not without reluctance. As all these powers, except France,
entertained sentiments very different from those of her
Britannic majesty, the conferences seemed calculated
rather to retard than accelerate a pacification. The
Queen of England had foreseen and provided against
these difficulties. Her great end was to free her subjects from the miseries attending an unprofitable war,
and to restore peace to Europe; and this aim she was
resolved to accomplish in spite of all opposition. She
had also determined to procure reasonable terms of accommodation for her allies, without, however, continuing to lavish the blood and treasure of her people in
supporting their extravagant demands. The emperor
obstinately insisted upon his claim to the whole Spanish
monarchy, refusing to give up the least tittle of his pretensions; and the Dutch adhered to the old preliminaries which Lewis had formerly rejected. The queen
saw that the liberties of Europe would be exposed to
much greater danger from an actual union of the imperial and Spanish crowns in one head of the house of
Austria, than from a bare possibility of Spain's being
united with France in one branch of the house of
Bourbon. She knew by experience the difficulty of de-
throning Philip, rooted as he was in the affections of a
brave and loyal people; and that a prosecution of this
design would serve no purpose but to protract the war,
and augment the grievances of the British nation. She
was well acquainted with the distresses of the French,
which she considered as pledges of their monarch's sincerity. She sought not the total ruin of that people,
already reduced to the brink of despair. The dictates
of true policy dissuaded her from contributing to her fur-

ther conquest in that kingdom, which would have proved the source of contention among the allies, depressed the house of Bourbon below the standard of importance which the balance of Europe required it should maintain, and aggrandize the States-General at the expense of Great Britain. As she had borne the chief burden of the war, she had a right to take the lead, and dictate a plan of pacification; at least she had a right to consult the welfare of her own kingdom, in delivering, by a separate peace, her subjects from those enormous loads which they could no longer sustain; and she was well enough aware of her own consequence to think she could not obtain advantageous conditions.

Such were the sentiments of the queen; and her ministers seem to have acted on the same principles, though perhaps party motives may have helped to influence their conduct. The allies concurred in opposing with all their might any treaty which could not gratify their different views of avarice, interest, and ambition. They practised a thousand little artifices to intimidate the queen, to excite a jealousy of Louis, to blacken the characters of her ministers, to raise and keep up a dangerous ferment among her people, by which her life and government were endangered. She could not fail to resent these efforts, which greatly perplexed her measures, and obstructed her design. Her ministers were sensible of the dangerous predicament in which they stood. The queen's health was much impaired; and the successor countenanced the opposite faction. In case of their sovereign's death, they had nothing to expect but prosecution and ruin for obeying her commands; they saw no hope of safety, except in renouncing their principles, and submitting to their adversaries; or else in taking such measures as would hasten the pacification, that the troubles of the kingdom might be appeased, and the people be satisfied with their conduct, before death should deprive them of their sovereign's protection. With this view they advised her to set on foot a private negotiation with Louis; to stipulate certain advantages for her own subjects in a concerted plan of peace; to enter into such mutual confidence with that monarch, as would anticipate all clandestine transactions to her prejudice,

The queen's measures obstructed by the allies.

and in some measure enable her to prescribe terms for her allies. The plan was judiciously formed, but executed with too much precipitation. The stipulated advantages were not such as she had a right to demand and insist upon; and without all doubt better might have been obtained, had not the obstinacy of the allies abroad, and the violent conduct of the whig faction at home, obliged the ministers to relax in some material points, and hasten the conclusion of the treaty.

The death of the dauphin and his son.

The articles being privately regulated between the two courts of London and Versailles, the English plenipotentiaries at Utrecht were furnished with general powers and instructions, being ignorant of the agreement which the queen had made with the French monarch touching the kingdom of Spain, which was indeed the basis of the treaty. This secret plan of negotiation, however, had well nigh been destroyed by some unforeseen events that were doubly afflicting to Louis. The dauphin had died of the small-pox in the course of the preceding year, and his title had been conferred upon his son, the Duke of Burgundy, who now expired on the last day of February, six days after the death of his wife, Mary Adelaide of Savoy. The parents were soon followed to the grave by their eldest offspring, the Duke of Bretagne, in the sixth year of his age; so that of the Duke of Burgundy's children none remained alive but the Duke of Anjou, the late French king, who was at that time a sickly infant. Such a series of calamities could not fail of being extremely shocking to Louis in his old age; but they were still more alarming to the Queen of England, who saw that nothing but the precarious life of an unhealthy child divided the two monarchies of France and Spain, the union of which she resolved by all possible means to prevent. She therefore sent the Abbé Gualtier to Paris, with a memorial, representing the danger to which the liberty of Europe would be exposed, should Philip ascend the throne of France; and demanding that his title should be transferred to his brother, the Duke of Berry, in consequence of his pure, simple, and voluntary renunciation.

The queen demands Philip's re-

Meanwhile the French plenipotentiaries at Utrecht were prevailed upon to deliver their proposals in writing

under the name of specific offers, which the allies re- CHAP.
XI.
1712.
nunciation
of the
crown of
France.
ceived with indignation. They were treated in England with universal scorn. Lord Halifax, in the House
of Peers, termed them trifling, arrogant, and injurious to
her majesty and her allies. An address was presented
to the queen, in which they expressed their resentment
against the insolence of France, and promised to assist
her with all their power in prosecuting the war, until a
safe and honourable peace should be obtained. The
plenipotentiaries of the allies were not less extravagant
in their specific demands than the French had been arrogant in their offers. In a word, the ministers seemed to
have been assembled at Utrecht, rather to start new
difficulties, and widen the breach, than to heal animosities, and concert a plan of pacification. They amused
one another with fruitless conferences, while the Queen
of Great Britain endeavoured to engage the States-
General in her measures, that they might treat with
France upon moderate terms, and give law to the rest
of the allies. She departed from some of her own pretensions, in order to gratify them with the possession of
some towns in Flanders. She consented to their being
admitted into a participation of some advantages in commerce; and ordered the English ministers at the congress to tell them that she would take her measures according to the return they should make on this occasion.
Finding them still obstinately attached to their first
chimerical preliminaries, she gave them to understand
that all her offers for adjusting the differences were
founded upon the express condition that they should
come in to her measures, and co-operate with her openly
and sincerely; but they had made such bad returns to
all her condescension towards them, that she looked upon
herself as released from all engagements. The ministers
of the allies had insisted upon a written answer to their
specific demands; and this the French plenipotentiaries
declined, until they should receive fresh instructions from
their master. Such was the pretence for suspending the
conferences; but the real bar to a final agreement between England and France was the delay of Philip's
renunciation, which at length, however, arrived, and produced a cessation of arms.

CHAP.
XI.

1712.
The Duke
of Ormond
takes the
command
of the Bri-
tish forces
in Flan-
ders.
In the mean time the Duke of Ormond, who was now invested with the supreme command of the British forces, received a particular order that he should not hazard an engagement. Louis had already undertaken for the compliance of his grandson. Reflecting on his own great age, he was shocked at the prospect of leaving his kingdom involved in a pernicious war during a minority, and determined to procure a peace at all events. The queen, knowing his motives, could not help believing his protestations, and resolved to avoid a battle, the issue of which might have considerably altered the situation of affairs, and consequently retarded the conclusion of the treaty. Preparations had been made for an early campaign. In the beginning of March, the Earl of Albemarle, having assembled a body of thirty-six battalions, marched towards Arras, which he reduced to a heap of ashes by a most terrible cannonading and bombardment. In May, the Duke of Ormond conferred with the deputies of the States-General at the Hague, and assured them that he had orders to act vigorously in the prosecution of the war. He joined Prince Eugene at Tournay; and, on the twenty-sixth day of May, the allied army, passing the Scheldt, encamped at Haspre and Solemnes. The imperial general proposed that they should attack the French army under Villars; but by this time the Duke was restrained from hazarding a siege or battle; a circumstance well known to the French commander, who therefore abated of his usual vigilance. It could not be long concealed from Prince Eugene and the deputies, who forthwith despatched an express to their principals on this subject, and afterwards presented a long memorial to the duke, representing the injury which the grand alliance would sustain from his obedience to such an order. He seemed to be extremely uneasy at his situation; and in a letter to Secretary St. John, expressed a desire that the queen would permit him to return to England.

Prince Eugene, notwithstanding the queen's order, which Ormond had not yet formally declared, invested the town of Quesnoy, and the duke furnished towards this enterprise seven battalions and nine squadrons of the foreign troops maintained by Great Britain. The Dutch deputies at Utrecht expostulating with the Bishop of Bristol upon the duke's refusing to act against the enemy, that prelate told them, that he had lately received an express, with a letter from her majesty, in which she complained, that as the States-General had not properly answered her advances, they ought not to be surprised, if she thought herself at liberty to enter into separate measures, in order to obtain a peace for her own conveniency. When they remonstrated against such conduct as contradictory to all the alliances subsisting between the queen and the States-General, the bishop declared his instructions further imported that, considering the conduct of the states towards her majesty, she thought herself disengaged from all alliances and engagements with their high mightinesses. The states and the ministers of the allies were instantly in commotion. Private measures were concerted with the Elector of Hanover, the Landgrave of Hesse-Cassel, and some other princes of the empire, concerning the troops belonging to those powers in the pay of Great Britain. The States-General wrote a long letter to the queen, and ordered their envoy at London to deliver it into her own hand. Count Zinzendorf, the emperor's plenipotentiary, despatched expresses to his master, to Prince Eugene, and to the imperial ambassador at London. The queen held a council at Kensington upon the subject of the letter; and a fresh order was sent to the Duke of Ormond, directing him to concur with the general of the allies in a siege.

On the twenty-eighth day of May, Lord Halifax, in Debate in the House of Peers, descanted upon the ill consequences of the duke's refusing to co-operate with Prince Eugene, this subject. and moved for an address, desiring her majesty would order the general to act offensively, in concert with her allies. The treasurer observed, it was prudent to avoid a battle on the eve of a peace, especially considering they had to do with an enemy so apt to break his word. The Earl of Wharton replied, this was a strong reason for keeping no measures with such an enemy. When Oxford declared, that the Duke of Ormond had received orders to join the allies in a siege, the Duke of Marlborough affirmed it was impossible to carry on a siege without either hazarding a battle, in case the enemy should attempt to relieve the place, or shamefully abandoning the enterprise. The Duke of Argyle having declared his opinion, that since the time of Julius Cæsar there had not been a greater captain than Prince Eugene of Savoy, observed that, considering the different interests of the House of Austria and of Great Britain, it might not consist with prudence to trust him with the management of the war, because a battle won or lost might entirely break off a negotiation of peace, which in all probability was near being concluded. He added, that two years before the confederates might have taken Arras and Cambray, instead of amusing themselves with the insignificant conquests of Aire, Bethune, and St. Venant. The Duke of Devonshire said he was, by proximity of blood, more concerned than any other in the reputation of the Duke of Ormond; and, therefore, could not help expressing his surprise, that any one would dare to make a nobleman of the first rank, and of so distinguished a character, the instrument of such proceedings. Earl Paulet answered, that nobody could doubt the Duke of Ormond's courage; but he was not like a certain general, who led troops to the slaughter, to cause a great number of officers to be knocked on the head, that he might fill his pockets by disposing of their commissions. The Duke of Marlborough was so deeply affected by this reflection, that though he suppressed his resentment in the House, he took the first opportunity to send Lord Mohun to the earl with a message, importing that he should be glad to come to an explanation with his lordship about some expressions he had used in that day's debate, and desiring his company to take the air in the country. The earl understood his meaning; but could not conceal his emotion from the observation of his lady, by whose means the affair was communicated to the Earl of Dartmouth, secretary of state. Two sentinels were immediately placed at his lordship's gate: the queen, by the channel of Lord Dartmouth, desired the Duke of Marlborough would proceed no farther in the quarrel; and he assured her he would punctually obey her majesty's commands. The Earl of Oxford assured the House that a separate peace was never intended; that such a peace would be so base, so knavish, and so villainous, that every one who served the queen knew they must answer it with their heads to the nation; but that it would appear to be a safe and glorious peace, much more to the honour and interest of the nation than the first preliminaries insisted upon by the allies. The question being put for adjourning, was, after a long debate, carried in the affirmative; but twenty lords entered a protest. The Earl of Strafford, who had returned from Holland, proposed that they should examine the negotiations of the Hague and Gertruydenberg before they considered that of Utrecht. He observed, that in the former negotiations the French ministers had conferred only with the pensionary, who communicated no more of it to the ministers of the allies than what was judged proper to let them know; so that the Dutch were absolute masters of the secret. He asserted that the States-General had consented to give Naples and Sicily to King Philip; a circumstance which proved that the recovery of the whole Spanish monarchy was looked upon as impracticable. He concluded with a motion for an address to her majesty, desiring that the papers relating to the negotiations of the Hague and Gertruydenberg should be laid before the House. This was carried without a division.

In the House of Commons, Mr. Pulteney moved for an address, acquainting her majesty that her faithful Commons were justly alarmed at the intelligence received from abroad, that her general in Flanders had declined acting offensively against France in concurrence with her allies; and beseeching her majesty, that he might receive speedy instructions to prosecute the war with the utmost vigour. This motion was rejected by a great majority. A certain member having insinuated, that the present negotiation had been carried on in a clandestine and treacherous manner, Mr. Secretary St. John said, he hoped it would not be accounted treachery to act for the good and advantage of Great Britain; that he gloried in the small share he had in the transaction; and whatever censure he might undergo for it, the bare satisfaction of acting in that view would be a sufficient recompense and comfort to him during the whole course of his life. The

A loyal address of the Commons.

House resolved that the Commons had an entire confidence in her majesty's promise to communicate to her Parliament the terms of the peace before it should be concluded; and that they would support her against all such persons, either at home or abroad, as should endeavour to obstruct the pacification. The queen thanked them heartily for this resolution, as being dutiful to her, honest to their country, and very seasonable at a time when so many artifices were used to obstruct a good peace, or to force one disadvantageous to Britain. They likewise presented an address, desiring they might have an account of the negotiations and transactions at the Hague and Gertruydenberg, and know who were then employed as her majesty's plenipotentiaries.

Philip promises to renounce the crown of France.

The ministry foreseeing that Philip would not willingly resign his hopes of succeeding to the crown of France, proposed an alternative, that, in case of his preferring his expectation of the crown of France to the present possession of Spain, this kingdom, with the Indies, should be forthwith ceded to the Duke of Savoy; that Philip, in the mean time, should possess the duke's hereditary dominions, and the kingdom of Sicily, together with Montserrat and Mantua; all which territories should be annexed to France at Philip's succession to that crown, except Sicily, which should revert to the house of Austria. Louis seemed to relish this expedient, which, however, was rejected by Philip, who chose to make the renunciation rather than quit the throne upon which he was established. The queen demanded, that the renunciation should be ratified in the most solemn manner by the states of France; but she afterwards waved this demand, in consideration of its being registered in the different Parliaments. Such forms are but slender securities against the power, ambition, and interest of princes. The marquis de Torcy frankly owned, that Philip's renunciation was of itself void, as being contrary to the fundamental laws and constitution of the French monarchy; but it was found necessary for the satisfaction of the English people. Every material article being now adjusted between the two courts, particularly those relating to the King of Spain, the commerce of Great Britain, and the

delivery of Dunkirk, a suspension of arms prevailed in
the Netherlands, and the Duke of Ormond acted in concert with Mareschal de Villars.

On the sixth day of June, the queen, going to the
House of Peers, communicated the plan of peace to her
Parliament, according to the promise she had made.
After having premised, that the making of peace and
war was the undoubted prerogative of the crown, and
hinted at the difficulties which had arisen both from the
nature of the affair, and numberless obstructions contrived by the enemies of peace, she proceeded to enumerate the chief articles to which both crowns had agreed,
without, however, concluding the treaty. She told them
she had secured the Protestant succession, which France
had acknowledged in the strongest terms; and that the
pretender would be removed from the French dominions:
that the Duke of Anjou should renounce for himself and
his descendants all claim to the crown of France; so that
the two monarchies would be for ever divided. She
observed, that the nature of this proposal was such as
would execute itself: that it would be the interest of
Spain to support the renunciation; and in France, the
persons entitled to the succession of that crown upon the
death of the dauphin were powerful enough to vindicate
their own right. She gave them to understand that a
treaty of commerce between England and France had
been begun, though not yet adjusted; but provision was
made, that England should enjoy the same privileges that
France granted to the most favoured nation: that the
French king had agreed to make an absolute cession of
the island of St. Christopher's, which had hitherto been
divided between the two nations: that he had also consented to restore the whole bay and straits of Hudson;
to deliver the island of Newfoundland, with Placentia;
to cede Annapolis, with the rest of Acadia or Nova
Scotia; to demolish the fortifications of Dunkirk; to leave
England in possession of Gibraltar, Port Mahon, and the
whole island of Minorca; to let the trade of Spain in the
West Indies be settled as it was in the reign of his late
Catholic majesty: she signified that she had obtained for
her subjects the assiento, or contract for furnishing the
Spanish West Indies with negroes, for the term of thirty

years, in the same manner as it had been enjoyed by the French. With respect to the allies, she declared, that France offered to make the Rhine the barrier of the empire; to yield Brisac, Fort Kehl, and Landau, and raze all the fortresses both on the other side of the Rhine and in the islands of that river: that the Protestant interest in Germany would be resettled on the footing of the treaty of Westphalia: that the Spanish Netherlands, the kingdoms of Naples and Sardinia, the duchy of Milan, and the places belonging to Spain on the coast of Tuscany might be yielded to his imperial majesty; but the disposition of Sicily was not yet determined: that the demands of the States-General with relation to commerce, and the barrier in the Low Countries, would be granted with a few exceptions, which might be compensated by other expedients: that no great progress had yet been made upon the pretensions of Portugal; but that those of Prussia would be admitted by France without much difficulty: that the difference between the barrier demanded by the Duke of Savoy in the year one thousand seven hundred and nine, and that which France now offered, was very inconsiderable: that the Elector Palatine should maintain his present rank among the electors; and that France would acknowledge the electoral dignity in the house of Hanover. Such were the conditions which the queen hoped would make some amends to her subjects for the great and unequal burden they had borne during the whole course of the war. She concluded with saying, she made no doubt but they were fully persuaded that nothing would be neglected on her part, in the progress of this negotiation, to bring the peace to a happy and speedy issue; and she expressed her dependence upon the entire confidence and cheerful concurrence of her Parliament.

Exceptions
taken to
some of the
articles in
the House
of Lords.
An address of thanks and approbation was immediately voted, drawn up, and presented to the queen by the Commons in a body. When the House of Lords took the speech into consideration, the Duke of Marlborough asserted, that the measures pursued for a year past were directly contrary to her majesty's engagements with the allies: that they sullied the triumphs and glories of her reign, and would render the English

name odious to all nations. The Earl of Strafford said, that some of the allies would not have shown such backwardness to a peace, had they not been persuaded and encouraged to carry on the war by a member of that illustrious assembly, who maintained a secret correspondence with them, and fed them with hopes that they would be supported by a strong party in England. In answer to this insinuation against Marlborough, Lord Cowper observed, that it could never be suggested as a crime in the meanest subject, much less in any member of that august assembly, to hold correspondence with the allies of the nation; such allies, especially, whose interest her majesty had declared to be inseparable from her own, in her speech at the opening of the session; whereas it would be a hard matter to justify and reconcile, either with our laws, or with the laws of honour and justice, the conduct of some persons, in treating clandestinely with the common enemy, without the participation of the allies. This was a frivolous argument. A correspondence with any person whatsoever becomes criminal, when it tends to foment the divisions of one's country, and arm the people against their sovereign. If England had it not in her power, without infringing the laws of justice and honour, to withdraw herself from a confederacy which she could no longer support, and treat for peace on her own bottom, then was she not an associate but a slave to the alliance. The Earl of Godolphin affirmed, that the trade to Spain was such a trifle as deserved no consideration; and that it would continually diminish, until it should be entirely engrossed by the French merchants. Notwithstanding these remonstrances against the plan of peace, the majority agreed to an address, in which they thanked the queen for her extraordinary condescension in communicating those conditions to her Parliament; and expressed an entire satisfaction with her conduct. A motion was made for a clause in the address, desiring her majesty would take such measures, in concert with her allies, as might induce them to join with her in a mutual guarantee. A debate ensued: the question was put, and the clause rejected. Several noblemen entered a pro-

1712.
A motion
for the
guarantee
of the
Protestant
succession
by the allies
rejected
in the
House of
Commons.

test, which was expunged from the journals of the House by the decision of the majority.

In the House of Commons, a complaint was exhibited against Bishop Fleetwood, who, in a preface to four sermons which he had published, took occasion to extol the last ministry, at the expense of the present administration. This piece was voted malicious and factious, tending to create discord and sedition among her majesty's subjects, and condemned to be burned by the hands of the common hangman. They presented an address to the queen, assuring her of the just sense they had of the indignity offered to her, by printing and publishing a letter from the States-General to her majesty; and desiring she would so far resent such insults as to give no answer for the future to any letters or memorials that should be thus ushered into the world, as inflammatory appeals to the public. Mr. Hambden moved for an address to her majesty, that she would give particular instructions to her plenipotentiaries, that, in the conclusion of the treaty of peace, the several powers in alliance with her majesty might be guarantees for the Protestant succession in the illustrious house of Hanover. The question being put was carried in the negative. Then the House resolved, that they had such confidence in the repeated declarations her majesty had made of her concern for assuring to these kingdoms the Protestant succession as by law established, that they could never doubt of her taking the proper measures for the security thereof; that the House would support her against faction at home and her enemies abroad; and did humbly beseech her, that she would be pleased to discountenance all those who should endeavour to raise jealousies between her majesty and her subjects, especially by misrepresenting her good intentions for the welfare of her people. The queen was extremely pleased with this resolution. When it was presented, she told them that they had shown themselves honest asserters of the monarchy, zealous defenders of the constitution, and real friends to the Protestant succession. She thought she had very little reason to countenance a compliment of supererogation to a prince who had caballed with the enemies of her administration. On the twenty-first day of June the queen closed the session with a speech, expressing her satisfaction at the addresses and supplies she had received: she observed that, should the treaty be broke off, their burdens would be at least continued, if not increased; that Britain would lose the present opportunity of improving her own commerce, and establishing a real balance of power in Europe; and that though some of the allies might be gainers by a continuance of the war, the rest would suffer in the common calamity. Notwithstanding the ferment of the people, which was now risen to a very dangerous pitch, addresses, approving the queen's conduct, were presented by the city of London and all the corporations in the kingdom that espoused the tory interest. At this juncture the nation was so wholly possessed by the spirit of party, that no appearance of neutrality or moderation remained.

During these transactions the trenches were opened before Quesnoy, and the siege carried on with uncommon vigour, under cover of the forces commanded by the Duke of Ormond. This nobleman, however, having received a copy of the articles signed by the Marquis de Torcy, and fresh instructions from the queen, signified to Prince Eugene and the Dutch deputies that the French king had agreed to several articles demanded by the queen, as the foundation of an armistice; and, among others, to put the English troops in immediate possession of Dunkirk; that he could therefore no longer cover the siege of Quesnoy, as he was obliged by his instructions to march with the British troops, and those in the queen's pay, and declare a suspension of arms as soon as he should be possessed of Dunkirk. He expressed his hope that they would readily acquiesce in these instructions, seeing their concurrence would act as the most powerful motive to induce the queen to take all possible care of their interests at the congress; and he endeavoured to demonstrate that Dunkirk, as a cautionary town, was a place of greater consequence to the allies than Quesnoy. The deputies desired he would delay his march five days, that they might have time to consult their principals, and he granted three days with-

CHAP. XI.

1712.

The Duke of Ormond declares to Prince Eugene that he can no longer cover the siege of Quesnoy.

out hesitation. Prince Eugene observed, that his marching off with the British troops, and the foreigners in the queen's pay, would leave the allies at the mercy of the enemy; but he hoped these last would not obey the duke's order. He and the deputies had already tampered with their commanding officers, who absolutely refused to obey the Duke of Ormond, alleging that they could not separate from the confederacy without express directions from their masters, to whom they had despatched couriers. An extraordinary assembly of the states was immediately summoned to meet at the Hague. The ministers of the allies were invited to the conferences. At length, the princes whose troops were in the pay of Britain assured them, that they would maintain them under the command of Prince Eugene for one month at their own expense, and afterwards sustain half the charge, provided the other half should be defrayed by the emperor and the States-General.

Irruption into France by General Grovestein. The Bishop of Bristol imparted to the other plenipotentiaries at Utrecht the concessions which France would make to the allies; and proposed a suspension of arms for two months, that they might treat in a friendly manner, and adjust the demands of all the confederates. To this proposal they made no other answer, but that they had no instructions on the subject. Count Zinzendorf, the first imperial plenipotentiary, presented a memorial to the States-General, explaining the danger that would result to the common cause from a cessation of arms; and exhorting them to persevere in their generous and vigorous resolutions. He proposed a renewal of the alliance for recovering the Spanish monarchy to the house of Austria, and a certain plan for prosecuting the war with redoubled ardour. Prince Eugene, in order to dazzle the confederates with some bold enterprise, detached Major-General Grovestein, with fifteen hundred cavalry, to penetrate into the heart of France. This officer, about the middle of June, advanced into Champagne, passed the Noire, the Maese, the Moselle, and the Saar, and retired to Traerbach with a rich booty, and a great number of hostages, after having extorted contributions as far as the gates of Metz, ravaged the country, and reduced a great number of villages and towns to ashes.

The consternation produced by this irruption reached the city of Paris: the King of France did not think himself safe at Versailles with his ordinary guards: all the troops in the neighbourhood of the capital were assembled about the palace. Villars sent a detachment after Grovestein, as soon as he understood his destination; but the other had gained a day's march of the French troops, which had the mortification to follow him so close that they found the flames still burning in the villages he had destroyed. By way of retaliation, Major-General Pasteur, a French partisan, made an excursion beyond Bergen-op-zoom, and ravaged the island of Tortola belonging to Zealand.

The Earl of Strafford having returned to Holland, proposed a cessation of arms to the States-General, by whom it was rejected. Then he proceeded to the army of the Duke of Ormond, where he arrived in a few days after the reduction of Quesnoy, the garrison of which were made prisoners of war on the fourth day of July. The officers of the foreign troops had a second time refused to obey a written order of the duke; and such a spirit of animosity began to prevail between the English and allies, that it was absolutely necessary to effect a speedy separation. Prince Eugene resolved to undertake the siege of Landrecy: a design is said to have been formed by the German generals to confine the duke, on pretence of the arrears that were due to them; and to disarm the British troops, lest they should join the French army. In the mean time a literary correspondence was maintained between the English General and the Mareschal de Villars. France having consented to deliver up Dunkirk, a body of troops was transported from England, under the command of Brigadier Hill, who took possession of the place on the seventh day of July: the French garrison retired to Winoxberg. On the sixteenth of the same month, Prince Eugene marched from his camp at Haspre, and was followed by all the auxiliaries in the British pay, except a few battalions of the troops of Holstein-Gottorp, and Walef's regiment of dragoons, belonging to the state of Liege.

Landrecy was immediately invested; while the Duke of Ormond, with the English forces, removed from

Château Cambresis, and encamping at Avensne-le-Secq, proclaimed by sound of trumpet a cessation of arms for two months. On the same day the like armistice was declared in the French army. The Dutch were so exasperated at the secession of the English troops, that the governors would not allow the Earl of Strafford to enter Bouchain, nor the British army to pass through Douay, though in that town they had left a great quantity of stores together with their general hospital. Prince Eugene and the Dutch deputies, understanding that the Duke of Ormond had begun his march towards Ghent, began to be in pain for that city, and sent Count Nassau Woodenburgh to him with a written apology, condemning and disavowing the conduct and commandants of Bouchain and Douay; but, notwithstanding these excuses, the English troops afterwards met with the same treatment at Tournay, Oudenarde, and Lisle: insults which were resented by the whole British nation. The Duke, however, pursued his march, and took possession of Ghent and Bruges for the Queen of England: then he reinforced the garrison of Dunkirk, which he likewise supplied with artillery and ammunition. His conduct was no less agreeable to his sovereign than mortifying to the Dutch, who never dreamed of leaving Ghent and Bruges in the hands of the English, and were now fairly outwitted and anticipated by the motions and expedition of the British general.

The loss of the British forces was soon severely felt in the allied army. Villars attacked a separate body of their troops encamped at Denain, under the command of the Earl of Albemarle. Their intrenchments were forced, and seventeen battalions either killed or taken. The earl himself and all the surviving officers were made prisoners. Five hundred waggons loaded with bread, twelve pieces of brass cannon, a large quantity of ammunition and provisions, a great number of horses, and a considerable booty, fell into the hands of the enemy: this advantage they gained in sight of Prince Eugene, who advanced on the other side of the Scheldt to sustain Albemarle; but the bridge over that river was broken down by accident, so that he was prevented from lending the least assistance. Villars immediately invested Merchiennes, where the principal stores of the allies were lodged. The place was surrendered on the last day of July; and the garrison, consisting of five thousand men, were conducted prisoners to Valenciennes. He afterwards undertook the siege of Douay; an enterprise, in consequence of which Prince Eugene abandoned his design on Landrecy, and marched towards the French, in order to hazard an engagement. The states, however, would not run the risk; and the prince had the mortification to see Douay reduced by the enemy. He could not even prevent their retaking Quesnoy and Bouchain, of which places they were in possession before the tenth day of October. The allies enjoyed no other compensation for their great losses but the conquest of Fort Knocque, which was surprised by one of their partisans.

CHAP. XI. 1712.

The British ministers at the congress continued to press the Dutch and other allies to join in the armistice; but they were deaf to the proposal, and concerted measures for a vigorous prosecution of the war. Then the Earl of Strafford insisted upon their admitting to the congress the plenipotentiaries of King Philip; but he found them equally averse to this expedient. In the beginning of August, Secretary St. John, now created Lord Viscount Bolingbroke, was sent to the court of Versailles incognito, to remove all obstructions to the treaty between England and France. He was accompanied by Mr. Prior, and the Abbé Gualtier, treated with the most distinguished marks of respect, caressed by the French king and the Marquis de Torcy, with whom he adjusted the principal interests of the Duke of Savoy and the Elector of Bavaria. He settled the time and manner of the renunciation, and agreed to a suspension of arms by sea and land for four months between the crowns of France and England: this was accordingly proclaimed at Paris and London. The negotiation being finished in a few days, Bolingbroke returned to England, and Prior remained as resident at the court of France. The States-General breathed nothing but war: the Pensionary Heinsius pronounced an oration in their assembly, representing the impossibility of concluding a peace without losing the fruits of all the blood and treasure they had expended. The conferences at Utrecht were

Progress of the conferences at Utrecht.

interrupted by a quarrel between the domestics of Menager and those of the Count de Rechteren, one of the
Dutch plenipotentiaries. The populace insulted the Earl
of Strafford and the Marquis del Borgo, minister of
Savoy, whose master was reported to have agreed to the
armistice. These obstructions being removed, the conferences were renewed, and the British plenipotentiaries
exerted all their rhetoric, both in public and private, to
engage the allies in the queen's measures. At length
the Duke of Savoy was prevailed upon to acquiesce in
the offers of France. Mr. Thomas Harley had been sent
ambassador to Hanover, with a view to persuade the
elector that it would be for his interest to co-operate
with her majesty: but that prince's resolution was
already taken. "Whenever it shall please God (said
he) to call me to the throne of Britain, I hope to act as
becomes me for the advantage of my people; in the
mean time, speak to me as to a German prince, and a
prince of the empire." Nor was she more successful in
her endeavours to bring over the King of Prussia to her
sentiments. In the mean time, Lord Lexington was
appointed ambassador to Madrid, where King Philip
solemnly swore to observe the renunciation, which was
approved and confirmed by the Cortez. The like renunciation to the crown of Spain was afterwards made by
the princes of France; and Philip was declared incapable of succeeding to the crown of that realm. The court
of Portugal held out against the remonstrances of England, until the Marquis de Bay invaded that kingdom at
the head of twenty thousand men, and undertook the
siege of Campo-Major, and they found they had no
longer any hope of being assisted by her Britannic
majesty. The Portuguese minister at Utrecht signed
the suspension of arms on the seventh day of November,
and excused this step to the allies as the pure effect of
necessity. The English troops in Spain were ordered to
separate from the army of Count Staremberg, and march
to the neighbourhood of Barcelona, where they were
embarked on board an English squadron commanded by
Sir John Jennings, and transported to Minorca.

The Duke
of Hamil-
ton and

The campaign being at an end in the Netherlands,
the Duke of Ormond returned to England, where the

party disputes were become more violent than ever. The
whigs affected to celebrate the anniversary of the late
king's birth-day, in London, with extraordinary rejoicings. Mobs were hired by both factions; and the whole
city was filled with riot and uproar. A ridiculous scheme
was contrived to frighten the lord treasurer with some
squibs in a bandbox, which the ministers magnified into
a conspiracy. The Duke of Hamilton having been appointed ambassador extraordinary to the court of France,
the whigs were alarmed on the supposition that this
nobleman favoured the pretender. Some dispute arising
between the duke and Lord Mohun, on the subject of a
lawsuit, furnished a pretence for a quarrel. Mohun,
who had been twice tried for murder, and was counted
a mean tool, as well as the hector of the whig party, sent
a message by General Macartney to the duke, challeng-
ing him to single combat. The principals met by appointment in Hyde-Park, attended by Macartney and
Colonel Hamilton. They fought with such fury that
Mohun was killed upon the spot, and the duke expired
before he could be conveyed to his own house. Macartney disappeared, and escaped in disguise to the continent. Colonel Hamilton declared upon oath before
the privy council, that when the principals engaged, he
and Macartney followed their example; that Macartney
was immediately disarmed; but the colonel seeing the
duke fall upon his antagonist, threw away the swords,
and ran to lift him up: that while he was employed in
raising the duke, Macartney, having taken up one of the
swords, stabbed his grace over Hamilton's shoulder, and
retired immediately. A proclamation was issued, promising a reward of five hundred pounds to those who
should apprehend or discover Macartney; and the Duchess of Hamilton offered three hundred pounds for the
same purpose. The tories exclaimed against this event
as a party duel: they treated Macartney as a cowardly
assassin; and affirmed that the whigs had posted others
of the same stamp all round Hyde-Park to murder the
Duke of Hamilton, in case he had triumphed over his
antagonist, and escaped the treachery of Macartney.
The whigs on the other hand affirmed, that it was altogether a private quarrel: that Macartney was entirely

innocent of the perfidy laid to his charge: that he afterwards submitted to a fair trial, at which Colonel Hamilton prevaricated in giving his evidence, and was contradicted by the testimony of divers persons who saw the combat at a distance. The Duke of Marlborough hearing himself accused as the author of those party mischiefs, and seeing his enemies grow every day more and more implacable, thought proper to retire to the continent, where he was followed by his duchess. His friend Godolphin had died in September, with the general character of an able, cool, dispassionate minister, who had rendered himself necessary to four successive sovereigns, and managed the finances with equal skill and integrity. The Duke of Shrewsbury was nominated ambassador to France, in the room of the Duke of Hamilton: the Duke d'Aumont arrived at London in the same quality from the court of Versailles; and about the same time the queen granted an audience to the Marquis de Monteleone, whom Philip had appointed one of his plenipotentiaries at the congress.

The States-General sign the barrier treaty.

In vain had the British ministers in Holland endeavoured to overcome the obstinacy of the States-General, by alternate threats, promises, and arguments. In vain did they represent that the confederacy against France could be no longer supported with any prospect of success: that the queen's aim had been to procure reasonable terms for her allies; but that their opposition to her measures prevented her from obtaining such conditions as she would have a right to demand in their favour, were they unanimous in their consultations. In November, the Earl of Strafford presented a new plan of peace, in which the queen promised to insist upon France's ceding to the states the city of Tournay, and some other places which they could not expect to possess, should she conclude a separate treaty. They now began to waver in their councils. The first transports of their resentment having subsided, they plainly perceived that the continuation of the war would entail upon them a burden which they could not bear, especially since the Duke of Savoy and the King of Portugal had deserted the alliance: besides, they were staggered by the affair of the new barrier, so much more advantageous

than that which France had proposed in the beginning
of the conferences. They were influenced by another
motive, namely, the apprehension of new mischiefs to the
empire from the King of Sweden, whose affairs seemed
to take a favourable turn at the Ottoman Porte, through
the intercession of the French monarch. The czar and
King Augustus had penetrated into Pomerania: the King
of Denmark had taken Staden, reduced Bremen, and laid
Hamburgh under contribution; but Count Steenbock,
the Swedish general, defeated the Danish army in Mecklenburgh, ravaged Holstein with great barbarity, and reduced the town of Altona to ashes. The grand signor
threatened to declare war against the czar, on pretence
that he had not performed some essential articles of the
late peace; but his real motive was an inclination to
support the King of Sweden. This disposition, however,
was defeated by a powerful party at the Porte, who were
averse to war. Charles, who still remained at Bender,
was desired to return to his own kingdom, and given to
understand that the sultan would procure him a safe
passage. He treated the person who brought this intimation with the most outrageous insolence; rejected
the proposal, fortified his house, and resolved to defend
himself to the last extremity. Being attacked by a considerable body of Turkish forces, he and his attendants
fought with the most frantic valour. They slew some
hundreds of the assailants; but at last the Turks set fire
to the house; so that he was obliged to surrender himself and his followers, who were generally sold for slaves.
He himself was conveyed under a strong guard to
Adrianople. Meanwhile the czar landed with an army
in Finland, which he totally reduced. Steenbock maintained himself in Tonningen until all his supplies were
cut off, and then he was obliged to deliver himself and
his troops prisoners of war. But this reverse was not
foreseen when the Dutch dreaded a rupture between
the Porte and the Muscovites, and were given to understand that the Turks would revive the troubles in Hungary. In that case, they knew the emperor would recall
great part of his troops from the Netherlands, where the
burden of the war must lie upon their shoulders. After
various consultations in their different assemblies, they

CHAP.
XI.

came in to the queen's measures, and signed the barrier treaty.

1712.
The other
allies be-
come more
tractable.

Then the plenipotentiaries of the four associated circles presented a remonstrance to the British ministers at Utrecht, imploring the queen's interposition in their favour, that they might not be left in the miserable condition to which they had been reduced by former treaties. They were given to understand, that if they should not obtain what they desired, they themselves would be justly blamed as the authors of their own disappointment: that they had been deficient in furnishing their proportion of troops and other necessaries; and left the whole burden of the war to fall upon the queen and the states in the Netherlands: that when a cessation was judged necessary, they had deserted her majesty to follow the chimerical projects of Prince Eugene; that while she prosecuted the war with the utmost vigour, they had acted with coldness and indifference; but when she inclined to peace, they began to exert themselves in prosecuting hostilities with uncommon eagerness; that, nevertheless, she would not abandon their interests, but endeavour to procure for them as good conditions as their preposterous conduct would allow her to demand. Even the emperor's plenipotentiaries began to talk in more moderate terms. Zinzendorf declared that his master was very well disposed to promote a general peace, and no longer insisted on a cession of the Spanish monarchy to the house of Austria. Philip's ministers, together with those of Bavaria and Cologn, were admitted to the congress: and now the plenipotentiaries of Britain acted as mediators for the rest of the allies.

The peace
with
France
signed at
Utrecht.

The pacification between France and England was retarded, however, by some unforeseen difficulties that arose in adjusting the commerce and the limits of the countries possessed by both nations in North America. A long dispute ensued; and the Duke of Shrewsbury and Prior held many conferences with the French ministry: at length it was compromised, though not much to the advantage of Great Britain; and the English plenipotentiaries received an order to sign a separate treaty. They declared to the ministers of the other powers, that they and some other plenipotentiaries were ready to sign their

respective treaties on the eleventh day of April. Count
Zinzendorf endeavoured to postpone this transaction until
he should be furnished with fresh instructions from
Vienna; and even threatened that if the states should
sign the peace contrary to his desire, the emperor would
immediately withdraw his troops from the Netherlands.
The ministers of Great Britain agreed with those of
France, that his imperial majesty should have time to
consider whether he would or would not accept the proposals: but this time was extended no farther than the
first day of June; nor would they agree to a cessation
of arms during that interval. Meanwhile the peace with
France was signed in different treaties by the plenipotentiaries of Great Britain, Savoy, Prussia, Portugal, and
the States-General. On the fourteenth day of the month
the British plenipotentiaries delivered to Count Zinzendorf, in writing, " Offers and demands of the French king
for making peace with the house of Austria and the
empire." The count and the ministers of the German
princes exclaimed against the insolence of France, which
had not even bestowed the title of Emperor on Joseph;
but wanted to impose terms upon them, with relation
to the Electors of Cologn and Bavaria.

The treaties of peace and commerce between England
and France being ratified by the Queen of England, the
Parliament was assembled on the ninth day of April.
The queen told them the treaty was signed, and that in
a few days the ratifications would be exchanged. She
said, what she had done for the Protestant succession,
and the perfect friendship subsisting between her and
the house of Hanover, would convince those who wished
well to both, and desired the quiet and safety of their
country, how vain all attempts were to divide them.
She left it entirely to the House of Commons to determine what force might be necessary for the security of
trade by sea, and for guards and garrisons. " Make
yourselves safe (said she) and I shall be satisfied. Next
to the protection of the Divine Providence, I depend
upon the loyalty and affection of my people. I want no
other guarantee." She recommended to their protection
those brave men who had exposed their lives in the service of their country, and could not be employed in time

CHAP.
XI.

1712.
Burnet.
Boyer.
Hare.
Lamberty.
Quincy.
Rousset.
Torcy.
Bolingbr.
Voltaire.
Tindal.
Mil. Hist.
History of
the Duke
of Marl-
borough.

1713.
Both
Houses of
Parliament
congratu-
lat the
queen on
the peace.

CHAP.
XI.

1713.

of peace. She desired they would concert proper measures for easing the foreign trade of the kingdom, for
improving and encouraging manufactures and the fishery,
and for employing the hands of idle people. She expressed her displeasure at the scandalous and seditious
libels which had been lately published. She exhorted
them to consider of new laws to prevent this licentiousness, as well as for putting a stop to the impious practice
of duelling. She conjured them to use their utmost endeavours to calm the minds of men at home, that the
arts of peace might be cultivated ; and that groundless
jealousies, contrived by a faction, and fomented by party
rage, might not effect that which their foreign enemies
could not accomplish. This was the language of a pious,
candid, and benevolent sovereign, who loved her subjects
with a truly parental affection. The Parliament considered her in that light. Each House presented her
with a warm address of thanks and congratulation, expressing, in particular, their inviolable attachment to the
Protestant succession in the illustrious house of Hanover.
The ratifications of the treaty being exchanged, the peace
was proclaimed on the fifth of May, with the usual cere-
monies, to the inexpressible joy of the nation in general.
It was about this period that the Chevalier de St. George
conveyed a printed remonstrance to the ministers at
Utrecht, solemnly protesting against all that might be
stipulated to his prejudice. The Commons, in a second
address, had besought her majesty to communicate to the
House in due time the treaties of peace and commerce
with France; and now they were produced by Mr. Benson,
chancellor of the exchequer.

Substance of the treaty with France.

By the treaty of peace the French king obliged himself
to abandon the pretender, and acknowledge the queen's
title and the Protestant succession; to raze the fortifications of Dunkirk within a limited time, on condition
of receiving an equivalent; to cede Newfoundland, Hudson's Bay, and St. Christopher's to England; but the
French were left in possession of Cape Breton, and at
liberty to dry their fish in Newfoundland. By the treaty
of commerce a free trade was established, according to
the tariff of the year one thousand six hundred and sixty-
four, except in some commodities that were subjected to

new regulations in the year sixteen hundred and ninety-nine. It was agreed, that no other duties should be imposed on the productions of France imported into England, than those that were laid on the same commodities from other countries; and, that commissioners should meet at London, to adjust all matters relating to commerce; as for the tariff with Spain, it was not yet finished. It was stipulated, that the emperor should possess the kingdom of Naples, the duchy of Milan, and the Spanish Netherlands: that the Duke of Savoy should enjoy Sicily, with the title of king: that the same title, with the island of Sardinia, should be allotted to the Elector of Bavaria, as an indemnification for his losses: that the States-General should restore Lisle and its dependencies: that Namur, Charleroy, Luxembourg, Ypres, and Newport should be added to the other places they already possessed in Flanders; and that the King of Prussia should have Upper Gueldre, in lieu of Orange and the other states belonging to that family in Franche-Comté. The King of Portugal was satisfied; and the first day of June was fixed as the period of time granted to the emperor for consideration.

A day being appointed by the Commons to deliberate upon the treaty of commerce, very just and weighty objections were made to the eighth and ninth articles, importing that Great Britain and France should mutually enjoy all the privileges in trading with each other that either granted to the most favoured nation; and that no higher customs should be exacted from the commodities of France, than those that were drawn from the same productions of any other people. The balance of trade having long inclined to the side of France, severe duties had been laid on all the productions and manufactures of that kingdom, so as almost to amount to a total prohibition. Some members observed that, by the treaty between England and Portugal, the duties charged upon the wines of that country were lower than those laid upon the wines of France; that should they now be reduced to an equality, the difference of freight was so great, that the French wines would be found much cheaper than those of Portugal; and, as they were more agreeable to the taste of the

Objections to the treaty of commerce.

nation in general, there would be no market for the
Portuguese wines in England: that should this be the
case, the English would lose their trade with Portugal,
the most advantageous of any traffic which they now
carried on; for it consumed a great quantity of their
manufactures, and returned a yearly sum of six hundred
thousand pounds in gold. Mr. Nathaniel Gould, formerly governor of the bank, affirmed, that as France
had, since the Revolution, encouraged woollen manufactures, and prepared at home several commodities
which formerly they drew from England; so the English
had learned to make silk stuffs, paper, and all manner
of toys, formerly imported from France: by which means
an infinite number of artificers were employed, and a
vast sum annually saved to the nation: but these people
would now be reduced to beggary, and that money lost
again to the kingdom, should French commodities of the
same kind be imported under ordinary duties, because
labour was much cheaper in France than in England,
consequently the British manufactures would be undersold and ruined. He urged, that the ruin of the silk
manufacture would be attended with another disadvantage. Great quantities of woollen cloths were vended
in Italy and Turkey, in consequence of the raw silk
which the English merchants bought up in those countries; and, should the silk manufacture at home be lost,
those markets for British commodities would fail of
course. Others alleged, that if the articles of commerce
had been settled before the English troops separated
from those of the confederates, the French king would
not have presumed to insist upon such terms, but have
been glad to comply with more moderate conditions. Sir
William Wyndham reflected on the late ministry for
having neglected to make an advantageous peace when
it was in their power. He said that Portugal would
always have occasion for the woollen manufactures and
the corn of England, and be obliged to buy them at all
events. After a violent debate, the House resolved, by
a great majority, that a bill should be brought in to make
good the eighth and ninth articles of the treaty of commerce with France. Against these articles, however,
the Portuguese minister presented a memorial, declaring

that, should the duties on French wines be lowered to the same level with those that were laid on the wines of Portugal, his master would renew the prohibition of the woollen manufactures, and other products of Great Britain. Indeed, all the trading part of the nation exclaimed against the treaty of commerce, which seems to have been concluded in a hurry, before the ministers fully understood the nature of the subject. This precipitation was owing to the fears that their endeavours after peace would miscarry, from the intrigues of the whig faction, and the obstinate opposition of the confederates.

The Commons having granted an aid of two shillings in the pound, proceeded to renew the duty on malt for another year, and extended this tax to the whole island, notwithstanding the warm remonstrances of the Scottish members, who represented it as a burden which their country could not bear. They insisted upon an express article of the union, stipulating, that no duty should be laid on the malt in Scotland during the war, which they affirmed was not yet finished, inasmuch as the peace with Spain had not been proclaimed. During the adjournment of the Parliament, on account of the Whitsun-holidays, the Scots of both Houses, laying aside all party distinctions, met and deliberated on this subject. They deputed the Duke of Argyle, the Earl of Mar, Mr. Lockhart, and Mr. Cockburn, to lay their grievances before the queen. They represented, that their countrymen bore with impatience the violation of some articles of the union; and that the imposition of such an insupportable burden as the malt-tax would, in all probability, prompt them to declare the union dissolved. The queen, alarmed at this remonstrance, answered, that she wished they might not have cause to repent of such a precipitate resolution; but she would endeavour to make all things easy. On the first day of June, the Earl of Findlater, in the House of Peers, represented that the Scottish nation was aggrieved in many instances: that they were deprived of a privy council, and subjected to the English laws in cases of treason: that their nobles were rendered incapable of being created British peers: and that now they were oppressed with the insupportable

burden of a malt-tax, when they had reason to expect
they should reap the benefit of peace : he therefore
moved, that leave might be given to bring in a bill for
dissolving the union, and securing the Protestant succession to the house of Hanover. Lord North and Grey
affirmed, that the complaints of the Scots were groundless ; that the dissolution of the union was impracticable ;
and he made some sarcastic reflections on the poverty of
that nation. He was answered by the Earl of Eglinton,
who admitted the Scots were poor, and therefore unable
to pay the malt-tax. The Earl of Ilay, among other
pertinent remarks upon the union, observed that when
the treaty was made, the Scots took it for granted that
the Parliament of Great Britain would never load them
with any imposition that they had reason to believe
grievous. The Earl of Peterborough compared the
union to a marriage. He said, that though England,
who must be supposed the husband, might in some instances prove unkind to the lady, she ought not immediately to sue for a divorce, the rather because she had
very much mended her fortune by the match. Ilay
replied, that marriage was an ordinance of God, and the
union no more than a political expedient. The other
affirmed, that the contract could not have been more
solemn, unless, like the ten commandments, it had come
from heaven : he inveighed against the Scots, as a people
that would never be satisfied : that would have all the
advantages resulting from the union, but would pay
nothing by their good will, although they had received
more money from England than the amount of all their
estates. To these animadversions the Duke of Argyle
made a very warm reply. "I have been reflected on
by some people (said he) as if I was disgusted, and had
changed sides : but I despise their persons as much as
I undervalue their judgment." He urged, that the malt-
tax in Scotland was like taxing land by the acre throughout England, because land was worth five pounds an acre
in the neighbourhood of London, and would not fetch so
many shillings in the remote counties. In like manner,
the English malt was valued at four times the price of
that which was made in Scotland : therefore the tax in
this country must be levied by a regiment of dragoons.

He owned he had a great share in making the union, with a view to secure the Protestant succession; but he was now satisfied this end might be answered as effectually if the union was dissolved; and, if this step should not be taken, he did not expect long to have either property left in Scotland, or liberty in England. All the whig members voted for the dissolution of that treaty which they had so eagerly promoted; while the tories strenuously supported the measure against which they had once argued with such vehemence. In the course of the debate, the lord treasurer observed, that although the malt-tax was imposed, it might be afterwards remitted by the crown. The Earl of Sunderland expressed surprise at hearing that noble lord broach a doctrine which tended to establish a despotic dispensing power, and arbitrary government. Oxford replied, his family had never been famous, as some others had been, for promoting and advising arbitrary measures. Sunderland, considering this expression as a sarcasm levelled at the memory of his father, took occasion to vindicate his conduct, adding, that in those days the other lord's family was hardly known. Much violent altercation was discharged. At length the motion for the bill was rejected by a small majority, and the malt bill afterwards passed with great difficulty.

Another bill being brought into the House of Commons for rendering the treaty of commerce effectual, such a number of petitions were delivered against it, and so many solid arguments advanced by the merchants who were examined on the subject, that even a great number of tory members were convinced of the bad consequence it would produce to trade, and voted against the ministry on this occasion; so that the bill was rejected by a majority of nine voices. At the same time, however, the House agreed to an address, thanking her majesty for the great care she had taken of the security and honour of her kingdoms in the treaty of peace; as also for having laid so good a foundation for the interest of her people in trade. They likewise besought her to appoint commissioners to treat with those of France, for adjusting such matters as should be necessary to be settled on the subject of commerce, that the treaty might be explained and perfected for the good and welfare of her people. The queen interpreted this address into a full approbation of the treaties of peace and commerce, and thanked them accordingly in the warmest terms of satisfaction and acknowledgment. The Commons afterwards desired to know what equivalent should be given for the demolition of Dunkirk; and she gave them to understand that this was already in the hands of his most Christian majesty: then they besought her, that she would not evacuate the towns of Flanders that were in her possession, until those who were entitled to the sovereignty of the Spanish Netherlands should agree to such articles for regulating trade as might place the subjects of Great Britain upon an equal footing with those of any other nation. The queen made a favourable answer to all their remonstrances. Such were the steps taken by the Parliament during this session with relation to the famous treaty of Utrecht, against which the whigs exclaimed so violently, that many well-meaning people believed it would be attended with the immediate ruin of the kingdom; yet, under the shadow of this very treaty, Great Britain enjoyed a long term of peace and tranquillity. Bishop Burnet was heated with an enthusiastic terror of the house of Bourbon. He declared to the queen in private, that any treaty by which Spain and the West Indies were left in the hands of King Philip must in a little time deliver all Europe into the hands of France: that, if any such peace was made, the queen was betrayed, and the people ruined: that in less than three years she would be murdered, and the fires would blaze again in Smithfield. This prelate lived to see his prognostic disappointed; therefore he might have suppressed this anecdote of his own conduct.

Violence of parties in England.

On the twenty-fifth day of June, the queen signified, in a message to the House of Commons, that her civil list was burdened with some debts incurred by several articles of extraordinary expense; and that she hoped they would empower her to raise such a sum of money upon the funds for that provision as would be sufficient to discharge the incumbrances, which amounted to five hundred thousand pounds. A bill was immediately prepared for raising this sum on the civil-list revenue, and

passed through both Houses with some difficulty. Both
Lords and Commons addressed the queen concerning the Chevalier de St. George, who had repaired to Lorraine. They desired she would press the duke of that name, and all the princes and states in amity with her, to exclude from their dominions the pretender to the imperial crown of Great Britain. A public thanksgiving for the peace was appointed, and celebrated with great solemnity; and on the sixteenth day of July the queen closed the session with a speech which was not at all agreeable to the violent whigs, because it did not contain one word about the pretender and the Protestant succession. From these omissions they concluded that the dictates of natural affection had biassed her in favour of the Chevalier de St. George. Whatever sentiments of tenderness and compassion she might feel for that unfortunate exile, the acknowledged son of her own father, it does not appear that she ever entertained a thought of altering the succession as by law established. The term of Sacheverel's suspension being expired, extraordinary rejoicings were made upon the occasion. He was desired to preach before the House of Commons, who thanked him for his sermon; and the queen promoted him to the rich benefice of St. Andrew's, Holborn. On the other hand, the Duke d'Aumont, ambassador from France, was insulted by the populace. Scurrilous ballads were published against him, both in the English and French languages. He received divers anonymous letters, containing threats of setting fire to his house, which was accordingly burned to the ground, though whether by accident or design he could not well determine. The magistracy of Dunkirk, having sent a deputation with an address to the queen, humbly imploring her majesty to spare the port and harbour of that town, and representing that they might be useful to her own subjects, the memorial was printed and dispersed, and the arguments it contained were answered and refuted by Addison, Steele, and Maynwaring. Commissioners were sent to see the fortifications of Dunkirk demolished. They were accordingly razed to the ground; the harbour was filled up; and the Duke d'Aumont returned to Paris in the month of November. The queen, by her remonstrances to the court of Versailles,

had procured the enlargement of one hundred and thirty-six Protestants from the galleys: understanding afterwards that as many more were detained on the same account, she made such application to the French ministry that they too were released. Then she appointed General Ross her envoy extraordinary to the King of France.

Proceedings of the Parliament of Ireland.

The Duke of Shrewsbury being nominated lord lieutenant of Ireland, assembled the Parliament of that kingdom on the twenty-fifth day of November, and found the two Houses still at variance, on the opposite principles of whig and tory. Allen Broderick being chosen speaker of the Commons, they ordered a bill to be brought in to attaint the pretender and all his adherents. They prosecuted Edward Lloyd for publishing a book entitled "Memoirs of the Chevalier de St. George;" and they agreed upon an address to the queen, to remove from the chancellorship Sir Constantine Phipps, who had countenanced the tories of that kingdom. The Lords, however, resolved, that Chancellor Phipps had, in his several stations, acquitted himself with honour and integrity. The two Houses of Convocation presented an address to the same purpose. They likewise complained of Mr. Molesworth for having insulted them, by saying, when they appeared in the castle of Dublin, "They that have turned the world upside down are come hither also;" and he was removed from the privy council. The Duke of Shrewsbury received orders to prorogue this Parliament, which was divided against itself, and portended nothing but domestic broils. Then he obtained leave to return to England, leaving Chancellor Phipps, with the Archbishops of Armagh and Tuam, justices of the kingdom.

New Parliament in England. Writers employed by both parties.

The Parliament of England had been dissolved; and the elections were managed in such a manner as to retain the legislative power in the hands of the tories; but the meeting of the new Parliament was delayed, by repeated prorogations, to the tenth day of December; a delay partly owing to the queen's indisposition, and partly to the contests among her ministers. Oxford and Bolingbroke were competitors for power, and rivals in reputation for ability. The treasurer's parts were deemed the more solid, the secretary's more shining; but both ministers

were aspiring and ambitious. The first was bent upon
maintaining the first rank in the administration, which
he had possessed since the revolution in the ministry;
the other disdained to act as a subaltern to the man whom
he thought he excelled in genius and equalled in importance. They began to form separate cabals, and adopt
different principles. Bolingbroke insinuated himself into
the confidence of Lady Masham, to whom Oxford had
given some cause of disgust. By this communication he
gained ground in the good opinion of his sovereign, while
the treasurer lost it in the same proportion. Thus she,
who had been the author of his elevation, was now used
as the instrument of his disgrace. The queen was sensibly affected with these dissensions, which she interposed
her advice and authority, by turns, to appease; but their
mutual animosity continued to rankle under an exterior
accommodation. The interest of Bolingbroke was powerfully supported by Sir Simon Harcourt, the chancellor,
Sir William Wyndham, and Mr. Secretary Bromley.
Oxford perceived his own influence was on the wane, and
began to think· of retirement. Meanwhile the Earl of
Peterborough was appointed ambassador to the King of
Sicily, and set out for Turin. The queen retired to
Windsor, where she was seized with a very dangerous
inflammatory fever. The hopes of the Jacobites visibly
rose : the public funds immediately fell : a great run was
made upon the bank, the directors of which were overwhelmed with consternation, which was not a little increased by the report of an armament equipped in the
ports of France. They sent one of their members to
represent to the treasurer the danger that threatened
the public credit. The queen being made acquainted
with these occurrences, signed a letter to Sir Samuel
Stancer, lord mayor of London, declaring that, now she
was recovered of her late indisposition, she would return
to the place of her usual residence, and open the Parliament on the sixteenth day of February. This intimation
she sent to her loving subjects of the city of London, to
the intent that all of them, in their several stations,
might discountenance those malicious rumours, spread
by evil-minded persons, to the prejudice of credit, and
the imminent hazard of the public peace and tranquillity.

CHAP. XI.

1713.

The queen's recovery, together with certain intelligence that the armament was a phantom, and the pretender still in Lorraine, helped to assuage the ferment of the nation, which had been industriously raised by party writings. Mr. Richard Steele published a performance, entitled "The Crisis," in defence of the Revolution and the Protestant establishment, and enlarging upon the danger of a popish successor. On the other hand, the hereditary right to the crown of England was asserted in a large volume, supposed to be written with a view to pave the way for the pretender's accession. One Bedford was apprehended, tried, convicted, and severely punished, as the publisher of this treatise.

Treaty of Rastadt between the emperor and France.

While England was harassed by these intestine commotions, the emperor, rejecting the terms of peace proposed by France, resolved to maintain the war at his own expense, with the assistance of the empire. His forces on the Rhine, commanded by Prince Eugene, were so much outnumbered by the French under Villars, that they could not prevent the enemy from reducing the two important fortresses of Landau and Fribourg. His imperial majesty hoped that the death of Queen Anne, or that of Louis XIV., would produce an alteration in Europe that might be favourable to his interest; and he depended upon the conduct and fortune of Prince Eugene for some lucky event in war. But finding himself disappointed in all these expectations, and absolutely unable to support the expense of another campaign, he hearkened to overtures of peace that were made by the Electors of Cologn and Palatine; and conferences were opened at the castle of Al-Rastadt, between Prince Eugene and Mareschal de Villars, on the twenty-sixth day of November. In the beginning of February these ministers separated, without seeming to have come to any conclusion: but all the articles being settled between the two courts of Vienna and Versailles, they met again the latter end of the month: the treaty was signed on the third day of March; and orders were sent to the governors and commanders on both sides to desist from all hostilities. By this treaty, the French king yielded to the emperor Old Brisac, with all its dependencies, Fribourg, the forts in the Brisgau and Black Forest, together with Fort Kehl.

He engaged to demolish the fortifications opposite to Huningen, the fort of Sellingen, and all between that and Fort Louis. The town and fortress of Landau were ceded to the King of France, who acknowledged the Elector of Hanover. The Electors of Bavaria and Cologn were restored to all their dignities and dominions. The emperor was put in immediate possession of the Spanish Netherlands; and the King of Prussia was permitted to retain the high quarters of Guelders. Finally, the contracting parties agreed that a congress should be opened on the first day of May, at Baden in Switzerland, for terminating all differences; and Prince Eugene and Mareschal de Villars were appointed their first plenipotentiaries.

The ratifications of the treaty between Great Britain and Spain being exchanged, the peace was proclaimed on the first day of March, in London; and the articles were not disagreeable to the English nation. The kingdoms of France and Spain were separated for ever. Philip acknowledged the Protestant succession, and renounced the pretender. He agreed to a renewal of the treaty of navigation and commerce concluded in the year one thousand six hundred and sixty-seven. He granted an exclusive privilege to the English for furnishing the Spanish West Indies with negroes, according to the assiento contract [a]. He ceded Gibraltar to England, as well as the Island of Minorca, on condition that the Spanish inhabitants should enjoy their estates and religion. He obliged himself to grant a full pardon to the Catalonians, with the possession of all their estates, honours, and privileges, and to yield the kingdom of Sicily to the Duke of Savoy. The new Parliament was opened by commission in February, and Sir Thomas Hanmer was chosen speaker of the House of Commons. On the second day of March, the queen being carried in a sedan to the House of Lords, signified to both Houses that she had obtained an honourable and advantageous peace for her own people, and for the greatest part of her allies; and

Marginal notes: Principal articles in the treaty between Great Britain and Spain. Meeting of the Parliament.

---

[a] The assiento contract stipulated, that from the first day of May, 1713, to the first of May, 1743, the company should transport into the West Indies one hundred and forty-four thousand negroes, at the rate of four thousand eight hundred negroes a year; and pay for each negro thirty-three pieces of eight and one-third, in full for all royal duties.

she hoped her interposition might prove effectual to complete the settlement of Europe. She observed, that some persons had been so malicious as to insinuate that the Protestant succession, in the house of Hanover, was in danger under her government; but that those who endeavoured to distract the minds of men with imaginary dangers could only mean to disturb the public tranquillity. She said that, after all she had done to secure the religion and liberties of her people, she could not mention such proceedings without some degree of warmth; and she hoped her Parliament would agree with her, that attempts to weaken her authority, or to render the possession of the crown uneasy to her, could never be proper means to strengthen the Protestant succession. Affectionate addresses were presented by the Lords, the Commons, and the Convocation: but the ill humour of party still subsisted, and was daily inflamed by new pamphlets and papers. Steele, supported by Addison and Halifax, appeared in the front of those who drew their pens in defence of whig principles; and Swift was the champion of the ministry.

The House of Lords take cognizance of a libel against the Scots.

The Earl of Wharton complained in the House of Lords of a libel entitled "The public spirit of the whigs set forth in their generous encouragement of the author of the Crisis." It was a sarcastic performance, imputed to Lord Bolingbroke and Swift, interspersed with severe reflections upon the union, the Scottish nation, and the Duke of Argyle in particular. The lord treasurer disclaimed all knowledge of the author, and readily concurred in an order for taking into custody John Morphew, the publisher, as well as John Barber, printer of the gazette, from whose house the copies were brought to Morphew. The Earl of Wharton said it highly concerned the honour of that august assembly to find out the villain who was author of that false and scandalous libel, that justice might be done to the Scottish nation. He moved that Barber and his servants might be examined: but, next day, the Earl of Mar, one of the secretaries of state, declared, that, in pursuance to her majesty's command, he had directed John Barber to be prosecuted. Notwithstanding this interposition, which was calculated to screen the offenders, the Lords presented an address,

beseeching her majesty to issue out her royal proclamation, promising a reward to any person who should discover the author of the libel, which they conceived to be
false, malicious, and factious, highly dishonourable and
scandalous to her majesty's subjects of Scotland, most
injurious to her majesty, and tending to the ruin of the
constitution.   In compliance with their request, a reward
of three hundred pounds was offered; but the author remained safe from all detection.

The Commons, having granted the supplies, ordered a Mr. Steele
bill to be brought in for securing the freedom of parlia- expelled
ments, by limiting the number of officers in the House of Com-
of Commons, and it passed through both Houses with mons.
little difficulty.   In March, a complaint was made of
several scandalous papers, lately published, under the
name of Richard Steele, esquire, a member of the House.
Sir William Wyndham observed, that some of that
author's writings, contained insolent, injurious reflections on the queen herself, and were dictated by the
spirit of rebellion.   Steele was ordered to attend in his
place : some paragraphs of his works were read ; and he
answered them with an affected air of self-confidence
and unconcern.   A day being appointed for his trial, he
acknowledged the writings, and entered into a more circumstantial defence.   He was assisted by Mr. Addison,
General Stanhope, and Mr. Walpole ; and attacked by
Sir William Wyndham, Mr. Foley, and the attorney-
general.   Whatever could be urged in his favour was
but little regarded by the majority, which voted that two
pamphlets, entitled "The Englishman," and "The Crisis,"
written by Richard Steele, esquire, were scandalous and
seditious libels; and that he should be expelled the
House of Commons.

The Lords, taking into consideration the state of the Precau-
nation, resolved upon addresses to the queen, desiring tions by the
they might know what steps had been taken for remov- the security
ing the pretender from the dominions of the Duke of of the Pro-
Lorraine: that she would impart to them a detail of the cession.
negotiations for peace, a recital of the instances which
had been made in favour of the Catalans, and an account
of the moneys granted by Parliament since the year one
thousand seven hundred and ten, to carry on the war in

Spain and Portugal. They afterwards agreed to other addresses, beseeching her majesty to lay before them the debts and state of the navy, the particular writs of Noli Prosequi granted since her accession to the throne, and a list of such persons as, notwithstanding sentence of outlawry or attainder, had obtained licences to return into Great Britain, or other of her majesty's dominions, since the Revolution. Having voted an application to the queen in behalf of the distressed Catalans, the House adjourned itself to the last day of March. As the minds of men had been artfully irritated by false reports of a design undertaken by France in behalf of the pretender, the ambassador of that crown at the Hague disowned it in a public paper, by command of his Most Christian Majesty. The suspicions of many people, however, had been too deeply planted by the arts and insinuations of the whig leaders, to be eradicated by this or any other declaration; and what served to rivet their apprehensions was a total removal of the whigs from all the employments, civil and military, which they had hitherto retained. These were now bestowed upon professed tories, some of whom were attached at bottom to the supposed heir of blood. At a time when the queen's views were maliciously misrepresented; when the wheels of her government were actually impeded, and her servants threatened with proscription by a powerful,

Boyer.
Burnet.
Tindal.
Torcy.
Boling-
broke.
Voltaire.

turbulent, and implacable faction; no wonder that she discharged the partisans of that faction from her service, and filled their places with those who were distinguished by a warm affection to the house of Stuart, and by a submissive respect for the regal authority. Those were steps which her own sagacity must have suggested; and which her ministers would naturally advise as necessary for their own preservation. The whigs were all in commotion, either apprehending, or affecting to apprehend, that a design was formed to secure the pretender's succession

An. 1714.

to the throne of Great Britain. Their chiefs held secret consultations with Baron Schutz, the resident from Hanover. They communicated their observations to the elector; they received his instructions: they maintained a correspondence with the Duke of Marlborough; and they concerted measures for opposing all efforts that

might be made against the Protestant succession upon
the death of the queen, whose health was by this time
so much impaired, that every week was believed to be
the last of her life. This conduct of the whigs was
resolute, active, and would have been laudable, had their
zeal been confined within the bounds of truth and moderation; but they, moreover, employed all their arts to excite and encourage the fears and jealousies of the people.

The House of Peers resounded with debates upon
the Catalans, the pretender, and the danger that
threatened the Protestant succession. With respect to
the Catalonians, they represented that Great Britain
had prevailed upon them to declare for the house of
Austria, with promise of support; and that these engagements ought to have been made good. Lord
Bolingbroke declared that the queen had used all her
endeavours in their behalf; and that the engagements
with them subsisted no longer than King Charles resided
in Spain. They agreed, however, to an address, acknowledging her majesty's endeavours in favour of the Catalans, and requesting she would continue her interposition
in their behalf. With respect to the pretender, the whig
lords expressed such a spirit of persecution and rancorous hate as would have disgraced the members of any,
even the lowest assembly of Christians. Not contented
with hunting him from one country to another, they
seemed eagerly bent upon extirpating him from the face
of the earth, as if they had thought it was a crime in him
to be born. The Earl of Sunderland declared, from the
information of the minister of Lorraine, that, notwithstanding the application of both Houses to her majesty,
during the last session, concerning the pretender's being
removed from Lorraine, no instances had yet been made
to the duke for that purpose. Lord Bolingbroke affirmed that he himself had made those instances, in the
queen's name, to that very minister before his departure
from England. The Earl of Wharton proposed a question; "Whether the Protestant succession was in danger
under the present administration?" A warm debate ensued, in which the Archbishop of York and the Earl of Anglesey joined in the opposition to the ministry. The
earl pretended to be convinced and converted by the

Debates in
the House
of Lords
concerning
the pre-
tender and
the Cata-
lans.

arguments used in the course of the debate. He owned he had given his assent to the cessation of arms, for which he took shame to himself, asking pardon of God, his country, and his conscience. He affirmed that the honour of his sovereign and the good of his country were the rules of his actions; but that, without respect of persons, should he find himself imposed upon, he durst pursue an evil minister from the queen's closet to the Tower, and from the Tower to the scaffold. This conversion, however, was much more owing to a full persuasion, that a ministry divided against itself could not long subsist, and that the Protestant succession was firmly secured. He therefore resolved to make a merit of withdrawing himself from the interests of a tottering administration, in whose ruin he might be involved. The Duke of Argyle charged the ministers with mal-administration, both within those walls and without: he offered to prove that the lord treasurer had yearly remitted a sum of money to the highland clans of Scotland, who were known to be entirely devoted to the pretender. He affirmed that the new-modelling of the army, the practice of disbanding some regiments out of their turn, and removing a great number of officers, on account of their affection to the house of Hanover, were clear indications of the ministry's designs: that it was a disgrace to the nation to see men, who had never looked an enemy in the face, advanced to the posts of several brave officers, who, after they had often exposed their lives for their country, were now starving in prison for debt, on account of their pay being detained. The treasurer, laying his hand upon his breast, said, he had on so many occasions given such signal proofs of affection to the Protestant succession, that he was sure no member of that august assembly did call it in question. He owned he had remitted, for two or three years past, between three and four thousand pounds to the highland clans; and he hoped the House would give him an opportunity to clear his conduct in that particular: with respect to the reformed officers, he declared he had given orders for their being immediately paid. The Protestant succession was voted out of danger by a small majority.

Lord Halifax proposed an address to the queen, that

she would renew her instances for the speedy removing
the pretender out of Lorraine; and that she would, in
conjunction with the States-General, enter into the
guarantee of the Protestant succession in the house of
Hanover. The Earl of Wharton moved, that in the
address her majesty should be desired to issue a proclamation, promising a reward to any person who should
apprehend the pretender dead or alive. He was seconded by the Duke of Bolton; and the House agreed
that an address should be presented. When it was reported by the committee, Lord North and Grey expatiated upon the barbarity of setting a price on any
one's head: he proved it was an encouragement to murder and assassination; contrary to the precepts of Christianity; repugnant to the law of nature and nations; inconsistent with the dignity of such an august assembly,
and with the honour of a nation famed for lenity and
mercy. He was supported by Lord Trevor, who moved
that the reward should be promised for apprehending
and bringing the pretender to justice, in case he should
land, or attempt to land, in Great Britain or Ireland.
The cruelty of the first clause was zealously supported
and vindicated by the Lords Cowper and Halifax; but
by this time the Earl of Anglesey and some others, who
had abandoned the ministry, were brought back to their
former principles, by promise of profitable employment;
and the mitigation was adopted by a majority of ten
voices. To this address, which was delivered by the
chancellor and the whig lords only, the queen replied in
these words: "My lords, it would be a real strengthening to the succession in the house of Hanover, as well as
a support to my government, that an end were put to
those groundless fears and jealousies which have been so
industriously promoted. I do not at this time see any
occasion for such a proclamation. Whenever I judge it to
be necessary, I shall give my orders for having it issued.
As to the other particulars of this address, I will give
proper directions therein." She was likewise importuned,
by another address, to issue out a proclamation against
all jesuits, popish priests, and bishops, as well as against
all such as were outlawed for adhering to the late King
James and the pretender. The House resolved, that no

person, not included in the articles of Limerick, and who
had borne arms in France and Spain, should be capable
of any employment civil or military; and that no person,
a natural-born subject of her majesty, should be capable
of sustaining the character of a public minister from any
foreign potentate.　These resolutions were aimed at Sir
Patrick Lawless, an Irish papist, who had come to England with a credential letter from King Philip, but now
thought proper to quit the kingdom.

A writ de-
manded for
the Elec-
toral
Prince of
Hanover,
as Duke of
Cambridge.
　　　Then the lords in the opposition made an attack upon
the treasurer, concerning the money he had remitted to
the Highlanders; but Oxford silenced his opposers by
asserting that in so doing he had followed the example
of King William, who, after he had reduced that people,
thought fit to allow yearly pensions to the heads of clans,
in order to keep them quiet. His conduct was approved
by the House; and Lord North and Grey moved, that
a day might be appointed for considering the state of
the nation with regard to the treaties of peace and commerce.　The motion was seconded by the Earl of Cla-
rendon; and the thirteenth day of April fixed for this
purpose.　In the mean time, Baron Schutz demanded
of the chancellor a writ for the Electoral Prince of Hanover to sit in the House of Peers as Duke of Cambridge,
intimating that his design was to reside in England.
The writ was granted with reluctance; but the prince's
design of coming to England was so disagreeable to the
queen, that she signified her disapprobation of such a
step in a letter to the Princess Sophia.　She observed
that such a method of proceeding would be dangerous
to the succession itself, which was not secure any other
way than as the prince who was in actual possession of
the throne maintained her authority and prerogative:
she said a great many people in England were seditiously
disposed; so she left her highness to judge what tumults they might be able to raise, should they have a
pretext to begin a commotion; she, therefore, persuaded
herself that her aunt would not consent to any thing
which might disturb the repose of her and her subjects.
At the same time she wrote a letter to the electoral
prince, complaining that he had formed such a resolution, without first knowing her sentiments on the sub-

ject, and telling him plainly, that nothing could be more
dangerous to the tranquillity of her dominions, to the
right of succession in the Hanoverian line, or more disagreeable to her, than such conduct at this juncture. A
third letter was written to the elector, his father; and
the treasurer took this opportunity to assure that prince
of his inviolable attachment to the family of Hanover.

The whig lords were dissatisfied with the queen's
answer to their address concerning the pretender; and
they moved for another address on the same subject,
which was resolved upon, but never presented. They
took into consideration the treaties of peace and commerce, to which many exceptions were taken; and much
sarcasm was expended on both sides of the dispute: but
at length the majority carried the question in favour of
an address, acknowledging her majesty's goodness in delivering them, by a safe, honourable, and advantageous
peace with France, from the burden of a consuming land
war, unequally carried on, and become at last impracticable. The House of Commons concurred in this address, after having voted that the Protestant succession
was out of danger; but these resolutions were not taken
without violent opposition, in which General Stanhope,
Mr. Lechmere, and Mr. Walpole chiefly distinguished
themselves. The letters which the queen had written
to the electoral house of Hanover were printed and published in England, with a view to inform the friends of
that family of the reasons which prevented the Duke of
Cambridge from executing his design of residing in
Great Britain. The queen considered this step as a personal insult, as well as an attempt to prejudice her in
the opinion of her subjects: she therefore ordered the
publisher to be taken into custody. At this period the
Princess Sophia died, in the eighty-fourth year of her
age; and her death was intimated to the queen by Baron
Bothmar, who arrived in England with the character of
envoy-extraordinary from the Elector of Hanover. This
princess was the fourth and youngest daughter of Frederick, Elector Palatine, King of Bohemia, and Elizabeth,
daughter of King James I. of England. She enjoyed
from nature an excellent capacity, which was finely cultivated; and was in all respects one of the most accom-

CHAP.
XI.

1714

plished princesses of the age in which she lived. At her death the court of England appeared in mourning; and the Elector of Brunswick was prayed for by name in the liturgy of the church of England. On the twelfth day of May, Sir William Wyndham made a motion for a bill to prevent the growth of schism, and for the further security of the church of England, as by law established. The design of it was to prohibit dissenters from teaching in schools and academies. It was accordingly prepared, and eagerly opposed in each House as a species of persecution. Nevertheless, it made its way through both, and received the royal assent: but the queen dying before it took place, this law was rendered ineffectual.

Another
against all
who should
list or be
enlisted in
a foreign
service.

Her majesty's constitution was now quite broken; one fit of sickness succeeded another: what completed the ruin of her health was the anxiety of her mind, occasioned partly by the discontents which had been raised and fomented by the enemies of her government; and partly by the dissensions among her ministers, which were now become intolerable. The council-chamber was turned into a scene of obstinate dispute and bitter altercation. Even in the queen's presence the treasurer and secretary did not abstain from mutual obloquy and reproach. Oxford advised moderate measures, and is said to have made advances towards a reconciliation with the leaders of the whig party. As he foresaw it would soon be their turn to domineer, such precautions were necessary for his own safety. Bolingbroke affected to set the whigs at defiance: he professed a warm zeal for the church: he soothed the queen's inclinations with the most assiduous attention. He and his coadjutrix insinuated that the treasurer was biassed in favour of the dissenters, and even that he acted as a spy for the house of Hanover. In the midst of these disputes and commotions the Jacobites were not idle. They flattered themselves that the queen in secret favoured the pretensions of her brother; and they depended on Bolingbroke's attachment to the same interest. They believed the same sentiments were cherished by the nation in general. They held private assemblies both in Great Britain and in Ireland. They concerted measures for turning the dissensions of the kingdom to the advantage of their cause.

They even proceeded so far as to enlist men for the service of the pretender. Some of these practices were discovered by the Earl of Wharton, who did not fail to sound the alarm. A proclamation was immediately published, promising a reward of five thousand pounds for apprehending the pretender whenever he should land or attempt to land in Great Britain. The Commons voted an address of thanks for the proclamation; and assured her majesty that they would cheerfully aid and assist her, by granting the sum of a hundred thousand pounds, as a further reward to any who should perform so great a service to her majesty and her kingdoms. The Lords likewise presented an address on the same subject. Lord Bolingbroke proposed a bill decreeing the penalties of high treason against those who should list or be enlisted in the pretender's service. The motion was approved, and the penalty extended to all those who should list or be enlisted in the service of any foreign prince or state, without a licence under the sign manual of her majesty, her heir, or successors.

On the second day of July, the Lords took into consideration the treaty of commerce with Spain; and a great number of merchants being examined at the bar of the House, declared, that unless the explanation of the third, fifth, and eighth articles, as made at Madrid after the treaty was signed, were rescinded, they could not carry on their commerce without losing five-and-twenty per cent. After a long debate, the House resolved to address the queen for all the papers relating to the negotiation of the treaty of commerce with Spain, with the names of the persons who advised her majesty to that treaty. To this address she replied, that understanding the three explanatory articles of the treaty were not detrimental to the trade of her subjects, she had consented to their being ratified with the treaty. The Earl of Wharton represented, that if so little regard was shown to the addresses of that august assembly to the sovereign, they had no business in that House. He moved for a remonstrance, to lay before her majesty the insuperable difficulties that attended the Spanish trade on the footing of the late treaty, and the House agreed to this motion. Another member moved, that the House should

The Parliament prorogued.

insist on her majesty's naming the person who advised
her to ratify the three explanatory articles. This was a
blow aimed at Arthur Moore, a member of the Lower
House, whom Lord Bolingbroke had consulted on the
subject of the treaty. He was screened by the majority
in Parliament; but a general court of the South Sea
Company resolved, upon a complaint exhibited by Captain Johnson, that Arthur Moore, while a director, was
privy to and encouraged the design of carrying on a
clandestine trade, to the prejudice of the corporation,
contrary to his oath, and in breach of the trust reposed in
him : that, therefore, he should be declared incapable of
being a director of, or having any employment in, this
company. The queen had reserved to herself the quarter part of the assiento contract, which she now gave up
to the company, and received the thanks of the Upper
House ; but she would not discover the names of those
who advised her to ratify the explanatory articles. On
the ninth day of July she thought proper to put an end
to the session, with a speech on the usual subjects. After
having assured them that her chief concern was to preserve the Protestant religion, the liberty of her subjects,
and to secure the tranquillity of her kingdoms, she concluded in these words : "But I must tell you plainly,
that these desirable ends can never be obtained, unless
you bring the same dispositions on your parts ; unless all
groundless jealousies, which create and foment divisions
among you, be laid aside; and unless you show the same
regard for my just prerogative, and for the honour of my
government, as I have always expressed for the rights of
my people."

The trea-
surer dis-
graced.
After the peace had thus received the sanction of the
Parliament, the ministers, being no longer restrained by
the tie of common danger, gave a loose to their mutual
animosity. Oxford wrote a letter to the queen, containing a detail of the public transactions; in the course of
which he endeavoured to justify his own conduct, and
expose the turbulent and ambitious spirit of his rival.
On the other hand, Bolingbroke charged the treasurer
with having invited the Duke of Marlborough to return
from his voluntary exile, and maintained a private correspondence with the house of Hanover. The Duke of

Shrewsbury likewise complained of his having presumed
to send orders to him in Ireland, without the privity of
her majesty and the council. In all probability his
greatest crime was his having given umbrage to the
favourite, Lady Masham. Certain it is, on the twenty-
seventh day of July, a very acrimonious dialogue passed
between that lady, the chancellor, and Oxford, in the
queen's presence. The treasurer affirmed he had been
wronged and abused by lies and misrepresentations; but
he threatened vengeance, declaring that he would leave
some people as low as he had found them when they
first attracted his notice. In the mean time he was removed from his employment, and Bolingbroke seemed
to triumph in the victory he had obtained. He laid his
account with being admitted as chief minister into the
administration of affairs; and is said to have formed a
design of a coalition with the Duke of Marlborough, who
at this very time embarked at Ostend for England.
Probably, Oxford had tried to play the same game, but
met with a repulse from the duke, on account of the implacable resentment which the duchess had conceived
against that minister.

Whatever schemes might have been formed, the fall Precautions taken
for secur-
ing the
peace of the
kingdom.
of the treasurer was so sudden, that no plan was established for supplying the vacancy occasioned by his disgrace. The confusion that incessantly ensued at court,
and the fatigue of attending a long cabinet council on
this event, had such an effect upon the queen's spirits
and constitution, that she declared she should not outlive
it, and was immediately seized with a lethargic disorder.
Notwithstanding all the medicines which the physicians
could prescribe, the distemper gained ground so fast, that
next day, which was the thirtieth of July, they despaired
of her life. Then the committee of the council assembled
at the Cockpit, adjourned to Kensington. The Dukes
of Somerset and Argyle, informed of the desperate situation in which she lay, repaired to the palace; and without being summoned, entered the council chamber. The
members were surprised at their appearance; but the
Duke of Shrewsbury thanked them for their readiness
to give their assistance at such a critical juncture, and
desired they would take their places. The physicians

having declared that the queen was still sensible, the council unanimously agreed to recommend the Duke of Shrewsbury as the fittest person to fill the place of lord treasurer. When this opinion was intimated to the queen, she said, they could not have recommended a person she liked better than the Duke of Shrewsbury. She delivered to him the white staff, bidding him use it for the good of her people. He would have returned the lord chamberlain's staff, but she desired he would keep them both; so that he was at one time possessed of the three greatest posts in the kingdom, under the titles of lord treasurer, lord chamberlain, and lord lieutenant of Ireland. No nobleman in England better deserved such distinguishing marks of his sovereign's favour. He was modest, liberal, disinterested, and a warm friend to his country. Bolingbroke's ambition was defeated by the vigour which the Dukes of Somerset and Argyle exerted on this occasion. They proposed, that all privy-counsellors in and about London should be invited to attend, without distinction of party. The motion was approved; and Lord Somers, with many other whig members, repaired to Kensington. The council being thus reinforced, began to provide for the security of the kingdom. Orders were immediately despatched to four regiments of horse and dragoons quartered in remote counties, to march up to the neighbourhood of London and Westminster. Seven of the ten British battalions in the Netherlands were directed to embark at Ostend for England, with all possible expedition; an embargo was laid upon all shipping; and directions given for equipping all the ships of war that could be soonest in a condition for service. They sent a letter to the Elector of Brunswick, signifying that the physicians had despaired of the queen's life, informing him of the measures they had taken, and desiring he would, with all convenient speed, repair to Holland, where he should be attended by a British squadron, to convey him to England, in case of her majesty's decease. At the same time they despatched instructions to the Earl of Strafford, to desire the States-General would be ready to perform the guarantee of the Protestant succession. The heralds at arms were kept in waiting with a troop of horse-guards, to proclaim the new king as soon as the throne

should become vacant. Precautions were taken to secure
the sea-ports, to overawe the Jacobites in Scotland, and
the command of the fleet was bestowed upon the Earl of
Berkley.

The queen continued to doze in a lethargic insensibility, Death and
with very short intervals, till the first day of August, in character
the morning, when she expired, in the fiftieth year of her of Queen
age, and in the thirteenth of her reign. Anne Stuart, Anne.
Queen of Great Britain, was in her person of the middle
size, well proportioned. Her hair was of the dark brown
colour, her complexion ruddy ; her features were regular,
her countenance was rather round than oval, and her
aspect more comely than majestic. Her voice was clear
and melodious, and her presence engaging. Her capacity
was naturally good, but not much cultivated by learning ;
nor did she exhibit any marks of extraordinary genius, or
personal ambition. She was certainly deficient in that
vigour of mind, by which a prince ought to preserve
his independence, and avoid the snares and fetters of
sycophants and favourites ; but whatever her weakness
in this particular might have been, the virtues of her
heart were never called in question. She was a pattern
of conjugal affection and fidelity, a tender mother, a warm
friend, an indulgent mistress, a munificent patron, a mild
and merciful prince, during whose reign no subject's
blood was shed for treason. She was zealously attached
to the church of England from conviction rather than
from prepossession, unaffectedly pious, just, charitable, and
compassionate. She felt a mother's fondness for her
people, by whom she was universally beloved with a
warmth of affection which even the prejudice of party
could not abate. In a word, if she was not the greatest,
she was certainly one of the best and most unblemished
sovereigns that ever sat upon the throne of England, and
well deserved the expressive though simple epithet of
"The good Queen Anne."

CHAPTER XII.

GEORGE I.

CHAP.
XII.

1714.
State of
parties in
Great
Britain.

IT may be necessary to remind the reader of the state of
party at this important juncture. The Jacobites had been
fed with hopes of seeing the succession altered by the
Earl of Oxford. These hopes he had conveyed to them
in a distant, undeterminate, and mysterious manner, without any other view than that of preventing them from
taking violent measures to embarrass his administration.
At least, if he actually entertained at one time any other
design, he had, long before his disgrace, laid it wholly

aside, probably from an apprehension of the danger with
which it must have been attended, and seemed bent upon
making a merit of his zeal for the house of Hanover;
but his conduct was so equivocal and unsteady, that he
ruined himself in the opinion of one party, without
acquiring the confidence of the other. The friends of
the pretender derived fresh hopes from the ministry of
Bolingbroke. Though he had never explained himself
on this subject, he was supposed to favour the heir of
blood, and known to be an implacable enemy to the
whigs, who were the most zealous advocates for the Protestant succession. The Jacobites promised themselves
much from his affection, but more from his resentment;
and they believed the majority of the tories would join
them on the same maxims. All Bolingbroke's schemes of
power were defeated by the promotion of the Duke of
Shrewsbury to the office of treasurer; and all his hopes
blasted by the death of the queen, on whose personal favour
he depended. The resolute behaviour of the Dukes of
Somerset and Argyle, together with the diligence and
activity of a council in which the whig interest had gained
the ascendancy, completed the confusion of the tories,
who found themselves without a head, divided, distracted,
and irresolute. Upon recollection, they saw nothing so eligible as silence, and submission to those measures which
they could not oppose with any prospect of success.
They had no other objection to the succession in the
house of Hanover but the fear of seeing the whig faction
once more predominant; yet they were not without hope
that their new sovereign, who was reputed a prince of
sagacity and experience, would cultivate and conciliate
the affection of the tories, who were the landholders and
proprietors of the kingdom, rather than declare himself
the head of a faction which leaned for support on those
who were enemies to the church and monarchy, on the
bank and the monied interest, raised upon usury, and
maintained by corruption. In a word, the whigs were
elated and overbearing; the tories abashed and humble;
the Jacobites eager, impatient, and alarmed at a juncture
which, with respect to them, was truly critical.

The queen had no sooner resigned her last breath than King
the privy council met, and the Archbishop of Canterbury, George
proclaimed.

the lord chancellor, and the Hanoverian resident, Kreyen-berg, produced the three instruments in which the Elector of Brunswick had nominated the persons* to be added as lords justices to the seven great officers of the realm. Orders were immediately issued for proclaiming King George, in England, Scotland, and Ireland. The regency appointed the Earl of Dorset to carry to Hanover the intimation of his majesty's accession, and attend him in his journey to England. They sent the general officers in whom they could confide to their respective posts: they reinforced the garrison of Portsmouth: they appointed Mr. Addison their secretary: while Boling-broke was obliged to stand at the door of the council-chamber with his bag and papers, and underwent every species of mortification. On the whole, King George ascended the throne of Great Britain in the fifty-fifth year of his age, without the least opposition, tumult, or sign of popular discontent; and the unprejudiced part of the nation was now fully persuaded that no design had ever been concerted by Queen Anne and her ministry in favour of the pretender. The mayor of Oxford received a letter, requiring him to proclaim the pretender. This being communicated to the vice-chancellor, a copy of it was immediately transmitted to Mr. Secretary Bromley, member of Parliament for the university; and the vice-chancellor offered a reward of one hundred pounds to any person who should discover the author. It was either the production of some lunatic, or a weak contrivance to fix an odium on that venerable body.

The civil list granted to his majesty by the Parliament.
The Parliament having assembled pursuant to the act which regulated the succession, the lord chancellor, on the fifth day of August, made a speech to both Houses in the name of the regency. He told them, that the privy council appointed by the Elector of Brunswick had proclaimed that prince, under the name of King George, as the lawful and rightful sovereign of these kingdoms; and that they had taken the necessary care to maintain the public peace. He observed, that the several branches

---

* These were the Dukes of Shrewsbury, Somerset, Bolton, Devonshire, Kent, Argyle, Montrose, and Roxburgh; the Earls of Pomfret, Anglesey, Carlisle, Nottingham, Abingdon, Scarborough, and Orford; Lord Viscount Townshend, and Lords Halifax and Cowper.

of the public revenue were expired by the demise of her late majesty; and recommended to the Commons the making such provision, in that respect, as might be requisite to support the honour and dignity of the crown. He likewise expressed his hope, that they would not be wanting in any thing that might conduce to the establishing and advancing of the public credit. Both Houses immediately agreed to addresses, containing the warmest expressions of duty and affection to their new sovereign, who did not fail to return such answers as were very agreeable to the Parliament of Great Britain. In the mean time the Lower House prepared and passed a bill, granting to his majesty the same civil list which the queen had enjoyed, with additional clauses for the payment of arrears due to the troops of Hanover which had been in the service of Great Britain; and for a reward of one hundred thousand pounds, to be paid by the treasury to any person who should apprehend the pretender in landing, or attempting to land, in any part of the British dominions. Mr. Craggs, who had been despatched to Hanover before the queen died, returning on the thirteenth day of August, with letters from the king to the regency, they went to the House of Peers; then the chancellor, in another speech to both Houses, intimated his majesty's great satisfaction in the loyalty and affection which his people had universally expressed at his accession. Other addresses were voted on this occasion. The Commons finished the bill for the civil list, and one for making some alterations in an act for a state lottery, which received the royal assent from the lords justices. Then the Parliament was prorogued:

Mr. Prior having notified the queen's death to the court of Versailles, Louis declared that he would inviolably maintain the treaty of peace concluded at Utrecht, particularly with relation to the settlement of the British crown in the house of Hanover. The Earl of Strafford having signified the same event to the states of Holland, and the resident of Hanover having presented them with a letter, in which his master claimed the performance of their guarantee, they resolved to perform their engagements, and congratulated his electoral highness on his accession to the throne of Great Britain. They invited

The electoral prince created Prince of Wales.

CHAP. XII.

1714.

him to pass through their dominions, and assured him that his interests were as dear to them as their own. The Chevalier de St. George no sooner received the news of the queen's death than he posted to Versailles, where he was given to understand that the King of France expected he should quit his territories immediately, and he was accordingly obliged to return to Lorraine. By this time Mr. Murray had arrived in England from Hanover, with notice that the king had deferred his departure for some days. He brought orders to the regency to prepare a patent for creating the prince royal Prince of Wales, and for removing Lord Bolingbroke from his post of secretary. The seals were taken from this minister by the Dukes of Shrewsbury and Somerset, and Lord Cowper, who at the same time sealed up all the doors of his office.

King George having vested the government of his German dominions in a council, headed by his brother Prince Ernest, set out with the electoral Prince from Herenhausen, on the thirty-first day of August; and in five days arrived at the Hague, where he conferred with the States-General. On the sixteenth day of September he embarked at Orange Poldar, under convoy of an English and Dutch squadron, commanded by the Earl of Berkley; and next day arrived at the Hope. In the afternoon the yacht sailed up the river; and his majesty with the prince were landed from a barge at Greenwich about six in the evening. There he was received by the Duke of Northumberland, captain of the life-guards, and the lords of the regency. From the landing-place he walked to his house in the park, accompanied by a great number of the nobility, and other persons of distinction, who had the honour to kiss the hand as they approached. When he retired to his bed-chamber, he sent for those of the nobility who had distinguished themselves by their zeal for his succession; but the Duke of Ormond, the lord chancellor, and Lord Trevor were not of the number. Next morning the Earl of Oxford presented himself with an air of confidence, as if he had expected to receive some particular mark of his majesty's favour; but he had the mortification to remain a considerable time undistinguished among the crowd; and then was permitted to kiss the king's hand, without being honoured with any other notice. On the other hand, his majesty expressed uncommon regard for the Duke of Marlborough, who had lately arrived in England, as well as for all the leaders of the whig party.

It was the misfortune of this prince, as well as a very great prejudice to the nation, that he had been misled into strong prepossessions against the tories, who constituted such a considerable part of his subjects. They were now excluded from all share of the royal favour, which was wholly engrossed by their enemies: these early marks of aversion, which he was at no pains to conceal, alienated the minds of many from his person and government, who would otherwise have served him with fidelity and affection. An instantaneous and total change was effected in all offices of honour and advantage. The Duke of Ormond was dismissed from his command, which the king restored to the Duke of Marlborough, whom he likewise appointed colonel of the first regiment of foot-guards, and master of the ordnance. The great seal was given to Lord Cowper; the privy seal to the Earl of Wharton; the government of Ireland to the Earl of Sunderland. The Duke of Devonshire was made steward of the household: Lord Townshend and Mr. Stanhope were appointed secretaries of state: the post of secretary for Scotland was bestowed upon the Duke of Montrose. The Duke of Somerset was constituted master of the horse; the Duke of St. Alban's captain of the band of pensioners; and the Duke of Argyle commander in chief of the forces in Scotland. Mr. Pulteney became secretary at war; and Mr. Walpole, who had already undertaken to manage the House of Commons, was gratified with the double place of paymaster to the army and to Chelsea-hospital. A new privy council was appointed, and the Earl of Nottingham declared president; but all affairs of consequence were concerted by a cabinet council, or junto, composed of the Duke of Marlborough, the Earls of Nottingham and Sunderland, the Lords Halifax, Townshend, and Somers, and General Stanhope. The regency had already removed Sir Constantine Phipps and the Archbishop of Armagh from the office of lords justices of Ireland, and filled their places in the regency

The tories totally excluded from the royal favour.

of that kingdom with the archbishop of Dublin and the
Earl of Kildare.   Allen Broderick was appointed chancellor: another privy council was formed, and the Duke
of Ormond was named as one of the members.   The
treasury and admiralty were put into commission; all
the governments were changed; and, in a word, the
whole nation was delivered into the hands of the whigs.
At the same time, the prince royal was declared Prince
of Wales, and took his place in council.   The king was
congratulated on his accession in addresses from the two
universities, and from all the cities and corporations in
the kingdom.   He expressed particular satisfaction at
these expressions of loyalty and affection.   He declared
in council his firm purpose to support and maintain the
churches of England and Scotland as they were by law
established: an aim which he imagined might be effectually accomplished, without impairing the toleration
allowed by law to Protestant dissenters, and so necessary to the trade and riches of the kingdom: he, moreover, assured them he would earnestly endeavour to
render property secure; the good effects of which were
nowhere so clearly seen as in this happy nation.   Before
the coronation he created some new peers, and others
were promoted to higher titles [b].   On the twentieth day of October, he was crowned in Westminster
Abbey with the usual solemnity, at which the Earl of
Oxford and Lord Bolingbroke assisted [c].   On that very
day the university of Oxford, in full convocation, unanimously conferred the degree of doctor of civil law on
Sir Constantine Phipps, with particular marks of honour
and esteem.   As the French king was said to protract
the demolition of Dunkirk, Mr. Prior received orders to
present a memorial to hasten this work, and to prevent
the canal of Mardyke from being finished.   The answer
which he received being deemed equivocal, this minister

[b] James, Lord Chandos, was created Earl of Caernarvon ; Lewis, Lord Rockingham, Earl of that name ; Charles, Lord Ossulston, Earl of Tankerville ; Charles,
Lord Halifax, Earl of Halifax ; Heneage, Lord Guernsey, Earl of Aylesford ;
John, Lord Hervey, Earl of Bristol ; Thomas, Lord Pelham, Earl of Clare ;
Henry, Earl of Thomond, in Ireland, Viscount Tadcaster ; James, Viscount Castleton, in Ireland, Baron Sanderson ; Bennet, Lord Sherrard, in Ireland, Baron
of Harborough ; Gervase, Lord Pierrepont, in Ireland, Baron Pierrepont, in the
county of Bucks ; Henry Boyle, Baron of Carleton, in the county of York ; Sir
Richard Temple, Baron of Cobham ; Henry, Lord Paget, Earl of Uxbridge.
[c] In the month of October the Princess of Wales arrived in England with her
two eldest daughters, the Princesses Anne and Amelia.

was recalled, and the Earl of Stair appointed ambassador to the court of France, where he prosecuted this affair with uncommon vigour. About the same time, General Cadogan was sent as plenipotentiary to Antwerp, to assist at the barrier treaty, negotiated there between the emperor and the States-General.

Meanwhile the number of the malecontents in Eng- land was considerably increased by the king's attachment to the whig faction. The clamour of the church's being in danger was revived; jealousies were excited; seditious libels dispersed; and dangerous tumults raised in different parts of the kingdom. Birmingham, Bristol, Chippenham, Norwich, and Reading were filled with licentious riot. The party cry was, "Down with the whigs! Sacheverel for ever!" Many gentlemen of the whig faction were abused; magistrates in towns, and justices in the country, were reviled and insulted by the populace in the execution of their office. The pretender took this opportunity to transmit, by the French mail, copies of a printed manifesto to the Dukes of Shrewsbury, Marlborough, Argyle, and other noblemen of the first distinction. In this declaration he mentioned the good intentions of his sister towards him, which were prevented by her deplorable death. He observed that his people, instead of doing him and themselves justice, had proclaimed for their king a foreign prince, contrary to the fundamental and incontestable laws of hereditary right, which their pretended acts of settlement could never abrogate. These papers being delivered to the secretaries of state, the king refused an audience to the Marquis de Lamberti, minister from the Duke of Lorraine, on the supposition that this manifesto could not have been prepared or transmitted without the knowledge and countenance of his master. The marquis having communicated this circumstance to the duke, that prince absolutely denied his having been privy to the transaction, and declared that the Chevalier de St. George came into Lorraine by the directions of the French king, whom the duke could not disoblige without exposing his territories to invasion. Notwithstanding this apology, the marquis was given to understand that he could not be admitted to an audience until the pretender should be removed from the dominions of his master: he, therefore, quitted the kingdom without further hesitation. Religion was still mingled in all political disputes. The high-churchmen complained that impiety and heresy daily gained ground, from the connivance, or at least the supine negligence, of the whig prelates. The Lower House of Convocation had, before the queen's death, declared that a book published by Dr. Samuel Clarke under the title of "The Scripture Doctrine of the Trinity," contained assertions contrary to the Catholic faith. They sent up extracts from this performance to the bishops; and the doctor wrote an answer to their objections. He was prevailed upon to write an apology, which he presented to the Upper House; but apprehending it might be published separately, and misunderstood, he afterwards delivered an explanation to the Bishop of London. This was satisfactory to the bishops; but the Lower House resolved, that it was no recantation of his heretical assertions. The disputes about the Trinity increasing, the archbishops and bishops received directions, which were published, for preserving unity in the church, the purity of the Christian faith concerning the holy Trinity, and for maintaining the peace and quiet of the state. By these every preacher was restricted from delivering any other doctrine than what is contained in the Holy Scriptures with respect to the Trinity; and from intermeddling in any affairs of state or government. The like prohibition was extended to those who should write, harangue, or dispute on the same subjects.

New Parliament.

The Parliament being dissolved, another was called by a very extraordinary proclamation, in which the king complained of the evil designs of men disaffected to his succession; and of their having misrepresented his conduct and principles. He mentioned the perplexity of public affairs, the interruption of commerce, and the heavy debts of the nation. He expressed his hope that his loving subjects would send up to Parliament the fittest persons to redress the present disorders; and that in the elections, they would have a particular regard to such as had expressed a firm attachment to the Protestant succession when it was in danger. It does not appear that the Protestant succession was ever in danger. How then was this declaration to be interpreted? People in general construed it into a design to maintain party distinctions, and encourage the whigs to the full exertion of their influence in the elections; into a renunciation of the tories; and as the first flash of that vengeance which was afterwards seen to burst upon the heads of the late ministry. When the Earl of Strafford returned from Holland, all his papers were seized by an order from the secretary's office. Mr. Prior was recalled from France, and promised to discover all he knew relating to the conduct of Oxford's administration. Uncommon vigour was exerted on both sides in the elections; but, by dint of the monied interest, which prevailed in most of the corporations through the kingdom, and the countenance of the ministry, which will always have weight with needy and venal electors, a great majority of whigs was returned both in England and Scotland.

When this new Parliament assembled on the seventeenth day of March at Westminster, Mr. Spencer Compton was chosen speaker of the Commons. On the twenty-first day of the month, the king appeared in the House of Lords, and delivered to the chancellor a written speech, which was read in presence of both Houses. His majesty thanked his faithful and loving subjects for that zeal and firmness they had shown in defence of the Protestant succession, against all the open and secret practices which had been used to defeat it. He told them that some conditions of the peace, essential to the security and trade of Great Britain, were not yet duly executed; and that the performance of the whole might be looked upon as precarious, until defensive alliances should be formed to guarantee the present treaties. He observed, that the pretender boasted of the assistance he expected in England, to repair his former disappointment; that great part of the national trade was rendered impracticable; and that the public debts were surprisingly increased ever since the fatal cessation of arms. He gave the Commons to understand that the branches of the revenue formerly granted for the support of the civil government were so far encumbered and alienated that the produce of the funds which remained, and had been granted to him, would fall short of what was at first designed for maintaining the honour and dignity of the crown; that as it was his and their happiness to see a Prince of Wales who might in due time succeed him on the throne, and to see him blessed with many children; these circumstances would naturally occasion an expense to which the nation had not been for many years accustomed ; and, therefore, he did not doubt but they would think of it with that affection which he had reason to hope from his Commons. He desired that no unhappy divisions of parties might divert them from pursuing the common interest of their country. He declared, that the established constitution in church and state should be the rule of his government; and that the happiness, ease, and prosperity of his people should be the chief care of his life. He concluded with expressing his confidence that with their assistance he should disappoint the designs of those who wanted to deprive him of that blessing which he most valued—the affection of his people.

Lord Bolingbroke withdraws himself to France.

Speeches suggested by a vindictive ministry better became the leader of an incensed party than the father and sovereign of a divided people. This declaration portended measures which it was the interest of the crown to avoid, and suited the temper of the majority in both Houses, which breathed nothing but destruction to their political adversaries. The Lords, in their address of thanks, professed their hope that his majesty, assisted by the Parliament, would be able to recover the reputation of the kingdom in foreign parts, the loss of which they hoped to convince the world by their actions was by no means to be imputed to the nation in general. The tories said this was an invidious reflection, calculated to mislead and inflame the people ; for the reputation of the kingdom had never been so high as at this very juncture. The Commons pretended astonishment to find that any conditions of the late peace should not yet be duly executed ; and that care was not taken to form such alliances as might have rendered the peace not precarious. They declared their resolution to inquire into these fatal miscarriages ; to trace out those measures whereon the pretender placed his hopes, and bring the authors of them to condign punishment. These addresses were not voted without opposition. In the House of Lords, the Dukes of Buckingham and Shrewsbury, the Earl of Anglesey, the Archbishop of York, and other peers, both secular and ecclesiastical, observed, that their address was injurious to the late queen's memory, and would serve only to increase those unhappy divisions that distracted the kingdom. In the Lower House, Sir William Wyndham, Mr. Bromley, Mr. Shippen, General Ross, Sir William Whitelock, and other members, took exceptions to passages of the same nature, in the address which the Commons had prepared. They were answered by Mr. Walpole, Mr. Pulteney, and Mr. Secretary Stanhope. These gentlemen took occasion to declare, that notwithstanding the endeavours which had been used to prevent a discovery of the late mismanagements, by conveying away several papers from the secretary's office, yet the government had sufficient evidence left to prove the late ministry the most corrupt that ever sat at the helm; that those matters would soon be laid before the House, when it would appear that a certain English general had acted in concert with, if not received orders from, Mareschal de Villars. Lord Bolingbroke, who had hitherto appeared in public, as usual, with remarkable serenity, and spoke in the House of Lords with great freedom and confidence, thought it was now high time to consult his personal safety. He accordingly withdrew to the continent, leaving a letter which was afterwards printed in his justification. In this paper, he declared he had received certain and repeated informations, that a resolution was taken to pursue him to the scaffold; that if there had been the least reason to hope for a fair and open trial, after having been already prejudged unheard by the two Houses of Parliament, he should not have declined the strictest examination. He challenged the most inveterate of his enemies to produce any one instance of criminal correspondence, or the least corruption in any part of the administration in which he was concerned. He said, if his zeal for the honour and dignity of his royal mistress and the true interest of his country had any where transported him to let slip a warm and unguarded expression, he hoped the most favourable interpretation would be put upon it. He affirmed, that he had served her majesty

Boyer.
Torcy.
Tindal.
Bolingbroke.
Voltaire.

CHAP.
XII.
1714.

faithfully and dutifully in that especially which she had most at heart, relieving her people from a bloody and expensive war; and that he had always been too much an Englishman to sacrifice the interest of his country to any foreign ally whatsoever.

1715.
Sir William
Wyndham
reprimand-
ed by the
speaker.

In the midst of all this violence against the late ministers, friends were not wanting to espouse their cause in the face of opposition; and even in some addresses to the king their conduct was justified. Nay, some individuals had courage enough to attack the present administration. When a motion was made in the House of Commons, to consider the king's proclamation for calling a new Parliament, Sir William Whitelock, member for the university of Oxford, boldly declared it was unprecedented and unwarrantable. Being called upon to explain himself, he made an apology. Nevertheless, Sir William Wyndham, rising up, said, the proclamation was not only unprecedented and unwarrantable, but even of dangerous consequence to the very being of Parliaments. When challenged to justify his charge, he observed, that every member was free to speak his thoughts. Some exclaimed, "The Tower! the Tower!" A warm debate ensued: Sir William being ordered to withdraw, was accompanied by one hundred and twenty-nine members; and those who remained in the House resolved that he should be reprimanded by the speaker. He was accordingly rebuked for having presumed to reflect on his majesty's proclamation, and having made an unwarrantable use of the freedom of speech granted by his majesty. Sir William said, he was not conscious of having offered any indignity to his majesty, or of having been guilty of a breach of privilege: that he acquiesced in the determination of the House; but had no thanks to give to those gentlemen who, under pretence of lenity, had subjected him to this censure.

Committee
of secresy.

On the ninth day of April, General Stanhope delivered to the House of Commons fourteen volumes, consisting of all the papers relating to the late negotiations of peace and commerce, as well as to the cessation of arms; and moved that they might be referred to a select committee of twenty persons, who should digest the substance of them under proper heads, and report them, with their observations, to the House. One more was added to the number of this secret committee, which was chosen by ballot, and met that same evening. Mr. Robert Walpole, original chairman, being taken ill, was succeeded in that place by Mr. Stanhope. The whole number was subdivided into three committees: to each a certain number of books was allotted; and they carried on the inquiry with great eagerness and expedition. Before this measure was taken, Dr. Gilbert Burnet, Bishop of Sarum, died of a pleuritic fever, in the seventy-second year of his age. Immediately after the committee had begun to act, the whig party lost one of their warmest champions, by the death of the Marquis of Wharton, a nobleman possessed of happy talents for the cabinet, the senate, and the common scenes of life; talents which a life of pleasure and libertinism did not prevent him from employing with surprising vigour and application. The Committee of the Lower House, taking the civil list into consideration, examined several papers relating to that revenue. The tories observed, that from the seven hundred thousand pounds granted annually to King William, fifty thousand pounds were allotted to the late queen, when Princess of Denmark, twenty thousand pounds to the Duke of Gloucester, and twice that sum, as a dowry, to James's queen: that near two hundred thousand pounds had been yearly deducted from the revenues of the late queen's civil list, and applied to other uses; notwithstanding which deduction, she had honourably maintained her family, and supported the dignity of the crown. In the course of the debate some warm altercation passed between Lord Guernsey and one of the members, who affirmed that the late ministry had used the whigs, and indeed the whole nation, in such a manner, that nothing they should suffer could be deemed hardship. At length the House agreed that the sum of seven hundred thousand pounds clear should be granted for the civil list during his majesty's life. A motion being made for an address against pensions, it was opposed by Mr. Walpole, and overruled by the majority. The lords passed the bill for regulating the land forces, with some amendments.

On the eighteenth day of May, Sir John Norris sailed

CHAP.
XII.

1715.
Sir John
Norris sent
with a fleet
to the
Baltic.

with a strong squadron to the Baltic, in order to protect the commerce of the nation, which had suffered from the King of Sweden, who caused all ships trading to those parts to be seized and confiscated. That prince had rejected the treaty of neutrality concerted by the allies for the security of the empire; and considered the English and Dutch as his enemies. The ministers of England and the States-General had presented memorials to the regency of Sweden; but finding no redress, they resolved to protect their trade by force of arms. After the Swedish general, Steenboch, and his army were made prisoners, Count Wellen concluded a treaty with the administrator of Holstein-Gottorp, by which the towns of Stetin and Wismar were sequestered into the hands of the King of Prussia; the administrator engaged to secure them, and all the rest of Swedish Pomerania, from the Poles and Muscovites; but, as the governor of Pomerania refused to comply with this treaty, those allies marched into the province, subdued the island of Rugen, and obliged Stetin to surrender. Then the governor consented to the sequestration, and paid to the Poles and Muscovites four hundred thousand rix-dollars, to indemnify them for the expense of the siege. The King of Sweden returning from Turkey, rejected the treaty of sequestration, and insisted upon Stetin's being restored, without his repaying the money. As this monarch likewise threatened to invade the electorate of Saxony, and chastise his false friend, King George, for the security of his German dominions, concluded a treaty with the King of Denmark, by which the duchies of Bremen and Verden, which had been taken from the Swedes in his absence, were made over to his Britannic majesty, on condition that he should immediately declare war against Sweden. Accordingly he took possession of the duchies in October; published a declaration of war against Charles in his German dominions; and detached six thousand Hanoverians to join the Danes and Prussians in Pomerania. These allies reduced the islands of Rugen and Uledon, and attacked the towns of Wismar and Stralsund, from which last place Charles was obliged to retire in a vessel to Schonen. He assembled a body of troops with which he proposed to pass the Sound

upon the ice, and attack Copenhagen, but was disappointed by a sudden thaw. Nevertheless, he refused to
return to Stockholm, which he had not seen for sixteen
years; but remained at Carlscroon, in order to hasten his
fleet for the relief of Wismar.

The spirit of discontent and disaffection seemed to gain
ground every day in England. Notwithstanding proclamations against riots, and orders of the justices for maintaining the peace, repeated tumults were raised by the
malecontents in the cities of London and Westminster.
Those who celebrated the anniversary of the king's birthday with the usual marks of joy and festivity were insulted by the populace; but next day, which was the
anniversary of the Restoration, the whole city was lighted
up with bonfires and illuminations, and echoed with the
sound of mirth and tumultuous rejoicing. The people
even obliged the life-guards, who patrolled through the
streets, to join in the cry of "High-church and Ormond!"
and in Smithfield they burned the picture of King
William. Thirty persons were imprisoned for being
concerned in these riots. One Bournois, a schoolmaster,
who affirmed that King George had no right to the
crown, was tried, and scourged through the city, with such
severity, that in a few days he expired in the utmost
torture. A frivolous incident served to increase the
popular ferment. The shirts allowed to the first regiment
of guards, commanded by the Duke of Marlborough, were
so coarse, that the soldiers could hardly be persuaded to
wear them. Some were thrown into the garden of the
king's palace, and into that which belonged to the Duke
of Marlborough. A detachment, in marching through
the city, produced them to the view of the shopkeepers
and passengers, exclaiming, "These are the Hanover
shirts." The court being informed of this clamour,
ordered those new shirts to be burned immediately; but
even this sacrifice, and an advertisement published by the
Duke of Marlborough in his own vindication, did not
acquit that general of suspicion that he was concerned in
this mean species of peculation. A reward of fifty pounds
was offered by the government to any person that would
discover one Captain Wright, who, by an intercepted
letter, appeared to be disaffected to King George; and

Mr. George Jefferies was seized at Dublin, with a packet, directed to Dr. Jonathan Swift, Dean of St. Patrick's. Several treasonable papers being found in this packet were transmitted to England; Jefferies was obliged to give bail for his appearance; and Swift thought proper to abscond.

Report of the secret committee.

The House of Lords, to demonstrate their abhorrence of all who should engage in conspiracies against their sovereign, rejected with indignation a petition presented to them in behalf of Blackburn, Casils, Barnarde, Meldrum, and Chambers, who had hitherto continued prisoners, for having conspired against the life of King William. On the ninth day of June, Mr. Walpole, as chairman of the secret committee, declared to the House of Commons that the report was ready; and in the mean time moved that a warrant might be issued by Mr. Speaker, for appprehending several persons, particularly Mr. Matthew Prior and Mr. Thomas Harley, who, being in the House, were immediately taken into custody. Then he recited the report, ranged under these different heads: the clandestine negotiation with Monsieur Menager; the extraordinary measures pursued to form the congress at Utrecht; the trifling of the French plenipotentiaries, by the connivance of the British ministers; the negotiation about the renunciation of the Spanish monarchy; the fatal suspension of arms; the seizure of Ghent and Bruges, in order to distress the allies and favour the French; the Duke of Ormond's acting in concert with the French General; the Lord Bolingbroke's journey to France, to negotiate a separate peace; Mr. Prior's and the Duke of Shrewsbury's negotiations in France; the precipitate conclusion of the peace at Utrecht. The report being read, Sir Thomas Hanmer moved that the consideration of it should be adjourned to a certain day; and that in the mean time the report should be printed for the perusal of the members: he was seconded by the tories; a debate ensued; and the motion was rejected by a great majority.

Resolutions to impeach Lord Bolingbroke, Earl of

This point being gained, Mr. Walpole impeached Henry Lord Viscount Bolingbroke of high-treason, and other high crimes and misdemeanours. Mr. Hungerford declared his opinion, that nothing mentioned in the re-

port, in relation to Lord Bolingbroke, amounted to high-
treason ; and General Ross expressed the same sentiment.
Then Lord Coningsby standing up, "the worthy chairman
(said he) has impeached the hand, but I impeach the head :
he has impeached the clerk, and I the justice : he has impeached the scholar, and I the master. I impeach Robert
Earl of Oxford and Earl Mortimer of high-treason, and
other crimes and misdemeanours." Mr. Auditor Harley,
the earl's brother, spoke in vindication of that minister.
He affirmed he had done nothing but by the immediate
command of his sovereign; that the peace was a good
peace, and approved as such by two Parliaments; and
that the facts charged to him in the report amounted only
to misdemeanours : if the sanction of a Parliament, which
is the representative and legislature of the nation, be not
sufficient to protect a minister from the vengeance of his
enemies, he can have no security. Mr. Auditor Foley,
the Earl's brother-in-law, made a speech to the same
purpose ; Sir Joseph Jekyll, a stanch whig, and member
of the secret committee, expressed his doubt, whether
they had sufficient matter or evidence to impeach the
earl of high-treason. Nevertheless, the House resolved
to impeach him, without a division. When he appeared
in the House of Lords next day, he found himself avoided
by his brother peers as infectious ; and retired with signs
of confusion. Prior and Harley having been examined
by such of the committee as were justices of the peace
for Middlesex, Mr. Walpole informed the House that
matters of such importance appeared in Prior's examination, that he was directed to move them for that member's
being closely confined. Prior was accordingly imprisoned,
and cut off from all communication. On the twenty-
first day of June, Mr. Secretary Stanhope impeached
James, Duke of Ormond, of high-treason and other high
crimes and misdemeanours. Mr. Archibald Hutchinson,
one of the commissioners of trade, spoke in favour of the
duke. He expatiated on his noble birth and qualifications : he enumerated the great services performed to
the crown and nation by his grace and his ancestors: he
observed, that in the whole course of his late conduct, he
had only obeyed the queen's commands ; and he affirmed
that all the allegations against him could not, in the

rigour of the law, be construed into high-treason. Mr. Hutchinson was seconded by General Lumley, who urged that the Duke of Ormond had on all occasions given signal proofs of his affection for his country, as well as of personal courage; and that he had generously expended the best part of his estate, by living abroad in a most noble and splendid manner, for the honour of his sovereign. Sir Joseph Jekyll said, if there was room for mercy, he hoped it would be shown to that noble, generous, and courageous peer, who had in a course of many years exerted those great accomplishments for the good and honour of his country; that, as the statute of Edward III., on which the charge of high-treason against him was to be grounded, had been mitigated by subsequent acts, the House ought not, in his opinion, to take advantage of that act against the duke, but only impeach him of high crimes and misdemeanours. General Ross, Sir William Wyndham, and the speakers of that party, did not abandon the duke in this emergency; but all their arguments and eloquence were lost upon the other faction, by which they were greatly outnumbered. The question being put, was carried for the impeachment of the Duke of Ormond, who perceiving every thing conducted by a furious spirit of revenge, and that he could not expect the benefit of an impartial trial, consulted his own safety, by withdrawing himself from the kingdom. On the twenty-second day of June, the Earl of Strafford was likewise impeached by Mr. Aislaby, for having advised the fatal suspension of arms, and the seizing of Ghent and Bruges; as well as for having treated the most serene house of Hanover with insolence and contempt. He was also defended by his friends, but overpowered by his enemies.

When the articles against the Earl of Oxford were read in the House, a warm debate arose upon the eleventh, by which he was charged with having advised the French king in what manner Tournay might be gained from the States-General. The question being put, whether this article amounted to high-treason, Sir Robert Raymond, formerly solicitor-general, maintained the negative, and was supported not only by Sir William Wyndham and the tories, but also by Sir Joseph Jekyll. This honest patriot said it was ever his prin-

ciple to do justice to every body, from the highest to
the lowest; and that it was the duty of an honest man
never to act by a spirit of party: that he hoped he
might pretend to have some knowledge of the laws of
the kingdom; and would not scruple to declare, that,
in his judgment, the charge in question did not amount
to high-treason. Mr. Walpole answered with great
warmth, that there were several persons both in and out
of the committee, who did not in the least yield to that
member in point of honesty, and who were superior to
him in the knowledge of the laws, yet were satisfied that
the charge specified in the eleventh article amounted
to high-treason. This point being decided against the
earl, and the other articles approved by the House,
Lord Coningsby, attended by the whig members, impeached the Earl of Oxford at the bar of the House of
Lords, demanding at the same time, that he might be
sequestered from Parliament, and committed to safe
custody. A motion was made, that the consideration
of the articles might be adjourned. After a short debate the articles were read; then the tory lords moved
that the judges might be consulted. The motion being
rejected, another was made, that the earl should be committed to safe custody; this occasioned another debate,
in which he himself spoke to the following purpose: that
the whole charge might be reduced to the negotiations
and conclusion of the peace; that the nation wanted a
peace, he said, nobody would deny; that the conditions
of the peace were as good as could be expected, considering the backwardness and reluctancy which some of the
allies showed to come in to the queen's measures; that
the peace was approved by two successive Parliaments;
that he had no share in the affair of Tournay, which was
wholly transacted by that unfortunate nobleman who had
thought fit to step aside: that, for his own part, he always acted by the immediate directions and commands
of the late queen, without offending against any known
law; and being justified by his own conscience, was unconcerned for the life of an insignificant old man; that,
if ministers of state, acting by the immediate commands
of their sovereign, are afterwards to be made account-
able for their proceedings, it might one day or other be

the case with all the members of that august assembly;
that he did not doubt their lordships, out of regard to
themselves, would give him an equitable hearing; and
that in the prosecution of the inquiry it would appear
he had merited not only the indulgence, but even the
favour of his government. "My lords (said he), I am
now to take my leave of your lordships, and of this
honourable House, perhaps for ever; I shall lay down
my life with pleasure in a cause favoured by my late
dear royal mistress. When I consider that I am to be
judged by the justice, honour, and virtue of my peers, I
shall acquiesce, and retire with great content; and, my
lords, God's will be done." The Duke of Shrewsbury
having acquainted the house that the earl was very much
indisposed with the gravel, he was suffered to remain at
his own house, in custody of the black rod; in his way
thither he was attended by a great multitude of people,
crying, "High-church, Ormond, and Oxford, for ever!"
Next day he was brought to the bar; where he received
a copy of the articles, and was allowed a month to prepare his answer. Though Dr. Mead declared, that if the
earl should be sent to the Tower his life would be in
danger, it was carried, on a division, that he should be
conveyed thither on the sixteenth day of July. During
the debate, the Earl of Anglesey observed that these impeachments were disagreeable to the nation; and that it
was to be feared such violent measures would make the
sceptre shake in the king's hands. This expression kindled the whole House into a flame. Some members
cried, "To the Tower!" some, "To order!" The Earl
of Sunderland declared, that if these words had been
spoken in another place he would have called the person
who spoke them to an account; in the mean time he
moved that the noble lord should explain himself. Anglesey, dreading the resentment of the House, was glad
to make an apology; which was accepted. The Earl of
Oxford was attended to the Tower by a prodigious concourse of people, who did not scruple to exclaim against
his persecutors. Tumults were raised in Staffordshire
and other parts of the kingdom, against the whig party,
which had depressed the friends of the church, and embroiled the nation. The House of Commons presented

an address to the king, desiring that the laws might be
vigorously executed against the rioters. They prepared
the proclamation act, decreeing, that if any persons, to
the number of twelve, unlawfully assembled, should continue together one hour after having been required to
disperse by a justice of peace or other officer, and heard
the proclamation against riots read in public, they should
be deemed guilty of felony without benefit of clergy.

When the king went to the House of Peers, on the The king
declares to
both
Houses
that a re-
bellion is
begun. twentieth day of July, to give the royal assent to this
and some other bills, he told both Houses that a rebellion was actually begun at home, and that the nation
was threatened with an invasion from abroad. He, therefore, expected that the Commons would not leave the
kingdom in a defenceless condition, but enable him to
take such measures as should be necessary for the public
safety. Addresses in the usual style were immediately presented by the Parliament, the convocation, the common
council and lieutenancy of London, and the two universities; but that of Oxford was received in the most contemptuous manner; and the deputies were charged with
disloyalty, on account of a fray which had happened between some recruiting officers and the scholars of the
university. The addresses from the kirk of Scotland,
and the dissenting ministers of London and Westminster,
met with a much more gracious reception. The Parliament forthwith passed a bill, empowering the king to
secure suspected persons, and to suspend the habeas
corpus act in that time of danger. A clause was added
to a money bill, offering the reward of one hundred thousand pounds to such as should seize the pretender dead
or alive. Sir George Byng was sent to take the command
of the fleet: General Earle repaired to his government
of Portsmouth: the guards were encamped in Hyde
Park: Lord Irwin was appointed governor of Hull, in
the room of Brigadier Sutton, who, together with Lord
Windsor, the Generals Ross, Webb, and Stuart, were
dismissed from the service. Orders were given for raising thirteen regiments of dragoons, and eight of infantry;
and the trained bands were kept in readiness to suppress
tumults. In the midst of these transactions the Commons added six articles to those exhibited against the

Earl of Oxford.   Lord Bolingbroke was impeached at
the bar of the House of Lords by Mr. Walpole.   Bills
being brought in to summon him and the Duke of Ormond to surrender themselves by the tenth of September, or, in default thereof, to attaint them of high-treason,
they passed both Houses, and received the royal assent.
On the last day of August, the Commons agreed to the
articles against the Earl of Strafford, which being presented to the House of Lords, the earl made a speech
in his own vindication.   He complained that his papers
had been seized in an unprecedented manner.   He said,
if he had in his letters or discourse dropped any unguarded expressions against some foreign ministers while
he had the honour to represent the crown of Great
Britain, he hoped they would not be accounted criminal
by a British House of Peers: he desired he might be
allowed a competent time to answer the articles brought
against him, and have duplicates of all the papers which
had either been laid before the committee of secresy, or
remained in the hands of government, to be used occasionally in his justification.   This request was vehemently
opposed by the leaders of the other party, until the Earl
of Ilay represented that, in all civilized nations, all courts
of judicature, except the inquisition, allowed the persons
arraigned all that was necessary for their justification;
and that the House of Peers of Great Britain ought not,
in this case, to do any thing contrary to that honour and
equity for which they were so justly renowned throughout
all Europe.   This observation made an impression on the
House, which resolved that the earl should be indulged
with copies of such papers as he might have occasion to
use in his defence.

The Duke
of Ormond
and Lord
Boling-
broke at-
tainted.

On the third day of September, Oxford's answer was
delivered to the House of Lords, who transmitted it to
the Commons.   Mr. Walpole, having heard it read, said
it contained little more than a repetition of what had
been suggested in some pamphlets and papers which had
been published in vindication of the late ministry: that
it was a false and malicious libel, laying upon his royal
mistress the blame of all the pernicious measures he had
led her into, against her own honour, and the good of
his country; that it was likewise a libel on the proceed-

ings of the Commons, since he endeavoured to clear those persons who had already confessed their guilt by flight. After some debate, the House resolved, that the answer of Robert Earl of Oxford should be referred to the committee appointed to draw up articles of impeachment, and prepare evidence against the impeached lords; and that the committee should prepare a replication to the answer. This was accordingly prepared, and sent up to the Lords. Then the committee reported, that Mr. Prior had grossly prevaricated on his examination, and behaved with great contempt of their authority. The Duke of Ormond and Lord Viscount Bolingbroke having omitted to surrender themselves within the time limited, the House of Lords ordered the earl-marshal to raze out of the list of peers their names and armorial bearings. Inventories were taken of their personal estates; and the duke's achievement, as knight of the garter, was taken down from St. George's chapel at Windsor. A man of candour cannot, without an emotion of grief and indignation, reflect upon the ruin of the noble family of Ormond, in the person of a brave, generous, and humane nobleman, to whom no crime was imputed but that of having obeyed the commands of his sovereign. About this period, the royal assent was given to an act for encouraging loyalty in Scotland. By this law, the tenant who continued peaceable while his lord took arms in favour of the pretender was invested with the property of the lands he rented: on the other hand, it was decreed that the lands possessed by any person guilty of high treason should revert to the superior of whom they were held, and be consolidated with the superiority; and that all entails and settlements of estates, since the first day of August, in favour of children, with a fraudulent intent to avoid the punishment of the law due to the offence of high-treason, should be null and void. It likewise contained a clause for summoning suspected persons to find bail for their good behaviour, on pain of being denounced rebels. By virtue of this clause all the heads of the Jacobite clans, and other suspected persons, were summoned to Edinburgh; and those who did not appear were declared rebels.

By this time the rebellion was actually begun in Scot-

CHAP.
XII.

1715.
Intrigues of
the Jacob-
ites.

land. The dissensions occasioned in that country by the union had never been wholly appeased. Even since the queen's death, addresses were prepared in different parts of Scotland against the union, which was deemed a national grievance; and the Jacobites did not fail to encourage this aversion. Though their hopes of dissolving that treaty were baffled by the industry and other arts of the revolutioners, who secured a majority of whigs in Parliament, they did not lay aside their designs of attempting something of consequence in favour of the pretender; but maintained a correspondence with the malecontents of England, a great number of whom were driven by apprehension, hard usage, and resentment, into a system of politics, which otherwise they would not have espoused. The tories finding themselves totally excluded from any share in the government and legislature, and exposed to the insolence and fury of a faction which they despised, began to wish in earnest for a revolution. Some of them held private consultations, and communicated with the Jacobites, who conveyed their sentiments to the Chevalier de St. George, with such exaggerations as were dictated by their own eagerness and extravagance. They assured the pretender that the nation was wholly disaffected to the new government; and, indeed, the clamours, tumults, and conversation of the people in general countenanced this assertion. They promised to take arms without further delay in his favour; and engaged that the tories should join him at his first landing in Great Britain. They, therefore, besought him to come over with all possible expedition, declaring that his appearance would produce an immediate revolution. The chevalier resolved to take the advantage of this favourable disposition. He had recourse to the French king, who had always been the refuge of his family. Louis favoured him in secret; and, notwithstanding his late engagements with England, cherished the ambition of raising him to the throne of Great Britain. He supplied him privately with sums of money, to prepare a small armament in the port of Havre, which was equipped in the name of Depine d'Anicaut; and, without all doubt, his design was to assist him more effectually, in proportion as the English should manifest their attachment to the

house of Stuart. The Duke of Ormond and Lord Bolingbroke, who had retired to France, finding themselves
condemned unheard, and attainted, engaged in the service of the chevalier, and corresponded with the tories of
England.

All these intrigues and machinations were discovered
and communicated to the court of London by the Earl
of Stair, who then resided as English ambassador at Paris.
He was a nobleman of unquestioned honour and integrity, generous, humane, discerning, and resolute. He
had signalized himself by his valour, intrepidity, and
other military talents, during the war in the Netherlands; and he now acted in another sphere with uncommon vigour, vigilance, and address. He detected the
chevalier's scheme while it was yet in embryo, and gave
such early notice of it as enabled the King of Great
Britain to take effectual measures for defeating the design. All the pretender's interest in France expired
with Louis XIV., that ostentatious tyrant, who had for
above half a century sacrificed the repose of Christendom
to his insatiate vanity and ambition. At his death, which
happened on the first day of September, the regency of
the kingdom devolved to the Duke of Orleans, who
adopted a new system of politics, and had already entered into engagements with the King of Great Britain.
Instead of assisting the pretender, he amused his agents
with mysterious and equivocal expressions, calculated to
frustrate the design of the expedition. Nevertheless,
the more violent part of the Jacobites in Great Britain
believed he was at bottom a friend to their cause, and
depended upon him for succour. They even extorted
from him a sum of money by dint of importunities, and
some arms; but the vessel was shipwrecked, and the
cargo lost upon the coast of Scotland.

The partisans of the pretender had proceeded too far
to retreat with safety, and, therefore, resolved to try their
fortune in the field. The Earl of Mar repaired to the
Highlands, where he held consultations with the Mar-
quisses of Huntley and Tullibardine; the Earls Marischal
and Southesk, the Generals Hamilton and Gordon, with
the chiefs of the Jacobite clans. Then he assembled
three hundred of his own vassals; proclaimed the pre-

tender at Castletown, and set up his standard at Braemar, on the sixth day of September. By this time the Earls of Home, Wintoun, and Kinnoul, Lord Deskford, and Lockhart of Carnwath, with other persons suspected of disaffection to the present government, were committed prisoners to the castle of Edinburgh; and Major-General Whetham marched with the regular troops which were in that kingdom to secure the bridge at Stirling. Before these precautions were taken, two vessels had arrived at Arbroath from Havre, with arms, ammunition, and a great number of officers, who assured the Earl of Mar, that the pretender would soon be with them in person. The death of Louis XIV. struck a general damp upon their spirits; but they laid their account with being joined by a powerful body in England. The Earl of Mar, by letters and messages, pressed the chevalier to come over without further delay. He, in the mean time, assumed the title of lieutenant-general of the pretender's forces, and published a declaration, exhorting the people to take arms for their lawful sovereign. This was followed by a shrewd manifesto, explaining the national grievances, and assuring the people of redress. Some of his partisans attempted to surprise the castle of Edinburgh; but were prevented by the vigilance and activity of Colonel Stuart, lieutenant-governor of that fortress. The Duke of Argyle set out for Scotland, as commander in chief of the forces in North Britain: the Earl of Sutherland set sail in the Queenborough ship of war for the North, where he proposed to raise his vassals for the service of government; and many other Scottish peers returned to their own country, in order to signalize their loyalty to King George.

Divers members of the Lower House taken into custody.

In England the practices of the Jacobites did not escape the notice of the ministry. Lieutenant-Colonel Paul was imprisoned in the gate-house for enlisting men in the service of the pretender. The titular Duke of Powis was committed to the Tower: Lords Lansdown and Duplin were taken into custody; and a warrant was issued for apprehending the Earl of Jersey. The king desired the consent of the Lower House to seize and detain Sir William Wyndham, Sir John Packington,

Mr. Edward Harvey of Combe, Mr. Thomas Forster, Mr. John Anstis, and Mr. Corbet Kynaston, who were members of the House, and suspected of favouring the invasion. The Commons unanimously agreed to the proposal, and presented an address, signifying their approbation. Harvey and Anstis were immediately secured. Forster, with the assistance of some popish lords, assembled a body of men in Northumberland: Sir John Packington being examined before the council was dismissed for want of evidence: Mr. Kynaston absconded: Sir William Wyndham was seized at his own house in Somersetshire by Colonel Huske and a messenger, who secured his papers: he found means, however, to escape from them; but afterwards surrendered himself, and, having been examined at the council-board, was committed to the Tower. His father-in-law, the Duke of Somerset, offered to become bound for his appearance; and being rejected as bail, expressed his resentment so warmly, that the king thought proper to remove him from the office of master of the horse. On the twenty-first day of September, the king went to the House of Lords, and passed the bills that were ready for the royal assent. Then the chancellor read his majesty's speech expressing his acknowledgment and satisfaction, in consequence of the uncommon marks of their affection he had received; and the Parliament adjourned to the sixth day of October.

The friends of the house of Stuart were very numerous in the western counties, and began to make preparations for an insurrection. They had concealed some arms and artillery at Bath, and formed a design to surprise Bristol; but they were betrayed and discovered by the emissaries of the government, which baffled all their schemes, and apprehended every person of consequence suspected of attachment to that cause. The university of Oxford felt the rod of power on this occasion. Major-General Pepper, with a strong detachment of dragoons, took possession of the city at daybreak, declaring he would use military execution on all students who should presume to appear without the limits of their respective colleges. He seized ten or eleven persons, among whom was one Lloyd, a coffeeman; and made prize of some horses and furniture belonging to Colonel Owen, and

The pretender proclaimed in the north of England by the Earl of Derwentwater and Mr. Forster.

other gentlemen. With this booty he retreated to Abingdon; and Handasyde's regiment of foot was afterwards quartered in Oxford, to overawe the university. The ministry found it more difficult to suppress the insurgents in the northern counties. In the month of October the Earl of Derwentwater and Mr. Forster took the field with a body of horse, and being joined by some gentlemen from the borders of Scotland, proclaimed the pretender at Warkworth, Morpeth, and Alnwick. Their first design was to seize the town of Newcastle, in which they had many friends; but they found the gates shut upon them, and retired to Hexham; while General Carpenter, having assembled a body of dragoons, resolved to march from Newcastle, and attack them before they should be reinforced. The rebels retiring northward to Wooller, were joined by two hundred Scottish horse under the Lord Viscount Kenmuir, and the Earls of Carnwath and Wintoun, who had set up the pretender's standard at Moffat, and proclaimed him in different parts of Scotland. The rebels thus reinforced advanced to Kelso, having received advice that they would be joined by Mackintosh, who had crossed the Forth with a body of Highlanders.

Mackintosh crosses the Frith of Forth into Lothian, and joins the English insurgents.

By this time the Earl of Mar was at the head of ten thousand men well armed. He had secured the pass of the Tay at Perth, where his head-quarters were established, and made himself master of the whole fruitful province of Fife, and all the sea-coast on that side of the Frith of Edinburgh. He selected two thousand five hundred men, commanded by Brigadier Mackintosh, to make a descent upon the Lothian side, and join the Jacobites in that county, or such as should take arms on the borders of England. Boats were assembled for this purpose; and notwithstanding all the precautions that could be taken by the king's ships in the Frith to prevent the design, above fifteen hundred chosen men made good their passage in the night, and landed on the coast of Lothian, having crossed an arm of the sea about sixteen miles broad, in open boats that passed through the midst of the king's cruisers. Nothing could be better concerted, or executed with more conduct and courage, than was this hazardous enterprise. They amused the king's ships with marches and counter-marches along the coast,

in such a manner that they could not possibly know
where they intended to embark. The Earl of Mar, in
the mean time, marched from Perth to Dumblaine, as if
he had intended to cross the Forth at Stirling-bridge;
but his real design was to divert the Duke of Argyle
from attacking his detachment which had landed in
Lothian. So far the scheme succeeded. The duke,
who had assembled some troops in Lothian, returned to
Stirling with the utmost expedition, after having secured
Edinburgh, and obliged Mackintosh to abandon his design on that city. This partisan had actually taken possession of Leith, from whence he retired to Seaton-house,
near Preston-Pans, which he fortified in such a manner
that he could not be forced without artillery. Here he
remained until he received an order to cross the Frith
from the Earl of Mar, to join Lord Kenmuir and the
English at Kelso, for which place he immediately began
his march, and reached it on the twenty-second day of
October, though a good number of his men had deserted
on the route.

The Lord Kenmuir, with the Earls of Wintoun, Niths- Who are
dale, and Carnwath, the Earl of Derwentwater, and attacked at
Mr. Forster, with the English insurgents, arriving at the and surren-
same time, a council of war was immediately called. der at dis-
Wintoun proposed that they should march immediately cretion.
into the western parts of Scotland and join General Gordon, who commanded a strong body of Highlanders in
Argyleshire. The English insisted upon crossing the
Tweed, and attacking General Carpenter, whose troops
did not exceed nine hundred dragoons. Neither scheme
was executed. They took the route to Jedburgh, where
they resolved to leave Carpenter on one side, and penetrate into England by the western border. The Highlanders declared they would not quit their own country;
but were ready to execute the scheme proposed by the
Earl of Wintoun. Means, however, were found to prevail upon one half of them to advance, while the rest
returned to the Highlands. At Brampton, Forster
opened his commission of general, which had been
sent to him from the Earl of Mar, and proclaimed
the pretender. They continued their march to Penrith,
where the sheriff, assisted by Lord Lonsdale and the

Bishop of Carlisle, had assembled the whole posse-comi-
tatus of Cumberland, amounting to twelve thousand
men, who dispersed with the utmost precipitation at the
approach of the rebels. From Penrith, Forster proceeded
by the way of Kendal and Lancaster to Preston, from
whence Stanhope's regiment of dragoons, and another of
militia, immediately retired; so that he took possession of
the place without resistance. General Willis marched
against the enemy with six regiments of horse and dragoons, and one battalion of foot commanded by Colonel
Preston. They had advanced to the bridge of Ribble
before Forster received intelligence of their approach.
He forthwith began to raise barricadoes, and put the
place in a posture of defence. On the twelfth day of
November, the town was briskly attacked in two different places; but the king's troops met with a very warm
reception, and were repulsed with considerable loss.
Next day General Carpenter arrived with a reinforcement of three regiments of dragoons, and the rebels
were invested on all sides. The Highlanders declared
they would make a sally sword in hand, and either cut
their way through the king's troops, or perish in the attempt, but they were overruled. Forster sent Colonel
Oxburgh with a trumpet to General Willis, to propose a
capitulation. He was given to understand that the general would not treat with rebels; but in case of their
surrendering at discretion, he would prevent his soldiers
from putting them to the sword, until he should receive
further orders. He granted them time to consider till
next morning, upon their delivering the Earl of Derwentwater and Mackintosh as hostages. When Forster submitted, this Highlander declared he could not promise
that the Scots would surrender in that manner. The
general desired him to return to his people, and he would
forthwith attack the town, in which case every man of
them should be cut to pieces. The Scottish nobleman
did not choose to run the risk, and persuaded the Highlanders to accept the terms that were offered. They accordingly laid down their arms, and were put under a
strong guard. All the noblemen and leaders were secured. Major Nairn, Captain Lockhart, Captain Shaftoe,
and Ensign Erskine, were tried by a court martial as

deserters, and executed. Lord Charles Murray, son of
the Duke of Athol, was likewise condemned for the same
crime, but reprieved. The common men were imprisoned at Chester and Liverpool, the noblemen and considerable officers were sent to London, conveyed through
the streets pinioned like malefactors, and committed to
the Tower and to Newgate.

The day on which the rebels surrendered at Preston
was remarkable for the battle of Dumblaine, fought between the Duke of Argyle and the Earl of Mar, who
commanded the pretender's forces. This nobleman had
retreated to his camp at Perth, when he understood the
duke was returned from Lothian to Stirling. But being
now joined by the northern clans under the Earl of Seaforth, and those of the west commanded by General
Gordon, who had signalized himself in the service of the
Czar of Muscovy, he resolved to pass the Forth, in order
to join his southern friends, that they might march together into England. With this view he advanced to
Auchterarder, where he reviewed his army, and rested
on the eleventh day of November. The Duke of Argyle,
apprised of his intention, and being joined by some regiments of dragoons from Ireland, determined to give
him battle in the neighbourhood of Dumblaine. On the
twelfth day of the month, Argyle passed the Forth at
Stirling, and encamped with his left at the village of
Dumblaine, and his right towards Sheriff-moor. The
Earl of Mar advanced within two miles of his camp,
and remained till daybreak in order of battle; his army
consisting of nine thousand effective men, cavalry as
well as infantry. In the morning the duke, understanding they were in motion, drew up his forces, which did
not exceed three thousand five hundred men, on the
heights to the north-east of Dumblaine; but he was out-
flanked both on the right and left. The clans that
formed part of the centre and right wing of the enemy,
with Glengary and Clanronald at their head, charged the
left of the king's army sword in hand, with such impetuosity, that in seven minutes both horse and foot
were totally routed with great slaughter; and General
Whetham, who commanded them, fled at full gallop to
Stirling, where he declared that the royal army was

totally defeated. In the mean time, the Duke of Argyle, who commanded in person on the right, attacked the left of the enemy, at the head of Stair's and Evans's dragoons, and drove them two miles before him, as far as the water of Allan : yet in that space they wheeled about, and attempted to rally ten times ; so that he was obliged to press them hard, that they might not recover from their confusion. Brigadier Wightman followed, in order to sustain him with three battalions of infantry ; while the victorious right wing of the rebels, having pursued Whetham a considerable way, returned to the field, and formed in the rear of Wightman to the amount of five thousand men. The Duke of Argyle, returning from the pursuit, joined Wightman, who had faced about and taken possession of some enclosures and mud-walls, in expectation of being attacked. In this posture both armies fronted each other till the evening, when the duke drew off towards Dumblaine, and the rebels retired to Ardoch, without mutual molestation. Next day the duke marching back to the field of battle, carried off the wounded, with four pieces of cannon left by the enemy, and retreated to Stirling. Few prisoners were taken on either side ; the number of the slain might be about five hundred of each army, and both generals claimed the victory. This battle was not so fatal to the Highlanders as the loss of Inverness, from which Sir John Mackenzie was driven by Simon Frazer Lord Lovat, who, contrary to the principles he had hitherto professed, secured this important post for the government ; by which means a free communication was opened with the north of Scotland, where the Earl of Sutherland had raised a considerable body of vassals. The Marquis of Huntley and the Earl of Seaforth were obliged to quit the rebel army in order to defend their own territories ; and in a little time submitted to King George : a good number of the Frazers declared with their chief against the pretender : the Marquis of Tullibardine withdrew from the army, to cover his own country ; and the clans, seeing no likelihood of another action, began to disperse, according to custom.

The government was now in a condition to send strong reinforcements to Scotland. Six thousand men that were claimed of the States-General, by virtue of the treaty, landed in England, and began their march for Edinburgh: General Cadogan set out for the same place, together with Brigadier Petit, and six other engineers; and a train of artillery was shipped at the Tower for that country, the Duke of Argyle resolving to drive the Earl of Mar out of Perth, to which town he had retired with the remains of his forces. The pretender having been amused with the hope of seeing the whole kingdom of England rise up as one man in his behalf; and the Duke of Ormond having made a fruitless voyage to the western coast, to try the disposition of the people, he was now convinced of the vanity of his expectation in that quarter; and, as he knew not what other course to take, he resolved to hazard his person among his friends in Scotland, at a time when his affairs in that kingdom were absolutely desperate. From Bretagne he posted through part of France in disguise, and embarking in a small vessel at Dunkirk, hired for that purpose, arrived on the twenty-second day of December at Peterhead with six gentlemen in his retinue, one of whom was the Marquis of Tinmouth, son to the Duke of Berwick. He passed through Aberdeen incognito, to Fetterosse, where he was met by the Earls of Mar and Marischal, and about thirty noblemen and gentlemen of the first quality. Here he was solemnly proclaimed: his declaration, dated at Commercy, was printed and circulated through all the parts in that neighbourhood; and he received addresses from the episcopal clergy, and the laity of that communion in the diocese of Aberdeen. On the fifth day of January, he made his public entry into Dundee; and on the seventh arrived at Scone, where he seemed determined to stay until the ceremony of his coronation should be performed. From thence he made an excursion to Perth, where he reviewed his forces. Then he formed a regular council; and published six proclamations; one for a general thanksgiving, on account of his safe arrival; another enjoining the ministers to pray for him in churches; a third establishing the currency of foreign coins; a fourth summoning the meeting of the convention of estates; a fifth ordering all sensible men to repair to his standard; and a sixth, fixing the twenty-third day of January for his coronation. He made a pathetic speech in a grand council, at which all the chiefs of his party assisted. They determined, however, to abandon the enterprise, as the king's army was reinforced by the Dutch auxiliaries, and they themselves were not only reduced to a small number, but likewise destitute of money, arms, ammunition, forage, and provision ; for the Duke of Argyle had taken possession of Burnt-island, and transported a detachment to Fife, so as to cut off Mar's communication with that fertile country.

He retires again to France.

Notwithstanding the severity of the weather, and a prodigious fall of snow, which rendered the roads almost impassable, the duke, on the twenty-ninth of January, began his march to Dumblaine, and next day reached Tullibardine, where he received intelligence that the pretender and his forces had, on the preceding day, retired towards Dundee. He forthwith took possession of Perth ; and then began his march to Aberbrothick in pursuit of the enemy. The Chevalier de St. George, being thus hotly pursued, was prevailed upon to embark on board a small French ship that lay in the harbour of Montrose. He was accompanied by the Earls of Mar and Melford, the Lord Drummond, Lieutenant-General Bulkley, and other persons of distinction, to the number of seventeen. In order to avoid the English cruisers, they stretched over to Norway, and coasting along the German and Dutch shores, arrived in five days at Graveline. General Gordon, whom the pretender had left commander in chief of the forces, assisted by the Earl Marischal, proceeded with them to Aberdeen, where he secured three vessels to sail northward, and take on board the persons who intended to make their escape to the continent. They then continued their march through Strathspey and Strath-down, to the hills of Badernoch, where the common people were quietly dismissed. This retreat was made with such expedition, that the Duke of Argyle, with all his activity, could never overtake their rear-guard, which consisted of a thousand horse, commanded by the Earl Marischal. Such was the issue of a rebellion that proved fatal to many noble families : a rebellion which, in all probability, would never have happened, had not the violent measures of a whig ministry kindled such a flame

of discontent in the nation as encouraged the partisans of
the pretender to hazard a revolt.

The Parliament of Ireland, which met at Dublin on the
twelfth day of November, seemed even more zealous, if
possible, than that of England for the present administration. They passed bills for recognising the king's title;
for the security of his person and government; for setting
a price on the pretender's head; and for attainting the
Duke of Ormond. They granted the supplies without
opposition. All those who had addressed the late queen
in favour of Sir Constantine Phipps, then Lord Chancellor
of Ireland, were now brought upon their knees and censured as guilty of a breach of privilege. They desired the
lords-justices would issue a proclamation against the
popish inhabitants of Limerick and Galway, who, pre-
suming upon the capitulation signed by King William,
claimed an exemption from the penalties imposed upon
other papists. They engaged in an association against
the pretender, and all his abettors. They voted the Earl
of Anglesey an enemy to the king and kingdom, because
he advised the queen to break the army, and prorogue the
late Parliament; and they addressed the king to remove
him from his council and service. The lords-justices
granted orders for apprehending the Earls of Antrim and
Westmeath, the Lords Netterville, Cahir, and Dillon, as
persons suspected of disaffection to the government.
Then they adjourned the two Houses.

The king in his speech to the English Parliament,
which met on the ninth of January, told them he had
reason to believe the pretender was landed in Scotland:
he congratulated them on the success of his arms in suppressing the rebellion; on the conclusion of the barrier
treaty between the emperor and the States-General,
under his guarantee; on a convention with Spain that
would deliver the trade of England to that kingdom from
the new impositions and hardships to which it was subjected in consequence of the late treaties. He likewise
gave them to understand, that a treaty for renewing all
former alliances between the crown of Great Britain and
the States-General was almost concluded; and he assured
the Commons he would freely give up all the estates that
should become forfeited to the crown by this rebellion,

to be applied towards defraying the extraordinary expense incurred on this occasion. The Commons, in their address of thanks, declared that they would prosecute, in the most vigorous and impartial manner, the authors of those destructive counsels which had drawn down such miseries upon the nation. Their resolutions were speedy, and exactly conformable to this declaration. They expelled Mr. Forster from the House. They forthwith impeached the Earls of Derwentwater, Nithsdale, Carnwath, and Wintoun ; Lords Widdrington, Kenmuir, and Nairn. These noblemen, being brought to the bar of the House of Lords, heard the articles of impeachment read on the tenth day of January, and were ordered to put in their answers on the sixteenth. The impeachments being lodged, the Lower House ordered a bill to be brought in for continuing the suspension of the habeas corpus act: then they prepared another to attaint the Marquis of Tullibardine, the Earls of Mar and Linlithgow, and Lord John Drummond. On the twenty-first day of January, the king gave the royal assent to the bill for continuing the suspension of the habeas corpus act. He told the Parliament that the pretender was actually in Scotland, heading the rebellion, and assuming the style and title of king of these realms : he demanded of the Commons such supply as might discourage any foreign power from assisting the rebels. On Thursday, the nineteenth day of January, all the impeached lords pleaded guilty to the articles exhibited against them, except the Earl of Wintoun, who petitioned for longer time, on various pretences. The rest received sentence of death on the ninth day of February, in the court erected in Westminster-hall, where the Lord Chancellor Cowper presided as lord high-steward on that occasion. The Countess of Nithsdale and Lady Nairn threw themselves at the king's feet, as he passed through the apartments of the palace, and implored his mercy in behalf of their husbands; but their tears and entreaties produced no effect. The council resolved that the sentence should be executed, and orders were given for that purpose to the lieutenant of the Tower, and the sheriffs of London and Middlesex.

The Countess of Derwentwater, with her sister, accompanied by the Duchesses of Cleveland and Bolton, and several other ladies of the first distinction, was introduced by the Dukes of Richmond and St. Alban's into the king's bedchamber, where she invoked his majesty's clemency for her unfortunate consort. She afterwards repaired to the lobby of the House of Peers, attended by the ladies of the other condemned lords, and above twenty others of the same quality, and begged the intercession of the House ; but no regard was paid to their petition. Next day they petitioned both Houses of Parliament. The Commons rejected their suit. In the Upper House, the Duke of Richmond delivered a petition from the Earl of Derwentwater, to whom he was nearly related, at the same time declaring that he himself should oppose his solicitation. The Earl of Derby expressed some compassion for the numerous family of Lord Nairn. Petitions from the rest were presented by other lords, moved by pity and humanity. Lord Townshend and others vehemently opposed their being read. The Earl of Nottingham thought this indulgence might be granted : the House assented to his opinion, and agreed to an address, praying his majesty would reprieve such of the condemned lords as should seem to deserve his mercy. To this petition the king answered, that on this, and all other occasions, he would do what he thought most consistent with the dignity of his crown and the safety of his people. The Earl of Nottingham, president of the council, his brother the Earl of Aylesbury, chancellor of the Duchy of Lancaster, his son Lord Finch, one of the lords of the treasury, his kinsman Lord Guernsey, master of the jewel-office, were altogether dismissed from his majesty's service. Orders were despatched for executing the Earls of Derwentwater and Nithsdale, and the Viscount of Kenmuir, immediately ; the others were respited to the seventh day of March. Nithsdale made his escape in woman's apparel, furnished and conveyed to him by his own mother. On the twenty-fourth day of February, Derwentwater and Kenmuir were beheaded on Tower-hill. The former was an amiable youth, brave, open, generous, hospitable, and humane. His fate drew tears from the spectators, and was a great misfortune to the country in which he lived. He gave bread to multi-

CHAP. XII.

1715.
The Earl of Derwentwater and Lord Kenmuir are beheaded.

tudes of people whom he employed on his estate; the poor, the widow, and the orphan, rejoiced in his bounty. Kenmuir was a virtuous nobleman, calm, sensible, resolute, and resigned. He was a devout member of the English church; but the other died in the faith of Rome: both adhered to their political principles. On the fifteenth day of March, Wintoun was brought to trial, and being convicted, received sentence of death.

When the king passed the land-tax bill, which was ushered in with a very extraordinary preamble, he informed both Houses of the pretender's flight from Scotland. In the beginning of April, a commission for trying the rebels met in the court of common-pleas, when bills of high treason were found against Mr. Forster, Mackintosh, and twenty of their confederates. Forster escaped from Newgate, and reached the continent in safety: the rest pleaded not guilty, and were indulged with time to prepare for their trials. The judges appointed to try the rebels at Liverpool found a considerable number guilty of high treason. Two-and-twenty were executed at Preston and Manchester: about a thousand prisoners submitted to the king's mercy, and petitioned for transportation. Pitts, the keeper of Newgate, being suspected of having connived at Forster's escape, was tried for his life at the Old Bailey, and acquitted. Notwithstanding this prosecution, which ought to have redoubled the vigilance of the jailors, Brigadier Mackintosh, and several other prisoners, broke from Newgate, after having mastered the keeper and turnkey, and disarmed the sentinel. The court proceeded with the trials of those that remained; and a great number were found guilty: four or five were hanged, drawn, and quartered at Tyburn: and among these was one William Paul, a clergyman, who, in his last speech, professed himself a true and sincere member of the church of England, but not of the revolution schismatical church, whose bishops had abandoned the king, and shamefully given up their ecclesiastical rights, by submitting to the unlawful, invalid, lay-deprivations authorized by the Prince of Orange.

Though the rebellion was extinguished, the flame of national dissatisfaction still continued to rage; the severities exercised against the rebels increased the general discontent: for now the danger was blown over, their humane passions began to prevail. The courage and fortitude with which the condemned persons encountered the pains of death in its most dreadful form, prepossessed many spectators in favour of the cause by which those unhappy victims were animated. In a word, persecution as usual extended the heresy. The ministry, perceiving this universal dissatisfaction, and dreading the revolution of a new Parliament, which might wrest the power from their faction, and retort upon them the violence of their own measures, formed a resolution equally odious and effectual to establish their administration. This was no other than a scheme to repeal the triennial act, and by a new law to extend the term of Parliaments to seven years. On the tenth day of April, the Duke of Devonshire represented, in the House of Lords, that triennial elections served to keep up party divisions; to raise and foment feuds in private families; to produce ruinous expenses, and give occasion to the cabals and intrigues of foreign princes: that it became the wisdom of such an august assembly to apply proper remedies to an evil that might be attended with the most dangerous consequences, especially in the present temper of the nation, as the spirit of rebellion still remained unconquered. He, therefore, proposed a bill for enlarging the continuance of Parliaments. He was seconded by the Earls of Dorset and Rockingham, the Duke of Argyle, Lord Townshend, and the other chiefs of that party. The motion was opposed by the Earls of Nottingham, Abingdon, and Paulet. They observed, that frequent Parliaments were required by the fundamental constitution of the kingdom, ascertained in the practice of many ages: that the members of the Lower House were chosen by the body of the nation, for a certain term of years, at the expiration of which they could be no longer representatives of the people, who, by the Parliament's protracting its own authority, would be deprived of the only remedy which they have against those who, through ignorance or corruption, betrayed the trust reposed in them: that the reasons in favour of such a bill were weak and frivolous: that, with respect to foreign alliances, no prince or state

could reasonably depend upon a people to defend their
liberties and interests, who should be thought to have
given up so great a part of their own; nor would it be
prudent in them to wish for a change in that constitution
under which Europe had of late been so powerfully supported : on the contrary, they might be deterred from
entering into any engagements with Great Britain, when
informed by the preamble of the bill, that the popish
faction was so dangerous as to threaten destruction to
the government; they would apprehend that the administration was so weak as to want so extraordinary a
provision for its safety; that the gentlemen of Britain
were not to be trusted; and that the good affections of
the people were restrained within the limits of the House
of Commons.   They affirmed that this bill, far from preventing the expense of elections, would rather increase
it, and encourage every species of corruption; for the
value of a seat would always be in proportion to the
duration of a Parliament; and the purchase would rise
accordingly : that a long Parliament would yield a greater
temptation, as well as a better opportunity to a vicious
ministry, to corrupt the members, than they could possibly have when the Parliaments were short and frequent:
that the same reasons urged for passing the bill to continue this Parliament for seven years would be at least
as strong, and, by the conduct of the ministry, might be
made much stronger before the end of that term, for
continuing, and even perpetuating, their legislative power,
to the absolute subversion of the third estate of the realm.
These arguments served only to form a decent debate,
after which the bill for septennial Parliaments passed
by a great majority; though twenty peers entered a protest.   It met with the same fate in the Lower House,
where many strong objections were stated to no purpose.
They were represented as the effects of party spleen ; and,
indeed, this was the great spring of action on both sides.
The question for the bill was carried in the affirmative;
and in a little time it received the royal sanction.

The Duke
of Argyle
disgraced.
The rebellion being utterly quelled, and all the suspected persons of consequence detained in safe custody,
the king resolved to visit his German dominions, where
he foresaw a storm gathering from the quarter of Sweden.

Charles XII. was extremely exasperated against the Elector of Hanover, for having entered into the confederacy against him in his absence, particularly for his having purchased the duchies of Bremen and Verden, which constituted part of his dominions; and he breathed nothing but revenge against the King of Great Britain. It was with a view to avert this danger, or prepare against it, that the king now determined upon a voyage to the continent. But as he was restricted from leaving his British dominion, by the act for the further limitation of the crown, this clause was repealed in a new bill that passed through both Houses without the least difficulty. On the twenty-sixth day of June, the king closed the session with a speech upon the usual topics, in which, however, he observed, that the numerous instances of mercy he had shown served only to encourage the faction of the pretender, whose partisans acted with such insolence and folly, as if they intended to convince the world that they were not to be reclaimed by gentle methods. He intimated his purpose of visiting his dominions in Germany; and gave them to understand, that he had constituted his beloved son, the Prince of Wales, guardian of the kingdom in his absence. About this period, General Macartney, who had returned to England at the accession of King George, presented himself to trial for the murder of the Duke of Hamilton. The deposition of Colonel Hamilton was contradicted by two park-keepers: the general was acquitted of the charge, restored to his rank in the army, and gratified with the command of a regiment. The king's brother, Prince Ernest, Bishop of Osnabruck, was created Duke of York and Albany, and Earl of Ulster. The Duke of Argyle, and his brother the Earl of Ilay, to whom his majesty owed, in a great measure, his peaceable accession to the throne, as well as the extinction of the rebellion in Scotland, were now dismissed from all their employments. General Carpenter succeeded the duke in the chief command of the forces in North Britain, and in the government of Port Mahon; and the Duke of Montrose was appointed lord register of Scotland in the room of the Earl of Ilay.

On the seventh day of July, the king embarked at Gravesend, landed on the ninth in Holland, through Triple alliance be-

CHAP.
XII.
1716.
tween Eng-
land,
France,
and Hol-
land.

which he passed incognito to Hanover, and from thence set out for Pyrmont. His aim was to secure his German dominions from the Swede, and Great Britain from the pretender. These two princes had already begun to form a design, in conjunction, of invading his kingdom. He knew the Duke of Orleans was resolved to ascend the throne of France, in case the young king, who was a sickly child, should die without male issue. The regent was not ignorant that Philip of Spain would powerfully contest that succession, notwithstanding his renunciation; and he was glad of an opportunity to strengthen his interest by an alliance with the maritime powers of England and Holland. The King of England sounded him on this subject, and found him eager to engage in such an association. The negotiation was carried on by General Cadogan for England, the Abbé du Bois for France, and the pensionary Heinsius for the States-General. The regent readily complied with all their demands. He engaged that the pretender should immediately depart from Avignon to the other side of the Alps, and never return to Lorraine or France on any pretence whatsoever: that no rebellious subjects of Great Britain should be allowed to reside in that kingdom: and that the treaty of Utrecht, with respect to the demolition of Dunkirk, should be fully executed, to the satisfaction of his Britannic majesty. The treaty contained a mutual guarantee of all the places possessed by the contracting powers; of the Protestant succession on the throne of England, as well as of that of the Duke of Orleans to the crown of France; and a defensive alliance, stipulating the proportion of ships and forces to be furnished to that power which should be disturbed at home or invaded from abroad. The English people murmured at this treaty. They said an unnecessary umbrage was given to Spain, with which the nation had great commercial connexions; and that on pretence of an invasion, a body of foreign troops might be introduced to enslave the kingdom.

Count Gyl-
lenburgh,
the Swed-
ish minis-
ter in Lon-
don, arrest-
ed.

His majesty was not so successful in his endeavours to appease the King of Sweden, who refused to listen to any overtures until Bremen and Verden should be restored. These the Elector of Hanover resolved to keep

as a fair purchase; and he engaged in a confederacy
with the enemies of Charles, for the maintenance of this
acquisition. Meanwhile his rupture with Sweden was
extremely prejudicial to the commerce of England, and
had well nigh entailed upon the kingdom another invasion, much more formidable than that which had so
lately miscarried. The ministers of Sweden resident at
London, Paris, and the Hague, maintained a correspondence with the disaffected subjects of Great Britain.
A scheme was formed for the Swedish king's landing on
this island with a considerable body of forces, where he
should be joined by the malecontents of the united
kingdom. Charles relished the enterprise, which flattered his ambition and revenge; nor was it disagreeable to the Czar of Muscovy, who resented the elector's
offer of joining the Swede against the Russians, provided
he would ratify the cession of Bremen and Verden.
King George, having received intimation of these intrigues, returned to England towards the end of January; and ordered a detachment of foot-guards to secure
Count Gyllenburgh, the Swedish minister, with all his
papers. At the same time, Sir Jacob Bancks and Mr.
Charles Cæsar were apprehended. The other foreign
ministers took the alarm, and remonstrated to the ministry upon this outrage committed against the law of
nations. The two secretaries, Stanhope and Methuen,
wrote circular letters to them, assuring them that in a
day or two they should be acquainted with the reasons
that induced the king to take such an extraordinary step.
They were generally satisfied with this intimation; but
the Marquis de Monteleone, ambassador from Spain,
expressed his concern, that no other way could be found
to preserve the peace of the kingdom without arresting
the person of a public minister, and seizing all his papers,
which were the sacred repositories of his master's secrets:
he observed, that in whatever manner these two facts
might seem to be understood, they very sensibly wounded
the law of nations. About the same time Baron Gortz,
the Swedish residentiary in Holland, was seized with his
papers at Arnheim, at the desire of King George, communicated to the states by Mr. Leathes, his minister at
the Hague. The baron owned he had projected the

invasion, a design that was justified by the conduct of King George, who had joined the princes in confederacy against the King of Sweden, without having received the least provocation; who had assisted the King of Denmark in subduing the duchies of Bremen and Verden, and then purchased them of the usurper; and who had, in the course of this very summer, sent a strong squadron of ships to the Baltic, where it joined the Danes and Russians against the Swedish fleet.

When the Parliament of Great Britain met on the twentieth day of February, the king informed them of the triple alliance he had concluded with France and Holland. He mentioned the projected invasion; told them he had given orders for laying before them copies of the letters which had passed between the Swedish ministers on that subject; and he demanded of the Commons such supplies as should be found necessary for the defence of the kingdom. By those papers it appeared that the scheme projected by Baron Gortz was very plausible, and even ripe for execution; which, however, was postponed until the army should be reduced, and the Dutch auxiliaries sent back to their own country. The letters being read in Parliament, both Houses presented addresses, in which they extolled the king's prudence in establishing such conventions with foreign potentates as might repair the gross defects, and prevent the pernicious consequences of the treaty of Utrecht, which they termed a treacherous and dishonourable peace; and they expressed their horror and indignation at the malice and ingratitude of those who had encouraged an invasion of their country. He likewise received an address of the same kind from the convention; another from the dissenting ministers; a third from the university of Cambridge; but Oxford was not so lavish of her compliments. At a meeting of the vice-chancellor and heads of that university, a motion was made for an address to the king, on the suppression of the late unnatural rebellion, his majesty's safe return, and the favour lately shown to the university, in omitting, at their request, the ceremony of burning in effigy the devil, the pope, the pretender, the Duke of Ormond, and the Earl of Mar, on the anniversary of his majesty's accession. Dr. Smallridge, Bishop

of Bristol, observed, that the rebellion had been long
suppressed; that there would be no end of addresses,
should one be presented every time his majesty returned
from his German dominions; that the late favour they
had received was overbalanced by a whole regiment now
quartered upon them; and that there was no precedent
for addressing a king upon his return from his German
dominions. The university thought they had reason to
complain of the little regard paid to their remonstrances,
touching a riot raised in that city by the soldiers there
quartered, on pretence that the anniversary of the prince's
birthday had not been celebrated with the usual rejoicings. Affidavits had been sent up to the council, which
seemed to favour the officers of the regiment. When
the House of Lords deliberated upon the mutiny bill,
by which the soldiers were exempted from arrests for
debts, complaint was made of their licentious behaviour
at Oxford, and a motion was made, that they should inquire into the riot. The Lords presented an address to
the king, desiring that the papers relating to that affair
might be laid before the House. These being perused,
were found to be recriminations between the Oxonians
and the officers of the regiment. A warm debate ensued,
during which the Earl of Abingdon offered a petition
from the vice-chancellor of the university, the mayor
and magistrates of Oxford, praying to be heard. One of
the court members observing that it would be irregular
to receive a petition while the House was in a grand
committee,- a motion was made, that the chairman should
leave the chair; but this being carried in the negative,
the debate was resumed, and the majority agreed to the
following resolutions: that the heads of the university,
and mayor of the city, neglected to make public rejoicings on the prince's birthday; that the officers having
met to celebrate that day, the house in which they had
assembled was assaulted, and the windows were broken
by the rabble; that this assault was the beginning and
occasion of the riots that ensued; that the conduct of
the major seemed well justified by the affidavits produced
on his part; that the printing and publishing the depositions, upon which the complaints relating to the riots
at Oxford were founded, while that matter was under

CHAP.
XII.
1716.
Annals.
State
Trials.
Deb. in
Parliam.
Tindal.
Voltaire.
1717.
The king
demands an
extraordi-
nary supply
of the Com-
mons.

the examination of the lords of the committee of the council, before they had time to come to any resolution touching the same, was irregular, disrespectful to his royal highness, and tending to sedition. An inquiry of this nature, so managed, did not much redound to the honour of such an august assembly.

The Commons passed a bill, prohibiting all commerce with Sweden, a branch of trade which was of the utmost consequence to the English merchants. They voted ten thousand seamen for the ensuing year; granted about a million for the maintenance of guards, garrisons, and land-forces; and passed the bill relating to mutiny and desertion. The House likewise voted four-and-twenty thousand pounds for the payment of four battalions of Munster and two of Saxe-Gotha, which the king had taken into his service, to supply the place of such as might be, during the rebellion, drawn from the garrisons of the States-General to the assistance of England. This vote, however, was not carried without a violent debate. The demand was inveighed against as an imposition, seeing no troops had ever served. A motion was made for an address, desiring that the instructions of those who concluded the treaties might be laid before the House; but this was overruled by the majority[d]. The supplies were raised by a land-tax of three shillings in the pound, and a malt-tax. What the Commons had given was not thought sufficient for the expenses of the year; therefore Mr. Secretary Stanhope brought a message from his majesty, demanding an extraordinary supply, that he might be the better enabled to secure his kingdoms against the danger with which they were threatened from Sweden; and he moved that a supply should be granted to his majesty for this purpose. Mr. Shippen observed, that it was a great misfortune that the king was as little acquainted with the parliamentary proceedings as with the language of the country; that the message was unparliamentary and unprecedented; and, in his opinion, penned

[d] This year was rendered famous by a complete victory which Prince Eugene obtained over the Turks at Peterwaradin upon the Danube. The battle was fought on the fifth day of August. The imperial army did not exceed sixty thousand men: that of the infidels amounted to one hundred and fifty thousand, commanded by the grand vizier, who was mortally wounded in the engagement. The infidels were totally defeated with the loss of all their tents, artillery, and baggage; so that the victors obtained an immense booty.

by some foreign minister: he said he had been often told
that his majesty had retrieved the honour and reputation
of the nation; a truth which appeared in the flourishing
condition of trade; but that the supply demanded seemed
to be inconsistent with the glorious advantages which his
majesty had obtained for the people. He was seconded by
Mr. Hungerford, who declared that for his part he could
not understand what occasion there was for new alliances; much less that they should be purchased with
money. He expressed his surprise that a nation so lately
the terror of France and Spain should now seem to fear
so inconsiderable an enemy as the King of Sweden. The
motion was supported by Mr. Boscawen, Sir Gilbert
Heathcote, and others; but some of the whigs spoke
against it; and Mr. Robert Walpole was silent. The
speaker and Mr. Smith, one of the tellers of the exchequer, opposed this unparliamentary way of demanding the
supply: the former proposed that part of the army should
be disbanded, and the money applied towards the making
good such new engagements as were deemed necessary.
After several successive debates, the resolution for a
supply was carried by a majority of four voices.

The ministry was now divided within itself. Lord
Townshend had been removed from the office of secretary
of state by the intrigues of the Earl of Sunderland; and
he was now likewise dismissed from the place of Lord-
Lieutenant of Ireland. Mr. Robert Walpole resigned
his posts of first commissioner of the treasury and chancellor of the exchequer: his example was followed by
Mr. Pulteney, secretary at war, and Mr. Methuen, secretary of state. When the affair of the supply was resumed
in the House of Commons, Mr. Stanhope made a motion
for granting two hundred and fifty thousand pounds for
that purpose. Mr. Pulteney observed, that having resigned his place, he might now act with the freedom becoming an Englishman: he declared against the manner
of granting the supply, as unparliamentary and unprecedented. He said he could not persuade himself that any
Englishman advised his majesty to send such a message;
but he doubted not the resolution of a British Parliament
would make a German ministry tremble. Mr. Stanhope
having harangued the House in vindication of the

Division
in the
ministry.

CHAP.
  XII.
 1717.

ministry, Mr. Smith answered every article of his speech: he affirmed, that if an estimate of the conduct of the ministry in relation to affairs abroad was to be made from a comparison of their conduct at home, they would not appear altogether so faultless as they were represented. "Was it not a mistake (said he) not to preserve the peace at home, after the king had ascended the throne with the universal applause and joyful acclamations of all his subjects? Was it not a mistake, upon the breaking out of the rebellion, not to issue a proclamation, to offer pardon to such as should return home peaceably, according to the custom on former occasions of the same nature? Was it not a mistake, after the suppression of the rebellion and the trial and execution of the principal authors of it, to keep up animosities and drive people to despair, by not passing an act of indemnity, by keeping so many persons under hard and tedious confinement; and by granting pardons to some, without leaving them any means to subsist? Is it not a mistake not to trust to a vote of Parliament for making good such engagements as his majesty should think proper to enter into; and instead of that, to insist on the granting this supply in such an extraordinary manner? Is it not a mistake to take this opportunity to create divisions, and render some of the king's best friends suspected and obnoxious? Is it not a mistake, in short, to form parties and cabals, in order to bring in a bill to repeal the act of occasional conformity?" A great number of members had agreed to this measure in private, though at this period it was not brought into the House of Commons. After a long debate the sum was granted. These were the first-fruits of Britain's being wedded to the interests of the continent. The Elector of Hanover quarrelled with the King of Sweden; and England was not only deprived of a necessary branch of commerce, but even obliged to support him in the prosecution of the war. The ministry now underwent a new revolution. The Earl of Sunderland and Mr. Addison were appointed secretaries of state: Mr. Stanhope became first commissioner of the treasury and chancellor of the exchequer.

The Commons pass the South-

On the sixth day of May, the king going to the House of Peers, gave the Parliament to understand that the

fleet under Sir George Byng, which had sailed to the
Baltic, to observe the motions of the Swedes, was safely
arrived in the Sound.   He said he had given orders for
the immediate reduction of ten thousand soldiers, as
well as directions to prepare an act of indemnity.   He
desired they would take proper measures for reducing the
public debts with a just regard to parliamentary credit;
and that they would go through the public business with
all possible despatch and unanimity.   Some progress had
already been made in deliberations upon the debt of the
nation, which was comprehended under the two heads
of redeemable and irredeemable incumbrances.   The
first had been contracted with a redeemable interest;
and these the public had a right to discharge: the others
consisted of long and short annuities granted for a greater
or less number of years, which could not be altered without the consent of the proprietors.   Mr. Robert Walpole
had projected a scheme for lessening the interest, and
paying the capital of those debts, before he resigned his
place in the exchequer.   He proposed, in the House of
Commons, to reduce the interest of redeemable funds,
and offer an alternative to the proprietors of annuities.
His plan was approved; but when he resigned his places,
the ministers made some small alterations in it, which
furnished him with a pretence for opposing the execution of the scheme.   In the course of the debate, some
warm altercation passed between him and Mr. Stanhope,
by which it appeared they had made a practice of selling
places and reversions.   Mr. Hungerford, standing up,
said he was sorry to see two such great men running
foul of one another; that, however, they ought to be
looked upon as patriots and fathers of their country;
and since they had by mischance discovered their naked-
ness, the other members ought, according to the custom
of the East, to turn their backs upon them, that they
might not be seen in such a shameful condition.   Mr.
Boscawen moved that the House would lay their commands upon them, that no further notice should be taken
of what had passed.   He was seconded by Mr. Methuen;
the House approved of the motion; and the speaker took
their word and honour that they should not prosecute
their resentment.   The money-corporations having agreed

to provide cash for such creditors as should be willing
to receive their principal, the House came to certain resolutions, on which were founded the three bills that
passed into laws, under the names of "the South-Sea
act, the bank act, and the general fund act." The original stock of the South-Sea company did not exceed
nine millions four hundred and seventy-one thousand
three hundred and twenty-five pounds; but the funds
granted being sufficient to answer the interest of ten
millions at six per cent. the company made up that sum
to the government, for which they received six hundred
thousand pounds yearly, and eight thousand pounds a
year for management. By this act they declared themselves willing to receive five hundred thousand pounds,
and the eight thousand for management. It was enacted, that the company should continue a corporation
until the redemption of their annuity, towards which not
less than a million should be paid at a time. They were
likewise required to advance a sum not exceeding two
millions, towards discharging the principal and interest
due on the four lottery funds of the ninth and tenth
years of Queen Anne. By the bank act the governors
and company declared themselves willing to accept an
annuity of eighty-eight thousand seven hundred and
fifty-one pounds, seven shillings, and ten pence halfpenny, or the principal of one million seven hundred
and seventy-five thousand twenty-seven pounds, seventeen shillings, and ten pence halfpenny, in lieu of the
present annuity, amounting to one hundred and six thousand five hundred and one pounds, thirteen shillings, and
five pence. They likewise declared themselves willing
to discharge, and deliver up to be cancelled, as many
exchequer-bills as amounted to two millions, and to
accept of an annuity of one hundred thousand pounds,
being after the rate of five per cent. redeemable after
one year's notice; to circulate the remaining exchequer-
bills at three per cent. and one penny per day. It was
enacted, that the former allowances should be continued
to Christmas, and then the bank should have for circu-
lating the two millions five hundred and sixty-one thousand and twenty-five pounds remaining exchequer-bills,
an annuity of seventy-six thousand eight hundred and

thirty pounds, fifteen shillings, at the rate of three pounds per cent. till redeemed, over and above the one penny a day for interest. By the same act the bank was required to advance a sum not exceeding two millions five hundred thousand pounds, towards discharging the national debt, if wanted, on condition that they should have five pounds per cent. for as much as they might advance, redeemable by Parliament. The general fund act recited the several acts of Parliament, for establishing the four lotteries in the ninth and tenth years of the late queen, and stated the annual produce of the several funds, amounting in all to seven hundred twenty-four thousand eight hundred forty-nine pounds, six shillings, and tenpence one fifth. This was the general fund; the deficiency of which was to be made good annually, out of the first aids granted by Parliament. For the regular payment of all such annuities as should be made payable by this act, it was enacted, that all the duties and revenues mentioned therein should continue for ever, with the proviso, however, that the revenues rendered by this act perpetual should be subject to redemption. This act contained a clause by which the sinking fund was established. The reduction of interest to five per cent. producing a surplus or excess upon the appropriated funds, it was enacted, that all the monies arising from time to time, as well for the surplus, by virtue of the acts for redeeming the funds of the bank and of the South-Sea company, as also for the surplus of the duties and revenues by this act appropriated to make good the general fund, should be appropriated and employed for the discharging the principal and interest of such national debt as was incurred before the twenty-fifth of December of the preceding year, in such manner as should be directed and appointed by any future act of Parliament, to be discharged out of the same, and for no other use, intent, or purpose whatsoever.

The Earl of Oxford, who had now remained almost two years a prisoner in the Tower, presented a petition to the House of Lords, praying that his imprisonment might not be indefinite. Some of the tory lords affirmed that the impeachment was destroyed and determined by the prorogation of Parliament, which superseded the whole pro-

Trial of the Earl of Oxford. Act of indemnity.

M 2

ceedings; but the contrary was voted by a considerable
majority.   The thirteenth day of June was fixed for the
trial; and the House of Commons made acquainted with
this determination. The Commons appointed a committee
to inquire into the state of the earl's impeachment; and,
in consequence of their report, sent a message to the
Lords, demanding longer time to prepare for trial.
Accordingly the day was prolonged to the twenty-fourth
of June; and the Commons appointed the committee,
with four hundred members, to be managers for making
good the articles of impeachment.   At the appointed
time, the Peers repaired to the court in Westminster-
hall, where Lord Cowper presided as lord steward.   The
Commons were assembled as a committee of the whole
House: the king, the rest of the royal family, and the
foreign ministers, assisted at the solemnity: the Earl of
Oxford was brought from the Tower: the articles of impeachment were read with his answers, and the replication
of the Commons.   Sir Joseph Jekyll standing up to make
good the first article, Lord Harcourt signified to their
lordships that he had a motion to make, and they adjourned to their own House.   There he represented, that
a great deal of time would be unnecessarily consumed in
going through all the articles of the impeachment: that
if the Commons would make good the two articles for
high treason, the Earl of Oxford would forfeit both life
and estate, and there would be an end of the matter;
whereas, to proceed in the method proposed by the
Commons, would draw the trial on to a prodigious length.
He therefore moved that the Commons might not be permitted to proceed, until judgment should be first given
upon the articles of high treason. He was supported by the
Earls of Anglesey and Nottingham, the Lord Trevor, and
a considerable number of both parties; and though opposed by the Earl of Sunderland, the Lords Coningsby and
Parker, the motion was carried in the affirmative. It produced a dispute between the two Houses. The Commons,
at a conference, delivered a paper, containing their reasons
for asserting it as their undoubted right to impeach a peer,
either for treason, or for high crimes and misdemeanours;
or, should they see occasion, to mix both in the same accusation.   The House of Lords insisted on their former

resolution; and in another conference delivered a paper, wherein they asserted it to be a right inherent in every court of justice to order and direct such methods of proceeding as it should think fit to be observed in all causes that fall under its cognizance. The Commons demanded a free conference, which was refused. The dispute grew more and more warm. The Lords sent a message to the Lower House, importing, that they intended presently to proceed on the trial of the Earl of Oxford. The Commons paid no regard to this intimation, but adjourned to the third day of July. The Lords, repairing to Westminster-hall, took their places, ordered the earl to be brought to the bar, and made proclamation for his accusers to appear. Having waited a quarter of an hour, they adjourned to their own House, where, after some debate, the earl was acquitted upon a division; then returning to the hall, they voted that he should be set at liberty. Oxford owed his safety to the dissensions among the ministers, and to the late change in the administration. In consequence of this, he was delivered from the persecution of Walpole; and numbered among his friends the Dukes of Devonshire and Argyle, the Earls of Nottingham and Ilay, and Lord Townshend. The Commons, in order to express their sense of his demerit, presented an address to the king, desiring he might be excepted out of the intended act of grace. The king promised to comply with their request; and in the mean time forbade the earl to appear at court. On the fifteenth day of July the Earl of Sunderland delivered in the House of Peers the act of grace, which passed through both Houses with great expedition. From this indulgence were excepted the Earl of Oxford, Mr. Prior, Mr. Thomas Harley, Mr. Arthur Moore, Crisp, Nodes, Obryan, Redmayne the printer, and Thompson; as also the assassinators in Newgate, and the clan of Macgregor in Scotland. By virtue of this act, the Earl of Carnwath, the Lords Widdrington and Nairn, were immediately discharged, together with all the gentlemen under sentence of death in Newgate, and those that were confined on account of the rebellion in the Fleet, the Marshalsea, and other prisons of the kingdom. The act of grace being prepared for the royal assent, the king went to the House of Peers on the fifteenth day of July,

Proceed-
ings in the
Convoca-
tion with
regard to
Dr. Hoad-
ley, Bishop
of Bangor.

and having given his sanction to all the bills that were ready, closed the session with a speech on the usual topics.

The proceedings in the Convocation turned chiefly upon two performances of Dr. Hoadley, Bishop of Bangor. One was entitled " A Preservative against the Principles and Practices of the Nonjurors:" the other was a sermon preached before the king, under the title of "The Nature of the Kingdom of Christ." An answer to this discourse was published by Dr. Snape, master of Eton college, and the Convocation appointed a committee to examine the bishop's two performances. They drew up a representation, in which the Preservative and the sermon were censured, as tending to subvert all government and discipline in the church of Christ; to reduce his kingdom to a state of anarchy and confusion; to impugn and impeach the royal supremacy in causes ecclesiastical, and the authority of the legislature to enforce obedience in matters of religion by civil sanctions. The government thought proper to put a stop to these proceedings by a prorogation: which, however, inflamed the controversy. A great number of pens were drawn against the bishop; but his chief antagonists were Dr. Snape and Dr. Sherlock, whom the king removed from the office of his chaplains; and the Convocation has not been permitted to sit and do business since that period.

CHAPTER XIII.

DURING these transactions, the negotiations of the North were continued against the King of Sweden, who had penetrated into Norway, and advanced towards Christianstadt, the capital of that kingdom. The czar had sent five-and-twenty thousand Russians to assist the allies in the reduction of Wismar, which he intended to bestow upon his niece, lately married to the Duke of Mecklenburgh-Schwerin; but, before his troops arrived, the place had surrendered, and the Russians were not admitted into the garrison; a circumstance which increased the misunderstanding between him and the King of Great Britain. Nevertheless, he consented to a project for making a descent upon Schonen, and actually took upon him the command of the allied fleet; though he was not at all pleased to see Sir John Norris in the Baltic, because he had formed designs against Denmark, which he knew

CHAP. XIII.

1717.
Difference between King George and the Czar of Muscovy.

the English squadron would protect. He suddenly desisted from the expedition against Schonen, on pretence that the season was too far advanced; and the King of Denmark published a manifesto, remonstrating against his conduct on this occasion. By this time Baron Gortz had planned a pacification between his master and the czar, who was discontented with all his German allies, because they opposed his having any footing in the empire. This monarch arrived at Amsterdam in December, whither he was followed by the czarina; and he actually resided at the Hague when King George passed through it, in returning to his British dominions; but he declined an interview with the King of England. When Gyllenburgh's letters were published in London, some passages seemed to favour the supposition of the czar's being privy to the conspiracy. His minister at the English court presented a long memorial, complaining that the king had caused to be printed the malicious insinuations of his enemies. He denied his having the least concern in the design of the Swedish king. He charged the court of England with having privately treated of a separate peace with Charles, and even with having promised to assist him against the czar, on condition that he would relinquish his pretensions to Bremen and Verden. Nevertheless he expressed an inclination to re-establish the ancient good understanding, and to engage in vigorous measures for prosecuting the war against the common enemy. The memorial was answered by the King of Great Britain, who assured the czar he should have reason to be fully satisfied, if he would remove the only obstacle to their mutual good understanding; in other words, withdraw the Russian troops from the empire. Notwithstanding these professions, the two monarchs were never perfectly reconciled.

The King of Sweden is killed at Frederickstadt.

The czar made an excursion to the court of France, where he concluded a treaty of friendship with the regent, at whose earnest desire he promised to recall his troops from Mecklenburgh. At his return to Amsterdam, he had a private interview with Gortz, who, as well as Gyllenburgh, had been set at liberty. Gortz undertook to adjust all difference between the czar and the King of Sweden within three months; and Peter engaged to suspend all operations against Sweden until that term should be expired. A congress was opened at Abo, between the Swedish and Russian ministers; but the conferences were afterwards removed to Aland. By this convention, the czar obliged himself to assist Charles in the conquest of Norway; and they promised to unite all their forces against the king of Great Britain, should he presume to interpose. Both were incensed against that prince; and one part of their design was to raise the pretender to the throne of England. Baron Gortz set out from Aland for Frederickstadt in Norway, with the plan of peace, but, before he arrived, Charles was killed by a cannon-ball from the town, as he visited the trenches, on the thirteenth of November. Baron Gortz was immediately arrested, and brought to the scaffold by the nobles of Sweden, whose hatred he had incurred by his insolence of behaviour. The death of Charles was fortunate for King George. Sweden was now obliged to submit: while the czar, the King of Denmark, and the Elector of Hanover, kept possession of what they had acquired in the course of the war.

Thus Bremen and Verden were secured to the House of Hanover: an acquisition towards which the English nation contributed by her money, as well as by her arms: an acquisition made in contradiction to the engagements into which England entered when King William became guarantee for the treaty of Travendahl; an acquisition that may be considered as the first link of a political chain by which the English nation was dragged back into expensive connexions with the continent. The king had not yet received the investiture of the duchies; and until that should be procured, it was necessary to espouse with warmth the interest of the emperor. This was another source of misunderstanding between Great Britain and Spain. Prince Eugene gained another complete victory over a prodigious army of the Turks at Belgrade, which was surrendered to him after the battle. The emperor had engaged in this war as an ally of the Venetians, whom the Turks had attacked and driven from the Morea. The pope considered it as a religious war against the infidels; and obtained repeated assurances from the King of Spain, that he would not undertake any thing against

Negotiation for the quadruple alliance.

the emperor, while he was engaged in such a laudable quarrel. Philip had even sent a squadron of ships and galleys to the assistance of the Venetians. In the course of this year, however, he equipped a strong armament, the command of which he bestowed on the Marquis de Lede, who sailed from Barcelona in July, and landing at Cagliari in Sardinia, which belonged to the emperor, made a conquest of the whole island. At the same time, the King of Spain endeavoured to justify these proceedings by a manifesto, in which he alleged that the archduke, contrary to the faith of treaties, encouraged and supported the rebellion of his subjects in Catalonia, by frequent succours from Naples, and other places; and that the Great-Inquisitor of Spain had been seized, though furnished with a passport from his holiness. He promised, however, to proceed no further, and suspend all operations, that the powers of Europe might have time and opportunity to contrive expedients for reconciling all differences, and securing the peace and balance of power in Italy: nay, he consented that this important affair should be left to the arbitration of King George and the States-General. These powers undertook the office. Conferences were begun between the ministers of the emperor, France, England, and Holland; and these produced, in the course of the following year, the famous quadruple alliance. In this treaty it was stipulated that the emperor should renounce all pretensions to the crown of Spain, and exchange Sardinia for Sicily, with the Duke of Savoy; that the succession to the Duchies of Tuscany, Parma, and Placentia, which the Queen of Spain claimed by inheritance, as Princess of the house of Farnese, should be settled on her eldest son, in case the present possessors should die without male issue. Philip, dissatisfied with this partition, continued to make formidable preparations by sea and land. The King of England and the Regent of France interposed their admonitions to no purpose. At length his Britannic majesty had recourse to more substantial arguments, and ordered a strong squadron to be equipped with all possible expedition [a].

[a] The pretender, who resided at Urbino, having received intelligence from Paris, that there was a design formed against his life, Pope Clement XI. gave

On the third day of November, the Princess of Wales CHAP.
XIII.
1717.
Proceed-
ings in Par-
liament. was delivered of a prince, the ceremony of whose baptism was productive of a difference between the grandfather and the father. The Prince of Wales intended that his uncle, the Duke of York, should stand godfather. The king ordered the Duke of Newcastle to stand for himself. After the ceremony, the prince expressed his resentment against this nobleman in very warm terms. The king ordered the prince to confine himself within his own apartments; and afterwards signified his pleasure that he should quit the palace of St. James's. He retired with the princess to a house belonging to the Earl of Grantham; but the children were detained at the palace. All peers and peeresses, and all privy-counsellors and their wives, were given to understand, that in case they visited the prince and princess, they should have no access to his majesty's presence; and all who enjoyed posts and places under both king and prince were obliged to quit the service of one or other, at their option. When the Parliament met on the twenty-first day of November, the king, in his speech, told both Houses that he had reduced the army to very near one half, since the beginning of the last session : he expressed his desire that all those who were friends to the present happy establishment might unanimously concur in some proper method for the greater strengthening the Protestant interest, of which, as the church of England was unquestionably the main support and bulwark, so would she reap the principal benefit of every advantage accruing from the union and mutual charity of all Protestants. After the addresses of thanks, which were couched in the usual style, the Commons proceeded to take into consideration the

directions that all foreigners in that neighbourhood, especially English, should be arrested. The Earl of Peterborough arriving at Bologna, with a few armed followers, was seized, with all his papers. Being interrogated, he said he came to pass some time in Italy for the benefit of the air. He was close confined for a whole month in Fort Urbino, and his attendants were sent to prison. Nothing appearing to justify the suspicion, he was dismissed with uncommon civility. The king demanding reparation for this insult, the pope wrote with his own hand a letter to an ally of Great Britain, declaring that the legate of Bologna had violently and unjustly, without the knowledge of his holiness, caused the Earl of Peterborough to be seized upon suspicions which proved to be ill-grounded. The cardinal legate sent a declaration to the English admiral in the Mediterranean, that he had asked forgiveness of his holiness, and now begged pardon of his Britannic majesty, for having unadvisedly arrested a peer of Great Britain on his travels.

CHAP.
XIII.

1717.

estimates and accounts, in order to settle the establishment of the army, navy, and ordnance.   Ten thousand
men were voted for the sea-service.   When the supply
for the army fell under deliberation, a very warm debate
ensued, upon the number of troops necessary to be maintained.   Sir William Wyndham, Mr. Shippen, and Mr.
Walpole, in a long elaborate harangue, insisted upon its
being reduced to twelve thousand.   They were answered
by Mr. Craggs, secretary at war, and Sir David Dalrymple.
Mr. Shippen, in the course of the debate, said the second
paragraph of the king's speech seemed rather to be calculated for the meridian of Germany than for Great Britain;
and it was a great misfortune that the king was a stranger
to our language and constitution.   Mr. Lechmere affirmed
this was a scandalous invective against the king's person
and government; and moved that he who uttered it
should be sent to the Tower.   Mr. Shippen, refusing to
retract or excuse what he had said, was voted to the
Tower by a great majority; and the number of standing forces was fixed at sixteen thousand three hundred
and forty-seven effective men.

James
Shepherd
executed
for a design
against the
king's life.
The Parlia-
ment pro-
rogued.

On account of the great scarcity of silver coin, occasioned by the exportation of silver, and the importation
of gold, a motion was made to put a stop to this growing
evil by lowering the value of gold specie.   The Commons
examined a representation which had been made to the
treasury by Sir Isaac Newton, master of the mint, on
this subject.   Mr. Caswell explained the nature of a
clandestine trade carried on by the Dutch and Ham-
burghers, in concert with the Jews of England and other
traders, for exporting the silver coin and importing gold,
which, being coined at the mint, yielded a profit of fifteen pence upon every guinea.   The House, in an address to the king, desired that a proclamation might be
issued, forbidding all persons to utter or receive guineas
at a higher rate than one-and-twenty shillings each.
His majesty complied with their request; but people
hoarding up their silver, in hopes that the price of it
would be raised, or in apprehension that the gold would
be lowered still farther, the two Houses resolved that
the standard of the gold and silver coins of the kingdoms
should not be altered in fineness, weight, or denomina-

tion; and they ordered a bill to be brought in, to prevent the melting down of the silver coin. At this period, one James Shepherd, a youth of eighteen, apprentice to a coach-maker, and an enthusiast in jacobitism, sent a letter to a nonjuring clergyman proposing a scheme for assassinating King George. He was immediately apprehended, owned the design, was tried, condemned, and executed at Tyburn. This was likewise the fate of the Marquis de Palleotti, an Italian nobleman, brother to the Duchess of Shrewsbury. He had, in a transport of passion, killed his own servant, and seemed indeed to be disordered in his brain. After he had received sentence of death, the king's pardon was earnestly solicited by his sister the duchess, and many other persons of the first distinction; but the common people became so clamorous, that it was thought dangerous to rescue him from the penalties of the law, which he accordingly underwent in the most ignominious manner. No subject produced so much heat and altercation in Parliament during this session as did the bill for regulating the land-forces, and punishing mutiny and desertion : a bill which was looked upon as an encroachment upon the liberties and constitution of England, inasmuch as it established martial law, which wrested from the civil magistrate the cognizance of crimes and misdemeanors committed by the soldiers and officers of the army : a jurisdiction inconsistent with the genius and disposition of the people. The dangers that might accrue from such a power were explained in the Lower House by Mr. Hutchinson, Mr. Harley, and Mr. Robert Walpole, which last, however, voted afterwards for the bill. In the House of Lords, it was strenuously opposed by the Earls of Oxford, Strafford, and Lord Harcourt. Their objections were answered by Lord Carteret. The bill passed by a great majority; but divers lords entered a protest. This affair being discussed, a bill was brought in for vesting in trustees the forfeited estates in Britain and Ireland, to be sold for the use of the public; for giving relief to lawful creditors, by determining the claims, and for the more effectual bringing into the respective exchequers the rents and profits of the estates till sold. The time of claiming was prolonged : the sum of twenty thousand pounds was

CHAP.
XIII.

1717.
Oldmixon.
Annals.
Lamberty.
Burchet.
Hist. Reg.
Tindal.
St. Trials.
Parlia.
Bolingbr.
Lives of the
Admirals.

reserved out of the sale of the estates in Scotland for erecting schools; and eight thousand pounds for building barracks in that kingdom. The king having signified, by a message to the House of Commons, that he had lately received such information from abroad as gave reason to believe that a naval force, employed where it should be necessary, would give weight to his endeavours; he therefore thought fit to acquaint the House with this circumstance, not doubting but that in case he should be obliged, at this critical juncture, to exceed the number of men granted this year for the sea-service, the House would provide for such exceeding. The Commons immediately drew up and presented an address, assuring his majesty that they would make good such exceedings of seamen as he should find necessary to preserve the tranquillity of Europe. On the twenty-first day of March, the king went to the House of Peers, and having passed the bills that were ready for the royal assent, ordered the Parliament to be prorogued [b].

The King of Spain, by the care and indefatigable diligence of his prime minister, Cardinal Alberoni, equipped a very formidable armament, which, in the beginning of June, set sail from Barcelona towards Italy; but the destination of it was not known. A strong squadron having been fitted out in England, the Marquis de Monteleone, ambassador from Spain, presented a memorial to the British ministry, importing that so powerful an armament in time of peace could not but give umbrage to the king his master, and alter the good intelligence that subsisted between the two crowns. In answer to this representation, the ministers declared that the king intended to send Admiral Byng with a powerful squadron into the Mediterranean, to maintain the neutrality in Italy. Meanwhile, the negotiations between the English and French ministers produced the quadruple alliance, by which King George and the regent prescribed a peace between the emperor, the King of Spain, and the King of Sicily, and undertook to compel Philip and

[b] Earl Cowper, lord chancellor, resigned the great seal, which was at first put in commission, but afterwards given to Lord Parker, as high chancellor. The Earl of Sunderland was made president of the council, and first commissioner of the treasury; Lord Stanhope and Mr. Craggs were appointed secretaries of state; Lord Stanhope and Lord Cadogan were afterwards created earls.

the Savoyard to submit to such conditions as they had
concerted with his imperial majesty. These powers were
allowed only three months to consider the articles, and
declare whether they would reject them, or acquiesce in
the partition. Nothing could be more contradictory to
the true interest of Great Britain than this treaty, which
destroyed the balance in Italy, by throwing such an accession of power into the hands of the house of Austria.
It interrupted the commerce with Spain, involved the
kingdom in an immediate war with that monarchy, and
gave rise to all the quarrels and disputes which have
arisen between England and Spain in the sequel. The
States-General did not approve of such violent measures,
and for some time kept aloof; but at length they acceded
to the quadruple alliance, which indeed was no other
than a very expensive compliment to the emperor, who
was desirous of adding Sicily to his other Italian dominions.

The King of England had used some endeavours to
compromise the difference between his imperial majesty
and the Spanish branch of the house of Bourbon. Lord
Stanhope had been sent to Madrid with a plan of pacification, which being rejected by Philip as partial and
iniquitous, the king determined to support his mediation by force of arms. Sir George Byng sailed from
Spithead on the fourth day of June, with twenty ships
of the line, two fire-ships, two bomb-vessels, and ample
instructions how to act on all emergencies. He arrived
off Cape St. Vincent on the thirtieth day of the month,
and despatched his secretary to Cadiz, with a letter to
Colonel Stanhope, the British minister at Madrid, desiring him to inform his Most Catholic Majesty of the
admiral's arrival in those parts, and lay before him this
article of his instructions: "You are to make instances
with both parties to cease from using any farther acts
of hostility; but in case the Spaniards do still insist,
with their ships of war and forces, to attack the kingdom of Naples, or other the territories of the emperor in
Italy, or to land in any part of Italy, which can only be
with a design to invade the emperor's dominions, against
whom only they have declared war by invading Sardinia;
or if they should endeavour to make themselves masters

of the kingdom of Sicily, which must be with a design to invade the kingdom of Naples; in which case you are, with all your power, to hinder and obstruct the same. If it should so happen, that at your arrival, with our fleet under your command, in the Mediterranean, the Spaniards should already have landed any troops in Italy in order to invade the emperor's territories, you shall endeavour amicably to dissuade them from persevering in such an attempt, and offer them your assistance, to help them to withdraw their troops, and put an end to all farther acts of hostility. But in case these your friendly endeavours should prove ineffectual, you shall, by keeping company with, or intercepting their ships or convoy, or, if it be necessary, by openly opposing them, defend the emperor's territories from any farther attempt." When Cardinal Alberoni perused these instructions, he told Colonel Stanhope with some warmth, that his master would run all hazards, and even suffer himself to be driven out of Spain, rather than recall his troops, or consent to a suspension of arms. He said the Spaniards were not to be frightened; and he was so well convinced that the fleet would do their duty, that in case of their being attacked by Admiral Byng, he should be in no pain for the success. Mr. Stanhope presenting him with a list of the British squadron, he threw it upon the ground with great emotion. He promised, however, to lay the admiral's letter before the king, and to let the envoy know his majesty's resolution. Such an interposition could not but be very provoking to the Spanish minister, who had laid his account with the conquest of Sicily, and for that purpose prepared an armament, which was altogether surprising, considering the late shattered condition of the Spanish affairs. But he seems to have put too much confidence in the strength of the Spanish fleet. In a few days he sent back the admiral's letter to Mr. Stanhope, with a note under it, importing, that the Chevalier Byng might execute the orders he had received from the king his master.

The admiral, in passing by Gibraltar, was joined by Vice-Admiral Cornwall, with two ships. He proceeded to Minorca, where he relieved the garrison of Port-Mahon. Then he sailed for Naples, where he arrived on the first day of August, and was received as a deliverer; for the Neapolitans had been under the utmost terror of an invasion from the Spaniards. Sir George Byng received intelligence from the viceroy, Count Daun, who treated him with the most distinguishing marks of respect, that the Spanish army, amounting to thirty thousand men, commanded by the Marquis de Lede, had landed in Sicily, reduced Palermo and Messina, and were then employed in the siege of the citadel belonging to this last city; that the Piedmontese garrison would be obliged to surrender, if not speedily relieved; that an alliance was upon the carpet between the emperor and the King of Sicily, which last had desired the assistance of the imperial troops, and agreed to receive them into the citadel of Messina. The admiral immediately resolved to sail thither, and took under his convoy a reinforcement of two thousand Germans for the citadel, under the command of General Wetzel. He forthwith sailed from Naples, and on the ninth day of August was in sight of the Faro of Messina. He despatched his own captain, with a polite message to the Marquis de Lede, proposing a cessation of arms in Sicily for two months, that the powers of Europe might have time to concert measures for restoring a lasting peace; and declaring, that should this proposal be rejected, he would, in pursuance of his directions, use all his force to prevent further attempts to disturb the dominions his master had engaged to defend. The Spanish general answered, that he had no power to treat, and consequently could not agree to an armistice, but should obey his orders, which directed him to reduce Sicily for his master the King of Spain. The Spanish fleet had sailed from the harbour of Messina on the day before the English squadron appeared. Admiral Byng supposed they had retired to Malta, and directed his course towards Messina, in order to encourage and support the garrison in the citadel. But, in doubling the point of Faro, he descried two Spanish scouts, and learned from the people of a felucca from the Calabrian shore, that they had seen from the hills the Spanish fleet lying-to in order of battle. The admiral immediately detached the German troops to Reggio, under convoy of two ships of war. Then he stood through the Faro after the Spanish scouts that led him to their main fleet, which before noon he descried in a line of battle, amounting to seven-and-twenty sail, large and small, besides two fire-ships, four bomb-vessels, and seven galleys. They were commanded in chief by Don Antonio de Castanita, under whom were the four Rear-Admirals Chacon, Mari, Guevara, and Cammock. At sight of the English squadron, they stood away at large, and Byng gave chase all the rest of the day. In the morning, which was the eleventh of August, Rear-Admiral de Mari, with six ships of war, the galleys, fire-ships, and bomb-ketches, separated from the main fleet, and stood in for the Sicilian shore. The English admiral detached Captain Walton with five ships in pursuit of them; and they were soon engaged. He himself continued to chase their main fleet; and about ten o'clock the battle began. The Spaniards seemed to be distracted in their councils, and acted in confusion. They made a running fight: yet the admirals behaved with courage and activity, in spite of which they were all taken, except Cammock, who made his escape with three ships of war and three frigates. In this engagement, which happened off Cape Passaro, Captain Haddock, of the Grafton, signalized his courage in an extraordinary manner. On the eighteenth the admiral received a letter from Captain Walton, dated off Syracuse, intimating that he had taken four Spanish ships of war, together with a bomb-ketch, and a vessel laden with arms; and that he had burned four ships of the line, a fire-ship, and a bomb-vessel[c]. Had the Spaniards followed the advice of Rear-Admiral Cammock, who was a native of Ireland, Sir George Byng would not have obtained such an easy victory. That officer proposed that they should remain at anchor in the road of Paradise, with their broadsides to the sea; in which case the English admiral would have found it a very difficult task to attack them; for the coast is so bold, that the largest ships could ride with a cable ashore; whereas farther out the currents are so various and rapid, that

[c] This letter is justly deemed a curious specimen of the laconic style.
"Sir,
"We have taken and destroyed all the Spanish ships and vessels which were upon the coast; the number as per margin. I am, &c.
"G. WALTON."

the English squadron could not have come to anchor, or lie near them in order of battle; besides, the Spaniards might have been reinforced from the army on shore, which would have raised batteries to annoy the assailants. Before King George had received an account of this engagement from the admiral, he wrote him a letter with his own hand, approving his conduct. When Sir George's eldest son arrived in England, with a circumstantial account of the action, he was graciously received, and sent back with plenipotentiary powers to his father, that he might negotiate with the several princes and states of Italy as he should see occasion. The son likewise carried the king's royal grant to the officers and seamen of all the prizes they had taken from the Spaniards. Notwithstanding this victory, the Spanish army carried on the siege of the citadel of Messina with such vigour, that the governor surrendered the place by capitulation on the twenty-ninth day of September. A treaty was now concluded at Vienna between the emperor and the Duke of Savoy. They agreed to form an army for the conquest of Sardinia in behalf of the duke; and in the mean time this prince engaged to evacuate Sicily; but until his troops could be conveyed from that island, he consented that they should co-operate with the Germans against the common enemy. Admiral Byng continued to assist the imperialists in Sicily during the best part of the winter, by scouring the seas of the Spaniards, and keeping the communication open between the German forces and the Calabrian shore, from whence they were supplied with provisions. He acted in this service with equal conduct, resolution, and activity. He conferred with the Viceroy of Naples and the other imperial generals about the operations of the ensuing campaign, and Count Hamilton was despatched to Vienna, to lay before the emperor the result of their deliberations; then the admiral set sail for Mahon, where his ships might be refitted, and put in a condition to take the sea in the spring.

The destruction of the Spanish fleet was a subject that employed the deliberations and conjectures of all the politicians in Europe. Spain exclaimed against the conduct of England, as inconsistent with the rules of good faith, for the observation of which she had always been so famous. The Marquis de Monteleone wrote a letter to Mr. Secretary Craggs, in which he expostulated with him upon such an unprecedented outrage. Cardinal Alberoni, in a letter to that minister, inveighed against it as a base unworthy action. He said the neutrality of Italy was a weak pretence, since every body knew that neutrality had long been at an end; and that the prince's guarantees of the treaty of Utrecht were entirely discharged from their engagements, not only by the scandalous infringements committed by the Austrians in the evacuation of Catalonia and Majorca; but also because the guarantee was no longer binding than till a peace was concluded with France. He taxed the British ministry with having revived and supported this neutrality, not by an amicable mediation, but by open violence, and artfully abusing the confidence and security of the Spaniards. This was the language of disappointed ambition. Nevertheless it must be owned, that the conduct of England, on this occasion, was irregular, partial, and precipitate.

Disputes in Parliament touching the admiral's attacking the Spanish fleet. The Parliament meeting on the eleventh day of November, the king, in his speech, declared that the court of Spain had rejected all his amicable proposals, and broke through their most solemn engagements, for the security of the British commerce. To vindicate, therefore, the faith of his former treaties, as well as to maintain those he had lately made, and to protect and defend the trade of his subjects, which had in every branch been violently and unjustly oppressed, it became necessary for his naval forces to check their progress: that notwithstanding the success of his arms, that court had lately given orders at all the ports of Spain and of the West Indies to fit out privateers against the English. He said he was persuaded that a British Parliament would enable him to resent such treatment; and he assured them that his good brother, the Regent of France, was ready to concur with him in the most vigorous measures. A strong opposition was made in both Houses to the motion for an address of thanks and congratulation proposed by Lord Carteret. Several peers observed, that such an address was, in effect, to approve a sea-fight which might be attended with dangerous consequences, and to give the sanction of that august assembly to measures which, upon examination, might appear either to clash with the law of nations, or former treaties, or to be prejudicial to the trade of Great Britain: that they ought to proceed with the utmost caution and maturest deliberation, in an affair wherein the honour as well as the interest of the nation were so highly concerned. Lord Strafford moved for an address, that Sir George Byng's instructions might be laid before the House. Earl Stanhope replied, that there was no occasion for such an address, since by his majesty's command he had already laid before the House the treaties, of which the late sea-fight was a consequence; particularly the treaty for a defensive alliance between the emperor and his majesty, concluded at Westminster on the twenty-fifth day of May, in the year one thousand seven hundred and sixteen; and the treaty of alliance for restoring and settling the public peace, signed at London on the twenty-second day of July. He affirmed, that the court of Spain had violated the treaty of Utrecht, and acted against the public faith in attacking the emperor's dominions, while he was engaged in a war against the enemies of Christendom; that they had rejected his majesty's friendly offices and offers for mediating an accommodation. He explained the cause of his journey to Spain, and his negotiations at Madrid. He added, it was high time to check the growth of the naval power of Spain, in order to protect and secure the trade of the British subjects, which had been violently oppressed by the Spaniards. After a long debate, the motion was carried by a considerable majority. The same subject excited disputes of the same nature in the House of Commons, where Lord Hinchingbroke moved, that in their address of thanks they should declare their entire satisfaction in those measures which the king had already taken for strengthening the Protestant succession, and establishing a lasting tranquillity in Europe. The members in the opposition urged, that it was unparliamentary and unprecedented, on the first day of the session, to enter upon particulars: that the business in question was of the highest importance, and deserved the most mature deliberation: that before they approved the measures which had been taken, they ought to examine the reasons on which those measures were founded. Mr. Robert Walpole affirmed, that the giving sanction, in the manner proposed, to the late measures, could have no other view than that of screening ministers, who were conscious of having begun a war against Spain, and now wanted to make it the Parliament's war. He observed, that instead of an entire satisfaction, they ought to express their entire dissatisfaction, with such conduct as was contrary to the law of nations, and a breach of the most solemn treaties. Mr. Secretary Craggs, in a long speech, explained the nature of the quadruple alliance, and justified all the measures which had been taken. The address, as moved by Lord Hinchingbroke, was at length carried, and presented to his majesty. Then the Commons proceeded to consider the supply. They voted thirteen thousand five hundred sailors; and twelve thousand four hundred and thirty-five men for the land-service. The whole estimate amounted to two millions two hundred and fifty-seven thousand five hundred eighty-one pounds, nineteen shillings. The money was raised by a land-tax, malt-tax, and lottery.

Act for-
strengthen-
ing the
Protestant
interest.

On the thirteenth day of December, Earl Stanhope declared, in the House of Lords, that, in order to unite the hearts of the well-affected to the present establishment, he had a bill to offer under the title of "An act for strengthening the Protestant interest in these kingdoms." It was accordingly read, and appeared to be a bill repealing the acts against occasional conformity, the growth of schism, and some clauses in the corporation and test acts. This had been concerted by the ministry in private meetings with the most eminent dissenters. The tory lords were astonished at this motion, for which they were altogether unprepared. Nevertheless, they were strenuous in their opposition. They alleged that the bill, instead of strengthening, would certainly weaken the church of England, by plucking off her best feathers, investing her enemies with power, and sharing with churchmen the civil and military employments of which they were then wholly possessed. Earl Cowper declared himself against that part of the bill by which some clauses of the test and corporation acts were repealed; because he looked upon those acts as the main bulwark of our excellent constitution in church and state, which ought to be inviolably preserved. The Earl of Ilay opposed the bill, because in his opinion it infringed the *pacta conventa* of the treaty of union, by which the bounds both of the church of England and of the church of Scotland were fixed and settled; and he was apprehensive, if the articles of the union were broken with respect to one church, it might afterwards be a precedent to break them with respect to the other. The Archbishop of Canterbury said the acts which by this bill would be repealed were the main bulwark and supporters of the English Church: he expressed all imaginable tenderness for well-meaning conscientious dissenters; but he could not forbear saying, some among that sect made a wrong use of the favour and indulgence shown to them at the Revolution, though they had the least share in that happy event: it was, therefore, thought necessary for the legislature to interpose, and put a stop to the scandalous practice of occasional conformity. He added, that it would be needless to repeal the act against schism, since no advantage had been taken of it to the prejudice of the dissenters. Dr. Hoadley, Bishop of Bangor, endeavoured to prove, that the occasional and schism acts were in effect persecuting laws; and that by admitting the principle of self-defence and self-preservation in matters of religion, all the persecutions maintained by the heathens against the professors of Christianity, and even the popish inquisition, might be justified. With respect to the power of which many clergymen appeared so fond and so zealous, he owned the desire of power and riches was natural to all men; but that he had learned, both from reason and from the gospel, that this desire must be kept within due bounds, and not intrench upon the rights and liberties of their fellow-creatures and countrymen. After a long debate, the House agreed to leave out some clauses concerning the test and corporation acts: then the bill was committed, and afterwards passed. In the Lower House it met with violent opposition, in spite of which it was carried by the majority.

The king, on the seventeenth day of December, sent a

CHAP.
XIII.

1718.
War de-
clared
against
Spain.

message to the Commons, importing, that all his endeavours to procure redress for the injuries done to his
subjects by the King of Spain having proved ineffectual,
he had found it necessary to declare war against that
monarch. When a motion was made for an address, to
assure the king they would cheerfully support him in the
prosecution of the war, Mr. Shippen and some other
members said, they did not see the necessity of involving
the nation in a war, on account of some grievances of
which the merchants complained, as these might be
amicably redressed. Mr. Stanhope assured the House,
that he had presented five-and-twenty memorials to the
ministry of Spain on that subject, without success. Mr.
Methuen accounted for the dilatory proceedings of the
Spanish court in commercial affairs, by explaining the
great variety of regulations in the several provinces and
ports of that kingdom. It was suggested, that the
ministry paid very little regard to the trade and interest
of the nation; inasmuch as it appeared by the answers
from a secretary of state to the letter of the Marquis de
Monteleone, that they would have overlooked the violation of the treaties of commerce, provided Spain had
accepted the conditions stipulated in the quadruple
alliance; for it was there expressly said, that his majesty,
the King of Great Britain, did not seek to aggrandize
himself by any new acquisitions, but was rather inclined
to sacrifice something of his own to procure the general
quiet and tranquillity of Europe. A member observed,
that nobody could tell how far that sacrifice would have
extended; but certainly it was a very uncommon stretch
of condescension. This sacrifice was said to be the cession of Gibraltar and Port-Mahon, which the Regent of
France had offered to the King of Spain, provided he
would accede to the quadruple alliance. Horatio Walpole observed, that the disposition of Sicily in favour of
the emperor was an infraction of the treaty of Utrecht;
and his brother exclaimed against the injustice of attacking the Spanish fleet before a declaration of war. Notwithstanding all these arguments and objections, the
majority agreed to the address; and such another was
carried in the Upper House without a division. The
declaration of war against Spain was published with the
usual solemnities; but this war was not a favourite of the

people, and therefore did not produce those acclamations
that were usual on such occasions.

Meanwhile Cardinal Alberoni employed all his intrigues, power, and industry, for the gratification of his revenge. He caused new ships to be built, the sea-ports to be put in a posture of defence, succours to be sent to Sicily, and the proper measures to be taken for the security of Sardinia. He, by means of the Prince de Cellamare, the Spanish ambassador at Paris, caballed with the malecontents of that kingdom, who were numerous and powerful. A scheme was actually formed for seizing the regent, and securing the person of the king. The Duke of Orleans owed the first intimation of this plot to King George, who gave him to understand, that a conspiracy was formed against his person and government. The regent immediately took measures for watching the conduct of all suspected persons; but the whole intrigue was discovered by accident. The Prince de Cellamare entrusted his despatches to the Abbé Portocarrero, and to a son of the Marquis de Monteleone. These emissaries set out from Paris in a post-chaise, and were overturned. The postilion overheard Portocarrero say, he would not have lost his portmanteau for a hundred thousand pistoles. The man at his return to Paris, gave notice to the government of what he had observed. The Spaniards, being pursued, were overtaken and seized at Poitiers, with the portmanteau, in which the regent found two letters that made him acquainted with the particulars of the conspiracy. The Prince de Cellamare was immediately conducted to the frontiers; the Duke of Maine, the Marquis de Pompadour, the Cardinal de Polignac, and many other persons of distinction, were committed to different prisons. The regent declared war against Spain on the twenty-ninth day of December; and an army of six-and-thirty thousand men began its march towards that kingdom in January, under the command of the Duke of Berwick.

Cardinal Alberoni had likewise formed a scheme in favour of the pretender. The Duke of Ormond, repairing to Madrid, held conferences with his eminence; and measures were concerted for exciting another insurrection in Great Britain. The Chevalier de St. George quitted Urbino by stealth; and embarking at Netteno, landed at

Cagliari in March.   From thence he took his passage to
Roses in Catalonia, and proceeded to Madrid, where he
was received with great cordiality, and treated as King
of Great Britain.   An armament had been equipped of
ten ships of war and transports, having on board six
thousand regular troops, with arms for twelve thousand
men.   The command of this fleet was bestowed on the
Duke of Ormond, with the title of captain-general of his
Most Catholic Majesty.   He was provided with declarations in the name of that king, importing, that for many
good reasons he had sent part of his land and sea forces
into England and Scotland, to act as auxiliaries to King
James.   His Britannic majesty, having received from the
Regent of France timely notice of this intended invasion,
offered, by proclamation, rewards to those that should
apprehend the Duke of Ormond, or any gentleman embarked in that expedition.   Troops were ordered to
assemble in the north, and in the west of England : two
thousand men were demanded of the States-General : a
strong squadron was equipped to oppose the Spanish
armament ; and the Duke of Orleans made a proffer to
King George of twenty battalions for his service.

Three hun-
dred Spa-
niards land
and are
taken in
Scotland.

His majesty having communicated to both Houses of
Parliament the repeated advices he had received touching this projected descent, they promised to support him
against all his enemies. They desired he would augment
his forces by sea and land ; and assured him they would
make good the extraordinary expense.   Two thousand
men were landed from Holland, and six battalions of
imperialists from the Austrian Netherlands.   The Duke
of Ormond sailed from Cadiz, and proceeded as far as
Cape Finisterre, where his fleet was dispersed and disabled by a violent storm, which entirely defeated the
purposed expedition.   Two frigates, however, arrived in
Scotland, with the Earls Marischal and Seaforth, the
Marquis of Tullibardine, some field officers, three hundred Spaniards, and arms for two thousand men.   They
were joined by a small body of Highlanders, and possessed themselves of Donan Castle.   Against these adventurers General Wightman marched with a body
of regular troops from Inverness.   They had taken possession of the pass at Glenshiel ; but, at the approach of
the king's forces, retired to the pass at Strachell, which

they resolved to defend. They were attacked and driven
from one eminence to another till night, when the Highlanders dispersed, and next day the Spaniards surrendered
themselves prisoners of war. Marischal, Seaforth, and
Tullibardine, with some officers, retired to one of the
western isles, in order to wait an opportunity of being
conveyed to the continent.

On the last day of February the Duke of Somerset
represented in the House of Lords, that the number of
peers being very much increased, especially since the
union of the two kingdoms, it seemed absolutely necessary to take effectual measures for preventing the inconveniences that might attend the creation of a great number of peers, to serve a present purpose; an expedient
which had been actually taken in the late reign. He
therefore moved that a bill should be brought in, to settle and limit the peerage, in such a manner, that the
number of English peers should not be enlarged beyond
six above the present number, which, upon failure of
male issue, might be supplied by new creations: that
instead of the sixteen elective peers from Scotland,
twenty-five should be made hereditary on the part of
that kingdom; and that this number, upon failure of
heirs male, should be supplied from the other members
of the Scottish peerage. This bill was intended as a
restraint upon the Prince of Wales, who happened to
be at variance with the present ministry. The motion
was supported by the Duke of Argyle, now lord steward
of the household, the Earls of Sunderland and Carlisle.
It was opposed by the Earl of Oxford, who said that
although he expected nothing from the crown, he would
never give his vote for lopping off so valuable a branch
of the prerogative, which enabled the king to reward
merit and virtuous actions. The debate was adjourned
to the second day of March, when Earl Stanhope delivered a message from the king, intimating, that as they
had under consideration the state of the British peerage,
he had so much at heart the settling it upon such a
foundation as might secure the freedom and constitution
of Parliaments in all future ages, that he was willing his
prerogative should not stand in the way of so great and
necessary a work. Another violent debate ensued be-

tween the two factions. The question here, as in almost every other dispute, was not, Whether the measure proposed was advantageous to the nation? but, Whether the tory or the whig interest should predominate in Parliament? Earl Cowper affirmed, that the part of the bill relating to the Scottish peerage was a manifest violation of the treaty of union, as well as a flagrant piece of injustice, as it would deprive persons of their right without being heard, and without any pretence or forfeiture on their part. He observed that the Scottish peers excluded from the number of the twenty-five would be in a worse condition than any other subjects in the kingdom; for they would be neither electing nor elected,

Annals.
Corbet.
Tindal.
Hist. Reg.
Deb. in
Parlia-
ment.
Lives of
the Ad-
mirals.

neither representing nor represented. These objections were overruled: several resolutions were taken agreeably to the motion; and the judges were ordered to prepare and bring in the bill. This measure alarmed the generality of Scottish peers, as well as many English commoners, who saw in the bill the avenues of dignity and title shut up against them; and they did not fail to exclaim against it, as an encroachment upon the fundamental maxims of the constitution. Treatises were written and published on both sides of the question; and a national clamour began to arise, when Earl Stanhope observed, in the House, that as the bill had raised strange apprehensions, he thought it advisable to postpone the further consideration of it till a more proper opportunity. It was accordingly dropped, and the Parliament prorogued on the eighteenth day of April, on which occasion his majesty told both Houses that the Spanish king had acknowledged the pretender.

1719.
Count
Merci as-
sumes the
command
of the im-
perial army
in Sicily.

The king having appointed lords justices to rule the kingdom in his absence, embarked in May for Holland, from whence he proceeded to Hanover, where he concluded a peace with Ulrica, the new Queen of Sweden. By this treaty Sweden yielded for ever to the royal and electoral house of Brunswick, the duchies of Bremen and Verden, with all their dependencies: King George obliged himself to pay a million of rix-dollars to the Queen of Sweden; and to renew, as King of Great Britain and Elector of Hanover, the alliances formerly subsisting between his predecessors and that kingdom. He like-

wise mediated a peace between Sweden and his former
allies, the Danes, the Prussians, and the Poles. The
czar, however, refused to give up his schemes of conquest.
He sent his fleet to the Scheuron or Batses of Sweden,
where his troops landing, to the number of fifteen thousand, committed dreadful outrages; but Sir John Norris,
who commanded an English squadron in those seas, having
orders to support the negotiations, and oppose any hostilities that might be committed, the czar, dreading the
fate of the Spanish navy, thought proper to recall his
fleet. In the Mediterranean, Admiral Byng acted with
unwearied vigour in assisting the imperialists to finish
the conquest of Sicily. The court of Vienna had agreed
to send a strong body of forces to finish the reduction of
that island; and the command in this expedition was
bestowed upon the Count de Merci, with whom Sir
George Byng conferred at Naples. This admiral supplied them with ammunition and artillery from the Spanish prizes. He took the whole reinforcement under
his convoy, and saw them safely landed in the Bay of
Patti, to the number of three thousand five hundred
horse, and ten thousand infantry. Count Merci, thinking himself more than a match for the Spanish forces
commanded by the Marquis de Lede, attacked him in a
strong camp at Franca-Villa, and was repulsed with the
loss of five thousand men, himself being dangerously
wounded in the action. Here his army must have perished
for want of provision, had they not been supplied by the
English navy.

Admiral Byng no sooner learned the bad success of
the attack at Franca-Villa than he embarked two battalions from the garrison of Melazzo, and about a thousand recruits, whom he sent under a convoy through the
Faro to Scheso-bay, in order to reinforce the imperial
army. He afterwards assisted at a council of war with
the German generals, who, in consequence of his advice,
undertook the siege of Messina. Then he repaired to
Naples, where he proposed to Count Gallas, the new
viceroy, that the troops destined for the conquest of
Sardinia should be first landed in Sicily, and co-operate
towards the conquest of that island. The proposal was
immediately despatched to the court of Vienna. In the

mean time the admiral returned to Sicily, and assisted
at the siege of Messina. The town surrendered; the
garrison retired into the citadel; and the remains of the
Spanish navy, which had escaped at Passaro, were now
destroyed in the Mole. The emperor approved of the
scheme proposed by the English admiral, to whom he
wrote a very gracious letter, intimating that he had despatched orders to the governor of Milan, to detach the
troops designed for Sardinia to Vado, in order to be
transported into Italy. The admiral charged himself
with the performance of this service. Having furnished
the imperial army before Messina with another supply
of cannon, powder, and shot, upon his own credit, he set
sail for Vado, where he surmounted numberless difficulties, started by the jealousy of Count Bonneval, who was
unwilling to see his troops, destined for Sardinia, now
diverted to another expedition, in which he could not
enjoy the chief command. At length Admiral Byng
saw the forces embarked, and convoyed them to Messina,
the citadel of which surrendered in a few days after their
arrival. By this time the Marquis de Lede had fortified
a strong post at Castro-Giovanne, in the centre of the
island; and cantoned his troops about Aderno, Palermo,
and Catanea. The imperialists could not pretend to
attack him in this situation, nor could they remain in
the neighbourhood of Messina, on account of the scarcity
of provisions. They would, therefore, have been obliged
to quit the island during the winter, had not the admiral
undertaken to transport them by sea to Trapani, where
they could extend themselves in a plentiful country. He
not only executed this enterprise, but even supplied them
with corn from Tunis, as the harvest of Sicily had been
gathered into the Spanish magazines. It was the second
day of March before the last embarkation of the imperial
troops were landed at Trapani.

The Spa-
nish troops
evacuate
Sicily.

The Marquis de Lede immediately retired with his
army to Alcamo, from whence he sent his mareschal de
camp to Count Merci and the English admiral, with overtures for evacuating Sicily. The proposals were not disagreeable to the Germans; but Sir George Byng declared
that the Spaniards should not quit the island while the
war continued, as he foresaw that these troops would be

employed against France or England. He agreed, however, with Count Merci, in proposing, that if the marquis
would surrender Palermo, and retire into the middle part
of the island, they would consent to an armistice for six
weeks, until the sentiments of their different courts should
be known. The marquis offered to surrender Palermo,
in consideration of a suspension of arms for three months;
but while this negotiation was depending, he received
advice from Madrid that a general peace was concluded.
Nevertheless, he broke off the treaty in obedience to a
secret order for that purpose. The King of Spain hoped
to obtain the restitution of St. Sebastian's, Fontarabia,
and other places taken in the course of the war, in exchange for the evacuation of Sicily. Hostilities were
continued until the admiral received advice from the
Earl of Stair at Paris that the Spanish ambassador at
the Hague had signed the quadruple alliance. By the
same courier packets were delivered to the Count de
Merci and the Marquis de Lede, which at last gave the
admiral and imperial general to understand that he
looked upon the peace as a thing concluded ; and was
ready to treat for a cessation of hostilities. They insisted upon his delivering up Palermo : on the other
hand, he urged that, as their masters were in treaty for
settling the terms of evacuating Sicily and Sardinia, he
did not think himself authorized to agree to a cessation,
except on condition that each party should remain on
the ground they occupied, and expect further orders
from their principals. After a fruitless interview between
the three chiefs at the Cassine de Rossignola, the imperial general resolved to undertake the siege of Palermo :
with this view he decamped from Alcamo on the eighteenth day of April, and followed the Marquis de Lede,
who retreated before him, and took possession of the
advantageous posts that commanded the passes into the
plain of Palermo ; but Count Merci, with indefatigable
diligence, marched over the mountains, while the admiral
coasted along shore, attending the motions of the army.
The Spanish general, perceiving the Germans advancing
into the plain, retired under the cannon of Palermo, and
fortified his camp with strong intrenchments. On the
second day of May the Germans took one of the enemy's

redoubts by surprise, and the Marquis de Lede ordered all his forces to be drawn out to retake this fortification: both armies were on the point of engaging, when a courier arrived in a felucca, with a packet for the marquis, containing full powers to treat and agree about the evacuation of the island, and the transportation of the army to Spain. He forthwith drew off his army, and sent a trumpet to the general and admiral, with letters informing them of the orders he had received. Commissioners were appointed on each side, the negotiations begun, and the convention signed in a very few days. The Germans were put in possession of Palermo, and the Spanish army marched to Tauromini, from whence they were transported to Barcelona.

Philip
obliged to
accede to
the qua-
druple al-
liance.

The admiral continued in the Mediterranean until he had seen the islands of Sicily and Sardinia evacuated by the Spaniards, and the mutual cessions executed between the emperor and the Duke of Savoy; in consequence of which, four battalions of Piedmontese troops were transported from Palermo to Sardinia, and took possession of Cagliari in the name of their master. In a word, Admiral Byng bore such a considerable share in this war of Sicily, that the fate of the island depended wholly on his courage, vigilance, and conduct. When he waited on his majesty at Hanover, he met with a very gracious reception. The king told him he had found out the secret of obliging his enemies as well as his friends; for the court of Spain had mentioned him in the most honourable terms, with respect to his candid and friendly deportment, in providing transports and other necessaries for the embarkation of their troops, and in protecting them from oppression. He was appointed treasurer of the navy, and rear-admiral of Great Britain: in a little time the king ennobled him, by the title of Viscount Torrington: he was declared a privy-counsellor; and afterwards made knight of the bath, at the revival of that order. During these occurrences in the Mediterranean, the Duke of Berwick advanced with the French army to the frontiers of Spain, where he took Fort Passage, and destroyed six ships of war that were on the stocks: then he reduced Fontarabia and St. Sebastian's, together with Port Antonio in the bottom of the bay of Biscay. In

this last exploit the French were assisted by a detachment of English seamen, who burnt two large ships unfinished, and a great quantity of naval stores. The King
of England, with a view to indemnify himself for the
expense of the war, projected the conquest of Corunna
in Biscay, and of Peru in South America. Four thousand
men, commanded by Lord Cobham, were embarked at
the Isle of Wight, and sailed on the twenty-first day of
September, under convoy of five ships of war, conducted
by Admiral Mighels. Instead of making an attempt upon
Corunna, they reduced Vigo with very little difficulty;
and Pont-a-Vedra submitted without resistance : here
they found some brass artillery, small arms, and military stores, with which they returned to England. In
the mean time, Captain Johnson, with two English ships
of war, destroyed the same number of Spanish ships in
the port of Ribadeo, to the eastward of Cape Ortegas ;
so that the naval power of Spain was totally ruined. The
expedition to the West Indies was prevented by the
peace. Spain being oppressed on all sides, and utterly
exhausted, Philip saw the necessity of a speedy pacification. He now perceived the madness of Alberoni's
ambitious projects. That minister was personally disagreeable to the emperor, the King of England, and the
Regent of France, who had declared they would hearken
to no proposals while he should continue in office : the
Spanish monarch, therefore, divested him of his employment, and ordered him to quit the kingdom in three
weeks. The Marquis de Beretti Landi, minister from
the court of Madrid at the Hague, delivered a plan of
pacification to the states; but it was rejected by the
allies ; and Philip was obliged at last to accede to the
quadruple alliance.

On the fourteenth day of November, King George Bill for
returned to England, and on the twenty-third opened securing
the session of Parliament with a speech, in which he told pendency
them that all Europe, as well as Great Britain, was on of Ireland
the point of being delivered from the calamities of war, crown of
by the influence of British arms and councils. He ex- Britain.
horted the Commons to concert proper means for lessening the debts of the nation; and concluded with a panegyric upon his own government. It must be owned he

had acted with equal vigour and deliberation in all the troubles he had encountered since his accession to the throne. The addresses of both Houses were as warm as he could desire. They in particular extolled him for having interposed in behalf of the Protestants of Hungary, Poland, and Germany, who had been oppressed by the practices of the popish clergy, and presented to him memorials, containing a detail of their grievances. He and all the other Protestant powers warmly interceded in their favour; but the grievances were not redressed. The peerage bill was now revived by the Duke of Buckingham; and, in spite of all opposition, passed through the House of Lords. It had been projected by Earl Stanhope, and eagerly supported by the Earl of Sunderland; therefore, Mr. Robert Walpole attacked it in the House of Commons with extraordinary vehemence. Here too it was opposed by a considerable number of whig members; and, after warm debates, rejected by a large majority. The next object that engrossed the attention of the Parliament was a bill for better securing the dependency of Ireland upon the crown of Great Britain. Maurice Annesley had appealed to the House of Peers in England from a decree of the House of Peers in Ireland, which was reversed. The British Peers ordered the barons of the exchequer in Ireland to put Mr. Annesley in possession of the lands he had lost by the decree in that kingdom. The barons obeyed this order; and the Irish House of Peers passed a vote against them, as having acted in derogation to the king's prerogative in his high court of Parliament in Ireland, as also of the rights and privileges of that kingdom, and of the Parliament thereof; they likewise ordered them to be taken into custody of the usher of the black rod; they transmitted a long representation to the king, demonstrating their right to the final judicature of causes; and the Duke of Leeds, in the Upper House, urged fifteen reasons to support the claim of the Irish Peers. Notwithstanding these arguments, the House of Lords in England resolved that the barons of the exchequer in Ireland had acted with courage, according to law in support of his majesty's prerogative, and with fidelity to the crown of Great Britain. They addressed the king to confer on them some marks

of his royal favour as a recompense for the ill usage they
had undergone. Finally, they prepared the bill, by
which the Irish House of Lords was deprived of all right
to pass sentence, affirm, or reverse any judgment or decree,
given or made, in any court within that kingdom. In the
House of Commons it was opposed by Mr. Pitt, Mr.
Hungerford, Lords Molesworth and Tyrconnel; but was
carried by the majority, and received the royal assent.

The king having recommended to the Commons the
consideration of proper means for lessening the national
debt, was a prelude to the famous South-Sea act, which
became productive of so much mischief and infatuation.
The scheme was projected by Sir John Blunt, who had
been bred a scrivener, and was possessed of all the cunning, plausibility, and boldness requisite for such an undertaking. He communicated his plan to Mr. Aislabie,
the chancellor of the exchequer, as well as to one of the
secretaries of state. He answered all their objections;
and the project was adopted. They foresaw their own
private advantage in the execution of the design, which
was imparted in the name of the South-Sea Company, of
which Blunt was a director, who influenced all their proceedings. The pretence for the scheme was to discharge
the national debt, by reducing all the funds into one.
The bank and South-Sea Company outbid each other.
The South-Sea Company altered their original plan, and
offered such high terms to government, that the proposals of the bank were rejected; and a bill was ordered
to be brought into the House of Commons, formed on
the plan presented by the South-Sea Company. While
this affair was in agitation, the stock of that company
rose from one hundred and thirty to near four hundred,
in consequence of the conduct of the Commons, who
had rejected a motion for a clause in the bill, to fix what
share in the capital stock of the company should be
vested in those proprietors of the annuities who might
voluntarily subscribe; or how many years' purchase in
money they should receive in subscribing, at the choice
of the proprietors. In the House of Lords, the bill was
opposed by Lords North and Grey, Earl Cowper, the
Dukes of Wharton, Buckingham, and other peers. They
affirmed it was calculated for enriching a few and im-

CHAP.
XIII.

1719.

South-Sea
act.

Annals.
Corbet.
Hist. Reg.
Tindal.
Lives of the
Admirals.

1720.

o 2

poverishing a great number; that it countenanced the fraudulent and pernicious practice of stock-jobbing, which diverted the genius of the people from trade and industry: that it would give foreigners the opportunity to double and treble the vast sums they had in the public funds; and they would be tempted to realize and withdraw their capital and immense gains to other countries; so that Great Britain would be drained of all its gold and silver; that the artificial and prodigious rise of the South-Sea stock was a dangerous bait, which might decoy many unwary people to their ruin, alluring them by a false prospect of gain to part with the fruits of their industry, to purchase imaginary riches: that the addition of above thirty millions capital would give such power to the South-Sea Company as might endanger the liberties of the nation; for by their extensive interest they would be able to influence most if not all the elections of the members; and consequently overrule the resolutions of the House of Commons. Earl Cowper urged, that in all public bargains the individuals in the administration ought to take care that they should be more advantageous to the state than to private persons; but that a contrary method had been followed in the contract made with the South-Sea Company; for, should the stocks be kept at the advanced price to which they had been raised by the oblique arts of stock-jobbing, either that company or its principal members would gain above thirty millions, of which no more than one-fourth part would be given towards the discharge of the national debts. He apprehended that the repurchase of annuities would meet with insuperable difficulties; and, in such case, none but a few persons who were in the secret, who had bought stocks at a low rate, and afterwards sold them at a high price, would in the end be gainers by the project. The Earl of Sunderland answered their objections. He declared that those who countenanced the scheme of the South-Sea Company had nothing in view but the advantage of the nation. He owned that the managers for that company had undoubtedly a prospect of private gain, either to themselves or to their corporation; but, he said, when the scheme was accepted, neither the one nor the other could foresee that the stocks would have risen to such a height; that if they had continued as they were, the public would have had the far greater share of the advantage accruing from the scheme; and should they be kept up to the present high price, it was but reasonable that the South-Sea Company should enjoy the profits procured to it by the wise management and industry of the directors, which would enable it to make large dividends, and thereby accomplish the purpose of the scheme. The bill passed without amendment or division; and on the seventh day of April received the royal assent. By this act the South-Sea Company was authorized to take in, by purchase or subscription, the irredeemable debts of the nation, stated at sixteen millions five hundred forty-six thousand four hundred eighty-two pounds, seven shillings, one penny farthing, at such times as they should find it convenient before the first day of March of the ensuing year, and without any compulsion on any of the proprietors, at such rates and prices as should be agreed upon between the company and the respective proprietors. They were likewise authorized to take in all the redeemable debts, amounting to the same sum as that of the irredeemables, either by purchase, by taking subscriptions, or by paying off the creditors. For the liberty of taking in the national debts, and increasing their capital stock accordingly, the company consented that their present and to be increased annuity should be continued at five per cent. till Midsummer, in the year one thousand seven hundred and twenty-seven; from thence to be reduced to four per cent. and be redeemable by Parliament. In consideration of this and other advantages expressed in the act, the company declared themselves willing to make such payments into the receipt of the exchequer as were specified for the use of the public, to be applied to the discharge of the public debts incurred before Christmas, in the year one thousand seven hundred and sixteen. The sums they were obliged to pay for the liberty of taking in the redeemable debts, four years and a half's purchase for all long and short annuities that should be subscribed, and one year's purchase for such long annuities as should not be subscribed, amounted on the execution of the act to about seven millions. For enabling the company to raise this sum, they were empowered to make calls for money from their members; to open books of subscription; to grant annuities redeemable by the company; to borrow money upon any contract or bill under their common seal, or on the credit of their capital stock; to convert the money demanded of their members into additional stock, without, however, making any addition to the company's annuities, payable out of the public duties. It was enacted, that out of the first monies arising from the sums paid by the company into the exchequer, such public debts, carrying interest at five per cent. incurred before the twenty-fifth day of December, in the year one thousand seven hundred and sixteen, founded upon any former act of Parliament, as were now redeemable, or might be redeemed before the twenty-fifth day of December, in the year one thousand seven hundred and twenty-two, should be discharged in the first place: that then all the remainder should be applied towards paying off so much of the capital stock of the company as should then carry an interest of five per cent. It was likewise provided that after Midsummer, in the year one thousand seven hundred and twenty-seven, the company should not be paid off in any sums being less than one million at a time.

Charters granted to the Royal and London Assurance offices.

The heads of the Royal Assurance and London Assurance Companies, understanding that the civil list was considerably in arrears, offered to the ministry six hundred thousand pounds towards the discharge of that debt, on condition of their obtaining the king's charter, with a parliamentary sanction, for the establishment of their respective companies. The proposal was embraced; and the king communicated it in a message to the House of Commons, desiring their concurrence. A bill was immediately passed, enabling his majesty to grant letters of incorporation to the two companies. It soon obtained the royal assent; and on the eleventh day of June, an end was put to the session. This was the age of interested projects, inspired by a venal spirit of adventure, the natural consequence of that avarice, fraud, and profligacy which the monied corporations had introduced. This of all others is the most unfavourable era for an historian. A reader of sentiment and imagination cannot be enter-

tained or interested by a dry detail of such transactions
as admit of no warmth, no colouring, no embellishment;
a detail which serves only to exhibit an inanimate picture
of tasteless vice and mean degeneracy.

By this time an alliance offensive and defensive was Treaty of
concluded at Stockholm between King George and the alliance
Queen of Sweden, by which his majesty engaged to send Sweden.
a fleet into the Baltic, to act against the Czar of Muscovy,
in case that monarch should reject reasonable proposals
of peace.   Peter loudly complained of the insolent interposition of King George, alleging that he had failed in
his engagements, both as Elector of Hanover and King
of Great Britain.   His resident at London presented a
long memorial on this subject, which was answered by
the British and Hanoverian ministry.   These recriminations served only to inflame the difference.   The czar
continued to prosecute the war, and at length concluded
a peace without a mediator.   At the instances, however,
of King George and the Regent of France, a treaty of
peace was signed between the Queen of Sweden and the
King of Prussia, to whom that princess ceded the city of
Stetin, the district between the rivers Oder and Pehnne,
with the isles of Wollin and Usedom.   On the other
hand, he engaged to join the King of Great Britain in
his endeavours to effect a peace between Sweden and
Denmark, on condition that the Danish king should restore to Queen Ulrica that part of Pomerania which he
had seized; he likewise promised to pay to that queen
two millions of rix-dollars; in consideration of the cessions
she had made.   The treaty between Sweden and Denmark was signed at Frederickstadt in the month of June,
through the mediation of the King of Great Britain, who
became guarantee for the Dane's keeping possession of
Sleswick.   He consented, however, to restore the Upper
Pomerania, the Isle of Rugen, the city of Wismar, and
whatever he had taken from Sweden during the war, in
consideration of Sweden's renouncing the exemption from
toll in the Sound, and the two Belts, and paying to Denmark six hundred thousand rix-dollars.

Sir John Norris had again sailed to the Baltic with a The Prince
strong squadron, to give weight to the king's mediation. of Hesse
When he arrived at Copenhagen he wrote a letter to ing of
Sweden.

Prince Dolgorouki, the czar's ambassador at the court of Denmark, signifying that he and the king's envoy at Stockholm were vested with full powers to act jointly or separately in quality of plenipotentiaries, in order to effect a peace between Sweden and Muscovy, in the way of mediation. The prince answered that the czar had nothing more at heart than peace and tranquillity; and in case his Britannic majesty had any proposals to make to that prince, he hoped the admiral would excuse him from receiving them, as they might be delivered in a much more compendious way. The English fleet immediately joined that of Sweden as auxiliaries; but they had no opportunity of acting against the Russian squadron, which secured itself in Revel. Ulrica, Queen of Sweden and sister to Charles XII., had married the Prince of Hesse, and was extremely desirous that he should be joined with her in the administration of the regal power. She wrote a separate letter to each of the four states, desiring they would confer on him the sovereignty; and after some opposition from the nobles, he was actually elected king of Sweden. He sent one of his general officers to notify his elevation to the czar, who congratulated him upon his accession to the throne: this was the beginning of a negotiation which ended in peace, and established the tranquillity of the north. In the midst of these transactions, King George set out from England for his Hanoverian dominions; but, before he departed from Great Britain, he was reconciled to the Prince of Wales, through the endeavours of the Duke of Devonshire and Mr. Walpole, who, with Earl Cowper, Lord Townshend, Mr. Methuen, and Mr. Pulteney, were received into favour, and reunited with the ministry. The Earls of Dorset and Bridgewater were promoted to the title of dukes; Lord Viscount Castleton was made an earl; Hugh Boscawen was created a baron, and Viscount Falmouth; and John Wallop, baron, and Viscount of Lymington.

Effects of the South-Sea scheme.

While the king was involved at Hanover in a labyrinth of negotiations, the South-Sea scheme produced a kind of national delirium in his English dominions. Blunt, the projector, had taken the hint of his plan from the famous Mississippi scheme formed by Law, which in the preceding year had raised such a ferment in France, and entailed ruin upon many thousand families of that kingdom. In the scheme of Law, there was something substantial. An exclusive trade to Louisiana promised some advantage; though the design was defeated by the frantic eagerness of the people. Law himself became the dupe of the regent, who transferred the burden of fifteen hundred millions of the king's debts to the shoulders of the subjects : while the projector was sacrificed as the scape-goat of political iniquity. The South-Sea scheme promised no commercial advantage of any consequence. It was buoyed up by nothing but the folly and rapaciousness of individuals, which became so blind and extravagant, that Blunt, with moderate talents, was able to impose upon the whole nation, and make tools of the other directors, to serve his own purposes, and those of a few associates. When this projector found that the South-Sea stock did not rise according to his expectation upon the bills being passed, he circulated a report that Gibraltar and Port Mahon would be exchanged for some places in Peru; by which means the English trade to the South-Sea would be protected and enlarged. This rumour, diffused by his emissaries, acted like a contagion. In five days the directors opened their books for a subscription of one million, at the rate of three hundred pounds for every hundred pounds capital. Persons of all ranks crowded to the house in such a manner, that the first subscription exceeded two millions of original stock. In a few days this stock advanced to three hundred and forty pounds ; and the subscriptions were sold for double the price of the first payment. Without entering into a detail of the proceedings, or explaining the scandalous arts that were practised to enhance the value of the stock, and decoy the unwary, we shall only observe that, by the promise of prodigious dividends, and other infamous arts, the stock was raised to one thousand ; and the whole nation infected with the spirit of stock-jobbing to an astonishing degree. All distinctions of party, religion, sex, character, and circumstances, were swallowed up in this universal concern, or in some such pecuniary project. Exchange-alley was filled with a strange concourse of statesmen and clergymen, churchmen and dissenters, whigs and tories, physicians, lawyers, tradesmen, and even with multitudes of females. All other professions and employments were utterly neglected; and the people's attention wholly engrossed by this and other chimerical schemes, which were known by the denomination of bubbles. New companies started up every day, under the countenance of the prime nobility. The Prince of Wales was constituted governor of the Welsh Copper Company: the Duke of Chandos appeared at the head of the York-buildings Company: the Duke of Bridgewater formed a third, for building houses in London and Westminster. About a hundred such schemes were projected and put in execution, to the ruin of many thousands. The sums proposed to be raised by these expedients amounted to three hundred millions sterling, which exceeded the value of all the lands in England. The nation was so intoxicated with the spirit of adventure, that people became a prey to the grossest delusion. An obscure projector, pretending to have formed a very advantageous scheme, which, however, he did not explain, published proposals for a subscription, in which he promised, that in one month the particulars of his project should be disclosed. In the mean time he declared that every person paying two guineas should be entitled to a subscription for one hundred pounds, which would produce that sum yearly. In one forenoon this adventurer received a thousand of these subscriptions; and in the evening set out for another kingdom. The king, before his departure, had issued a proclamation against these unlawful projects; the lords justices afterwards dismissed all the petitions that had been presented for charters and patents; and the Prince of Wales renounced the company of which he had been elected governor. The South-Sea scheme raised such a flood of eager avidity and extravagant hope, that the majority of the directors were swept along with it even contrary to their own sense and inclination; but Blunt and his accomplices still directed the stream.

The bubble breaks.　　The infatuation prevailed till the eighth day of September, when the stock began to fall. Then did some of the adventurers awake from their delirium. The number of the sellers daily increased. On the twenty-ninth

day of the month the stock had sunk to one hundred
and fifty : several eminent goldsmiths and bankers, who
had lent great sums upon it, were obliged to stop payment and abscond. The ebb of this portentous tide was
so violent that it bore down every thing in its way; and
an infinite number of families were overwhelmed with
ruin. Public credit sustained a terrible shock : the nation
was thrown into a dangerous ferment; and nothing was
heard but the ravings of grief, disappointment, and despair. Some principal members of the ministry were
deeply concerned in these fraudulent transactions: when
they saw the price of stock sinking daily, they employed
all their influence with the bank to support the credit of
the South-Sea Company. That corporation agreed, though
with reluctance, to subscribe into the stock of the South-
Sea Company, valued at four hundred per cent., three
millions five hundred thousand pounds, which the company was to repay to the bank on Lady-day and Michael-
mas of the ensuing year. This transaction was managed
by Mr. Robert Walpole, who, with his own hand, wrote
the minute of agreement, afterwards known by the name
of the bank contract. Books were opened at the bank
to take in a subscription for the support of public credit;
and considerable sums of money were brought in. By
this expedient the stock was raised at first, and those
who contrived it seized the opportunity to realize. But
the bankruptcy of goldsmiths and the Sword-blade Company, from the fall of South-Sea stock, occasioned such
a run upon the bank, that the money was paid away
faster than it could be received from the subscription.
Then the South-Sea stock sunk again; and the directors
of the bank, finding themselves in danger of being involved in that company's ruin, renounced the agreement,
which, indeed, they were under no obligation to perform, for it was drawn up in such a manner as to be no
more than the rough draft of a subsequent agreement,
without due form, penalty, or clause of obligation. All
expedients having failed, and the clamours of the people
daily increasing, expresses were despatched to Hanover,
representing the state of the nation, and pressing the
king to return. He accordingly shortened his intended

CHAP.
XIII.

1720.
A secret
committee
appointed
by the
House of
Commons.

stay in Germany, and arrived in England on the eleventh
day of November.

The Parliament being assembled on the eighth day of
December, his majesty expressed his concern for the unhappy turn of affairs, which had so deeply affected the
public credit at home : he earnestly desired the Commons
to consider of the most effectual and speedy methods to
restore the national credit, and fix it upon a lasting establishment. The Lower House was too much interested
in the calamity to postpone the consideration of that
subject. The members seemed to lay aside all party
distinctions, and vie with each other in promoting an
inquiry, by which justice might be done to the injured
nation. They ordered the directors to produce an account of all their proceedings. Sir Joseph Jekyll moved,
that a select committee might be appointed, to examine
the particulars of this transaction. Mr. Walpole, now
paymaster of the forces, observed, that such a method
would protract the inquiry, while the public credit lay
in a bleeding condition. He told the House he had
formed a scheme for restoring public credit; but before
he would communicate this plan, desired to know whether the subscriptions of public debts and incumbrances,
money subscriptions, and other contracts made with the
South-Sea Company, should remain in the present state.
After a warm debate, the question was carried in the
affirmative, with this addition, "Unless altered for the
ease and relief of the proprietors, by a general court of
the South-Sea Company, or set aside in due course of
law." Next day Walpole produced his scheme, to en-
graft nine millions of South-Sea stock into the bank of
England, and the like sum into the East India Company,
on certain conditions. The House voted, that proposals
should be received from the bank, and those two companies, on this subject. These being delivered, the Commons resolved, that an engrossment of nine millions of
the capital stock of the South-Sea Company, into the
capital stock of the bank and East India Company, as
proposed by these companies, would contribute very much
to the restoring public credit. A bill upon this resolution was brought in, passed through both Houses, and

received the royal assent. Another bill was enacted into
a law, for restraining the sub-governor, deputy-governor,
directors, treasurer, under-treasurer, cashier, secretary,
and accountants, of the South-Sea Company, from quit-
ting the kingdom, till the end of the next session of Parliament; and for discovering their estates and effects, so
as to prevent them from being transported or alienated.
A committee of secrecy was chosen by ballot, to examine
all the books, papers, and proceedings, relating to the
execution of the South-Sea act.

The Lords were not less eager than the Commons to
prosecute this inquiry, though divers members in both
Houses were deeply involved in the guilt and infamy of
the transaction. Earl Stanhope said the estates of the
criminals, whether directors or not directors, ought to be
confiscated, to repair the public losses. He was seconded
by Lord Carteret, and even by the Earl of Sunderland.
The Duke of Wharton declared he would give up the
best friend he had, should he be found guilty. He observed, that the nation had been plundered in a most
flagrant and notorious manner; therefore, they ought to
find out and punish the offenders severely without respect to persons. The sub and deputy-governors, the
directors and officers of the South-Sea Company were
examined at the bar of the House. Then a bill was
brought in, disabling them to enjoy any office in that
company, or in the East India Company, or in the bank
of England. Three brokers were likewise examined, and
made great discoveries. Knight, the treasurer of the
South-Sea Company, who had been entrusted with the
secrets of the whole affair, thought proper to withdraw
himself from the kingdom. A proclamation was issued
to apprehend him; and another for preventing any of
the directors from escaping out of the kingdom. At
this period the secret committee informed the House of
Commons, that they had already discovered a train of
the deepest villany and fraud that hell ever contrived to
ruin a nation, which in due time they would lay before
the House: in the mean while they thought it highly
necessary to secure the persons of some of the directors
and principal officers of the South-Sea Company, as well
as to seize their papers. An order was made to secure

CHAP.
XIII.

1720.the books and papers of Knight, Surman, and Turner.
The persons of Sir George Caswell, Sir John Blunt, Sir
John Lambert, Sir John Fellowes, and Mr. Grigsby, were
taken into custody. Sir Theodore Jansen, Mr. Sawbridge,
Sir Robert Chaplain, and Mr. Eyles, were expelled the
House, and apprehended. Mr. Aislabie resigned his employments of chancellor of the exchequer and lord of the
treasury; and orders were given to remove all directors
of the South-Sea Company from the places they possessed
under the government.

Death of
Earl Stan-
hope and
Mr.Craggs,
both secre-
taries of
state.

The Lords, in the course of their examination, discovered that large portions of South-Sea stock had been
given to several persons in the administration and House
of Commons, for promoting the passing of the South-
Sea act. The House immediately resolved, that this
practice was a notorious and most dangerous species of
corruption; that the directors of the South-Sea Company having ordered great quantities of their stock to
be bought for the service of the company, when it was
at a very high price, and on pretence of keeping up the
price of stock; and at the same time several of the
directors, and other officers belonging to the company,
having, in a clandestine manner, sold their own stock to
the company, such directors and officers were guilty of a
notorious fraud and breach of trust, and their so doing
was one great cause of the unhappy turn of affairs, that
had so much affected public credit. Many other resolutions were taken against that infamous confederacy, in
which, however, the innocent were confounded with the
guilty. Sir John Blunt refusing to answer certain in-
terrogations, a violent debate arose about the manner in
which he should be treated. The Duke of Wharton
observed, that the government of the best princes was
sometimes rendered intolerable to their subjects by bad
ministers: he mentioned the example of Sejanus, who
had made a division in the imperial family, and rendered
the reign of Claudius hateful to the Romans. Earl Stanhope, conceiving this reflection was aimed at him, was
seized with a transport of anger. He undertook to vindicate the ministry; and spoke with such vehemence as
produced a violent headache, which obliged him to retire.
He underwent proper evacuations, and seemed to re-

cover; but next day, in the evening, he became lethargic, and being seized with a suffocation, instantly expired. The king deeply regretted the loss of this favourite minister, which was the more unfortunate as it happened at such a critical conjuncture; and he appointed Lord Townshend to fill his place of secretary. Earl Stanhope was survived but a few days by the other secretary, Mr. Craggs, who died of the small-pox on the sixteenth day of February. Knight, the cashier of the South-Sea Company, being seized at Tirlemont, by the vigilance of Mr. Gandot, secretary to Mr. Leathes, the British resident at Brussels, was confined in the citadel of Antwerp. Application was made to the court of Vienna, that he should be delivered to such persons as might be appointed to receive him; but he had found means to interest the states of Brabant in his behalf. They insisted upon their privilege granted by charter, that no person apprehended for any crime in Brabant should be tried in any other country. The House of Commons expressed their indignation at this frivolous pretence: instances were renewed to the emperor: and in the mean time Knight escaped from the citadel of Antwerp.

The committee of secrecy found that, before any subscription could be made, a fictitious stock of five hundred and seventy-four thousand pounds had been disposed of by the directors, to facilitate the passing the bill. Great part of this was distributed among the Earl of Sunderland, Mr. Craggs, senior, the Duchess of Kendal, the Countess of Platen and her two nieces, Mr. Secretary Craggs, and Mr. Aislabie, chancellor of the exchequer. In consequence of the committee's report, the House came to several severe though just resolutions against the directors and officers of the South-Sea Company; and a bill was prepared for the relief of the unhappy sufferers. Mr. Stanhope, one of the secretaries of the treasury, charged in the report with having large quantities of stock and subscriptions, desired that he might have an opportunity to clear himself. His request was granted; and the affair being discussed, he was cleared by a majority of three voices. Fifty thousand pounds in stock had been taken by Knight for the use of the Earl of Sunderland. Great part of the House entered eagerly into this

CHAP. XIII.

1720.

The estates of the directors of the South-Sea Company are confiscated.

inquiry; and a violent dispute ensued. The whole strength of the ministry was mustered in his defence. The majority declared him innocent: the nation in general was of another opinion. He resigned his place of first commissioner in the treasury, which was bestowed upon Mr. Robert Walpole; but he still retained the confidence of his master. With respect to Mr. Aislabie, the evidence appeared so strong against him, that the Commons resolved, he had promoted the destructive execution of the South-Sea scheme, with a view to his own exorbitant profit, and combined with the directors in their pernicious practices, to the ruin of public credit. He was expelled the House, and committed to the Tower. Mr. Craggs, senior, died of the small-pox, before he underwent the censure of the House. Nevertheless, they resolved that he was a notorious accomplice with Robert Knight, and some of the directors, in carrying on their scandalous practices; and, therefore, that all the estate of which he was possessed, from the first day of December in the preceding year, should be applied towards the relief of the unhappy sufferers in the South-Sea Company. The directors, in obedience to the order of the House, delivered in inventories of their estates, which were confiscated by act of Parliament, towards making good the damages sustained by the company, after a certain allowance was deducted for each, according to his conduct and circumstances.

Oldmixon.
Annals.
Hist. Reg.
Polit. State
Deb. in
Parliam.
Tindal.

1721.
Proceedings of the Commons with respect to the stock of the South-Sea Company.
The delinquents being thus punished by the forfeiture of their fortunes, the House converted their attention to means for repairing the mischiefs which the scheme had produced. This was a very difficult task, on account of the contending interests of those engaged in the South-Sea Company, which rendered it impossible to relieve some but at the expense of others. Several wholesome resolutions were taken, and presented with an address to the king, explaining the motives of their proceedings. On the twenty-ninth day of July, the Parliament was prorogued for two days only. Then his majesty, going to the House of Peers, declared that he had called them together again so suddenly, that they might resume the consideration of the state of public credit. The Commons immediately prepared a bill upon the resolutions

they had taken. The whole capital stock, at the end of the year one thousand seven hundred and twenty, amounted to about thirty-seven millions eight hundred thousand pounds. The stock allotted to all the proprietors did not exceed twenty-four millions five hundred thousand pounds; the remaining capital stock belonged to the company in their corporate capacity. It was the profit arising from the execution of the South-Sea scheme; and out of this the bill enacted, that seven millions should be paid to the public. The present act likewise directed several additions to be made to the stock of the proprietors, out of that possessed by the company in their own right; it made a particular distribution of stock, amounting to two millions two hundred thousand pounds; and upon remitting five millions of the seven to be paid to the public, annihilated two millions of their capital. It was enacted that, after these distributions, the remaining capital stock should be divided among all the proprietors. This dividend amounted to thirty-three pounds six shillings and eight-pence per cent., and deprived the company of eight millions nine hundred thousand pounds. They had lent above eleven millions on stock unredeemed; of which the Parliament discharged all the debtors, upon their paying ten per cent. Upon this article the company's loss exceeded six millions nine hundred thousand pounds; for many debtors refused to make any payment. The proprietors of the stock loudly complained of their being deprived of two millions; and the Parliament in the sequel revived that sum which had been annihilated. While this affair was in agitation, petitions from counties, cities, and boroughs, in all parts of the kingdom, were presented to the House, crying for justice against the villany of the directors. Pamphlets and papers were daily published on the same subject; so that the whole nation was exasperated to the highest pitch of resentment. Nevertheless, by the wise and vigorous resolutions of the Parliament, the South-Sea company was soon in a condition to fulfil their engagements with the public; the ferment of the people subsided; and the credit of the nation was restored.

CHAPTER XIV.

CHAP. XIV. — 1721. Bill against atheism and immorality postponed.

DURING the infatuation produced by this infamous scheme, luxury, vice, and profligacy, increased to a shocking degree of extravagance. The adventurers, intoxicated by their imaginary wealth, pampered themselves with the rarest dainties, and the most expensive wines that could be imported: they purchased the most sumptuous furniture, equipage, and apparel, though without taste or discernment: they indulged their criminal passions to the most scandalous excess: their discourse was the language of pride, insolence, and the most ridiculous ostentation: they affected to scoff at religion and morality; and even to set Heaven at defiance. The Earl of Nottingham complained in the House of Lords of the growth of atheism, profaneness, and immorality; and a bill was brought in for suppressing blasphemy and pro-

faneness. It contained several articles seemingly calculated to restrain the liberty granted to nonconformists
by the laws of the last session; for that reason it met
with violent opposition. It was supported by the Archbishop of Canterbury, the Earl of Nottingham, Lords
Bathurst and Trevor, the Bishops of London, Winchester, and Lichfield and Coventry. One of these said, he
verily believed the present calamity occasioned by the
South-Sea project was a judgment of God on the blasphemy and profaneness of the nation. Lord Onslow
replied, "That noble peer must then be a great sinner,
for he has lost considerably by the South-Sea scheme."
The Duke of Wharton, who had rendered himself famous
by his wit and profligacy, said he was not insensible of
the common opinion of the town concerning himself,
and gladly seized this opportunity of vindicating his
character, by declaring he was far from being a patron
of blasphemy, or an enemy to religion. On the other
hand, he could not but oppose the bill, because he conceived it to be repugnant to the holy scripture. Then
pulling an old family Bible from his pocket, he quoted
several passages from the epistles of St. Peter and St.
Paul; concluding with a desire that the bill might be
thrown out. The Earl of Peterborough declared, that
though he was for a parliamentary king, yet he did not
desire to have a parliamentary God, or a parliamentary
religion; and should the House declare for one of this
kind, he would go to Rome, and endeavour to be chosen
a cardinal; for he had rather sit in the conclave than
with their lordships upon those terms. After a vehement debate, the bill was postponed to a long day, by a
considerable majority.

The season was far advanced before the supplies were
granted; and at length they were not voted with that
cheerfulness and good humour which the majority had
hitherto manifested on such occasions. On the sixteenth
day of June, the king sent a message to the House of
Commons, importing that he had agreed to pay a subsidy to the crown of Sweden, and he hoped they would
enable him to make good his engagements. The leaders
of the opposition took fire at this intimation. They
desired to know whether this subsidy, amounting to

Session
closed.

seventy-two thousand pounds, was to be paid to Sweden over and above the expense of maintaining a strong squadron in the Baltic. Lord Molesworth observed that, by our late conduct, we were become the allies of the whole world, and the bubbles of all our allies; for we were obliged to pay them well for their assistance. He affirmed that the treaties which had been made with Sweden, at different times, were inconsistent and contradictory: that our late engagements with that crown were contrary to the treaties subsisting with Denmark, and directly opposite to the measures formerly concerted with the Czar of Muscovy. He said, that in order to engage the czar to yield what he had gained in the course of the war, the King of Prussia ought to give up Stetin, and the Elector of Hanover restore Bremen and Verden: that, after all, England had no business to intermeddle with the affairs of the empire: that we reaped little or no advantage by our trade to the Baltic, but that of procuring naval stores: he owned that hemp was a very necessary commodity, particularly at this juncture; but he insisted, that if due encouragement were given to some of our plantations in America, we might be supplied from thence at a much cheaper rate than from Sweden and Norway. Notwithstanding these arguments, the Swedish supply was granted; and in about three weeks, their complaisance was put to another proof. They were given to understand, by a second message, that the debts of the civil list amounted to five hundred and fifty thousand pounds; and his majesty hoped they would empower him to raise that sum upon the revenue, as he proposed it should be replaced in the civil list, and reimbursed by a deduction from the salaries and wages of all officers, as well as from the pensions and other payments from the crown. A bill was prepared for this purpose, though not without warm opposition; and, at the same time, an act passed for a general pardon. On the tenth day of August, the king closed the session with a speech, in which he expressed his concern for the sufferings of the innocent, and a just indignation against the guilty, with respect to the South-Sea scheme. These professions were judged necessary to clear his own character, which had incurred the suspicion of some people,

who whispered, that he was not altogether free from connexions with the projectors of that design; that the emperor had, at his desire, refused to deliver up Knight;
and that he favoured the directors and their accomplices.

Lords Townshend and Carteret were now appointed
secretaries of state; and the Earl of Ilay was vested with
the office of lord privy-seal of Scotland. In June the
treaty of peace between Great Britain and Spain was
signed at Madrid. The contracting parties engaged to
restore mutually all the effects seized and confiscated
on both sides. In particular, the King of England
promised to restore all the ships of the Spanish fleet
which had been taken in the Mediterranean, or the
value of them, if they were sold. He likewise promised, in a secret article, that he would no longer interfere in the affairs of Italy; and the King of Spain
made an absolute cession of Gibraltar and Port-Mahon.
At the same time, a defensive alliance was concluded
between Great Britain, France, and Spain. All remaining difficulties were referred to a congress at Cambray,
where they hoped to consolidate a general peace, by determining all differences between the emperor and his
Catholic majesty. In the mean time, the powers of Great
Britain, France, and Spain, engaged, by virtue of the
present treaty, to grant to the Duke of Parma a particular protection for the preservation of his territories and
rights, and for the support of his dignity. It was also
stipulated, that the States-General should be invited to
accede to this alliance. The congress at Cambray was
opened; but the demands on both sides were so high
that it proved ineffectual. In the mean time, the peace
between Russia and Sweden was concluded, on condition that the czar should retain Livonia, Ingria, Estonia,
part of Carelia, and of the territory of Wyburg, Riga,
Revel, and Nerva, in consideration of his restoring part
of Finland, and paying two millions of rix-dollars to the
King of Sweden. The personal animosity subsisting
between King George and the czar seemed to increase.
Bastigif, the Russian resident at London, having presented a memorial that contained some unguarded expressions, was ordered to quit the kingdom in a fortnight.
The czar published a declaration at Petersburgh, com-

plaining of this outrage, which, he said, ought naturally
to have engaged him to use reprisals; but, as he perceived it was done without any regard to the concerns
of England, and only in favour of the Hanoverian interest, he was unwilling that the English nation should
suffer for a piece of injustice in which they had no share.
He, therefore, granted to them all manner of security,
and free liberty to trade in all his dominions. To finish
this strange tissue of negotiations, King George concluded
a treaty with the Moors of Africa, against which the
Spaniards loudly exclaimed.

Plague at
Marseilles.
In the course of this year, Pope Clement XI. died;
and the Princess of Wales was delivered of a prince,
baptized by the name of William Augustus, the late
Duke of Cumberland. A dreadful plague raging at
Marseilles, a proclamation was published, forbidding any
person to come into England, from any part of France
between the Bay of Biscay and Dunkirk, without cer-
tificates of health. Other precautions were taken to
guard against contagion. An act of Parliament had
passed in the preceding session, for the prevention of
infection, by building pest-houses, to which all infected
persons, and all persons of an infected family, should be
conveyed; and, by drawing trenches and lines round any
city, town, or place infected. The king, in his speech at
opening the session of Parliament, on the nineteenth
day of October, intimated the pacification of the north,
by the conclusion of the treaty between Muscovy and
Sweden. He desired the House of Commons to consider of means for easing the duties upon the imported
commodities used in the manufactures of the kingdom.
He observed, that the nation might be supplied with
naval stores from our own colonies in North America;
and that their being employed in this useful and advantageous branch of commerce would divert them from
setting up manufactures which directly interfered with
those of Great Britain. He expressed a desire that,
with respect to the supplies, his people might reap some
immediate benefit from the present circumstances of
affairs abroad; and he earnestly recommended to their
consideration means for preventing the plague, particularly by providing against the practice of smuggling.

One of the first objects that attracted the attention of the Upper House was the case of John Law, the famous projector. The resentment of the people on account of his Mississippi scheme had obliged him to leave France. He retired to Italy, and was said to have visited the pretender at Rome. From thence he repaired to Hanover, and returned to England from the Baltic, in the fleet commanded by Sir John Norris. The king favoured him with a private audience : he kept open house, and was visited by great numbers of persons of the first quality. Earl Coningsby represented in the House of Lords, that he could not but entertain some jealousy of a person who had done so much mischief in a neighbouring kingdom, who, being immensely rich, might do a great deal more hurt here, by tampering with those who were grown desperate, in consequence of being involved in the calamity occasioned by the fatal imitation of his pernicious projects. He observed, that this person was the more dangerous, as he had renounced his natural affection to his country, his allegiance to his lawful sovereign, and his religion, by turning Roman Catholic. Lord Carteret replied, that Mr. Law had, many years ago, the misfortune to kill a gentleman in a duel; but, having at last received the benefit of the king's clemency, and the appeal lodged by the relations of the deceased being taken off, he was come over to plead his majesty's pardon. He said there was no law to keep an Englishman out of his country; and, as Mr. Law was a subject of Great Britain, it was not even in the king's power to hinder him from coming over. After some dispute, the subject was dropped, and this great projector pleaded his pardon in the King's Bench, according to the usual form.

The ministry had by this time secured such a majority in both Houses, as enabled them to carry any point without the least difficulty. Some chiefs of the opposition they had brought over to their measures, and amongst the rest Lord Harcourt, who was created a viscount, and gratified with a pension of four thousand pounds. Nevertheless they could not shut the mouths of the minority, who still preserved the privilege of complaining. Great debates were occasioned by the navy-debt, which was in-

CHAP.
XIV.

1721.
Debates in
the House
of Lords.
about Mr.
Law the
projector.

Sentiments
of some
lords
touching
the war
with Spain.

creased to one million seven hundred thousand pounds. Some members in both Houses affirmed that such extraordinary expense could not be for the immediate service of Great Britain; but in all probability, for the preservation of foreign acquisitions. The ministers answered, that near two-thirds of the navy-debts were contracted in the late reign; and the Parliament acquiesced in this declaration; but in reality, the navy-debt had been unnecessarily increased, by keeping seamen in pay during the winter, and sending fleets to the Mediterranean and Baltic, in order to support the interests of Germany. The Duke of Wharton moved that the treaty with Spain might be laid before the House. The Earl of Sunderland said it contained a secret article which the King of Spain desired might not be made public, until after the treaty of Cambray should be discussed. The question was put, and the duke's motion rejected. The Earl of Strafford asserted, that as the war with Spain had been undertaken without necessity or just provocation, so the peace was concluded without any benefit or advantage: that, contrary to the law of nations, the Spanish fleet had been attacked without any declaration of war; even while a British minister and a secretary of state were treating amicably at Madrid: that the war was neither just nor politic, since it interrupted one of the most valuable branches of the English commerce, at a time when the nation groaned under the pressure of heavy debts, incurred by the former long expensive war. He, therefore, moved for an address to his majesty, desiring that the instructions given to Sir George Byng, now Lord Torrington, should be laid before the House. This motion being likewise, upon the question, rejected, a protest was entered. They voted an address, however, to know in what manner the king had disposed of the ships taken from the Spaniards. Disputes arose also from the bill to prevent infection. Earl Cowper represented, that the removal of persons to a lazaret, or pest-house, by order of the government, and the drawing lines and trenches round places infected, were powers unknown to the British constitution; inconsistent with the lenity of a free government, such as could never be wisely or usefully put in practice; the more odious, because copied

from the arbitrary government of France; and impracticable, except by military compulsion. These obnoxious
clauses were accordingly repealed, though not without
great opposition. Indeed, nothing can be more absurd
than a constitution that will not admit of just and necessary laws and regulations to prevent the dire consequences of the worst of all calamities. Such restrictions,
instead of favouring the lenity of a free government,
would be the most cruel imposition that could be laid on
a free people, as it would act in diametrical opposition
to the great principle of society, which is the preservation
of the individual.

The quakers having presented a petition to the House Petition of the quakers.
of Commons, praying that a bill might be brought in for
omitting, in their solemn affirmation, the words " In the The Parliament dissolved.
presence of Almighty God," the House complied with
their request; but the bill gave rise to a very warm
debate among the Peers. Dr. Atterbury, Bishop of Rochester, said he did not know why such a distinguished
mark of indulgence should be allowed to a set of people
who were hardly Christians. He was supported by the
Archbishop of York, the Earl of Strafford, and Lords
North and Grey. A petition was presented against the
bill by the London clergy, who expressed a serious concern lest the minds of good men should be grieved and
wounded, and the enemies of Christianity triumph, when
they should see such condescensions made by a Christian
legislature, to a set of men who renounce the divine
institutions of Christ, particularly that by which the
faithful are initiated into his religion, and denominated
Christians. The petition, though presented by the Archbishop of York, was branded by the ministry as a seditious
libel, and rejected by the majority. Then, upon a motion
by the Earl of Sunderland, the House resolved that such
lords as might enter protestations with reasons should do
it before two o'clock on the next sitting day, and sign
them before the House rises. The supplies being granted,
and the business of the session despatched as the court Annals.
was pleased to dictate, on the seventh day of March the Hist. Reg. Debates in
Parliament was prorogued. In a few days it was dis- Parliament.
solved, and another convoked by proclamation. In the Pol. State.
election of members for the new Parliament, the ministry Tindal.

CHAP.
XIV.

1722.

Rumours
of a con-
spiracy.
The Bishop
of Roches-
ter is com-
mitted to
the Tower.

exerted itself with such success, as returned a great majority in the House of Commons, extremely well adapted
for all the purposes of their administration[a].

In the beginning of May, the king is said to have
received from the Duke of Orleans full and certain information of a fresh conspiracy formed against his person
and government. A camp was immediately formed in
Hyde-park. All military officers were ordered to repair
to their respective commands. Lieutenant-General
Macartney was despatched to Ireland to bring over some
troops from that kingdom. Some suspected persons
were apprehended in Scotland: the states of Holland
were desired to have their auxiliary or guarantee troops
in readiness to be embarked; and Colonel Churchill was
sent to the court of France with a private commission.
The apprehension raised by this supposed plot affected
the public credit. South-Sea stock began to fall; and
crowds of people called in their money from the bank.
Lord Townshend wrote a letter to the mayor of London,
by the king's command, signifying his majesty's having
received unquestionable advices, that several of his subjects had entered into a wicked conspiracy, in concert
with traitors abroad, for raising a rebellion in favour of
a popish pretender: but that he was firmly assured the
authors of it neither were nor would be supported by any
foreign power. This letter was immediately answered
by an affectionate address from the court of aldermen;
and the example of London was followed by many other
cities and boroughs. The king had determined to visit
Hanover, and actually settled a regency, in which the
Prince of Wales was not included; but now this intended
journey was laid aside: the court was removed to Kensington, and the prince retired to Richmond. The Bishop
of Rochester having been seized, with his papers, was
examined before a committee of the council, who com-

---

[a] The Earl of Sunderland died in April, having incurred a great load of popular
odium, from his supposed connexions with the directors of the South-Sea company. He was a minister of abilities, but violent, impetuous, and headstrong. His
death was soon followed by that of his father-in-law, the great Duke of Marlborough, whose faculties had been for some time greatly impaired. He was interred in Westminster-abbey with such profusion of funeral pomp, as evinced the
pride and ostentation, much more than the taste and concern, of those who directed his obsequies. He was succeeded as master of the ordnance, and colonel
of the first regiment of foot guards, by Earl Cadogan.

mitted him to the Tower for high-treason. The Earl of CHAP.
Orrery, Lords North and Grey, Mr. Cochran, and Mr. XIV.
Smith, from Scotland, and Mr. Christopher Layer, a young 1722.
gentleman of the Temple, were confined in the same place.
Mr. George Kelly, an Irish clergyman, Mr. Robert Cotton,
of Huntingdonshire, Mr. Bingley, Mr. Fleetwood, Neynoe, an Irish priest, and several persons, were taken into
custody; and Mr. Shippen's house was searched. After
Bishop Atterbury had remained a fortnight in the Tower,
Sir Constantine Phipps presented a petition to the court
at the Old Bailey, in the name of Mrs. Morris, that prelate's daughter, praying that, in consideration of the
bishop's ill state of health, he might be either brought to
a speedy trial, bailed, or discharged; but this was overruled. The churchmen through the whole kingdom
were filled with indignation at the confinement of a
bishop, which they said was an outrage upon the church
of England and the episcopal order. Far from concealing their sentiments on this subject, the clergy ventured to offer up public prayers for his health, in almost
all the churches and chapels of London and Westminster. In the mean time the king, attended by the
Prince of Wales, made a summer progress through the
western counties.

The new Parliament being assembled on the ninth New Par-
day of October, his majesty made them acquainted with liament.
the nature of the conspiracy. He said the conspirators
had, by their emissaries, made the strongest instances for
succours from foreign powers; but were disappointed
in their expectations. That, nevertheless, confiding in
their numbers, they had resolved once more upon their
own strength to attempt the subversion of his government. He said they had provided considerable sums of
money: engaged great numbers of officers from abroad,
secured large quantities of arms and ammunition; and
had not the plot been timely discovered, the whole nation, and particularly the city of London, would have
been involved in blood and confusion. He expatiated
upon the mildness and integrity of his own government;
and inveighed against the ingratitude, the implacability,
and madness of the disaffected, concluding with an assu-

rance, that he would steadily adhere to the constitution in church and state, and continue to make the laws of the realm the rule and measure of all his actions. Such addresses were presented by both Houses as the fears and attachments of the majority may be supposed to have dictated on such an occasion. A bill was brought into the House of Lords for suspending the habeas corpus act for a whole year; but they were far from being unanimous in agreeing to such an unusual length of time. By this suspension they, in effect, vested the ministry with a dictatorial power over the liberties of the people.

Declaration of the pretender.

The opposition in the House of Commons was so violent, that Mr. Robert Walpole found it necessary to alarm their apprehensions by a dreadful story of a design to seize the bank and exchequer, and to proclaim the pretender on the Royal Exchange. Their passions being inflamed by this ridiculous artifice, they passed the bill, which immediately received the royal assent. The Duke of Norfolk being brought from Bath, was examined before the council, and committed to the Tower, on suspicion of high treason. On the sixteenth day of November, the king sent to the House of Peers the original and printed copy of a declaration signed by the pretender. It was dated at Lucca, on the twentieth day of September, in the present year, and appeared to be a proposal addressed to the subjects of Great Britain and Ireland, as well as to all foreign princes and states. In this paper, the Chevalier de St. George, having mentioned the late violation of the freedom of elections, conspiracies invented to give a colour to new oppressions, infamous informers, and the state of proscription in which he supposed every honest man to be, very gravely proposed, that if King George would relinquish to him the throne of Great Britain, he would, in return, bestow upon him the title of king in his native dominions, and invite all other states to confirm it; he likewise promised to leave to King George his succession to the British dominions secure, whenever, in due course, his natural right should take place. The Lords unanimously resolved, that this declaration was a false, insolent, and traitorous libel; and ordered it to be burned at the Royal Exchange.

The Commons concurred in these resolutions. Both
Houses joined in an address, expressing their utmost
astonishment and indignation at the surprising insolence
of the pretender; and assuring his majesty, they were
determined to support his title to the crown with their
lives and fortunes.   The Commons prepared a bill for
raising one hundred thousand pounds upon the real and
personal estates of all Papists, or persons educated in the
popish religion, towards defraying the expenses occasioned
by the late rebellion and disorders.   This bill, though
strenuously opposed by some moderate members as a
species of persecution, was sent up to the House of Lords,
together with another, obliging all persons, being Papists,
in Scotland, and all persons in Great Britain refusing or
neglecting to take the oaths appointed for the security
of the king's person and government, to register their
names and real estates.   Both these bills passed through
the Upper House without amendments, and received the
royal sanction.

Mr. Layer being brought to his trial at the King's
Bench, on the twenty-first day of November, was convicted of having enlisted men for the pretender's service,
in order to stir up a rebellion, and received sentence of
death.   He was reprieved for some time, and examined
by a committee of the House of Commons; but he either
could not, or would not, discover the particulars of the
conspiracy, so that he suffered death at Tyburn, and his
head was fixed up at Temple Bar.   Mr. Pulteney, chairman of the committee, reported to the House, that from
the examination of Layer and others, a design had been
formed by persons of figure and distinction at home, in
conjunction with traitors abroad, for placing the pretender
on the throne of these realms: that their first intention
was to procure a body of foreign troops to invade the
kingdom at the time of the late elections; but that the
conspirators being disappointed in this expectation, resolved to make an attempt at the time that it was
generally believed the king intended to go to Hanover,
by the help of such officers and soldiers as could pass
into England unobserved from abroad, under the command of the late Duke of Ormond, who was to have
landed in the river with a great quantity of arms, pro-

Report of
the secret
committee.

vided in Spain for that purpose; at which time the
Tower was to have been seized. That this scheme being
also defeated by the vigilance of the government, they
deferred their enterprise till the breaking up of the camp;
and, in the mean time, employed their agents to corrupt
and seduce the officers and soldiers of the army : that
it appeared from several letters and circumstances, that
the late Duke of Ormond, the Duke of Norfolk, the Earl
of Orrery, Lords North and Grey, and the Bishop of
Rochester, were concerned in this conspiracy ; that their
acting agents were Christopher Layer and John Plunket,
who travelled together to Rome ; Dennis Kelly, George
Kelly, and Thomas Carte, nonjuring clergymen, Neynoe,
the Irish priest, who by this time was drowned in the river
Thames, in attempting to make his escape from the
messenger's house, Mrs. Spilman, alias Yallop, and John
Sample.

Bill of
pains and
penalties
against the
Bishop of
Rochester.

This pretended conspiracy, in all likelihood, extended
no farther than the first rudiments of a design that was
never digested into any regular form; otherwise the persons said to be concerned in it must have been infatuated
to a degree of frenzy; for they were charged with having
made application to the Regent of France, who was well
known to be intimately connected with the King of
Great Britain. The House of Commons, however, resolved, that it was a detestable and horrid conspiracy for
raising a rebellion, seizing the Tower and the city of
London, laying violent hands upon the persons of his
most sacred majesty and the Prince of Wales, in order
to subvert our present happy establishment in church and
state, by placing a popish pretender upon the throne;
that it was formed and carried on by persons of figure
and distinction, and their agents and instruments, in conjunction with traitors abroad. Bills were brought in, and
passed, for inflicting pains and penalties against John
Plunket and George Kelly, who were by these acts to
be kept in close custody during his majesty's pleasure, in
any prison in Great Britain; and that they should not
attempt to escape on pain of death, to be inflicted upon
them and their assistants. Mr. Yonge made a motion
for a bill of the same nature against the Bishop of Rochester. This was immediately brought into the House,

though Sir William Wyndham affirmed there was no
evidence against him but conjectures and hearsay. The
bishop wrote a letter to the speaker, importing, that
though conscious of his own innocence, he should decline
giving the house any trouble that day, contenting himself with the opportunity of making his defence before
another, of which he had the honour to be a member.
Counsel being heard for the bill, it was committed to a
grand committee on the sixth day of April, when the
majority of the tory members quitted the House. It was
then moved, that the bishop should be deprived of his
office and benefice, and banished the kingdom for ever.
Mr. Lawson and Mr. Oglethorpe spoke in his favour.

CHAP.
XIV.
1722.
Annals.
Tindal.
Debates in
Parlia-
ment.
Pol. State.

The bill being passed and sent up to the Lords, the
bishop was brought to his trial before them on the ninth
of May. Himself and his counsel having been heard, the
Lords proceeded to consider the articles of the bill.
When they read it a third time, a motion was made to
pass it, and then a long and warm debate ensued. Earl
Paulet demonstrated the danger and injustice of swerv-
ing in such an extraordinary manner from the fixed rules
of evidence. The Duke of Wharton having summed up
the depositions, and proved the insufficiency of them,
concluded with saying, that, let the consequences be
what they would, he hoped such a hellish stain would
never sully the lustre and glory of that illustrious House,
as to condemn a man without the least evidence. Lord
Bathurst spoke against the bill with equal strength and
eloquence. He said, if such extraordinary proceedings
were countenanced, he saw nothing remaining for him
and others to do, but to retire to their country-houses,
and there, if possible, quietly enjoy their estates within
their own families, since the least correspondence, the
least intercepted letter, might be made criminal. He
observed, that Cardinal Mazarin boasted, that if he had
but two lines of any man's writing, he could, by means
of a few circumstances, attested by witnesses, deprive
him of his life at his pleasure. Turning to the bench of
bishops, who had been generally unfavourable to Dr. Atterbury, he said he could hardly account for the inveterate hatred and malice some persons bore the learned
and ingenious Bishop of Rochester, unless they were in-

1723.
Who is de-
prived, and
driven into
perpetual
exile.

toxicated with the infatuation of some savage Indians, who believed they inherited not only the spoils, but even the abilities of any great enemy whom they had killed in battle. The bill was supported by the Duke of Argyle, the Earl of Seafield, and Lord Lechmere, which last was answered by Earl Cowper. This nobleman observed, that the strongest argument urged in behalf of the bill was necessity: but that, for his part, he saw no necessity that could justify such unprecedented and such dangerous proceedings, as the conspiracy had above twelve months before been happily discovered, and the effects of it prevented : that besides the intrinsic weight and strength of the government, the hands of those at the helm had been still further fortified by the suspension of the habeas corpus act, and the additional troops which had been raised. He said the known rules of evidence, as laid down at first, and established by the law of the land, were the birthright of every subject in the nation, and ought to be constantly observed, not only in the inferior courts of judicature, but also in both Houses of Parliament, till altered by the legislature ; that the admitting of the precarious and uncertain evidence of the clerks of the post-office was a very dangerous precedent. In former times (said he) it was thought very grievous that in capital cases a man should be affected by similitude of hands ; but here the case is much worse, since it is allowed that the clerks of the post-office should carry the similitude of hands four months in their minds. He applauded the bishop's noble deportment, in declining to answer before the House of Commons, whose proceeding in this unprecedented manner, against a lord of Parliament, was such an encroachment on the prerogative of the peerage, that if they submitted to it, by passing the bill, they might be termed the last of British peers, for giving up their ancient privileges. The other party were not so solicitous about answering reasons, as eager to put the question, when the bill passed, and a protest was entered. By this act the bishop was deprived of all offices, benefices, and dignities, and rendered incapable of enjoying any for the future : he was banished the realm, and subjected to the pains of death in case he should return, as were all persons who should

correspond with him during his exile. Dr. Friend, the CHAP.
celebrated physician, who was a member of the House ⌐ XIV. ¬
of Commons, and had exerted himself strenuously in 1723.
behalf of the bishop, was now taken into custody, on
suspicion of treasonable practices.

The next object that excited the resentment of the Proceed-
Commons was the scheme of a lottery, to be drawn at ings against
Harburgh, in the king's German dominions. The House cerned in
appointed a committee to inquire into this and other the lottery
lotteries at that time on foot in London. The scheme burgh.
was published, on pretence of raising a subscription for
maintaining a trade between Great Britain and the king's
territories on the Elbe; but it was a mysterious scene of
iniquity, which the committee, with all their penetration,
could not fully discover. They reported, however, that
it was an infamous, fraudulent undertaking, whereby
many unwary persons had been drawn in, to their great
loss: that the manner of carrying it on had been a manifest violation of the laws of the kingdom: that the
managers and agents of this lottery had, without any
authority for so doing, made use of his majesty's royal
name, thereby to give countenance to the infamous project, and induce his majesty's subjects to engage or be
concerned therein. A bill was brought in to suppress
this lottery, and to oblige the managers of it to make
restitution of the money they had received from the con-
tributors. At the same time the House resolved, that
John Lord Viscount Barrington had been notoriously
guilty of promoting, abetting, and carrying on that fraudulent undertaking; for which offence he should be expelled the House. The court of Vienna having erected
an East India Company at Ostend, upon a scheme formed
by one Colebrook, an English merchant, Sir Nathaniel
Gould represented to the House of Commons the great
detriment which the English East India Company had
already received, and were likely further to sustain, by
this Ostend company. The House immediately resolved,
that for the subjects of this kingdom to subscribe, or be
concerned in encouraging any subscription, to promote
an East India Company now erecting in the Austrian
Netherlands, was a high crime and misdemeanour; and
a law was enacted for preventing British subjects from

engaging in that enterprise. By another act, relating to the South-Sea Company, the two millions of stock which had been annihilated were revived, added to the capital, and divided among the proprietors. A third law passed, for the more effectual execution of justice in a part of Southwark, called the Mint, where a great number of debtors had taken sanctuary, on the supposition that it was a privileged place. On the twenty-seventh day of May the session was closed, with a speech that breathed nothing but panegyric, acknowledgment, and affection to a Parliament which had complied with all his majesty's wishes.

Affairs of the continent.

His majesty, having ennobled the son of Mr. Robert Walpole, in consideration of the father's services, made a good number of church promotions. He admitted the imprisoned lords and gentlemen to bail; granted a pardon to Lord Bolingbroke; and ordered the Bishop of Rochester to be conveyed to the continent. Then he himself set out for Hanover, leaving the administration of his kingdoms in the hands of a regency, Lord Harcourt being one of the justices. The king was attended by the two secretaries, Lords Townshend and Carteret, who were counted able negotiators. The affairs of the continent had begun to take a new turn. The interests and connexions of the different princes were become perplexed and embarrassed; and King George resolved to unravel them by dint of negotiation. Understanding that a treaty was on the carpet between the czar and the King of Sweden, favourable to the Duke of Holstein's pretensions to Sleswick, the possession of which the Elector of Hanover had guaranteed to Denmark, his majesty began to be in pain for Bremen and Verden. The Regent of France and the King of Spain had now compromised all differences; and their reconciliation was cemented by a double marriage between Philip's sons and the regent's daughters. The former proposed new treaties to England; but insisted upon the restitution of Gibraltar and Port Mahon, as well as upon the king's openly declaring against the Ostend company. His Britannic majesty was apprehensive that should the emperor be hard pressed on that subject, he might join the czar and the King of Sweden, and promote their designs in favour of the Duke of Holstein. On the other hand, all the Italian powers exclaimed against the treaty of London. The pope had protested against any thing that might have been decided at Cambray to the prejudice of his right. Memorials to the same effect had been presented by the King of Sardinia, the Dukes of Tuscany, Parma, and Modena. France and Spain were inclined to support these potentates against the house of Austria. Europe seemed to be on the eve of a new war. King George was entangled in such a variety of treaties and interests that he knew not well how to extricate himself from the troublesome engagements he had contracted. By declaring for the emperor he must have countenanced the new establishment at Ostend, which was so prejudicial to his British subjects, and incurred the resentment of France, Spain, and their allies of Italy. In renouncing the interest of the emperor he would have exposed his German dominions. In vain he exhorted the emperor to relax in his disputes with Spain, and give up the Ostend company, which was so detrimental and disagreeable to his faithful allies : the court of Vienna promised in general to observe the treaties which it had concluded, but declined entering into any particular discussion ; so that all his majesty's endeavours issued in contracting closer connexions with Prussia and Denmark. All those negotiations carried on, all those treaties concluded by King George, with almost every prince and state in Christendom, which succeeded one another so fast, and appear, at first view, so intricate and unaccountable, were founded upon two simple and natural principles, namely, the desire of ascertaining his acquisitions as Elector of Hanover, and his resolution to secure himself against the disaffection of his British subjects, as well as the efforts of the pretender.

Great Britain at this period enjoyed profound tranquillity. Ireland was a little ruffled by an incident which seemed to have been misrepresented to the people of that kingdom. William Wood had obtained a patent for furnishing Ireland with copper currency, in which it was deficient. A great clamour was raised against this coin. The Parliament of that kingdom, which met in September, resolved, that it would be prejudicial to the

Clamour in Ireland on account of Wood's coinage.

Q 2

revenue, destructive of trade, and of dangerous consequence to the rights of the subject: that the patent had
been obtained by misrepresentation: that the halfpence
wanted weight: that, even if the terms of the patent
had been complied with, there would have been a great
loss to the nation: that granting the power of coinage
to a private person had ever been highly prejudicial to
the kingdom, and would at all times be of dangerous
consequence. Addresses from both Houses were presented to the king on this subject. The affair was referred to the lords of the privy-council of England. They
justified the conduct of the patentee, upon the report of
Sir Isaac Newton and other officers of the Mint, who had
made an assay and trial of Wood's halfpence, and found
he had complied with the terms of the patent. They
declared that this currency exceeded in goodness, fineness, and value of metal, all the copper money which had
been coined for Ireland, in the reigns of King Charles II.,
King James II., King William and Queen Mary. The
privy-council likewise demonstrated, that his majesty's
predecessors had always exercised the undoubted prerogative of granting patents for copper coinage in Ireland to private persons: that none of these patents had
been so beneficial to the kingdom as this granted to
William Wood, who had not obtained it in an unprecedented manner, but after a reference to the attorney
and solicitor-general, and after Sir Isaac Newton had
been consulted in every particular: finally, they proved,
by a great number of witnesses, that there was a real
want of such money in Ireland. Notwithstanding this
decision, the ferment of the Irish nation was industriously
kept up by clamour, pamphlets, papers, and lampoons,
written by Dean Swift and other authors; so that Wood
voluntarily reduced his coinage from the value of one
hundred thousand to forty thousand pounds. Thus the
noise was silenced. The Commons of Ireland passed an
act for accepting the affirmation of the quakers instead
of an oath; and voted three hundred and forty thousand
pounds towards discharging the debt of the nation, which
amounted to about double that sum.

Death of
the Duke of
Orleans.
    In the month of October, England lost a worthy no-
bleman in the death of Earl Cowper, who had twice

discharged the office of lord chancellor, with equal discernment and integrity. He was profoundly skilled in
the laws of his country; in his apprehension quick and
penetrating; in his judgment clear and determinate.
He possessed a manly eloquence; his manner was agreeable, and his deportment graceful. This year was likewise remarkable for the death of the Duke of Orleans,
Regent of France, who, since the decease of Louis XIV.,
had ruled that nation with the most absolute authority.
He was a prince of taste and spirit, endowed with shining
talents for empire, which he did not fail to display, even
in the midst of effeminate pursuits and idle debauchery.
From the infirm constitution of the infant king, he had
conceived hopes of ascending the throne, and taken his
measures accordingly; but the young monarch's health
began to be established, and all the duke's schemes were
defeated by an apoplexy, of which he died, in the fiftieth
year of his age, after having nominated the Duke of
Bourbon as prime minister. King George immediately
received assurances of the good disposition of the French
court to cultivate and even improve the good understanding so happily established between France and
Great Britain. The king arrived in England on the
eighteenth day of December; and on the ninth day of
January the Parliament was assembled. His majesty,
in his speech, recommended to the Commons the care
of the public debts; and he expressed his satisfaction at
seeing the sinking fund improved and augmented, so as
to put the debt of the nation into a method of being
speedily and gradually discharged.

This was the repeated theory of patriotism, which, An act for
unhappily for the subjects, was never reduced to prac- lessening
tice: not but that a beginning of such a laudable work debts.
was made in this very session, by an act for lessening
the public debts. This law provided that the annuities
at five per cent. charged on the general fund by a former act, except such as had been subscribed into the
South-Sea, together with the unsubscribed blanks of the
lottery in the year one thousand seven hundred and fourteen, should be paid off at Lady-day of the year next
ensuing, with the money arising from the sinking fund.
The ministry, however, did not persevere in this path of

CHAP.
XIV.

1724.

Oldmixon.
Pol. State.
Hist. Reg.
Annals of
K. George.
Mem. Hist.
Tindal.

Philip,
King of
Spain, ab-
dicates the
throne.

prudent economy. The Commons granted all the supplies that were demanded. They voted ten thousand
seamen; and the majority, though not without violent
opposition, agreed to maintain four thousand additional
troops, which had been raised in the preceding year; so
that the establishment of the land-forces amounted to
eighteen thousand two hundred and sixty-four. The
expense of the year was defrayed by a land-tax and malt-
tax. The Commons, having despatched the supply, took
into consideration a grievance arising from protections
granted by foreign ministers, peers, and members of
Parliament, under which profligate persons used to screen
themselves from the prosecution of their just creditors.
The Commons resolved, that all protections granted by
members of that House should be declared void, and
immediately withdrawn. The Lords made a declaration
to the same purpose, with an exception of menial servants,
and those necessarily employed about the estates of peers[b].
On the twenty-fourth day of April, his majesty closed
the session in the usual manner, made some alterations
in the disposition of the great offices of state, and sent
Mr. Horatio Walpole as ambassador-extraordinary to
the court of France.

In the beginning of this year, Philip, King of Spain,
retiring with his queen to the monastery of St. Ildefonso,
sent the Marquis of Grimaldi, his principal secretary of
state, to his son Louis, Prince of Asturias, with a solemn
renunciation of the crown, and a letter of advice, in
which he exhorted him to cultivate the Blessed Virgin
with the warmest devotion; and put himself and his
kingdoms under her protection. The renunciation was
published through the whole monarchy of Spain; and
the council of Castile resolved, that Louis might assume

[b] The Duke of Newcastle was now appointed secretary of state; the Duke of
Grafton, lord chamberlain; and Lord Carteret, lord lieutenant of Ireland.
    The king instituted a professorship for the modern languages in each university.
    In the month of May died Robert Harley, Earl of Oxford and Earl Mortimer,
who had been a munificent patron of genius and literature; and completed a very
valuable collection of manuscripts.
    The practice of inoculation for the small-pox was by this time introduced into
England from Turkey. Prince Frederick, the two Princesses Amelia and Carolina, the Duke of Bedford and his sister, with many other persons of distinction,
underwent this operation with success.
    Dr. Henry Sacheverel died in June, after having bequeathed five hundred pounds
to the late Bishop of Rochester.

the reins of government without assembling the Cortez.
The English minister at Paris was instructed to interpose in behalf of the French Protestants, against whom
a severe edict had been lately published; but his remonstrances produced no effect. England, in the mean
time, was quite barren of such events as deserve a place
in history. The government was now firmly established
on the neck of opposition, and commerce flourished
even under the load of grievous impositions.

The next Parliament, which met on the twelfth day
of November, seemed to be assembled for no other purpose than that of establishing funds for the expense of
the ensuing year: yet the session was distinguished by
a remarkable incident; namely, the trial of the Earl of
Macclesfield, lord chancellor of England. This nobleman had connived at certain venal practices touching
the sale of places, and the money of suitors deposited
with the masters of chancery, so as to incur the general
reproach of the nation. He found it necessary to resign the great seal in the beginning of January. On the
ninth day of the ensuing month, the king sent a message
to the Commons, importing, that his majesty, having
reason to apprehend that the suitors in the court of
chancery were in danger of losing a considerable sum
of money, from the insufficiency of some of the masters,
thought himself obliged, in justice and compassion to
the said sufferers, to take the most speedy and proper
method the law would allow for inquiring into the state
of the masters' accounts, and securing their effects for
the benefit of the suitors; and his majesty having had
several reports laid before him in pursuance of the directions he had given, had ordered the reports to be
communicated to the House, that they might have as
full and as perfect a view of this important affair as the
shortness of the time, and the circumstances and nature
of the proceedings, would admit.

These papers being taken into consideration, Sir
George Oxenden observed, that enormous abuses had
crept into the high court of chancery: that the crimes
and misdemeanours of the late lord chancellor were
many and various, but might be reduced to the following heads: that he had embezzled the estates and effects

of many widows, orphans, and lunatics: that he had raised the offices of masters in chancery to an exorbitant price; trusting in their hands large sums of money belonging to suitors, that they might be enabled to comply with his exorbitant demands; and that in several cases he had made divers irregular orders. He therefore moved, that Thomas Earl of Macclesfield should be impeached of high crimes and misdemeanours. Mr. Pulteney moved, that this affair might be left to the consideration of a select committee. Sir William Wyndham asserted, that in proceeding by way of impeachment upon reports from above, they would make a dangerous precedent; and seem to give up the most valuable of their privileges, the inquest after state criminals. The question being put, it was carried for the impeachment. The earl was accordingly impeached at the bar of the Upper House: a committee was appointed to prepare articles; and a bill was brought in, to indemnify the masters in chancery from the penalties of the law, upon discovering what considerations they had paid for their admission to their respective offices. The trial lasted twenty days: the earl was convicted of fraudulent practices, and condemned in a fine of thirty thousand pounds, with imprisonment until that sum should be paid. He was immediately committed to the Tower, where he continued about six weeks; but upon producing the money he was discharged; and Sir Peter King, now created Baron of Oakham, succeeded him in the office of chancellor.

*Annals.
Hist. Mem.
Deb. in
Parliam.
Tindal.*

*Debates
about the
debts of the
civil list.*

His majesty, on the 8th day of April, gave the House of Commons to understand, that having been engaged in some extraordinary expenses, he hoped he should be enabled to raise a sum of money, by making use of the funds lately established for the payment of the civil list annuities, in order to discharge the debts contracted in the civil government. Mr. Pulteney, cofferer of the household, moved for an address, that an account should be laid before the House of all moneys paid for secret service, pensions, and bounties, from the twenty-fifth day of March, in the year one thousand seven hundred and one, to the twenty-fifth of the same month in the present year. This address being voted, a motion was made to consider the king's message. Mr. Pulteney urged that this consideration should be postponed until the House should have examined the papers that were the subject of the address. He expressed his surprise, that a debt amounting to above five hundred thousand pounds should be contracted in three years; he said, he did not wonder that some persons should be so eager to make good the deficiencies of the civil list, since they and their friends enjoyed such a share of that revenue; and he desired to know whether this was all that was due, or whether they should expect another reckoning? This gentleman began to be dissatisfied with the measures of the ministry; and his sarcasms were aimed at Mr. Walpole, who undertook to answer his objections. The Commons took the message into consideration, and passed a bill enabling his majesty to raise a sum, not exceeding one million, by exchequer bills, loans, or otherwise, on the credit of the deductions of sixpence per pound, directed by an act of Parliament of the seventh year of his majesty, and of the civil list revenues, at an interest not exceeding three pounds per cent. till repayment of the principal.

On the twentieth day of April, a petition was presented to the House by Lord Finch, in behalf of Henry St. John, late Viscount Bolingbroke, praying that the execution of the law with respect to his forfeitures might be suspended, as a pardon had suspended it with respect to his life. Mr. Walpole signified to the House, by his majesty's command, that, seven years before, the petitioner had made his humble application and submission to the king, with assurances of duty, allegiance, and fidelity: that, from his behaviour since that time, his majesty was convinced of his being a fit object of his mercy; and consented to his petitioning the House. The petition being read, Mr. Walpole declared himself fully satisfied that the petitioner had sufficiently atoned for his past offences; and therefore deserved the favour of that House, so far as to enable him to enjoy the family inheritance that was settled upon him, which he could not do by virtue of his majesty's pardon, without an act of Parliament. Lord Finch moved that a bill might be brought in for this purpose, and was warmly opposed by Mr. Methuen, comptroller of the household, who repre-

sented Bolingbroke as a monster of iniquity. His remonstrance was supported by Lord William Paulet, and
Mr. Onslow; nevertheless, the bill was prepared, passed
through both Houses, and received the royal assent. An
act being passed for disarming the Highlanders of Scotland; another for regulating elections within the city of
London; a third for reducing the interest of several
bank annuities, together with some bills of a private
nature, the Parliament was prorogued in May, after the
king had, in the warmest terms of acknowledgment,
expressed his approbation of their conduct. Then he
appointed lords-justices to govern the nation in his absence; and set out in June for his German dominions[c].

Treaty of
alliance be-
tween the
courts of
Vienna and
Madrid.
The tide of political interests on the continent had
begun to flow in a new channel, so as to render ineffectual the mounds which his Britannic majesty had raised
by his multiplicity of negotiations. Louis, the Spanish
monarch, dying soon after his elevation to the throne,
his father Philip resumed the crown which he had resigned; and gave himself up implicitly to the conduct
of his queen, who was a princess of indefatigable intrigue
and insatiate ambition. The infanta, who had been married
to Louis XV. of France, was so disagreeable to her husband, that the whole French nation began to be apprehensive of a civil war in consequence of his dying without
male issue; he therefore determined, with the advice of
his council, to send back the infanta, as the nuptials had
not been consummated; and she was attended to Madrid
by the Marquis de Monteleone. The Queen of Spain
resented this insult offered to her daughter; and in revenge dismissed Mademoiselle de Beaujolois, one of
the regent's daughters, who had been betrothed to her
son Don Carlos. As the congress at Cambray had
proved ineffectual, she offered to adjust her differences
with the emperor, under the sole mediation of Great

[c] On the fifth day of December the Princess of Wales was delivered of a prin-
cess, christened by the name of Louisa, and afterwards married to the King of
Denmark. She died December the nineteenth, one thousand seven hundred and
fifty-one.
Immediately after the session of Parliament, the king revived the order of the
Bath, thirty-eight in number, including the sovereign.
William Bateman was created Baron of Calmore in Ireland, and Viscount
Bateman; and Sir Robert Walpole, who had been one of the revived knights of
the Bath, was now honoured with the order of the Garter.

Britain. This was an honour which King George declined. He was averse to any undertaking that might interrupt the harmony subsisting between him and the court of Versailles; and he had taken umbrage at the emperor's refusing to grant the investiture of Bremen and Verden, except upon terms which he did not choose to embrace. The peace between the courts of Vienna and Madrid which he refused to mediate was effected by a private negotiation, under the management of the Duke de Ripperda, a native of the States-General, who had renounced the Protestant religion, and entered into the service of his Catholic majesty. By two treaties, signed at Vienna in the month of April, the emperor acknowledged Philip as King of Spain and the Indies, and promised that he would not molest him in the possession of those dominions that were secured to him by the treaty of Utrecht. Philip renounced all pretensions to the dominions in Italy and the Netherlands, adjudged to the emperor by the treaty of London: Charles granted the investiture of the dukedoms of Tuscany, Parma, and Placentia, to the eldest son of the Queen of Spain, in default of heirs in the present possessors, as masculine fiefs of the empire. Spain became guarantee of the Austrian succession, according to the pragmatic sanction, by which the dominions of that house were settled on the emperor's heirs general, and declared to be a perpetual, indivisible, and inseparable feoffment to the primogeniture. By the commercial treaty of Vienna, the Austrian subjects were entitled to advantages in trade with Spain, which no other nation enjoyed. His Catholic majesty guaranteed the Ostend East India company; and agreed to pay an annual subsidy of four millions of piastres to the emperor. Great sums were remitted to Vienna: the imperial forces were augmented to a formidable number; and other powers were solicited to engage in this alliance, to which the court of Petersburgh actually acceded.

The King of Great Britain took the alarm. The emperor and he had for some time treated each other with manifest coolness. He had reason to fear some attempts upon his German dominions, and projected a defensive treaty with France and Prussia. This alliance, limited

to the term of fifteen years, was negotiated and concluded at Hanover in the month of September.   It implied a mutual guarantee of the dominions possessed by
the contracting parties, their rights and privileges, those
of commerce in particular, and an engagement to procure
satisfaction to the Protestants of Thorn, who had lately
been oppressed by the Catholics, contrary to the treaty
of Oliva.   The king, having taken these precautions at
Hanover, set out on his return for England; embarked
at Helvoetsluys in the middle of December; and, after
having been exposed to the fury of a dreadful storm, was
landed with great difficulty at Rye, from whence he proceeded by land to London.   The Parliament meeting on
the twentieth day of the next month, he gave them to
understand that the distressed condition of some of their
Protestant brethren abroad, and the negotiations and
engagements contracted by some foreign powers, which
seemed to have laid the foundation of new troubles and
disturbances in Europe, and to threaten his subjects with
the loss of several of the most advantageous branches of
their trade, had obliged him to concert with other powers
such measures as might give a check to the ambitious
views of those who were endeavouring to render themselves formidable, and put a stop to the further progress
of such dangerous designs.   He told them, that the
enemies of his government were already very busy, by
their instruments and emissaries in those courts whose
measures seemed most to favour their purposes, in soli-
citing and promoting the cause of the pretender.   One
sees at first sight, that the interests of Germany dictated
the treaty of Hanover; but, in order to secure the approbation of Great Britain, upon which the support of
this alliance chiefly depended, it was judged necessary
to insert the articles relating to commerce and the Protestant religion, as if the engagement had been contracted purely for the advantage and glory of England.
In a word, the ministry began now to ring the changes
upon a few words that have been repeated ever since,
like cabalistical sounds, by which the nation has been
enchanted into a very dangerous connexion with the
concerns of the continent.   They harangued, they insisted upon the machinations of the disaffected, the

designs of a popish pretender, the Protestant interest, and
the balance of power, until these expressions became
absolutely terms of ridicule with every person of common sense and reflection. The people were told that
the emperor and the King of Spain, exclusive of the
public treaties concluded at Vienna, had entered into
private engagements, importing, that the imperialists
should join the Spaniards in recovering Gibraltar and
Port Mahon by force of arms, in case the King of England should refuse to restore them amicably, according to
a solemn promise he had made; that a double marriage
should take place between the two infants of Spain and
the two Archduchesses of Austria; and that means should
be taken to place the pretender on the throne of Great
Britain.

CHAP.
XIV.
1725.

When the treaties of Vienna and Hanover fell under
consideration of the House of Commons, Horatio Walpole,
afterwards termed, in derision, "the balance master,"
opened the debate with a long unanimated oration, giving
a detail of the affairs of Europe since the treaty of Utrecht.
He enumerated the barrier treaty, the convention for executing that treaty, the defensive alliance with the emperor, the other with the most Christian king and the
States-General, another convention, the quadruple alliance, the congress at Cambray, the treaty of Hanover,
and that of Vienna. He explained the nature of each
engagement. He said, the main design of the treaty of
commerce concluded between the emperor and Spain
was to countenance and support the East India Company established at Ostend, which interfered so essen-
tially with the East India Companies of England and
Holland, and was directly contrary to several solemn
treaties still in force. He enlarged upon the danger to
which the balance of power would be exposed, should
the issue male of this projected marriage between the
houses of Austria and Spain ever possess the imperial
dignity and the kingdom of Spain together. The reader
will take notice, that this very man was one of those
who exclaimed against that article of the treaty of
Utrecht, which prevented the power of those two houses
from being immediately united in the person of the
emperor. He did not forget to expatiate upon the

Approved
in Parlia-
ment.

CHAP.
XIV.
1725.

pretended secret engagement concerning Gibraltar and Minorca, and the king's pious concern for the distressed Protestants of Thorn in Poland.   In vain did Mr. Shippen urge, that the treaty of Hanover would engage the British nation in a war for the defence of the king's German dominions, contrary to an express provision made in the act of limitation.   These arguments had lost all weight.   The opposition was so inconsiderable, that the ministry had no reason to be in pain about any measure they should propose.   An address was voted and delivered to his majesty, approving the alliance he had concluded at Hanover, in order to obviate and disappoint the dangerous views and consequences of the treaty of peace betwixt the emperor and the King of Spain; and promising to support his majesty against all insults and attacks that should be made upon any of his territories, though not belonging to the crown of Great Britain. An address of the same kind was presented by the House of Lords in a body.   A bill was brought in, empowering the commissioners of the treasury to compound with Mr. Richard Hampden, late treasurer of the navy, for a debt he owed to the crown, amounting to eight-and-forty thousand pounds.   This deficiency was occasioned by his embarking in the South-Sea scheme.   The king recommended his petition; and the House complied with his request, in consideration of his great-grandfather, the famous John Hampden, who made such a noble stand against the arbitrary measures of the first Charles.

Riots in Scotland on account of the malt-tax.

The malt-tax was found so grievous to Scotland, that the people refused to pay it, and riots were excited in different parts of the kingdom.   At Glasgow, the populace, armed with clubs and staves, rifled the house of Daniel Campbell, their representative in Parliament, who had voted for the bill : and maltreated some excisemen who attempted to take an account of the malt.   General Wade, who commanded the forces in Scotland, had sent two companies of soldiers, under the command of Captain Bushel, to prevent or appease any disturbance of this nature.   That officer drew up his men in the street, where they were pelted with stones by the multitude, which he endeavoured to disperse by firing among them without shot.   This expedient failing, he ordered his

men to load their pieces with ball; and at a time when
the magistrates were advancing towards him in a body
to assist him with their advice and influence, he commanded the soldiers to fire four different ways, without
the sanction of the civil authority. About twenty persons were killed or wounded on this occasion. The
people seeing so many victims fall, were exasperated beyond all sense of danger. They began to procure arms,
and breathed nothing but defiance and revenge. Bushel
thought proper to retreat to the castle of Dunbarton, and
was pursued above five miles by the enraged multitude.
General Wade being informed of this transaction, assembled a body of forces; and being accompanied by
Duncan Forbes, lord advocate, took possession of Glasgow. The magistrates were apprehended, and conveyed
prisoners to Edinburgh, where the lords justiciary, having
taken cognizance of the affair, declared them innocent;
so that they were immediately discharged. Bushel was
tried for murder, convicted, and condemned; but instead
of undergoing the penalties of the law, he was indulged
with a pardon, and promoted in the service. Daniel
Campbell having petitioned the House of Commons that
he might be indemnified for the damage he had sustained
from the rioters, a bill was passed in his favour, granting
him a certain sum to be raised from an imposition laid
upon all the beer and ale brewed in the city of Glasgow.
The malt-tax was so sensibly felt in Scotland, that the
convention of the royal burghs presented a remonstrance
against it, as a grievous burden, which their country could
not bear: petitions to the same purpose were delivered
to the Commons from different shires of that kingdom [d].
On the twenty-fourth day of March the king sent a message to the House by Sir Paul Methuen, desiring an extraordinary supply, that he might be able to augment his
maritime force, and concert such other measures as should
be necessary in the present conjuncture. A debate ensued; but the majority complied with the demand. Some

CHAP.
XIV.
1725.

Oldmixon
Annals.
Debates in
Parlia-
ment.
Historical
Memoirs.
Tindal.

[d] The Duke of Wharton, having consumed his fortune in riot and extravagance,
repaired to the court of Vienna, from whence he proceeded to Rome, and offered
his service to the pretender. There he received the order of the garter, and the
title of Duke of Northumberland. He was sent by the Chevalier de St. George
with credentials to the court of Madrid, where he abjured the Protestant religion, married a lady of the Queen of Spain's bedchamber, and obtained the rank
and appointment of a lieutenant-colonel in the Spanish service.

CHAP. members in the Upper House complained that the mes-
XIV.   sage was not sent to both Houses of Parliament, and this
1725. suggestion gave rise to another debate, in which Lord
Bathurst and others made some melancholy reflections
upon the state of insignificance to which the peers of
England were reduced. Such remarks, however, were
very little minded by the ministry, who had obtained a
complete victory over all opposition. The supplies, ordinary and extraordinary, being granted, with every thing
else which the court thought proper to ask, and several
bills passed for the regulation of civil economy, the king
dismissed the Parliament on the twenty-fourth day of
May.

A small   By this time Peter the Czar of Muscovy was dead, and
squadron   his Empress Catharine had succeeded him on the Russian
sent to the throne. This princess had begun to assemble forces in
Baltic.   the neighbourhood of Petersburgh; and to prepare a
formidable armament for a naval expedition. King
George, concluding that her design was against Sweden,
sent a strong squadron into the Baltic, under the
command of Sir Charles Wager, in order to anticipate
her views upon his allies. The English fleet being
joined at Copenhagen by a Danish squadron, alarmed
the court of Russia, which immediately issued orders for
reinforcing the garrisons of Wibourg, Cronstadt, Revel,
and Riga. The English admiral having had an audience
of his Swedish majesty, steered towards Revel, and sent
thither a lieutenant, with a letter from the King of Great
Britain to the czarina. This was an expostulation, in
which his majesty observed, that he and his allies could
not fail of being alarmed at her great preparations by sea
and land. He complained that measures had been taken
at her court in favour of the pretender : that his repeated
instances for establishing a lasting friendship with the
crown of Russia had been treated with neglect; and he
gave her to understand, that he had ordered his admiral to
prevent her ships from coming out of her harbours, should
she persist in her resolution to execute the designs she
had projected. The czarina, in her answer to the king,
expressed her surprise that she had not received his majesty's letter until his fleet was at anchor before Revel,
since it would have been more agreeable to the custom

established among sovereigns, and to the amity which had so long subsisted between her kingdoms and the crown of Great Britain, to expostulate with her on her armament, and expect her answer, before he had proceeded to such an offensive measure. She assured him that nothing was farther from her thoughts than any design to disturb the peace of the North; and with regard to the pretender, it was a frivolous and stale accusation, which had been frequently used as a pretext to cover all the unkind steps lately taken against the Russian empire. Sir Charles Wager continued in his station until he received certain intelligence that the Russian galleys were laid up in their winter harbour: then he set sail for the coast of Denmark, from whence he returned to England in the month of November.

King George, that he might not seem to convert all his attention to the affairs of the North, had equipped two other squadrons, one of which was destined for the West Indies, under the command of Admiral Hosier; the other, conducted by Sir John Jennings, having on board a body of land-forces, sailed from St. Helen's on the twentieth day of July, entered the bay of St. Antonio, then visited Lisbon, from whence he directed his course to the Bay of Bulls, near Cadiz, and cruized off Cape St. Mary's, so as to alarm the coast of Spain, and fill Madrid with consternation. Yet he committed no act of hostility; but was treated with great civility by the Spanish governor of Cadiz, who supplied him with refreshments. Rear-Admiral Hosier, with seven ships of war, had sailed in April for the Spanish West Indies, with instructions to block up the galleons in the ports of that country; or, should they presume to come out, to seize and bring them to England. Before his arrival at the Bastimentos, near Porto-Bello, the treasure, consisting of above six millions sterling, had been unloaded, and carried back to Panama, in pursuance of an order sent by an advice-boat which had the start of Hosier. This admiral lay inactive on that station, until he became the jest of the Spaniards. He returned to Jamaica, where he found means to reinforce his crews; then he stood over to Carthagena. The Spaniards had by this time seized the English South-Sea ship at La Vera Cruz, together with all the vessels and

Admiral Hosier's expedition to the West Indies.

effects belonging to that company. Hosier in vain demanded restitution; he took some Spanish ships by way
of reprisal, and continued cruizing in those seas until the
greater part of his men perished deplorably by the dis-
eases of that unhealthy climate, and his ships were totally ruined by the worms. This brave officer, being
restricted by his orders from obeying the dictates of his
courage, seeing his best officers and men daily swept off
by an outrageous distemper, and his ships exposed to
inevitable destruction, is said to have died of a broken
heart; while the people of England loudly clamoured
against this unfortunate expedition, in which so many
lives were thrown away, and so much money expended,
without the least advantage to the nation. It seems to
have been a mean piratical scheme to rob the court of
Spain of its expected treasure, even while a peace subsisted between the two nations. The ministry of Great
Britain, indeed, alleged, that the Spanish king had entered into engagements in favour of the pretender.

The Dukes of Ormond and Wharton, and the Earl
Marischal, were certainly at Madrid; and the Duke de
Ripperda, now prime minister of Spain, dropped some
expressions to the English envoy that implied some such
design, which, however, the court of Madrid positively
denied. Ripperda, as a foreigner, fell a sacrifice to the
jealousy of the Spanish ministers. He was suddenly dismissed from his employments, with a pension of three
thousand pistoles. He forthwith took refuge in the
house of Vandermeer, the Dutch ambassador, who was
unwilling to be troubled with such a guest. He therefore conveyed the duke in his coach to the house of
Colonel Stanhope, the British minister, whose protection
he craved and obtained. Nevertheless, he was dragged
from thence by force, and committed prisoner to the
castle of Segovia. He afterwards made his escape, and
sheltered himself in England from the resentment of his
Catholic majesty. Colonel Stanhope complained of this
violation of the law of nations, which the Spanish ministers
endeavoured to excuse. Memorials and letters passed
between the two courts, and every thing tended to a
rupture. The King of Spain purchased ships of war;
began to make preparations for some important under-

taking; and assembled an army of twenty thousand men at St. Roch, on pretence of rebuilding the old castle of Gibraltar. Meanwhile the States-General and the King of Sweden acceded to the treaty of Hanover; but the King of Prussia, though his majesty's son-in-law, was detached from the alliance by the emperor, with whom he contracted new engagements.

On the seventeenth day of January, the British Par- liament was opened with a long elaborate speech, import- ing, that the proceedings and transactions of the emperor and King of Spain, and the secret offensive alliance con- cluded between them, had laid the foundation of a most exorbitant and formidable power; that they were directly levelled against the most valuable and darling interests and privileges of the English nation, which must either give up Gibraltar to Spain, and acquiesce in the emperor's usurped exercise of commerce, or resolve vigorously to defend their undoubted rights against those reciprocal en- gagements, contracted in defiance and violation of all national faith, and the most solemn treaties. He assured them that one of those secret articles was the placing the pretender on the throne of Great Britain; and another, the conquest of Gibraltar and Port Mahon. He affirmed that those combinations extended themselves into Russia; and that the English fleet seasonably prevented such de- signs as would have opened a way to the invasion of these kingdoms. He exhorted the Commons to grant such supplies as should be necessary for the defence of their country, and for making good his engagements with the allies of Great Britain. He told them, that the King of Spain had ordered his minister residing in England to quit the kingdom; and that he had left a memorial little short of a declaration, in which he insisted upon the restitution of Gibraltar. He did not fail to touch the energetic strings which always moved their passions; the balance of power in Europe, the security of the British commerce, the designs of a popish pretender, the present happy establishment, the religion, liberties, and properties of a protestant people. Such addresses of thanks were penned in both Houses as the ministers were pleased to dictate; yet not without opposition from a minority, which was far from being formidable, though headed by chiefs of uncommon talents and resolution. The Commons voted twenty thousand seamen, besides six-and-twenty thousand three hundred and eighty-three men for the land-service; and, to defray the extraordinary expense, a land-tax of four shillings in the pound was granted.

Debate in
the House
of Lords
upon the
approach-
ing rupture
with the
emperor
and Spain.

The House of Lords having taken into consideration the letters and memorials between the ministers of Great Britain, France, and Spain, and the papers relating to the accession of the States-General in the treaty of Hanover, a warm debate ensued. Lord Bathurst took notice, that the accession of the States-General to the treaty was upon condition that this their act should be approved and ratified by the King of Great Britain, the most Christian king, and the king of Prussia; but that the minister of his Prussian majesty had refused to sign the act of accession, which was therefore of no effect: that if the court of France should, for the same reason, think itself disengaged from the Hanover alliance, Britain alone would be obliged to bear the burden of an expensive war against two of the greatest potentates of Europe. He said he could not see any just reason for a rupture with Spain: that, indeed, the Duke de Ripperda might have dropped some indiscreet expressions; he was known to be a man of violent temper; and he had been solemnly disavowed by his Catholic majesty; that, in the memorial left by the Spanish ambassador, he imputed the violent state of affairs between the two crowns to the ministers of England; and mentioned a positive promise made by the King of Great Britain for the restitution of Gibraltar: that methods of accommodation might be tried before the kingdom engaged in a war, which must be attended with dangerous consequences: that the nation was loaded with a debt of fifty millions; and, in order to maintain such a war, would be obliged to raise seven millions yearly; an annual sum by which the people would soon be exhausted. He observed, that in some papers laid before the House, mention was made of great sums distributed in divers places, to bring certain measures to bear. He declared, that for his own part, he had touched neither Spanish nor English gold: he was neither a Spaniard nor a Frenchman, but a true Englishman, and so long as he had the honour to sit in that House, he would speak and act for the good of his country. He, therefore, desired their lordships seriously to consider the matter before them, which was of the last consequence and importance to the whole nation. He said nothing could be gained by the war, should it prove successful; and every thing would be lost should it prove unprosperous. He was answered by Lord Townshend, who affirmed that his majesty had received positive and certain information with respect to the secret article of alliance between the Courts of Vienna and Madrid, in favour of the pretender, though the safety of the state did not permit him to lay these advices before the Parliament. After much altercation, the majority resolved, that the measures his majesty had thought fit to take were honourable, just, and necessary for preventing the execution of the dangerous engagements entered into in favour of the pretender; for preserving the dominions belonging to the crown of Great Britain, by solemn treaties, and particularly those of Gibraltar and the isle of Minorca; and for maintaining to his people their most valuable rights and privileges of commerce, and the peace and tranquillity of Europe. Seventeen lords entered a protest against this resolution. Disputes of the same nature arose from the same subject in the Lower House. Lord Townshend had affirmed in the House of Peers, that no promise of restoring Gibraltar had been made; Sir Robert Walpole owned such a promise in the House of Commons; a motion was made for an address, desiring these engagements might be laid before the House: another member moved for a copy of the memorial presented by Mr. Pointz to the King of Sweden, and for the secret offensive article between the courts of Vienna and Madrid; a third motion was made to address the king for such memorials and representations from the courts of Sweden and Denmark, as induced him, in the course of the preceding year, to send a squadron to the Baltic. In the account of the money granted for the service of the last year, there was an article of one hundred and twenty-five thousand pounds charged in general terms, as issued out for other engagements and expences, over and above such as were specified. Mr. Pulteney moved for an address on this subject; but each of these motions was rejected on a division; and the majority concurred in an address of thanks to his majesty, for the great wisdom of his conduct. They expressed the most implicit confidence in his goodness and discretion; they promised to support him in all such further measures as he should find necessary and expedient for preventing a rupture, as well as for consulting the honour and advantage of these kingdoms.

Memorial
of Mr.
Palms, the
imperialre-
sident at
London.
His majesty's speech gave such umbrage to the court of Vienna, that Mr. Palms, the imperial resident at London, was ordered to present a warm memorial to the king, and afterwards to publish it to the whole nation. In this bold remonstrance, the king was charged with having declared from the throne, as certain and undoubted facts, several things that were either wrested, misrepresented, or void of all foundation. The memorialist affirmed, that the treaty of Vienna was built on the quadruple alliance; that the treaty of commerce was calculated to promote the mutual and lawful advantages of the subjects of both parties, agreeably to the law of nations, and in no respect prejudicial to the British nation. He declared that there was no offensive alliance concluded between the two crowns; that the supposed article relating to the pretender was an absolute falsehood : that the insinuation with respect to the siege of Gibraltar was equally untrue, his master having made no engagements with the King of Spain but such as were specified in the treaty communicated to his Britannic majesty. He said, however, the hostilities notoriously committed in the West Indies and elsewhere against the King of Spain, in violation of treaties, seemed to justify that prince's undertaking the siege of Gibraltar. Finally, he demanded, in the name of his imperial majesty, suitable reparation for the injury his honour had sustained from such calumnious imputations. Both Houses of Parliament expressed their indignation at the insolence of this memorial in an address to his majesty; and Mr. Palms was ordered to depart the kingdom. Virulent declarations were presented by the ministers of the emperor and the King of Great Britain to the diet of the empire at Ratisbon; and such personal reflections retorted be-

tween these two potentates, that all hope of reconciliation vanished.

King George, in order to secure himself against the
impending storm, entered into more strict engagements
with the French king; and agreed to pay fifty thousand
pounds for three years to the King of Sweden, in consideration of that prince's holding in readiness a body of
ten thousand troops for the occasions of the alliance. He
concluded a fresh treaty with the King of Denmark, who
promised to furnish a certain number of auxiliaries, on
account of a large subsidy granted by the King of France.
The proportions of troops to be sent into the field in case
of a rupture were ascertained. His Britannic majesty
engaged for four-and-twenty thousand men, and a strong
squadron to be sent into the Baltic. He made a convention with the Prince of Hesse-Cassel, who undertook
to provide eight thousand infantry and four thousand
horse, in consideration of seventy-four thousand pounds,
to be paid by Great Britain immediately, and fifty thousand pounds more in case the troops should be required,
besides their pay and subsistence. Such was the fruit of
all the alliances so industriously planned since the accession of King George to the throne of Great Britain. In
the day of his trouble, the King of Prussia, who had
espoused his daughter, deserted his interest; and the
States-General stood aloof. For the security of his German dominions, he had recourse to the King of France,
who was a precarious ally; to the kings of Sweden and
Denmark, and the Principality of Hesse Cassel: but
none of these powers would contribute their assistance
without being gratified with exorbitant subsidies, though
the danger was common, and the efforts ought to have
been equal. Instead of allies, they professed themselves
mercenaries. Great Britain paid them for the defence
of their own dominions: she moreover undertook to
maintain a powerful fleet for their safety. Is there any
Briton so weak as to think, or so foolhardy as to affirm,
that this was a British quarrel?

For the support of those expensive treaties, Mr.
Scroope, secretary of the treasury, moved in the House
of Commons, that in the malt-tax bill they should insert
a clause of appropriation, empowering the king to apply

such sums as should be necessary for defraying the expenses and engagements which had been or should be made before the twenty-fifth day of September, in concerting such measures as he should think most conducive to the security of trade, and restoring the peace of Europe. To little purpose did the members in the opposition urge, that this method of asking and granting supplies was unparliamentary: that such a clause would render ineffectual that appropriation of the public money, which the wisdom of all Parliaments had thought a necessary security against misapplication, which was the more to be feared, as no provision was made to call any person to account for the money that should be disposed of by virtue of this clause; that great sums had already been granted: that such an unlimited power ought never to be given in a free government: that such confidence in the crown might, through the influence of evil ministers, be attended with the most dangerous consequences: that the constitution could not be preserved but by a strict adherence to those essential parliamentary forms of granting supplies upon estimates, and of appropriating these supplies to services and occasions publicly avowed and judged necessary: that such clauses, if not seasonably checked, would become so frequent, as in time to lodge in the crown and in the ministers an absolute and uncontrollable power of raising money upon the people, which by the constitution is, and with safety can only be, lodged in the whole legislature. The motion was carried, the clause added, and the bill passed through the other House without amendment, though not without opposition. Notwithstanding this vote of credit, Sir William Yonge moved, that towards the supply granted to the king, the sum of three hundred and seventy thousand pounds should be raised by loans on exchequer bills, to be charged on the surplus of the duties on coal and culm, which was reserved for the Parliament's disposal. Though this motion was vigorously opposed by Sir Joseph Jekyl and Mr. Pulteney, as a dangerous deviation from several votes and acts of Parliament, by which the exceedings of the public funds were appropriated to the discharge of the national debt, or to the increase of the sinking fund, it was carried by the majority.

On the fifteenth day of May the Parliament was prorogued, after the king had acknowledged their zeal, liberality, and despatch; and given them to understand that
the siege of Gibraltar was actually begun. The trenches
were opened before this fortress on the eleventh day of
February, by the Condé de las Torres, at the head of
twenty thousand men. The place was well provided for
a defence; and the old Earl of Portmore, who was governor, embarked with a reinforcement from England,
under convoy of a fleet commanded by Sir Charles
Wager. He arrived at Gibraltar in the beginning of
April, where he landed the troops, with a great quantity
of ammunition, warlike stores, and four-and-twenty pieces
of cannon. At the same time, five hundred men arrived
from Minorca; so that the garrison amounted to six
thousand, plentifully supplied with fresh provisions from
the coasts of Barbary, and treated the efforts of the besiegers with great contempt. The States-General, being
apprehensive of an attempt upon their barrier in the Netherlands, desired the king would hold in readiness the
ten thousand auxiliaries stipulated in the treaty. These
were immediately prepared for embarkation, and the
forces of England were augmented with thirty new raised
companies. Sir John Norris set sail with a powerful
fleet for the Baltic, and was joined by a Danish squadron:
but the czarina dying on the seventeenth day of May, he
had no occasion to commit hostilities, as the Russian
armament was laid aside.

Meanwhile the powers at variance, though extremely
irritated against each other, were all equally averse to a
war that might again embroil all Europe. The King of
France interposed his mediation, which was conducted
by the Duke de Richelieu, his ambassador at Vienna.
Plans and counterplans of pacification were proposed
between the two crowns and the allies. At length, all
parties agreed to twelve preliminary articles, which were
signed in May at Paris, by the ministers of the Hanover
alliance, and afterwards at Vienna, by the imperial and
Spanish ambassadors. These imported, that hostilities
should immediately cease: that the charter of the Ostend
company should be suspended for seven years: and that
a congress should in four months be opened at Aix-la-

CHAP.
XIV.

1727.

Chapelle, for adjusting all differences, and consolidating the peace of Europe. This congress was afterwards transferred to Soissons, for the conveniency of the French minister, whose presence was necessary at court. The siege of Gibraltar was raised, after it had lasted four months, during which the Spaniards lost a great number of men by sickness, while the garrison sustained very little damage. The court of Madrid, however, started some new difficulties, and for some time would not consent to the restitution of the South-Sea ship, which had been detained at La Vera Cruz, in the West Indies; so that Sir Charles Wager continued to cruise on the coast of Spain; but these objections were removed in the sequel.

Death and character of George I. King of Great Britain.

King George, having appointed a regency, embarked at Greenwich on the third day of June, and landing in Holland on the seventh, set out on his journey to Hanover. He was suddenly seized with a paralytic disorder on the road; he forthwith lost the faculty of speech, became lethargic, and was conveyed in a state of insensibility to Osnabruck. There he expired on Sunday, the eleventh day of June, in the sixty-eighth year of his age, and in the thirteenth of his reign[e].—George I. was plain

---

[e] George I. married the Princess Sophia Dorothy, daughter and heiress of the Duke of Zell, by whom he had King George II. and the late Queen of Prussia. The king's body was conveyed to Hanover, and interred among his ancestors. From the death of Charles II. to this period, England had made a considerable figure in every branch of literature. Dr. Atterbury and Dr. Clarke distinguished themselves in divinity; Mr. Whiston wrote in defence of Arianism; John Locke shone forth the great restorer of human reason; the Earl of Shaftesbury raised an elegant, though feeble system of moral philosophy; Berkley, afterwards Bishop of Cloyne in Ireland, surpassed all his contemporaries in subtilty and variety in metaphysical arguments, as well as in the art of deduction; Lord Bolingbroke's talents as a metaphysician have been questioned since his posthumous works appeared; great progress was made in mathematics and astronomy, by Wallis, Halley, and Flamstead; the art of medicine owed some valuable improvement to the classical Dr. Friend, and the elegant Dr. Mead. Among the poets of this era we number John Phillips, author of a didactic poem called Cyder, a performance of real merit; he lived and died in obscurity; William Congreve, celebrated for his comedies, which are not so famous for strength of character and power of humour, as for wit, elegance, and regularity; Vanbrugh, who wrote with more nature and fire, though with far less art and precision; Steele, who in his comedies successfully engrafted modern characters on the ancient drama; Farquhar, who drew his pictures from fancy rather than from nature, and whose chief merit consists in the agreeable pertness and vivacity of his dialogue; Addison, whose fame as a poet greatly exceeded his genius, which was cold and enervate, though he yielded to none in the character of an essayist, either for style or matter; Swift, whose muse seems to have been mere misanthropy; he was a cynic rather than a poet, and his natural dryness and sarcastic severity would have been unpleasing, had not he qualified them by adopting the extravagant humour of Lucian and Rabelais; Prior, lively, familiar, and amusing; Rowe, solemn, florid, and declamatory; Pope, the prince of lyric poetry, unrivalled in satire, ethics, and polished versification; the agreeable Parnell; the wild, the witty, and the whimsical Garth; Gay, whose fables may vie

and simple in his person and address ; grave and composed in his deportment, though easy, familiar, and facetious in his hours of relaxation.   Before he ascended the
throne of Great Britain, he had acquired the character
of a circumspect general, a just and merciful prince, a
wise politician, who perfectly understood, and steadily
pursued, his own interest.   With these qualities, it cannot be doubted but that he came to England extremely well disposed to govern his new subjects according to the maxims of the British·constitution, and
the genius of the people ; and if ever he seemed to
deviate from these principles, we may take it for granted
that he was misled by the venal suggestions of a ministry
whose power and influence were founded on corruption.

with those of La Fontaine, in native humour, ease, and simplicity, and whose
genius for pastoral was truly original.   Dr. Bentley stood foremost in the list of
critics and commentators.   Sir Christopher Wren raised some noble monuments
of architecture.   The most remarkable political writers were Davenant, Hare,
Swift, Steele, Addison, Bolingbroke, and Trenchard.

CHAPTER XV.

GEORGE II.

CHAP. AT the accession of George II. the nation had great
XV. reason to wish for an alteration of measures. The pub-
1727. lic debt, notwithstanding the boasted economy and ma-
George II.
cends the nagement of the ministers; notwithstanding the sinking
rone of fund, which had been extolled as a growing treasure
reat
ritain. sacred to the discharge of national incumbrances, was
now increased to fifty millions two hundred sixty-one
thousand two hundred and six pounds, nineteen shillings,
eight-pence three farthings. The kingdom was bewil-
dered in a labyrinth of treaties and conventions, by which
it stood engaged in pecuniary subsidies to many powers
upon the continent, with whom its real interests could
never be connected. The wealth of the nation had been
lavished upon those foreign connexions, upon unneces-

sary wars, and fruitless expeditions. Dangerous encroachments had been made upon the constitution by the repeal of the act for triennial Parliaments; by frequent suspensions of the habeas-corpus act upon frivolous occasions; by repealing clauses in the act of settlement; by votes of credit; by habituating the people to a standing army; and, above all, by establishing a system of corruption, which at all times would secure a majority in Parliament. The nature of prerogative, by which the liberties of the nation had formerly been often endangered, was now so well understood, and so securely restrained, that it could no longer be used for the same oppressive purposes: besides, an avowed extension of the prerogative required more ability, courage, and resolution, than the present ministry could exert. They understood their own strength, and had recourse to a more safe and effectual expedient. The vice, luxury, and prostitution of the age, the almost total extinction of sentiment, honour, and public spirit, had prepared the minds of men for slavery and corruption. The means were in the hands of the ministry; the public treasure was at their devotion: they multiplied places and pensions, to increase the number of their dependents: they squandered away the money of the nation without taste, discernment, decency, or remorse; they enlisted an army of the most abandoned emissaries, whom they employed to vindicate the worst measures, in the face of truth, common sense, and common honesty; and they did not fail to stigmatize as Jacobites, and enemies to the government, all those who presumed to question the merit of their administration.

The supreme direction of affairs was not yet engrossed by a single minister. Lord Townshend had the reputation of conducting the external transactions relating to treaties and negotiations. He is said to have understood that province, though he did not always follow the dictates of his own understanding. He possessed an extensive fund of knowledge; and was well acquainted with the functions of his office. The Duke of N. his colleague, was not remarkable for any of these qualifications: he owed his promotion to his uncommon zeal for the illustrious house of Hanover, and to the strength of

Character of the principal persons concerned in the ministry.

his interest in Parliament, rather than to his judgment, precision, or any other intellectual merit. Lord C. who may be counted an auxiliary, though not immediately concerned in the administration, had distinguished himself in the character of envoy at several courts in Europe. He had attained an intimate knowledge of all the different interests and connexions subsisting among the powers of the continent; and he infinitely surpassed all the ministers in learning and capacity. He was, indeed, the only man of genius employed under this government. He spoke with ease and propriety; his conceptions were just and lively; his inferences bold, his counsels vigorous and warm. Yet he depreciated his talents, by acting in a subordinate character to those whom he despised; and seemed to look upon the pernicious measures of a bad ministry with silent contempt rather than with avowed detestation. The interior government of Great Britain was chiefly managed by Sir Robert W. a man of extraordinary talents, who had from low beginnings raised himself to the head of the treasury. Having obtained a seat in the Lower House, he declared himself one of the most forward partisans of the whig faction. He was endued with a species of eloquence, which, though neither nervous nor eloquent, flowed with great facility, and was so plausible on all subjects, that even when he misrepresented the truth, whether from ignorance or design, he seldom failed to persuade that part of his audience for whose hearing his harangue was chiefly intended. He was well acquainted with the nature of the public funds, and understood the whole mystery of stock-jobbing. This knowledge produced a connexion between him and the money corporations, which served to enhance his importance. He perceived the bulk of mankind were actuated by a sordid thirst of lucre; he had sagacity enough to convert the degeneracy of the times to his own advantage; and on this, and this alone, he founded the whole superstructure of his subsequent administration. In the late reign he had, by dint of speaking decisively to every question, by boldly impeaching the conduct of the tory ministers, by his activity in elections, and engaging as a projector in the schemes of the monied interest, become a leading member in the

House of Commons. By his sufferings under the tory Parliament, he attained the rank of a martyr to his party: his interest, his reputation, and his presumption daily increased: he opposed Sunderland as his rival in power, and headed a dangerous defection from the ministry, which evinced the greatness of his influence and authority. He had the glory of being principally concerned in effecting a reconciliation between the late king and the Prince of Wales: then he was re-associated in the administration with additional credit; and, from the death of the Earls of Sunderland and Stanhope, he had been making long strides towards the office of prime minister. He knew the maxims he had adopted would subject him to the hatred, the ridicule, and reproach of some individuals, who had not yet resigned all sentiments of patriotism, nor all views of opposition; but the number of these was inconsiderable, when compared to that which constituted the body of the community; and he would not suffer the consideration of such antagonists to come in competition with his schemes of power, affluence, and authority. Nevertheless, low as he had humbled anti-ministerial association, it required all his artifice to elude, all his patience and natural phlegm to bear, the powerful arguments that were urged, and the keen satire that was exercised against his measures and management, by a few members in the opposition. Sir William Wyndham possessed all the energy of elocution: Mr. Shippen was calm, intrepid, shrewd, and sarcastic: Mr. Hungerford, sly, insinuating, and ironical. Mr. W. P. inherited from nature a good understanding, which he had studiously cultivated. He was one of the most learned members in the House of Commons, extremely well qualified to judge of literary productions; well read in history and politics; deeply skilled in the British constitution, the detail of government, and the nature of the finances. He spoke with freedom, fluency, and uncommon warmth of declamation, which was said to be the effect of personal animosity to Sir R. W. with whom he had been formerly connected.

An express arriving on the fourteenth day of June, with an account of the king's death, his late majesty King George II. repaired from Richmond, where he Debates in Parliament concerning the civil-list.

received this intelligence, to Leicester-house; and the members of the privy-council being assembled, were sworn anew. The king declared his firm purpose to preserve the constitution in church and state, and to cultivate those alliances which his father had made with foreign princes. At the same time, he took and subscribed the oath for the security of the church of Scotland, as required by the act of union. Next day he was proclaimed King of Great Britain. The Parliament assembled in pursuance of the act made for that purpose; but was immediately prorogued by commission to the twenty-seventh day of the month. All the great officers of state continued in their places : Sir Robert Walpole kept possession of the treasury; and the system of politics which the late king had established underwent no sort of alteration. The king, in his speech to both Houses at the opening of the session, professed a fixed resolution to merit the love and affection of his people, by maintaining them in the full enjoyment of their religious and civil rights. He promised to lessen the public expense as soon as the circumstances of affairs would permit: he observed to the Commons, that the grant of the greatest part of the civil-list revenues was now determined; and that it would be necessary for them to make a new provision for the support of him and his family: lastly, he recommended it to both Houses to despatch the business that should be necessarily brought before them, as the season of the year and the circumstances of time required their presence in the country. Addresses of condolence and congratulation being drawn up and presented, the Commons, in a committee of the whole House, took into consideration a motion for a supply to his majesty. Sir Robert Walpole, having observed that the annual sum of seven hundred thousand pounds granted to and settled on the late king had fallen short every year, and that his present majesty's expenses were likely to increase, by reason of the largeness of his family, moved, that the entire revenues of the civil-list, which produced about eight hundred thousand pounds per annum, should be settled on the king during his life. Mr. Shippen opposed this motion, as inconsistent with the trust reposed in them as representatives of the people, who ought to be very frugal in exercising the right of giving away the public money. He said the sum of seven hundred thousand pounds was not obtained for his late majesty without a long and solemn debate; and every member who contended for it at that time allowed it to be an ample royal revenue: that, although his majesty's family should be enlarged, a circumstance which had been urged as one reason for the motion, he presumed the appointments of Prince Frederick would be much inferior to those settled on his present majesty when he was Prince of Wales: besides, it was to be hoped that many personal, many particular expenses in the late reign, especially those for frequent journeys to Hanover, would be discontinued, and entirely cease. He observed, that the civil-list branches in the queen's reign did not often exceed the sum of five hundred and fifty thousand pounds: nevertheless, she called upon her Parliament but once, in a reign of thirteen years, to pay the debts contracted in her civil government; and these were occasioned by the unparalleled instances of her piety and generosity. She gave the first-fruits and tenths, arising to nineteen thousand pounds a year, as an augmentation of the maintenance of the poor clergy. She bestowed five thousand pounds per annum out of the post-office on the Duke of Marlborough: she suffered seven hundred pounds to be charged weekly on the same office for the service of the public: she expended several hundred thousand pounds in building the castle of Blenheim: she allowed four thousand pounds annually to Prince Charles of Denmark: she sustained great losses by the tin contract: she supported the poor Palatines: she exhibited many other proofs of royal bounty: and immediately before her death she had formed a plan of retrenchment, which would have reduced her yearly expenses to four hundred and fifty-nine thousand nine hundred and forty-one pounds. He affirmed, that a million a year would not be sufficient to carry on the exorbitant expenses so often and so justly complained of in the House of Commons: that, over and above the yearly allowance of seven hundred thousand pounds, many occasional taxes, many excessive sums were raised, and all sunk in the bottomless gulf of secret service.

CHAP.
XV.

1727.

Two hundred and fifty thousand pounds were raised in defiance of the ancient parliamentary methods, to secure the kingdom from a Swedish invasion: then the two insurance offices were erected and paid near three hundred thousand pounds for their charters: our enmity with Sweden being changed into alliance, a subsidy of seventy-two thousand pounds was implicitly granted to fulfil some secret engagements with that crown; four-and-twenty thousand pounds were given for burning merchant ships arrived from infected places, though the goods which ought to have been destroyed for the public safety, were afterwards privately sold: a sum of five hundred thousand pounds was demanded, and granted, for paying the debts of the civil-list; and his majesty declared, by message, he was resolved to retrench his expenses for the future. Notwithstanding this resolution, in less than four years, a new demand of the like sum was made and granted, to discharge new incumbrances: the Spanish ships of war which Admiral Byng took in the Mediterranean were sold for a considerable sum of money: one hundred and twenty-five thousand pounds were granted in the last session, to be secretly disposed of for the public utility; and there was still a debt in the civil government, amounting to above six hundred thousand pounds. He took notice, that this amazing extravagance happened under the conduct of persons pretending to surpass all their predecessors in the knowledge and care of the public revenue; that as none of these sums had been accounted for, they were, in all probability, employed in services not fit to be owned. He said, he heartily wished that time, the great discoverer of hidden truths and concealed iniquities, might produce a list of all such as had been perverted from their public duty by private pensions; who had been the hired slaves and the corrupt instruments of a profuse and vain-glorious administration. He proposed, that instead of granting an addition to the civil-list, they should restrict that revenue to a certain sum, by concluding the question with these words, "in like manner as they were granted and continued to his late majesty, so as to make up the clear yearly sum of seven hundred thousand pounds." To these particulars, which were indeed unanswerable, no reply was made. Even this mark of decency was laid aside as idle and superfluous. The House agreed to the motion; and a bill was brought in for the better support of his majesty's household. The Commons, having received a message from the king, desiring they would make a further provision for the queen his consort, resolved, that in case she should survive his majesty, the sum of one hundred thousand pounds should be settled upon her for life, charged upon the revenues of the civil-list, together with his majesty's palace of Somerset-house, and Richmond Old-park. A bill was formed on this resolution, which, as well as the other, passed both Houses; and received the royal assent on the seventeenth day of July, when the king, in a speech to both Houses, expressed his satisfaction with their conduct; and congratulated them upon the wealth and glory of the nation, by which they had acquired such weight in holding the balance of Europe. Then the lord chancellor prorogued the Parliament to the twenty-ninth day of August; but on the seventh of that month a proclamation was issued for dissolving this, and convoking another.

In the interim, some changes were made in different departments of civil economy. Lord Viscount Torrington was placed at the head of the Admiralty: the Earl of Westmoreland was appointed first lord-commissioner of trade and plantations. Philip Dormer Stanhope, Earl of Chesterfield, a nobleman remarkable for his wit, eloquence, and polished manners, was nominated ambassador at the Hague. The privy-council being dissolved, another was appointed of the members then present. The Duke of Devonshire was dignified with the place of president; and the Duke of St. Alban's was appointed master of the horse. On the eleventh day of October the coronation of the king and queen was performed at Westminster-Abbey, with the usual solemnity [a]. By

Changes and promotions.

a King George II. ascended the throne in the forty-fourth year of his age. On the second day of September, 1705, he espoused the Princess Wilhelmina Charlotte Caroline, daughter to John Frèderick, Marquis of Brandenburgh Anspach, by whom he had two sons, Frederick Louis, Prince of Wales, born at Hanover, on the thirty-first day of January, 1707, and William Augustus, born at London, on the fifteenth day of April, 1721. She had likewise borne four princesses, namely, Anne, Amelia, Caroline, Mary, and was afterwards delivered of Louisa, married in the sequel to the King of Denmark.

CHAP.
XV.

1727.

this time the courts of France and Spain were perfectly reconciled: all Europe was freed from the calamities of war: and the peace of Great Britain suffered no interruption, except from some transient tumults among the tinners of Cornwall, who, being provoked by a scarcity of corn, rose in arms and plundered the granaries of that county.

New Parliament.

The elections in England and Scotland for the Parliament having succeeded on the new system according to the wishes of the ministry, the two Houses met on the twenty-third day of January, when the Commons unanimously chose for their speaker Arthur Onslow, esquire, knight of the shire for Surrey, a gentleman of extensive knowledge, worth, and probity; grave, eloquent, venerable, and every way qualified for the discharge of that honourable and important office. The king, in his speech to this new Parliament, declared, that by the last advices from abroad, he had reason to hope the difficulties which had hitherto retarded the execution of the preliminaries, and the opening of the congress, would soon be entirely removed: in the mean time he represented the absolute necessity of continuing the preparations which had hitherto secured the nation, and prevented an open rupture in Europe. He promised, that his first care should be to reduce, from time to time, the expense of the public, as often, and as soon as the interest and safety of his people would permit such reduction. He expressed an earnest desire of seeing the foundation laid of an effectual scheme for the increase and encouragement of seamen in general, that they might be invited rather than compelled into the service of their country. Finally, he recommended unanimity, zeal, and despatch of the public business. Those speeches, penned by the minister, were composed with a view to soothe the minds of the people into an immediate concurrence with the measures of the government; but without any intention of performing those promises of economy, reformation, and national advantage. The two Houses seemed to vie with each other in expressions of applause and affection to his majesty. The Lords, in their address, hailed him as the best of kings, and the true father of his country. The Commons expressed the warmest sense of gratitude for

the blessings they enjoyed in his reign, though it was not
yet eight months old. They approved of all his transactions; promised to support him in all his undertakings;
and declared they would cheerfully grant whatever
supplies should be wanted for the public service. Having
considered the estimates which were laid before them by
order of his majesty, they voted two-and-twenty thousand
nine hundred and fifty-five men for guards and garrisons;
and fifteen thousand seamen for the service of the ensuing
year. They granted two hundred and thirty thousand
nine hundred and twenty-three pounds for the maintenance of twelve thousand Hessian troops; a subsidy of
fifty thousand pounds to the King of Sweden; and half
that sum to the Duke of Brunswick Wolfenbuttel [b].
The expense of the year amounted to four millions, raised
by a land-tax of three shillings in the pound, a malt-tax,
and by borrowing of the bank one million seven hundred
and fifty thousand pounds, for which annuities to the
amount of seventy thousand pounds, to be raised by
duties on coals imported into the city of London, were
granted to that corporation.

All these sums, however, were not granted without
question. The number of land-forces occasioned a debate; and the Hessian auxiliaries were not allowed without dispute and opposition. When they deliberated on
the loan of the bank, Mr. W. Pulteney observed, that
the shifting of funds was but perpetuating taxes, and
putting off the evil day: that notwithstanding the great
merit which some persons had built on the sinking fund,
it appeared that the national debt had been increased
since the setting up that pompous project. Some warm
altercation passed between him and Sir Robert Walpole
on this subject. The lord-mayor, aldermen, and common-
council of London, presented a petition, setting forth, that
the duties already laid upon coals and culm, imported
into London, affected the trade of that city only; that
the inequality of the burden was a great discouragement
to their manufactures, and a hardship upon all the trading

*Violent dis-
pute con-
cerning the
national
debt.*

[b] Nothing could be a greater burlesque upon negotiation than this treaty of
alliance concluded with the petty Duke of Wolfenbuttel, who very gravely guarantees to his Britannic majesty the possession of his three kingdoms, and obliges
himself to supply his majesty with five thousand men, in consideration of an
annual subsidy of five-and-twenty thousand pounds for four years.

inhabitants. The petition was rejected, and the tax imposed. The House having addressed the king for a particular and distinct account of the distribution of two hundred and fifty thousand pounds, charged to have been issued for securing the trade and navigation of the kingdom, and preserving and restoring the peace of Europe, he declined granting their request, but signified in general, that part of the money had been issued and disbursed by his late majesty, and the remainder by himself, for carrying on the same necessary services, which required the greatest secresy. Such a message in the reign of King William would have raised a dangerous flame in the House of Commons. Mr. W. Pulteney inveighed against such a vague and general way of accounting for the public money, as tending to render Parliaments altogether insignificant, to cover embezzlements, and to screen corrupt and rapacious ministers. The Commons having taken into consideration the state of the national debt, examined the accounts, and interrogated the proper officers. A motion was made by a court member, that it appeared the moneys already issued and applied towards discharging the national debts, together with a sum to be issued at Lady-day, amounted to six millions six hundred and forty-eight thousand seven hundred and sixty-two pounds, five shillings, one penny, one farthing. In vain did the leaders of the opposition expose the fallacious tendency of this motion. In vain did they demonstrate the fraudulent artifice used in drawing up the accounts: the motion was carried; and several resolutions were taken on the state of the national debts. In the particular account of these debts, upon which the House resolved to form a representation to his majesty, an article of three hundred thousand pounds relating to the duty upon wrought plate was totally omitted. This extraordinary omission being discovered, gave rise to a very warm debate, and to very severe reflections against those who superintended the public accounts. This error being rectified, a committee appointed for the purpose drew up the representation, containing a particular detail of the national debts discharged and incurred since the twenty-fifth day of December, in the year one thousand seven hundred and sixteen, with a state of the sinking

fund and of the public credit. The draft being approved
by the House, was presented to the king, who received it graciously. He took this opportunity of saying, that the provision made for gradually discharging the national debts was now become so certain and considerable, that nothing but some unforeseen event could alter or diminish it : a circumstance that afforded the fairest prospect of seeing the old debts discharged without any necessity of incurring new incumbrances.

This answer, fraught with many other expressions of fatherly tenderness for his people, paved the way for a *Vote of credit.* message to the House, demanding a vote of credit to fulfil certain engagements entered into, and concerted, with the advice and concurrence of the last Parliament, for securing the trade and navigation of the kingdom, and for restoring and preserving the peace of Europe. Though a debate ensued upon this message, the majority resolved, that an address should be presented to his majesty, declaring the duty and fidelity of the Commons, their entire confidence in his royal care and goodness, and their readiness to enable his majesty to fulfil his engagements. A vote of credit passed accordingly. During this session, the Peers were chiefly employed in examining copies of several treaties and alliances which the king submitted to their perusal; they likewise prepared a bill for amending the statute of limitation, which, however, did not pass into a law: they considered the state of the national debt, a subject fruitful of debates; they passed the mutiny bill, and those that were sent up from the Commons, touching the supplies; together with an act, obliging ships arriving from infected places to perform quarantine; and some others of a more private nature. These bills having received the royal assent, the king closed the session on the twenty-eighth day of May, when he thanked the Commons for the effectual supplies they had raised, and in particular, for having empowered him to borrow five hundred thousand pounds for the discharge of wages due to the seamen employed in the navy.

England was at this period quite barren of remarkable *A double marriage between the houses* events. The king's uncle, Ernest Augustus, Prince of Brunswick, Duke of York, and Bishop of Osnabruck, died

CHAP.
XV.

1728.
of Spain
and Por-
tugal.
on the third day of August, and was succeeded in the
bishopric by the Elector of Cologn, according to the pac-
tum by which Osnabruck is alternately possessed by the
house of Brunswick and that Elector. In the beginning
of December, his majesty's eldest son, Prince Frederick,
arrived in England from Hanover, where he had hitherto
resided, was introduced into the privy-council, and created
Prince of Wales. Signior Como, resident from the Duke
of Parma, was ordered to quit the kingdom, because his
master paid to the pretender the honours due to the
King of Great Britain. The congress opened at Soissons,
for determining all disputes among the powers of Europe,
proved ineffectual. Such difficulties occurred in settling
and reconciling so many different pretensions and interests, that the contracting parties in the alliance of Hanover proposed a provisional treaty, concerning which no
definitive answer was given as yet by the courts of
Vienna and Madrid. The fate of Europe, therefore,
continued in suspense: the English fleet lay inactive and
rotting in the West Indies; the sailors perished miserably,
without daring to avenge their country's wrongs; while
the Spanish cruisers committed depredations with impunity on the commerce of Great Britain. The court of
Spain, at this juncture, seemed cold and indifferent with
regard to a pacification with England. It had renewed
a good understanding with France, and now strengthened
its interest by a double alliance of marriage with the
royal family of Portugal. The infanta of this house was
betrothed to the Prince of Asturias; while the Spanish
infanta, formerly affianced to the French king, was now
matched with the Prince of Brazil, eldest son of his Portuguese majesty. In the month of January, the two
courts met in a wooden house built over the little river
Coya, that separates the two kingdoms, and there the
princesses were exchanged.

Liberality
of the
Commons.
The Parliament of Great Britain meeting according to
their last prorogation on the twenty-first day of January,
the king in his speech communicated the nature of the
negotiation at the congress. He demanded such supplies
as might enable him to act vigorously in concert with
his allies, provided his endeavours to establish an advantageous peace should miscarry; and he hinted that

the dilatory conduct of the courts of Vienna and Madrid proceeded in a great measure from the hopes that were given of creating discontents and divisions among the subjects of Great Britain. This suggestion was a ministerial artifice to inflame the zeal and resentment of the nation, and intimidate the members in the opposition. Accordingly the hint was pursued, and in the addresses from both Houses, which could not fail of being agreeable, considering the manner in which they were dictated, particular notice was taken of this article: both Peers and Commons expressed their detestation and abhorrence of those who, by such base and unnatural artifices, suggested the means of distressing their country, and clamoured at the inconveniences which they themselves had occasioned. In these addresses, likewise, the Parliament congratulated his majesty on the arrival of the Prince of Wales in his British dominions; and the Commons sent a particular compliment to his royal highness on that occasion. The estimates having been examined in the usual form, the House voted fifteen thousand seamen for the ensuing year: but the motion for continuing the same number of land-forces which had been allowed in the preceding year was not carried without dispute. All the arguments against a standing army in time of peace, as inconsistent with the British constitution, and dangerous to the liberties of the people, were repeated with great vivacity by Mr. Shippen, and Mr. W. Pulteney. These, however, were answered, and represented as absurd, by Mr. Horatio Walpole and Mr. D., two staunch adherents of the minister. The first had, in despite of nature, been employed in different negotiations: he was blunt, awkward, and slovenly; an orator without eloquence, an ambassador without dignity, and a plenipotentiary without address. The other had natural parts and acquired knowledge; spoke with confidence; and in dispute was vain, sarcastic, petulant, and verbose.

The subsidies to Sweden, Hesse-Cassel, and Wolfen-buttel, were continued, notwithstanding the remonstrances of Sir Joseph Jekyll, Mr. Lutwyche, and Mr. Pulteney; which last observed, that as the Landgrave of Hesse-Cassel, and the Duke of Brunswick-Wolfen-buttel, usually maintained a certain number of troops in

Debates on the subsidies of Hesse-Cassel and Wolfen-buttel.

their pay, it was but reasonable that Great Britain should defray no more than the expense of the additional forces which those powers had raised in consequence of their conventions with the King of England. Sir Robert Walpole perceiving that this remark made an impression on the House, thought it necessary to vindicate his measure. He expatiated upon the wisdom of the late king, in concluding the Hanover alliance. He affirmed, that the convention with Hesse-Cassel had prevented a war in the empire, for which the court of Vienna had made great preparations: that the emperor had not only augmented his own forces by the help of Spanish subsidies, but also retained the troops of three electors; and if he had not been overawed by the Hessians, would certainly have rejected the preliminaries, and all other advances towards a pacification: that, therefore, they ought not to grudge an expense which had already proved so beneficial to the tranquillity of Europe. Sir Joseph Jekyll replied, that whatever gloss might be put upon such measures, they were repugnant to the maxims by which England in former times had steered and squared its conduct with relation to its interest abroad: that the navy was the natural strength of Great Britain—its best defence and security; but if, in order to avoid a war, they should be so free-hearted as to buy and maintain the forces of foreign princes, they were never likely to see an end of such extravagant expenses. This gentleman, who exercised the office of master of the rolls, had approved himself a zealous defender of whig principles, was an able lawyer, a sensible speaker, and a conscientious patriot. The supplies were raised by a continuation of the land-tax, the duties upon malt, cyder, and perry, an additional imposition on unmalted corn used in distilling, and by sale of annuities to the bank not exceeding fifty thousand pounds per annum.

Committee for inspecting the gaols.

Petitions were delivered to the House of Commons from the merchants of London, Liverpool, and Bristol, complaining of the interruptions they had suffered in their trade for several years, by the depredations of the Spaniards in the West Indies. These being considered, the House ordered the Lords of the Admiralty to produce the other memorials of the same kind which they

had received, that they might be laid before the congress
at Soissons: then they addressed his majesty for copies
of all the letters and instructions which had been sent to
Admiral Hosier, and those who succeeded him in the
command of the West India squadron. Mr. Oglethorpe
having been informed of shocking cruelties and oppressions exercised by gaolers upon their prisoners, moved
for an examination into these practices, and was chosen
chairman of a committee appointed to inquire into the
state of the gaols of the kingdom. They began with
the Fleet-prison, which they visited in a body: there
they found Sir William Rich, baronet, loaded with irons,
by order of Bambridge the warden, to whom he had
given some slight cause of offence. They made a discovery of many inhuman barbarities, which had been
committed by that ruffian, and detected the most iniquitous scenes of fraud, villainy, and extortion. When
the report was made by the committee, the House unanimously resolved, that Thomas Bambridge, acting warden
of the Fleet, had wilfully permitted several debtors to
escape; had been guilty of the most notorious breaches
of trust, great extortions, and the highest crimes and
misdemeanours in the execution of his office; that he
had arbitrarily and unlawfully loaded with irons, put
into dungeons, and destroyed prisoners for debt, under
his charge, treating them in the most barbarous and cruel
manner, in high violation and contempt of the laws of
the kingdom. John Huggins, esquire, who had been
warden of the Fleet-prison, was subjected to a resolution
of the same nature. The House presented an address
to the king, desiring he would direct his attorney-general forthwith to prosecute these persons and their accomplices, who were committed prisoners to Newgate.
A bill was brought in, disabling Bambridge to execute
the office of warden; another for the better regulating
the prison of the Fleet, and for more effectually preventing and punishing arbitrary and illegal practices of
the warden of the said prison [c].

Other merchants complained by petition of the losses

CHAP.
XV.
1728.

Address
touching
the Spanish
depreda-
tions.

[c] It afterwards appeared that some of the members of this inquest were actuated
by other motives than those they professed; and the committee was suffered to
sink into oblivion.

sustained by the Spaniards. The House, in a grand
committee, deliberated on this subject, inquired into
the particulars, examined evidence, and drew up an address to the king, desiring his majesty would be graciously pleased to use his utmost endeavours for preventing such depredations; for procuring just and reasonable
satisfaction; and for securing to his subjects the free
exercise of commerce and navigation to and from the
British colonies in America. The king assured them
he would use his best endeavours to answer the desires
and expectations of his people, in an affair of so much
importance; and they, in another address, thanked him
for his gracious answer. They did not, however, receive
such a satisfactory reply to a former address, touching
the sum of sixty thousand pounds that had been stated
in the public account, without specification of the particular uses to which it was applied. His majesty gave
them to understand that the money had been issued and
disbursed for secret services; and that a distinct and
particular account of the distribution of it could not be
given without a manifest prejudice to the public. A
bill was prepared for the more effectual preventing
bribery and corruption in elections for members of Parliament; and it passed through the House without opposition; but their attention was chiefly employed upon
the Spanish depredations, which had raised a great
clamour through the whole kingdom, and excited very
warm disputes in Parliament; for they were generally
reputed the fruits of negligence, incapacity, or want of
vigour in the ministers. The Commons having made
further progress in the inquiry, and received fresh petitions from the merchants, passed some resolutions, in
which the Spaniards were accused of having violated
the treaties subsisting between the two crowns; and with
having treated inhumanly the masters and crews of ships
belonging to Great Britain. They justified the instructions given to Admiral Hosier, to seize and detain the
flota and galleons of Spain, until justice and satisfaction
should be rendered to his majesty and his allies; nay,
even declared that such seizure would have been just,
prudent, and necessary, tending to prevent an open
rupture, and to preserve the peace and tranquillity of

Europe. They again addressed the king to use his endeavours to procure satisfaction; and he promised to
comply with their request.

Mr. Scroope, member for Bristol, moved for an address entreating his majesty to order an account of the
produce of the civil-list revenues for one year to be laid
before the House. The address was presented, the account produced, and the House, in a grand committee,
took this affair into consideration. The courtiers affirmed that they fell short of the eight hundred thousand pounds settled upon his majesty; and Mr. Scroope
proposed that the sum of one hundred and fifteen thousand pounds should be granted to the king on account
of those deficiencies and arrears. The motion was vigorously opposed by Mr. Pulteney and other members.
They expressed their surprise that it should be made so
late in the session, when no further demand of money
could be reasonably expected; and they said it was the
more extraordinary, because it appeared in the former
session, from the examination of the accounts then before the House, that the revenues of the civil-list produced yearly a much greater sum than that for which
they were given. Mr. Pulteney moved, that the accounts and papers should be referred to the examination
of a select committee, properly empowered to investigate
the truth. The ministers opposed this motion; and the
question being put, it passed in the negative. The majority voted the sum demanded; and in a bill for settling the price of imported corn, they inserted the resolution for granting to his majesty the sum of one hundred and fifteen thousand pounds, on account of arrears
due on the civil-list revenues.

A sum
voted to the
king on ac-
count of
arrears due
on the civil-
list re-
venue.

The House of Lords having prepared a bill for the
more effectual punishment of forgery, which was passed
into a law, and ordered the judges to bring in another
on the report of a committee appointed to consider the
case of imprisoned debtors, at length deliberated upon
the state of the nation, particularly the positive demand
made by the court of Spain for the restitution of Gibraltar, grounded on a letter written by the late king to
his Catholic majesty. From a copy of the letter laid before the House, it plainly appeared that King George I.

had consented to this restitution. A motion being made for a resolution, importing, that for the honour of his majesty, and the preservation and security of the trade and commerce of the kingdom, effectual care should be taken in the present treaty that the King of Spain should renounce all claim and pretension to Gibraltar and Minorca, in plain and strong terms: a debate ensued, and the question being put, passed in the negative, though not without a protest. Then the majority resolved, that the House did entirely rely upon his majesty, that he would, for maintaining the honour and securing the trade of this kingdom, take effectual care in the present treaty to preserve his undoubted right to Gibraltar and Minorca. When the House examined the papers relating to the Spanish depredations, many severe reflections were uttered against the conduct of the ministry; and the motion was made, to resolve that Hosier's expedition was an unreasonable burden on the nation: but this too was rejected, and occasioned another protest. Nor did the clause in the corn bill, for granting one hundred and fifteen thousand pounds to his majesty, pass through the House of Peers without warm opposition. Divers lords alleged, that, instead of a deficiency in the civil-list revenues, there was a considerable surplus; that this was a new grant, and a new burden on the people; that the nation was loaded, not to complete, but to augment the sum designed for the civil-list; and this at a time when the public debts were increased; when the taxes were heavily felt in all parts of the country; when the foreign trade of Britain was encumbered and diminished; when her manufactures were decayed, her poor multiplied, and she was surrounded by many other national calamities. They observed, that if the produce of the civil list revenue should not amount to the yearly sum of eight hundred thousand pounds, the deficiency must be made good to his majesty by the public; whereas no provision was made, by which, if the produce of these revenues should exceed that sum, the surplus could accrue to the benefit of the public: that, by this precedent, not only real deficiencies were to be made good, but also supplies were to be given for arrears standing out at the end of the year, which should come on before the supplies could be granted, though the supply given to make good arrears in one year would certainly increase the surplusages in another: that the revenues of the civil-list were variable in their own nature; and even when there is a deficiency in the produce, there might be arrears in the receipt: these might be easily increased by the management of designing ministers, by private directions to receivers, and by artful methods of stating accounts. All these arguments, and other objections equally strong and plausible, against this unconscionable and unparliamentary motion, served only to evince the triumph of the ministry over shame and sentiment, their contempt of public spirit, and their defiance of national reproach[d].

The king had, on the twenty-fourth day of March, given the royal assent to five bills; and on the fourteenth day of May, the same sanction was given to thirty other bills, including an act, enabling the queen to be regent in the kingdom during his majesty's absence, without taking the oaths, and another for the relief of insolvent debtors. At the same time two-and-thirty private bills were passed: then the king expressed his approbation of the Parliament, signified his intention of visiting his German dominions, and ordered the chancellor to prorogue both Houses. His majesty having appointed the queen regent of the realm, set out for Hanover, on the seventeenth day of May, in order to remove a petty misunderstanding which had happened between that electorate and the court of Berlin. Some Hanoverian subjects had been pressed or decoyed into the service of Prussia; and the regents of Hanover had seized certain Prussian officers by way of reprisal. The whole united kingdom of Great Britain at this juncture enjoyed uninterrupted repose; and commerce continued to increase, in spite of all restriction and discouragement. The people of Ireland found themselves happy under the government of Lord Carteret; and their Parliament, assembling in the month of September, approved themselves the fathers of their country. They established funds for

CHAP.
XV.

1728.

1729.
Wise conduct of the Irish Parliament.

[d] The peers that distinguished themselves in the opposition were, Beaufort, Strafford, Craven, Foley, Lichfield, Scarsdale, Gower, Mountjoy, Plymouth, Bathurst, Northampton, Coventry, Oxford and Mortimer, Willoughby de Broke, Boyle, and Warrington.

CHAP.
XV.

1729.

the discharge of their national debt, and for maintaining the expense of government; they enacted wholesome laws for the encouragement of manufactures, trade, and agriculture; and they formed wise regulations in different branches of civil economy. Some time after this session, which was conducted with so much harmony and patriotism, Lord Carteret returned to England, and was succeeded by the Duke of Dorset in the government of that kingdom. In the month of May, Charles Lord Townshend resigned the seals, which were given to Colonel Stanhope, now created Earl of Harrington; so that Sir R. W. now reigned without a rival. James Earl of Waldegrave was appointed ambassador to the court of France, which about that time was filled with joy by the birth of a dauphin.

Abdication of the King of Sardinia. Death of Pope Benedict XIII.

In the month of September, Victor Amadeus, king of Sardinia, resigned his crown to his son Charles Emanuel, Prince of Piedmont. The father reserved to himself a revenue of one hundred thousand pistoles per annum, retired to the castle of Chamberry, and espoused the Countess Dowager of St. Sebastian, who declined the title of queen, but assumed that of Marchioness of Somerive. Though the congress of Soissons proved abortive, conferences were begun at Seville between the plenipotentiaries of England, France, and Spain; and a treaty was concluded on the ninth day of November, not only without the concurrence of the emperor, but even contrary to his right, as established by the quadruple alliance. On this subject he communicated an imperial commissorial decree to the states of the empire assembled in the diet at Ratisbon, which was answered by the French minister de Chavigny. In October, Peter II., Czar of Muscovy, and grandson of Peter I. died in the fifteenth year of his age, at Moscow, and was succeeded on the Russian throne by the Princess Anne Ivanowna, second daughter of John Alexowitz, elder brother of the first Peter, and widow of Frederick William Duke of Courland. The following month was rendered remarkable by the death of Pope Benedict XIII., in whose room Cardinal Laurence Corsini was raised to the pontificate, and assumed the name of Clement XII.

Substance of the king's

The British Parliament assembling on the thirteenth day of January, the king gave them to understand, that the peace of Europe was now established by the treaty CHAP XV. of Seville, built upon the foundation of former treaties, and tending to render more effectual what the contract- 1729. speech to ing powers in the quadruple alliance were before engaged both to see performed. He assured them that all former con- Houses. ventions made with Spain in favour of the British trade and navigation were renewed and confirmed: that the free, uninterrupted exercise of their commerce was re- stored: that the court of Spain had agreed to an ample restitution and reparation for unlawful seizures and de- predations: that all rights, privileges, and possessions, belonging to him and his allies, were solemnly re-esta- blished, confirmed, and guaranteed; and that not one concession was made to the prejudice of his subjects. He told them he had given orders for reducing a great number of his land-forces, and for laying up great part of the fleet; and observed that there would be a con- siderable saving in the expense of the current year. After both Houses had presented their addresses of thanks and congratulation to the king on the peace of Seville, the Lords took that treaty into consideration, and it did not pass inquiry without severe animadversion.

The Lords in the opposition excepted to the article Objections to the treaty of by which the merchants of Great Britain were obliged to make proof of their losses at the court of Spain. They Seville in the Hous- said this stipulation was a hardship upon British subjects, of Lords. and dishonourable to the nation: that few would care to undertake such a troublesome and expensive journey, especially as they had reason to apprehend their claims would be counterbalanced by the Spaniards; and, after all, they would have no more than the slender comfort of hoping to obtain that redress by commissaries which they had not been able to procure by plenipotentiaries. They thought it very extraordinary that Great Britain should be bound to ratify and guarantee whatever agree- ment should be made between the King of Spain and the Dukes of Parma and Tuscany, concerning the gar- risons once established in their countries; that the Eng- lish should be obliged to assist in effectuating the in- troduction of six thousand Spanish troops into the towns of Tuscany and Parma, without any specification of the methods to be taken, or the charge to be incurred in giving that assistance; that they should guarantee for ever, not only to Don Carlos, but even to all his successors, the possession of the estates of Tuscany and Parma; a stipulation which in all probability would involve Great Britain in endless quarrels and disputes, about a country with which they had no concern. They affirmed that the treaty of Seville, instead of confirming other treaties, was contradictory to the quadruple alliance, particularly in the article of introducing Spanish troops into Tuscany and Parma, in the room of neutral forces stipulated by the former alliance; and agreeing that they should there remain until Don Carlos and his successors should be secure and exempt from all events. They complained that these alterations, from the tenor of the quadruple alliance, were made without the concurrence of the emperor, and even without inviting him to accede; an affront which might alienate his friendship from England, and hazard the loss of such an ancient, powerful, and faithful ally: they declared that throughout the whole treaty there seemed to be an artful omission of any express stipulation, to secure Great Britain in her right to Gibraltar and Minorca. Such was the substance of the objections made to the peace: then Lord Bathurst moved for a resolution, that the agreement on the treaty of Seville, to secure the succession of Don Carlos to the duchies of Tuscany, Parma, and Placentia, with Spanish troops, was a manifest violation of the fifth article of the quadruple alliance, tending to involve the nation in a dangerous and expensive war, and to destroy the balance of power in Europe. The question was put, and the motion rejected. Such too was the fate of two other motions, to resolve that Great Britain's right of sovereignty, dominion, possession, and claim to Gibraltar and Minorca were not ascertained by the treaty of Seville; and that the stipulations in that treaty for repairing the losses of the British merchants were insufficient and precarious. The majority, far from stigmatizing this transaction, resolved, that the treaty did contain all necessary stipulations for maintaining and securing the honour, dignity, rights, and possessions of the crown: that all due care was taken therein for the support of the trade of the kingdom, and for repairing the losses

sustained by the British merchants. On these resolutions an address of approbation was founded; but when
a motion was made for an address to his majesty, that
he would order to be laid before the House a list of all
pensions payable to the crown, it was immediately resolved in the negative. Divers contests of the same
kind arose upon the mutiny bill, the pension bill, and the
maintenance of the twelve thousand Hessians; but the
ministry bore down all opposition, though their triumphs
were clogged with vigorous protests, which did not fail
to make impression upon the body of the people.

Nor was the success of the court interest in the House
of Commons altogether pure, and free from exception
and dispute. When the charge of the land-forces fell
under the consideration of the Commons, and Mr. Henry
Pelham, secretary at war, moved that the number of
effective men for the land-service of the ensuing year
should be fixed at seventeen thousand seven hundred
and nine, Mr. Pulteney insisted upon its being reduced
to twelve thousand. Mr. Shippen affirmed, that Mr.
Pelham's motion was a flat negative to the address for
which he voted on the first day of the session, as it
plainly implied a distrust of the validity of the late
treaty, which he then assured the House would immediately produce all the blessings of an absolute peace,
and deliver the kingdom from the apprehensions and
inconveniences of a war. He said the motion tended
directly towards the establishment of an army in Great
Britain, which he hoped would never be so far German-
ized, as tamely to submit to a military government. He
observed, that the nation could have no occasion for all
the troops that were demanded, considering the glorious
scene of affairs which was now opened to all Europe.
"They are not necessary (said he) to awe Spain into a
firm adherence to its own treaty; they are not necessary
to force the emperor into an immediate accession; nor
are they in any sort necessary for the safety of his majesty's person and government. Force and violence are
the resort of usurpers and tyrants only; because they
are, with good reason, distrustful of the people whom
they oppress; and because they have no other security
for the continuance of their unlawful and unnatural

Opposition
in the
Lower
House to a
standing
army.

dominion than what depends entirely on the strength of their armies." The motion, however, was carried in the affirmative.

Bill prohibiting loans to foreign princes or states.

Another warm debate was excited by a bill which the courtiers brought in, to prevent any subjects of Great Britain from advancing sums of money to foreign princes or states, without having obtained licence from his majesty, under his privy-seal, or some greater authority. The minister pretended that this law was proposed to disable the emperor, who wanted to borrow a great sum of the English merchants, from raising and maintaining troops to disturb the tranquillity of Europe. The bill contained a clause, empowering the king to prohibit by proclamation all such loans of money, jewels, or bullion: the attorney-general was empowered to compel, by English bill, in the court of exchequer, the effectual discovery, on oath, of any such loans; and it was enacted, that in default of an answer to any such bill the court should decree a limited sum against the person refusing to answer. Mr. Daniel Pulteney, a gentleman of uncommon talents and ability, and particularly acquainted with every branch of commerce, argued strenuously against this bill, as a restraint upon trade that would render Holland the market of Europe, and the mart of money to the nations of the continent. He said that by this general prohibition, extending to all princes, states, or potentates, the English were totally disabled from assisting their best allies: that among others, the King of Portugal frequently borrowed money of the English merchants residing within his dominions: that while the licensing power remained in the crown, the licences would be issued through the hands of the minister, who by this new trade might gain twenty, thirty, or forty thousand a year: that the bill would render the exchequer a court of inquisition; and that whilst it restrained our merchants from assisting the princes and powers of Europe, it permitted our stock-jobbers to trade in their funds without interruption. Other arguments of equal weight were enforced by Mr. Barnard, a merchant of London, who perfectly understood trade in all its branches, spoke with judgment and precision, and upon all occasions steadily adhered to the interests and liberties of his country. After having explained his reasons, he declared he should never consent to a bill which he deemed a violation of our fundamental laws, a breach of our dearest liberties, and a very terrible hardship on mankind. Sir William Wyndham distinguished himself on the same side of the question : the bill was vindicated by Sir Robert Walpole, Mr. Pelham, and Sir Philip York, attorney-general ; and being supported by the whole weight of ministerial influence, not only passed through the House, but was afterwards enacted into a law.

The subsidies were continued to the Landgrave of Hesse-Cassel and the Duke of Brunswick-Wolfenbuttel, in spite of all that could be urged against these extraneous encumbrances ; and the supply for the ensuing year was granted according to the estimates which the ministry thought proper to produce, amounting to about two millions two hundred and eighty thousand pounds. It must be owned, however, for the credit of this session, that the House appropriated one million of the surpluses arising from the sinking fund towards the discharge of the national debt ; and by another act extinguished the duties upon salt, by which expedient the subject was eased of a heavy burden, not only in being freed from the duty, but also from a considerable charge of salaries given to a great number of officers employed to collect this imposition. They likewise encouraged the colony of Carolina with an act, allowing the planters and traders of that province to export rice directly to any part of Europe southward of Cape Finisterre ; and they permitted salt from Europe to be imported into the colony of New York. The term of the exclusive trade granted by act of Parliament to the East India Company drawing towards a period, many considerable merchants and others made application for being incorporated and vested with the privilege of trading to those countries, proposing to lay that branch of trade open to all the subjects of Great Britain on certain conditions. In consideration of an act of Parliament for this purpose, they offered to advance three millions two hundred thousand pounds, for redeeming the fund and trade of the present East India Company. This proposal was rejected ; and the exclusive privilege vested in the Company was, by act of Parliament, protracted to the year one thousand seven hundred and sixty-six, upon the following conditions: that they should pay into the exchequer the sum of two hundred thousand pounds towards the supplies of the year, without interest or addition to their capital stock: that the annuity or yearly fund of one hundred and sixty thousand pounds, payable to them from the public, should be reduced to one hundred and twenty-eight thousand: that after the year one thousand seven hundred and sixty-six, their right to the exclusive trade should be liable to be taken away by Parliament, on three years' notice, and repayment of their capital.

1730.
The em-
peror re-
sents the
treaty of
Seville.
On the fifteenth day of May the king went to the House of Peers, and closed the session. In his speech he expressed his joy, that notwithstanding all the clamours which were raised, the Parliament had approved of those matters which fell under their consideration; a circumstance which, he said, could not fail to inspire all mankind with a just detestation of those incendiaries, who, by scandalous libels, laboured to alienate the affections of his people; to fill their minds with groundless jealousies and unjust complaints, in dishonour of him and his government, and in defiance of the sense of both Houses of Parliament[*]. The emperor was so much incensed at the insult offered to him in the treaty of Seville, with respect to the garrisons of Tuscany and Parma, that he prohibited the subjects of Great Britain from trading in his dominions: he began to make preparations for war, and actually detached bodies of troops to Italy, with such despatch as had been very seldom exerted by the house of Austria. Yet the article of which he complained was not so much a real injury as an affront put upon the head of the empire; for the eventual succession to those Italian duchies had been secured to the infant,

---

[*] In the course of this session the Commons passed a bill for making more effectual the laws in being, for disabling persons from being chosen members of Parliament who enjoyed any pension during pleasure, or for any number of years, or any offices holden in trust for them, by obliging all persons hereafter to be chosen to serve for the Commons in Parliament, to take the oath therein mentioned. In all probability this bill would not have made its way through the House of Commons, had not the minister been well assured it would stick with the Upper House, where it was rejected at the second reading, though not without violent opposition.

Don Carlos, by the quadruple alliance; and all that the emperor required was that this prince should receive the investiture of them as fiefs of the empire.

In Great Britain, this year was not distinguished by any transactions of great moment. Seven chiefs of the Cherokee nations of Indians in America were brought to England by Sir Alexander Cumin. Being introduced to the king, they laid their crown and regalia at his feet; and by an authentic deed acknowledged themselves subjects to his dominion, in the name of all their compatriots, who had vested them with full powers for this purpose. They were amazed and confounded at the riches and magnificence of the British court: they compared the king and queen to the sun and moon, the princes to the stars of heaven, and themselves to nothing. They gave their assent in the most solemn manner to articles of friendship and commerce, proposed by the lords commissioners for trade and plantations; and being loaded with presents of necessaries, arms, and ammunition, were reconveyed to their own country, which borders on the province of South Carolina. In the month of September a surprising revolution was effected at Constantinople, without bloodshed or confusion. A few mean janissaries displayed a flag in the streets, exclaiming that all true Mussulmen ought to follow them, and assist in reforming the government. They soon increased to the number of one hundred thousand, marched to the seraglio, and demanded the grand vizir, the kiaja, and captain pacha. These unhappy ministers were immediately strangled. Their bodies being delivered to the insurgents were dragged through the streets, and afterwards thrown to the dogs to be devoured. Not contented with this sacrifice, the revolters deposed the Grand Signior Achmet, who was confined to the same prison from whence they brought his nephew Machmut, and raised this last to the throne, after he had lived seven-and-twenty years in confinement.

Seven
Indian
chiefs arrive n
England.
Revolution
at Constantinople.

England was at this period infested with robbers, assassins, and incendiaries, the natural consequences of degeneracy, corruption, and the want of police in the interior government of the kingdom. This defect, in a great measure, arose from an absurd notion, that laws necessary to prevent those acts of cruelty, violence, and rapine, would be incompatible with the liberty of British subjects; a notion that confounds all distinctions between liberty and brutal licentiousness, as if that freedom was desirable, in the enjoyment of which people find no security for their lives or effects. The peculiar depravity of the times was visible even in the conduct of those who preyed upon the commonwealth. Thieves and robbers were now become more desperate and savage than ever they had appeared since mankind was civilized. In the exercise of their rapine, they wounded, maimed, and even murdered the unhappy sufferers, through a wantonness of barbarity. They circulated letters demanding sums of money from certain individuals, on pain of reducing their houses to ashes, and their families to ruin; and even set fire to the house of a rich merchant in Bristol, who had refused to comply with their demand. The same species of villany was practised in different parts of the kingdom; so that the government was obliged to interpose, and offer a considerable reward for discovering the ruffians concerned in such execrable designs.

Bill against pensioners sitting as members in the House of Commons.

In the speech with which the king opened the session of parliament on the twenty-first day of January, he told them, that the present critical conjuncture seemed in a very particular manner to deserve their attention: that as the transactions then depending in the several courts of Europe were upon the point of being determined, the great event of peace or war might be very much affected by their first resolutions, which were expected by different powers with great impatience. He said, the continuance of that zeal and vigour with which they had hitherto supported him and his engagements must at this time be of the greatest weight and importance, both with regard to his allies, and to those who might be disposed, before the season of action, to prevent, by an accommodation, the fatal consequences of a general rupture. The former scene was repeated. Both Houses, in their addresses, promised to support his majesty, in all his engagements; yet the members in the opposition demonstrated the absurdity of promising to fulfil engagements before they could possibly know whether or not they were for the service of Great Britain. Another bill was

brought into the House of Commons, to prevent pensioners from sitting as members of Parliament; and after
a third reading, carried up to the Lords for their concurrence. When the supply fell under consideration,
the debates were renewed upon the subsidies to the
Landgrave of Hesse-Cassel and the Duke of Wolfen-
buttel, which, however, were continued; and every article was granted according to the estimates given in for
the expense of the ensuing year. Two petitions being
presented to the Commons, representing the delays of
justice, occasioned by the use of the Latin tongue in
proceedings at law, a bill was brought in for changing
this practice, and enacting that all those processes and
pleadings should be entered in the English language.
Though one would imagine that very little could be advanced against such a regulation, the bill met with warm
opposition, on pretence that it would render useless the
ancient records which were written in that language,
and introduce confusion and delay of justice, by altering the established form and method of pleading: in
spite of these objections, it passed through both Houses,
and obtained the royal assent. A great number of
merchants from different parts of the kingdom having
repeated their complaints of depredations and cruelties
committed by the Spaniards in the West Indies, their
petitions were referred to the consideration of a grand
committee. Their complaints upon examination appeared to be well founded. The House presented an
address to the king, desiring his majesty would be graciously pleased to continue his endeavours to prevent
such depredations for the future; to procure full satisfaction for the damages already sustained; and to secure
to the British subjects the full and uninterrupted exercise
of their trade and navigation to and from the British
colonies in America. The bill against pensions produced a warm debate in the House of Lords, where it
was violently opposed by the Dukes of Newcastle and
Argyle, the Earl of Ilay, and Dr. Sherlock, Bishop of
Bangor. This prelate, in a remarkable speech, represented it as a scheme to enlarge the power of the House
of Commons, and to break the balance between the
powers essential to the constitution, so as, sooner or

later, to prove the ruin of the whole. The great barrier provided against bribery and corruption by this bill consisted in an oath to be imposed on all members of the Lower House, by which they must have solemnly sworn and declared, that they had not directly, nor indirectly, any pension during pleasure, or for any number of years, or any office in part or in the whole, held for them, or for their benefit, by any persons whatsoever; and that they would not accept any such pensions or offices, without signifying the same to the House within fourteen days after they should be received or accepted. The bill was vindicated as just and necessary by the Earls of Winchelsea and Strafford, Lord Bathurst, and Lord Carteret, who had by this time joined as an auxiliary in the opposition [f].

The House of Peers proceeded to consider the state of the national debt; they read a bill for the free importation of wool from Ireland into England, which was fiercely opposed and laid aside, contrary to all the rules of sound policy. They passed the bill for carrying on proceedings at law in the English language; and a fruitless motion was made by Lord Bathurst for an address, to desire his majesty would give directions for discharging the Hessian troops that were in the pay of Great Britain. On the seventh day of May the Parliament was prorogued, after the king had given them to understand, that all apprehensions of war were now happily removed by a treaty signed at Vienna between him and the emperor. He said it was communicated to the courts of France and Spain, as parties to the treaty of Seville, the execution of which it principally regarded; and that it was likewise submitted to the consideration of the States-General. He observed, that the conditions and engage-

---

[f] Nothing was heard within doors in Parliament but sarcastic repartee and violent declamation between the two parties, who did not confine their altercation to these debates, but took the field against each other in periodical papers and occasional pamphlets. The paper called the Craftsman had already risen into high reputation all over England, for the wit, humour, and solid reasoning it contained. Some of the best writers in the opposition, including Lord Bolingbroke and Mr. P., made use of this vehicle to convey their animadversions upon the minister, who, on his side, employed the most wretched scribblers to defend his conduct. It was in consequence of two political pamphlets, written in opposition to each other, by Lord Hervey and Mr. P. and some recrimination they produced in the House of Commons, that his lordship challenged the other to single combat, and had well nigh lost his life in the duel, which was fought in Hyde-Park.

ments into which he had entered on this occasion were
agreeable to that necessary concern which the British
nation must always have for the security and preservation of the balance of power in Europe; and that this
happy turn, duly improved with a just regard to former
alliances, yielded a favourable prospect of seeing the
public tranquillity re-established.

In the month of January the Duke of Parma died,
after having made a will in which he declared his duchess
was three months advanced in her pregnancy; entreating the allied powers of Europe to have compassion upon
his people, and defer the execution of their projects until
his consort should be delivered. In case the child should
be still-born, or die after the birth, he bequeathed his
dominions and allodial estates to the infant Don Carlos
of Spain, and appointed five regents to govern the duchy.
Notwithstanding this disposition, a body of imperial
troops immediately took possession of Parma and Placentia, under the command of General Stampa, who
declared they should conduct themselves with all possible regularity and moderation, and leave the administration entirely to the regents whom the duke had
appointed. They publicly proclaimed in the market-
place that they took possession of these duchies for the
infant Don Carlos; and that if the duchess-dowager
should not be delivered of a prince, the said infant might
receive the investiture from the emperor whenever he
would, provided he should come without an army.
Though these steps seemed to threaten an immediate
war, the King of Great Britain and the States-General
interposed their mediation so effectually with the Court
of Vienna, that the emperor desisted from the prosecution of his design; and on the sixteenth day of March
concluded at Vienna a treaty with his Britannic Majesty,
by which he consented to withdraw his troops from
Parma and Placentia. He agreed that the king of Spain
might take possession of these places in favour of his son
Don Carlos, according to the treaty of Seville. He likewise agreed, that the Ostend Company, which had given
such umbrage to the maritime powers, should be totally
dissolved, on condition that the contracting powers concerned in the treaty of Seville should guarantee the

CHAP.
XV.
1731.

pragmatic sanction, or succession of the Austrian hereditary dominions to the heirs female of the emperor, in
case he should die without male issue. The Dutch minister residing at the imperial court did not subscribe this
treaty, because, by the maxims received in that republic,
and the nature of her government, he could not be vested
with full powers so soon as it would have been necessary;
nevertheless the States-General were, by a separate article,
expressly named as a principal contracting party.

Don Carlos
takes pos-
session of
his terri-
tories.

On the twenty-second day of July a new treaty was
signed at Vienna between the emperor and the kings of
Great Britain and Spain, tending to confirm the former.
In August, a treaty of union and defensive alliance between the electorates of Saxony and Hanover was executed at Dresden. The court of Spain expressing some
doubts with regard to the pregnancy of the Duchess of
Parma, she underwent a formal examination by five
midwives of different nations, in presence of the elder
duchess dowager, several ladies of quality, three physicians, and a surgeon; and was declared with child:
nevertheless, after having kept all Europe in suspense
for six months, she owned she had been deceived; and
General Stampa, with the imperial forces, took formal
possession of the duchies of Parma and Placentia. Spain
and the Great Duke of Tuscany having acceded to the
last treaty of Vienna, the crown of Great Britain engaged to equip an armament that should convoy Don
Carlos to his new dominions. Accordingly, Sir Charles
Wager sailed with a strong squadron from Portsmouth
on the twenty-sixth day of August; and in September
arrived at Barcelona, where, being joined by the Spanish
fleet and transports, they sailed together to Leghorn;
from whence the admiral returned to England. Don
Carlos passed through part of France, and embarking at
Antibes on board of the Spanish galleys, arrived at Leghorn in December. Then the imperial general withdrew
his forces into the Milanese, and the infant took possession of his new territories.

France dis-
tracted by
religious
disputes.

During these transactions France was distracted by
religious disputes, occasioned by the bull Unigenitus
thundered against the doctrines of Jansenius; a bull
which had produced a schism in the Gallican church,

and well nigh involved that country in civil war and confusion. It was opposed by the Parliaments and lay tri-
bunals of the kingdom ; but many bishops, and the Jesuits
in general, were its most strenuous assertors. All the
artifices of priestcraft were practised on both sides to inflame the enthusiasm, and manage the superstition, of
the people. Pretended miracles were wrought at the
tomb of Abbé Paris, who had died without accepting the
bull, consequently was declared damned by the abettors of
that constitution. On the other hand, the Jesuits exerted
all their abilities and industry in preaching against the
Jansenists ; in establishing an opinion of their superior
sanctity ; and inspiring a spirit of quietism among their
votaries, who were transported into the delirium of possession, illumination, and supernatural converse. These
arts were often used for the most infamous purposes.
Female enthusiasts were wrought up to such a violence
of agitation, that nature fainted under the struggle, and
the pseudo-saint seized this opportunity of violating the
chastity of his penitent. Such was said to be the case
of Mademoiselle la Cadière, a young gentlewoman of
Toulon, abused in this manner by the lust and villany
of Père Girard, a noted Jesuit, who underwent a trial
before the Parliament of Aix, and very narrowly escaped
the stake.

The Parliament of Great Britain meeting on the thir- The minis-
teenth day of January, the king in his speech declared, try violently op-
that the general tranquillity of Europe was restored and posed in
established by the last treaty of Vienna ; and Don Carlos Parliament.
was actually possessed of Parma and Placentia : that six
thousand Spaniards were quietly admitted and quartered
in the duchy of Tuscany, to secure, by the express consent and agreement of the great duke, the reversion of
his dominions ; and that a family convention was made
between the courts of Spain and Tuscany, for preserving
mutual peace and friendship in the two houses. He
told the Commons, that the estimates for the service of
the current year would be considerably less than those
of former years. He recommended unanimity : he observed that his government had no security but what
was equally conducive to their happiness, and to the
protection of his people : that their prosperity had no

foundation but in the defence and support of his government. "Our safety," said he, "is mutual, and our interests are inseparable." The opposition to the court measures appears to have been uncommonly spirited during the course of this session. The minister's motions were attacked with all the artillery of elocution. His principal emissaries were obliged to task their faculties to their full exertion, to puzzle and perplex where they could not demonstrate and convince, to misrepresent what they could not vindicate, and to elude the arguments which they could not refute. In the House of Commons Lord Hervey, lately appointed vice-chamberlain of his majesty's household, made a motion for an address of thanks, in which they should declare their entire approbation of the king's conduct, acknowledge the blessings they enjoyed under his government, express their confidence in the wisdom of his councils, and declare their readiness to grant the necessary supplies. This member, son to the Earl of Bristol, was a nobleman of some parts, which, however, were more specious than solid. He condescended to act as a subaltern to the minister, and approved himself extremely active in forwarding all his designs, whether as a secret emissary or public orator; in which last capacity he appears to have been pert, frivolous, and frothy. His motion was seconded by Mr. Clutterbuck, and opposed by Sir Wilfred Lawson, Mr. Shippen, Mr. W. Pulteney, Sir William Wyndham, and Mr. Oglethorpe. They did not argue against a general address of thanks; but exposed the absurdity and bad tendency of expressions which implied a blind approbation of all the measures of the ministry. Sir Wilfred Lawson observed, that notwithstanding the great things we had done for the crown of Spain, and the favours we had procured for the royal family of that kingdom, little or no satisfaction had as yet been received for the injuries our merchants had sustained from that nation. Mr. Pulteney took notice, that the nation, by becoming guarantee to the pragmatic sanction, laid itself under an obligation to assist the Austrian family when attacked by any potentate whatever, except the grand signior: that they might be attacked when it would be much against the interest of the kingdom to engage itself in a war upon any foreign account: that it might one day be for the interest of the nation to join against them, in order to preserve the balance of Europe, the establishing of which had already cost England such immense sums of money. He insisted upon the absurdity of concluding such a number of inconsistent treaties; and concluded with saying, that if affairs abroad were now happily established, the ministry which conducted them might be compared to a pilot, who, though there was a clear, safe, and straight channel into port, yet took it in his head to carry the ship a great way about, through sands, rocks, and shallows; who, after having lost a great number of seamen, destroyed a great deal of tackle and rigging, and subjected the owners to an enormous expense, at last by chance hits the port and triumphs in his good conduct. Sir William Wyndham spoke to the same purpose. Mr. Oglethorpe, a gentleman of unblemished character, brave, generous, and humane, affirmed that many other things related more nearly to the honour and interest of the nation than did the guarantee of the pragmatic sanction. He said he wished to have heard that the new works at Dunkirk had been entirely razed and destroyed: that the nation had received full and complete satisfaction for the depredations committed by the natives of Spain: that more care was taken in disciplining the militia, on whose valour the nation must chiefly depend in case of invasion; and that some regard had been shown to the oppressed Protestants in Germany. He expressed his satisfaction to find that the English were not so closely united to France as formerly; for he had generally observed, that when two dogs were in a leash together, the stronger generally ran away with the weaker; and this he was afraid had been the case between France and Great Britain. The motion was vigorously defended by Mr. Pelham, paymaster of the forces, and brother to the Duke of Newcastle, a man whose greatest fault was his being concerned in supporting the measures of a corrupt ministry. In other respects he was liberal, candid, benevolent, and even attached to the interest of his country, though egregiously mistaken in his notions of government. On this occasion he asserted that it was no way inconsistent

CHAP.
XV.

1731.

with the honour or dignity of that House to thank his majesty in the most particular terms for every thing he had been pleased to communicate in his speech from the throne : that no expressions of approbation in the address could be any way made use of to prevent an inquiry into the measures which had been pursued, when the treaties should be laid before the House. He said, at the opening of a session the eyes of all Europe were turned towards Great Britain, and from the Parliament's first resolves all the neighbouring powers ¡judged of the unanimity that would ensue between his majesty and the representatives of his people : that their appearing ¡jealous or diffident of his majesty's conduct would weaken his influence upon the councils of foreign states and potentates, and perhaps put it out of his power to rectify any false step that might have been made by his ministers. His arguments were reinforced by a long speech from Mr. H. Walpole. The question was put, the motion carried, and the address presented.

Debate on a standing army.

The next subject of debate was the number of landforces. When the supply fell under consideration, Sir W. Strickland, secretary at war, moved that the same number which had been maintained in the preceding year should be continued in pay. On the other hand, Lord Morpeth, having demonstrated the danger to which the liberties of the nation might be exposed, by maintaining a numerous standing army in time of peace, made a motion that the number should be reduced to twelve thousand. A warm debate ensuing, was managed in favour of the first motion by Lord Hervey, Sir Robert Walpole and his brother, Mr. Pelham, and Sir Philip York, attorney-general. This gentleman was counted a better lawyer than a politician, and shone more as an advocate at the bar than as an orator in the House of Commons. The last partisan of the ministry was Sir William Yonge, one of the lords commissioners of the treasury ; a man who rendered himself serviceable and necessary, by stooping to all compliances, running upon every scent, and haranguing on every subject with an even, uninterrupted, tedious flow of dull declamation, composed of assertions without veracity, conclusions from false premises, words without meaning, and language without propriety. Lord Morpeth's motion was espoused by Mr. Watkin Williams Wynne, a gentleman of an ancient family and opulent fortune in Wales, brave, open, hospitable, and warmly attached to the ancient constitution and hierarchy; he was supported by Mr. Walter Plumer, who spoke with weight, precision, and severity, by Sir W. Wyndham, Mr. Shippen, Mr. W. Pulteney, and Mr. Barnard. The courtiers argued that it was necessary to maintain such a number of land-forces as might defeat the designs of malecontents, secure the interior tranquillity of the kingdom, defend it from external assaults, overawe its neighbours, and enable it to take vigorous measures in case the peace of Europe should be re-embroiled. They affirmed, the science of war was so much altered, and required so much attention, that no dependence was to be placed upon a militia: that all nations were obliged to maintain standing armies, for their security against the encroachments of neighbouring powers: that the number of troops in Great Britain was too inconsiderable to excite the jealousy of the people even under an ambitious monarch: that his majesty never entertained the least thought of infringing the liberties of his subjects: that it could not be supposed that the officers, among whom were many gentlemen of family and fortune, would ever concur in a design to enslave their country; and that the forces now in pay could not be properly deemed a standing army, inasmuch as they were voted and maintained from year to year by the Parliament, which was the representative of the people. To these arguments the members in the opposition replied, that a standing force in time of peace was unconstitutional, and had been always thought dangerous: that a militia was as capable of discipline as a standing army, and would have more incentives to courage and perseverance: that the civil magistrate was able to preserve the peace of the country: that the number of the malecontents was altogether contemptible, though it might be considerably augmented by maintaining a standing army, and other such arbitrary measures: that other nations had been enslaved by standing armies; and howsoever they might find themselves necessitated to depend upon a military force for security against encroaching neighbours, the case was very different with regard to Great Britain, for the defence of which nature had provided in a peculiar manner: that this provision was strengthened and improved by a numerous navy, which secured her the dominion on the sea; and, if properly disposed, would render all invasion impracticable, or at least ineffectual: that the land-army of Great Britain, though sufficient to endanger the liberties of an unarmed people, could not possibly secure such an extent of coast, and therefore could be of very little service in preventing an invasion: that though they had all imaginable confidence in his majesty's regard for the liberty of his subjects, they could not help apprehending, that should a standing army become part of the constitution, another prince of more dangerous talents, and more fatal designs, might arise and employ it for the worst purposes of ambition: that though many officers were gentlemen of honour and probity, these might be easily discarded, and the army gradually moulded into a quite different temper. By these means, practised in former times, an army had been new modelled to such a degree, that they turned their swords against the Parliament, for whose defence they had been raised, and destroyed the constitution both in church and state: that with respect to its being wholly dependent on the Parliament, the people of England would have reason to complain of the same hardship, whether a standing army should be declared at once indispensable, or regularly voted from year to year, according to the direction of the ministry: that the sanction of the legislature, granted to measures which in themselves are unconstitutional, burdensome, odious, and repugnant to the genius of the nation, instead of yielding consolation, would serve only to demonstrate, that the most effectual method of forging the chains of national slavery would be that of ministerial influence operating upon a venal Parliament. Such were the reasons urged against a standing army, of what number soever it might be composed: but the expediency of reducing the number from about eighteen thousand to twelve thousand was insisted upon as the natural consequence of his majesty's declaration, by which they were given to understand that the

peace of Europe was established; and that he had nothing so much at heart as the ease and prosperity of his
people. It was suggested, that if eighteen thousand
men were sufficient on the supposed eve of a general
war in Europe, it was surely reasonable to think that a
less number would suffice when peace was perfectly
re-established. Whatever effect these reasons had upon
the body of the nation, they made no converts in the
House, where the majority resolved that the standing army should be maintained without reduction.
Mr. Plumer complained, that the country was oppressed
by an arbitrary method of quartering soldiers, in an undue
proportion, upon those publicans who refused to vote in
elections according to the direction of the ministry.
Mr. Pulteney asserted, that the money raised for the subsistence of eighteen thousand men in England would
maintain sixty thousand French or Germans, or the same
number of almost any other people on the continent.
Sir William Wyndham declared, that eighteen thousand
of the English troops in the late war were maintained
on less than two-thirds of the sum now demanded for
the like number: but no regard was paid to these allegations.

The next object of importance that attracted the notice
of the House was the state of the Charitable Corporation.
This company was first erected in the year one thousand
seven hundred and seven. Their professed intention was
to lend money at legal interest to the poor, upon small
pledges; and to persons of better rank upon an in-
dubitable security of goods impawned. Their capital was
at first limited to thirty thousand pounds; but, by licences
from the crown, they increased it to six hundred thousand pounds, though their charter was never confirmed
by act of Parliament. In the month of October, George
Robinson, esquire, member for Marlow, the cashier, and
John Thompson, warehouse-keeper of the corporation, disappeared in one day. The proprietors, alarmed at this
incident, held several general courts, and appointed a
committee to inspect the state of their affairs. They reported, that for a capital of above five hundred thousand
pounds no equivalent was found; inasmuch as their effects
did not amount to the value of thirty thousand, the

remainder having been embezzled by means which they could not discover. The proprietors, in a petition to the House of Commons, represented that by the most notorious breach of trust in several persons to whom the care and management of their affairs were committed, the corporation had been defrauded of the greatest part of their capital; and that many of the petitioners were reduced to the utmost degree of misery and distress: they therefore prayed, that as they were unable to detect the combinations of those who had ruined them, or to bring the delinquents to justice, without the aid of the power and authority of Parliament, the House would vouchsafe to inquire into the state of the corporation and the conduct of their managers, and give such relief to the petitioners as to the House should seem meet. The petition was graciously received, and a secret committee appointed to proceed on the inquiry. They soon discovered a most iniquitous scene of fraud, which had been acted by Robinson and Thompson, in concert with some of the directors, for embezzling the capital and cheating the proprietors. Many persons of rank and quality were concerned in this infamous conspiracy: some of the first characters in the nation did not escape suspicion and censure. Sir Robert Sutton and Sir Archibald Grant were expelled the House of Commons, as having had a considerable share in those fraudulent practices: a bill was brought in to restrain them and other delinquents from leaving the kingdom, or alienating their effects. In the mean time, the committee received a letter from Signior John Angelo Belloni, an eminent banker at Rome, giving them to understand, that Thompson was secured in that city, with all his papers, and confined to the castle of St. Angelo; and that the papers were transmitted to his correspondent at Paris, who would deliver them up, on certain conditions stipulated in favour of the prisoner. This letter was considered as an artifice to insinuate a favourable opinion of the pretender, as if he had taken measures for securing Thompson, from his zeal for justice, and affection for the English people. On this supposition, the proposals were rejected with disdain; and both Houses concurred in an order that the letter should be burned at the Royal Exchange, by the hands

of the common hangman. The Lower House resolved,
that it was an insolent and audacious libel, absurd and
contradictory; that the whole transaction was a scandalous artifice, calculated to delude the unhappy, and
to disguise and conceal the wicked practices of the professed enemies to his majesty's person, crown, and dignity.

No motion, during this session, produced such a warm
contest as did that of Sir Robert Walpole, when, after
a long preamble, he proposed that the duties on salt,
which about two years before had been abolished, should
now be revived, and granted to his majesty, his heirs, and
successors, for the term of three years. In order to
sweeten this proposal, he declared that the land-tax for
the ensuing year should be reduced to one shilling in
the pound. All the members of the country party were
immediately in commotion. They expressed their surprise at the grossness of the imposition. They observed
that two years had scarce elapsed since the king, in a
speech from the throne, had exhorted them to abolish
some of the taxes that were the most burdensome to the
poor: the House was then of opinion, that the tax upon
salt was the most burdensome and the most pernicious to
the trade of the kingdom, of all the impositions to which
the poor were subjected, and therefore it was taken off;
but that no good reason could be produced for altering
their opinion so suddenly, and resolving to grind the faces
of the poor, in order to ease a few rich men of the landed
interest. They affirmed, that the most general taxes are
not always the least burdensome : that after a nation is
obliged to extend their taxes farther than the luxuries
of their country, those taxes that can be raised with the
least charge to the public are the most convenient and
easiest to the people ; but they ought carefully to avoid
taxing those things which are necessary for the subsistence of the poor. The price of all necessaries being thus
enhanced, the wages of the tradesman and manufacturer
must be increased ; and where these are high, the manufacturers will be undersold by those of cheaper countries.
The trade must of consequence be ruined ; and it is not
to be supposed that the landed gentleman would choose
to save a shilling in the pound from the land-tax, by
means of an expedient that would ruin the manufacturers
of his country, and decrease the value of his own fortune.

They alleged that the salt-tax particularly affected the poor, who could not afford to eat fresh provisions; and that, as it formerly occasioned murmurs and discontents among the lower class of people, the revival of it would, in all probability, exasperate them into open sedition. They observed, that while it was exacted in England, a great number of merchants sent their ships to Ireland to be victualled for their respective voyages; that, since it had been abolished, many experiments had been successfully tried with salt for the improvement of agriculture, which would be entirely defeated by the revival of this imposition. They suggested that the land-tax was raised at a very small expense, and subject to no fraud, whereas that upon salt would employ a great number of additional officers in the revenue, wholly depending upon the ministry, whose influence in elections they would proportionably increase. They even hinted, that this consideration was one powerful motive for proposing the revival of an odious tax, which was in effect an excise, and would be deemed a step towards a general excise upon all sorts of provisions. Finally, they demonstrated that the salt-tax introduced numberless frauds and perjuries in different articles of traffic. Sir Robert Walpole endeavoured to obviate all these objections in a long speech, which was minutely answered and refuted in every article by Mr. Pulteney. Nevertheless, the question being put, the minister's motion was carried in the affirmative, and the duty revived: yet, before the bill passed, divers motions were made, and additional clauses proposed, by the members in the opposition. New debates were raised on every new objection, and the courtiers were obliged to dispute their ground by inches.

Mr. Pulteney's name struck out of the list of privy-councillors.

The pension bill was revived, and for the third time rejected in the House of Lords. A bill for the encouragement of the sugar colonies passed through the Lower House with great difficulty, but was lost among the Peers: another, for the better securing the freedom of Parliaments, by further qualifying members to sit in the House of Commons, was read the third time and thrown out upon the question. A committee had been appointed to inquire into a sale of the estate which had belonged to the late Earl of Derwentwater. It appeared by the report, that the sale had been fraudulent: a bill was prepared to make it void: Dennis Bond, esquire, and Serjeant Birch, commissioners for the sale of the forfeited estates, were declared guilty of notorious breach of trust, and expelled the House, of which they were members: George Robinson, esquire, underwent the same sentence, on account of the part he acted in the Charitable Corporation, as he and Thompson had neglected to surrender themselves, according to the terms of a bill which had passed for that purpose. During this session, five members of Parliament were expelled for the most sordid acts of knavery; a sure sign of national degeneracy and dishonour. All the supplies were granted, and, among other articles, the sum of two-and-twenty thousand six hundred and ninety-four pounds, seven shillings, and sixpence, for the agio or difference of the subsidies payable to the crown of Denmark, in pursuance of the treaty subsisting between the late king and that monarch; but this was not obtained without a violent dispute. Mr. Pulteney, who bore a considerable share in all these debates, became in a little time so remarkable as to be thought worthy of a very particular mark of his majesty's displeasure. The king, on the first day of July, called for the council-book, and with his own hand struck the name of William Pulteney, esquire, out of the list of privy-councillors; his majesty further ordered him to be put out of all the commissions of the peace. The several lord lieutenants, from whom he had received deputations, were commanded to revoke them; and the lord chancellor and secretaries of state were directed to give the necessary orders for that purpose.

Nor did the House of Peers tamely and unanimously submit to the measures of the ministry. The pension bill being read, was again rejected, and a protest entered. A debate arose about the number of standing forces; and the Earl of Chesterfield argued for the court motion. The Earl of Oxford moved that they might be reduced to twelve thousand effective men. The Earl of Winchelsea observed, that a standing army rendered ministers of state more daring than otherwise they would be, in contriving and executing projects that were grievous to the people: schemes that never could enter into the heads of any but those who were drunk with excess of

The king sets out for Hanover.

power. The Marquis of Tweeddale, in reasoning against such a number as the ministry proposed, took occasion to observe, that not one shilling of the forfeited estates was ever applied to the use of the public: he likewise took notice, that the eighteen thousand men, demanded as a standing force, were modelled in such a manner, that they might be speedily augmented to forty thousand men on any emergency. The Duke of Argyle endeavoured to demonstrate the danger of depending for the safety of the kingdom upon an undisciplined militia, a fleet, or an army of auxiliaries. Then he represented the necessity of having recourse to a regular army in case of invasion; and after all acknowledged, that the number proposed was no way sufficient for that purpose. All his arguments were answered and refuted in an excellent speech by Lord Carteret: nevertheless, victory declared for the minister. The Parliament having granted every branch of the supply, towards the payment of which they borrowed a sum from the sinking-fund, and passed divers other acts for the encouragement of commerce and agriculture, the king, on the first day of June, gave the royal assent to the bills that were prepared, and closed the session, after having informed both Houses that the States-General had acceded to the treaty of Vienna; that he had determined to visit his German dominions, and to leave the queen regent in his absence. He accordingly set out for Hanover in the beginning of June. By this time the pragmatic sanction was confirmed by the diet of the empire, though not without a formal protest by the Electors Palatine, Bavaria, and Saxony.

CHAPTER XVI.

THE most remarkable incident that distinguished this year in England was a very uncommon instance of suicide; an act of despair so frequent among the English, that in other countries it is objected to them as a national reproach. Though it may be generally termed the effect of lunacy proceeding from natural causes operating on the human body, in some few instances it seems to have been the result of cool deliberation. Richard Smith, a bookbinder, and prisoner for debt within the liberties of

the King's Bench, persuaded his wife to follow his example in making away with herself, after they had murdered their little infant. This wretched pair were in
the month of April found hanging in their bedchamber,
at about a yard's distance from each other; and in a
separate apartment the child lay dead in a cradle. They
left two papers enclosed in a short letter to their land-
lord, whose kindness they implored in favour of their
dog and cat. They even left money to pay the porter
who should carry the enclosed papers to the person for
whom they were addressed. In one of these the husband
thanked that person for the marks of friendship he had
received at his hands; and complained of the ill offices
he had undergone from a different quarter. The other
paper, subscribed by the husband and wife, contained
the reasons which induced them to act such a tragedy
on themselves and their offspring. This letter was
altogether surprising for the calm resolution, the good
humour, and the propriety, with which it was written.
They declared, that they withdrew themselves from
poverty and rags; evils that, through a train of unlucky
accidents, were become inevitable. They appealed to
their neighbours for the industry with which they had
endeavoured to earn a livelihood. They justified the
murder of their child, by saying it was less cruelty to
take her with them, than to leave her friendless in the
world, exposed to ignorance and misery. They professed
their belief and confidence in an Almighty God, the
fountain of goodness and beneficence, who could not
possibly take delight in the misery of his creatures:
they, therefore, resigned up their lives to him without
any terrible apprehensions: submitting themselves to
those ways which, in his goodness, he should appoint
after death. These unfortunate suicides had been always
industrious and frugal, invincibly honest, and remarkable
for conjugal affection.

Trustees having been appointed by charter to superin-
tend a new settlement in Georgia, situated to the southward of Carolina in America, Mr. Oglethorpe, as general,
and governor of the province, embarked at Gravesend,
with a number of poor families to plant that colony. The
King of Spain having equipped a very powerful arma-

ment, the fleet sailed on the fourth day of June from the road of Alicant, under the command of the Count de Montemar, and arrived on the coast of Barbary in the neighbourhood of Oran, where a considerable body of troops was landed without much opposition. Next day, however, they were attacked by a numerous army of Moors, over whom they obtained a complete victory. The bey or governor of Oran immediately retired with his garrison, and the Spaniards took possession of the place, from which they had been driven in the year one thousand seven hundred and eight. The strong fort of Mazalaquivir was likewise surrendered to the victors at the first summons; so that this expedition answered all the views with which it had been projected. Victor Amadeus, the abdicated King of Sardinia, having, at the instigation of his wife, engaged in some intrigues, in order to re-ascend the throne, his son, the reigning king, ordered his person to be seized at Montcalier, and conveyed to Rivoli, under a strong escort. His wife, the Marchioness de Spigno, was conducted to Seva. The old king's confessor, his physician, and eight-and-forty persons of distinction were imprisoned. The citadel of Turin was secured with a strong garrison; and new instructions were given to the governor and senate of Chamberri. The dispute which had long subsisted between the King of Prussia and the young Prince of Orange, touching the succession to the estates possessed by King William III. as head of the house of Orange, was at last accommodated by a formal treaty signed at Berlin and Dierin. The Dutch were greatly alarmed about this time with an apprehension of being overwhelmed by an inundation, occasioned by worms, which were said to have consumed the piles and timber-work that supported their dykes. They prayed and fasted with uncommon zeal, in terror of this calamity, which they did not know how to avert in any other manner. At length they were delivered from their fears by a hard frost, which effectually destroyed those dangerous animals. About this time, Mr. Dieden, plenipotentiary from the Elector of Hanover, received, in the name of his master, the investiture of Bremen and Verden from the hands of the emperor.

CHAP.
XVI.

1732.
Meeting of
the Parlia-
ment.
The history of England at this period cannot be very
interesting, as it chiefly consists in an annual revolution
of debates in Parliament; debates, in which the same
arguments perpetually recur on the same subjects. When
the session was opened on the sixteenth day of January,
the king declared, that the situation of affairs, both at
home and abroad, rendered it unnecessary for him to lay
before the two Houses any other reasons for calling them
together but the ordinary despatch of the public business,
and his desire of receiving their advice in such affairs as
should require the care and consideration of Parliament.
The motion made in the House of Commons for an address of thanks implied, that they should express their
satisfaction at the present situation of affairs both at
home and abroad. The motion was carried, notwithstanding the opposition of those who observed, that the
nation had very little reason to be pleased with the
present posture of affairs; that the French were employed
in fortifying and restoring the harbour of Dunkirk, contrary to the faith of the most solemn treaties; that the
British merchants had received no redress for the depredations committed by the Spaniards; that the commerce
of England daily decreased; that no sort of trade throve
but the traffic of 'Change-alley, where the most abo-
minable frauds were practised; and that every session of
Parliament opened a new scene of villany and imposition.

Address to
the king
touching
the Spanish
depreda-
tions.
The pension bill was once more revived, and lost again
in the House of Peers. All the reasons formerly advanced against a standing army were now repeated;
and a reduction of the number insisted upon with such
warmth, that the ministerial party were obliged to have
recourse to the old phantom of the pretender. Sir Ar-
cher Croft said a continuation of the same number of
forces was the more necessary, because, to his knowledge,
popery was increasing very fast in the country; for, in
one parish which he knew, there were seven popish
priests; and that the danger from the pretender was the
more to be feared, because they did not know but he
was then breeding his son a Protestant. Sir Robert Walpole observed, that a reduction of the army was the chief
thing wished for and desired by all the Jacobites in the
kingdom: that no reduction had ever been made but

what gave fresh hopes to that party, and encouraged them to raise tumults against the government; and he did not doubt but that, if they should resolve to reduce any part of the army, there would be post-horses employed that very night to carry the good news beyond sea to the pretender. His brother Horatio added, that the number of troops then proposed was absolutely necessary to support his majesty's government, and would be necessary as long as the nation enjoyed the happiness of having the present illustrious family on the throne. The futility, the self-contradiction, and the ridiculous absurdity of these suggestions were properly exposed: nevertheless, the army was voted without any reduction. Sir Wilfred Lawson having made a motion for an address to the king, to know what satisfaction had been made by Spain for the depredations committed on the British merchants, it was after a violent debate approved, and the address presented. The king in answer to this remonstrance gave them to understand, that the meeting of the commissioners of the two crowns had been so long delayed by unforeseen accidents, that the conferences were not opened till the latter end of the preceding February: and that as the courts of London and Madrid had agreed that the term of three years stipulated for finishing the commission should be computed from their first meeting, a perfect account of their proceedings could not as yet be laid before the House of Commons. A bill had been long depending for granting encouragement to the sugar colonies in the West Indies; but, as it was founded upon a prohibition that would have put a stop to all commerce between the French islands and the British settlements in North America, it met with a very warm opposition from those who had the prosperity of those northern colonies at heart. But the bill being patronized and supported by the court interest, surmounted all objections; and afterwards passed into a law. While the Commons deliberated upon the supply, Sir Robert Walpole moved, that five hundred thousand pounds should be issued out of the sinking fund for the service of the ensuing year. Sir William Wyndham, Mr. Pulteney, and Sir John Barnard, expatiated upon the iniquity of pillaging a sacred deposit, solemnly appropriated to the discharge of the national debt. They might have demonstrated the egregious folly of a measure, by which the public, for a little temporary ease, lost the advantage of the accumulating interest which would have arisen from the sinking fund if properly managed and reserved. All objections vanished before the powers of ministerial influence, which nothing now could check but the immediate danger of popular commotion. Such hazardous interposition actually defeated a scheme which had been adopted by the minister, and even before its appearance alarmed all the trading part of the nation.

The excise scheme proposed by Sir Robert Walpole.
The House having resolved itself into a committee, to deliberate upon the most proper methods for the better security and improvement of the duties and revenues charged upon tobacco and wines, all the papers relating to these duties were submitted to the perusal of the members: the commissioners of the customs and excise were ordered to attend the House, the avenues of which were crowded with multitudes of people; and the members in the opposition waited impatiently for a proposal in which they thought the liberties of their country so deeply interested. In a word, there had been a call of the House on the preceding day. The session was frequent and full; and both sides appeared ready and eager for the contest when Sir Robert Walpole broached his design. He took notice of the arts which had been used to prejudice the people against his plan before it was known. He affirmed that the clamours occasioned by these prejudices had originally risen from smugglers and fraudulent dealers, who had enriched themselves by cheating the public; and that these had been strenuously assisted and supported by another set of men, fond of every opportunity to stir up the people of Great Britain to mutiny and sedition. He expatiated on the frauds that were committed in that branch of the revenue arising from the duties on tobacco; upon the hardships to which the American planters were subjected by the heavy duties payable on importation, as well as by the ill usage they had met with from their factors and correspondents in England, who, from being their servants, were now become their masters; upon the injury done to the fair trader; and the loss sustained by the public with

respect to the revenue. He asserted that the scheme he was about to propose would remove all these inconveniences, prevent numberless frauds, perjuries, and false entries, and add two or three hundred thousand pounds per annum to the public revenue. He entered into a long detail of frauds practised by the knavish dealers in those commodities: he recited the several acts of Parliament that related to the duties on wine and tobacco: he declared he had no intention to promote a general excise: he endeavoured to obviate some objections that might be made to his plan, the nature of which he at length explained. He proposed to join the laws of excise to those of the customs: that the further subsidy of three farthings per pound charged upon imported tobacco should be still levied at the custom-house, and payable to his majesty's civil-list as heretofore: that then the tobacco should be lodged in warehouses, to be appointed for that purpose by the commissioners of the excise: that the keeper of each warehouse, appointed likewise by the commissioners, should have one lock and key, and the merchant-importer have another: and that the tobacco should be thus secured until the merchant should find vent for it, either by exportation or home consumption : that the part designed for exportation should be weighed at the custom-house, discharged of the three farthings per pound which had been paid at its first importation, and then exported without further trouble : that the portion destined for home consumption should, in presence of the warehouse-keeper, be delivered to the purchaser, upon his paying the inland duty of fourpence per pound weight to the proper officer appointed to receive it ; by which means the merchant would be eased of the inconvenience of paying the duty upon importation, or of granting bonds and finding sureties for the payment, before he had found a market for the commodity ; that all penalties and forfeitures, so far as they formerly belonged to the crown, should for the future be applied to the use of the public : that appeals in this, as well as in all other cases relating to the excise, should be heard and determined by two or three of the judges, to be named by his majesty ; and in the country by the judge of assize upon the next circuit, who should hear and determine such appeals in the most

CHAP.
XVI.

summary manner, without the formality of proceedings in courts of law or equity.

1732.
Opposition
to the
scheme.

Such was the substance of the famous excise scheme, in favour of which Sir Robert Walpole moved, that the duties and subsidies on tobacco should from and after the twenty-fourth day of June cease and determine. The debate which ensued was managed and maintained by all the able speakers on both sides of the question. Sir Robert Walpole was answered by Mr. Perry, member for the city of London. Sir Paul Methuen joined in the opposition. Sir John Barnard, another representative of London, distinguished himself in the same cause. He was supported by Mr. Pulteney, Sir William Wyndham, and other patriots. The scheme was espoused by Sir Philip Yorke, appointed lord chief justice of the king's bench, and ennobled in the course of the ensuing year. Sir Joseph Jekyll approved of the project, which was likewise strenuously defended by Lord Hervey, Sir Thomas Robinson, Sir William Yonge, Mr. Pelham, and Mr. Winnington, which last excelled all his contemporaries of the ministry in talents and address. Those who argued against the scheme accused the minister of having misrepresented the frauds, and made false calculations. With respect to the supposed hardships under which the planters were said to labour, they affirmed that no planter had ever dreamed of complaining, until instigated by letters and applications from London : that this scheme, far from relieving the planters, would expose the factors to such grievous oppression, that they would not be able to continue the trade, consequently the planters would be entirely ruined ; and, after all, it would not prevent those frauds against which it was said to be provided : that from the examination of the commissioners of the customs, it appeared that those frauds did not exceed forty thousand pounds per annum, and might in a great measure be abolished, by a due execution of the laws in being ; consequently this scheme was unnecessary, would be ineffectual in augmenting the revenue, destructive to trade, and dangerous to the liberties of the subject, as it tended to promote a general excise, which was in all countries considered as a grievous oppression. They suggested that it would produce an additional swarm of excise-officers and warehouse-keepers, appointed and paid by the treasury, so as to multiply the dependents on the crown, and enable it still further to influence the freedom of elections: that the traders would become slaves to excisemen and warehouse-keepers, as they would be debarred all access to their commodities, except at certain hours, when attended by those officers: that the merchant, for every quantity of tobacco he could sell, would be obliged to make a journey, or send a messenger to the office for a permit, which could not be obtained without trouble, expense, and delay: and that, should a law be enacted in consequence of this motion, it would in all probability be some time or other used as a precedent for introducing excise laws into every branch of the revenue; in which case the liberty of Great Britain would be no more. In the course of this debate, Sir Robert Walpole took notice of the multitudes which had beset all the approaches to the House. He said it would be an easy task for a designing seditious person to raise a tumult and disorder among them: that gentlemen might give them what name they should think fit, and affirm they were come as humble suppliants; but he knew whom the law called sturdy beggars: and those who brought them to that place could not be certain but that they might behave in the same manner. This insinuation was resented by Sir John Barnard, who observed that merchants of character had a right to come down to the court of requests, and lobby of the House of Commons, in order to solicit their friends and acquaintance against any scheme or project which they might think prejudicial to their commerce: that when he came into the House, he saw none but such as deserved the appellation of sturdy beggars as little as the honourable gentleman himself, or any gentleman whatever. After a warm dispute the motion was carried by a majority of sixty-one voices. Several resolutions were founded on the proposal: and to these the House agreed, though not without another violent contest. The resolutions produced a bill, against which petitions were preferred by the lord mayor, aldermen, and common council of London, the city of Coventry, and Nottingham. A motion was made that counsel

should be heard for the city of London; but it was rejected by the majority, and the petitions were ordered
to lie upon the table. Had the minister encountered
no opposition but that which appeared within doors, his
project would have certainly been carried into execution: but the whole nation was alarmed, and clamoured
loudly against the excise bill. The populace still crowded
around Westminster-hall, blocking up all the avenues
to the House of Commons. They even insulted the persons of those members who had voted for the ministry
on this occasion; and Sir Robert Walpole began to be
in fear of his life. He, therefore, thought proper to
drop the design, by moving that the second reading of
the bill might be postponed till the twelfth day of June.
Then, complaint being made of the insolence of the
populace, who had maltreated several members, divers
resolutions were taken against those tumultuous crowds,
and their abettors; these resolves were communicated
to the lord mayor of London, the sheriff of Middlesex,
and the high-bailiff of Westminster. Some individuals
were apprehended in the court of requests, as having
fomented the disturbances; but they were soon released.
The miscarriage of the bill was celebrated with public
rejoicings in London and Westminster; and the minister
was burned in effigy by the populace. After the miscarriage of the excise scheme, the House unanimously
resolved to inquire into the frauds and abuses in the
customs; and a committee of twenty-one persons was
chosen by ballot for this purpose.

Bill for a dower to the princess royal.

The subsequent debates of this session were occasioned
by a bill to prevent the infamous practice of stock-jobbing, which with great difficulty made its way to the
House of Lords, who proposed some amendments, in
consequence of which it was laid aside; and succeeded
by another bill establishing a lottery, to raise five hundred thousand pounds for the relief of those who had
suffered by the charitable corporation. After having
undergone some alterations, it passed through both
Houses, and obtained the royal assent. The king, by a
message to Parliament, had signified his intention to give
the princess royal in marriage to the Prince of Orange,
promising himself their concurrence and assistance, that

he might be enabled to bestow such a portion with his eldest daughter as should be suitable to the occasion. The Commons immediately resolved, that out of the moneys arising from the sale of lands in the island of St. Christopher's, his majesty should be empowered to apply fourscore thousand pounds, as a marriage dower for his daughter; and a clause for this purpose was inserted in the bill, for enabling his majesty to apply five hundred thousand pounds out of the sinking fund for the service of the current year.

The opposition in the House of Lords was still more animated, though ineffectual. The debates chiefly turned upon the pension bill, the number of land-forces, and a motion made by Lord Bathurst for an account of the produce of the forfeited estates which had belonged to the directors of the South-Sea Company. The trustees for these estates had charged themselves' with a great sum of money, and the lords in the opposition thought they had a right to know how it had been disposed. The ministry had reasons to stifle this inquiry; and therefore opposed it with all their vigour. Nevertheless, the motion was carried, after a warm dispute, and the directors of the South-Sea Company were ordered to lay the accounts before the House. From this it appeared that the large sums of money arising from the forfeited estates had been distributed among the proprietors by way of dividend, even before recourse was had to Parliament for directions in what manner that produce should be applied : Lord Bathurst therefore moved for a resolution of the House, that the disposal of this money by way of dividend, without any order or direction of a general court for that purpose, was a violation of the act of Parliament made for the disposal thereof, and a manifest injustice done to the proprietors of that stock. The Duke of Newcastle, in order to gain time, moved, that as the account was confused, and almost unintelligible, the present directors of the company might be ordered to lay before the House a further and more distinct account of the manner in which the money had been disposed. A violent contest ensued, in the course of which the House divided, and of fifty-seven peers who voted for the delay, forty-six were such as enjoyed preferment in the

CHAP.
XVI.

1733.

Debates in
the House
of Lords
concerning
the estates
of the late
directors of
the South-
Sea com-
pany.

x 2

church, commissions in the army, or civil employments under the government. At length Lord Bathurst waved his motion for that time: then the House ordered that the present and former directors of the South-Sea Company, together with the late inspectors of their accounts, should attend and be examined. They were accordingly interrogated, and gave so little satisfaction, that Lord Bathurst moved for a committee of inquiry; but the question being put, was carried in the negative: yet a very strong protest was entered by the lords in the opposition. The next subject of altercation was the bill for misapplying part of the produce of the sinking fund. It was attacked with all the force of argument, wit, and declamation, by the Earl of Strafford, Lords Bathurst and Carteret, and particularly by the Earl of Chesterfield, who had by this time resigned his staff of lord-steward of the household, and renounced all connexion with the ministry. Lord Bathurst moved for a resolution, importing that in the opinion of the House, the sinking fund ought for the future to be applied, in time of peace and public tranquillity, to the redemption of those taxes which were most prejudicial to the trade, most burdensome on the manufactures, and most oppressive on the poor of the nation. This motion was overruled, and the bill adopted by the majority. On the eleventh day of June, the king gave the royal assent to the bills that were prepared, and closed the session with a speech, in which he took notice of the wicked endeavours that had been lately used to inflame the minds of the people, by the most unjust misrepresentations.

Double
election of
a King of
Poland.

Europe was now involved in fresh troubles by a vacancy on the throne of Poland. Augustus died at Warsaw in the end of January, and the neighbouring powers were immediately in commotion. The Elector of Saxony, son to the late king, and Stanislaus, whose daughter was married to the French monarch, declared themselves candidates for the Polish throne. The emperor, the czarina, and the King of Prussia, espoused the interest of the Saxons; the King of France supported the pretensions of his father-in-law. The foreign ministers at Warsaw forthwith began to form intrigues among the electors: the Marquis de Monti, ambassador from France, exerted himself so successfully that he soon gained over the primate, and a majority of the Catholic dietines, to the interests of Stanislaus; while the imperial and Russian troops hovered on the frontiers of Poland. The French king no sooner understood that a body of the emperor's forces was encamped at Silesia, than he ordered the Duke of Berwick to assemble an army on the Rhine, and take measures for entering Germany, in case the imperialists should march into Poland. A French fleet set sail for Dantzic, while Stanislaus travelled through Germany in disguise to Poland, and concealed himself in the house of the French ambassador at Warsaw. As the day of election approached, the imperial, Russian, and Prussian ministers delivered in their several declarations, by way of protest against the contingent election of Stanislaus, as a person proscribed, disqualified, depending upon a foreign power, and connected with the Turks and other infidels. The Russian General Lasci entered Poland at the head of fifty thousand men : the diet of the election was opened with the usual ceremony on the twenty-fifth day of August. Prince Viesazowski, chief of the Saxon interest, retired to the other side of the Vistula with three thousand men, including some of the nobility who adhered to that party. Nevertheless, the primate proceeded to the election : Stanislaus was unanimously chosen king ; and appeared in the electoral field, where he was received with loud acclamations. The opposite party soon increased to ten thousand men ; protested against the election, and joined the Russian army, which advanced by speedy marches. King Stanislaus finding himself unable to cope with such adversaries, retired with the primate and French ambassador to Dantzic, leaving the Palatine of Kiow at Warsaw. This general attacked the Saxon palace, which was surrendered upon terms : then the soldiers and inhabitants plundered the houses belonging to the grandees who had declared for Augustus, as well as the hotel of the Russian minister. In the mean time, the Poles, who had joined the Muscovites, finding it impracticable to pass the Vistula before the expiration of the time fixed for the session of the diet, erected a kelo at Cracow, where the Elector of Saxony was chosen and proclaimed by the Bishop of

CHAP.
XVI.

1733.

Cracow, King of Poland, under the name of Augustus III. on the sixth day of October. They afterwards passed the river, and the Palatine of Kiow retiring towards Cracow, they took possession of Warsaw, where in their turn they plundered the palaces and houses belonging to the opposite party.

The Kings of France, Spain, and Sardinia join against the emperor.

During these transactions, the French king concluded a treaty with Spain and Sardinia, by which those powers agreed to declare war against the emperor. Manifestos were published reciprocally by all the contracting powers. The Duke of Berwick passed the Rhine in October, and undertook the siege of fort Kehl, which in a few days was surrendered on capitulation ; then he repassed the river and returned to Versailles. The king of Sardinia having declared war against the emperor, joined a body of French forces commanded by Mareschal de Villars, and drove the imperialists out of the Milanese. His imperial majesty, dreading the effects of such a powerful confederacy against him, offered to compromise all differences with the crown of Spain, under the mediation of the King of Great Britain ; and Mr. Keen, the British minister at Madrid, proposed an accommodation. Philip expressed his acknowledgments to the King of England, declaring, however, that the emperor's advances were too late ; and that his own resolutions were already taken. Nevertheless, he sent orders to the Count de Montijo, his ambassador at London, to communicate to his Britannic majesty the motives which had induced him to take these resolutions. In the mean time he detached a powerful armament to Italy, where they invested the imperial fortress of Aula, the garrison of which was obliged to surrender themselves prisoners of war. The republic of Venice declared she would take no share in the disputes of Italy ; the States-General signed a neutrality with the French king for the Austrian Netherlands, without consulting the emperor or the king of Great Britain ; and the English councils seemed to be altogether pacific.

The Prince of Orange arrives in England.

In November the Prince of Orange arrived at Greenwich, in order to espouse the princess royal : but the marriage was postponed on account of his being taken ill ; and he repaired to Bath, in Somersetshire, to drink

the waters for the recovery of his strength. Henrietta,
the young Duchess of Marlborough, dying about this
time, the title devolved to her sister's son, the Earl of
Sunderland. Lord King resigning his office of chancellor,
it was conferred upon Mr. Talbot, solicitor-general, together with the title of baron; a promotion that reflected
honour upon those by whom it was advised. He possessed the spirit of a Roman senator, the elegance of an
Atticus, and the integrity of a Cato. At the meeting of
the Parliament in January, the king told them, in his
speech, that though he was no way engaged in the war
which had begun to rage in Europe, except by the good
offices he had employed among the contending powers,
he could not sit regardless of the present events, or be
unconcerned for the consequences of a war undertaken
and supported by such a powerful alliance. He said, he
had thought proper to take time to examine the facts
alleged on both sides, and to wait the result of the
councils of those powers that were more immediately
interested in the consequences of the rupture. He declared he would concert with his allies, more particularly
with the States-General of the United Provinces, such
measures as should be thought most advisable for their
common safety, and for restoring the peace of Europe.
In the mean time, he expressed his hope that they would
make such provision as should secure his kingdom, rights,
and possessions from all dangers and insults, and maintain the respect due to the British nation. He said, that
whatever part it might in the end be most reasonable
for him to act, it would in all views be necessary, when
all Europe was preparing for arms, to put his kingdoms
in a posture of defence. The motion for an address of
thanks produced, as usual, a debate in both Houses, which,
it must be owned, appears to have proceeded from a spirit
of cavilling, rather than from any reasonable cause of
objection.

The House of Commons resolved to address his ma- Altercation in the House of Commons.
jesty for a copy of the treaty of Vienna. Sir John Rush-
out moved for another, desiring that the letters and instructions relating to the execution of the treaty of Seville
should be submitted to the inspection of the Commons;
but after a hard struggle, it was overruled. The next

motion was made by Mr. Sandys, a gentleman who had for some time appeared strenuous in the opposition, and wrangled with great perseverance. He proposed that the House should examine the instructions which had been given to the British minister in Poland some years before the death of King Augustus, that they might be the better able to judge of the causes which produced this new rupture among the powers of Europe. The motion being opposed by all the court members, a contest ensued, in the course of which Mr. Pulteney compared the ministry to an empiric, and the constitution of England to his patient. This pretender in physic (said he) being consulted, tells the distempered person, there were but two or three ways of treating his disease: and he was afraid that none of them would succeed. A vomit might throw him into convulsions that would occasion immediate death; a purge might bring on a diarrhœa that would carry him off in a short time: and he had been already bled so much, and so often, that he could bear it no longer. The unfortunate patient, shocked at this declaration, replies, "Sir, you have always pretended to be a regular doctor, but now I find you are an arrant quack. I had an excellent constitution when I first fell into your hands, but you have quite destroyed it: and now I have no other chance for saving my life, but by calling for the help of some regular physician." In the debate, the members on both sides seemed to wander from the question, and indulged themselves with ludicrous personalities. Mr. H. Walpole took occasion to say, that the opposition treated the ministry as he himself was treated by some of his acquaintance with respect to his dress. "If I am in plain clothes (said he) then they call me a slovenly, dirty fellow; and if by chance I wear a laced suit, they cry, What, shall such an awkward fellow wear fine clothes?" He continued to sport in this kind of idle buffoonery. He compared the present administration to a ship at sea. As long as the wind was fair, and proper for carrying us to our destined port, the word was "Steady, steady!" but when the wind began to shift and change, the word was necessarily altered to "Thus, thus, and no nearer." The motion was overpowered by the majority; and this was the fate of several other pro-

posals made by the members in the opposition. Sir John
Barnard presented a petition from the druggists, and other dealers in tea, complaining of the insults and oppression to which they were subjected by the excise laws, and imploring relief. Sir John and Mr. Perry, another of the city members, explained the grievous hardships which those traders sustained, and moved that the petition might be referred to the consideration of the whole House. They were opposed by Mr. Winnington, Sir W. Yonge, and other partisans of the ministry; and these skirmishes brought on a general engagement of the two parties, in which every weapon of satire, argument, reason, and truth, was wielded against that odious, arbitrary, and oppressive method of collecting the public revenue. Nevertheless the motion in favour of the sufferers was rejected.

When the Commons deliberated upon the supply, Mr. Andrews, deputy-paymaster of the army, moved for an addition of eighteen hundred men to the number of land-forces which had been continued since the preceding year. The members in the opposition disputed this small augmentation with too much heat and eagerness. It must be acknowledged, they were by this time irritated into such personal animosity against the minister, that they resolved to oppose all his measures, whether they might or might not be necessary for the safety and advantage of the kingdom. Nor indeed were they altogether blamable for acting on this maxim, if their sole aim was to remove from the confidence and councils of their sovereign a man whose conduct they thought prejudicial to the interests and liberties of their country. They could not, however, prevent the augmentation proposed ; but they resolved, if they could not wholly stop the career of the ministry, to throw in such a number of rubs as should at least retard their progress. The Duke of Bolton and Lord Cobham had been deprived of the regiments they commanded, because they refused to concur in every project of the administration. It was in consequence of their dismission, that Lord Morpeth moved for a bill to prevent any commission-officer, not above the rank of a colonel, from being removed, unless by a court-martial, or by address of either House of Par-

CHAP.
XVI.

1733.

liament. Such an attack on the prerogative might have succeeded in the latter part of the reign of the first Charles; but at this juncture could not fail to miscarry; yet it was sustained with great vigour and address. When the proposal was set aside by the majority, Mr. Sandys moved for an address to the king, desiring to know who advised his majesty to remove the Duke of Bolton and Lord Cobham from their respective regiments. He was seconded by Mr. Pulteney and Sir William Wyndham: but the ministry, foreseeing another tedious dispute, called for the question, and the motion was carried in the negative. The next source of contention was a bill for securing the freedom of Parliament, by limiting the number of officers in the House of Commons. It was read a first and second time; but, when a motion was made for its being committed, it met with a powerful opposition, and produced a warm debate that issued in a question, which, like the former, passed in the negative. A clergyman having insinuated in conversation that Sir William Milner, baronet, member for York, received a pension from the ministry, the House took cognizance of this report; the clergyman acknowledged at the bar that he might have dropped such a hint from hearsay. The accused member protested, upon his honour, that he never did, nor ever would receive, place, pension, gratuity, or reward from the court, either directly or indirectly, for voting in Parliament, or upon any other account whatever. The accusation was voted false and scandalous, and the accuser taken into custody; but in a few days he was discharged upon his humble petition, and his begging pardon of the member whom he had calumniated. The duty on salt was prolonged for eight years; and a bill passed against stock-jobbing.

Motion for the repeal of the septennial act.

But the subject which of all others employed the eloquence and abilities on both sides to the most vigorous exertion, was a motion made by Mr. Bromley, who proposed that a bill should be brought in for repealing the septennial act, and for the more frequent meeting and calling of Parliaments. The arguments for and against septennial Parliaments have already been stated. The ministry now insisted upon the increase of Papists and Jacobites, which rendered it dangerous to weaken the hands of the government: they challenged the opposition to produce one instance in which the least encroachment had been made on the liberties of the people since the septennial act took place; and they defied the most ingenious malice to prove that his present majesty had ever endeavoured to extend any branch of the prerogative beyond its legal bounds. Sir John Hinde Cotton affirmed, that in many parts of England the Papists had already begun to use all their influence in favour of those candidates who were recommended by the ministers as members in the ensuing Parliament. With respect to his majesty's conduct, he said he would not answer one word; but as to the grievances introduced since the law was enacted for septennial Parliaments, he thought himself more at liberty to declare his sentiments. He asserted, that the septennial law itself was an encroachment on the rights of the people; a law passed by a Parliament that made itself septennial. He observed, that the laws of treason with regard to trials were altered since that period: that in former times a man was tried by a jury of his neighbours, within the county where the crimes alleged against him were said to be committed; but by an act of a septennial Parliament he might be removed and tried in any place where the crown, or rather the ministry, could find a jury proper for their purpose; where the prisoner could not bring any witnesses in his justification, without an expense which, perhaps, his circumstances would not bear. He asked, if the riot act was not an encroachment on the rights of the people? An act by which a little dirty justice of the peace, the meanest and vilest tool a minister can use, who, perhaps, subsists by his being in the commission, and may be deprived of that subsistence at the pleasure of his patron, had it in his power to put twenty or thirty of the best subjects in England to immediate death, without any trial or form but that of reading a proclamation. "Was not the fatal South-Sea scheme (said he) established by the act of a septennial Parliament? And can any man ask, whether that law was attended with any inconvenience? To the glorious catalogue I might have added the late excise bill, if it had passed into a law;

CHAP.
XVI.

1733.
Conclusion
of a re-
markable
speech
by Sir W.
Wyndham.

but, thank Heaven, the septennial Parliament was near expiring before that famous measure was introduced."

Sir William Wyndham concluded an excellent speech, that spoke him the unrivalled orator, the uncorrupted Briton, and the unshaken patriot, in words to this effect: " Let us suppose a man abandoned to all notions of virtue and honour, of no great family, and but a mean fortune, raised to be chief minister of state by the concurrence of many whimsical events; afraid, or unwilling, to trust any but creatures of his own making; lost to all sense of shame and reputation; ignorant of his country's true interest; pursuing no aim but that of aggrandizing himself and his favourites; in foreign affairs trusting none but those who, from the nature of their education, cannot possibly be qualified for the service of their country, or give weight and credit to their negotiations. Let us suppose the true interest of the nation, by such means, neglected or misunderstood, her honour tarnished, her importance lost, her trade insulted, her merchants plundered, and her sailors murdered ; and all these circumstances overlooked, lest his administration should be endangered. Suppose him next possessed of immense wealth, the plunder of the nation, with a Parliament chiefly composed of members whose seats are purchased, and whose votes are bought at the expense of the public treasure. In such a Parliament, suppose all attempts made to inquire into his conduct, or to relieve the nation from the distress which has been entailed upon it by his administration. Suppose him screened by a corrupt majority of his creatures, whom he retains in daily pay, or engages in his particular interest by distributing among them those posts and places which ought never to be bestowed upon any but for the good of the public. Let him plume himself upon his scandalous victory, because he has obtained a Parliament like a packed jury, ready to acquit him at all adventures. Let us suppose him domineering with insolence over all the men of ancient families, over all the men of sense, figure, or fortune, in the nation; as he has no virtue of his own, ridiculing it in others, and endeavouring to destroy or corrupt it in all. With such a minister, and such a Parliament, let us suppose a case which I hope will never happen: a prince upon the throne, uninformed, ignorant, and unacquainted with the inclinations and true interest of his people, weak, capricious, transported with unbounded ambition, and possessed with insatiable avarice. I hope such a case will never occur; but as it possibly may, could any greater curse happen to a nation, than such a prince on the throne, advised, and solely advised, by such a minister, and that minister supported by such a Parliament? The nature of mankind cannot be altered by human laws; the existence of such a prince or such a minister, we cannot prevent by act of Parliament; but the existence of such a Parliament I think we may prevent; as it is much more likely to exist, and may do more mischief while the septennial law remains in force, than if it were repealed: therefore, I am heartily for its being repealed." Notwithstanding the most warm, the most nervous, the most pathetic remonstrances in favour of the motion, the question was put, and it was suppressed by mere dint of number.

The triumph of the ministry was still more complete in the success of a message delivered from the crown in the latter end of the session, when a great many members of the other party had retired to their respective habitations in the country. Sir Robert Walpole delivered this commission to the House, importing that his majesty might be enabled to augment his forces, if occasion should require such an augmentation, between the dissolution of this Parliament and the election of another. Such an important point, that was said to strike at the foundation of our liberties, was not tamely yielded; but, on the contrary, contested with uncommon ardour. The motion for taking the message into consideration was carried in the affirmative; and an address presented to the king, signifying their compliance with his desire. In consequence of a subsequent message they prepared and passed a bill, enabling his majesty to settle an annuity of five thousand pounds for life on the princess royal, as a mark of his paternal favour and affection.

The opposition in the House of Peers kept pace with that in the House of Commons, and was supported with equal abilities, under the auspices of the Lords Bathurst and Carteret, the Earls of Chesterfield and Abingdon. The Duke of Marlborough made a motion for a bill to regulate the army, equivalent to that which had been rejected in the Lower House; and it met with the same fate after a warm dispute. Then Lord Carteret moved for an address to the king, that he would be graciously pleased to acquaint the House who advised his majesty to remove the Duke of Bolton and Lord Viscount Cobham from their respective regiments; and what crimes were laid to their charge. This proposal was likewise rejected, at the end of a debate in which the Duke of Argyle observed, that two lords had been removed, but only one soldier lost his commission. Such a great majority of the Scottish representatives had always voted for the ministry, since the accession of the late king, and so many of these enjoyed places and preferments in the gift of the crown, that several attempts were made by the lords in the opposition to prevent for the future the ministerial influence from extending itself to the elections of North Britain. Accordingly two motions for this purpose were made by the Earl of Marchmont and the Duke of Bedford; and sustained by the Earls of Chesterfield, Winchelsea, and Stair, Lords Willoughby de Broke, Bathurst, and Carteret. They were opposed by the Dukes of Newcastle and Argyle, the Earl of Cholmondeley, Earl Paulet, Lord Hervey, now called up by writ to the House of Peers, and Lord Talbot. The question being put on both, they were of course defeated; and the Earl of Stair was deprived of his regiment of dragoons, after having performed the most signal services to the royal family, and exhausted his fortune in supporting the interest and dignity of the crown. Strenuous protests were entered against the decision of the majority concerning the king's message, demanding a power to augment his forces during the recess of Parliament; as also against a bill for enabling his majesty to apply the sum of one million two hundred thousand pounds out of the sinking-fund for the service of the current year. The business of the session being despatched, the king repaired to the House of Lords on the sixteenth day of April, and having passed all the bills that were ready for the royal assent, took leave of this Parliament, with the warmest acknowledgment of their zeal, duty, and affection. It was at first prorogued, then dissolved, and another convoked by the same proclamation. On the fourteenth day of March, the nuptials of the Prince of Orange and the princess royal were solemnized with great magnificence ; and this match was attended with addresses of congratulation to his majesty from different parts of the kingdom.

CHAP.
XVI.
1734.

The powers at war upon the continent acted with surprising vigour. The Russian and Saxon army invested the city of Dantzic, in hopes of securing the person of King Stanislaus. The town was strong, the garrison numerous, and, animated by the examples of the French and Poles, made a very obstinate defence. For some time they were supplied by sea with recruits, arms, and ammunition. On the eleventh day of May a reinforcement of fifteen hundred men was landed from two French ships of war and some transports under fort Wechselmunde, which was so much in want of provisions that they were not admitted ; they therefore re-embarked, and sailed back to Copenhagen. But afterwards a larger number was landed in the same place, and attacked the Russian intrenchments, in order to force their way into the city. They were repulsed in this attempt, but retired in good order. At length the Russian fleet arrived, under the command of Admiral Gordon ; and now the siege was carried on with great fury. Fort Wechselmunde was surrendered ; the French troops capitulated, and were embarked in the Russian ships, to be conveyed to some port in the Baltic. Stanislaus escaped in the disguise of a peasant to Marienwarder in the Prussian territories. The city of Dantzic submitted to the dominion of Augustus III., King of Poland, and was obliged to defray the expense of the war to the Russian general, Count de Munich, who had assumed the command after the siege was begun. The Polish lords at Dantzic signed an act of submission to King Augustus, who, on the tenth day of July, arrived at the convent of Oliva. There a council was held in his presence. The recusant noblemen took the oath which he proposed.

Dantzic besieged by the Russians.

CHAP. XVI.

1734.
Philips-
burgh
taken by
the French.
Don Carlos
takes pos-
session of
Naples.

Then a general amnesty was proclaimed; and the king set out on his return to Dresden.

On the Rhine the French arms bore down all resistance. The Count de Belleisle besieged and took Traerbach. The Duke of Berwick, at the head of sixty thousand men, invested Philipsburgh, while Prince Eugene was obliged to remain on the defensive in the strong camp at Heilbron, waiting for the troops of the empire. On the twelfth day of June, the Duke of Berwick, in visiting the trenches, was killed by a cannon-ball, and the command devolved upon the Marquis d'Asfeldt, who carried on the operations of the siege with equal vigour and capacity. Prince Eugene being joined by the different reinforcements he expected, marched towards the French lines; but found them so strong that he would not hazard an attack; and such precautions taken, that with all his military talents he could not relieve the besieged. At length General Watgenau, the governor, capitulated, after having made a noble defence, and obtained the most honourable conditions. Prince Eugene retired to Heidelberg; and the campaign ended about the beginning of October. The imperial arms were not more successful in Italy. The Infant Don Carlos had received so many invitations from the Neapolitan nobility, that he resolved to take possession of that kingdom. He began his march in February, at the head of the Spanish forces; published a manifesto, declaring he was sent by his father to relieve the kingdom of Naples from the oppression under which it groaned; and entered the capital amidst the acclamations of the people; while the Count de Visconti, the German viceroy, finding himself unable to cope with the invaders, thought proper to retire, after having thrown succours into Gaeta and Capua. When he arrived at Nocera, he began to assemble the militia, with intent to form a camp at Barletta. The Count de Montemar marched with a body of forces against this general, and obtained over him a complete victory at Bitonto in Apuglia, on the twenty-fifth of May, when the imperialists were entirely routed, and a great number of principal officers taken prisoners. Don Carlos being proclaimed, and acknowledged King of Naples, created the Count de Montemar Duke of Bitonto; reduced Gaeta, and all other parts of the king- dom which were garrisoned with imperial troops; and resolved to subdue the island of Sicily. About twenty thousand troops being destined for this expedition were landed in the road of Solanto in August, under the command of the new Duke of Bitonto, who, being favoured by the natives, proceeded in his conquests with great rapidity. The people acknowledged Don Carlos as their sovereign, and took arms in support of his government; so that the imperial troops were driven before them, and the Spaniards possessed the whole kingdom, except Messina, Syracuse, and Trepani, when the infant determined to visit the island in person.

While Don Carlos was thus employed in the conquest of Naples and Sicily, the imperialists were hard pressed in Lombardy by the united forces of France and Piedmont, commanded by the King of Sardinia and the old Mareschal Duke de Villars. In the month of January they undertook the siege of Tortona, which they reduced; while the troops of the emperor began to pour in great numbers into the Mantuan. In the beginning of May, Count Merci, who commanded them, passed the Po in the face of the allies, notwithstanding all the skill of Villars, obliged him to retreat from the banks of that river, and took the Castle of Colorno. The old French general, being taken ill, quitted the army, and retired to Turin, where in a little time he died; and the King of Sardinia retiring to the same place, the command of the allied forces devolved upon the Mareschal de Coigny. The confederates were posted at Sanguina, and the imperialists at Sorbola, when the Count de Merci made a motion to San Prospero, as if he intended either to attack the enemy, or take possession of Parma. The Mareschal de Coigny forthwith made a disposition for an engagement; and, on the twenty-ninth day of June, the imperial general having passed the Parma, began the attack with great impetuosity. He charged in person at the head of his troops, and was killed soon after the battle began. Nevertheless, the prince of Wirtemberg assuming the command, both armies fought with great obstinacy, from eleven in the forenoon till four in the

The impe-
rialists are
again
worsted at
Guastalla.
An edict in
France
compelling
the British
subjects in
that king-
dom to en-
list in the
French
army.

afternoon, when the imperialists retired towards Monte Cirugalo, leaving five thousand men dead on the field of battle, and among these many officers of distinction. The loss of the allies was very considerable, and they reaped no solid fruits from their victory.

The imperial forces retreated to Reggio, and from thence moved to the plains of Carpi, on the right of the Secchia, where they received some reinforcements : then General Count Konigsegg, arriving in the camp, took upon himself the command of the army. His first step was to take post at Quingentolo, by which motion he secured Mirandola, that was threatened with a siege. On the fifteenth of February he forded the river Secchia, and surprised the quarters of Mareschal de Broglio, who escaped in his shirt with great difficulty. The French retired with such precipitation, that they left all their baggage behind, and above two thousand were taken prisoners. They posted themselves under Guastalla, where, on the nineteenth day of the month, they were vigorously attacked by the imperialists, and a general engagement ensued. Konigsegg made several desperate efforts to break the French cavalry, upon which, how- ever, he could make no impression. The infantry on both sides fought with uncommon ardour for six hours, and the field was covered with carnage. At length the imperial general retreated to Lazara, after having lost above five thousand men, including the Prince of Wir- temberg, the Generals Valpareze and Colminero, with many other officers of distinction : nor was the damage sustained by the French greatly inferior to that of the Germans, who repassed the Po, and took post on the banks of the Oglio. The allies crossed the same river, and the Marquis de Mallebois was sent with a detachment to attack Mirandola ; but the imperialists, marching to the relief of the place, compelled him to abandon the enter- prise : then he rejoined his army, which retired under the walls of Cremona, to wait for succours from Don Carlos. So little respect did the French court pay to the British nation at this juncture, that in the month of November, an edict was published at Paris, commanding all the British subjects in France, who were not actually in employment, from the age of eighteen to fifty, to quit

the kingdom in fifteen days, or enlist in some of the
Irish regiments, on pain of being treated as vagabonds,
and sent to the galleys. This edict was executed with
the utmost rigour. The prisons of Paris were crowded
with the subjects of Great Britain, who were surprised
and cut off from all communication with their friends,
and must have perished by cold and hunger, had not
they been relieved by the active charity of the Jansenists. The Earl of Waldegrave, who then resided at
Paris as ambassador from the King of Great Britain,
made such vigorous remonstrances to the French ministry
upon this unheard-of outrage against a nation with which
they had been so long in alliance, that they thought
proper to set the prisoners at liberty, and publish another edict, by which the meaning of the former was
explained away.

While these transactions occurred on the continent,
the King of Great Britain augmented his land-forces;
and warm contests were maintained through the whole
united kingdom in electing representatives for the new
Parliament. But in all these struggles the ministerial
power predominated; and the new members appeared
with the old complexion. The two Houses assembled
on the fourteenth day of January, and Mr. Onslow was
re-elected speaker. The leaders of both parties in all
debates were the self-same persons who had conducted
those of the former Parliament; and the same measures
were pursued in the same manner. The king, in his
speech at the opening of the session, gave them to understand, that he had concerted with the States-General
of the united provinces such measures as were thought
most advisable for their common safety, and for restoring the peace of Europe: that they had considered on
one side the pressing applications made by the imperial
court both in England and Holland for obtaining succours against the powers at war with the House of Austria; and, on the other side, the repeated professions
made by the allies of their sincere disposition to put an
end to the present troubles upon honourable and solid
terms; that he and the States-General had concurred in
a resolution to employ their joint and earnest instances
to bring matters to a speedy and happy accommodation:

that their good offices were at length accepted; and in a short time a plan would be offered to the consideration of all parties engaged in the war, as a basis for a general negotiation for peace. He told them he had used the power vested in him by the last Parliament with great moderation; and concluded a treaty with the crown of Denmark of great importance in the present conjuncture. He observed, that whilst many of the principal powers of Europe were actually engaged in a war, Great Britain must be more or less affected with the consequences; and as the best concerted measures are liable to uncertainty, the nation ought to be prepared against all events. He therefore expressed his hope, that his good subjects would not repine at the necessary means of procuring the blessings of peace and universal tranquillity, or of putting him in a condition to act that part which it might be necessary and incumbent upon him to take. The address of thanks produced a dispute as usual, which ended with an acquiescence in the motion. The House, in a grand committee on the supply, resolved, that thirty thousand seamen should be employed for the service of the ensuing year; and that the land-forces should be augmented to the number of twenty-five thousand seven hundred and forty-four effective men. But these resolutions were not taken without dispute and division. The minister's opponents not only reproduced all the reasons which had been formerly advanced against a standing army, but they opposed this augmentation with extraordinary ardour, as a huge stride towards the establishment of arbitrary power. They refuted those fears of external broils on which the ministry pretended to ground the necessity of such an augmentation; and they exposed the weak conduct of the administration, in having contributed to destroy the balance of power, by assisting Spain against the emperor in Italy, so as to aggrandize the house of Bourbon.

Debate on
a subsidy
to Den-
mark.

Sir William Wyndham moved, that the estimate of the navy for the ensuing year might be referred to a select committee. He expressed his surprise, that notwithstanding the vast sums which had been yearly raised, and the long continuance of the peace, the people had not been quite delivered of any one tax incurred in the preceding war. He said, he could not comprehend how it was possible to find pretences for exposing the nation to such exorbitant charges; and he took notice of some unconscionable articles in the account of the navy debt that lay upon the table. He was seconded by Mr. Sandys, and supported by Sir Joseph Jekyll and Mr. Pulteney; but, after some debate, the motion was carried in the negative. When the new treaty with Denmark fell under consideration in a grand committee, Mr. H. Walpole moved, that the sum of fifty-six thousand two hundred and fifty pounds should be granted to his majesty as a subsidy to the Dane, pursuant to the said treaty, for the service of the ensuing year. The demand did not meet with immediate compliance. All the leaders in the opposition exclaimed against the subsidy as unnecessary and unreasonable. They observed, that as the English had no particular interest of their own for inducing them to engage in the present war, but only the danger to which the balance of power might be exposed by that event; and as all the powers of Europe were as much, if not more, interested than the English in the preservation of that balance, should it ever be really endangered, they would certainly engage in its defence without receiving any valuable consideration from Great Britain; but should the English be always the first to take the alarm upon any rupture, and offer bribes and pensions to all the princes in Europe, the whole charge of preserving that balance would fall upon Great Britain: every state would expect a gratification from her, for doing that which it would otherwise be obliged to do for its own preservation: even the Dutch might at last refuse to assist in trimming this balance, unless Britain should submit to make the grand pensionary of Holland a pensionary of England, and take a number of their forces into English pay. The debate having had its free course, the question was put, and the motion approved by the majority. The ministry allowed a bill to be brought in for limiting the number of officers in the House of Commons; but at the second reading it was rejected upon a division, after a learned debate, in which it appeared that the opposition had gained a valuable auxiliary in the person of Lord Polwarth, son to the Earl of Marchmont,

CHAP.
XVI.

1734.

Petition
of some
Scottish no-
blemen to
the House
of Peers.

a nobleman of elegant parts, keen penetration, and uncommon vivacity, who spoke with all the fluency and
fervour of elocution.

The minority in the House of Lords were not less
vigilant and resolute in detecting and opposing every
measure which they thought would redound to the prejudice of their country. But the most remarkable object
that employed their attention during this session was a
very extraordinary petition, subscribed by the Dukes of
Hamilton, Queensberry, and Montrose, the Earls of Dun-
donald, Marchmont, and Stair, representing that undue
influence had been used for carrying on the election of
the sixteen peers for Scotland. The Duke of Bedford,
who delivered their petition to the House, proposed a
day for taking it into consideration; and to this they
agreed. It was afterwards moved, that the consideration
of it should be adjourned to a short day, before which
the petitioners should be ordered to declare whether they
intended to controvert the last election of all the sixteen
peers, or the election of any, and which of them. This
affair was of such an unprecedented nature, that the
House seemed to be divided in opinion about the manner
in which they ought to proceed. The partisans of the
ministry would have willingly stifled the inquiry in the
beginning; but the petitioners were so strenuously supported in their claim to some notice, by the Earls of
Chesterfield, Abingdon, and Strafford, the Lords Bathurst
and Carteret, that they could not dismiss it at once with
any regard to decorum. The order of the House, according to the motion explained above, being communicated by the lord chancellor to the petitioners, they
waited on him with a declaration, importing that they did
not intend to controvert the election or return of the
sixteen peers for Scotland; but they thought it their
duty to lay before their lordships the evidence of such
facts and undue methods as appeared to them to be dangerous to the constitution; and might in future elections
equally affect the right of the present sixteen peers, as
that of the other peers of Scotland, if not prevented by a
proper remedy. This declaration being repeated to the
House, the Duke of Devonshire made a motion, that the
petitioners might be ordered to lay before the House, in

writing, instances of those undue methods and illegal practices upon which they intended to proceed, and the names of the persons they suspected to be guilty. He was warmly opposed by the country party; and a long debate ensued; after which the question was carried in favour of the motion, and the order signified to the petitioners. Next day their answer was read to the House to this effect; that as they had no intention to state themselves accusers, they could not take upon them to name particular persons who might have been concerned in those illegal practices; but who they were would undoubtedly appear to their lordships upon their taking the proper examinations; nevertheless, they did humbly acquaint their lordships, that the petition was laid before them upon information, that the list of the sixteen peers for Scotland had been framed, previous to the election, by persons in high trust under the crown: that this list was shown to peers, as a list approved by the crown; and was called the king's list, from which there was to be no variation, unless to make way for one or two particular peers, on condition they should conform to measures: that peers were solicited to vote for this list, without the liberty of making any alteration: that endeavours were used to engage peers to vote for this list by promise of pensions, and offices civil and military to themselves and relations, as well as by offers of money: that sums were given for this purpose: that pensions, offices, and releases of debts owing to the crown, were actually granted to peers who concurred in voting for this list, and to their relations: that on the day of election a battalion of his majesty's troops were drawn up in the Abbey-court of Edinburgh, contrary to custom, and without any apparent cause but that of overawing the electors. This answer gave rise to another violent dispute; but the majority voted it unsatisfactory, and the petition was rejected, though the resolution was clogged with a vigorous protest.

Notwithstanding this discouragement, the Earl of Abingdon moved, that although the petition was dismissed, an inquiry might be set on foot touching an affair of such consequence to the liberties of the kingdom. The Earl of Ilay declaring his belief that no such

CHAP.
XVI.

1735.
wrongous
imprison-
ment.

illegal methods had been practised, the other produced a pamphlet, entitled " The Protests of a great Number of noble Lords, entered by them at the last Election of Peers for Scotland." Exceptions being taken to a pamphlet, as an object unworthy of their notice, Lord Bathurst exhibited an authentic copy of those protests, extracted from the journal of that election, signed by the two principal clerks, and witnessed by two gentlemen then attending in the lobby. These were accordingly read, and plainly demonstrated the truth of the allegations contained in the petition. Nothing could be more scandalous, arrogant, and shamefully flagrant than the conduct and deportment of those who acted the part of understrappers to the ministry on this occasion. But all this demonstration, adorned and enforced by the charms and energy of eloquence, was like preaching in a desert. A motion was made for adjourning, and carried in the affirmative : a protest was entered, and the whole affair consigned to oblivion. Divers other motions were made successively by the lords in the opposition, and rejected by the invincible power of a majority. The uninterrupted success of the ministry did not, however, prevent them from renewing the struggle as often as an opportunity offered. They disputed the continuation of the salt-tax, and the bill for enabling the king to apply the sum of one million out of the sinking-fund for the service of the current year, though success did not attend their endea-vours. They supported with all their might a bill sent up from the Commons, explaining and amending an act of the Scottish Parliament, for preventing wrongous imprisonment, and against undue delays in trials. This was all the natives of Scotland had in lieu of the habeas corpus act, though it did not screen them from oppression. Yet the Earl of Ilay undertook to prove they were on a footing with their neighbours of England in this respect; and the bill was thrown out on a division. The session was closed on the fifteenth of May, when the king, in his speech to both Houses, declared that the plan of pacification concerted between him and the States-General had not produced the desired effect. He thanked the Commons for the supplies they had granted with such cheerfulness and despatch. He signified his

intention to visit his German dominions; and told them
he should constitute the queen regent of the realm in
his absence. Immediately after the prorogation his
majesty embarked for Holland, in his way to Hanover.

By this time the good understanding between the
courts of Madrid and Lisbon was destroyed by a remarkable incident. The Portuguese ambassador at Madrid
having allowed his servants to rescue a criminal from the
officers of justice, all the servants concerned in that
rescue were dragged from his house to prison, by the
Spanish king's order, with circumstances of rigour and
disgrace. His Portuguese majesty being informed of
this outrage, ordered reprisals to be made upon the
servants of the Spanish ambassador at Lisbon. The two
ministers withdrew abruptly to their respective courts.
The two monarchs expressed their mutual resentment.
The King of Spain assembled a body of troops on the
frontiers of Portugal; and his Portuguese majesty had
recourse to the assistance of King George. Don Marcos
Antonio d'Alzeveda was despatched to London with the
character of envoy extraordinary; and succeeded in his
commission according to his wish. In a little time after
the king's departure from England, Sir John Norris
sailed from Spithead, with a powerful squadron, in order
to protect the Portuguese against the Spaniards; and on
the ninth day of June arrived at Lisbon, where he was
welcomed as a deliverer. Mr. Keene, the British envoy
at the court of Spain, had communicated to his Catholic
majesty the resolution of his master to send a powerful
squadron to Lisbon, with orders to guard that coast from
insults, and secure the Brazil fleet, in which the merchants
of Great Britain were deeply interested. Don Joseph
Patinho, minister of his Catholic majesty, delivered a
memorial to Mr. Keene, representing that such an expedition would affect the commerce of Spain, by intimi-
dating foreign merchants from embarking their merchandise in the flota. But in all probability, it prevented a
rupture between the two crowns, and disposed the King
of Spain to listen to terms of accommodation.

The powers in alliance against the House of Austria,
having rejected the plan of pacification concerted by the
King of Great Britain and the States-General, Mr. Wal-

CHAP.
XVI.

1735.
ror and
King of
France.

pole, ambassador at the Hague, presented a memorial to their high mightinesses, desiring they would, without loss of time, put themselves in a posture of defence by an augmentation of their forces at sea and land; that they might take such vigorous steps in concert with Great Britain, as the future conjuncture of affairs might require. But before they would subject themselves to such expense, they resolved to make further trial of their influence with the powers in alliance against the emperor; and conferences were renewed with the ministers of those allies. The affairs of Poland became more and more unfavourable to the interest of Stanislaus; for though a great number of the Polish nobility engaged in a confederacy to support his claim, and made repeated efforts in his behalf, the Palatine of Kiow submitted to Augustus; and even his brother the primate, after having sustained a long imprisonment and many extraordinary hardships, was obliged to acknowledge that prince his sovereign. In Italy the arms of the allies still continued to prosper. Don Carlos landed in Sicily, and reduced the whole island, almost without opposition; while the imperialists were forced to abandon all the territories they possessed in Italy, except the Mantuan. The emperor being equally unable to cope with the French armies on the Rhine, implored succours of the czarina, who sent thirty thousand men to his assistance. This vigorous interposition, and the success of Augustus in Poland, disposed the court of Versailles to a pacification. A secret negotiation was begun between France and the house of Austria; and the preliminaries were signed without the concurrence or knowledge of Spain, Sardinia, and the maritime powers. In these articles it was stipulated, that France should restore all the conquests she had made in Germany: that the reversion of the dukedom of Tuscany should be vested in the Duke of Lorraine: that Lorraine should be allotted to king Stanislaus; and after his death be united to the crown of France: that the emperor should possess the Milanese, the Mantuan, and Parma: that the King of Sardinia should enjoy Vigevano and Novara: that Don Carlos should be acknowledged King of Naples and Sicily, and retain the island of Elba, with all the Spanish territories on the coast of Tuscany; and that France should guarantee the pragmatic sanction.

CHAP.
XVI.
1735.
Proceed-
ings in
Parlia-
ment.

The King of Great Britain returned from Hanover to England in the month of November; and on the fifteenth day of January opened the session of Parliament. On this occasion he congratulated them on the near prospect of a general peace in Europe, in consequence of the preliminary articles in which the emperor and the King of France had agreed; and of which he had expressed his approbation, as they did not differ in any essential point from the plan of pacification which he and the States-General had offered to the belligerent powers. He told them that he had already ordered a considerable reduction to be made in his forces both by sea and land; but at the same time observed, it would be necessary to continue some extraordinary expense, until a more perfect reconciliation should be established among the several powers of Europe. An address of thanks was unanimously voted, presented, and graciously received. After the House had received several petitions from different counties and gentlemen, complaining of undue influence in elections for members of Parliament, it proceeded to consider of the supply, and Sir Charles Wager moving that fifteen thousand seamen should be employed for the service of the ensuing year, the proposal was approved without opposition. But this was not the case with a motion made by Mr. Pulteney, "That the ordinary estimate of the navy should be referred to a select committee." The ministry discouraged all such prying measures: a debate was produced, the House divided, and the motion was rejected. Such was the fate of a motion for raising the supplies within the year, made by Mr. Sandys, and supported by Sir John Barnard, Mr. Willimot, and other patriots, who demonstrated, that this was a speedy and practicable expedient for discharging the national debt, lowering the interest of money, reducing the price of labour, and encouraging a spirit of commerce.

The bill for limiting the number of officers in the House of Commons was again revived. The king was empowered to borrow six hundred thousand pounds, chargeable on the sinking-fund, for the service of the

CHAP.
XVI.

1735.
Another
for the
relief of
Quakers in
the article
of tithes.

1736.

ensuing year, though this power was not easily granted;
and the House resolved to lay a duty of twenty shillings
per gallon on all spirituous liquors, after it had appeared
to the committee appointed for that purpose, that those
spirits were pernicious to the health and morals of the
people. To this resolution was added another, which
amounted to a total prohibition, namely, that fifty pounds
should be yearly paid to his majesty for a licence to be
annually taken out by every person who should vend,
barter, or utter any such spirituous liquors. Mr. Walter
Plumer, in a well-concerted speech, moved for the repeal of some clauses in the test act : these he represented
as a species of persecution, in which Protestant dissenters
were confounded with the Roman Catholics and enemies
to the establishment. He was sustained by Lord Polwarth and Mr. Heathcote ; but Sir Robert Walpole was
joined by Mr. Shippen against the motion as dangerous
to the established church ; and the question being put,
it was carried in the negative. When Sir Joseph Jekyll
presented to the House, according to order, a bill founded
on the resolutions they had taken against spirituous
liquors, Sir Robert Walpole acquainted them, by his
majesty's command, that as the alterations proposed to
be made by that bill in the duties charged upon all
spirituous liquors might, in a great degree, affect some
part of the civil-list revenues, his majesty, for the sake
of remedying so great an evil as was intended by that
bill to be prevented, did consent to accept any other
revenue of equal value, to be settled and appropriated in
lieu of his interest in the said duties. The bill was read
a second time, and consigned to a committee of the whole
House ; but that for limiting the number of officers in the
House of Commons was thrown out at the second reading. Petitions against the bill touching the retail of
spirituous liquors were presented by the traders to the
British sugar colonies, by the merchants of Bristol and
Liverpool, representing the hardships to which they would
be exposed by a law which amounted to a prohibition of
rum and spirits distilled from molasses. In consequence
of these remonstrances, a mitigating clause was inserted
in favour of the composition known by the name of
punch, and distillers were permitted to exercise any other

employment. The sum of seventy thousand pounds was
voted for making good the deficiencies that might happen in the civil-list by this bill, which at length passed through the House, though not without reiterated disputes and warm altercation. Violent opposition was likewise made to a bill for the relief of the people called Quakers, who offered a petition, representing, that though from motives of conscience they refused the payment of tithes, church-rates, oblations, and ecclesiastical dues, they were exposed to grievous sufferings by prosecution in the exchequer, ecclesiastical, and other courts, to the imprisonment of their persons, and the ruin of them and their families. A bill being prepared for their relief, was read and printed: then petitions were preferred against it by the clergy of Middlesex, and of many other parts of the kingdom. Counsel was heard in behalf of these petitioners, and several alterations proposed in the bill, which, after long and repeated debates, surmounted all opposition, and was sent up to the Lords.

In the month of February the king had sent two Mortmain members of the privy-council to the Prince of Wales, act. with a message, proposing a marriage between his royal highness and the Princess of Saxegotha. The proposal being agreeable to the prince, the marriage was celebrated on the twenty-seventh day of April. Upon this occasion Mr. Pulteney moved for an address of congratulation to his majesty, and was supported by Mr. George Lyttelton and Mr. William Pitt, who seized this opportunity of pronouncing elegant panegyrics on the Prince of Wales and his amiable consort. These two young members soon distinguished themselves in the House by their eloquence and superior talents. The attention of the House was afterwards converted to a bill for the preventing of smuggling; and another for explaining the act for the more effectual preventing of bribery and corruption in the election of members to serve in Parliament. Both made their way through the Lower House, and were sent up to the Lords for their concurrence. The number of land-forces voted for the service of the current year was reduced to seventeen thousand seven hundred and four effective men. The supplies were raised by the malt-tax and land-tax at two shillings in the pound, additional duties on mum, cider, and perry, stamped vellum, parchment, and paper; and by an act empowering his majesty to borrow six hundred thousand pounds from the sinking-fund. In this session the Parliament repealed the old statutes of England and Scotland against conjuration, witchcraft, and dealing with evil spirits. The Commons likewise prepared a bill to restrain the disposition of lands in mortmain, whereby they became unalienable. Against this measure petitions were presented by the two universities, the colleges of Eton, Winchester, and Westminster, and divers hospitals that subsisted by charitable donations. In favour of the universities and colleges a particular exempting clause was inserted. Several other amendments were made in the bill, which passed through both Houses, and obtained the royal assent. Among the acts passed in this session, was one for naturalizing her royal highness the Princess of Wales; and another for building a bridge across the Thames from New Palace-yard, in the city of Westminster, to the opposite shore in the county of Surrey. The points chiefly debated in the House of Lords were the address of thanks for his majesty's speech, the mortmain bill, the Quakers' bill, which was thrown out, and that for the prevention of smuggling, which did not pass without division and protest. On the twentieth day of May the king closed the session with a speech, in which he told both Houses, that a further convention, touching the execution of the preliminaries, had been made and communicated to him by the emperor and Most Christian king; and that negotiations were carrying on by the several powers engaged in the late war, in order to settle a general pacification. He expressed great concern at seeing such seeds of dissatisfaction sown among his people: he protested it was his desire, and should be his care, to preserve the present constitution in church and state as by law established: he recommended harmony and mutual affection among all Protestants of the nation, as the great security of that happy establishment; and signified his intention to visit his German dominions. Accordingly the Parliament was no sooner prorogued than he set out for Hanover, after having appointed the queen regent in his absence.

Such a degree of licentiousness prevailed over the whole nation, that the kingdom was filled with tumult and riots, which might have been prevented by proper regulations of the civil government in the due execution of the laws. The most remarkable of these disturbances happened at Edinburgh, on the seventh day of September. John Porteous, who commanded the guard paid by that city, a man of brutal disposition and abandoned morals, had, at the execution of a smuggler, been provoked by some insults from the populace to order his men, without using the previous formalities of the law, to fire with shot among the crowd; by which precipitate order several innocent persons lost their lives. Porteous was tried for murder, convicted, and received sentence of death; but the queen, as guardian of the realm, thought proper to indulge him with a reprieve. The common people of Edinburgh resented this lenity shown to a criminal, who was the object of their detestation. They remembered that pardons had been granted to divers military delinquents in that country, who had been condemned by legal trial. They seemed to think those were encouragements to oppression: they were fired by a national jealousy; they were stimulated by the relations and friends of those who had been murdered; and they resolved to wreak their vengeance on the author of that tragedy, by depriving him of life on the very day which the judges had fixed for his execution. Thus determined, they assembled in different bodies, about ten o'clock at night. They blocked up the gates of the city, to prevent the admission of the troops that were quartered in the suburbs. They surprised and disarmed the town guards; they broke open the prison doors; dragged Porteous from thence to the place of execution; and, leaving him hanging by the neck on a dyer's pole, quietly dispersed to their several habitations. This exploit was performed with such conduct and deliberation as seemed to be the result of a plan formed by some persons of consequence; it therefore became the object of a very severe inquiry.

During this summer a rupture happened between the Turks and the Russians, which last reduced the city of Asoph, on the Black Sea, and overran the greatest part of Crim Tartary. The czarina declared war against the

Ottoman Porte, because the Tartars of the Crimea had made incursions upon her frontiers; and when she complained of these disorders to the vizir, she received no satisfaction; besides, a large body of Tartars had, by order of that minister, marched through the Russian provinces in despite of the empress, and committed terrible havoc in their route. The emperor was obliged to engage as a party in this war, by a treaty offensive and defensive, which he had many years before concluded with the czarina. Yet, before he declared himself, he joined the maritime powers in offering his mediation to the sultan, who was very well disposed to peace; but the czarina insisted upon her retaining Asoph, which her forces had reduced; and this preliminary article being rejected, as dishonourable to the Ottoman empire, the court of Vienna began to make preparations for war. By this time all the belligerent powers in Italy had agreed to the preliminaries of peace concluded between the emperor and France. The Duke of Lorraine had espoused the emperor's eldest daughter, the Archduchess Maria Theresa, and ceded Lorraine to France, even before he succeeded to Tuscany. Don Carlos was crowned King of Sicily; Stanislaus abdicated the crown of Poland; and Augustus was universally acknowledged sovereign of that kingdom. The preliminaries were approved and accepted by the diet of the empire: the King of Spain sent orders for his troops to evacuate Tuscany; and the provinces in Italy yielded to the House of Austria. Prince Eugene, who had managed the interests of the emperor on this occasion, did not live to see the happy fruits of this negotiation. He died at Vienna in April, at the age of seventy-three, leaving behind him the character of an invincible hero and consummate politician. He was not long survived by Count Staremberg, another imperial general, who ranked next to the prince in military reputation. About the same time Great Britain sustained a national loss in the death of Lord Chancellor Talbot, who, by his worth, probity, and acquired accomplishments, had dignified the great office to which he had been raised. He died universally lamented, in the month of February, at the age of fifty-two, and was succeeded on the bench by Lord Hardwicke.

The king being indisposed, in consequence of having been fatigued by a very tempestuous passage from Holland, the Parliament was prorogued from the twenty-first day of January to the first of February, and then the session was opened by commission. The lord chancellor, as one of the peers authorized by this commission, made a speech in his majesty's name to both Houses. With respect to foreign affairs, he told them, that the respective acts of cession being exchanged, and orders given for the evacuation and possession of the several countries and places by the powers concerned, according to the allotment and disposition of the preliminary articles, the great work of re-establishing the general tranquillity was far advanced: that, however, common prudence called upon them to be very attentive to the final conclusion of the new settlement. He said, his majesty could not, without surprise and concern, observe the many contrivances and attempts carried on, in various shapes and in different parts of the nation, tumultuously to resist and obstruct the execution of the laws, and to violate the peace of the kingdom. He observed, that the consideration of the height to which these audacious practices might rise, if not timely suppressed, afforded a melancholy prospect, and required particular attention, lest they should affect private persons in the quiet enjoyment of their property, as well as the general peace and good order of the whole. After the Commons had agreed to an address, and heard counsel on some controverted elections, they proceeded to take the supply into consideration. They voted ten thousand men for the sea-service. They continued for the land-service the same number they had maintained in times of tranquillity, amounting to seventeen thousand seven hundred and four: but this measure was not adopted without opposition; the money was raised by the land and malt-taxes, reinforced with one million granted out of the sinking-fund.

The chief subject of contention that presented itself in the course of this session, was a motion which Mr. Pulteney made for an address to his majesty, that he would be pleased to settle one hundred thousand pounds a year upon the Prince of Wales. He represented that

CHAP. XVI.

1736.

The session of Parliament opened by commission.

Motion in both Houses for a settlement on the Prince of Wales.

such provision was conformable to the practice of ancient
time: that what he proposed had been enjoyed by his
present majesty in the lifetime of his father; and that
a settlement of this nature was reasonable and necessary
to ascertain the independency of the apparent heir to
the crown. The motion was vigorously opposed by Sir
Robert Walpole, as an encroachment on the prerogative;
as an officious intermeddling in the king's family affairs;
and as an effort to set his majesty and the prince at variance. But a misunderstanding, it seems, had already
happened in the royal family. The minister in the midst
of his harangue told the House, by his majesty's command, that on the preceding day the king had sent a
message to the prince by several noblemen of the first
quality, importing that his majesty had given orders for
settling a jointure upon the Princess of Wales, suitable
to her high rank and dignity, which he would in a proper
time lay before Parliament, in order to be rendered
more certain and effectual: that although his royal highness had not thought fit, by any application to his majesty, to desire that his allowance of fifty thousand pounds
might be rendered less precarious, the king, to prevent
the bad consequences which he apprehended might follow from the undutiful measures which his majesty was
informed the prince had been advised to pursue, would
grant to his royal highness, for his majesty's life, the said
fifty thousand pounds per annum, to be issued out of the
civil-list revenues, over and above the prince's revenues
arising from the duchy of Cornwall, which his majesty
thought a very competent allowance, considering his own
numerous issue, and the great expense which did and
must necessarily attend an honourable provision for the
whole royal family; that the prince, by a verbal answer,
desired their lordships to lay him with all humility at
his majesty's feet; to assure him that he did, and ever
should, retain the utmost duty for his royal person: that
he was very thankful for any instance of his majesty's
goodness to him or to the princess, and particularly for
his majesty's gracious intention of settling a jointure
upon her royal highness; but that, as to the message,
the affair was now out of his hands, and therefore he
could give no answer to it: that his royal highness

afterwards used many dutiful expressions towards his
majesty, adding, "Indeed, my lords, it is in other hands,
and I am sorry for it;" or words to that effect. Sir
Robert Walpole then endeavoured to demonstrate, that
the annual sum of fifty thousand pounds was as much
as the king could afford to allow for the prince's maintenance; and he expatiated upon the bad consequences
that might ensue, if the son should be rendered altogether independent of the father.

These suggestions did not pass unanswered. Sir
Robert Walpole had asserted, that the Parliament had
no right to interfere in the creation or maintenance of
a Prince of Wales; and that in the case of Richard II.,
who, upon the death of his father, the Black Prince, was
created Prince of Wales, in consequence of an address
or petition from Parliament, that measure was in all probability directed by the king himself. In answer to this
assertion it was observed, that probably the king would
not have been so forward in creating his grandson Prince
of Wales, if he had not been forced into this step by
his Parliament; for Edward in his old age fell into a
sort of love dotage, and gave himself entirely up to the
management of his mistress, Alice Pierce, and his second son, the Duke of Lancaster; a circumstance that
raised a most reasonable jealousy in the Black Prince,
at that time on his death-bed, who could not but be
anxious about the safety and right of his only son, whom
he found he was soon to leave a child in the hands of a
doting grandfather, and an ambitious, aspiring uncle.
The supporters of the motion observed, that the allowance of fifty thousand pounds was not sufficient to defray
the prince's yearly expense, without allotting one shilling
for acts of charity and munificence; and that the several
deductions for land-taxes and fees reduced it to forty-
three thousand pounds. They affirmed that his whole
income, including the revenues of the duchy of Cornwall,
did not exceed fifty-two thousand pounds a year, though,
by his majesty's own regulation, the expense of the
prince's household amounted to sixty-three thousand.
They proved, that the produce of the civil-list exceeded
nine hundred thousand pounds, a sum above one hundred thousand pounds a year more than was enjoyed by

his late majesty; and that, in the first year of the late king, the whole expense of his household and civil government did not much exceed four hundred and fifty thousand pounds a year. They observed, that the Parliament added one hundred and forty thousand pounds annually for acts of charity and bounty, together with the article of secret service money; and allowed one hundred thousand pounds for the maintenance of the Prince of Wales: that the article of secret service money had prodigiously increased in the late reign: by an account which happened to be laid before the Parliament, it appeared that vast sums of money had been given for purposes which nobody understood, and to persons whom nobody knew. In the beginning of the following session several members proposed that this extraordinary account should be taken into consideration; but the inquiry was warded off by the other party, who declared that the Parliament could not examine any account which had been presented to a former session. The debate was fierce and long; and ended in a division, by which the motion was rejected. A motion of the same nature was made by Lord Carteret in the House of Peers, and gave rise to a very keen dispute, maintained by the same arguments, and issuing in the same termination.

Scheme by Sir John Barnard for reducing the interest of the national debt.
The next remarkable contest was occasioned by a motion of Sir R. Walpole, who proposed that the sum of one million should be granted to his majesty, towards redeeming the like sum of the increased capital of the South-Sea Company, commonly called South-Sea annuities. Several members argued for the expediency of applying this sum to the payment of the debt due to the bank, as a part of that incumbrance was saddled with an interest of six per cent., whereas the interest paid for the other sums that constituted the public debt did not exceed four per cent. Many plausible arguments were offered on both sides of the question; and at length the motion was carried in the affirmative. The House having resolved itself into a committee to consider of the national debt, Sir John Barnard made a motion, for enabling his majesty to raise money either by the sale of annuities, or by borrowing at an interest not exceed-

ing three per cent., to be applied towards redeeming the
South-Sea annuities; and that such of the said annui- tants as should be inclined to subscribe their respective annuities should be preferred to all others. He said, that even those public securities which bore an interest of three per cent. only were sold at a premium in Change- alley; he was therefore persuaded, that all those who were willing to give a premium for a three per cent. security would gladly lend their money to the govern- ment at the same interest, should books of subscription be opened for that purpose, with an assurance that no part of the principal should be paid off for fourteen years. He expatiated upon the national advantages that would accrue from a reduction of interest. From easy and obvious calculations he inferred, that in a very little time the interest upon all the South-Sea annuities would be reduced from four to three per cent. without any danger to public credit, or breach of public faith: that then the produce of the sinking-fund would amount to fourteen hundred thousand pounds per annum, to be applied only towards redeeming the capital of the seve- ral trading companies: he proved that this measure would bring every one of them so much within the power of Parliament, that they would be glad to accept of three per cent. interest on any reasonable terms; in which case the sinking-fund would rise to one million six hundred thousand pounds per annum. Then the Parliament might venture to annihilate one half of it, by freeing the people from the taxes upon coals, candles, soap, leather, and such other impositions as lay heavy upon the poor labourers and manufacturers: the remaining part of the sinking-fund might be applied towards the discharge of those annuities and public debts which bore an interest of three per cent. only, and afterwards towards dimin- ishing the capitals of the several trading companies, till the term of fourteen years should be expired; then the sinking fund would again amount to above a million yearly, which would be sufficient for paying them off, and freeing the nation entirely from all its incumbrances. This salutary scheme was violently opposed by Alder- man Heathcote, and other partisans of the ministry: yet all their objections were refuted; and, in order to defeat the project, they were obliged to have recourse to arti-

fice. Mr. Winnington moved, that all the public creditors, as well as the South-Sea annuitants, should be
comprehended. Sir John Barnard demonstrated, that
it might be easy for the government to borrow money
at three per cent. sufficient for paying off such of the
proprietors of four-and-twenty millions as were not willing to accept of that interest, but it would be extremely
difficult to borrow enough to satisfy the proprietors of
four-and-forty millions, who might choose to have their
principal rather than such an interest. Nevertheless,
resolutions were founded on this and other alterations of
the original scheme; and a bill was immediately prepared. It produced many other debates, and was at last
postponed by dint of ministerial influence. The same
venerable patriot, who projected this scheme, moved
that as soon as the interest of all the national redeemable debt should be reduced to three per cent. the House
would take off some of the heavy taxes which oppressed
the poor and the manufacturers; but this motion was rejected by the majority.

The last disputes of this session were excited by a bill
sent down from the Lords for punishing the magistrates
and city of Edinburgh, on account of the murder of John
Porteous. In the beginning of the session Lord Carteret
recapitulated the several tumults and riots which had
lately happened in different parts of the kingdom. He
particularly insisted upon the atrocious murder of Captain
Porteous, as a flagrant insult upon the government, and
a violation of the public peace, so much the more dangerous, as it seemed to have been concerted and executed
with deliberation and decency. He suspected that some
citizens of Edinburgh had been concerned in the murder,
not only from this circumstance, but likewise because,
notwithstanding the reward of two hundred pounds,
which had been offered by proclamation for the discovery
of any person who acted in that tragedy, not one individual had as yet been detected. He seemed to think
that the magistrates had encouraged the riot, and that
the city had forfeited its charter; and he proposed a
minute inquiry into the particulars of the affair. He was
seconded by the Duke of Newcastle and the Earl of
Ilay; though this last nobleman differed in opinion from
him with respect to the charter of the city, which, he

said, could not be justly forfeited by the fault of the magistracy. The Lords resolved, that the magistrates and
other persons from whom they might obtain the necessary
information concerning this riot should be ordered to
attend; and that an address should be presented to
his majesty, desiring that the different accounts and
papers relating to the murder of Captain Porteous might
be submitted to the perusal of the House. These docu-
ments being accordingly examined, and all the witnesses
arrived, including three Scottish judges, a debate arose
about the manner in which these last should be interrogated, whether at the bar, at the table, or on the wool-
sacks. Some Scottish lords asserted that they had a
right to be seated next to the judges of England; but
after a long debate this claim was rejected, and the
judges of Scotland appeared at the bar in their robes.
A bill was brought in to disable Alexander Wilson,
Esquire, lord provost of Edinburgh, from enjoying any
office or place of magistracy in the city of Edinburgh, or
elsewhere in Great Britain; for imprisoning the said
Alexander Wilson; for abolishing the guard of that city;
and for taking away the gates of the Nether-bow-port,
so as to open a communication between the city and
suburbs, in which the king's troops are quartered. The
Duke of Argyle, in arguing against this bill, said he could
not think of a proceeding more harsh or unprecedented
than the present, as he believed there was no instance of
the whole weight of parliamentary indignation, for such
he called a proceeding by a bill *ex post facto*, falling upon
any single person, far less upon any community, for
crimes that were within the reach of the inferior courts
of justice; for this reason he observed, that if the lord
provost and citizens of Edinburgh should suffer in the
terms of the present bill, they would suffer by a cruel,
unjust, and fantastical proceeding; a proceeding of which
the worst use might be made, if ever the nation should
have the misfortune to fall under a partial, self-interested
administration. He told them he sat in the Parliament
of Scotland when that part of the treaty of union relating
to the privileges of the royal burghs was settled on the
same footing as religion; that is, they were made un-
alterable by any subsequent Parliament of Great Britain.

Notwithstanding the eloquence and warmth of his remonstrance, the bill was sent down to the House of
Commons, where it produced a violent contest. The
Commons set on foot a severe scrutiny into the particular
circumstances that preceded and attended the murder of
Porteous: from the examination of the witnesses, it appeared that no freeman or citizen of Edinburgh was concerned in the riot, which was chiefly composed of country
people, excited by the relations of some unhappy persons
whom Porteous and his men had slain at the execution
of the smuggler; and these were assisted by prentice-
boys, and the lowest class of vagabonds that happened to
be at Edinburgh : that the lord provost had taken all
the precautions to prevent mischief that his reflection
suggested ; that he even exposed his person to the rage
of the multitude, in his endeavour to disperse them ; and
that, if he had done amiss, he erred from want of judgment, rather than from want of inclination to protect
the unhappy Porteous. It likewise appeared that Mr.
Lindsay, member for the city of Edinburgh, had gone in
person to General Moyle, commander of the forces in
North Britain, informed him of the riot, implored his
immediate assistance, and promised to conduct his troops
into the city ; and that his suit was rejected, because he
could not produce a written order from the magistracy,
which he neither could have obtained in such confusion,
nor ventured to carry about his person through the
midst of an enraged populace. The Scottish members
exerted themselves with uncommon vivacity in defence
of their capital. They were joined by Sir John Barnard,
Lord Cornbury, Mr. Shippen, and Mr. Oglethorpe. Lord
Polwarth declared, that if any gentleman would show
where one argument in the charge against the lord provost
and the city of Edinburgh had been proved, he would
that instant give his vote for the commitment of the bill.
He said, if gentlemen would lay their hands upon their
hearts, and ask themselves whether they would have
voted in this manner had the case of Edinburgh been
that of the city of Bristol, York, or Norwich, he was persuaded they would have required that every tittle of the
charge against them should have been fully and unde-
niably proved. Some amendments and mitigations being

inserted in the bill, it passed the House, was sent back
to the Lords, who agreed to the alterations, and then received the royal assent.

The next effort of the minister was obliquely levelled
at the liberty of the press, which it was much for his
interest to abridge. The errors of his conduct, the mystery of that corruption which he had so successfully reduced to a system, and all the blemishes of his administration, had been exposed and ridiculed, not only in
political periodical writings produced by the most eminent hands, but likewise in a succession of theatrical
pieces, which met with uncommon success among the
people. He either wanted judgment to distinguish men
of genius, or could find none that would engage in his
service : he therefore employed a set of wretched authors,
void of understanding and ingenuity. They undertook
the defence of his ministry, and answered the animadversions of his antagonists. The match was so extremely
unequal, that, instead of justifying his conduct, they exposed it to additional ridicule and contempt, and he saw
himself in danger of being despised by the whole nation.
He resolved to seize the first opportunity to choke those
canals through which the torrent of censure had flowed
upon his character. The manager of a playhouse communicated to him a manuscript farce, entitled the Golden
Rump, which was fraught with treason and abuse upon the
government, and had been presented to the stage for
exhibition. This performance was produced in the House
of Commons. The minister descanted upon the insolence,
the malice, the immorality, and the seditious calumny,
which had been of late propagated in theatrical pieces.
A bill was brought in to limit the number of playhouses;
to subject all dramatic writers to the inspection of the lord
chamberlain ; and to compel them to take out a licence
for every production before it could appear on the stage.
Notwithstanding a vigorous opposition, this bill passed
through both Houses with extraordinary despatch, and
obtained the royal sanction. In this debate the Earl of
Chesterfield distinguished himself by an excellent speech,
that will ever endear his character to all the friends of
genius and literature, to all those who are warmed with
zeal for the liberties of their country. " Our stage (said

he) ought certainly to be kept within due bounds; but, for this purpose, our laws as they stand at present are sufficient. If our stage-players at any time exceed those bounds, they ought to be prosecuted; they may be punished. We have precedents, we have examples of persons punished for things less criminal than some pieces which have been lately represented: a new law must, therefore, be unnecessary; and in the present case it cannot be unnecessary without being dangerous. Every unnecessary restraint is a fetter upon the legs, is a shackle upon the hands of liberty. One of the greatest blessings we enjoy, one of the greatest blessings a people can enjoy, is liberty. But every good in this life has its allay of evil. Licentiousness is the allay of liberty. It is an ebullition, an excrescence; it is a speck upon the eye of the political body, which I can never touch but with a gentle, with a trembling hand; lest I destroy the body, lest I injure the eye, upon which it is apt to appear. If the stage becomes at any time licentious, if a play appears to be a libel upon the government, or upon any particular man, the king's courts are open: the law is sufficient to punish the offender. If poets and players are to be restrained, let them be restrained as other subjects are, by the known laws of their country: if they offend, let them be tried as every Englishman ought to be, by God and their country. Do not let us subject them to the arbitrary will and pleasure of any one man. A power lodged in the hands of a single man to judge and determine without limitation, control, or appeal, is a sort of power unknown to our laws, inconsistent with our constitution. It is a higher, a more absolute power than we trust even to the king himself; and, therefore, I must think we ought not to vest any such power in his majesty's lord chamberlain." His arguments had no effect, though the House admired his elocution; and the playhouse bill passed into a law. On the twenty-first day of June the king made a short speech to both Houses, and the lord chancellor prorogued the Parliament.

CHAPTER XVII.

A CONGRESS had been opened at Niemerow, in Poland, to compromise the differences between the czarina and the grand signor; but this proving ineffectual, the emperor declared war against the Turks, and demanded assistance from the diet of the empire. He concerted the operations of the campaign with the Empress of Muscovy. It was agreed that the imperialists, under Count Seckendorf, should attack Widin, in Servia, while the Russians, commanded by Count de Munich, should penetrate to the Ukraine, and besiege Oczakow, on the Boristhenes. They accordingly advanced against this place, which was garrisoned by twenty thousand men; and on the side of the Boristhenes defended by eighteen galleys. The

CHAP.
XVII.

1737.

The Russians take Oczakow.

Muscovites carried on their approaches with such impetuosity and perseverance, that the Turks were terrified
at their valour, and in a few days capitulated. Among
those who signalized themselves by uncommon marks of
prowess in these attacks was General Keith, now field-
marshal in the Prussian service, who was dangerously
wounded on this occasion. Meanwhile Count Seckendorf, finding it impossible to reduce Widin without a
squadron of ships on the Danube, turned his arms against
Nissa, which was surrendered to him on the eight-and-
twentieth day of July; but this was the farthest verge
of his good fortune. The Turks attacked the post which
the imperialists occupied along the Danube. They took
the fort of Padudil, burned the town of Ilas in Wallachia, and plundered the neighbouring villages. The
Prince of Saxe-Hildburghausen, who had invested Bag-
nalack in Bosnia, was defeated, and obliged to repass
the Saave. Count Seckendorf was recalled to Vienna;
and the command of the army devolved upon Count
Philippi. Count Kevenhuller was obliged to retreat
from Servia; and Nissa was retaken by the Mussulmen.
The conferences at Niemerow were broken off; and the
Turkish plenipotentiaries returned to Constantinople.

Death of
Gaston de
Medicis,
Duke of
Tuscany.

The kingdom of Poland now enjoyed the most perfect
repose under the dominion of Augustus. Ferdinand,
the old Duke of Courland, dying without issue, the succession was disputed by the Teutonic order and the
kingdom of Poland, while the states of Courland claimed
a right of election, and sent deputies to Petersburg, imploring the protection of the czarina. A body of Russian
troops immediately entered that country; and the states
elected the Count de Biron, high chamberlain to the
Empress of Muscovy. The Elector of Cologn, as grand
master of the Teutonic order, protested against this election; but the King of Poland agreed to it, on certain
conditions settled at Dantzic with the commissaries of
the new duke and those of the czarina. In the month of
July, John Gaston de Medicis, Great Duke of Tuscany,
died at Florence; and the Prince de Craon took possession of his territories, in the name of the Duke of
Lorraine, to whom the emperor had already granted the
eventual investiture of that duchy.

In England, the attention of the public was attracted by an open breach in the royal family. The Princess of Wales had advanced to the very last month of her pregnancy before the king and queen were informed of her being with child. She was twice conveyed from Hampton-court to the palace of St. James's, when her labour-pains were supposed to be approaching; and at length was delivered of a princess in about two hours after her arrival. The king, being apprised of this event, sent a message by the Earl of Essex to the prince, expressing his displeasure at the conduct of his royal highness, as an indignity offered to himself and the queen. The prince deprecated his majesty's anger in several submissive letters, and implored the queen's mediation. The princess joined her entreaties to those of his royal highness; but all their humility and supplication proved ineffectual. The king, in another message sent by the Duke of Grafton, observed, that the prince had removed the princess twice in the week immediately preceding the day of her delivery from the place of his majesty's residence, in expectation of her labour; and both times, on his return, industriously concealed from the knowledge of the king and queen every circumstance relating to this important affair: that at last, without giving any notice to their majesties, he had precipitately hurried the princess from Hampton-court, in a condition not to be named: that the whole tenor of his conduct, for a considerable time, had been so entirely void of all real duty to the king, that his majesty had reason to be highly offended with him. He gave him to understand, that until he should withdraw his regard and confidence from those by whose instigation and advice he was directed and encouraged in his unwarrantable behaviour to his majesty and the queen, and return to his duty, he should not reside in the palace: he therefore signified his pleasure that he should leave St. James's with all his family, when it could be done without prejudice or inconvenience to the princess. In obedience to this order the prince retired to Kew, and made other efforts to be re-admitted into his majesty's favour, which, however, he could not retrieve. Whatever might have been his design in concealing so long from the king and queen the pregnancy of the princess, and afterwards hurrying her from place to place in such a condition, to the manifest hazard of her life, his majesty had certainly cause to be offended at this part of his conduct; though the punishment seems to have been severe, if not rigorous; for he was not even admitted into the presence of the queen his mother, to express his duty to her, in her last moments, to implore her forgiveness, and receive her last blessing. She died of a mortification in her bowels, on the twentieth day of November, in the fifty-fifth year of her age, regretted as a princess of uncommon sagacity, and as a pattern of conjugal virtue.

Dispute in
Parliament
about the
standing
army.

The king opened the session of Parliament on the twenty-fourth day of January, with a short speech, recommending the despatch of the public business with prudence and unanimity. Each House presented a warm address of condolence on the queen's death, with which he seemed to be extremely affected. Though the House of Commons unanimously sympathized with the king in his affliction, the minister still met with contradiction in some of his favourite measures. One would imagine that all the arguments for and against a standing army in time of peace had been already exhausted; but, when it was moved that the same number of land-forces which they had voted in the preceding year should be continued in pay for the ensuing year, the dispute was renewed with surprising vivacity, and produced some reasons which had not been suggested before. The adherents of the minister fairly owned, that if the army should be disbanded, or even considerably reduced, they believed the tory interest would prevail; that the present number of forces was absolutely necessary to maintain the peace of the kingdom, which was filled with clamour and discontent, as well as to support the whig interest; and that they would vote for keeping up four times the number, should it be found expedient for that purpose. The members in the opposition replied, that this declaration was a severe satire on the ministry, whose conduct had given birth to such a spirit of discontent. They said it was in effect a tacit acknowledgment, that what they called the whig interest was no more than an inconsiderable party, which had engrossed the administration by indirect methods; which acted contrary to the sense of the nation; and depended for support upon a military power, by which the people in general were overawed, and consequently enslaved.   They affirmed, that the discontent of which the ministry complained was in a great measure owing to that very standing army, which perpetuated their taxes, and hung over their heads as the instruments of arbitrary power and oppression. Lord Polwarth explained the nature of whig principles, and demonstrated that the party which distinguished itself by this appellation no longer retained the maxims by which the whigs were originally characterized.   Sir John Hynde Cotton, who spoke with the courage and freedom of an old English baron, declared he never knew a member of that House, who acted on true whig principles, vote for a standing army in time of peace: "I have heard of whigs (said he) who opposed all unlimited votes of credit: I have heard of whigs who looked upon corruption as the greatest curse that could befall any nation: I have heard of whigs who esteemed the liberty of the press to be the most valuable privilege of a free people, and triennial Parliaments as the greatest bulwark of their liberties; and I have heard of a whig administration which has resented injuries done to the trade of the nation, and revenged insults offered to the British flag."   The ministry triumphed as usual, and the same number of forces was continued.

Ever since the treaty of Seville, the Spaniards in America had almost incessantly insulted and distressed the commerce of Great Britain.   They disputed the right of English traders to cut logwood in the bay of Campeachy, and gather salt on the island of Tortugas; though that right was acknowledged by implication in all the treaties which had been lately concluded between the two nations.   The captains of their armed vessels, known by the name of guarda-costas, had made a practice of boarding and plundering British ships, on pretence of searching for contraband commodities, on which occasions they had behaved with the utmost insolence, cruelty, and rapine.   Some of their ships of war had actually attacked a fleet of English merchant ships at the island of Tortugas, as if they had been at open enmity with England.   They

Spanish depredations.

had seized and detained a great number of British vessels, imprisoned their crews, and confiscated their cargoes, in violation of treaties, in defiance of common justice and humanity. Repeated memorials were presented to the court of Spain by the British ambassador at Madrid. He was amused with evasive answers, vague promises of inquiry, and cedulas of instructions sent to the Spanish governors in America, to which they paid no sort of regard. Not but that the Spaniards had reason to complain, in their turn, of the illicit commerce which the English traders from Jamaica and other islands carried on with their subjects on the continent of South America; though this could not justify the depredations and cruelties which the commanders of the guarda-costas had committed, without provocation or pretence.

Motives of the minister for avoiding a war.

The merchants of England loudly complained of these outrages; the nation was fired with resentment, and cried for vengeance; but the minister appeared cold, phlegmatic, and timorous. He knew that a war would involve him in such difficulties as must of necessity endanger his administration. The treasure which he now employed for domestic purposes must in that case be expended in military armaments: the wheels of that machine on which he had raised his influence would no longer move: the opposition would of consequence gain ground, and the imposition of fresh taxes, necessary for the maintenance of the war, would fill up the measure of popular resentment against his person and ministry. Moved by these considerations, he industriously endeavoured to avoid a rupture, and to obtain some sort of satisfaction by dint of memorials and negotiations, in which he betrayed his own fears to such a degree, as animated the Spaniards to persist in their depredations, and encouraged the court of Madrid to disregard the remonstrances of the British ambassador. But this apprehension of war did not proceed from Spain only: the two branches of the house of Bourbon were now united by politics as well as by consanguinity: and he did not doubt that, in case of a rupture with Spain, they would join their forces against Great Britain. Petitions were delivered to the House by merchants from different parts of the kingdom, explaining the repeated violences to which they had been exposed, and imploring relief of the Parliament. These were referred to a committee of the whole House; and an order was made to admit the petitioners, if they should think fit, to be heard by themselves or by counsel. Sir John Barnard moved for an address to the king, that all the memorials and papers relating to the Spanish depredations should be laid before the House; and this, with some alteration proposed by Sir Robert Walpole, was actually presented. In compliance with this request, an enormous multitude of letters and memorials was produced.

The House, in a grand committee, proceeded to hear counsel for the merchants, and examine evidence; by which it appeared that amazing acts of wanton cruelty and injustice had been perpetrated by Spaniards on the subjects of Great Britain. Mr. Pulteney expatiated upon these circumstances of barbarity. He demonstrated, from treaties, the right of the British traders to the logwood of Campeachy, and to the salt of Tortugas : he exposed the pusillanimity of the minister, and the futility of his negotiations : he moved for such resolutions as would evince the resentment of an injured nation, and the vigour of a British Parliament. These were warmly combated by Sir Robert Walpole, who affirmed, they would cramp the ministers in their endeavours to compromise these differences : that they would frustrate their negotiations, intrench upon the king's prerogative, and precipitate the nation into an unnecessary and expensive war. Answers produced replies, and a general debate ensued. A resolution was reported; but the question being put for re-committing it, was carried in the negative. The House, however, agreed to an address, beseeching his majesty to use his endeavours to obtain effectual relief for his injured subjects, to convince the court of Spain that his majesty could no longer suffer such constant and repeated insults and injuries to be carried on, to the dishonour of his crown, and to the ruin of his trading subjects; and assuring him, that in case his royal and friendly instances with the catholic king should miscarry, the House would effectually support his majesty in taking such measures as honour and justice should make it necessary

Address to the king on the subject of the depredations.

CHAP.
XVII.
for him to pursue.   To this address the king made a favourable answer.

1738.
Bill for se-
curing the
trade of his
majesty's
subjects in
America.
The next important subject on which both sides exercised their talents, was a bill prepared and brought in by Mr. Pulteney, for the more effectual securing the trade of his majesty's subjects in America.   This was no other than the revival of part of two acts passed in the reign of queen Anne, by which the property of all prizes taken from the enemy was vested in the captors; while the sovereign was empowered to grant commissions or charters to any persons or societies, for taking any ships, goods, harbours, lands, or fortifications of the nation's enemies in America, and for holding and enjoying the same as their own property and estate for ever.   The ministry endeavoured to evade the discussion of this bill, by amusing the House with other business, until an end should be put to the session.   A mean artifice was practised with this view; and some severe altercation passed between Sir Robert Walpole and Mr. Pulteney.   At length the bill was read, and gave rise to a very long and warm contest, in which the greatest orators of both sides found opportunities to display their eloquence and satire. Mr. Pulteney defended the bill with all the ardour of paternal affection; but, notwithstanding his warmest endeavours, it was rejected upon a division.

Debates in
the House
of Lords.
When the mutiny bill was sent up to the House of Lords, a long debate arose upon the number of troops voted for the ensuing year.   Lord Carteret explained the situation of affairs in almost every nation of Europe with great conciseness and precision.   He demonstrated the improbability of a rupture between Great Britain and any power against which a land army could be of any service.   He examined the domestic circumstances of the nation; and proved, that whatever discontents there might be in the kingdom, there was little or no disaffection, and no seeming design to overturn or disturb the government.   In answer to an argument, that such a number of regular forces was necessary for preventing or quelling tumults, and for enabling the civil magistrate to execute the laws of his country, he expressed his hope that he should never see the nation reduced to such

unfortunate circumstances: he said, a law which the civil power was unable to execute, must either be in itself oppressive, or such a one as afforded a handle for oppression. In arguing for a reduction of the forces, he took notice of the great increase of the national expense. He observed, that before the Revolution, the people of England did not raise above two millions for the whole of the public charge; but now what was called the current expense, for which the Parliament annually provided, exceeded that sum; besides the civil-list, the interest due to the public creditors, and the sinking-fund, which, added together, composed a burden of six millions yearly. The Earl of Chesterfield, on the same subject, affirmed, that slavery and arbitrary power were the certain consequences of keeping up a standing army for any number of years. It is the machine by which the chains of slavery are riveted upon a free people. They may be secretly prepared by corruption; but, unless a standing army protected those that forged them, the people would break them asunder, and chop off the polluted hands by which they were prepared. By degrees a free people must be accustomed to be governed by an army; by degrees that army must be made strong enough to hold them in subjection. England had for many years been accustomed to a standing army, under pretence of its being necessary to assist the civil power; and by degrees the number and strength of it have been increasing. At the accession of the late king it did not exceed six thousand: it soon amounted to double that number, which has been since augmented under various pretences. He therefore concluded, that slavery, under the disguise of an army for protecting the liberties of the people, was creeping in upon them by degrees; if no reduction should be made, he declared he should expect in a few years to hear some minister, or favourite of a minister, terrifying the House with imaginary plots and invasions, and making the tour of Europe in search of possible dangers, to show the necessity of keeping up a mercenary standing army, three times as numerous as the present. In spite of these suggestions, the standing army maintained its ground. The same noblemen, assisted by Lord Bathurst, distinguished themselves in a debate upon the Spanish depre-

A a 2

dations, which comprehended the same arguments that were used in the House of Commons. They met with the same success in both. Resolutions equivalent to those of the Lower House were taken: an address was presented; and his majesty assured them he would repeat, in the most pressing manner, his instances at the court of Spain in order to obtain satisfaction and security for his subjects trading to America. This assurance was renewed in his speech at the close of the session, on the twentieth of May, when the Parliament was prorogued.

Birth of Prince George. Admiral Haddock sails with a squadron to the Mediterranean.

At this period the Princess of Wales was delivered of a son, who was baptized by the name of George, now King of Great Britain. His birth was celebrated with uncommon rejoicings: addresses of congratulation were presented to the king by the two universities, and by almost all the cities and communities of the kingdom. But the Prince of Wales still laboured under the displeasure of his majesty, who had ordered the lord chamberlain to signify in the gazette, that no person who visited the prince should be admitted to the court of St. James's. His royal highness was divested of all the external marks of royalty, and lived like a private gentleman, cultivating the virtues of a social life, and enjoying the best fruits of conjugal felicity. In the latter end of this month, Rear-Admiral Haddock set sail with a strong squadron for the Mediterranean, which it was hoped would give weight to the negotiation of the British minister at the court of Madrid. The act to discourage the retail of spirituous liquors had incensed the populace to such a degree as occasioned numberless tumults in the cities of London and Westminster. They were so addicted to the use of that pernicious compound, known by the appellation of gin or geneva, that they ran all risks rather than forego it entirely; and so little regard was paid to the law by which it was prohibited, that in less than two years twelve thousand persons within the bills of mortality were convicted of having sold it illegally. Nearly one-half of that number were cast in the penalty of one hundred pounds; and three thousand persons paid ten pounds each, for an exemption from the disgrace of being committed to the house of correction.

The war maintained by the emperor and the czarina

against the Ottoman Porte had not yet produced any de-
cisive event. Count Seckendorf was disgraced and con-
fined on account of his ill success in the last campaign.
General Doxat was tried by a council of war at Belgrade,
and condemned to death, for having surrendered to the
enemy the town of Nissa, in which he commanded. The
diet of the empire granted a subsidy of fifty Roman
months to the emperor, who began to make vigorous
preparations for the ensuing campaign; but, in the mean
time, Ragotski, Vaivode of Transylvania, revolted against
the house of Austria, and brought a considerable army
into the field, under the protection of the grand signor.
He was immediately proclaimed a rebel, and a price set
upon his head by the court of Vienna. The Turks taking
the field early, reduced the fort of Usitz and Meadia,
and undertook the siege of Orsova, which, however, they
abandoned at the approach of the imperial army, com-
manded by the Grand Duke of Tuscany, assisted by
Count Konigsegg. The Turks, being reinforced, marched
back, and attacked the imperialists, by whom they were
repulsed after an obstinate engagement. The Germans,
notwithstanding this advantage, repassed the Danube;
and then the infidels made themselves masters of Orsova,
where they found a fine train of artillery, designed for
the siege of Widin. By the conquest of this place the
Turks laid the Danube open to their galleys and vessels;
and the Germans retired under the cannon of Belgrade.
In the Ukraine, the Russians under General Count
Munich obtained the advantage over the Turks in two
engagements; and General Lacy routed the Tartars of
the Crimea; but they returned in greater numbers, and
harassed the Muscovites in such a manner, by inter-
cepting their provisions and destroying the country, that
they were obliged to abandon the lines of Precops.

In the month of October, an affair of very small im-
portance produced a rupture between the King of
Denmark and the Elector of Hanover. A detachment
of Hanoverians took by assault the castle of Steinhorst,
belonging to the privy counsellor Wederkop, and de-
fended by thirty Danish dragoons, who had received
orders to repel force by force. Several men were killed
on both sides before the Hanoverians could enter the

CHAP.
XVII.
1738.
Progress of
the war
against the
Turks.

Dispute
and rupture
between
Hanover
and Den-
mark.

place, when the garrison was disarmed and conducted to
the frontiers. This petty dispute, about a small territory,
which did not yield the value of one thousand pounds a
year, had well nigh involved Hanover in a war, which, in
all probability, Great Britain must have maintained; but
this dispute was compromised by a convention between
the Kings of England and Denmark.

Sir Robert
Walpole
extols the
convention
in the
House of
Commons.

The session of Parliament was opened on the first day
of February, when the king in his speech to both Houses
gave them to understand, that a convention was concluded
and ratified between him and the King of Spain, who
had obliged himself to make reparation to the British
subjects for their losses, by certain stipulated payments:
the plenipotentiaries were named and appointed for regulating, within a limited time, all those grievances and
abuses which had hitherto interrupted the commerce of
Great Britain in the American seas; and for settling all
matters of dispute, in such a manner as might for the
future prevent and remove all new causes and pretences
of complaint. The motion for an address of approbation
was disputed as usual. Though the convention was not
yet laid before the House, the nature of it was well
known to the leaders of the opposition. Sir William
Wyndham observed, that if the ministry had made the
resolutions taken by the Parliament in the last session
the foundation of their demands; if they had discovered
a resolution to break off all treating, rather than depart
from the sense of Parliament; either a defensive treaty
might have been obtained, or by this time the worst
would have been known; but, by what appeared from
his majesty's speech, the convention was no other than a
preliminary; and, in all probability, a very bad preliminary. He supposed the minister had ventured to clothe
some of his creatures with full powers to give up the
rights of the nation; for they might do it if they durst.
Sir Robert Walpole, in answer to these suggestions,
affirmed, that the ministry had on this occasion obtained
more than ever on like occasions was known to be obtained: that they had reconciled the peace of their
country with her true interest: that this peace was attended with all the advantages that the most successful
arms could have procured: that future ages would con-

sider this as the most glorious period of our history, and
do justice to the counsels that produced the happy event,
which every gentleman divested of passion and prejudice
was ready to do: and which he believed the present age,
when rightly informed, would not refuse. In a word, he
extolled his own convention with the most extravagant
encomiums.

The House resolved to address the king, that copies
of all the memorials, representations, letters and papers,
presented to his majesty, or his secretary of state, relating to depredations, should be submitted to the perusal
of the House; but some members in the opposition were
not contented with this resolution. Then Mr. Sandys,
who may be termed the "motion maker," moved for an
address, desiring that the House might inspect all letters
written, and instructions given by the secretaries of state,
or commissioners of the Admiralty, to any of the British
governors in America, or any commander-in-chief, or
captains of his majesty's ships of war, or his majesty's
minister at the court of Spain, or any of his majesty's
consuls in Europe, since the treaty of Seville, relating to
the losses which the British subjects had sustained by
means of depredations committed by the subjects of
Spain in Europe and America. This was an unreasonable proposal, suggested by the spirit of animosity and
faction. Mr. H. Walpole justly observed, that a compliance with such an address might lay open the most
private transactions of the cabinet, and discover secrets
that ought, for the good of the kingdom, to be concealed.
It would discover to the court of Spain the *ultimatum* of
the king's demands and concessions, and the nation would
thereby be deprived of many advantages which it might
reap, were no such discovery made. He said, that as
soon as the differences betwixt the two courts should
arrive at such a crisis, and not before, the consuls were
instructed to give notice to the merchants, that they
might retire in time with their effects; but should such
instructions come to the knowledge of the Spaniards, it
would be a kind of watch-word to put them on their
guard, and unavoidably occasion the ruin of many thousands of British subjects. Certain it is, no government
could act either in external or domestic affairs with

Motion for
an address,
that the
representa-
tions, let-
ters, &c.,
relating to
the Spanish
depreda-
tions,
should be
laid before
the House.

CHAP.
XVII.

1738.proper influence, dignity, and despatch, if every letter
and instruction relating to an unfinished negotiation
should be exposed to the view of such a numerous assembly, composed of individuals actuated by motives in
themselves diametrically opposite.   The motion being
rejected by the majority, the same gentleman moved
again for an address, that his majesty would give directions for laying before the House copies of such memorials or representations as had been made, either to the
King of Spain or to his ministers, since the treaty of
Seville, relating to the depredations committed in Europe
or America.   A debate ensued; and, upon a division,
the question passed in the negative.

Petitions
against the
convention.

The House, in a committee of supply, voted twelve
thousand seamen for the service of the ensuing year,
and the standing army was continued without reduction,
though powerfully attacked by the whole strength of the
opposition.   The Commons likewise ordered an address
to his majesty, for the copies of several memorials since
the treaty of Seville, touching the rights of Great Britain,
or any infraction of treaties which had not been laid
before them.   These were accordingly submitted to the
inspection of the House.   By this time the convention
itself was not only presented to the Commons, but also
published for the information of the people.   Divers
merchants, planters, and others trading to America, the
cities of London and Bristol, the merchants of Liverpool, and owners of sundry ships which had been seized
by the Spaniards, offered petitions against the convention, by which the subjects of Spain were so far from
giving up their groundless and unjustifiable practice of
visiting and searching British ships sailing to and from
the British plantations, that they appeared to have
claimed the power of doing it as a right; for they insisted that the differences which had arisen concerning
it should be referred to plenipotentiaries, to be discussed
by them without even agreeing to abstain from such
visitation and search during the time that the discussion
of this affair might last.   They therefore prayed, that
they might have an opportunity of being heard, and
allowed to represent the great importance of the British
trade to and from the plantations in America; the clear

indisputable right which they had to enjoy it, without being stopped, visited, or searched by the Spaniards, on any pretence whatsoever; and the certain inevitable destruction of all the riches and strength derived to Great Britain from that trade, if a search of British ships sailing to and from their own plantations should be tolerated upon any pretext, or under any restrictions, or even if the freedom of this navigation should continue much longer in a state of uncertainty. These petitions were referred to the committee appointed to consider of the convention. Another remonstrance was likewise presented by the trustees for establishing the colony of Georgia, setting forth, that the King of Spain claimed that colony as part of his territories; and that by the convention, the regulation of the limits of Carolina and Florida was referred to the determination of plenipotentiaries; so that the colony of Georgia, which undoubtedly belonged to the crown of Great Britain, was left in dispute, while the settlers remained in the most precarious and dangerous situation. It was moved, that the merchants should be heard by their counsel; but the proposal was strenuously opposed by the ministry, and rejected upon a division.

This famous convention, concluded at the Pardo on the fourteenth day of January, imported, that within six weeks, to be reckoned from the day on which the ratifications were exchanged, two ministers plenipotentiaries should meet at Madrid, to confer, and finally regulate the respective pretensions of the two crowns, with relation to the trade and navigation in America and Europe, and to the limits of Florida and Carolina, as well as concerning other points which remained likewise to be adjusted, according to the former treaties subsisting between the two nations: that the plenipotentiaries should finish their conferences within the space of eight months: that in the mean time no progress should be made in the fortifications of Florida and Carolina: that his Catholic majesty should pay to the King of Great Britain the sum of ninety-five thousand pounds, for a balance due to the crown and subjects of Great Britain, after deduction made of the demands of the crown and subjects of Spain: that this sum should be employed for the satis-

faction, discharge, and payment of the demands of the
British subjects upon the crown of Spain: that this reciprocal discharge, however, should not extend or relate
to the accounts and differences which subsisted and were
to be settled between the crown of Spain and the Assiento company, nor to any particular or private contracts
that might subsist between either of the two crowns, or
their ministers, with the subjects of the other; or between the subjects and subjects of each nation respec-
tively: that his Catholic majesty should cause the sum
of ninety-five thousand pounds to be paid at London
within four months, to be reckoned from the day on
which the ratifications were exchanged. Such was the
substance of that convention, which alarmed and provoked the merchants and traders of Great Britain,
excited the indignation of all those who retained any
regard for the honour of their country, and raised a
general cry against the minister who stood at the helm
of administration.

The eyes of the whole kingdom were now turned
upon the House of Commons. The two contending
parties summoned their whole force for the approaching
dispute: on the day appointed for considering the convention, four hundred members had taken their seats
by eight in the morning. In a committee of the whole
House, certain West India merchants and planters were
heard against the convention; so that this and the following day were employed in reading papers and obtaining information. On the eighth day of March, Mr. H.
Walpole, having launched out in the praise of that agreement, moved for an address of approbation to his majesty. He was seconded by Mr. Campbell, of Pembroke-
shire; and the debate began with extraordinary ardour.
He who first distinguished himself in the lists was Sir
Thomas Sanderson, at that time treasurer to the Prince
of Wales, afterwards Earl of Scarborough. All the officers and adherents of his royal highness had joined the
opposition; and he himself on this occasion sat in the
gallery, to hear the debate on such an important transaction. Sir Thomas Sanderson observed, that the
Spaniards by the convention, instead of giving us reparation, had obliged us to give them a general release.

They had not allowed the word satisfaction to be so much as once mentioned in the treaty. Even the Spanish pirate who had cut off the ear of Captain Jenkins [a], and used the most insulting expression towards the person of the king—an expression which no British subject could decently repeat—an expression which no man that had a regard for his sovereign could ever forgive—even this fellow lived to enjoy the fruits of his rapine, and remained a living testimony of the cowardly tameness and mean submission of Great Britain, of the triumphant haughtiness and stubborn pride of Spain. Lord Gage, one of the most keen, spirited, and sarcastic orators in the House, stated in this manner the account of the satisfaction obtained from the court of Spain by the convention: the losses sustained by the Spanish depredations amounted to three hundred and forty thousand pounds; the commissary, by a stroke of his pen, reduced this demand to two hundred thousand pounds; then forty-five thousand were struck off for prompt payment: he next allotted sixty thousand pounds as the remaining part of a debt pretended to be due to Spain, for the destruction of her fleet by Sir George Byng, though it appeared by the instructions on the table, that Spain had been already amply satisfied on that head: these deductions reduced the balance to ninety-five thousand pounds; but the King of Spain insisted upon the South-Sea Company's paying immediately the sum of sixty-eight thousand pounds, as a debt due to him on one head of accounts, though, in other

a Captain Jenkins was master of a Scottish merchant-ship. He was boarded by the captain of a Spanish guarda-costa, who treated him in the most barbarous manner. The Spaniards, after having rummaged his vessel for what they called contraband commodities, without finding any thing to justify their search, insulted Jenkins with the most opprobrious invectives. They tore off one of his ears, bidding him carry it to his king, and tell him they would serve him in the same manner should an opportunity offer: they tortured him with the most shocking cruelty, and threatened him with immediate death. This man was examined at the bar of the House of Commons, and being asked by a member what he thought when he found himself in the hands of such barbarians! "I recommended my soul to God," said he, "and my cause to my country." The behaviour of this brave seaman, the sight of his ear, which was produced, with his account of the indignities which had been offered to the nation and sovereign of Great Britain, filled the whole House with indignation. Jenkins was afterwards employed in the service of the East India Company: he approved himself worthy of his good fortune in a long engagement with the pirate Angria, during which he behaved with extraordinary courage and conduct, and saved his own ship, with three others that were under his convoy.

articles, his Catholic majesty was indebted to the company a million over and above this demand: the remainder to be paid by Spain did not exceed seven-and-
twenty thousand pounds, from which she insisted upon
deducting whatever she might have already given in
satisfaction for any of the British ships that had been
taken; and on being allowed the value of the St. Theresa,
a Spanish ship which had been seized in the port of
Dublin. Mr. W. Pitt, with an energy of argument
and diction peculiar to himself, declaimed against the
convention, as insecure, unsatisfactory, and dishonourable
to Great Britain. He said the great national objection,
the searching of British ships, was not admitted, indeed,
in the preamble; but stood there as the reproach of the
whole, as the strongest evidence of the fatal submission
that followed: on the part of Spain, an usurpation,
an inhuman tyranny claimed and exercised over the
American seas; on the part of England, an undoubted
right, by treaties, and from God and nature, declared and
asserted in the resolutions of Parliament, were now referred to the discussion of plenipotentiaries, upon one
and the same equal foot. This undoubted right was to
be discussed and regulated; and if to regulate be to
prescribe rules, as in all construction it is, that right was,
by the express words of the convention, to be given up
and sacrificed; for it must cease to be any thing from
the moment it is submitted to limitation. Mr. Lyttelton,
with equal force and fluency, answered the speech of
Mr. H. Walpole. "After he had used many arguments
to persuade us to peace (said he), to any peace, good or
bad, by pointing out the dangers of a war, dangers I by
no means allow to be such as he represents them, he
crowned all those terrors with the name of the pretender. It would be the cause of the pretender. The
pretender would come. Is the honourable gentleman
sensible what this language imports? The people of
England complain of the greatest wrongs and indignities: they complain of the interruption, the destruction,
of their trade; they think the peace has left them in a
worse condition than before; and, in answer to all these
complaints, what are they told? Why, that their continuing to suffer all this, is the price they must pay to

keep the king and his family on the throne of these realms. If this were true, it ought not to be owned; but it is far from truth; the very reverse is true. Nothing can weaken the family, nothing shake the establishment, but such measures as these, and such language as this." He affirmed, that if the ministers had proceeded conformably to the intentions of Parliament, they would either have acted with vigour, or have obtained a real security in an express acknowledgment of our right not to be searched as a preliminary, *sine qua non*, to our treating at all. Instead of this, they had referred it to plenipotentiaries. "Would you, sir, (said he,) submit to a reference, whether you may travel unmolested from your house in town to your house in the country? Your right is clear and undeniable, why would you have it discussed? but much less would you refer it, if two of your judges belonged to a gang which has often stopped and robbed you in your way thither before."—The ministers, in vindication of the convention, asserted, that the satisfaction granted by Spain was adequate to the injury received; that it was only the preliminary of a treaty which would remove all causes of complaint; that war was always expensive and detrimental to a trading nation, as well as uncertain in its events; that France and Spain would certainly join their forces in case of a rupture with Great Britain; that there was not one power in Europe upon which the English could depend for effectual assistance; and that war would favour the cause and designs of a popish pretender. The House, upon a division, agreed to the address; but when a motion was made for its being recommitted, the two parties renewed the engagement with redoubled eagerness and impetuosity. Sir William Wyndham and Mr. Pulteney poured all the thunder of their eloquence against the insolence of Spain and the concessions of the British ministry. Sir Robert Walpole exerted all his fortitude and dexterity in defence of himself and his measures, and the question being put, the resolutions for the address were carried by a small majority.

Then Sir William Wyndham, standing up, made a pathetic remonstrance upon this determination. "This Secession of the chief

CHAP.
XVII.

1738.
members
in the op-
position.

address (said he) is intended to convince mankind, that the treaty under our consideration is a reasonable and an honourable treaty. But if a majority of twenty-eight in such a full house should fail of that success; if the people should not implicitly resign their reason to a vote of this House, what will be the consequence? Will not the Parliament lose its authority? Will it not be thought, that even in the Parliament we are governed by a faction? and what the consequence of this may be, I leave to those gentlemen to consider, who are now to give their vote for this address: for my own part I will trouble you no more, but with these my last words, I sincerely pray to Almighty God, who has so often wonderfully protected these kingdoms, that he will graciously continue his protection over them, by preserving us from that impending danger which threatens the nation from without, and likewise from that impending danger which threatens our constitution from within." The minister was on this occasion deserted by his usual temper, and even provoked into personal abuse. He declared, that the gentleman who was now the mouth of his opponents, had been looked upon as the head of those traitors, who twenty-five years before conspired the destruction of their country and of the royal family, in order to set a popish pretender upon the throne; that he was seized by the vigilance of the then government, and pardoned by its clemency; but all the use he had ungratefully made of that clemency, was to qualify himself according to law, that he and his party might some time or other have an opportunity to overthrow all law. He branded them all as traitors, and expressed his hope that their behaviour would unite all the true friends of the present happy establishment. To such a degree of mutual animosity were both sides inflamed, that the most eminent members in the minority actually retired from Parliament; and were by the nation in general revered as martyrs to the liberty of the people.

Debate in
the House
of Lords
upon an
address to
his majesty
touching
the conven-
tion.

The dispute occasioned by the convention in the House of Lords was maintained with equal warmth, and perhaps with more abilities. After this famous treaty had been considered, Lord Carteret suggested, that possibly one of the contracting powers had presented a protest or declaration, importing that she acceded to such or such a measure, only upon condition that the terms of that protest or declaration should be made good. He said, that until his mind should be free from the most distant suspicion that such a paper might exist in the present case, he could not form a just opinion of the transaction himself, nor communicate to their lordships any light which might be necessary for that purpose. The adherents to the ministry endeavoured to evade his curiosity in this particular by general assertions; but he insisted on his suspicion with such perseverance, that at length the ministry produced the copy of a declaration made by the King of Spain before he ratified the convention, signifying that his Catholic majesty reserved to himself, in its full force, the right of being able to suspend the assiento of negroes, in case the company should not pay within a short time the sum of sixty-eight thousand pounds sterling, owing to Spain on the duty of negroes, or on the profit of the ship Caroline; that under the validity and force of this protest, the signing of the said convention might be proceeded on, and in no other manner. In the debate that ensued, Lord Carteret displayed a surprising extent of political knowledge, recommended by all the graces of elocution, chaste, pure, dignified, and delicate. Lord Bathurst argued against the articles of convention with his usual spirit, integrity, and good sense, particularly animated by an honest indignation which the wrongs of his country had inspired. The Earl of Chesterfield attacked this inglorious measure with all the weight of argument, and all the poignancy of satire. The Duke of Argyle, no longer a partisan of the ministry, inveighed against it as infamous, treacherous, and destructive, with all the fire, impetuosity, and enthusiasm of declamation. It was defended with unequal arms by the Duke of Newcastle, the Earl of Cholmondeley, Lord Hervey, the lord chancellor, the Bishop of Salisbury, and in particular by the Earl of Ilay, a nobleman of extensive capacity and uncommon erudition; remarkable for his knowledge of the civil law, and seemingly formed by nature for a politician; cool, discerning, plausible, artful, and enterprising, staunch to the minister, and invariably true to his own interest. The dispute was learned, long, and obstinate; but ended

as usual in the discomfiture of those who had stigmatized
the treaty. The house agreed to an address, in which they
thanked his majesty for his gracious condescension in laying before them the convention. They acknowledged
his great prudence in bringing the demands of his subjects for their past losses, which had been so long depending, to a final adjustment; in procuring an express stipulation for a speedy payment; and in laying a foundation
for accomplishing the great and desirable ends of obtaining future security, and preserving the peace between
the two nations. They declared their confidence in his
royal wisdom, that in the treaty to be concluded, in pursuance of the convention, proper provisions would be
made for the redress of the grievances of which the nation
had so justly complained : they assured his majesty, that
in case his just expectations should not be answered, the
House would heartily and zealously concur in all such
measures as should be necessary to vindicate his majesty's
honour, and to preserve to his subjects the full enjoyment of all those rights to which they were entitled by
treaty and the law of nations. This was a hard-won victory. At the head of those who voted against the address we find the Prince of Wales. His example was
followed by six dukes, two-and-twenty earls, four vis-
counts, eighteen barons, four bishops; and their party

1739.   was reinforced by sixteen proxies. A spirited protest was
entered, and subscribed by nine-and-thirty peers, comprehending all the noblemen of the kingdom who were most
eminent for their talents, integrity, and virtue.

Message
from the
throne
touching a
subsidy to
Denmark,
and a power
to augment
the forces
of the king-
dom.

A message having been delivered to the House from
his majesty, importing that he had settled nine-and-thirty
thousand pounds per annum on the younger children of
the royal family; and desiring their lordships would
bring in a bill to enable his majesty to make that provision good out of the hereditary revenues of the crown;
some lords in the opposition observed, that the next heir
to the crown might look upon this settlement as a mort-
gage of his revenue, which a Parliament had no power
to make : that formerly no daughter of the royal family
was ever provided for by Parliament, except the eldest,
and that never was by way of annuity, but an express
provision of a determinate sum of money paid by way

of dowry. These objections were overruled; and the House complied with his majesty's request. Then the Duke of Newcastle produced a subsidy-treaty, by which his majesty obliged himself to pay to the King of Denmark seventy thousand pounds per annum, on condition of the Dane's furnishing to his Britannic majesty a body of six thousand men when demanded. At the same time, his grace delivered a message from the king, desiring the House would enable him to fulfil this engagement; and also to raise what money and troops the exigency of affairs, during the approaching recess, might require. Another vehement dispute arose from this proposal. With respect to the treaty, Lord Carteret observed, that no use could be made of the Danish troops in any expedition undertaken against Spain, because it was stipulated in the treaty, that they should not be used either in Italy, or on board of the fleet, or be transported in whole or in part beyond sea, after they should have marched out of the territories of Denmark, except for the defence of the kingdoms of Great Britain and Ireland: nay, should France join against the English, the Danes could not act against that power or Spain, except as part of an army formed in Germany or Flanders. This body of Danes may be said, therefore, to have been retained for the defence and protection of Hanover; or, if the interest of Britain was at all consulted in the treaty, it must have been in preventing the Danes from joining their fleets to those of France and Spain. Then he argued against the second part of the message with great vivacity. He said nothing could be more dangerous to the constitution than a general and unlimited vote of credit. Such a demand our ancestors would have heard with amazement, and rejected with scorn. He affirmed that the practice was but of modern date in England; that it was never heard of before the Revolution; and never became frequent until the nation was blessed with the present wise administration. He said, if ever a general vote of credit and confidence should become a customary compliment from the Parliament to the crown at the end of every session, or as often as the minister might think fit to desire it, Parliaments would grow despicable in the eyes of the people; then a proclamation might be easily

CHAP.
XVII.

1739.

substituted in its stead, and happy would it be for the nation if that should be sufficient; for when a Parliament ceases to be a check upon ministers, it becomes an useless and unnecessary burden on the people. The representatives must always be paid some way or other: ·if their wages are not paid openly and surely by their respective constituents, as they were formerly, a majority of them may in future times be always ready to accept of wages from the administration, and these must come out of the pockets of the people. The Duke of Argyle and the Earl of Chesterfield enlarged upon the same topics. Nevertheless, the House complied with the message; and presented an address, in which they not only approved of the treaty with Denmark, but likewise assured his majesty they would concur with his measures, and support him in fulfilling his engagements, as well as in making such further augmentation of his forces by sea and land, as he should think necessary for the honour, interest, and safety of these kingdoms.

Parliament prorogued.

The same message being communicated to the Commons, they voted seventy thousand five hundred and-eighty-three pounds for the subsidy to Denmark, and five hundred thousand pounds for augmenting the forces on any emergency. As Great Britain stood engaged by the convention to pay to the crown of Spain the sum of sixty thousand pounds in consideration of the ships taken and destroyed by Sir George Byng, which sum was to be applied to the relief of the British merchants who had suffered by the Spanish depredations, the Commons inserted in a bill a clause providing for this sum to be paid by the Parliament. When the bill was read in the House of Lords, a motion was made by Lord Bathurst for an address, to know whether Spain had paid the money stipulated by the convention, as the time limited for the payment of it was now expired. The Duke of Newcastle, by his majesty's permission, acquainted the House that it was not paid, and that Spain had as yet given no reason for the non-payment. Then a day was appointed to consider the state of the nation, when Lord Carteret moved for a resolution, that the failure of Spain in this particular was a breach of the convention, a high indignity to his majesty, and an injustice to the nation;

but, after a warm debate, this motion was overruled by CHAP.
the majority. The minister, in order to atone in some XVII.
measure for the unpopular step he had taken in the con- 1739.
vention, allowed a salutary law to pass for the encouragement of the woollen manufacture, and two bills in
behalf of the sugar colonies : one permitting them for a
limited time to export their produce directly to foreign
parts, under proper restrictions ; and the other making
more effectual provisions for securing the duties laid
upon the importation of foreign sugars, rum, and molasses, into Great Britain, and his majesty's plantations
in America. The supplies being voted, the funds established, and the crown gratified in every particular, the
king closed the session with a speech on the fourteenth
day of June, when the chancellor in his majesty's name
prorogued the Parliament[b].

Letters of marque and reprisal were granted against The King
the Spaniards; a promotion was made of general officers; of Spain
the troops were augmented; a great fleet was assembled manifesto.
at Spithead ; a reinforcement sent out to Admiral Haddock ; and an embargo laid on all merchant-ships out-
ward bound. Notwithstanding these preparations of war,
Mr. Keene, the British minister at Madrid, declared to
the court of Spain that his master, although he had permitted his subjects to make reprisals, would not be understood to have broken the peace ; and that this permission
would be recalled as soon as his Catholic majesty should
be disposed to make the satisfaction which had been so
justly demanded. He was given to understand, that the
King of Spain looked upon those reprisals as acts of
hostility ; and that he hoped, with the assistance of
heaven and his allies, he should be able to support a
good cause against his adversaries. He published a

[b] Among the laws enacted in the course of this session was an act against
gaming, which had become universal through all ranks of people, and likely to
prove destructive of all morals, industry, and sentiment. Another bill passed,
for granting a reward to Joanna Stevens, on her discovering, for the benefit of
the public, a nostrum for the cure of persons afflicted with the stone ; a medicine
which has by no means answered the expectations of the legislature.
In the House of Lords, complaint was made by Lord Delawar of a satire, entitled Manners, written by Mr. Whitehead ; in which some characters of distinction were severely lashed, in the true spirit of poetry. It was voted a libel : a
motion was made to take the author into custody ; but he having withdrawn himself, the resentment of the House fell upon R. Dodsley, the publisher of the work,
who was committed to the usher of the black-rod, though Lord Carteret, the
Earl of Abingdon, and Lord Talbot, spoke in his behalf.

manifesto in justification of his own conduct, complaining that Admiral Haddock had received orders to cruize
with his squadron between the capes St. Vincent and
St. Mary, in order to surprise the Assogue ships; that
letters of reprisal had been published at London in an in-
decent style, and even carried into execution in different
parts of the world.   He excused his non-payment of the
ninety-five thousand pounds stipulated in the convention,
by affirming that the British court had first contravened
the articles of that treaty, by the orders sent to Haddock;
by continuing to fortify Georgia; by reinforcing the
squadron at Jamaica; and by eluding the payment of
the sixty-eight thousand pounds due to Spain from the
South-Sea Company, on the assiento for negroes.   The
French ambassador at the Hague declared that the king
his master was obliged by treaties to assist his Catholic
majesty by sea and land, in case he should be attacked;
he dissuaded the States-General from espousing the
quarrel of Great Britain; and they assured him they
would observe a strict neutrality, though they could not
avoid furnishing his Britannic majesty with such succours
as he could demand, by virtue of the treaties subsisting
between the two powers.   The people of England were
inspired with uncommon alacrity at the near prospect of
war, for which they had so long clamoured; and the
ministry, seeing it unavoidable, began to be earnest and
effectual in their preparations.

The em-
peror and
czarina
conclude a
peace with
the Turks.

The events of war were still unfavourable to the emperor.   He had bestowed the command of his army upon
Veldt-Mareschal Count Wallis, who assembled his forces
in the neighbourhood of Belgrade; and advanced towards
Crotska, where he was attacked by the Turks with such
impetuosity and perseverance, that he was obliged to give
ground, after a long and obstinate engagement, in which
he lost above six thousand men.   The Earl of Crawford,
who served as a volunteer in the imperial army, signalized
his courage in an extraordinary manner on this occasion,
and received a dangerous wound, of which he never perfectly recovered.   The Turks were afterwards worsted at
Jabouka; nevertheless, their grand army invested Belgrade on the side of Servia, and carried on the operations
of the siege with extraordinary vigour.   The emperor,

dreading the loss of this place, seeing his finances exhausted, and his army considerably diminished, consented to a negotiation for peace, which was transacted under the mediation of the French ambassador at the Ottoman Porte. The Count de Neuperg, as imperial plenipotentiary, signed the preliminaries on the first day of September. They were ratified by the emperor, though he pretended to be dissatisfied with the articles; and declared that his minister had exceeded his powers. By this treaty the house of Austria ceded to the grand signor, Belgrade, Sabatz, Servia, Austrian Wallachia, the isle and fortress of Orsova, with the fort of St. Elizabeth; and the contracting powers agreed that the Danube and the Saave should serve as boundaries to the two empires. The emperor published a circular letter, addressed to his ministers at all the courts in Europe, blaming Count Wallis for the bad success of the last campaign, and disowning the negotiations of Count Neuperg; nay, these two officers were actually disgraced, and confined in different castles. This, however, was no other than a sacrifice to the resentment of the czarina, who loudly complained that the emperor had concluded a separate peace, contrary to his engagements with the Russian empire. Her general, Count Munich, had obtained a victory over the Turks at Choczim, in Moldavia, and made himself master of that place, in which he found two hundred pieces of artillery; but the country was so ruined by the incursions of the Tartars, that the Muscovites could not subsist in it during the winter. The czarina, finding herself abandoned by the emperor, and unable to cope with the whole power of the Ottoman empire, took the first opportunity of putting an end to the war upon honourable terms. After a short negotiation, the conferences ended in a treaty, by which she was left in possession of Asoph, on condition that its fortifications should be demolished; and the ancient limits were re-established between the two empires.

A rupture between Great Britain and Spain was now become inevitable. The English squadron in the Mediterranean had already made prize of two rich Caracca ships. The king had issued orders for augmenting his land-forces and raising a body of marines; and a great

Preparations for war in England.

number of ships of war were put in commission. Admiral Vernon had been sent to the West Indies, to assume the command of the squadron in those seas, and to annoy the trade and settlements of the Spaniards. This gentleman had rendered himself considerable in the House of Commons, by loudly condemning all the measures of the ministry, and bluntly speaking his sentiments, whatever they were, without respect of persons, and sometimes without any regard to decorum. He was counted a good officer, and this boisterous manner seemed to enhance his character. As he had once commanded a squadron in Jamaica, he was perfectly well acquainted with those seas; and in a debate upon the Spanish depredations, he chanced to affirm, that Porto Bello, on the Spanish main, might be easily taken; nay, he even undertook to reduce it with six ships only. This offer was echoed from the mouths of all the members in the opposition. Vernon was extolled as another Drake or Raleigh: he became the idol of a party, and his praise resounded from all corners of the kingdom. The minister, in order to appease the clamours of the people on this subject, sent him as commander-in-chief to the West Indies. He was pleased with an opportunity to remove such a troublesome censor from the House of Commons; and, perhaps, he was not without hope, that Vernon would disgrace himself and his party, by failing in the exploit he had undertaken. His Catholic majesty having ordered all the British ships in his harbours to be seized and detained, the King of England would keep measures with him no longer, but denounced war against him on the twenty-third day of October. Many English merchants began to equip privateers, and arm their trading vessels, to protect their own commerce, as well as to distress that of the enemy. The session of Parliament was opened in November, when the king, in his speech to both Houses, declared that he had augmented his forces by sea and land, pursuant to the power vested in him by Parliament for the security of his dominions, the protection of trade, and the annoyance of the enemy; and he expressed his apprehension, that the heats and animosities which had been industriously fomented throughout the kingdom, encouraged Spain to act in such a manner as rendered it necessary for him to have recourse to arms. In answer to this speech, affectionate addresses were presented by both Houses, without any considerable opposition.

The seceding members had again resumed their seats in the House of Commons; and Mr. Pulteney thought proper to vindicate the extraordinary step which they had taken. He said, they thought that step was necessary, as affairs then stood, for clearing their characters to posterity from the imputation of sitting in an assembly, where a determined majority gave a sanction to measures evidently to the disgrace of his majesty and the nation. He observed, that their conduct was so fully justified by the declaration of war against Spain, that any further vindication would be superfluous; for every assertion contained in it had been almost in the same words insisted upon by those who opposed the convention: "Every sentence in it (added he) is an echo of what was said in our reasonings against that treaty: every positive truth which the declaration lays down was denied with the utmost confidence by those who spoke for the convention; and since that time there has not one event happened which was not then foreseen and foretold." He proposed, that in maintaining the war, the Spanish settlements in the West Indies should be attacked; and that the ministry should not have the power to give up the conquests that might be made. He said he heartily wished, for his majesty's honour and service, that no mention had been made of heats and animosities in the king's speech; and gave it as his opinion, that they should take no notice of that clause in their address. He was answered by Sir Robert Walpole, who took occasion to say, he was in no great concern lest the service of his majesty or the nation should suffer by the absence of those members who had quitted the House: he affirmed, the nation was generally sensible, that the many useful and popular acts which passed towards the end of the last session were greatly forwarded and facilitated by the secession of those gentlemen; and, if they were returned only to oppose and perplex, he should not be at all sorry to see them secede again.

Mr. Pulteney revived the bill which he had formerly

CHAP.
XVII.

1739.
Pension-
bill revived
and lost.
prepared for the encouragement of seamen. After a
long dispute, and eager opposition by the ministry, it
passed both Houses, and obtained the royal assent.
Mr. Sandys, having observed that there could be no
immediate use for a great number of forces in the kingdom, and explained how little service could be expected
from raw and undisciplined men, proposed an address to
the king, desiring that the body of marines should be
composed of drafts from the old regiments; that as few
officers should be appointed as the nature of the case
would permit; and he expressed his hope that the House
would recommend this method to his majesty, in tender
compassion to his people, already burdened with many
heavy and grievous taxes. This scheme was repugnant
to the intention of the ministry, whose aim was to increase the number of their dependents, and extend their
parliamentary interest, by granting a great number of
commissions. The proposal was, therefore, after a long
debate, rejected by the majority. Motions were made
for an inquiry into the conduct of those who concluded
the convention, but they were overruled. The pension
bill was revived, and so powerfully supported by the eloquence of Sir William Wyndham, Mr. Pulteney, and
Mr. Lyttelton, that it made its way through the Commons
to the Upper House, where it was again lost, upon a
division, after a very long debate. As the seamen of
the kingdom expressed uncommon aversion to the service of the government, and the fleet could not be manned
without great difficulty, the ministry prepared a bill, which
was brought in by Sir Charles Wager, for registering all
seamen, watermen, fishermen, and lightermen throughout his majesty's dominions. Had this bill passed into
a law, a British sailor would have been reduced to the
most abject degree of slavery: had he removed from a
certain district allotted for the place of his residence, he
would have been deemed a deserter, and punished accordingly; he must have appeared, when summoned, at
all hazards, whatever might have been the circumstances
of his family, or the state of his private affairs: had he
been encumbered with debt, he must either have incurred the penalties of this law, or lain at the mercy of
his creditors: had he acquired by industry, or received

by inheritance, an ample fortune, he would have been liable to be torn from his possessions, and subjected to hardships which no man would endure but from the sense of fear or indigence. The bill was so vigorously opposed by Sir John Barnard and others, as a flagrant encroachment on the liberties of the people, that the House rejected it on the second reading.

The king having by message communicated to the House his intention of disposing the Princess Mary in marriage to Prince Frederick of Hesse; and expressing his hope, that the Commons would enable him to give a suitable portion to his daughter, they unanimously resolved to grant forty thousand pounds for that purpose; and presented an address of thanks to his majesty, for having communicated to the House this intended marriage. On the thirteenth day of March a ship arrived from the West Indies, despatched by Admiral Vernon, with an account of his having taken Porto Bello, on the isthmus of Darien, with six ships only, and demolished all the fortifications of the place. The Spaniards acted with such pusillanimity on this occasion, that their forts were taken almost without bloodshed. The two Houses of Parliament joined in an address of congratulation upon the success of his majesty's arms; and the nation in general was wonderfully elated by an exploit which was magnified much above its merit. The Commons granted every thing the crown thought proper to demand. They provided for eight-and-twenty thousand land forces, besides six thousand marines. They enabled his majesty to equip a very powerful navy; they voted the subsidy to the King of Denmark; and they empowered their sovereign to defray certain extraordinary expenses not specified in the estimates. To answer these uncommon grants, they imposed a land-tax of four shillings in the pound; and enabled his majesty to deduct twelve hundred thousand pounds from the sinking fund; in a word, the expense of the war, during the course of the ensuing year, amounted to about four millions. The session was closed on the twenty-ninth day of April, when the king thanked the Commons for the supplies they had so liberally granted, and recommended union and moderation to both Houses.

Porto Bello taken by Admiral Vernon.

During the greatest part of this winter, the poor had been grievously afflicted in consequence of a severe frost, which began at Christmas, and continued till the latter end of February. The river Thames was covered with such a crust of ice that a multitude of people dwelled upon it in tents, and a great number of booths were erected for the entertainment of the populace. The navigation was entirely stopped : the watermen and fishermen were disabled from earning a livelihood : the fruits of the earth were destroyed by the cold, which was so extreme that many persons were chilled to death; and this calamity was the more deeply felt, as the poor could not afford to supply themselves with coals and fuel, which were advanced in price, in proportion to the severity and continuance of the frost. The lower class of labourers who worked in the open air, were now deprived of all means of subsistence : many kinds of manufacture were laid aside, because it was found impracticable to carry them on. The price of all sorts of provisions rose almost to a dearth ; even water was sold in the streets of London. In this season of distress, many wretched families must have perished by cold and hunger, had not those of opulent fortunes been inspired with a remarkable spirit of compassion and humanity. Nothing can more redound to the honour of the English nation than did those instances of benevolence and well-conducted charity which were then exhibited. The liberal hand was not only opened to the professed beggar, and the poor that owned their distress; but uncommon pains were taken to find out and relieve those more unhappy objects, who, from motives of false pride or ingenuous shame, endeavoured to conceal their misery. These were assisted almost in their own despite. The solitary habitations of the widow, the fatherless, and the unfortunate, were visited by the beneficent, who felt for the woes of their fellow-creatures; and, to such as refused to receive a portion of the public charity, the necessaries of life were privately conveyed, in such a manner as could least shock the delicacy of their dispositions.

In the beginning of May the King of Great Britain set out for Hanover, after having appointed a regency,

and concerted vigorous measures for distressing the enemy.
In a few days after his departure, the espousals of the
Princess Mary were celebrated by proxy, the Duke of
Cumberland representing the Prince of Hesse; and in
June the princess embarked for the continent. About the
same time, a sloop arrived in England with despatches
from Admiral Vernon, who, since his adventure at Porto
Bello, had bombarded Carthagena, and taken the fort of
San Lorenzo, on the river of Chagre, in the neighbourhood of his former conquest. This month was likewise
marked by the death of his Prussian majesty, a prince
by no means remarkable for great or amiable qualities.
He was succeeded on the throne by Frederick his eldest
son, the late king of that realm, who has so eminently
distinguished himself as a warrior and legislator. In
August, the King of Great Britain concluded a treaty
with the Landgrave of Hesse, who engaged to furnish
him with a body of six thousand men for four years, in
consideration of an annual subsidy of two hundred and
fifty thousand crowns.

Meanwhile, preparations of war were vigorously carried on by the ministry in England. They had wisely
resolved to annoy the Spaniards in their American possessions. Three ships of war, cruising in the bay of
Biscay, fell in with a large Spanish ship of the line
strongly manned, and took her after a very obstinate
engagement; but the assogue ships arrived, with the
treasure, in Spain, notwithstanding the vigilance of the
English commanders, who were stationed in a certain
latitude to intercept that flota. One camp was formed
on Hounslow-heath; and six thousand marines lately
levied were encamped on the Isle of Wight, in order to
be embarked for the West Indies. Intelligence being
received, that a strong squadron of Spanish ships of war
waited at Ferrol for orders to sail to their American settlements, Sir John Norris sailed with a powerful fleet from
Spithead, to dispute their voyage; and the Duke of Cumberland served in person as a volunteer in this expedition; but after divers fruitless efforts, he was, by contrary winds, òbliged to lie inactive for the greatest part
of the summer in Torbay; and, upon advice that the
French and Spanish squadrons had sailed to the West

CHAP.
XVII.

1740.

Indies in conjunction, the design against Ferrol was wholly laid aside. In September, a small squadron of ships, commanded by Commodore Anson, set sail for the South-Sea, in order to act against the enemy on the coast of Chili and Peru, and co-operate occasionally with Admiral Vernon across the isthmus of Darien. The scheme was well laid, but ruined by unnecessary delays and unforeseen accidents. But the hopes of the nation centred chiefly in a formidable armament designed for the northern coast of New Spain, and his Catholic majesty's other settlements on that side of the Atlantic. Commissions had been issued for raising a regiment of four battalions in the English colonies of North America, that they might be transported to Jamaica, and join the forces from England. These, consisting of the marines, and detachments from some old regiments, were embarked in October at the Isle of Wight, under the command of Lord Cathcart, a nobleman of approved honour, and great experience in the art of war; and they sailed under convoy of Sir Chaloner Ogle, with a fleet of seven-and-twenty ships of the line, besides frigates, fire-ships, bomb-ketches, and tenders. They were likewise furnished with hospital-ships, and store-ships, laden with provisions, ammunition, all sorts of warlike implements, and every kind of convenience. Never was an armament more completely equipped; and never had the nation more reason to hope for extraordinary success.

Death of
the em-
peror and
czarina.

On the twentieth day of October, Charles VI. Emperor of Germany, the last prince of the house of Austria, died at Vienna, and was succeeded in his hereditary dominions by his eldest daughter, the Archduchess Maria Theresa, married to the Grand Duke of Tuscany. Though this princess succeeded as Queen of Hungary, by virtue of the pragmatic sanction guaranteed by all the powers in Europe, her succession produced such contests as kindled a cruel war in the empire. The young King of Prussia was no sooner informed of the emperor's death, than he entered Silesia at the head of twenty thousand men; seized certain fiefs to which his family laid claim; and published a manifesto, declaring that he had no intention to contravene the pragmatic sanction. The Elector of Bavaria refused to acknowledge the arch-

duchess as Queen of Hungary and Bohemia; alleging,
that he himself had pretensions to those countries, as the
descendant of the Emperor Ferdinand I., who was head
of the German branch of the house of Austria. Charles
VI. was survived but a few days by his ally, the Czarina
Anne Iwanowna, who died in the forty-fifth year of her
age, after having bequeathed her crown to Iwan, or John,
the infant son of her niece, the Princess Anne of Mecklenburgh, who had been married to Anthony Ulrick,
Duke of Brunswick Lunenbourg-Bevern. She appointed
the Duke of Courland regent of the empire, and even
guardian of the young czar, though his own parents were
alive; but this disposition was not long maintained.

The King of Great Britain having returned to Eng- Proceed-
land from his German dominions, the session of Parlia- ings in Parliament was opened in November. His majesty assured ment.
them, on this occasion, that he was determined to prose-
secute the war vigorously, even though France should
espouse the cause of Spain, as her late conduct seemed
to favour this supposition. He took notice of the emperor's death, as an event which in all likelihood would
open a new scene of affairs in Europe; he therefore recommended to their consideration the necessary supplies
for putting the nation in such a posture, that it should
have nothing to fear from any emergency. Finally, he
desired them to consider of some proper regulations for
preventing the exportation of corn, and for more effectual methods to man the fleet at this conjuncture. The
Commons, after having voted an address of thanks,
brought in a bill for prohibiting the exportation of corn
and provisions, for a limited time, out of Great Britain,
Ireland, and the American plantations. This was a measure calculated to distress the enemy, who were supposed
to be in want of these necessaries. The French had
contracted for a very large quantity of beef and pork in
Ireland for the use of their own and the Spanish navy;
and an embargo had been laid upon the ships of that
kingdom. The bill met with a vigorous opposition; yet
the House unanimously resolved, that his majesty should
be addressed to lay an immediate embargo upon all ships
laden with corn, grain, starch, rice, beef, pork, and other

provisions to be exported to foreign parts. They likewise resolved that the thanks of the House should be
given to Vice-Admiral Vernon, for the services he had
done to his king and country in the West Indies. One
William Cooley was examined at the bar of the House,
and committed to prison, after having owned himself
author of a paper, entitled "Considerations upon the
Embargo on Provision of Victual." The performance
contained many shrewd and severe animadversions upon
the government, for having taken a step which, without
answering the purpose of distressing the enemy, would
prove a grievous discouragement to trade, and ruin all
the graziers of Ireland. Notwithstanding the arguments
used in this remonstrance, and several petitions that were
presented against the corn-bill, it passed by mere dint of
ministerial influence. The other party endeavoured, by
various motions, to set on foot an inquiry into the orders,
letters, and instructions, which had been sent to Admiral
Vernon and Admiral Haddock; but all such investiga-
tions were carefully avoided.

Seamen's
bill.

A very hot contest arose from a bill which the ministry brought in under the specious title of "A bill for
the encouragement and increase of seamen, and for the
better and speedier manning his majesty's fleet." This
was a revival of the oppressive scheme which had been
rejected in the former session; a scheme by which the
justices of the peace were empowered to issue warrants
to constables and headboroughs, to search by day or
night for such seafaring men as should conceal themselves within their respective jurisdictions. These
searchers were vested with authority to force open doors
in case of resistance; and encouraged to this violence by
a reward for every seaman they should discover; while
the unhappy wretches so discovered were dragged into
the service, and their names entered in a register to be
kept at the navy or the admiralty office. Such a plan
of tyranny did not pass uncensured. Every exception-
able clause produced a warm debate, in which Sir John
Barnard, Mr. Pulteney, Mr. Sandys, Lord Gage, Mr. Pitt,
and Mr. Lyttelton, signalized themselves nobly in de-
fending the liberties of their fellow-subjects. Mr. Pitt

having expressed a laudable indignation at such a large CHAP.
stride towards despotic power, in justification of which XVII.
nothing could be urged but the plea of necessity, Mr. H. 1740.
Walpole thought proper to attack him with some personal sarcasms. He reflected upon his youth; and observed that the discovery of truth was very little promoted
by pompous diction and theatrical emotion. These insinuations exposed him to a severe reply. Mr. Pitt,
standing up again, said, " He would not undertake to
determine whether youth could be justly imputed to any
man as a reproach; but he affirmed, that the wretch,
who, after having seen the consequences of repeated
errors, continues still to blunder, and whose age has only
added obstinacy to stupidity, is surely the object of either
abhorrence or contempt, and deserves not that his gray
head should secure him from insults; much more is he
to be abhorred, who, as he has advanced in age, has re-
ceded from virtue, and becomes more wicked with less
temptation; who prostitutes himself for money which he
cannot enjoy; and spends the remains of his life in the
ruin of his country." Petitions were presented from the
city of London, and county of Gloucester, against the
bill, as detrimental to the trade and navigation of the
kingdom, by discouraging rather than encouraging sailors,
and destructive to the liberties of the subject; but they
were both rejected as insults upon the House of Commons.
After very long debates, maintained on both sides with
extraordinary ardour and emotion, the severe clauses were
dropped, and the bill passed with amendments.

But the most remarkable incident of this session was Discontents
an open and personal attack upon the minister, who was against
become extremely unpopular all over the kingdom. The try.
people were now more than ever sensible of the grievous
taxes under which they groaned; and saw their burdens
daily increasing. No effectual attempt had as yet been
made to annoy the enemy. Expensive squadrons had
been equipped, had made excursions, and returned without striking a blow. The Spanish fleet had sailed first
from Cadiz, and then from Ferrol, without any interruption from Admiral Haddock, who commanded the
British squadron in the Mediterranean, and who was
supposed to be restricted by the instructions he had

received from the ministry, though in fact his want of success was owing to accident. Admiral Vernon had written from the West Indies to his private friends, that he was neglected, and in danger of being sacrificed. Notwithstanding the numerous navy which the nation maintained, the Spanish privateers made prize of the British merchant-ships with impunity. In violation of treaties, and in contempt of that intimate connexion which had been so long cultivated between the French and English ministry, the King of France had ordered the harbour and fortifications of Dunkirk to be repaired; his fleet had sailed to the West Indies, in conjunction with that of Spain; and the merchants of England began to tremble for Jamaica: finally, commerce was in a manner suspended, by the practice of pressing sailors into the service, and by the embargo which had been laid upon ships, in all the ports of Great Britain and Ireland. These causes of popular discontent, added to other complaints which had been so long repeated against the minister, exaggerated and inculcated by his enemies with unwearied industry, at length rendered him so universally odious, that his name was seldom or never mentioned with decency, except by his own dependents.

Motion for removing Sir Robert Walpole from his majesty's councils and presence for ever. The country party in Parliament seized this opportunity of vengeance. Mr. Sandys went up to Sir Robert Walpole in the House, and told him, that on Friday next he should bring a charge against him in public. The minister seemed to be surprised at this unexpected intimation; but, after a short pause, thanked him politely for this previous notice, and said he desired no favour, but fair play[c]. Mr. Sandys, at the time which he had appointed for this accusation, stood up, and in a studied speech entered into a long deduction of the minister's misconduct. He insisted upon the discontents of the nation, in consequence of the measures which had been for many years pursued at home and abroad. He professed his belief that there was not a gentleman in the House who did not know that one single person in the

---

[c] Upon this occasion he misquoted Horace. " As I am not conscious of any crime, (said he,) I do not doubt of being able to make a proper defence." *Nil conscire sibi, nulli pallescere culpæ.* He was corrected by Mr. Pulteney; but insisted upon his being in the right, and actually laid a wager on the justness of his quotation.

administration was the chief, if not the sole adviser and promoter of all those measures. "This (added he) is known without doors, as well as within; therefore, the discontents, the reproaches, and even the curses of the people are all directed against that single person. They complain of present measures; they have suffered by past measures; they expect no redress; they expect no alteration or amendment, whilst he has a share in directing or advising our future administration. These, sir, are the sentiments of the people in regard to that minister: these sentiments we are in honour and duty bound to represent to his majesty; and the proper method for doing this, as established by our constitution, is to address his majesty to remove him from his councils." He then proceeded to explain the particulars of the minister's misconduct in the whole series of his negotiations abroad. He charged him with having endeavoured to support his own interest, and to erect a kind of despotic government, by the practice of corruption; with having betrayed the interest and honour of Great Britain in the late convention; with having neglected to prosecute the war against Spain; and he concluded with a motion for an address to the king, that he would be pleased to remove Sir Robert Walpole from his presence and councils for ever. He was answered by Mr. Pelham, who undertook to defend or excuse all the measures which the other had condemned; and acquitted himself as a warm friend and unshaken adherent. Against this champion Sir John Barnard entered the lists, and was sustained by Mr. Pulteney, who, with equal spirit and precision, pointed out and exposed all the material errors and mal-practices of the administration. Sir Robert Walpole spoke with great temper and deliberation in behalf of himself. With respect to the article of bribery and corruption, he said, if any one instance had been mentioned; if it had been shown that he ever offered a reward to any member of either House, or ever threatened to deprive any member of his office or employment, in order to influence his voting in Parliament, there might have been some ground for this charge; but when it was so generally laid, he did not know what he could say to it, unless to deny it as generally and as positively

CHAP.
XVII.

1740.

as it had been asserted.—Such a declaration as this, in the hearing of so many persons, who not only knew, but subsisted by his wages of corruption, was a strong proof of the minister's being dead to all sense of shame, and all regard to veracity. The debate was protracted by the court members till three o'clock in the morning, when, about sixty of the opposite party having retired, the motion was rejected by a considerable majority.

Debate on the mutiny bill.

A bill was brought in for prohibiting the practice of insuring ships belonging to the enemies of the nation; but it was vigorously opposed by Sir John Barnard and Mr. Willimot, who demonstrated that this kind of traffic was advantageous to the kingdom; and the scheme was dropped. Another warm contest arose upon a clause of the mutiny bill, relating to the quartering of soldiers upon innkeepers and publicans, who complained of their being distressed in furnishing those guests with provisions and necessaries at the rates prescribed by law or custom. There were not wanting advocates to expatiate upon the nature of this grievance, which, however, was not redressed. A new trade was at this time opened with Persia, through the dominions of the czar, and vested with an exclusive privilege in the Russian company, by an act of Parliament. The Commons voted forty thousand seamen for the service of the ensuing year, and about thirty thousand men for the establishment of land-forces. They provided for the subsidies granted to the King of Denmark and the Landgrave of Hesse-Cassel; and took every step which was suggested for the ease and the convenience of the government.

Proceedings in the House of Lords.

The parties in the House of Lords were influenced by the same motives which actuated the Commons. The Duke of Argyle, who had by this time resigned all his places, declared open war against the ministry. In the beginning of the session, the king's speech was no sooner reported by the chancellor, than this nobleman stood up, and moved that a general address of thanks should be presented to his majesty, instead of a recapitulation of every paragraph of the king's speech, re-echoed from the Parliament to the throne, with expressions of blind approbation, implying a general concurrence with all the measures of the minister. He spoke on this subject with

an astonishing impetuosity of eloquence, that rolled like
a river which had overflowed its banks and deluged the
whole adjacent country. The motion was supported by
Lord Bathurst, Lord Carteret, the Earl of Chesterfield,
and Lord Gower, who, though they displayed all the
talents of oratory, were outvoted by the opposite party,
headed by the Duke of Newcastle, the Earl of Cholmondeley, Lord Hervey, and the Lord Chancellor. The
motion was rejected, and the address composed in the
usual strain. The same motions for an inquiry into
orders and instructions, which had miscarried in the
Lower House, were here repeated with the same bad
success : in the debates which ensued, the young Earls
of Halifax and Sandwich acquired a considerable share
of reputation, for the strength of argument and elocution
with which they contended against the adherents of the
ministry. When the House took into consideration the
state of the army, the Duke of Argyle having harangued
with equal skill and energy on military affairs, proposed
that the forces should be augmented by adding new
levies to the old companies, without increasing the
number of officers ; as such an augmentation served only
to debase the dignity of the service, by raising the lowest
of mankind to the rank of gentlemen ; and to extend
the influence of the minister, by multiplying his depend-
ants. He therefore moved for a resolution, that the
augmenting the army by raising regiments, as it is the
most unnecessary and most expensive method of augmentation, was also the most dangerous to the liberties of the
nation. This proposal was likewise overruled, after a
short though warm contention. This was the fate of all
the other motions made by the lords in the opposition,
though the victory of the courtiers was always clogged
with a nervous and spirited protest. Two days were expended in the debate produced by Lord Carteret's motion
for an address, beseeching his majesty to remove Sir
Robert Walpole from his presence and councils for ever.
The speech that ushered in this memorable motion would
not have disgraced a Cicero. It contained a retrospect of
all the public measures which had been pursued since the
Revolution. It explained the nature of every treaty,
whether right or wrong, which had been concluded under

c c 2

the present administration. It described the political connexions subsisting between the different powers in Europe. It exposed the weakness, the misconduct, and the iniquity of the minister, both in his foreign and domestic transactions. It was embellished with all the ornaments of rhetoric, and warmed with a noble spirit of patriotic indignation. The Duke of Argyle, Lord Bathurst, and his other colleagues, seemed to be animated with uncommon fervour, and even inspired, by the subject. A man of imagination, in reading their speeches, will think himself transported into the Roman senate, before the ruin of that republic. Nevertheless, the minister still triumphed by dint of numbers; though his victory was dearly purchased. Thirty peers entered a vigorous protest; and Walpole's character sustained such a rude shock from this opposition, that his authority seemed to be drawing near a period. Immediately after this contest was decided, the Duke of Marlborough moved for a resolution, that any attempt to inflict any kind of punishment on any person, without allowing him an opportunity to make his defence, or without any proof of any crime or misdemeanour committed by him, is contrary to natural justice, the fundamental laws of the realm, and the ancient established usage of Parliament; and is a high infringement of the liberties of the subject. It was seconded by the Duke of Devonshire and Lord Lovel; and opposed by Lord Gower, as an intended censure on the proceedings of the day. This sentiment was so warmly espoused by Lord Talbot, who had distinguished himself in the former debate, that he seemed to be transported beyond the bounds of moderation. He was interrupted by the Earl of Cholmondeley, who charged him with having violated the order and decorum which ought to be preserved in such an assembly. His passion was inflamed by this rebuke: he declared himself an independent lord; a character which he would not forfeit for the smiles of a court, the profit of an employment, or the reward of a pension: he said, when he was engaged on the side of truth, he would trample on the insolence that should command him to suppress his sentiments.—On a division, however, the motion was carried.

In the beginning of April, the king, repairing to the

House of Peers, passed some acts that were ready for the royal assent. Then, in his speech to both Houses, he gave them to understand, that the Queen of Hungary had made a requisition of the twelve thousand men stipulated by treaty; and that he had ordered the subsidy-troops of Denmark and Hesse-Cassel to be in readiness to march to her assistance. He observed, that in this complicated and uncertain state of affairs, many incidents might arise, and render it necessary for him to incur extraordinary expenses for maintaining the pragmatic sanction, at a time when he could not possibly have recourse to the advice and assistance of his Parliament. He therefore demanded of the Commons such a supply as might be requisite for these ends; and promised to manage it with all possible frugality. The Lower House, in their address, approved of all his measures; declared they would effectually support him against all insults and attacks that might be made upon any of his territories, though not belonging to the crown of Great Britain; and that they would enable him to contribute, in the most effectual manner, to the support of the Queen of Hungary Sir Robert Walpole moved, that an aid of two hundred thousand pounds should be granted to that princess. Mr. Shippen protested against any interposition in the affairs of Germany. He expressed his dislike of the promise which had been made to defend his majesty's foreign dominions; a promise, in his opinion, inconsistent with that important and inviolable law, the act of settlement; a promise which, could it have been foreknown, would perhaps have for ever precluded from the succession that illustrious family to which the nation owed such numberless blessings, such continued felicity. The motion however passed, though not without further opposition; and the House resolved that three hundred thousand pounds should be granted to his majesty, to enable him effectually to support the Queen of Hungary. Towards the expense of this year, a million was deducted from the sinking-fund; and the land-tax continued at four shillings in the pound. The preparations for this war had already cost five millions. The session was closed on the twenty-fifth day of April, when the king took his leave of this Parliament, with warm expressions of tenderness and

CHAP.
XVII.

1740.
Close of the last session of this Parliament.

satisfaction. Henry Bromley, Stephen Fox, and John Howe, three members of the Lower House, who had signalized themselves in defence of the minister, were now ennobled, and created Barons of Montfort, Ilchester, and Chedworth. A camp was formed near Colchester; and the king, having appointed a regency, set out in May for his German dominions [d].

[d] Sir William Wyndham died in the preceding year, deeply regretted as an orator, a patriot, and a man, the constant asserter of British liberty, and one of the chief ornaments of the English nation. In the course of the same year, General Oglethorpe, governor of Georgia, had, with some succours obtained from the colony of Carolina, and a small squadron of the king's ships, made an attempt upon Fort Augustine, the capital of Spanish Florida ; and actually reduced some small forts in the neighbourhood of the place ; but the Carolinians withdrawing in disgust, dissensions prevailing among the sea-officers, the hurricane months approaching, and the enemy having received a supply and reinforcements, he abandoned the enterprise, and returned to Georgia.

CHAPTER XVIII.

THE ARMY UNDER LORD CATHCART AND SIR CHALONER OGLE PROCEEDS TO THE WEST INDIES.—NATURE OF THE CLIMATE ON THE SPANISH MAIN.—ADMIRAL VERNON SAILS TO CARTHAGENA.—ATTACK OF FORT LAZAR.—EXPEDITION TO CUBA.—RUPTURE BETWEEN THE QUEEN OF HUNGARY AND THE KING OF PRUSSIA. —BATTLE OF MOLWITZ.—THE KING OF GREAT BRITAIN CONCLUDES A TREATY OF NEUTRALITY WITH FRANCE FOR THE ELECTORATE OF HANOVER.—A BODY OF FRENCH FORCES JOINS THE ELECTOR OF BAVARIA.—HE IS CROWNED KING OF BOHEMIA AT PRAGUE.—FIDELITY OF THE HUNGARIANS.—WAR BETWEEN RUSSIA AND SWEDEN.—REVOLUTION IN RUSSIA.—THE SPANISH AND FRENCH SQUADRONS PASS UNMOLESTED BY THE ENGLISH ADMIRAL IN THE MEDITERRANEAN.—INACTIVITY OF THE NAVAL POWER OF GREAT BRITAIN.—OBSTINATE STRUGGLE IN ELECTING MEMBERS IN THE NEW PARLIAMENT.—REMARKABLE MOTION IN THE HOUSE OF COMMONS BY LORD NOEL SOMERSET.—THE COUNTRY PARTY OBTAIN A MAJORITY IN THE HOUSE OF COMMONS.—SIR ROBERT WALPOLE CREATED EARL OF ORFORD. —CHANGE IN THE MINISTRY.—INQUIRY INTO THE ADMINISTRATION OF SIR ROBERT WALPOLE.—OBSTRUCTED BY THE NEW MINISTRY.—REPORTS OF THE SECRET COMMITTEE.—THE ELECTOR OF BAVARIA CHOSEN EMPEROR.—THE KING OF PRUSSIA GAINS THE BATTLE OF CZASLAU.—TREATY AT BRESLAU.—THE FRENCH TROOPS RETIRE UNDER THE CANNON OF PRAGUE.—A FRESH BODY SENT WITH THE MARESCHAL DE MAILLEBOIS TO BRING THEM OFF.—EXTRAORDINARY RETREAT OF M. DE BELLEISLE.—THE KING OF GREAT BRITAIN FORMS AN ARMY IN FLANDERS.—PROGRESS OF THE WAR BETWEEN RUSSIA AND SWEDEN.—THE KING OF SARDINIA DECLARES FOR THE HOUSE OF AUSTRIA.—MOTIONS OF THE SPANIARDS IN ITALY AND SAVOY.—CONDUCT OF ADMIRAL MATTHEWS IN THE MEDITERRANEAN.— OPERATIONS IN THE WEST INDIES.—THE ATTENTION OF THE MINISTRY TURNED CHIEFLY ON THE AFFAIRS OF THE CONTINENT.—EXTRAORDINARY MOTION IN THE HOUSE OF LORDS BY EARL STANHOPE.—WARM AND OBSTINATE DEBATE ON THE REPEAL OF THE GIN ACT.—BILL FOR QUIETING CORPORATIONS.—CONVENTION BETWEEN THE EMPEROR AND THE QUEEN OF HUNGARY.—DIFFERENCE BETWEEN THE KING OF PRUSSIA AND THE ELECTOR OF HANOVER.—THE KING OF GREAT BRITAIN OBTAINS A VICTORY OVER THE FRENCH AT DETTINGEN.—TREATY OF WORMS.—CONCLUSION OF THE CAMPAIGN.—AFFAIRS IN THE NORTH.—BATTLE OF CAMPO-SANTO.—TRANSACTIONS OF THE BRITISH FLEET IN THE MEDITERRANEAN. —UNSUCCESSFUL ATTEMPTS UPON THE SPANISH SETTLEMENTS IN THE WEST INDIES.

THE British armament had by this time proceeded to action in the West Indies. Sir Chaloner Ogle, who sailed from Spithead, had been overtaken by a tempest in the bay of Biscay, by which the fleet, consisting of about one hundred and seventy sail, were scattered and dispersed. Nevertheless, he prosecuted his voyage, and anchored with a view to provide wood and water in the

CHAP. XVIII.

1741. The army under Lord Cathcart and Sir Chaloner Ogle pro-

CHAP.
XVIII.

1741.
ceeds to the
West In-
dies.

neutral island of Dominica, where the intended expedition sustained a terrible shock in the death of the gallant
Lord Cathcart, who was carried off by a dysentery. The
loss of this nobleman was the more severely felt, as the
command of the land-forces devolved upon General
Wentworth, an officer without experience, authority,
or resolution. As the fleet sailed along the island of
Hispaniola, in its way to Jamaica, four large ships of
war were discovered; and Sir Chaloner detached an
equal number of his squadron to give them chase, while
he himself proceeded on his voyage. As those strange
ships refused to bring to, Lord Augustus Fitzroy, the
commodore of the four British ships, saluted one of
them with a broadside, and a smart engagement ensued.
After they had fought during the best part of the night,
the enemy hoisted their colours in the morning, and appeared to be part of the French squadron, which had
sailed from Europe, under the command of the Marquis
d'Antin, with orders to assist the Spanish Admiral de
Torres, in attacking and distressing the English ships
and colonies. War was not yet declared between France
and England; therefore hostilities ceased: the English
and French commanders complimented each other; excused themselves mutually for the mistake which had
happened; and parted as friends, with a considerable
loss of men on both sides.

Nature of
the climate
on the Spa-
nish main.

In the mean time Sir Chaloner Ogle arrived at Jamaica, where he joined Vice-Admiral Vernon, who now
found himself at the head of the most formidable fleet
and army that ever visited those seas, with full power
to act at discretion. The conjoined squadrons consisted
of nine-and-twenty ships of the line, with almost an
equal number of frigates, fire-ships, and bomb-ketches,
well manned, and plentifully supplied with all kinds
of provisions, stores, and necessaries. The number of
seamen amounted to fifteen thousand; that of the land-
forces, including the American regiment of four battalions, and a body of negroes enlisted at Jamaica, did
not fall short of twelve thousand. Had this armament
been ready to act in the proper season of the year, under
the conduct of wise, experienced officers, united in councils, and steadily attached to the interest and honour

of their country, the Havannah and the whole island CHAP. XVIII. of Cuba might have been easily reduced; the whole treasure of the Spanish West Indies would have been 1741. intercepted; and Spain must have been humbled into the most abject submission. But several unfavourable circumstances concurred to frustrate the hopes of the public. The ministry had detained Sir Chaloner Ogle at Spithead without any visible cause, until the season for action was almost exhausted; for, on the continent of New Spain, the periodical rains begin about the end of April; and this change in the atmosphere is always attended with epidemical distempers, which render the climate extremely unhealthy; besides, the rain is so excessive, that for the space of two months no army can keep the field.

Sir Chaloner Ogle arrived at Jamaica on the ninth Admiral Vernon sails to Carthagena. day of January; and Admiral Vernon did not sail on his intended expedition till towards the end of the month. Instead of directing his course to the Havannah, which lay to leeward, and might have been reached in less than three days, he resolved to beat up against the wind to Hispaniola, in order to observe the motions of the French squadron commanded by the Marquis d'Antin. The fifteenth day of February had elapsed before he received certain information that the French admiral had sailed for Europe, in great distress, for want of men and provisions, which he could not procure in the West Indies. Admiral Vernon, thus disappointed, called a council of war, in which it was determined to proceed for Carthagena. The fleet being supplied with wood and water at Hispaniola, set sail for the continent of New Spain, and on the fourth of March anchored in Playa Grande, to the windward of Carthagena. Admiral de Torres had already sailed to the Havannah; but Carthagena was strongly fortified, and the garrison reinforced by the crews of a small squadron of large ships commanded by Don Blas de Leso, an officer of experience and reputation. Here the English admiral lay inactive till the ninth, when the troops were landed on the island of Tierra Bomba, near the mouth of the harbour, known by the name of Boca-chica, or Little-mouth, which was surprisingly fortified with castles, batteries, booms,

chains, cables, and ships of war. The British forces
erected a battery on shore, with which they made a
breach in the principal fort, while the admiral sent in
a number of ships to divide the fire of the enemy, and
co-operate with the endeavours of the army. Lord
Aubrey Beauclerc, a gallant officer, who commanded
one of these ships, was slain on this occasion. The
breach being deemed practicable, the forces advanced to
the attack; but the forts and batteries were abandoned;
the Spanish ships that lay athwart the harbour's mouth
were destroyed or taken; the passage was opened, and
the fleet entered without further opposition. Then the
forces were re-embarked with the artillery, and landed
within a mile of Carthagena, where they were opposed
by about seven hundred Spaniards, whom they obliged to
retire. The admiral and general had contracted a hearty
contempt for each other, and took all opportunities of
expressing their mutual dislike: far from acting vigorously in concert, for the advantage of the community,
they maintained a mutual reserve, and separate cabals;
and each proved more eager for the disgrace of his rival,
than zealous for the honour of the nation.

Attack of
Fort Lazar.
The general complained that the fleet lay idle while
his troops were harassed and diminished by hard duty
and distemper. The admiral affirmed, that his ships
could not lie near enough to batter the town of Carthagena: he upbraided the general with inactivity and want
of resolution to attack the fort of St. Lazar, which commanded the town, and might be taken by scalade.
Wentworth, stimulated by these reproaches, resolved to
try the experiment. His forces marched up to the
attack; but the guides being slain, they mistook their
route, and advanced to the strongest part of the fortification, where they were moreover exposed to the fire of
the town. Colonel Grant, who commanded the grena-
diers, was mortally wounded: the scaling ladders were
found too short: the officers were perplexed for want
of orders and directions: yet the soldiers sustained a severe fire for several hours with surprising intrepidity, and
at length retreated, leaving about six hundred killed or
wounded on the spot. Their number was now so much
reduced, that they could no longer maintain their footing

on shore; besides, the rainy season had begun with such
violence, as rendered it impossible for them to live in
camp : they were, therefore, re-embarked ; and all hope
of further success immediately vanished. The admiral,
however, in order to demonstrate the impracticability of
taking the place by sea, sent in the Gallicia, one of the
Spanish ships which had been taken at Boca-chica, to
cannonade the town, with sixteen guns mounted on one
side, like a floating battery. This vessel, manned by
detachments of volunteers from different ships, and commanded by Captain Hoare, was warped into the inner
harbour, and moored before day, at a considerable distance from the walls, in very shallow water. In this
position she stood the fire of several batteries for some
hours, without doing or sustaining much damage: then
the admiral ordered the men to be brought off in boats,
and the cables to be cut; so that she drove with the
sea-breeze upon a shoal, where she was soon filled
with water. This exploit was absurd, and the inference
which the admiral drew from it altogether fallacious: he
said it plainly proved that there was not depth of water
in the inner harbour sufficient to admit large ships near
enough to batter the town with any prospect of success.
This, indeed, was the case in that part of the harbour to
which the Gallicia was conducted; but a little farther to
the left, he might have stationed four or five of his largest
ships abreast, within pistol-shot of the walls; and if this
step had been taken, when the land-forces marched to
the attack of St. Lazar, in all probability the town would
have been surrendered.

After the re-embarkation of the troops, the distempers Expedition
to Cuba.
peculiar to the climate and season began to rage with
redoubled fury ; and great numbers of those who escaped
the vengeance of the enemy perished by a more painful
and inglorious fate. Nothing was heard but complaints
and execrations : the groans of the dying, and the service
for the dead : nothing was seen but objects of woe, and
images of dejection. The conductors of this unfortunate
expedition agreed in nothing but the expediency of a
speedy retreat from this scene of misery and disgrace.
The fortifications of the harbour were demolished, and
the fleet returned to Jamaica.—The miscarriage of this

expedition, which had cost the nation an immense sum of money, was no sooner known in England, than the kingdom was filled with murmurs and discontent, and the people were depressed in proportion to that sanguine hope by which they had been elevated. Admiral Vernon, instead of undertaking any enterprise which might have retrieved the honour of the British arms, set sail from Jamaica with the forces in July, and anchored at the south-east part of Cuba, in a bay on which he bestowed the appellation of Cumberland Harbour. The troops were landed, and encamped at the distance of twenty miles further up the river, where they remained totally inactive, and subsisted chiefly on salt and damaged provisions, till the month of November, when being considerably diminished by sickness, they were put on board again, and reconveyed to Jamaica. He was afterwards reinforced from England by four ships of war, and about three thousand soldiers; but he performed nothing worthy of the reputation he had acquired; and the people began to perceive that they had mistaken his character.

Rupture
between
the Queen
of Hungary
and the
King of
Prussia.

The affairs on the continent of Europe were now more than ever embroiled. The King of Prussia had demanded of the court of Vienna part of Silesia, by virtue of old treaties of co-fraternity, which were either obsolete or annulled; and promised to assist the queen with all his forces, in case she should comply with his demand; but this being rejected with disdain, he entered Silesia at the head of an army, and prosecuted his conquests with great rapidity. In the mean time the Queen of Hungary was crowned at Presburgh, after having signed a capitulation, by which the liberties of that kingdom were confirmed; and the grand duke, her consort, was, at her request, associated with her for ten years in the government. At the same time the states of Hungary refused to receive a memorial from the Elector of Bavaria. During these transactions, his Prussian majesty made his public entrance into Breslau, and confirmed all the privileges of the inhabitants. One of his generals surprised the town and fortress of Jablunka, on the confines of Hungary: Prince Leopold of Anhalt-Dessau, who commanded another army, which formed the blockade of Great Glogau on the Oder, took the place by scalade, made the Generals Wallis and Reyski prisoners, with a thousand men that were in garrison: here, likewise, the victor found the military chest, fifty pieces of brass cannon, and a great quantity of ammunition.

The Queen of Hungary had solicited the maritime powers for assistance, but found them fearful and backward. Being obliged, therefore, to exert herself with the more vigour, she ordered Count Neuperg to assemble a body of forces, and endeavour to stop the progress of the Prussians in Silesia. The two armies encountered each other in the neighbourhood of Neiss, at a village called Molwitz; and, after an obstinate dispute, the Austrians were obliged to retire, with the loss of four thousand men, killed, wounded, or taken. The advantage was dearly purchased by the King of Prussia. His kinsman, Frederick, Margrave of Brandenburgh, and Lieutenant-General Schuylemberg, were killed in the engagement, together with a great number of general officers, and about two thousand soldiers. After this action, Brieg was surrendered to the Prussian, and he forced the important pass of Fryewalde, which was defended by four thousand Austrian hussars. The English and Dutch ministers, who accompanied him in his progress, spared no pains to effect an accommodation; but the two sovereigns were too much irritated against each other to acquiesce in any terms that could be proposed. The Queen of Hungary was incensed to find herself attacked, in the day of her distress, by a prince to whom she had given no sort of provocation; and his Prussian majesty charged the court of Vienna with a design either to assassinate, or carry him off by treachery; a design which was disowned with expressions of indignation and disdain. Count Neuperg being obliged to abandon Silesia, in order to oppose the Bavarian arms in Bohemia, the King of Prussia sent thither a detachment to join the elector, under the command of Count Deslau, who, in his route, reduced Glatz and Neiss, almost without opposition; then his master received the homage of the Silesian states at Breslau, and returned to Berlin. In December the Prussian army was distributed in winter-quarters in Moravia, after having taken Olmutz, the capital of that province; and in March his Prussian

majesty formed a camp of observation in the neighbourhood of Magdeburgh.

1741.
The King
of Great
Britain
concludes
a treaty of
neutrality
with
France
for the
electorate
of Hanover.
The Elector of Hanover was alarmed at the success of
the King of Prussia, in apprehension that he would become too formidable a neighbour. A scheme was said
to have been proposed to the court of Vienna for attacking that prince's electoral dominions, and dividing
the conquest; but it never was put in execution. Nevertheless, the troops of Hanover were augmented: the
auxiliary Danes and Hessians in the pay of Great Britain
were ordered to be in readiness to march; and a good
number of British forces encamped and prepared for embarkation. The subsidy of three hundred thousand
pounds granted by Parliament, was remitted to the Queen
of Hungary; and every thing seemed to presage the
vigorous interposition of his Britannic majesty. But in
a little time after his arrival at Hanover, that spirit of
action seemed to flag, even while her Hungarian majesty
tottered on the verge of ruin. France resolved to seize
this opportunity of crushing the house of Austria. In
order to intimidate the Elector of Hanover, Mareschal
Maillebois was sent with a numerous army into Westphalia; and this expedient proved effectual. A treaty of
neutrality was concluded; and the King of Great Britain
engaged to vote for the Elector of Bavaria at the ensuing
election of an emperor. The design of the French court
was to raise this prince to the imperial dignity, and furnish him with such succours as should enable him to deprive the Queen of Hungary of her hereditary dominions.

A body
of French
forces join
the Elector
of Bavaria.
While the French minister at Vienna endeavoured to
amuse the queen with the strongest assurances of his
master's friendship, a body of five-and-thirty thousand
men began their march for Germany, in order to join the
Elector of Bavaria: another French army was assembled
upon the Rhine; and the Count de Belleisle, being provided with large sums of money, was sent to negotiate
with different electors. Having thus secured a majority
of voices, he proceeded to Munich, where he presented
the Elector of Bavaria with a commission, appointing him
generalissimo of the French troops marching to his assistance; and now the treaty of Nymphenburgh was concluded. The French king engaged to assist the elector

with his whole power, towards raising him to the imperial
throne : the elector promised, that after his elevation he
would never attempt to recover any of the towns or provinces of the empire which France had conquered : that
he would in his imperial capacity renounce the barrier-
treaty ; and agree that France should irrevocably retain
whatever places she should subdue in the Austrian Netherlands. The next step of Belleisle was to negotiate
another treaty between France and Prussia, importing,
that the Elector of Bavaria should possess Bohemia,
Upper Austria, and the Tyrolese: that the King of
Poland should be gratified with Moravia and Upper
Silesia; and that his Prussian majesty should retain
Lower Silesia, with the town of Neiss and the county of
Glatz. These precautions being taken, the Count de
Belleisle repaired to Frankfort in quality of ambassador
and plenipotentiary from France, at the imperial diet of
election. It was in this city that the French king published a declaration, signifying, that as the King of Great
Britain had assembled an army to influence the approaching election of an emperor, his most Christian
majesty, as guarantee of the treaty of Westphalia, had
ordered some troops to advance towards the Rhine, with
a view to maintain the tranquillity of the Germanic body,
and secure the freedom of the imperial election.

In July, the Elector of Bavaria being joined by the He is
crowned
French forces under Mareschal Broglio, surprised the King of
imperial city of Passau, upon the Danube ; and entering Bohemia
at Prague.
Upper Austria, at the head of seventy thousand men,
took possession of Lintz, where he received the homage
of the states of that country. Understanding that the
garrison of Vienna was very numerous, and that Count
Palfi had assembled thirty thousand Hungarians in the
neighbourhood of this capital, he made no further progress in Austria, but marched into Bohemia, where he
was reinforced by a considerable body of Saxons, under
the command of Count Rutowski, natural son to the late
King of Poland. By this time his Polish majesty had
acceded to the treaty of Nymphenburgh, and declared
war against the Queen of Hungary, on the most frivolous
pretences. The Elector of Bavaria advanced to Prague,
which was taken in the night by scalade ; an achieve-

CHAP. ment in which Maurice Count of Saxe, another natural
XVIII. son of the King of Poland, distinguished himself at the
1741. head of the French forces. In December the Elector of
Bavaria made his public entry into his capital, where he
was proclaimed King of Bohemia, and inaugurated with
the usual solemnities; then he set out for Frankfort, to
be present at the diet of election.

Fidelity of   At this period the Queen of Hungary saw herself
the Hunga- abandoned by all her allies, and seemingly devoted to de-
rians. struction. She was not, however, forsaken by her courage;
nor destitute of good officers and an able ministry. She
retired to Presburgh, and, in a pathetic Latin speech to
the states, expressed her confidence in the loyalty and
valour of her Hungarian subjects. The nobility of that
kingdom, touched with her presence and distress, assured
her, unanimously, that they would sacrifice their lives
and fortunes in her defence. The ban being raised, that
brave people crowded to her standard; and the diet expressed their resentment against her enemy by a public
edict, excluding for ever the electoral house of Bavaria
from the succession to the crown of Hungary: yet,
without the subsidy she received from Great Britain,
their courage and attachment would have proved ineffectual. By this supply she was enabled to pay her army,
erect magazines, complete her warlike preparations, and
put her strong places in a posture of defence. In December, her generals, Berenclau and Mentzel, defeated
Count Thoring, who commanded eight thousand men, at
the pass of Scardingen, and opening their way into Bavaria, laid the whole country under contribution: while
Count Khevenhuller retook the city of Lintz, and drove
the French troops out of Austria. The grand signor
assured the Queen of Hungary, that, far from taking advantage of her troubles, he should seize all opportunities
to convince her of his friendship: the pope permitted
her to levy a tenth on the revenues of the clergy within
her dominions, and even to use all the church-plate
for the support of the war.

War be-   As the czarina expressed an inclination to assist this
tween
Russia and unfortunate princess, the French court resolved to find
Sweden. her employment in another quarter. They had already
gained over to their interest Count Gyllenburgh, prime

minister and president of the chancery in Sweden. A
dispute happening between him and Mr. Burnaby, the
British resident at Stockholm, some warm altercation
passed : Mr. Burnaby was forbid the court, and published
a memorial in his own vindication; on the other hand,
the King of Sweden justified his conduct in a rescript
sent to all the foreign ministers. The King of Great
Britain had proposed a subsidy-treaty to Sweden, which,
from the influence of French counsels, was rejected.
The Swedes having assembled a numerous army in Finland, and equipped a large squadron of ships, declared
war against Russia upon the most trifling pretences; and
the fleet, putting to sea, commenced hostilities by blocking up the Russian ports in Livonia. A body of eleven
thousand Swedes, commanded by General Wrangle, having advanced to Willmenstrand, were in August attacked and defeated by General Lasci, at the head of
thirty thousand Russians. Count Lewenhaupt, who commanded the main army of the Swedes, resolved to take
vengeance for this disgrace, after the Russian troops had
retired into winter-quarters. In December he marched
towards Wybourg; but receiving letters from the Prince
of Hesse-Hombourg and the Marquis de la Chetardie,
the French ambassador at Petersburgh, informing him
of the surprising revolution which had just happened in
Russia, and proposing a suspension of hostilities, he retreated with his army in order to wait for further instructions; and the two courts agreed to a cessation of
arms for three months.

The Russians had been for some time discontented Revolution in Russia.
with their government. The late czarina was influenced
chiefly by German counsels, and employed a great number of foreigners in her service. These causes of discontent produced factions and conspiracies; and when
they were discovered, the empress treated the authors of
them with such severity as increased the general disaffection. Besides, they were displeased at the manner in
which she had settled the succession. The Prince of
Brunswick-Lunenburgh Bevern, father to the young
czar, was not at all agreeable to the Russian nobility;
and his consort, the Princess Anne of Mecklenburgh,
having assumed the reins of government during her son's

minority, seemed to follow the maxims of her aunt, the late czarina.   The Russian grandees and generals, therefore, turned their eyes upon the Princess Elizabeth, who was daughter of Peter the Great, and the darling of the empire.   The French ambassador gladly concurred in a project for deposing a princess who was well affected to the house of Austria.   General Lasci approved of the design, which was chiefly conducted by the Prince of Hesse-Hombourg, who, in the reigns of the Empress Catherine and Peter II. had been generalissimo of the Russian army.   The good-will and concurrence of the troops being secured, two regiments of guards took possession of all the avenues of the imperial palace at Petersburgh.   The Princess Elizabeth, putting herself at the head of one thousand men, on the fifth day of December entered the winter-palace, where the Princess of Mecklenburgh and the infant czar resided. She advanced into the chamber where the princess and her consort lay, and desired them to rise and quit the palace, adding that their persons were safe, and that they could not justly blame her for asserting her right.   At the same time the Counts Osterman, Golofkin, Mingden, and Munich, were arrested; their papers and effects were seized, and their persons conveyed to Schlisselbourg, a fortress on the Neva.   Early in the morning the senate assembling, declared all that had passed since the reign of Peter II. to be usurpation; and that the imperial dignity belonged of right to the Princess Elizabeth: she was immediately proclaimed Empress of all the Russias, and recognized by the army in Finland. She forthwith published a general act of indemnity: she created the Prince of Hesse-Hombourg generalissimo of her armies: she restored the Dolgorucky family to their honours and estates: she recalled and rewarded all those who had been banished for favouring her pretensions: she mitigated the exile of the Duke of Courland, by indulging him with a maintenance more suitable to his rank: she released General Wrangle, Count Wasaburgh, and the other Swedish officers, who had been taken at the battle of Willmenstrand; and the Princess Anne of Mecklenburgh, with her consort and children, were sent under a strong guard to Riga, the capital of Livonia.

Amidst these tempests of war and revolution, the States-General wisely determined to preserve their own tranquillity. It was doubtless their interest to avoid the dangers and expense of a war, and to profit by that stagnation of commerce which would necessarily happen among their neighbours that were at open enmity with each other; besides, they were overawed by the declarations of the French monarch on one side; by the power, activity, and pretensions of his Prussian majesty on the other; and they dreaded the prospect of a stadtholder at the head of their army. These at least were the sentiments of many Dutch patriots, reinforced by others that acted under French influence. But the Prince of Orange numbered among his partisans and adherents many persons of dignity and credit in the commonwealth: he was adored by the populace, who loudly exclaimed against their governors, and clamoured for a war, without ceasing. This national spirit, joined to the remonstrances and requisitions made by the courts of Vienna and London, obliged the states to issue orders for an augmentation of their forces; but these were executed so slowly, that neither France nor Prussia had much cause to take umbrage at their preparations. In Italy, the King of Sardinia declared for the house of Austria: the republic of Genoa was deeply engaged in the French interest: the pope, the Venetians, and the dukedom of Tuscany were neutral: the King of Naples resolved to support the claim of his family to the Austrian dominions in Italy, and began to make preparations accordingly. His mother, the Queen of Spain, had formed a plan for erecting these dominions into a monarchy for her second son Don Philip; and a body of fifteen thousand men, being embarked at Barcelona, were transported to Orbitello, under the convoy of the united squadrons of France and Spain. While Admiral Haddock, with twelve ships of the line, lay at anchor in the bay of Gibraltar, the Spanish fleet passed the straits in the night, and was joined by the French squadron from Toulon. The British admiral, sailing from Gibraltar, fell in with them in a few days, and found both squadrons drawn up in line of battle. As he bore down upon the Spanish fleet, the French admiral sent

CHAP.
XVIII.

1741.
The Spanish and French squadrons pass unmolested by the English admiral in the Mediterranean.

D d 2

CHAP.
XVIII.

1741.

a flag of truce, to inform him that, as the French and Spaniards were engaged in a joint expedition, he should be obliged to act in concert with his master's allies. This interposition prevented an engagement. The combined fleet amounting to double the number of the English squadron, Admiral Haddock was obliged to desist, and proceeded to Port Mahon, leaving the enemy to prosecute their voyage without molestation. The people of England were incensed at this transaction, and did not scruple to affirm, that the hands of the British admiral were tied up by the neutrality of Hanover[a].

Inactivity of the naval power of Great Britain.

The court of Madrid seemed to have shaken off that indolence and phlegm which had formerly disgraced the councils of Spain. They no sooner learned the destination of Commodore Anson, who had sailed from Spithead in the course of the preceding year, than they sent Don Pizarro, with a more powerful squadron, upon the same voyage, to defeat his design. He accordingly steered the same course, and actually fell in with one or two ships of the British armament, near the straits of Magellan; but he could not weather a long and furious tempest through which Mr. Anson proceeded into the South-Sea. One of the Spanish ships perished at sea: another was wrecked on the coast of Brazil: and Pizarro bore away for the Rio de la Plata, where he arrived with the three remaining ships in a shattered condition, after having lost twelve hundred men by sickness and famine. The Spaniards exerted the same vigilance and activity in Europe. Their privateers were so industrious and successful, that in the beginning of this year they had taken, since the commencement of the war, four hundred and seven ships belonging to the subjects of Great Britain, valued at near four millions of piastres.

---

[a] In the month of July two ships of Haddock's squadron falling in with three French ships of war, Captain Barnet, the English commodore, supposing them to be Spanish register ships, fired a shot in order to bring them to; and they refusing to comply with this signal, a sharp engagement ensued: after they had fought several hours, the French commander ceased firing, and thought proper to come to an explanation, when he and Barnet parted with mutual apologies.

In the course of this year a dangerous conspiracy was discovered at New York, in North America. One Hewson, a low publican, had engaged several negroes in a design to destroy the town, and massacre the people. Fire was set to several parts of the city; nine or ten negroes were apprehended, convicted, and burned alive. Hewson, with his wife, and a servant maid privy to the plot, were found guilty and hanged, though they died protesting their innocence.

The traders had, therefore, too much cause to complain, considering the formidable fleets which were maintained for the protection of commerce. In the course of the summer, Sir John Norris had twice sailed towards the coast of Spain, at the head of a powerful squadron, without taking any effectual step for annoying the enemy, as if the sole intention of the ministry had been to expose the nation to the ridicule and contempt of its enemies. The inactivity of the British arms appears the more inexcusable, when we consider the great armaments which had been prepared. The land-forces of Great Britain, exclusive of the Danish and Hessian auxiliaries, amounted to sixty thousand men; and the fleet consisted of above one hundred ships of war, manned by fifty-four thousand sailors.

The general discontent of the people had a manifest influence upon the election of members for the new Parliament, which produced one of the most violent contests between the two parties which had happened since the Revolution. All the adherents of the Prince of Wales concurred with the country party, in opposition to the ministry; and the Duke of Argyle exerted himself so successfully among the shires and boroughs of Scotland, that the partisans of the ministry could not secure six members out of the whole number returned from North Britain. They were, however, much more fortunate in the election of the sixteen peers, who were chosen literally according to the list transmitted from court. Instructions were delivered by the constituents to a great number of members returned for cities and counties, exhorting and requiring them to oppose a standing army in time of peace; to vote for the mitigation of excise laws, for the repeal of septennial Parliaments, and for the limitation of placemen in the House of Commons. They likewise insisted upon their examining into the particulars of the public expense, and endeavouring to redress the grievances of the nation. Obstinate struggles were maintained in all parts of the united kingdom with uncommon ardour and perseverance: and such a national spirit of opposition prevailed, that, notwithstanding the whole weight of ministerial

Obstinate struggle in electing members in the new Parliament.

CHAP.
XVIII.

1741.
Remark-
able motion
in the
House of
Commons
by Lord
Noel So-
merset.

influence, the country interest seemed to preponderate in the new Parliament.

The king returned to England in the month of October; and on the first day of December the session was opened. Mr. Onslow being rechosen speaker was approved of by his majesty, who spoke in the usual style to both Houses. He observed, that the former Parliament had formed the strongest resolutions in favour of the Queen of Hungary, for the maintenance of the pragmatic sanction; for the preservation of the balance of power, and the peace and liberties of Europe; and that if the other powers which were under the like engagements with him had answered the just expectations so solemnly given, the support of the common cause would have been attended with less difficulty. He said he had endeavoured, by the most proper and early applications, to induce other powers that were united with him by the ties of common interest, to concert such measures as so important and critical a conjuncture required: that where an accommodation seemed necessary, he had laboured to reconcile princes whose union would have been the most effectual means to prevent the mischiefs which had happened, and the best security for the interest and safety of the whole. He owned his endeavours had not hitherto produced the desired effect; though he was not without hope, that a just sense of approaching danger would give a more favourable turn to the counsels of other nations. He represented the necessity of putting the kingdom in such a posture of defence as would enable him to improve all opportunities of maintaining the liberties of Europe, and defeat any attempts that should be made against him and his dominions; and he recommended unanimity, vigour, and despatch. The House of Commons having appointed their several committees, the speaker reported the king's speech; and Mr. Herbert moved for an address of thanks, including an approbation of the means by which the war had been prosecuted. The motion being seconded by Mr. Trevor, Lord Noel Somerset stood up and moved, that the House would in their address desire his majesty not to engage these kingdoms in a war for the preservation of his foreign dominions. He was supported by that CHAP. incorruptible patriot, Mr. Shippen, who declared he was neither ashamed nor afraid to affirm, that thirty years had made no change in any of his political opinions. He said he was grown old in the House of Commons; that time had verified the predictions he had formerly uttered; and that he had seen his conjectures ripened into knowledge. "If my country (added he) has been so unfortunate as once more to commit her interest to men who propose to themselves no advantage from their trust but that of selling it, I may, perhaps, fall once more under censure for declaring my opinion, and be once more treated as a criminal, for asserting what they who punish me cannot deny; for maintaining that Hanoverian maxims are inconsistent with the happiness of this nation; and for preserving the caution so strongly inculcated by those patriots who framed the act of settlement, and conferred upon the present royal family their title to the throne." He particularized the instances in which the ministry had acted in diametrical opposition to that necessary constitution; and he insisted on the necessity of taking some step to remove the apprehensions of the people, who began to think themselves in danger of being sacrificed to the security of foreign dominions. Mr. Gibbon, who spoke on the same side of the question, expatiated upon the absurdity of returning thanks for the prosecution of a war which had been egregiously mismanaged. "What! (said he) are our thanks to be solemnly returned for defeats, disgrace, and losses, the ruin of our merchants, the imprisonment of our sailors, idle shows of armaments, and useless expenses?" Sir Robert Walpole, having made a short speech in defence of the first motion for an address, was answered by Mr. Pulteney, who seemed to be animated with a double proportion of patriot indignation. He asserted, that from a review of that minister's conduct since the beginning of the dispute with Spain, it would appear that he had been guilty not only of single errors, but of deliberate treachery: that he had always co-operated with the enemies of his country, and sacrificed to his private interest the happiness and honour of the British nation. He then entered into a detail of that conduct against which he had so often

CHAP.
XVIII.

1741.

declaimed; and being transported by an overheated imagination, accused him of personal attachment and affection to the enemies of the kingdom. A charge that was
doubtless the result of exaggerated animosity, and served
only to invalidate the other articles of imputation that
were much better founded. His objections were overruled; and the address, as at first proposed, was presented
to his majesty.

The coun-
try party
obtain a
majority in
the House
of Com-
mons.

This small advantage, however, the minister did not
consider as a proof of his having ascertained an undoubted
majority in the House of Commons. There was a great
number of disputed elections; and the discussion of these
was the point on which the people had turned their eyes,
as the criterion of the minister's power and credit. In
the first, which was heard at the bar of the House, he
carried his point by a majority of six only; and this he
looked upon as a defeat rather than a victory. His
enemies exulted in their strength, as they knew they
should be joined, in matters of importance, by several
members who voted against them on this occasion. The
inconsiderable majority that appeared on the side of the
administration plainly proved that the influence of the
minister was greatly diminished, and seemed to prognos-
ticate his further decline. This consideration induced
some individuals to declare against him as a setting sun,
from whose beams they could expect no further warmth.
His adherents began to tremble; and he himself had
occasion for all his art and equanimity. The court interest was not sufficient to support the election of their
own members for Westminster. The high-bailiff had
been guilty of some illegal practices at the poll; and
three justices of the peace had, on pretence of preventing
riots, sent for a military force to overawe the election.
A petition presented by the electors of Westminster
was taken into consideration by the House; and the
election was declared void by a majority of four voices.
The high-bailiff was taken into custody: the officer who
ordered the soldiers to march, and the three justices
who signed the letter, in consequence of which he
acted, were reprimanded on their knees at the bar of
the House.

The country party maintained the advantage they had

gained in deciding upon several other controverted elections; and Sir Robert Walpole tottered on the brink of ruin. He knew that the majority of a single vote would at any time commit him prisoner to the Tower, should ever the motion be made: and he saw that his safety could be effected by no other expedient but that of dividing the opposition. Towards the accomplishment of this purpose he employed all his credit and dexterity. His emissaries did not fail to tamper with those members of the opposite party who were the most likely to be converted by their arguments. A message was sent by the Bishop of Oxford to the Prince of Wales, importing, that if his royal highness would write a letter of condescension to the king, he and all his counsellors should be taken into favour; that fifty thousand pounds should be added to his revenue; four times that sum be disbursed immediately for the payment of his debts; and suitable provision be made in due time for all his followers. The prince declined this proposal. He declared that he would accept no such conditions while Sir Robert Walpole continued to direct the public affairs: that he looked upon him as a bar between his majesty and the affections of his people; as the author of the national grievances both at home and abroad; and as the sole cause of that contempt which Great Britain had incurred in all the courts of Europe. His royal highness was now chief of this formidable party, revered by the whole nation—a party which had gained the ascendancy in the House of Commons; which professed to act upon the principles of public virtue; which demanded the fall of an odious minister, as a sacrifice due to an injured people; and declared that no temptation could shake their virtue; that no art could dissolve the cement by which they were united. Sir Robert Walpole, though repulsed in his attempt upon the Prince of Wales, was more successful in his other endeavours. He resolved to try his strength once more in the House of Commons, in another disputed election; and had the mortification to see the majority augmented to sixteen voices. He declared he would never more sit in that House; and next day, which was the third of February, the king adjourned both Houses of Parliament to the

CHAP.
XVIII.

1741.
Sir Robert
Walpole
created
Earl of
Orford.

Change in
the minis-
try.

eighteenth day of the same month.   In this interim, Sir
Robert Walpole was created Earl of Orford, and resigned
all his employments.

At no time of his life did he acquit himself with such
prudential policy as he now displayed. He found means
to separate the parts that composed the opposition, and
to transfer the popular odium from himself to those who
had professed themselves his keenest adversaries.   The
country party consisted of the tories, reinforced by discontented whigs, who had either been disappointed in
their own ambitious views, or felt for the distresses of
their country, occasioned by a weak and worthless administration. The old patriots, and the whigs whom they
had joined, acted upon very different, and, indeed, upon
opposite principles of government : and therefore they
were united only by the ties of convenience. A coalition
was projected between the discontented whigs, and those
of the same denomination who acted in the ministry.
Some were gratified with titles and offices ; and all were
assured that in the management of affairs a new system
would be adopted, according to the plan they themselves
should propose. The court required nothing of them, but
that the Earl of Orford should escape with impunity. His
place of chancellor of the exchequer was bestowed upon
Mr. Sandys, who was likewise appointed a lord of the
treasury ; and the Earl of Wilmington succeeded him as
first commissioner of that board. Lord Harrington being
dignified with the title of Earl, was declared president
of the council ; and in his room Lord Carteret became
secretary of state. The Duke of Argyle was made master-
general of the ordnance, colonel of his majesty's royal
regiment of horse-guards, field-marshal and commander-
in-chief of all the forces in South Britain ; but, finding
himself disappointed in his expectations of the coalition,
he in less than a month renounced all these employments. The Marquis of Tweeddale was appointed secretary of state for Scotland, a post which had been long
suppressed ; Mr. Pulteney was sworn of the privy-council,
and afterwards created Earl of Bath. The Earl of Winchelsea and Nottingham was preferred to the head of
the Admiralty, in the room of Sir Charles Wager ; and
after the resignation of the Duke of Argyle, the Earl of

Stair was appointed field-marshal of all his majesty's
forces, as well as ambassador extraordinary to the States-
General. On the seventeenth day of February the
Prince of Wales, attended by a numerous retinue of his
adherents, waited on his majesty, who received him graciously, and ordered his guards to be restored. Lord
Carteret and Mr. Sandys were the first who embraced
the offers of the court, without the consent or privity
of any other leaders in the opposition, except that of
Mr. Pulteney; but they declared to their friends, they
would still proceed upon patriot principles; that they
would concur in promoting an inquiry into past measures;
and in enacting necessary laws to secure the constitution
from the practices of corruption. These professions were
believed, not only by their old coadjutors in the House
of Commons, but also by the nation in general. The
reconciliation between the king and the Prince of Wales,
together with the change in the ministry, were celebrated
with public rejoicings all over the kingdom; and immediately after the adjournment nothing but concord appeared in the House of Commons.

But this harmony was of short duration. It soon ap- Inquiry
peared that those who had declaimed the loudest for the into the
liberties of their country had been actuated solely by the tion of Sir
most sordid, and even the most ridiculous, motives of Robert
self-interest. Jealousy and mutual distrust ensued be- Walpole.
tween them and their former confederates. The nation
complained that, instead of a total change of men and
measures, they saw the old ministry strengthened by this
coalition; and the same interest in Parliament predo-
minating with redoubled influence. They branded the
new converts as apostates and betrayers of their country;
and in the transport of their indignation, they entirely
overlooked the old object of their resentment. That a
nobleman of pliant principles, narrow fortune, and unbounded ambition, should forsake his party for the bland-
ishments of affluence, power, and authority, will not
appear strange to any person acquainted with the human
heart; but the sensible part of mankind will always reflect with amazement upon the conduct of a man who,
seeing himself idolized by his fellow-citizens as the first
and firmest patriot in the kingdom, as one of the most

shining ornaments of his country, could give up all his popularity, and incur the contempt or detestation of mankind, for the wretched consideration of an empty. title, without office, influence, or the least substantial appendage. One cannot, without an emotion of grief, contemplate such an instance of infatuation; one cannot but lament that such glory should have been so weakly forfeited; that such talents should have been lost to the cause of liberty and virtue. Doubtless he flattered himself with the hope of one day directing the councils of his sovereign; but this was never accomplished, and he remained a solitary monument of blasted ambition. Before the change in the ministry, Mr. Pulteney moved that the several papers relating to the conduct of the war, which had been laid before the House, should be referred to a select committee, who should examine strictly into the particulars, and make a report to the House of their remarks and objections. The motion introduced a debate; but, upon a division, was rejected by a majority of three voices. Petitions having been presented by the merchants of London, Bristol, Liverpool, Glasgow, and almost all the trading towns in the kingdom, complaining of the losses they had sustained by the bad conduct of the war, the House resolved itself into a committee, to deliberate on these remonstrances. The articles of the London petition were explained by Mr. Glover, an eminent merchant of that city. Six days were spent in perusing papers and examining witnesses: then the same gentleman summed up the evidence, and in a pathetic speech endeavoured to demonstrate that the commerce of Great Britain had been exposed to the insults and rapine of the Spaniards, not by inattention or accident, but by one uniform and continued design. This inquiry being resumed after the adjournment, copies of instructions to admirals and captains of cruising ships were laid before the House: the Commons passed several resolutions, upon which a bill was prepared for the better protecting and securing the trade and navigation of the kingdom. It made its way through the Lower House, but was thrown out by the Lords. The pension-bill was revived, and sent up to the Peers, where it was again rejected; Lord Carteret voting against that very measure

which he had so lately endeavoured to promote. On the
ninth day of March, Lord Limerick made a motion for
appointing a committee to inquire into the conduct of
affairs for the last twenty years : he was seconded by Sir
John St. Aubyn, and supported by Mr. Velters Cornwall,
Mr. Phillips, Mr. W. Pitt, and Lord Percival, the new
member for Westminster, who had already signalized
himself by his eloquence and capacity. The motion was
opposed by Sir Charles Wager, Mr. Pelham, and Mr.
Henry Fox, surveyor-general to his majesty's works,
and brother to Lord Ilchester. Though the opposition
was faint and frivolous, the proposal was rejected by a
majority of two voices. Lord Limerick, not yet discouraged, made a motion, on the twenty-third day of March,
for an inquiry into the conduct of Robert Earl of Orford
for the last ten years of his administration; and after a
sharp debate, it was carried in the affirmative. The
House resolved to choose a secret committee by ballot;
and in the mean time presented an address to the king,
assuring him of their fidelity, zeal, and affection.

Sir Robert Godschall having moved for leave to bring
in a bill to repeal the act for septennial Parliaments, he
was seconded by Sir John Barnard; but warmly opposed
by Mr. Pulteney and Mr. Sandys; and the question
passed in the negative. The committee of secrecy being
chosen, began to examine evidence, and Mr. Paxton,
solicitor to the treasury, refusing to answer such ques-
tions as were put to him, Lord Limerick, chairman of
the committee, complained to the House of his obstinacy.
He was first taken into custody; and still persisting in
his refusal, committed to Newgate. Then his lordship
moved, that leave should be given to bring in a bill for
indemnifying evidence against the Earl of Orford; and
it was actually prepared by a decision of the majority.
In the House of Lords it was vigorously opposed by Lord
Carteret, and as strenuously supported by the Duke of
Argyle; but fell upon a division, by the weight of superior numbers. Those members in the House of Commons who heartily wished that the inquiry might be prosecuted, were extremely incensed at the fate of this bill.
A committee was appointed to search the journals of the
Lords for precedents : their report being read, Lord

Marginal notes:

CHAP.
XVIII.

1741.

1742.

Obstructed
by the new
ministry.

Strange, son of the Earl of Derby, moved for a resolution, "that the Lords refusing to concur with the Commons of Great Britain, in an indemnification necessary to the effectual carrying on the inquiry now depending in Parliament, is an obstruction to justice, and may prove fatal to the liberties of this nation." This motion, which was seconded by Lord Quarendon, son of the Earl of Lichfield, gave rise to a warm debate; and Mr. Sandys declaimed against it, as a step that would bring on an immediate dissolution of the present form of government. It is really amazing to see with what effrontery some men can shift their maxims, and openly contradict the whole tenor of their former conduct. Mr. Sandys did not pass uncensured : he sustained some severe sarcasms on his apostasy from Sir John Hynde Cotton, who refuted all his objections; nevertheless, the motion passed in the negative. Notwithstanding this great obstruction, purposely thrown in the way of the inquiry, the secret committee discovered many flagrant instances of fraud and corruption in which the Earl of Orford had been concerned. It appeared that he had granted fraudulent contracts for paying the troops in the West Indies : that he had employed iniquitous arts to influence elections : that for secret service, during the last ten years, he had touched one million four hundred fifty-three thousand four hundred pounds of the public money : that above fifty thousand pounds of this sum had been paid to authors and printers of newspapers and political tracts written in defence of the ministry; that on the very day which preceded his resignation, he had signed orders on the civil-list revenues for above thirty-thousand pounds; but as the cash remaining in the exchequer did not much exceed fourteen thousand pounds, he had raised the remaining part of the thirty thousand by pawning the orders to a banker. The committee proceeded to make further progress in their scrutiny, and had almost prepared a third report, when they were interrupted by the prorogation of Parliament.

Reports of the secret committee.

The ministry finding it was necessary to take some step for conciliating the affection of the people, gave way to a bill for excluding certain officers from seats in the House of Commons. They passed another for encouraging the linen manufacture; a third for regulating the trade of the plantations; and a fourth to prevent the marriage of lunatics. They voted forty thousand seamen and sixty-two thousand five hundred landmen for the service of the current year. They provided for the subsidies to Denmark and Hesse-Cassel, and voted five hundred thousand pounds to the Queen of Hungary. The expense of the year amounted to near six millions, raised by the land-tax at four shillings in the pound, by the malt-tax, -by one million from the sinking fund, by annuities granted upon it for eight hundred thousand pounds, and a loan of one million six hundred thousand pounds from the bank. In the month of July, John Lord Gower was appointed keeper of his majesty's privy-seal; Allen Lord Bathurst was made captain of the band of pensioners; and on the fifteenth day of the month, Mr. Pulteney took his seat in the House of Peers as Earl of Bath. The king closed the session in the usual way, after having given them to understand that a treaty of peace was concluded between the Queen of Hungary and the King of Prussia, under his mediation; and that the late successes of the Austrian arms were in a great measure owing to the generous assistance afforded by the British nation.

By this time great changes had happened in the affairs of the continent. The Elector of Bavaria was chosen emperor of Germany at Frankfort on the Maine, and crowned by the name of Charles VII. on the twelfth day of February. Thither the imperial diet was removed from Ratisbon: they confirmed his election, and indulged him with a subsidy of fifty Roman months, amounting to about two hundred thousand pounds sterling. In the mean time, the Austrian General Khevenhuller ravaged his electorate, and made himself master of Munich, the capital of Bavaria; he likewise laid part of the palatinate under contribution, in resentment for that elector's having sent a body of his troops to reinforce the imperial army. In March, Count Saxe, with a detachment of French and Bavarians, reduced Egra; and the Austrians were obliged to evacuate Bavaria, though they afterwards returned. Khevenhuller took post in the neighbourhood of Passau, and detached General Bernclau to Dinglesing on the Iser, to observe the motions of the enemy, who were now become extremely formidable. In May, a detachment of French and Bavarians advanced to the castle of Hilkersbergh on the Danube, with a view to take possession of a bridge over the river: the Austrian garrison immediately marched out to give them battle, and a severe action ensued, in which the imperialists were defeated.

The King of Prussia gains the battle at Czaslau. Treaty at Breslau.

In the beginning of the year the Queen of Hungary had assembled two considerable armies in Moravia and Bohemia. Prince Charles of Lorraine, at the head of fifty thousand men, advanced against the Saxons and Prussians, who thought proper to retire with precipitation from Moravia, which they had invaded. Then the prince took the route to Bohemia; and Mareschal Broglio, who commanded the French forces in that country, must have fallen a sacrifice, had not the King of Prussia received a strong reinforcement, and entered that kingdom before his allies could be attacked. The two armies advanced towards each other; and on the seventeenth of May joined battle at Czaslau, where the Austrians at first gained a manifest advantage, and penetrated as far as the Prussian baggage: then the irregulars began to plunder so eagerly, that they neglected every other consideration. The Prussian infantry took this opportunity to rally: the battle was renewed, and, after a very obstinate contest, the victory was snatched out of the hands of the Austrians, who were obliged to retire, with the loss of five thousand men killed, and twelve hundred taken by the enemy. The Prussians paid dear for the honour of remaining on the field of battle; and from the circumstances of this action the king is said to have conceived a disgust to the war. When the Austrians made such progress in the beginning of the engagement, he rode off with great expedition, until he was recalled by a message from his general, the Count de Schwerin, assuring his majesty that there was no danger of a defeat. Immediately after this battle, he discovered an inclination to accommodate all differences with the Queen of Hungary. The Earl of Hyndford, ambassador from the court of Great Britain, who accompanied him in this campaign, and was vested with full powers by her Hungarian majesty, did not fail to cultivate this favourable disposition; and on the first day of June, a treaty of peace between the two powers was concluded at Breslau. The queen ceded to his Prussian majesty the Upper and Lower Silesia, with the county of Glatz in Bohemia; and he charged himself with the payment of the sum lent by the merchants of London to the late emperor, on the Silesian revenues. He likewise engaged to observe a strict neutrality during the war, and to withdraw his forces from Bohemia in fifteen days after the ratification of the treaty, in which were comprehended the King of Great Britain, Elector of Hanover, the Czarina, the King of Denmark, the States-General, the house of Wolfenbuttel, and the King of Poland, Elector of Saxony, on certain conditions, which were accepted.

The King of Prussia recalled his troops; while Mare- The French troops retire under the cannon of Prague. schal Broglio, who commanded the French auxiliaries in that kingdom, and the Count de Belleisle, abandoned their magazines and baggage, and retired with precipitation under the cannon of Prague. There they intrenched themselves in an advantageous situation; and Prince Charles being joined by the other body of Austrians, under Prince Lobkowitz, encamped in sight of them, on the hills of Girinsnitz. The Grand Duke of Tuscany arrived in the Austrian army, of which he took the command; and the French generals offered to surrender Prague, Egra, and all the other places they possessed in Bohemia, provided they might be allowed to march off with their arms, artillery, and baggage. The proposal was rejected, and Prague invested on all sides about the end of July. Though the operations of the siege were carried on in an awkward and slovenly manner, the place was so effectually blocked up, that famine must have compelled the French to surrender at discretion, had not very extraordinary efforts been made for their relief. The emperor had made advances to the Queen of Hungary. He promised that the French forces should quit Bohemia, and evacuate the empire; and he offered to renounce all pretensions to the kingdom of Bohemia, on condition that the Austrians would restore Bavaria; but these conditions were declined by the court of Vienna. The King of France was no sooner apprised of the con-

1742.
A fresh
body sent
with the
Mareschal
de Maille-
bois to
bring them
off.

dition to which the Generals Broglio and Belleisle were reduced, than he sent orders to Mareschal Maillebois, who commanded his army on the Rhine, to march to their relief. His troops were immediately put in motion; and when they reached Amberg in the Upper Palatinate, were joined by the French and imperialists from Bavaria. Prince Charles of Lorraine, having received intelligence of their junction and design, left eighteen thousand men to maintain the blockade of Prague, under the command of General Festititz, while he himself, with the rest of his army, advanced to Haydon on the frontiers of Bohemia. There he was joined by Count Khevenhuller, who from Bavaria had followed the enemy, now commanded by Count Seckendorff, and the Count de Saxe. Seckendorff, however, was sent back to Bavaria, while Mareschal Maillebois entered Bohemia on the twenty-fifth day of September: but he marched with such precaution that Prince Charles could not bring him to an engagement. Meanwhile, Festititz, for want of sufficient force, was obliged to abandon the blockade of Prague; and the French generals being now at liberty, took post at Leut-maritz. Maillebois advanced as far as Kadan; but seeing the Austrians possessed of all the passes of the mountains, he marched back to the Palatinate, and was miserably harassed in his retreat by Prince Charles, who had left a strong body with Prince Lobkowitz, to watch the motions of Belleisle and Broglio.

Extraordi-
nary re-
treat of
M. de
Belleisle.

These generals, seeing themselves surrounded on all hands, returned to Prague, from whence Broglio made his escape in the habit of a courier, and was sent to command the army of Maillebois, who was by this time disgraced. Prince Lobkowitz, who now directed the blockade of Prague, had so effectually cut off all communication between that place and the adjacent country, that in a little time the French troops were reduced to great extremity, both from the severity of the season and the want of provision. They were already reduced to the necessity of eating horse-flesh and unclean animals; and they had no other prospect but that of perishing by famine or war, when their commander formed the scheme of a retreat, which was actually put in execution. Having taken some artful precautions to deceive the enemy, he, in the middle of December, departed from Prague at midnight, with about fourteen thousand men, thirty pieces of artillery, and some of the principal citizens as hostages for the safety of nine hundred soldiers whom he had left in garrison. Notwithstanding the difficulties he must have encountered at that season of the year, in a broken and unfrequented road, which he purposely chose, he marched with such expedition, that he had gained the passes of the mountains before he was overtaken by the horse and hussars of Prince Lobkowitz. The fatigue and hardships which the miserable soldiers underwent are inexpressible. A great number perished in the snow, and many hundreds, fainting with weariness, cold, and hunger, were left to the mercy of the Austrian irregulars, consisting of the most barbarous people on the face of the earth. The Count de Belleisle, though tortured with the hip-gout, behaved with surprising resolution and activity. He caused himself to be carried in a litter to every place where he thought his presence was necessary, and made such dispositions, that the pursuers never could make an impression upon the body of his troops; but all his artillery, baggage, and even his own equipage, fell into the hands of the enemy. On the twenty-ninth day of December he arrived at Egra, from whence he proceeded to Alsace without further molestation; but, when he returned to Versailles, he met with a very cold reception, notwithstanding the gallant exploit which he had performed. After his escape, Prince Lobkowitz returned to Prague, and the small garrison which Belleisle had left in that place surrendered upon honourable terms; so that this capital reverted to the house of Austria.

The King of Great Britain, resolving to make a power- *The King of Great Britain forms an army in Flanders.* ful diversion in the Netherlands, had in the month of April ordered sixteen thousand effective men to be embarked for that country; but, as this step was taken without any previous concert with the States-General, the Earl of Stair, destined to the command of the forces in Flanders, was in the mean time appointed ambassador extraordinary and plenipotentiary to their high mightinesses, in order to persuade them to co-operate vigorously in the plan which his Britannic majesty had formed; a plan by which Great Britain was engaged as a principal

CHAP.   in a foreign dispute, and entailed upon herself the whole
XVIII. burden of an expensive war, big with ruin and disgrace.
1742.   England, from being the umpire, was now become a party
in all continental quarrels; and instead of trimming the
balance of Europe, lavished away her blood and treasure
in supporting the interest and allies of a puny electorate
in the north of Germany. The King of Prussia had been
at variance with the Elector of Hanover. The duchy of
Mecklenburgh was the avowed subject of dispute; but
his Prussian majesty is said to have had other more provoking causes of complaint, which, however, he did not
think proper to divulge. The King of Great Britain
found it convenient to accommodate these differences.
In the course of this summer, the two powers concluded
a convention, in consequence of which the troops of Hanover evacuated Mecklenburgh, and three regiments of
Brandenburgh took possession of those bailiwicks that
were mortgaged to the King of Prussia. The Elector
of Hanover being now secured from danger, sixteen
thousand troops of that country, together with the six
thousand auxiliary Hessians, began their march for the
Netherlands; and about the middle of October arrived
in the neighbourhood of Brussels, where they encamped.
The Earl of Stair repaired to Ghent, where the British
forces were quartered: a body of Austrians was assembled; and though the season was far advanced, he seemed
determined upon some expedition: but all of a sudden
the troops were sent into winter-quarters. The Austrians retired to Luxembourg; the English and Hessians
remained in Flanders; and the Hanoverians marched
into the county of Liege, without paying any regard to
the bishop's protestation.

Progress of   The States-General had made a considerable augment-
the war be- ation of their forces by sea and land; but, notwithstand-
tween Rus- ing the repeated instances of the Earl of Stair, they
sia and   resolved to adhere to their neutrality: they dreaded the
Sweden.   neighbourhood of the French; and they were far from
being pleased to see the English get footing in the
Netherlands. The friends of the house of Orange began
to exert themselves: the states of Groningen and West
Friesland protested, in favour of the prince, against the
promotion of foreign generals which had lately been

made; but his interest was powerfully opposed by the provinces of Zealand and Holland, which had the greatest weight in the republic. The revolution in Russia did not put an end to the war with Sweden. These two powers had agreed to an armistice of three months, during which the czarina augmented her forces in Finland. She likewise ordered the Counts Osterman and Munich, with their adherents, to be tried: they were condemned to death, but pardoned on the scaffold, and sent in exile to Siberia. The Swedes, still encouraged by the intrigues of France, refused to listen to any terms of accommodation, unless Carelia, and the other conquests of the Czar Peter, should be restored. The French court had expected to bring over the new empress to their measures; but they found her as well disposed as her predecessor to assist the house of Austria. She remitted a considerable sum of money to the Queen of Hungary; and at that same time congratulated the Elector of Bavaria on his elevation to the imperial throne. The ceremony of her coronation was performed in May, with great solemnity, at Moscow; and in November she declared her nephew, the Duke of Holstein-Gottorp, her successor, by the title of Grand Prince of all the Russias. The cessation of arms being expired, General Lasci reduced Fredericksheim, and obliged the Swedish army, commanded by Count Lewenhaupt, to retire before him, from one place to another, until at length they were quite surrounded near Helsingfors. In this emergency, the Swedish general submitted to a capitulation, by which his infantry were transported by sea to Sweden; his cavalry marched by land to Abo; and his artillery and magazines remained in the hands of the Russians. The King of Sweden being of an advanced age, the diet assembled in order to settle the succession; and the Duke of Holstein-Gottorp, as grandson to the eldest sister to Charles XII., was declared next heir to the crown. A courier was immediately despatched to Moscow, to notify to the duke this determination of the diet; and this message was followed by a deputation; but when they understood that he had embraced the religion of the Greek church, and been acknowledged successor to the throne of Russia, they annulled his election for Sweden, and

CHAP. resolved that the succession should not be re-established,
XVIII. until a peace should be concluded with the czarina.
1742. Conferences were opened at Abo for this purpose. In
the mean time, the events of the war had been so long
unfortunate for Sweden, that it was absolutely necessary
to appease the indignation of the people with some sacri-
.fice. The Generals Lewenhaupt and Bodenbrock were
tried by a court-martial for misconduct: being found
guilty, and condemned to death, they applied to the
diet, by which the sentence was confirmed. The term
of the subsidy-treaty between Great Britain and Denmark
expiring, his Danish majesty refused to renew it; nor
would he accede to the peace of Breslau. On the other
hand, he became subsidiary to France, with which also
he concluded a new treaty of commerce.

The King The court of Versailles were now heartily tired of
of Sardinia maintaining the war in Germany, and had actually made
declares for equitable proposals of peace to the Queen of Hungary,
the House by whom they were rejected. Thus repulsed, they re-
of Austria. doubled their preparations; and endeavoured, by advantageous offers, to detach the King of Sardinia from the interest of the house of Austria. This prince had espoused
a sister to the grand duke, who pressed him to declare
for her brother, and the Queen of Hungary promised
to gratify him with some territories in the Milanese:
besides, he thought the Spaniards had already gained
too much ground in Italy; but, at the same time, he
was afraid of being crushed between France and Spain,
before he could be properly supported. He therefore
temporized, and protracted the negotiation, until he was
alarmed at the progress of the Spanish arms in Italy,
and fixed in his determination by the subsidies of Great
Britain. The Spanish army assembled at Rimini, under
the Duke de Montemar; and being joined by the Neapolitan forces, amounted to sixty thousand men, furnished
with a large train of artillery. About the beginning of
May they entered the Bolognese: then the King of
Sardinia declaring against them, joined the Austrian
army commanded by Count Traun; marched into the
duchy of Parma; and understanding that the Duke of
Modena had engaged in a treaty with the Spaniards, dis-
possessed that prince of his dominions. The Duke de

Montemar, seeing his army diminished by sickness and desertion, retreated to the kingdom of Naples, and was followed by the King of Sardinia as far as Rimini.

Here he received intelligence that Don Philip, third son of his Catholic majesty, had made an irruption into Savoy with another army of Spaniards, and already taken possession of Chamberri, the capital. He forthwith began his march for Piedmont. Don Philip abandoned Savoy at his approach, and retreating into Dauphiné, took post under the cannon of Fort Barreaux. The king pursued him thither, and both armies remained in sight of each other till the month of December, when the Marquis de Minas, an active and enterprising general, arrived from Madrid, and took upon him the command of the forces under Don Philip. This general's first exploit was against the castle of Aspremont, in the neighbourhood of the Sardinian camp. He attacked it so vigorously, that the garrison was obliged to capitulate in four-and-forty hours. The loss of this important post compelled the king to retire into Piedmont, and the Spaniards marched back into Savoy, where they established their winter-quarters. In the mean time, the Duke de Montemar, who directed the other Spanish army, though the Duke of Modena was nominal generalissimo, resigned his command to Count Gages, who attempted to penetrate into Tuscany; but was prevented by the vigilance of Count Traun, the Austrian general. In December he quartered his troops in the Bolognese and Romagna; while the Austrians and Piedmontese were distributed in the Modenese and Parmesan. The pope was passive during the whole campaign: the Venetians maintained their neutrality, and the King of the two Sicilies was overawed by the British fleet in the Mediterranean.

The new ministry in England had sent out Admiral Matthews to assume the command of this squadron, which had been for some time conducted by Lestock, an inferior officer, as Haddock had been obliged to resign his commission on account of his ill state of health. Matthews was likewise invested with the character of minister-plenipotentiary to the King of Sardinia and the states of Italy. Immediately after he had taken possession of his command, he ordered Captain Norris to de-

CHAP.
XVIII.

1742.stroy five Spanish galleys which had put into the bay of St. Tropez; and this service was effectually performed. In May he detached Commodore Rowley, with eight sail, to cruise off the harbour of Toulon; and a great number of merchant-ships belonging to the enemy fell into his hands. In August he sent Commodore Martin with another squadron into the bay of Naples to bombard that city, unless his Sicilian majesty would immediately recall his troops which had joined the Spanish army, and promise to remain neuter during the continuance of the war. Naples was immediately filled with consternation; the king subscribed to these conditions; and the English squadron rejoined the admiral in the road of Hieres, which he had chosen for his winter station. Before this period he had landed some men at St. Remo, in the territories of Genoa, and destroyed the magazines that were erected for the use of the Spanish army. He had likewise ordered two of his cruisers to attack a Spanish ship of the line, which lay at anchor in the port of Ajaccio, in the island of Corsica: but the Spanish captain set his men on shore, and blew up his ship, rather than she should fall into the hands of the English.

Operations in the West Indies. In the course of this year Admiral Vernon and General Wentworth made another effort in the West Indies. They had in January received a reinforcement from England, and planned a new expedition, in concert with the governor of Jamaica, who accompanied them in their voyage. Their design was to disembark the troops at Porto Bello, and march across the isthmus of Darien, to attack the rich town of Panama. They sailed from Jamaica on the ninth day of March, and on the twenty-eighth arrived at Porto Bello. There they held a council of war, in which it was resolved that, as the troops were sickly, the rainy season begun, and several transports not yet arrived, the intended expedition was become impracticable. In pursuance of this determination the armament immediately returned to Jamaica, exhibiting a ridiculous spectacle of folly and irresolution[b]. In August, a ship of war was sent from

[b] In May, two English frigates, commanded by Captain Smith and Captain Stuart, fell in with three Spanish ships of war, near the island of St. Christopher's. They forthwith engaged, and the action continued till night, by the favour of which the enemy retired to Porto Rico, in a shattered condition.   [In

thence, with about three hundred soldiers, to the small
island of Rattan, in the bay of Honduras, of which they
took possession.   In September, Vernon and Wentworth received orders to return to England with such
troops as remained alive: these did not amount to a
tenth part of the number which had been sent abroad
in that inglorious service.   The inferior officers fell ig-
nobly by sickness and despair, without an opportunity
of signalizing their courage, and the commanders lived
to feel the scorn and reproach of their country.   In
the month of June the new colony of Georgia was invaded by an armament from St. Augustine, commanded
by Don Marinel de Monteano, governor of that fortress.
It consisted of six-and-thirty ships, from which four
thousand men were landed at St. Simon's; and began
their march for Frederica.   General Oglethorpe, with
a handful of men, took such wise precautions for opposing their progress, and harassed them in their march
with such activity and resolution, that, after two of their
detachments had been defeated, they retired to their
ships, and totally abandoned the enterprise.

In England the merchants still complained that their
commerce was not properly protected, and the people
clamoured against the conduct of the war.   They said
their burdens were increased to maintain quarrels with
which they had no concern; to defray the enormous expense of inactive fleets and pacific armies.   Lord C. had
by this time insinuated himself into the confidence of his
sovereign, and engrossed the whole direction of public
affairs.   The war with Spain was now become a secondary
consideration, and neglected accordingly; while the
chief attention of the new minister was turned upon the
affairs of the continent.   The dispute with Spain concerned Britain only.   The interests of Hanover were
connected with the troubles of the empire.   By pursuing this object he soothed the wishes of his master,
and opened a more ample field for his own ambition.
He had studied the policy of the continent with peculiar
eagerness.   This was the favourite subject of his reflec-

CHAP.
XVIII.
1742.

The atten-
tion of the
ministry
turned
chiefly on
the affairs
of the con-
tinent.

In the month of September the Tilbury ship of war, of sixty guns, was acci-
dentally set on fire, and destroyed, off the island of Hispaniola, on which occasion
one hundred and twenty-seven men perished; the rest were saved by Captain
Hoare, of the Defiance, who happened to be on the same cruise.

tion, upon which he thought and spoke with a degree of enthusiasm. The intolerable taxes, the poverty, the ruined commerce of his country, the iniquity of standing armies, votes of credit, and foreign connexions, upon which he had so often expatiated, were now forgotten, or overlooked. He saw nothing but glory, conquest, and acquired dominion. He set the power of France at defiance; and, as if Great Britain had felt no distress, but teemed with treasure which she could not otherwise employ, he poured forth her millions with a rash and desperate hand, in purchasing beggarly allies, and maintaining mercenary armies. The Earl of Stair had arrived in England towards the end of August, and conferred with his majesty. A privy-council was summoned; and in a few days that nobleman returned to Holland. Lord Carteret was sent with a commission to the Hague in September; and when he returned, the baggage of the king and the Duke of Cumberland, which had been shipped for Flanders, was ordered to be brought on shore. The Parliament met on the sixteenth day of November, when his majesty told them, that he had augmented the British forces in the Low Countries with sixteen thousand Hanoverians and the Hessian auxiliaries, in order to form such a force, in conjunction with the Austrian troops, as might be of service to the common cause at all events. He extolled the magnanimity and fortitude of the Queen of Hungary, as well as the resolute conduct of the King of Sardinia, and that prince's strict adherence to his engagements, though attacked in his own dominions. He mentioned the requisition made by Sweden, of his good offices for procuring a peace between that nation and Russia, the defensive alliances which he had concluded with the czarina, and with the King of Prussia, as events which could not have been expected, if Great Britain had not manifested a seasonable spirit and vigour, in defence and assistance of her ancient allies, and in maintaining the liberties of Europe. He said the honour and interest of his crown and kingdoms, the success of the war with Spain, the re-establishment of the balance and tranquillity of Europe, would greatly depend on the prudence and vigour of their resolutions. The Marquis of Tweeddale moved for an address of thanks, which was opposed by the Earl of Chesterfield, for the reasons so often urged on the same occasion; but supported by Lord C. on his new adopted maxims, with those specious arguments which he could at all times produce, delivered with amazing serenity and assurance. The motion was agreed to, and the address presented to his majesty. About this period a treaty of mutual defence and guarantee between his majesty and the King of Prussia was signed at Westminster. In the House of Commons Mr. Lyttelton made a motion for reviving the place-bill; but it was opposed by a great number of members who had formerly been strenuous advocates for this measure, and rejected upon a division. This was also the fate of a motion made to renew the inquiry into the conduct of Robert Earl of Orford. As many strong presumptions of guilt had appeared against him in the reports of the secret committee, the nation had reason to expect that this proposal would have been embraced by a great majority; but several members, who in the preceding session had been loud in their demands of justice, now shamefully contributed their talents and interest in stifling the inquiry.

When the House of Lords took into consideration the several estimates of the expense occasioned by the forces in the pay of Great Britain, Earl Stanhope, at the close of an elegant speech, moved for an address, to beseech and advise his majesty, that, in compassion to his people, loaded already with such numerous and heavy taxes, such large and growing debts, and greater annual expenses than the nation at any time before had ever sustained, he would exonerate his subjects of the charge and burden of those mercenaries who were taken into the service last year, without the advice or consent of Parliament. The motion was supported by the Earl of Sandwich, who took occasion to speak with great contempt of Hanover, and, in mentioning the royal family, seemed to forget that decorum which the subject required. He had, indeed, reason to talk with asperity on the contract by which the Hanoverians had been' taken into the pay of Great Britain. Levy-money was charged to the account, though they were engaged for one year only, and though not a single regiment

Extraordinary motion in the House of Lords by Earl Stanhope.

had been raised on this occasion: they had been levied for the security of the electorate; and would have been maintained if England had never engaged in the affairs of the continent. The Duke of Bedford enlarged upon the same subject. He said it had been suspected, nor was the suspicion without foundation, that the measures of the English ministry had long been regulated by the interest of his majesty's electoral territories: that these had been long considered as a gulf into which the treasures of Great Britain had been thrown: that the state of Hanover had been changed, without any visible cause, since the accession of its princes to the throne of England: affluence had begun to wanton in their towns, and gold to glitter in their cottages, without the discovery of mines, or the increase of their commerce; and new dominions had been purchased, of which the value was never paid from the revenues of Hanover. The motion was hunted down by the new minister, the patriot Lord Bathurst, and the Earl of Bath, which last nobleman declared, that he considered it as an act of cowardice and meanness to fall passively down the stream of popularity, to suffer his reason and integrity to be overborne by the noise of vulgar clamours, which had been raised against the measures of government by the low arts of exaggeration, fallacious reasonings, and partial representations. This is the very language which Sir Robert Walpole had often used against Mr. Pulteney and his confederates in the House of Commons. The associates of the new secretary pleaded the cause of Hanover, and insisted upon the necessity of a land-war against France, with all the vehemence of declamation. Their suggestions were answered; their conduct was severely stigmatized by the Earl of Chesterfield, who observed, that the assembling an army in Flanders, without the concurrence of the States-General, or any other power engaged by treaty, or bound by interest, to support the Queen of Hungary, was a rash and ridiculous measure: the taking sixteen thousand Hanoverians into British pay, without consulting the Parliament, seemed highly derogatory to the rights and dignity of the great council of the nation, and a very dangerous precedent to future times: that these troops could not be employed against the emperor,

whom they had already recognized: that the arms and
wealth of Britain alone were altogether insufficient to
raise the house of Austria to its former strength, dominion, and influence: that the assembling an army in
Flanders would engage the nation as principals in an
expensive and ruinous war, with a power which it ought
not to provoke, and could not pretend to withstand in
that manner: that while Great Britain exhausted herself almost to ruin, in pursuance of schemes founded
on engagements to the Queen of Hungary, the Electorate of Hanover, though under the same engagements,
and governed by the same prince, did not appear to
contribute any thing as an ally to her assistance, but
was paid by Great Britain for all the forces it had sent
into the field, at a very exorbitant price: that nothing
could be more absurd and iniquitous than to hire these
mercenaries, while a numerous army lay inactive at
home, and the nation groaned under such intolerable
burdens. " It may be proper (added he) to repeat what
may be forgotten in the multitude of other objects, that
this nation, after having exalted the Elector of Hanover
from a state of obscurity to the crown, is condemned to
hire the troops of that electorate to fight their own
cause; to hire them at a rate which was never demanded
before; and to pay levy-money for them, though it is
known to all Europe that they were not raised for this
occasion." All the partisans of the old ministry joined
in the opposition to Earl Stanhope's motion, which was
rejected by the majority. Then the Earl of Scarborough
moved for an address, to approve of the measures which
had been taken on the continent; and this was likewise
carried by dint of numbers. It was not however a very
eligible victory: what they gained in Parliament they
lost with the people. The new ministers became more
odious than their predecessors; and the people began to
think public virtue was an empty name.

But the most severe opposition they underwent was
in their endeavours to support a bill which they had
concerted, and which had passed through the House of
Commons with great precipitation: it repealed certain
duties on spirituous liquors, and licences for retailing
these liquors; and imposed others at an easier rate. When

those severe duties, amounting almost to a prohibition, were imposed, the populace of London were sunk into the most brutal degeneracy, by drinking to excess the pernicious spirit called gin, which was sold so cheap that the lowest class of the people could afford to indulge themselves in one continued state of intoxication, to the destruction of all morals, industry, and order. Such a shameful degree of profligacy prevailed, that the retailers of this poisonous compound set up painted boards in public, inviting people to be drunk for the small expense of one penny ; assuring them they might be dead drunk for two-pence, and have straw for nothing. They accordingly provided cellars and places strewed with straw, to which they conveyed those wretches who were overwhelmed with intoxication. In these dismal caverns they lay until they had recovered some use of their faculties, and then they had recourse to the same mischievous potion ; thus consuming their health and ruining their families, in hideous receptacles of the most filthy vice, resounding with riot, execration, and blasphemy. Such beastly practices too plainly denoted a total want of all police and civil regulations, and would have reflected disgrace upon the most barbarous community. In order to restrain this evil, which was become intolerable, the legislature enacted that law which we have already mentioned. But the populace soon broke through all restraint. Though no licence was obtained, and no duty paid, the liquor continued to be sold in all corners of the streets : informers were intimidated by the threats of the people ; and the justices of the peace, either from indolence or corruption, neglected to put the law in execution. The new ministers foresaw that a great revenue would accrue to the crown from a repeal of this act ; and this measure they thought they might the more decently take, as the law had proved ineffectual ; for it appeared that the consumption of gin had considerably increased every year since those heavy duties were imposed. They therefore pretended that, should the price of the liquor be moderately raised, and licences granted at twenty shillings each to the retailers, the lowest class of people would be debarred the use of it to excess ; their morals would of consequence be mended ; and a considerable

sum of money might be raised for the support of the
war, by mortgaging the revenue arising from the duty
and the licences.   Upon these maxims the new bill was
founded, and passed through the Lower House without
opposition; but among the Peers it produced the most
obstinate dispute which had happened since the beginning
of this Parliament.   The first assault it sustained was
from Lord Hervey, who had been divested of his post of
privy-seal, which was bestowed on Lord Gower; and
these two noblemen exchanged principles from that instant.   The first was hardened into a sturdy patriot; the
other suppled into an obsequious courtier.   Lord Hervey
on this occasion made a florid harangue upon the pernicious effects of that destructive spirit they were about
to let loose upon their fellow-creatures.   Several prelates
expatiated on the same topics; but the Earl of Chesterfield attacked the bill with the united powers of reason,
wit, and ridicule.   Lord Carteret, Lord Bathurst, and
the Earl of Bath, were numbered among its advocates;
and shrewd arguments were advanced on both sides of
the question.   After very long, warm, and repeated debates, the bill passed without amendments, though the
whole bench of bishops voted against it; and we cannot
help owning that it has not been attended with those
dismal consequences which the lords in the opposition
foretold.   When the question was put for committing
this bill, and the Earl of Chesterfield saw the bishops
join in his division, " I am in doubt (said he) whether
I have not got on the other side of the question; for I
have not had the honour to divide with so many lawn
sleeves for several years."

By the report of the secret committee it appeared Bill for
that the then minister had commenced prosecutions quieting
against the mayors of boroughs who opposed his influence tions.
in the elections of members of Parliament. These prosecutions were founded on ambiguities in charters, or trivial
informalities in the choice of magistrates. An appeal on
such a process was brought into the House of Lords;
and this evil falling under consideration, a bill was prepared for securing the independency of corporations; but
as it tended to diminish the influence of the ministry,
they argued against it with their usual eagerness and

success; and it was rejected on a division. The mutiny bill and several others passed through both Houses. The Commons granted supplies to the amount of six millions, raised by the land-tax, the malt-tax, duties on spirituous liquors and licences, and a loan from the sinking-fund. In two years the national debt had suffered an increase of two millions four hundred thousand pounds. On the twenty-first day of April the session was closed in the usual manner. The king, in his speech to both Houses, told them that, at the requisition of the Queen of Hungary, he had ordered his army, in conjunction with the Austrians, to pass the Rhine for her support and assistance: that he continued one squadron of ships in the Mediterranean, and another in the West Indies. He thanked the Commons for the ample supplies they had granted; and declared it was the fixed purpose of his heart to promote the true interest and happiness of his kingdoms. Immediately after the prorogation of Parliament he embarked for Germany, accompanied by the Duke of Cumberland, Lord Carteret, and other persons of distinction.

Convention between the empe- ror and the Queen of Hungary.

At this period the Queen of Hungary seemed to triumph over all her enemies. The French were driven out of Bohemia and part of the Upper Palatinate; and their forces under Mareschal Broglio were posted on the Danube. Prince Charles of Lorraine, at the head of the Austrian army, entered Bavaria; and in April obtained a victory over a body of Bavarians at Braunau: at the same time, three bodies of Croatians penetrating through the passes of the Tyrolese, ravaged the whole country to the very gates of Munich. The emperor pressed the French general to hazard a battle; but he refused to run the risk, though he had received a strong reinforcement from France. His imperial majesty, thinking himself unsafe in Munich, retired to Augsburgh: Mareschal Seckendorf retreated with the Bavarian troops to Ingoldstadt, where he was afterwards joined by Mareschal Broglio, whose troops had in this retreat been pursued and terribly harassed by the Austrian cavalry and hussars. Prince Charles had opened a free communication with Munich, which now for the third time fell into the hands of the Queen of Hungary. Her arms likewise reduced

Friedberg and Landsperg, while Prince Charles continued
to pursue the French to Donawert, where they were
joined by twelve thousand men from the Rhine. Broglio
still avoided an engagement, and retreated before the
enemy to Hailbron. The emperor being thus abandoned
by his allies, and stripped of all his dominions, repaired
to Frankfort, where he lived in indigence and obscurity.
He now made advances towards an accommodation with
the Queen of Hungary. His general, Seckendorf, had
an interview with Count Khevenhuller at the convent of
Lowersconfield, where a convention was signed. This
treaty imported, that the emperor should remain neuter
during the continuance of the present war : and that his
troops should be quartered in Franconia; that the Queen
of Hungary should keep possession of Bavaria till the
peace: that Braunau and Scarding should be delivered
up to the Austrians : that the French garrison of Ingoldstadt should be permitted to withdraw, and be replaced
by Bavarians; but that the Austrian general should be
put in possession of all the artillery, magazines, and
warlike stores belonging to the French, which should be
found in the place. The governors of Egra and Ingoldstadt refusing to acquiesce in the capitulation, the Austrians had recourse to the operations of war; and both
places were reduced. In Ingoldstadt they found all the
emperor's domestic treasure, jewels, plate, pictures,
cabinets, and curiosities, with the archives of the house
of Bavaria, the most valuable effects belonging to the
nobility of that electorate, a prodigious train of artillery,
and a vast quantity of provisions, arms, and ammunition.

The French king, baffled in all the efforts he had
hitherto made for the support of the emperor, ordered
his minister at Frankfort to deliver a declaration to the
diet, professing himself extremely well pleased to hear
they intended to interpose their mediation for terminating the war. He said, he was no less satisfied with
the treaty of neutrality which the emperor had concluded
with the Queen of Hungary; an event of which he was
no sooner informed, than he had ordered his troops to
return to the frontiers of his dominions, that the Germanic body might be convinced of his equity and moderation. To this declaration the Queen of Hungary

answered in a rescript, that the design of France was to embarrass her affairs, and deprive her of the assistance of her allies: that the Elector of Bavaria could not be considered as a neutral party in his own cause: that the mediation of the empire could only produce a peace either with or without the concurrence of France: that in the former case no solid peace could be expected; in the latter, it was easy to foresee that France would pay no regard to a peace in which she should have no concern. She affirmed, that the aim of the French king was solely to gain time to repair his losses, that he might afterwards revive the troubles of the empire. The Elector of Mentz, who had favoured the emperor, was now dead, and his successor inclined to the Austrian interest. He allowed this rescript to be entered in the journal of the diet, together with the protests which had been made when the vote of Bohemia was suppressed in the late election. The emperor complained in a circular letter of this transaction, as a stroke levelled at his imperial dignity; and it gave rise to a warm dispute among the members of the Germanic body. Several princes resented the haughty conduct, and began to be alarmed at the success, of the house of Austria; while others pitied the deplorable situation of the emperor. The Kings of Great Britain and Prussia, as Electors of Hanover and Brandenburgh, espoused opposite sides in this contest. His Prussian majesty protested against the investiture of the duchy of Saxe Lawenburgh, claimed by the King of Great Britain: he had an interview with General Seckendorf at Anspach; and was said to have privately visited the emperor at Frankfort.

The King of Great Britain obtains a victory over the French at Dettingen.

The troops which the King of Great Britain had assembled in the Netherlands, began their march for the Rhine in the latter end of February; and in May they encamped near Hoech on the river Mayne, under the command of the Earl of Stair. This nobleman sent Major-General Bland to Frankfort, with a compliment to the emperor, assuring him, in the name of his Britannic majesty, that the respect owing to his dignity should not be violated, nor the place of his residence disturbed. Notwithstanding this assurance, the emperor retired to Munich, though he was afterwards compelled.

to return, by the success of the Austrians in Bavaria.
The French king, in order to prevent the junction of the
British forces with Prince Charles of Lorraine, ordered
the Mareschal de Noailles to assemble sixty thousand
men upon the Mayne ; while Coigny was sent into Alsace
with a numerous army, to defend that province, and oppose Prince Charles, should he attempt to pass the Rhine.
The Mareschal de Noailles, having secured the towns of
Spire, Worms, and Oppenheim, passed the Rhine in the
beginning of June, and posted himself on the east side
of that river, above Frankfort. The Earl of Stair advanced towards him, and encamped at Killenbach, between the river Mayne and the forest of D'Armstadt;
from this situation he made a motion to Aschaffenburgh,
with a view to secure the navigation of the Upper Mayne ;
but he was anticipated by the enemy, who lay on the
other side of the river, and had taken possession of the
posts above, so as to intercept all supplies. They were
posted on the other side of the river, opposite to the
allies, whose camp they overlooked ; and they found
means, by their parties and other precautions, to cut off
the communication by water between Frankfort and the
confederates. The Duke of Cumberland had already
come to make his first campaign, and his majesty arrived
in the camp on the ninth day of June. He found his
army, amounting to about forty thousand men, in danger
of starving : he received intelligence that a reinforcement of twelve thousand Hanoverians and Hessians had
reached Hanau ; and he resolved to march thither, both
with a view to effect a junction, and to procure provision'
for his forces. With this view he decamped on the
twenty-sixth day of June. He had no sooner quitted
Aschaffenburgh than it was seized by the French general : he had not marched above three leagues, when he
perceived the enemy, to the number of thirty thousand,
had passed the river farther down, at Selingenstadt, and
were drawn up in order of battle at the village of Dettingen, to dispute his passage. Thus he found himself
cooped up in a very dangerous situation. The enemy
had possessed themselves of Aschaffenburgh behind, so
as to prevent his retreat : his troops were confined in a
narrow plain, bounded by hills and woods on the right,

flanked on the left by the river Mayne, on the opposite side of which the French had erected batteries that annoyed the allies on their march : in the front a considerable part of the French army was drawn up, with a narrow pass before them, the village of Dettingen on their right, a wood on their left, and a morass in the centre. Thus environed, the confederates must either have fought at a very great disadvantage, or surrendered themselves prisoners of war, had not the Duke de Gramont, who commanded the enemy, been instigated by the spirit of madness to forego these advantages. He passed the defile, and advancing towards the allies, a battle ensued. The French horse charged with great impetuosity, and some regiments of British cavalry were put in disorder; but the infantry of the allies behaved with such intrepidity and deliberation, under the eye of their sovereign, as soon determined the fate of the day : the French were obliged to give way, and repass the Mayne with great precipitation, having lost about five thousand men killed, wounded, or taken. Had they been properly pursued before they recollected themselves from their first confusion, in all probability they would have sustained a total overthrow. The Earl of Stair proposed that a body of cavalry should be detached on this service; but his advice was overruled. The loss of the allies in this action amounted to two thousand men. The Generals Clayton and Monroy were killed : the Duke of Cumberland, who exhibited uncommon proofs of courage, was shot through the calf of the leg : the Earl of Albemarle, General Huske, and several other officers of distinction, were wounded. The king exposed his person to a severe fire of cannon as well as musketry : he rode between the first and second lines with his sword drawn, and encouraged the troops to fight for the honour of England. Immediately after the action he continued his march to Hanau, where he was joined by the reinforcement. The Earl of Stair sent a trumpeter to Mareschal de Noailles, recommending to his protection the sick and wounded that were left on the field of battle; and these the French general treated with great care and tenderness. Such generosity softens the rigours of war, and does honour to humanity.

The two armies continued on different sides of the river till the twelfth day of July, when the French general receiving intelligence that Prince Charles of Lorraine had approached the Neckar, he suddenly retired and repassed the Rhine between Worms and Oppenheim. The King of Great Britain was visited by Prince Charles and Count Khevenhuller at Hanau, where the future operations of the campaign were regulated. On the twenty-seventh day of August, the allied army passed the Rhine at Mentz, and the king fixed his headquarters in the episcopal palace at Worms. Here the forces lay encamped till the latter end of September, when they advanced to Spire, where they were joined by twenty-thousand Dutch auxiliaries from the Netherlands. Mareschal Noailles having retreated into Upper Alsace, the allies took possession of Germersheim, and demolished the intrenchments which the enemy had raised on the Queich; then they returned to Mentz, and in October were distributed into winter-quarters, after an inactive campaign that redounded very little to the honour of those by whom the motions of the army were conducted. In September a treaty had been concluded at Worms between his Britannic majesty, the King of Sardinia, and the Queen of Hungary. She engaged to maintain thirty thousand men in Italy: the King of Sardinia obliged himself to employ forty thousand infantry and five thousand horse, in consideration of his commanding the combined army, and receiving an annual subsidy of two hundred thousand pounds from Great Britain. As a further gratification, the queen yielded to him the city of Placentia, with several districts in the duchy of Pavia, and in the Novarese; and all her right and pretensions to Final, at present possessed by the republic at Genoa, which they hoped would give it up on being repaid the purchase-money, amounting to three hundred thousand pounds. This sum the King of England promised to disburse; and moreover to maintain a strong squadron in the Mediterranean, the commander of which should act in concert with his Sardinian majesty. Finally, the contracting powers agreed that Final should be constituted a free port, like that of Leghorn. Nothing could be more unjust than this treaty, by which the Genoese were negotiated out of their property. They had purchased the marquisate of Final of the late emperor for a valuable consideration, and the purchase had been guaranteed by Great Britain. It could not, therefore, be expected that they would part with this acquisition to a prince whose power they thought already too formidable; especially, on condition of its being made a free port, to the prejudice of their own commerce. They presented remonstrances against this article by their ministers at the courts of London, Vienna, and Turin; and, as very little regard was paid to their representations, they threw themselves into the arms of France and Spain for protection.

Conclusion of the campaign.

After the battle of Dettingen, Colonel Mentzel, at the head of a large body of irregulars belonging to the Queen of Hungary, made an irruption into Lorraine, part of which they ravaged without mercy. In September, Prince Charles, with the Austrian army, entered the Brisgaw, and attempted to pass the Rhine; but Mareschal Coigny had taken such precautions for guarding it on the other side, that he was obliged to abandon his design, and marching back into the Upper Palatinate, quartered his troops in that country, and in Bavaria. By this time the Earl of Stair had solicited and obtained leave to resign his command. He had for some time thought himself neglected; and was unwilling that his reputation should suffer on account of measures in which he had no concern. In October the King of Great Britain returned to Hanover, and the army separated. The troops in British pay marched back to the Netherlands, and the rest took the route to their respective countries. The States-General still wavered between their own immediate interest and their desire to support the house of Austria. At length, however, they supplied her with a subsidy, and ordered twenty thousand men to march to her assistance, notwithstanding the intrigues of the Marquis de Fenelon, the French ambassador at the Hague, and the declaration of the King of Prussia, who disapproved of this measure, and refused them a passage through his territories to the Rhine.

Affairs in the north.

Sweden was filled with discontents, and divided into factions. The Generals Bodenbrock and Lewenhaupt were beheaded, having been sacrificed as scape-goats for the ministry. Some unsuccessful efforts by sea and land were made against the Russians. At last the peace of Abo was concluded; and the Duke of Holstein-Utin, uncle to the successor of the Russian throne, was chosen as next heir to the crown of Sweden. A party had been formed in favour of the Prince of Denmark ; and the order of the peasants actually elected him as successor. The debates in the college of nobles rose to a very dangerous degree of animosity, and were appeased by an harangue in Swedish verse, which one of the senators pronounced. The peasants yielded the point, and the succession was settled on the Duke of Holstein. Denmark, instigated by French counsels, began to make preparations for war against Sweden; but a body of Russian auxiliaries arriving in that kingdom, under the command of General Keith, and the czarina declaring she would assist the Swedes with her whole force, the King of Denmark thought proper to disarm. It had been an old maxim of French policy to embroil the courts of the north, that they might be too much employed at home to intermeddle in the affairs of Germany, while France was at war with the house of Austria. The good understanding between the czarina and the Queen of Hungary was at this period destroyed, in consequence of a conspiracy which had been formed by some persons of distinction at the court of Petersburgh, for removing the Empress Elizabeth, and recalling the Princess Anne to the administration. This design being discovered, the principal conspirators were corporally punished, and sent in exile to Siberia. The Marquis de Botta, the Austrian minister, who had resided at the court of the czarina, was suspected of having been concerned in the plot; though the grounds of this suspicion did not appear till after he was recalled, and sent as ambassador to the court of Berlin. The empress demanded satisfaction of the Queen of Hungary, who appointed commissioners to inquire into his conduct, and he was acquitted; but the czarina was not at all satisfied of his innocence. In February a defensive treaty of alliance was concluded between this princess and the King of Great Britain.

By this time France was deprived of her ablest

CHAP.
XVIII.

1743.
Battle of
Campo-
Santo.

minister, in the death of the Cardinal de Fleury, who had for many years managed the affairs of that kingdom. He is said to have possessed a lively genius, and an insinuating address; to have been regular in his deportment, and moderate in his disposition; but at the same time he has been branded as deceitful, dissembling, and vindictive. His scheme of politics was altogether pacific: he endeavoured to accomplish his purposes by raising and fomenting intrigues at foreign courts: he did not seem to pay much regard to the military glory of France; and he too much neglected the naval power of that kingdom. Since Broglio was driven out of Germany, the French court affected uncommon moderation. They pretended that their troops had only acted as auxiliaries while they remained in the empire: being, however, apprehensive of an irruption into their own dominions, they declared, that those troops were no longer to be considered in that light, but as subjects acting in the service of France. The campaign in Italy proved unfavourable to the Spaniards. In the beginning of February, Count Gages, who commanded the Spanish army in the Bolognese, amounting to four-and-twenty thousand men, passed the Penaro, and advanced to Campo-Santo, where he encountered the imperial and Piedmontese forces, commanded by the Counts Traun and Aspremont. The strength of the two armies was nearly equal. The action was obstinate and bloody, though indecisive. The Spaniards lost about four thousand men killed, wounded, or taken. The damage sustained by the confederates was not quite so great. Some cannon and colours were taken on both sides; and each claimed the victory. Count Gages repassed the Penaro, retreated suddenly from Bologna, and marched to Rimini in the ecclesiastical state, where he fortified his camp in an advantageous situation, after having suffered severely by desertion. Count Traun remained inactive in the Modenese till September, when he resigned his command to Prince Lobkowitz. This general entered the Bolognese in October, and then advanced towards Count Gages, who, with his forces, now reduced to seven thousand, retreated to Fano; but afterwards took possession of Pesaro, and fortified all the passes of the river Foglia.

The season was far advanced before the Spanish troops, commanded by Don Philip, in Savoy, entered upon action. In all probability, the courts of Versailles and Madrid carried on some private negotiation with the King of Sardinia. This expedient failing, Don Philip decamped from Chamberri in the latter end of August, and defiling through Dauphiné towards Briançon, was joined by the Prince of Conti, at the head of twenty thousand French auxiliaries. Thus reinforced, he attacked the Piedmontese lines at Chateau-Dauphiné; but was repulsed in several attempts, and obliged to retreat with considerable loss. The French established their winter-quarters in Dauphiné and Provence; and the Spaniards maintained their footing in Savoy.

The British fleet, commanded by Admiral Matthews, Transac-tions of the British fleet in the Mediterranean. overawed all the states that bordered on the Mediterranean. This officer, about the end of June, understanding that fourteen xebecks, laden with artillery and ammunition for the Spanish army, had arrived at Genoa, sailed thither from the road of Hieres, and demanded of the republic that they would either oblige these vessels with the stores to quit their harbour, or sequester their lading until a general peace should be established. After some dispute, it was agreed that the cannon and stores should be deposited in the castle of Bonifacio, situated on a rock at the south end of Corsica; and that the xebecks should have leave to retire without molestation. The Corsicans had some years before revolted, and shaken off the dominion of the Genoese, under which their island had remained for many centuries. They found themselves oppressed, and resolved to assert their freedom. They conferred the sovereign authority on a German adventurer, who was solemnly proclaimed by the name of King Theodore. He had supplied them with some arms and ammunition, which he had brought from Tunis; and amused them with promises of being assisted by foreign powers in retrieving their independency; but as these promises were not performed, they treated him so roughly, that he had thought proper to quit the island, and they submitted again to their old masters. The troubles of Corsica were now revived. Theodore revisited his kingdom,

CHAP.
XVIII.

1743.

and was recognized by the principal chiefs of the island. He published a manifesto: he granted a general pardon to all his subjects who should return to their obedience: he pretended to be countenanced and supported by the King of Great Britain and the Queen of Hungary. He was certainly thought a proper instrument to perplex and harass the Genoese, and was supplied at this juncture with a sum of money to purchase arms for the Corsicans; but a change soon happened in the British ministry, and then he was suffered to relapse into his original obscurity. Admiral Matthews, though he did not undertake any expedition of importance against the maritime towns of Spain, continued to assert the British empire at sea through the whole extent of the Mediterranean. The Spanish army under Don Philip was no sooner in motion, than the English admiral ordered some troops and cannon to be disembarked for the security of Villa-Franca. Some stores having been landed at Civita Vecchia, for the use of the Spanish forces under Count Gages, Matthews interpreted this transaction into a violation of the neutrality which the pope had professed; and sent thither a squadron to bombard the place. The city of Rome was filled with consternation; and the pope had recourse to the good offices of his Sardinian majesty, in consequence of which the English squadron was ordered to withdraw. The captains of single cruising ships, by their activity and vigilance, wholly interrupted the commerce of Spain; cannonaded and burned some towns on the sea-side; and kept the whole coast in continual alarm [c].

In the West Indies some unsuccessful efforts were

---

[c] In May a dreadful plague broke out at Messina in Sicily. It was imported in cotton and other commodities brought from the Morea; and swept off such a multitude of people, that the city was almost depopulated: all the galley slaves, who were employed in burying the dead, perished by the contagion; and this was the fate of many priests and monks who administered to those who were infected. The dead bodies lay in heaps in the streets, corrupting the air, and adding fresh fuel to the rage of the pestilence. Numbers died miserably, for want of proper attendance and necessaries; and all was horror and desolation. At the beginning of winter it ceased, after having destroyed near fifty thousand inhabitants of Messina, and of the garrisons in the citadel and castle. It was prevented from spreading in Sicily by a strong barricado drawn from Melazzo to Taormina; but it was conveyed to Reggio in Calabria, by the avarice of a broker of that place, who bought some goods at Messina. The King of Naples immediately ordered lines to be formed, together with a chain of troops, which cut off all communication between that place and the rest of the continent.

made by an English squadron, commanded by Commodore Knowles. He attacked La Gueira on the coast of Caraccas, in the month of February; but met with such a warm reception, that he was obliged to desist, and make the best of his way for the Dutch island Curaçoa, where he repaired the damage he had sustained. His ships being refitted, he made another attempt upon Porto Cavallo in April, which like the former miscarried. Twelve hundred marines being landed in the neighbourhood of that place, were seized with such a panic that it was found necessary to re-embark them without delay. Then the commodore abandoned the enterprise, and sailed back to his station at the Leeward Islands, without having added much to his reputation, either as to conduct or resolution. On the continent of America the operations of the war were very inconsiderable. General Oglethorpe having received intelligence that the Spaniards prepared for another invasion from St. Augustine, assembled a body of Indians, as a reinforcement to part of his own regiment, with the highlanders and rangers, and in the spring began his march, in order to anticipate the enemy. He encamped for some time in the neighbourhood of St. Augustine, by way of defiance; but they did not think proper to hazard an engagement; and as he was in no condition to undertake a siege, he returned to Georgia. In October the Princess Louisa, youngest daughter of his Britannic majesty, was married by proxy, at Hanover, to the Prince Royal of Denmark, who met her at Altona, and conducted her to Copenhagen.

CHAP.
XVIII.

1743.
Unsuccessful attempts
upon the
Spanish
settlements
in the West
Indies.

CHAPTER XIX.

CHAP.
XIX.

1743.
Debate in
Parliament
against the
Hanove-
rian troops.

THE discontents of England were artfully inflamed by
anti-ministerial writers, who not only exaggerated the
burdens of the people, and drew frightful pictures of the
distress and misery which, they said, impended over the
nation, but also employed the arts of calumny and misrepresentation, to excite a jealousy and national quarrel
between the English and Hanoverians. They affirmed
that in the last campaign the British general had been
neglected and despised ; while the counsels of foreign
officers, greatly inferior to him in capacity, quality, and
reputation, had been followed, to the prejudice of the
common cause : that the British troops sustained daily

insults from their own mercenaries, who were indulged
with particular marks of royal favour: that the sovereign himself appeared at Dettingen in a Hanoverian
scarf; and that his electoral troops were of very little
service in that engagement. Though the most material
of these assertions were certainly false, they made a
strong impression on the minds of the people, already
irritated by the enormous expense of a continental war
maintained for the interests of Germany. When the
Parliament met in the beginning of December, a motion
was made in the House of Peers, by the Earl of Sandwich, for an address, beseeching his majesty to discontinue
the Hanoverian troops in British pay, in order to remove
the popular discontent, and stop the murmurs of the
English troops abroad. He was supported by the Duke
of Bedford, the Earl of Chesterfield, and all the leaders
in the opposition, who did not fail to enumerate, and
insist upon all the circumstances we have mentioned.
They moreover observed, that better troops might be
hired at a smaller expense: that it would be a vain and
endless task to exhaust the national treasure, in enriching
a hungry and barren electorate : that the popular dissatisfaction against these mercenaries was so general, and
raised to such violence, as nothing but their dismission
could appease: that if such hirelings should be thus
continued from year to year, they might at last become
a burden entailed upon the nation, and be made sub-
servient, under some ambitious prince, to purposes destructive of British liberty. These were the suggestions
of spleen and animosity; for, granting the necessity of a
land war, the Hanoverians were the most natural allies
and auxiliaries which Great Britain could engage and
employ. How insolent soever some few individual generals of that electorate might have been in their private
deportment, certain it is, their troops behaved with great
sobriety, discipline, and decorum; and in the day of
battle did their duty with as much courage and alacrity
as any body of men ever displayed on the like occasion.
The motion was rejected by the majority; but, when the
term for keeping them in the British pay was nearly expired, and the estimates for their being continued the

ensuing year were laid before the House, the Earl of
Sandwich renewed his motion. The lord chancellor, as
speaker of the House, interposing, declared, that by their
rules a question once rejected could not be revived during
the same session. A debate ensued, and the second motion
was overruled. The Hanoverian troops were voted in the
House of Commons: nevertheless, the same nobleman
moved in the Upper House, that the continuing sixteen
thousand Hanoverians in British pay was prejudicial to
his majesty's true interest, useless to the common cause,
and dangerous to the welfare and tranquillity of the
nation. He was seconded by the Duke of Marlborough,
who had resigned his commission in disgust; and the
proposal gave birth to another warm dispute; but victory declared, as usual, for the ministry.

Supplies
granted.

In the House of Commons they sustained divers attacks. A motion was made for laying a duty of eight
shillings in the pound on all places and pensions. Mr.
Grenville moved for an address, to beseech his majesty,
that he would not engage the British nation any further
in the war on the continent, without the concurrence of
the States-General on certain stipulated proportions of
force and expense, as in the late war. These proposals
begat vigorous debates, in which the country party were
always foiled by dint of superior numbers. Such was
the credit and influence of the ministry in Parliament,
that although the national debt was increased by above
six millions since the commencement of the war, the
Commons indulged them with an enormous sum for the
expense of the ensuing year. The grants specified in the
votes amounted to six millions and a half: to this sum
were added three millions and a half paid to the sinking
fund in perpetual taxes; so that this year's expense rose
to ten millions. The funds established for the annual
charge were the land and malt taxes; one million paid
by the East India company for the renewal of their
charter, twelve hundred thousand pounds by annuities,
one million from the sinking-fund, six-and-thirty thousand
pounds from the coinage, and six hundred thousand
pounds by a lottery; an expedient which for some time
had been annually repeated, and which, in a great mea-

sure, contributed to debauch the morals of the public, by introducing a spirit of gaming, destructive of all industry and virtue.

The dissensions of the British Parliament were suddenly suspended by an event that seemed to unite both parties in the prosecution of the same measures. This was the intelligence of an intended invasion. By the parliamentary disputes, the loud clamours, and the general dissatisfaction of the people in Great Britain, the French ministry were persuaded that the nation was ripe for a revolt. This belief was corroborated by the assertions of their emissaries in different parts of Great Britain and Ireland. These were Papists and Jacobites of strong prejudices and warm imaginations, who saw things through the medium of passion and party, and spoke rather from extravagant zeal than from sober conviction. They gave the court of Versailles to understand, that if the Chevalier de St. George, or his eldest son, Charles Edward, should appear at the head of a French army in Great Britain, a revolution would instantly follow in his favour. This intimation was agreeable to Cardinal de Tencin, who, since the death of Fleury, had borne a share in the administration of France. He was of a violent enterprising temper. He had been recommended to the purple by the Chevalier de St. George, and was seemingly attached to the Stuart family. His ambition was flattered with the prospect of giving a king to Great Britain; of performing such eminent service to his benefactor, and of restoring to the throne of their ancestors a family connected by the ties of blood with all the greatest princes of Europe. The ministry of France foresaw, that even if this aim should miscarry, a descent upon Great Britain would make a considerable diversion from the continent in favour of France, and embroil and embarrass his Britannic majesty, who was the chief support of the House of Austria and all its allies. Actuated by these motives, he concerted measures with the Chevalier de St. George at Rome, who, being too much advanced in years to engage personally in such an expedition, agreed to delegate his pretensions and authority to his son Charles, a youth of promising talents, sage, secret, brave, and enterprising, amiable in his person, grave, and

even reserved in his deportment.   He approved himself
in the sequel composed and moderate in success, wonderfully firm in adversity; and though tenderly nursed
in all the delights of an effeminate country and gentle
climate, patient, almost beyond belief, of cold, hunger,
and fatigue.   Such was the adventurer now destined to
fill the hope which the French ministry had conceived,
from the projected invasion of Great Britain.

A French
squadron
sails up the
English
channel.
Count Saxe was appointed by the French king commander of the troops designed for this expedition, which
amounted to fifteen thousand men.   They began their
march to Picardy, and a great number of vessels was
assembled for their embarkation at Dunkirk, Calais, and
Boulogne. It was determined that they should be landed
in Kent, under convoy of a strong squadron equipped at
Brest, and commanded by Monsieur de Roquefeuille, an
officer of experience and capacity.   The Chevalier de St.
George is said to have required the personal service of
the Duke of Ormond, who excused himself on account
of his advanced age: be that as it will, Prince Charles
departed from Rome about the end of December, in the
disguise of a Spanish courier, attended by one servant
only, and furnished with passports by Cardinal Aquaviva.
He travelled through Tuscany to Genoa, from whence
he proceeded to Savona, where he embarked for Antibes, and, prosecuting his journey to Paris, was indulged
with a private audience of the French king; then he set
out incognito for the coast of Picardy.   The British ministry being apprized of his arrival in France, at once
comprehended the destination of the armaments prepared at Brest and Boulogne.   Mr. Thomson, the English resident at Paris, received orders to make a remonstrance to the French ministry, on the violation of those
treaties by which the pretender to the crown of Great
Britain was excluded from the territories of France. But
he was given to understand, that his Most Christian Majesty would not explain himself on that subject, until
the King of England should have given satisfaction on
the repeated complaints which had been made to him,
touching the infractions of those very treaties which had
been so often violated by his orders.   In the month of
January, M. de Roquefeuille sailed from Brest, directing

his course up the English channel with twenty ships of war. They were immediately discovered by an English cruiser, which ran into Plymouth; and the intelligence was conveyed by land to the board of Admiralty. Sir John Norris was forthwith ordered to take the command of the squadron at Spithead, with which he sailed round to the Downs, where he was joined by some ships of the line from Chatham, and then he found himself at the head of a squadron considerably stronger than that of the enemy.

Several regiments marched to the southern coast of England: all governors and commanders were ordered to repair immediately to their respective posts: the forts at the mouths of the Thames and Medway were put in a posture of defence; and directions were issued to assemble the Kentish militia, to defend the coast in case of an invasion. On the fifteenth day of February the king sent a message to both Houses of Parliament, intimating the arrival of the pretender's son in France, the preparations at Dunkirk, and the appearance of a French fleet in the English channel. They joined in an address, declaring their indignation and abhorrence of the design formed in favour of a popish pretender; and assuring his majesty, that they would, with the warmest zeal and unanimity, take such measures as would enable him to frustrate and defeat so desperate and insolent an attempt. Addresses of the same kind were presented by the city of London, both universities, the principal towns of Great Britain, the clergy, the dissenting ministers, the quakers, and almost all the corporations and communities of the kingdom. A requisition was made of the six thousand auxiliaries, which the States-General were by treaty obliged to furnish on such occasions; and these were granted with great alacrity and expedition. The Earl of Stair, forgetting his wrongs, took this opportunity of offering his services to government, and was invested with the chief command of the forces in Great Britain. His example was followed by several noblemen of the first rank. The Duke of Montague was permitted to raise a regiment of horse; and orders were sent to bring over six thousand of the British troops from Flanders, in case the invasion should actually take place. His majesty

CHAP. XIX.

1743.

The kingdom is put in a posture of defence.

was, in another address from Parliament, exhorted to augment his forces by sea and land : the habeas corpus act was suspended for six months, and several persons of distinction were apprehended on suspicion of treasonable practices : a proclamation was issued for putting the laws in execution against papists and nonjurors, who were commanded to retire ten miles from London ; and every precaution was taken which seemed necessary for the preservation of the public tranquillity.

The design of the French defeated. War between France and England.

Meanwhile the French court proceeded with their preparations at Boulogne and Dunkirk, under the eye of the young pretender ; and seven thousand men were actually embarked. M. de Roquefeuille sailed up the channel as far as Dungeness, a promontory on the coast of Kent, after having detached M. de Barreil, with five ships, to hasten the embarkation at Dunkirk. While the French admiral anchored off Dungeness, he perceived, on the twenty-fourth day of February, the British fleet under Sir John Norris, doubling the South Foreland from the Downs ; and though the wind was against him, taking the opportunity of the tide to come up and engage the French squadron. Roquefeuille, who little expected such a visit, could not be altogether composed, considering the great superiority of his enemies ; but the tide failing, the English admiral was obliged to anchor two leagues short of the enemy. In this interval, M. de Roquefeuille called a council of war, in which it was determined to avoid an engagement, weigh anchor at sunset, and make the best of their way to the place from whence they had set sail. This resolution was favoured by a very hard gale of wind, which began to blow from the north-east, and carried them down the channel with incredible expedition. But the same storm which, in all probability, saved their fleet from destruction, utterly disconcerted the design of invading England. A great number of their transports were driven ashore and destroyed, and the rest were so damaged that they could not be speedily repaired. The English were now masters at sea, and their coast was so well guarded that the enterprise could not be prosecuted with any probability of success. The French generals nominated to serve in this expedition returned to Paris, and the young pretender resolved to wait a more favourable opportunity. In the mean time he remained in Paris, or that neighbourhood, incognito, and almost totally neglected by the court of France. Finding himself in this disagreeable situation, and being visited by John Murray of Broughton, who magnified the power of his friends in Great Britain, he resolved to make some bold effort, even without the assistance of Louis, in whose sincerity he had no faith, and forthwith took proper measures to obtain exact information touching the number, inclinations, and influence of his father's adherents in England and Scotland. The French king no longer preserved any measures with the court of London: the British resident at Paris was given to understand, that a declaration of war must ensue; and this was actually published on the twentieth day of March. The King of Great Britain was taxed with having dissuaded the court of Vienna from entertaining any thoughts of an accommodation; with having infringed the convention of Hanover; with having exercised piracy upon the subjects of France, and with having blocked up the harbour of Toulon. On the thirty-first day of March, a like denunciation of war against France was published at London, amidst the acclamations of the people.

The Commons of England, in order to evince their loyalty, brought in a bill, denouncing the penalties of high treason against those who should maintain correspondence with the sons of the pretender. In the Upper House, Lord Hardwicke, the chancellor, moved, that a clause should be inserted, extending the crime of treason to the posterity of the offenders, during the lives of the pretender's sons. The motion, which was supported by the whole strength of the ministry, produced a warm debate, in which the Duke of Bedford, the Earl of Chesterfield, the Lords Talbot and Hervey, argued against it in the most pathetic manner, as an illiberal expedient, contrary to the dictates of humanity, the law of nature, the rules of common justice, and the precepts of religion; an expedient that would involve the innocent with the guilty, and tend to the augmentation of ministerial power, for which purpose it was undoubtedly calculated. Notwithstanding these suggestions, the clause was carried in the affirmative, and the bill sent back to the Commons,

CHAP. XIX.

1743.

1744 Bill against those who should correspond with the sons of the pretender.

G g 2

where the amendment was vigorously opposed by Lord Strange, Lord Guernsey, Mr. W. Pitt, and other members, by whom the original bill had been countenanced [*]: the majority, however, declared for the amendment, and the bill obtained the royal assent.   The session of Parliament was closed in May, when the king told them, that the French had made vast preparations on the side of the Netherlands ; and that the States-General had agreed to furnish the succours stipulated by treaties.

Naval engagement off Toulon.

By this time an action had happened in the Mediterranean, between the British fleet commanded by Admiral Matthews, and the combined squadrons of France and Spain, which had been for some time blocked up in the harbour of Toulon.   On the ninth day of February they were perceived standing out of the road, to the number of four-and-thirty sail : the English admiral immediately weighed from Hieres bay ; and on the eleventh, part of the fleets engaged.   Matthews attacked the Spanish admiral, Don Navarro, whose ship, the Real, was a first rate, mounted with above a hundred guns.   Rear-Admiral Rowley singled out M. de Court, who commanded the French squadron ; and a very few captains followed the example of their commanders : but Vice-Admiral Lestock, with his whole division, remained at a great distance astern : and several captains who were immediately under the eye of Matthews, behaved in such a manner as reflected disgrace upon their country.   The whole transaction was conducted without order or deliberation.   The French and Spaniards would have willingly avoided an engagement, as the British squadron was superior to them in strength and number.   M. de Court, therefore, made the best of his way towards the Straits' mouth, probably with intention to join the Brest squadron ; but he had orders to protect the Spanish fleet ; and as they sailed heavily, he was obliged to wait for them at the hazard of maintaining a battle with the English.   Thus circumstanced, he made sail and lay-to by turns ; so that the British admiral could not engage them in proper order ;

[*] The opposition had sustained a heavy blow in the death of the Duke of Argyle, a nobleman of shining qualifications for the senate and the field, whose character would have been still more illustrious, had not some parts of his conduct subjected him to the suspicion of selfishness and inconstancy.   He was succeeded in that title by his brother, Archibald, Earl of Ilay.

and as they outsailed his ships, he began to fear they
would escape him altogether, should he wait for Vice-
Admiral Lestock, who was so far astern. Under this
apprehension he made the signal for engaging, while that
for the line of battle was still displayed; and this incon-
sistency naturally introduced confusion. The fight was
maintained with great vivacity by the few who engaged.
The Real being quite disabled, and lying like a wreck
upon the water, Mr. Matthews sent a fire-ship to destroy
her; but the expedient did not take effect. The ship
ordered to cover this machine did not obey the signal;
so that the captain of the fire-ship was exposed to the
whole fire of the enemy. Nevertheless, he continued to
advance until he found the vessel sinking; and being
within a few yards of the Real, he set fire to the fusees.
The ship was immediately in flames, in the midst of
which he and his lieutenant, with twelve men, perished.
This was likewise the fate of a Spanish launch, which had
been manned with fifty sailors, to prevent the fire-ship
from running on board the Real. One ship of the line
belonging to the Spanish squadron struck to Captain
Hawke, who sent a lieutenant to take possession of her:
she was afterwards retaken by the French squadron; but
was found so disabled that they left her deserted, and
she was next day burned by order of Admiral Matthews.
At night the action ceased; and the admiral found his
own ship so much damaged that he moved his flag into
another. Captain Cornwall fell in the engagement, after
having exhibited a remarkable proof of courage and intrepidity; but the loss of men was very inconsiderable.
Next day the enemy appeared to leeward, and the admiral gave chase till night, when he brought to, that he
might be joined by the ships astern. They were perceived again on the thirteenth at a considerable distance,
and pursued till the evening. In the morning of the
fourteenth, twenty sail of them were seen distinctly, and
Lestock with his division had gained ground of them
considerably by noon; but Admiral Matthews displayed
the signal for leaving off chase, and bore away for Port
Mahon, to repair the damage he had sustained. Meanwhile the combined squadrons continued their course
towards the coast of Spain. M. de Court, with his divi-

sion, anchored in the road of Alicant; and Don Navarro sailed into the harbour of Carthagena. Admiral Matthews, on his arrival at Minorca, accused Lestock of having misbehaved on the day of action; suspended him from his office, and sent him prisoner to England, where, in his turn, he accused his accuser. Long before the engagement, these two officers had expressed the most virulent resentment against each other. Matthews was brave, open, and undisguised; but proud, imperious, and precipitate. Lestock had signalized his courage on many occasions, and perfectly understood the whole discipline of the navy; but he was cool, cunning, and vindictive. He had been treated superciliously by Matthews, and in revenge took advantage of his errors and precipitation. To gratify this passion he betrayed the interest and glory of his country; for it is not to be doubted but that he might have come up in time to engage; and in that case, the fleets of France and Spain would in all likelihood have been destroyed: but he intrenched himself within the punctilios of discipline, and saw with pleasure his antagonist expose himself to the hazard of death, ruin, and disgrace. Matthews himself, in the sequel, sacrificed his duty to his resentment, in restraining Lestock from pursuing and attacking the combined squadrons on the third day after the engagement, when they appeared disabled, and in manifest disorder, and would have fallen an easy prey, had they been vigorously attacked. One can hardly, without indignation, reflect upon these instances, in which a community has so severely suffered from the personal animosity of individuals. The miscarriage of Toulon became the subject of a parliamentary inquiry in England. The Commons, in an address to the throne, desired that a court-martial might be appointed to try the delinquents. By this time Lestock had accused Matthews, and all the captains of his division who misbehaved on the day of battle. The court-martial was constituted, and proceeded to trial. Several commanders of ships were cashiered: Vice-Admiral Lestock was honourably acquitted; and Admiral Matthews rendered incapable of serving for the future in his majesty's navy. All the world knew that Lestock kept aloof, and that Matthews rushed into the hottest part of the engagement.

Yet the former triumphed on his trial, and the latter
narrowly escaped the sentence of death for cowardice
and misconduct. Such decisions are not to be accounted
for, except from prejudice and faction.

The war in Germany, which had been almost extinguished in the last campaign, began to revive, and raged
with redoubled violence. The emperor had solicited
the mediation of his Britannic majesty for compromising
the differences between him and the court of Vienna.
Prince William of Hesse-Cassel had conferred with the
King of England on this subject; and a negotiation was
begun at Hanau. The emperor offered to dismiss the
French auxiliaries, provided the Austrians would evacuate his hereditary dominions. Nay, Prince William
and Lord Carteret, as plenipotentiaries, actually agreed
to preliminaries, by which his imperial majesty engaged
to renounce the alliance of France, and throw himself
into the arms of the maritime powers; to resign all pretensions to the succession of the house of Austria; and
to revive the vote of Bohemia in the electoral college;
on condition of his being re-established in the possession
of his dominions, recognized as emperor by the Queen
of Hungary, and accommodated with a monthly subsidy
for his maintenance, as his own territories were exhausted and impoverished by the war. By a separate
article, the King of Great Britain promised to furnish
him with three hundred thousand crowns, and to interpose his good offices with the Queen of Hungary, that
his electoral dominions should be favourably treated.
These preliminaries, though settled, were not signed.
The court of Vienna was unwilling to part with their
conquests in Bavaria and the Upper Palatinate. The
queen trusted too much to the valour of her troops, and
the wealth of her allies, to listen to such terms of accommodation; and whatever arguments were used by
the King of Great Britain, certain it is the negotiation
was dropped, on pretence that the articles were disapproved by the ministry of England. The emperor, environed with distress, renewed his application to the
King of Great Britain; and even declared that he would
refer his cause to the determination of the maritime
powers; but all his advances were discountenanced; and

the treaty of Worms dispelled all hope of accommodation. In this manner did the British ministry reject
the fairest opportunity that could possibly occur of terminating the war in Germany with honour and advantage,
and of freeing their country from that insufferable burden
of expense under which she groaned.

Treaty of
Frankfort.

The inflexibility of the house of Austria and its chief
ally proved serviceable to the emperor. The forlorn
situation of this unfortunate prince excited the compassion of divers princes: they resented the insolence
with which the head of the empire had been treated by
the court of Vienna ; and they were alarmed at the increasing power of a family noted for pride, tyranny, and
ambition. These considerations gave rise to the treaty
of Frankfort, concluded in May between the emperor,
the King of Prussia, the King of Sweden as Landgrave
of Hesse-Cassel, and the Elector Palatine. They engaged to preserve the constitution of the empire, according to the treaty of Westphalia, and to support the emperor in his rank and dignity. They agreed to employ
their good offices with the Queen of Hungary, that she
might be induced to acknowledge the emperor, to restore
his hereditary dominions, and give up the archives of the
empire that were in her possession. They guaranteed
to each other their respective territories; the disputes
about the succession of the late emperor they referred
to the decision of the states of the empire : they promised
to assist one another in case of being attacked ; and they
invited the King of Poland, the Elector of Cologn, and
the Bishop of Liege, to accede to this treaty. Such was
the confederacy that broke all the measures which had
been concerted between the King of Great Britain and
her Hungarian majesty, for the operations of the campaign. In the mean time, the French king declared
war against this princess, on pretence that she was obstinately deaf to all terms of accommodation, and determined to carry the war into the territories of France.
In her counter-declaration she taxed Louis with having
infringed the most solemn engagement, with respect to
the pragmatic sanction ; with having spirited up different
pretenders, to lay claim to the succession of the late
emperor ; with having endeavoured to instigate the com-

mon enemy of Christendom against her; and with having
acted the incendiary in the north of Europe, that the
czarina might be prevented from assisting the house of
Austria, while his numerous armies overspread the empire,
and desolated her hereditary countries. These recriminations were literally true. The houses of Bourbon and
Austria have, for many centuries, been the common dis-
turbers and plagues of Europe.

The King of France, though in himself pacific and
unenterprising, was stimulated by his ministry to taste
the glory of conquest in the Netherlands, where he had
assembled an army of one hundred and twenty thousand
men, provided with a very formidable train of artillery.
The chief command was vested in the Mareschal Count
de Saxe, who possessed great military talents, and proved
to be one of the most fortunate generals of the age in
which he lived. The allied forces, consisting of English,
Hanoverians, Dutch, and Austrians, to the number of
seventy thousand effective men, were in the month of
May assembled in the neighbourhood of Brussels, from
whence they marched towards Oudenarde, and posted
themselves behind the Schelde, being unable to retard
the progress of the enemy. The French monarch, attended by his favourite ladies, with all the pomp of
eastern luxury, arrived at Lisle on the twelfth day of the
same month; and in the adjacent plain reviewed his
army. The States-General, alarmed at his preparations,
had, in a conference with his ambassador at the Hague,
expressed their apprehensions, and entreated his most
Christian majesty would desist from his design of attacking their barrier. Their remonstrances having proved
ineffectual, they now sent a minister to wait upon that
monarch, to enforce their former representations, and repeat their entreaties; but no regard was paid to his request. The French king told him, he was determined
to prosecute the war with vigour, as his moderation
hitherto had served to no other purpose but that of rendering his enemies more intractable. Accordingly, his
troops invested Menin, which was in seven days surrendered upon capitulation. Ypres, Fort Knock, and
Furnes, underwent the same fate; and on the twenty-

Progress of
the French
king in the
Nether-
lands.

1744.
Prince
Charles of
Lorraine
passes the
Rhine.

ninth day of June the King of France entered Dunkirk in triumph.

He had taken such precautions for the defence of Alsace, which was guarded by considerable armies under the command of Coigny and Seckendorff, that he thought he had nothing to fear from the Austrians in that quarter: besides, he had received secret assurances that the King of Prussia would declare for the emperor; so that he resolved to pursue his conquests in the Netherlands. But all his measures were defeated by the activity of Prince Charles of Lorraine, and his officers, who found means to pass the Rhine, and oblige the French and Bavarian generals to retire to Lampertheim, that they might cover Strasburgh. The Austrians made themselves masters of Haguenau and Saverne; they secured the passes of Lorraine; and laid all the country of Lower Alsace under contribution. The King of France was no sooner apprized of the prince's having passed the Rhine, and penetrated into this province, than he sent off a detachment of thirty thousand men from his army in Flanders to reinforce that under the Mareschal de Coigny; and he himself began his journey from the Rhine, that he might in person check the progress of the enemy; but this design was anticipated by a severe distemper that overtook him at Mentz in Lorraine. The physicians despaired of his life. The queen, with her children, and all the princes of the blood, hastened from Versailles to pay their last duties to their dying sovereign, who, as a true penitent, dismissed his concubines, and began to prepare himself for death: yet the strength of his constitution triumphed over the fever, and his recovery was celebrated all over his dominions with uncommon marks of joy and affection.

The King
of Prussia
makes an
irruption
into Bo-
hemia.

In the mean time the schemes of the Austrian general were frustrated by the King of Prussia, who, in the month of August, entered the electorate of Saxony, at the head of a numerous army. There he declared, in a public manifesto, that his aims were only to re-establish the peace of the empire, and to support the dignity of its head. He assured the inhabitants that they might depend upon his protection, in case they should remain

quiet; but threatened them with fire and sword should
they presume to oppose his arms. In a rescript, addressed
to his ministers at foreign courts, he accused the Queen
of Hungary of obstinacy, in refusing to acknowledge the
emperor, and restore his hereditary dominions: he said
he had engaged in the league of Frankfort, to hinder the
head of the empire from being oppressed : that he had
no intention to violate the peace of Breslau, or enter as
. a principal into this war: he affirmed that his design was
to act as auxiliary to the emperor, and establish the quiet
of Germany. He penetrated into Bohemia, and undertook the siege of Prague, the governor of which surrendered himself and his garrison prisoners of war on the
sixteenth day of September. He afterwards reduced
Tabor, Bodweis, and Teyn, and, in a word, subdued the
greatest part of the kingdom; the Austrian forces in that
country being in no condition to stop his progress.
Nevertheless, he was soon obliged to relinquish his conquests. Prince Charles of Lorraine was recalled from
Alsace, and repassed the Rhine in the face of the French
army, commanded by the Mareschals de Coigny, Noailles,
and Belleisle. Then he marched to the Danube, laid
the Upper Palatinate under contribution, and entering
Bohemia, joined the troops under Bathiani at Merotitz.
The King of Poland, Elector of Saxony, at this juncture,
declared in favour of her Hungarian majesty. A convention for the mutual guarantee of their dominions had
been signed between those two powers in December;
and now Prince Charles of Lorraine was reinforced by
twenty thousand Saxon troops, under the conduct of
the Duke of Saxe-Wessenfels. The combined army was
superior to that of his Prussian majesty, whom they resolved to engage. But he retired before them, and
having evacuated all the places he had garrisoned in
Bohemia, retreated with precipitation into Silesia. There
his troops were put into winter-quarters; and he himself
returned to Berlin, extremely mortified at the issue of
the campaign.

During these transactions, Count Seckendorff marched
into Bavaria, at the head of a strong army, drove the
Austrians out of the electorate, and the emperor regained
possession of Munich, his capital, on the twenty-second

Campaign
in Bavaria
and Flan-
ders.

day of October. In August, the French army passed the Rhine at Fort Louis, and invested the strong and important city of Fribourg, defended by General Demnitz, at the head of nine thousand veterans. The King of France arrived in the camp on the eleventh day of October, and the siege was carried on with uncommon vigour. The Austrian governor made incredible efforts in the defence of the place, which he maintained until it was reduced to a heap of ruins, and one half of the garrison destroyed. At length, however, they were obliged to surrender themselves prisoners of war, after the trenches had been open five-and-forty days, during which they had killed above fifteen thousand of the besiegers. With this conquest the French king closed the campaign, and his army was cantoned along the Rhine, under the inspection of the Count de Maillebois. By the detachments drawn from the French army in Flanders, Count Saxe had found himself considerably weaker than the confederates: he threw up strong intrenchments behind the Lys, where he remained on the defensive, until he was reinforced by the Count de Clermont, who commanded a separate body on the side of Newport. The allies, to the number of seventy thousand, passed the Schelde, and advanced towards Helchin; but the enemy being so advantageously posted that they could not attack him with any prospect of advantage, they filed on in sight of Tournay; and on the eighth day of August encamped in the plains of Lisle, in hope of drawing Count Saxe from the situation in which he was so strongly fortified. Here they foraged for several days, and laid the open country under contribution: however, they made no attempt on the place itself, which in all probability would have fallen into their hands, had they invested it at their first approach, for then there was no other garrison but two or three battalions of militia: but Count Saxe soon threw in a considerable reinforcement. The allies were unprovided with a train of battering cannon; and their commanders would not deviate from the usual form of war. Besides, they were divided in their opinions, and despised one another. General Wade, who commanded the English and Hanoverians, was a vain, weak man, without confidence, weight, or authority; and the Austrian general, the Duke d'Aremberg, was a proud rapacious glutton, devoid of talents and sentiment. After having remained for some time in sight of Lisle, and made a general forage without molestation, they retired to their former camp on the Schelde, from whence they soon marched into winter quarters. Count Saxe at length quitted his lines; and by way of retaliation sent out detachments to ravage the Low Countries to the very gates of Ghent and Bruges. The conduct of the allied generals was severely censured in England, and ridiculed in France, not only in private conversation, but also on their public theatres, where it became the subject of farces and pantomimes.

The campaign in Italy produced divers vicissitudes of fortune. The King of Naples, having assembled an army, joined Count Gages, and published a manifesto in vindication of his conduct, which was a direct violation of the neutrality he had promised to observe. He maintained that his moderation had been undervalued by the courts of London and Vienna; that his frontiers were threatened with the calamities of war; and that the Queen of Hungary made no secret of her intention to invade his dominions. This charge was not without foundation. The emissaries of the house of Austria en deavoured to excite a rebellion in Naples, which Prince Lobkowitz had orders to favour by an invasion. This general was encamped at Monte Rotundo, in the neighbourhood of Rome, when, in the month of June, the confederates advanced to Velletri. While the two armies remained in sight of each other, Prince Lobkowitz detached a strong body of forces, under Count Soro and General Gorani, who made an irruption into the province of Abruzzo, and took the city of Aquilla, where they distributed a manifesto, in which the Queen of Hungary exhorted the Neapolitans to shake off the Spanish yoke, and submit again to the house of Austria. This step, however, produced little or no effect, and the Austrian detachment retired at the approach of the Duke of Vieuville, with a superior number of forces. In August, Count Brown, at the head of an Austrian detachment, surprised Velletri in the night; and the King of the Two Sicilies, with the Duke of Modena, were in the utmost danger of being taken. They escaped by a postern with great difficulty, and repaired to the quarters of Count Gages, who performed the part of a great general on this occasion. He rallied the fugitives, dispelled the panic and confusion which had begun to prevail in his camp, and made a disposition for cutting off the retreat of the Austrians. Count Brown, finding himself in danger of being surrounded, thought proper to secure his retreat, which he effected with great art and gallantry, carrying off a prodigious booty. Three thousand Spaniards are said to have fallen in this action; and eight hundred men were taken, with some standards and colours. Count Mariani, a Neapolitan general, was among the prisoners. The Austrians lost about six hundred men; and General Novati fell into the hands of the enemy; but the exploit produced no consequence of importance. The heats of autumn proved so fatal to the Austrians, who were not accustomed to the climate, that Prince Lobkowitz saw his army mouldering away, without any possibility of its being recruited: besides, the country was so drained that he could no longer procure subsistence. Impelled by these considerations, he meditated a retreat. On the eleventh day of November he decamped from Faiola, marched under the walls of Rome, passed the Tiber at Ponte Molle, formerly known by the name of Pons Milvius, which he had just time to break down behind him when the vanguard of the Spaniards and Neapolitans appeared. Part of his rear-guard, however, was taken, with Count Soro who commanded it, at Nocera; and his army suffered greatly by desertion. Nevertheless, he continued his retreat with equal skill and expedition, passed the mountains of Gubio, and by the way of Viterbo reached the Bolognese. The pope was altogether passive. In the beginning of the campaign he had caressed Lobkowitz; and now he received the King of the Two Sicilies with marks of the warmest affection. That prince having visited the chief curiosities of Rome, returned to Naples, leaving part of his troops under the command of Count Gages.

Battle of Coni.   Fortune likewise favoured his brother Don Philip, in Savoy and Piedmont. He was, early in the season, joined at Antibes by the French army, under the con-

duct of the Prince of Conti. In the latter end of March
the combined forces passed the Var, reduced the castle
of Aspremont, and entered the city of Nice, without
opposition. In April, they attacked the King of Sardinia, who, with twenty thousand men, was strongly intrenched among the mountains of Villa Franca. The
action was obstinate and bloody; but their numbers and
perseverance prevailed. He was obliged to abandon his
posts, and embark on board of the British squadron, which
transported him and his troops to Vado. The intention of Don Philip was to penetrate through the territories of Genoa into the Milanese; but Admiral Matthews, who hovered with a strong squadron on that coast,
sent a message to the republic, declaring that, should
the combined army be suffered to pass through her dominions, the King of Great Britain would consider such
a step as a breach of their neutrality. The senate, intimidated by this intimation, entreated the princes to
desist from their design, and they resolved to choose
another route. They defiled towards Piedmont, and
assaulted the strong post of Chateau Dauphiné, defended by the King of Sardinia in person. After a
desperate attack, in which they lost four thousand men,
the place was taken: the garrison of Demont surrendered at discretion, and the whole country of Piedmont
was laid under contribution. His Sardinian majesty
was not in a condition to hazard a battle; and therefore posted himself at Saluzzes, in order to cover his
capital. The combined army advanced to the strong
and important town of Coni, which was invested in the
beginning of September. Baron Leutrum the governor
made an obstinate defence, and the situation of the
place was such as rendered the siege difficult, tedious,
and bloody. The King of Sardinia being reinforced
by ten thousand Austrians, under General Pallavicini,
advanced to its relief, and a battle ensued. The action
was maintained with great vigour on both sides, till
night, when his majesty, finding it impracticable to force
the enemy's intrenchments, retired in good order to his
camp at Murasso. He afterwards found means to throw
a reinforcement and supply of provisions into Coni; and
the heavy rains that fell at this period not only retarded,

but even dispirited the besiegers. Nevertheless, the princes persisted in their design, notwithstanding a dearth of provisions, and the approach of winter, till the latter end of November, when the Chevalier de Soto entered the place with six hundred fresh men. This incident was no sooner known than the princes abandoned their enterprise; and, leaving their sick and wounded to the mercy of the Piedmontese, marched back to Demont. Having dismantled the fortifications of this place, they retreated with great precipitation to Dauphiné, and were dreadfully harassed by the Vaudois and light troops in the service of his Sardinian majesty, who now again saw himself in possession of Piedmont. The French troops were quartered in Dauphiné; but Don Philip still maintained his footing in Savoy, the inhabitants of which he fleeced without mercy.

Return of
Commo-
dore Anson.
Sir John
Balchen
perishes at
sea.

After the action at Toulon, nothing of consequence was achieved by the British squadron in the Mediterranean; and indeed the naval power of Great Britain was, during the summer, quite inactive. In the month of June, Commodore Anson returned from his voyage of three years and nine months, in which he had surrounded the terraqueous globe. We have formerly observed that he sailed with a small squadron to the South Sea, in order to annoy the Spanish settlements of Chili and Peru. Two of his large ships having been separated from him in a storm before he weathered Cape Horn, had put in at Rio de Janeiro, on the coast of Brazil, from whence they returned to Europe. A frigate, commanded by Captain Cheap, was shipwrecked on a desolate island in the South Sea. Mr. Anson having undergone a dreadful tempest, which dispersed his fleet, arrived at the island of Juan Fernandez, where he was joined by the Gloucester, a ship of the line, a sloop, and a pink loaded with provisions. These were the remains of his squadron. He made prize of several vessels; took and burned the little town of Payta; set sail from the coast of Mexico, for the Philippine Isles: and in this passage the Gloucester was abandoned and sunk: the other vessels had been destroyed for want of men to navigate them, so that nothing now remained but the commodore's own ship, the Centurion, and that but very indifferently manned; for the crews had been horribly thinned by sickness. Incredible were the hardships and misery they sustained from the shattered condition of the ships and the scorbutic disorder, when they reached the plentiful island of Tinian, where they were supplied with the necessary refreshments. Thence they prosecuted their voyage to the river of Canton in China, where the commodore ordered the ship to be sheathed, and found means to procure a reinforcement of sailors. The chief object of his attention was the rich annual ship that sails between Acapulco in Mexico, and Manilla, one of the Philippine Islands. In hopes of intercepting her, he set sail from Canton, and steered his course back to the straits of Manilla, where she actually fell into his hands, after a short but vigorous engagement. The prize was called Nuestra Signora de Cabodonga, mounted with forty guns, manned with six hundred sailors, and loaded with treasure and effects to the value of three hundred and thirteen thousand pounds sterling: with this windfall he returned to Canton, from whence he proceeded to the Cape of Good Hope, and prosecuted his voyage to England, where he arrived in safety. Though this fortunate commander enriched himself by an occurrence that may be termed almost accidental, the British nation was not indemnified for the expense of the expedition; and the original design was entirely defeated. Had the Manilla ship escaped the vigilance of the English commodore, he might have been, at his return to England, laid aside as a superannuated captain, and died in obscurity; but his great wealth invested him with considerable influence, and added lustre to ·his talents. He soon became the oracle which was consulted in all naval deliberations; and the king raised him to the dignity of a peerage. In July, Sir John Balchen, an admiral of approved valour and great experience, sailed from Spithead with a strong squadron, in quest of an opportunity to attack the French fleet at Brest, under the command of M. de Rochambault. In the bay of Biscay he was overtaken by a violent storm, that dispersed the ships, and drove them up the English channel. Admiral Stewart, with the greater part of them, arrived at Plymouth; but Sir John Balchen's own ship, the Victory, which was counted the most beautiful first-rate in the world, foundered at sea; and this brave commander perished, with all his officers, volunteers, and crew, amounting to eleven hundred choice seamen. On the fourth day of October, after the siege of Fribourg, the Marshal Duke de Belleisle, and his brother, happened, in their way to Berlin, to halt at a village in the forest of Hartz, dependent on the Electorate of Hanover. There they were apprehended by the bailiff of the place, and conducted as prisoners to Osterode; from whence they were removed to Stade on the Elbe, where they embarked for England. They resided at Windsor till the following year, when they were allowed the benefit of the cartel which had been established between Great Britain and France at Frankfort, and released accordingly, after they had been treated by the British nobility with that respect and hospitality which was due to their rank and merit [b].

Revolution in the British ministry. Session of Parliament.
The dissensions in the British cabinet were now ripened into another revolution in the ministry. Lord Carteret, who was by this time Earl Granville, in consequence of his mother's death, had engrossed the royal favour so much, that the Duke of N—— and his brother are said to have taken umbrage at his influence and greatness. He had incurred the resentment of those who were distinguished by the appellation of patriots, and entirely forfeited his popularity. The two brothers were very powerful by their parliamentary interest; they knew their own strength, and engaged in a political alliance with the leading men in the opposition, against the prime minister and his measures. This coalition was dignified with the epithet of "The Broad Bottom," as if it had been established on a true constitutional foundation, comprehending individuals of every class, without distinction of party. The appellation, however, which they assumed was afterwards converted into a term of derision. The Earl of Granville, perceiving the gathering storm, and foreseeing the impossibility of withstanding such an opposition in Parliament, wisely avoided the impending

[b] Mr. Pope, the celebrated poet, died in the month of June. In October, the old Duchess of Marlborough resigned her breath, in the eighty-fifth year of her age, immensely rich, and very little regretted, either by her own family, or the world in general.

danger and disgrace, by a voluntary resignation of his employments. The Earl of Harrington succeeded him as secretary of state. The Duke of Bedford was appointed first lord of the admiralty, and the Earl of Chesterfield declared lord lieutenant of Ireland. The Lords Gower and Cobham were re-established in the offices they had resigned : Mr. Lyttelton was admitted as a commissioner of the treasury : even Sir John Hynde Cotton accepted of a place at court; and Sir John Philips sat at the board of trade and plantations, though he soon renounced this employment. This was rather a change of men than of measures, and turned out to the ease and advantage of the sovereign; for his views were no longer thwarted by an obstinate opposition in Parliament. The session was opened on the twenty-eighth day of November, in the usual manner. The Commons unanimously granted about six millions and a half for the service of the ensuing year, to be raised by the land, the malt, and the salt taxes, the sinking fund, and an additional duty on wines. In January, the Earl of Chesterfield set out for the Hague, with the character of ambassador extraordinary, to persuade, if possible, the States-General to engage heartily in the war. About the same time, a treaty of quadruple alliance was signed at Warsaw, by the Queen of Hungary, the King of Poland, and the maritime powers. This was a mutual guarantee of the dominions belonging to the contracting parties : but his Polish majesty was paid for his concurrence with an annual subsidy of one hundred and fifty thousand pounds, two thirds of which were defrayed by England, and the remainder was disbursed by the United Provinces[c].

The business of the British Parliament being discussed, the session was closed in the beginning of May, and, immediately after the prorogation, the king set out for Hanover. The death of the Emperor Charles VII. which happened in the month of January, had entirely changed the face of affairs in the empire, and all the

1745
Death of
the Empe-
ror Charles
VII.
Accommo-
dation be-
tween the
Queen of
Hungary
and the
young
Elector of
Bavaria.

[c] Robert, Earl of Orford, late prime minister, died in March, after having for a very short time enjoyed a pension of four thousand pounds granted by the crown, in consideration of his past services. Though he had for such a length of time directed the application of the public treasure, his circumstances were not affluent ; he was liberal in his disposition, and had such a number of rapacious dependents to gratify, that little was left for his own private occasions.

princes of Germany were in commotion. The Grand
Duke of Tuscany, consort to her Hungarian majesty, was
immediately declared a candidate for the imperial crown;
while his pretensions were warmly opposed by the French
king and his allies. The court of Vienna, taking advantage of the late emperor's death, sent an army to
invade Bavaria in the month of March, under the conduct of General Bathiani, who routed the French and
Palatine troops at Psiffenhoven; took possession of Rain;
surrounded and disarmed six thousand Hessians in the
neighbourhood of Ingoldstadt; and drove the Bavarian
forces out of the electorate. The young elector was
obliged to abandon his capital, and retire to Augsburgh,
where he found himself in danger of losing all his dominions. In this emergency he yielded to the earnest
solicitations of the empress his mother, enforced by the
advice of his uncle, the Elector of Cologn, and of his
general, Count Seckendorff, who exhorted him to be
reconciled to the court of Vienna. A negotiation was
immediately begun at Fuessen, where, in April, the treaty
was concluded. The queen consented to recognize the
imperial dignity, as having been vested in the person of
his father; to acknowledge his mother as empress dowager; to restore his dominions, with all the fortresses,
artillery, stores, and ammunition which she had taken:
on the other hand, he renounced all claim to the succession of her father, and became guarantee of the pragmatic sanction: he acknowledged the validity of the
electoral vote of Bohemia in the person of the queen;
and engaged to give his voice for the grand duke, at the
ensuing election of the King of the Romans. Until that
should be determined, both parties agreed that Ingoldstadt should be garrisoned by neutral troops; and that
Braunau and Schardingen, with all the country lying between the Inn and the Saltza, should remain in the queen's
possession, though without prejudice to the civil government, or the elector's revenue. In the mean time he
dismissed the auxiliaries that were in his pay, and they
were permitted to retire without molestation.

The King
of Prussia
gains two
-ive
The court of Vienna had now secured the votes of all
the electors, except those of Brandenburgh and the Palatinate. Nevertheless, France assembled a powerful army

in the neighbourhood of Frankfort, in order to influence the election. But the Austrian army, commanded by the grand duke in person, marched thither from the Danube; and the Prince of Conti was obliged to repass the Rhine at Nordlingen. Then the grand duke repaired to Frankfort, where, on the second day of September, he was by a majority of voices declared King of the Romans and Emperor of Germany. Meanwhile the King of Prussia had made great progress in the conquest of Silesia. The campaign began in January, when the Hungarian insurgents were obliged to retire into Moravia. In the following month the Prussian General Lehwald defeated a body of twelve thousand Austrians, commanded by General Helsrich; the town of Ratibor was taken by assault; and the king entered Silesia, in May, at the head of seventy thousand men. Prince Charles of Lorraine, being joined by the Duke of Saxe-Wessenfels and twenty thousand Saxons, penetrated into Silesia by the defiles of Landshut, and were attacked by his Prussian majesty in the plains of Striegan, near Friedberg. The battle was maintained from morning till noon, when the Saxons giving way, Prince Charles was obliged to retire with the loss of twelve thousand men, and a great number of colours, standards, and artillery. This victory, obtained on the fourth day of June, complete as it was, did not prove decisive; for, though the victor transferred the seat of the war into Bohemia, and maintained his army by raising contributions in that country, the Austrians resolved to hazard another engagement. Their aim was to surprise him in his camp at Sohr, which they attacked on the thirtieth of September, at daybreak, but they met with such a warm reception, that, notwithstanding their repeated efforts during the space of four hours, they were repulsed with considerable damage, and retreated to Jaromire, leaving five thousand killed upon the spot, besides two thousand that were taken, with many standards, and twenty pieces of cannon. The loss of this battle was in a great measure owing to the avarice of the irregulars, who, having penetrated into the Prussian camp, began to pillage with great eagerness, giving the king an opportunity to rally his disordered troops, and restore the battle: nevertheless, they

CHAP.
XIX.

1745.
battles at
Friedberg
and Sohr,
over the
Austrian
and Saxon
forces.

CHAP.
XIX.

1745.

Treaty of
Dresden.
The Grand
Duke of
Tuscany
elected
Emperor of
Germany.

retired with the plunder of his baggage, including his military chest, the officers of his chancery, his own secretary, and all the papers of his cabinet.

After this action, his Prussian majesty returned to Berlin, and breathed nothing but peace and moderation. In August he had signed a convention with the King of Great Britain, who became guarantee of his possessions in Silesia, as yielded by the treaty of Breslau; and he promised to vote for the Grand Duke of Tuscany at the election of an emperor. This was intended as the basis of a more general accommodation. But he now pretended to have received undoubted intelligence that the King of Poland and the Queen of Hungary had agreed to invade Brandenburgh with three different armies; and that, for this purpose, his Polish majesty had demanded of the czarina the succours stipulated by treaty between the two crowns. Alarmed, or seemingly alarmed, at this information, he solicited the maritime powers to fulfil their engagements, and interpose their good offices with the court of Petersburgh. Yet, far from waiting for the result of these remonstrances, he made a sudden irruption into Lusatia, took possession of Gorlitz, and obliged Prince Charles of Lorraine to retire before him into Bohemia. Then he entered Leipsic, and laid Saxony under contribution. The King of Poland, unable to resist the torrent, quitted his capital, and took refuge in Prague. His troops, reinforced by a body of Austrians, were defeated at Pirna on the fifteenth day of December; and his Prussian majesty became master of Dresden without further opposition. The King of Poland, thus deprived of his hereditary dominions, was fain to acquiesce in such terms as the conqueror thought proper to impose; and the treaty of Dresden was concluded under the mediation of his Britannic majesty. By this convention the King of Prussia retained all the contributions he had levied in Saxony; and was entitled to a million of German crowns, to be paid by his Polish majesty at the next fair of Leipsic. He and the Elector Palatine consented to acknowledge the grand duke as Emperor of Germany; and this last confirmed to his Prussian majesty certain privileges *de non evocando*, which had been granted by the late emperor, with regard to some territories possessed by the King of Prussia, though not belonging to the electorate of Brandenburgh. Immediately after the ratification of this treaty, the Prussian troops evacuated Saxony; and the peace of Germany was restored.

Though the French king could not prevent the eleva- tion of the grand duke to the imperial throne, he resolved to humble the house of Austria by making a conquest of the Netherlands. A prodigious army was there assembled, under the auspices of Mareschal Count de Saxe; and his most Christian majesty, with the dauphin, arriving in the camp, they invested the strong town of Tournay on the thirtieth day of April. The Dutch garrison consisted of eight thousand men, commanded by the old Baron Dorth, who made a vigorous defence. The Duke of Cumberland assumed the chief command of the allied army assembled at Soignies: he was assisted with the advice of the Count Konigseg, an Austrian general, and the Prince of Waldeck, commander of the Dutch forces. Their army was greatly inferior in number to that of the enemy; nevertheless, they resolved to march to the relief of Tournay. They accordingly advanced to Leuse; and on the twenty-eighth day of April took post at Maulbre, in sight of the French army, which was encamped on an eminence, from the village of Antoine to a large wood beyond Vezon, having Fontenoy in their front. Next day was employed by the allies in driving the enemy from some outposts, and clearing the defiles through which they were obliged to advance to the attack; while the French completed their batteries, and made the most formidable preparations for their reception. On the thirtieth day of April, the Duke of Cumberland, having made the proper dispositions, began his march to the enemy at two o'clock in the morning: a brisk cannonade ensued; and about nine both armies were engaged. The British infantry drove the French beyond their lines; but the left wing failing in the attack on the village of Fontenoy, and the cavalry forbearing to advance on the flanks, they measured back their ground with some disorder, from the prodigious fire of the French batteries. They rallied, however, and returning to the charge with redoubled ardour, repulsed the enemy to their camp with great slaughter; but, being

wholly unsupported by the other wing, and exposed both
in front and flank to a dreadful fire, which did great execution, the duke was obliged to make the necessary dispositions for a retreat about three o'clock in the afternoon; and this was effected in tolerable order. The
battle was fought with great obstinacy, and the carnage
on both sides was very considerable. The allies lost
about twelve thousand men, including a good number
of officers; among these were Lieutenant-General Campbell, and Major-General Ponsonby. The victory cost the
French almost an equal number of lives; and no honour
was lost by the vanquished. Had the allies given battle
on the preceding day, before the enemy had taken their
measures, and received all their reinforcements, they
might have succeeded in their endeavours to relieve
Tournay. Although the attack was generally judged
rash and precipitate, the British and Hanoverian troops
fought with such intrepidity and perseverance, that if
they had been properly sustained by the Dutch forces,
and their flanks covered by the cavalry, the French, in
all likelihood, would have been obliged to abandon their
enterprise. The Duke of Cumberland left his sick and
wounded to the humanity of the victors; and retiring to
Aeth, encamped in an advantageous situation at Lessines.
The garrison of Tournay, though now deprived of all hope
of succour, maintained the place to the twenty-first day
of June, when the governor obtained an honourable
capitulation. After the conquest of this frontier, which
was dismantled, the Duke of Cumberland, apprehending the enemy had a design upon Ghent, sent a detachment of four thousand men to reinforce the garrison of
that city; but they fell into an ambuscade at Pas-du-
mêle; and were killed or taken, except a few dragoons
that escaped to Ostend: on that very night, which was
the twelfth of June, Ghent was surprised by a detachment of the French army. Then they invested Ostend,
which, though defended by an English garrison, and
open to the sea, was, after a short siege, surrendered by
capitulation on the fourteenth day of August. Dendermonde, Oudenarde, Newport, and Aeth underwent
the same fate; while the allied army lay intrenched beyond the canal of Antwerp. The French king, having

subdued the greatest part of the Austrian Netherlands, returned to Paris, which he entered in triumph.

The campaign in Italy was unpropitious to the Queen of Hungary and the King of Sardinia. Count Gages passed the Apennines, and entered the state of Lucca; from thence he proceeded by the eastern coast of Genoa to Lestride-Levante. The junction of the two armies was thus accomplished, and reinforced with ten thousand Genoese: meanwhile Prince Lobkowitz decamped from Modena and took post at Parma; but he was soon succeeded by Count Schuylemberg, and sent to command the Austrians in Bohemia. The Spaniards entered the Milanese without further opposition. Count Gages, with thirty thousand men, took possession of Serravalle; and advancing towards Placentia, obliged the Austrians to retire under the cannon of Tortona; but when Don Philip, at the head of forty thousand troops, made himself master of Acqui, the King of Sardinia and the Austrian general, unable to stem the torrent, retreated behind the Tanaro. The strong citadel of Tortona was taken by the Spaniards, who likewise reduced Parma and Placentia; and forcing the passage of the Tanaro, compelled his Sardinian majesty to take shelter on the other side of the Po. Then Pavia was won by scalade; and the city of Milan submitted to the infant, though the Austrian garrison still maintained the citadel; all Piedmont, on both sides of the Po, as far as Turin, was reduced, and even that capital threatened with a siege; so that by the month of October the territories belonging to the house of Austria, in Italy, were wholly subdued, and the King of Sardinia stripped of all his dominions; yet he continued firm and true to his engagements, and deaf to all proposals of a separate accommodation.

The naval transactions of Great Britain were in the course of this year remarkably spirited. In the Mediterranean, Admiral Rowley had succeeded Matthews in the command; Savona, Genoa, Final, St. Remo, with Bastia, the capital of Corsica, were bombarded; several Spanish ships were taken; but he could not prevent the safe arrival of their rich Havannah squadron at Corunna. Commodore Barnet, in the East Indies, made prize of several French ships richly laden ; and Commodore Townshend, in the latitude of Martinico, took about thirty merchant-ships belonging to the enemy, under convoy of four ships of war, two of which were destroyed. The English privateers likewise met with uncommon success. But the most important achievement was the conquest of Louisbourg on the isle of Cape Breton, in North America; a place of great consequence, which the French had fortified at a prodigious expense. The scheme of reducing this fortress was planned in Boston, recommended by their general assembly, and approved by his majesty, who sent instructions to Commodore Warren, stationed off the Leeward Islands, to sail for the northern parts of America, and to co-operate with the forces of New England in this expedition. A body of six thousand men was formed under the conduct of Mr. Pepperel, a trader of Piscataquay, whose influence was extensive in that country, though he was a man of little or no education, and utterly unacquainted with military operations. In April Mr. Warren arrived at Canso with ten ships of war; and the troops of New England, being embarked in transports, sailed immediately for the isle of Cape Breton, where they landed without opposition. The enemy abandoned their grand battery, which was detached from the town; and the immediate seizure of it contributed in a good measure to the success of the enterprise. While the American troops, reinforced by eight hundred marines, carried on their approaches by land, the squadron blocked up the place by sea in such a manner that no succours could be introduced. A French ship of the line, with some smaller vessels destined for the relief of the garrison, were intercepted and taken by the British cruisers ; and, indeed, the reduction of Louisbourg was chiefly owing to the vigilance and activity of Mr. Warren, one of the bravest and best officers in the service of England. The operations of the siege were wholly conducted by the engineers and officers who commanded the British marines; and the Americans, being ignorant of war, were contented to act under their directions. The town being considerably damaged by the bombs and bullets of the besiegers, and the garrison despairing of relief, the governor capitulated on the seventeenth day of June, when the city of Louisbourg and the isle of Cape Breton were surrendered to his Britannic majesty. The garrison and inhabitants engaged that they would not bear arms for twelve months against Great Britain or her allies; and being embarked in fourteen cartel ships, were transported to Rochefort. In a few days after the surrender of Louisbourg, two French East India ships, and another from Peru, laden with treasure, sailed into the harbour, on the supposition that it still belonged to France, and were taken by the English squadron.

The news of this conquest being transmitted to Eng- land, Mr. Pepperel was preferred to the dignity of a baronet of Great Britain, and congratulatory addresses were presented to the king on the success of his majesty's arms. The possession of Cape Breton was doubtless a valuable acquisition to Great Britain. It not only distressed the French in their fishery and navigation, but removed all fears of encroachment and rivalship from the English fishers on the banks of Newfoundland. It freed New England from the terrors of a dangerous neighbour, overawed the Indians of that country, and secured the possession of Acadia to the crown of Great Britain. The plan of this conquest was originally laid by Mr. Auchmuty, judge-advocate of the court of Admiralty in New England. He demonstrated that the reduction of Cape Breton would put the English in sole possession of the fishery of North America, which would annually return to Great Britain two millions sterling for the manufactures yearly shipped to the plantations: employ many thousand families that were otherwise unserviceable to the public; increase the shipping and mariners; extend navigation; cut off all communication between France and Canada by the river St. Laurence; so that Quebec would fall of course into the hands of the English, who might expel the French entirely from America, open a correspondence with the remote Indians, and render themselves masters of the profitable fur trade, which was now engrossed by the enemy. The natives of New England acquired great glory from the success of this enterprise. Britain, which had in some instances behaved like a stepmother to her own colonies, was now convinced of their importance, and treated those as brethren whom she had too long considered as aliens and rivals. Circumstanced as the nation is, the legislature cannot too tenderly cherish the interests of the British plantations in America. They are inhabited by a brave, hardy, industrious people, animated with an active spirit of commerce, inspired with a noble zeal for liberty and independence. The trade of Great Britain, clogged with heavy taxes and impositions, has for some time languished in many valuable branches. The French have undersold our cloths, and spoiled our markets in the Levant. Spain is no longer supplied as usual with the commodities of England : the exports to Germany must be considerably diminished by the misunderstanding between Great Britain and the house of Austria; consequently, her greatest resource must be in her communication with her own colonies, which consume her manufactures, and make immense returns in sugar, rum, tobacco, fish, timber, naval stores, iron, furs, drugs, rice, and indigo. The southern plantations likewise produce silk; and, with due encouragement, might furnish every thing that could be expected from the most fertile soil and the happiest climate. The continent of North America, if properly cultivated, will prove an inexhaustible fund of wealth and strength to Great Britain; and perhaps it may become the last asylum of British liberty. When the nation is enslaved by domestic despotism or foreign dominion; when her substance is wasted, her spirit broken, and the laws and constitution of England are no more; then those colonies, sent off by our fathers, may receive and entertain their sons as hapless exiles and ruined refugees.

Project of an insurrection in Great Britain.

While the continent of Europe and the isles of America were thus exposed to the ravages of war, and subjected to such vicissitudes of fortune, Great Britain underwent a dangerous convulsion in her own bowels. The son of the Chevalier de St. George, fired with ambition, and animated with the hope of ascending the throne of his ancestors, resolved to make an effort for that purpose, which, though it might not be crowned with success, should at least astonish all Christendom. The Jacobites in England and Scotland had promised,

that if he would land in Britain at the head of a regular
army, they would supply him with provisions, carriages,
and horses, and a great number of them declared they
would take up arms and join his standard; but they disapproved of his coming over without forces, as a dangerous enterprise, that would in all probability end in
the ruin of himself and all his adherents. This advice,
including an exact detail of his father's interest, with the
dispositions of his particular friends in every town and
county, was transmitted to London in January, in order
to be forwarded to Prince Charles; but the person with
whom it was entrusted could find no safe method of
conveyance; so that he sent it back to Scotland, from
whence it was despatched to France; but before it reached
Paris, Charles had left that kingdom. Had the paper
come to his hands in due time, perhaps he would not
have embarked in the undertaking, though he was stimulated to the attempt by many concurring motives. Certain it is, he was cajoled by the sanguine misrepresentations of a few adventurers, who hoped to profit by the
expedition. They assured him that the whole nation was
disaffected to the reigning family; that the people could
no longer bear the immense load of taxes, which was
daily increasing; and that the most considerable persons
of the kingdom would gladly seize the first opportunity
of crowding to his standard. On the other hand, he
knew the British government had taken some effectual
steps to alienate the friends of his house from the principles they had hitherto professed. Some of them had
accepted posts and pensions; others were preferred in
the army; and the Parliament were so attached to the
reigning family, that he had nothing to hope from their
deliberations. He expected no material succour from the
court of France: he foresaw that delay would diminish
the number of his adherents in Great Britain; and therefore resolved to seize the present occasion, which in
many respects was propitious to his design. Without
doubt, had he been properly supported, he could not
have found a more favourable opportunity of exciting
an intestine commotion in Great Britain; for Scotland
was quite unfurnished with troops; King George was in
Germany; the Duke of Cumberland, at the head of the

British army, was employed in Flanders, and a great part of the Highlanders were keen for insurrection. Their natural principles were on this occasion stimulated by the suggestions of revenge. At the beginning of the war a regiment of those people had been formed, and transported with the rest of the British troops to Flanders. Before they were embarked a number of them deserted with their arms, on pretence that they had been decoyed into the service by promises and assurances that they should never be sent abroad: and this was really the case. They were overtaken by a body of horse, persuaded to submit, brought back to London pinioned like malefactors, and tried for desertion. Three were shot to death *in terrorem;* and the rest were sent in exile to the plantations. Those who suffered were persons of some consequence in their own country; and their fate was deeply resented by the clans to which they belonged. It was considered as a national outrage; and the Highlanders, who are naturally vindictive, waited impatiently for an opportunity of vengeance.

The eldest son of the Chevalier de St. George lands in Scotland.

The young pretender being furnished with a sum of money, and a supply of arms, on his private credit, without the knowledge of the French court, wrote letters to his friends in Scotland, explaining his design and situation, intimating the place where he intended to land, communicating a private signal, and assuring them he should be with them by the middle of June. These precautions being taken, he embarked on board of a small frigate at Port St. Nazaire, accompanied by the Marquis of Tullibardine, Sir Thomas Sheridan, Sir John Macdonald, with a few other Irish and Scottish adventurers; and setting sail on the fourteenth of July, was joined off Belleisle by the Elizabeth, a French ship of war, mounted with sixty-six guns, as his convoy[d]. Their design was to sail round Ireland, and land in the western part of Scotland; but falling in with the Lion, an English ship of the line, a very obstinate and bloody action ensued. The Elizabeth was so disabled that she could not prosecute the voyage, and with difficulty reached

[d] The Elizabeth, a king's ship, was procured as a convoy by the interest of Mr. Walsh, an Irish merchant at Nantes; and on board of her fifty French young gentlemen embarked as volunteers.

the harbour of Brest; but the Lion was shattered to such a degree, that she floated like a wreck upon the water. The disaster of the Elizabeth was a great misfortune to the adventurer, as by her being disabled he lost a great quantity of arms, and about one hundred able officers, who were embarked on board of her for the benefit of his expedition. Had this ship arrived in Scotland, she could easily have reduced Fort William, situate in the midst of the clans attached to the Stuart family. Such a conquest, by giving lustre to the prince's arms, would have allured many to his standard, who were indifferent in point of principle, and encouraged a great number of Highlanders to join him who were restricted by the apprehension, that their wives and families would be subject to insults from the English garrison of this fortress. Prince Charles, in the frigate, continued his course to the western isles of Scotland. After a voyage of eighteen days, he landed on a little island between Barra and South Inst, two of the Hebrides; then he re-embarked, and in a few days arrived at Borodale in Arnsacy, on the confines of Lochnannach, where he was in a little time joined by a considerable number of hardy mountaineers, under their respective chiefs or leaders. On the nineteenth day of August, the Marquis of Tullibardine erected the pretender's standard at Glensinnan. Some of those, however, on whom Charles principally depended now stood aloof, either fluctuating in their principles, astonished at the boldness of the undertaking, or startled at the remonstrances of their friends, who did not fail to represent, in aggravated colours, all the dangers of embarking in such a desperate enterprise. Had the government acted with proper vigour when they received intelligence of his arrival, the adventurer must have been crushed in embryo before any considerable number of his adherents could have been brought together; but the lords of the regency seemed to slight the information, and even to suspect the integrity of those by whom it was conveyed. They were soon convinced of their mistake. Prince Charles, having assembled about twelve hundred men, encamped in the neighbourhood of Fort William; and immediately hostilities were commenced. A handful of

CHAP.
XIX.

1745.

Keppoch's clan, commanded by Major Donald Mac
Donald, even before they joined the pretender, attacked
two companies of new raised soldiers, who, with their
officer, were disarmed after an obstinate dispute: another captain of the king's forces, falling into their
hands, was courteously dismissed with one of the pretender's manifestoes, and a passport for his personal safety.
The administration was now effectually alarmed. The
lords of the regency issued a proclamation, offering a reward of thirty thousand pounds to any person who should
apprehend the prince adventurer. The same price was
set upon the head of the Elector of Hanover, in a proclamation published by the pretender. A courier was
despatched to Holland to hasten the return of his majesty, who arrived in England about the latter end of
August. A requisition was made of the six thousand
Dutch auxiliaries; and several British regiments were
recalled from the Netherlands. A loyal address was
presented to the king by the city of London; and the
merchants of this metropolis resolved to raise two regiments at their own expense. Orders were issued to
keep the trained bands in readiness; to array the militia
of Westminster; and instructions to the same effect were
sent to all the lords-lieutenants of the counties throughout the kingdom. The principal noblemen of the nation made a tender of their services to their sovereign;
and some of them received commissions to levy regiments towards the suppression of the rebellion. Bodies
of volunteers were incorporated in London, and many
other places; associations were formed, large contributions raised in different towns, counties, and communities; and a great number of eminent merchants in
London agreed to support the public credit, by receiving, as usual, bank-notes in payment for the purposes
of traffic. The Protestant clergy of all denominations
exerted themselves with extraordinary ardour in preaching against the religion of Rome and the pretender;
and the friends of the government were encouraged,
animated, and confirmed in their principles, by several
spiritual productions published for the occasion.

Takes pos-
session of
Edinburgh.

In a word, the bulk of the nation seemed unanimously
bent upon opposing the enterprise of the pretender, who,

nevertheless, had already made surprising progress. His arrival in Scotland was no sooner confirmed, than Sir John Cope, who commanded the troops in that kingdom, assembled what force he could bring together, and advanced against the rebels. Understanding, however, that they had taken possession of a strong pass, he changed his route, and proceeded northwards as far as Inverness, leaving the capital and southern parts of North Britain wholly exposed to the incursions of the enemy. The Highlanders forthwith marched to Perth, where the Chevalier de St. George was proclaimed King of Great Britain, and the public money seized for his use: the same steps were taken at Dundee and other places. Prince Charles was joined by the nobleman who assumed the title of Duke of Perth, the Viscount Strathallan, Lord Nairn, Lord George Murray, and many persons of distinction, with their followers. The Marquis of Tullibardine, who had accompanied him from France, took possession of Athol, as heir of blood to the titles and estates which his younger brother enjoyed in consequence of his attainder; and met with some success in arming the tenants for the support of that cause which he avowed. The rebel army being considerably augmented, though very ill provided with arms, crossed the Forth in the neighbourhood of Stirling, and advanced towards Edinburgh, where they were joined by Lord Elcho, son of the Earl of Wemys, and other persons of some distinction. On the sixteenth day of September Charles summoned the town to surrender. The inhabitants were divided by faction and distracted by fear: the place was not in a posture for defence, and the magistrates would not expose the people to the uncertain issue of an assault. Several deputations were sent from the town to the pretender, in order to negotiate terms of capitulation. In the mean time, one of the gates being opened for the admission of a coach, Cameron of Lochiel, one of the most powerful of the highland chiefs, rushed into the place with a party of his men, and secured it without opposition. Next morning the whole rebel army entered, and their prince took possession of the royal palace of Holyrood-house in the suburbs. Then he caused his father to be proclaimed at the market-

CHAP.
XIX.
1745.

cross: there also the manifesto was read, in which the Chevalier de St. George declared his son Charles regent of his dominions, promised to dissolve the union, and redress the grievances of Scotland. His being in possession of the capital encouraged his followers, and added reputation to his arms: but the treasure belonging to the two banks of that kingdom had been previously conveyed into the castle, a strong fortress, with a good garrison, under the command of General Guest, an old officer of experience and capacity.

Defeats Sir
John Cope
at Preston
Pans.

During these transactions, Sir John Cope marched back from Inverness to Aberdeen, where he embarked with his troops, and on the seventeenth day of September landed at Dunbar, about twenty miles to the eastward of Edinburgh. Here he was joined by two regiments of dragoons, which had retired with precipitation from the capital at the approach of the highland army. With this reinforcement his troops amounted to near three thousand men; and he began his march to Edinburgh, in order to give battle to the enemy. On the twentieth day of the month he encamped in the neighbourhood of Preston Pans, having the village of Tranent in his front, and the sea in his rear. Early next morning he was attacked by the young pretender, at the head of about two thousand four hundred Highlanders half armed, who charged them sword in hand with such impetuosity, that in less than ten minutes after the battle began, the king's troops were broken and totally routed. The dragoons fled in the utmost confusion at the first onset; the general officers having made some unsuccessful efforts to rally them, thought proper to consult their own safety by an expeditious retreat towards Coldstream on the Tweed. All the infantry were either killed or taken; and the colours, artillery, tents, baggage, and military chests, fell into the hands of the victor, who returned in triumph to Edinburgh. Never was victory more complete, or obtained at a smaller expense; for not above fifty of the rebels lost their lives in the engagement. Five hundred of the king's troops were killed on the field of battle, and among these Colonel Gardiner, a gallant officer, who disdained to save his life at the expense of his honour. When abandoned by his own regiment of dragoons, he alighted from his horse, joined the infantry, and fought on foot, until he fell covered with wounds in sight of his own threshold. Prince Charles bore his good fortune with moderation. He prohibited all rejoicings for the victory he had obtained : the wounded soldiers were treated with humanity; and the officers were sent into Fife and Angus, where they were left at liberty on their parole, which the greater part of them shamefully broke in the sequel. From this victory the pretender reaped manifold and important advantages. His followers were armed, his party encouraged, and his enemies intimidated. He was supplied with a train of field-artillery, and a considerable sum of money, and saw himself possessed of all Scotland, except the fortresses, the reduction of which he could not pretend to undertake without proper implements and engineers. After the battle he was joined by a small detachment from the Highlands; and some chiefs, who had hitherto been on the reserve, began to exert their influence in his favour. But he was not yet in a condition to take advantage of that consternation which his late success had diffused through the kingdom of England.

Charles continued to reside in the palace of Holyrood- house [*], and took measures for cutting off the communication between the castle and the city. General Guest declared that he would demolish the city, unless the blockade should be raised, so as that provision might be carried into the castle. After having waited the return of an express which he had found means to despatch to court, he began to put his threats into execution by firing upon the town. Some houses were beaten down, and several persons killed even at the market-cross. The citizens, alarmed at this disaster, sent a deputation to the prince, entreating him to raise the blockade; and he complied with their request. He levied a regiment in Edinburgh and the neighbourhood. He imposed taxes; seized the merchandise that was deposited in the king's warehouses at Leith, and other places; and compelled

[*] While he resided at Edinburgh, some of the presbyterian clergy continued to preach in the churches of that city, and publicly prayed for King George, without suffering the least punishment or molestation. One minister in particular, of the name of Mac Vicar, being solicited by some Highlanders to pray for their prince, promised to comply with their request, and performed his promise in words to this effect : " And as for the young prince, who is come hither in quest of an earthly crown, grant, O Lord, that he may speedily receive a crown of glory."

the city of Glasgow to accommodate him with a large sum, to be repaid when the peace of the kingdom should be re-established. The number of his followers daily increased; and he received considerable supplies of money, artillery, and ammunition, by single ships that arrived from France, where his interest seemed to rise in proportion to the success of his arms. The greater and richer part of Scotland was averse to his family and pretensions; but the people were unarmed and undisciplined, consequently passive under his dominion. By this time, however, the prince-pretender was joined by the Earl of Kilmarnock, the Lords Elcho, Balmerino, Ogilvie, Pitsligo; and the eldest son of Lord Lovat had begun to assemble his father's clan, in order to reinforce the victor, whose army lay encamped at Duddingston, in the neighbourhood of Edinburgh. Kilmarnock and Balmerino were men of broken and desperate fortune: Elcho and Ogilvie were sons to the Earls of Wemys and Airly; so that their influence was far from being extensive. Pitsligo was a nobleman of very amiable character, as well as of great personal interest; and great dependence was placed upon the power and attachment of Lord Lovat, who had entered into private engagements with the Chevalier de St. George, though he still wore the mask of loyalty to the government, and disavowed the conduct of his son when he declared for the pretender. This old nobleman is the same Simon Fraser whom we have had occasion to mention as a partisan and emissary of the court of St. Germain's, in the year one thousand seven hundred and three. He had renounced his connexions with that family, and in the rebellion immediately after the accession of King George I. approved himself a warm friend to the Protestant succession. Since that period he had been induced, by disgust and ambition, to change his principles again, and was in secret an enthusiast in Jacobitism. He had greatly augmented his estate, and obtained a considerable interest in the Highlands, where, however, he was rather dreaded than beloved. He was bold, enterprising, vain, arbitrary, rapacious, cruel, and deceitful; but his character was chiefly marked by a species of low cunning and dissimulation, which, however, overshot his purpose, and contributed to his own

ruin. While Charles resided at Edinburgh, the Marquis
de Guilles arrived at Montrose, as envoy from the French king, with several officers, some cannon, and a considerable quantity of small arms for the use of that adventurer[f].

While the young pretender endeavoured to improve the advantages he had gained, the ministry of Great Britain took every possible measure to retard his progress. Several powerful chiefs in the Highlands were attached to the government, and exerted themselves in its defence. The Duke of Argyle began to arm his vassals; but not before he had obtained the sanction of the legislature. Twelve hundred men were raised by the Earl of Sutherland: the Lord Rae brought a considerable number to the field: the Grants and Monroes appeared under their respective leaders for the service of his majesty: Sir Alexander Macdonald declared for King George, and the Laird of Macleod sent two thousand hardy islanders from Skie to strengthen the same interest. These gentlemen, though supposed to be otherwise affected, were governed and directed by the advice of Duncan Forbes, president of the college of justice at Edinburgh, a man of extensive knowledge, agreeable manners, and unblemished integrity. He procured commissions for raising twenty independent companies, and some of these he bestowed upon individuals who were either attached by principle, or engaged by promise, to the pretender. He acted with indefatigable zeal for the interest of the reigning family; and greatly injured an opulent fortune in their service. He confirmed several chiefs who began to waver in their principles: some he actually converted by the energy of his arguments, and brought over to the assistance of the government which they had determined to oppose: others he persuaded to remain quiet, without taking any share in the present troubles. Certain it is, this gentleman, by his industry and address, prevented the insurrection of ten thousand Highlanders, who would otherwise have joined the pretender; and, therefore, he may be said to have been one great cause of that adventurer's miscarriage. The Earl of Loudon repaired to Inverness, where he completed

Precautions taken in England.

---

[f] He solicited, and is said to have obtained of the Chevalier de St. George, the patent of a duke, and a commission for being lord lieutenant of all the Highlands.

his regiment of Highlanders; directed the conduct of the clans who had taken arms in behalf of his majesty; and, by his vigilance, overawed the disaffected chieftains of that country, who had not yet openly engaged in the rebellion. Immediately after the defeat of Cope, six thousand Dutch troops[g] arrived in England, and three battalions of guards, with seven regiments of infantry, were recalled from Flanders, for the defence of the kingdom. They forthwith began their march to the north, under the command of General Wade, who received orders to assemble an army, which proceeded to Newcastle. The Parliament meeting on the sixteenth day of October, his majesty gave them to understand that an unnatural rebellion had broken out in Scotland, towards the suppression of which he craved their advice and assistance. He found both Houses cordial in their addresses, and zealous in their attachment to his person and government. The Commons forthwith suspended the habeas corpus act; and several persons were apprehended on suspicion of treasonable practices. Immediately after the session was opened, the Duke of Cumberland arrived from the Netherlands, and was followed by another detachment of dragoons and infantry. The train-bands of London were reviewed by his majesty; the county regiments were completed; the volunteers in different parts of the kingdom employed themselves industriously in the exercise of arms; and the whole English nation seemed to rise up as one man against this formidable invader. The government being apprehensive of a descent from France, appointed Admiral Vernon to command a squadron in the Downs, to observe the motions of the enemy by sea, especially in the harbours of Dunkirk and Boulogne; and his cruisers took several ships laden with soldiers, officers, and ammunition, destined for the service of the pretender in Scotland.

The prince pretender reduces Carlisle, and penetrates as far as Derby. Consternation of the miners.

This enterprising youth, having collected about five thousand men, resolved to make an irruption into England, which he accordingly entered by the west border

g They were composed of the forces who had been in garrison at Tournay and Dendermonde when those places were taken, and engaged by capitulation that they should not perform any military function before the first day of January, in the year 1747; so they could not have acted in England without the infringement of a solemn treaty.

on the sixth day of November. Carlisle was invested, and in less than three days surrendered: the keys were delivered to him at Brampton, by the mayor and aldermen on their knees. Here he found a considerable quantity of arms : his father was proclaimed King of Great Britain, and himself regent, by the magistrates in their formalities. General Wade being apprised of his progress, decamped from Newcastle, and advanced across the country as far as Hexham, though the fields were covered with snow, and the roads almost impassable. There he received intelligence that Carlisle was reduced, and forthwith returned to his former station. In the mean time orders were issued for assembling another army in Staffordshire, under the command of Sir John Ligonier. Prince Charles, notwithstanding this formidable opposition, determined to proceed. He had received assurances from France, that a considerable body of troops would be landed on the southern coast of Britain, to make a diversion in his favour; and he never doubted but that he should be joined by all the English malecontents, as soon as he could penetrate into the heart of the kingdom. Leaving a small garrison in the castle of Carlisle, he advanced to Penrith, marching on foot in the highland garb, at the head of his forces ; and continued his route through Lancaster and Preston to Manchester, where, on the twenty-ninth day of the month, he established his head-quarters. There he was joined by about two hundred Englishmen, who were formed into a regiment, under the command of Colonel Townley. The inhabitants seemed to receive him with marks of affection, and his arrival was celebrated by illuminations, and other public rejoicings. His supposed intention was to prosecute his march by the way of Chester into Wales, where he hoped to find a great number of adherents; but all the bridges over the river Mersey being broken down, he chose the route to Stockport, and forded the river at the head of his division, though the water rose to his middle. He passed through Macclesfield and Congleton ; and on the fourth day of December entered the town of Derby, in which his army was quartered, and his father proclaimed with great formality. He had now advanced within one hundred miles of the capital, which

was filled with terror and confusion. Wade lingered in
Yorkshire: the Duke of Cumberland had assumed the
command of the other army assembled in the neighbourhood of Lichfield. He had marched from Stafford to
Stone; so that the rebels, in turning off from Ashbourne
to Derby, had gained a march between him and London.
Had Charles proceeded in his career with that expedition
which he had hitherto used, he might have made himself
master of the metropolis, where he would have been cer-
tainlyᵢjoined by a considerable number of his well-wishers,
who waited impatiently for his approach: yet this exploit could not have been achieved without hazarding an
engagement, and running the risk of being enclosed
within three armies, each greatly superior to his own in
number and artillery. Orders were given for forming a
camp on Finchley-common, where the king resolved to
take the field in person, accompanied by the Earl of
Stair, field-mareschal, and commander-in-chief of the
forces in South Britain. Some Romish priests were apprehended: the militia of London and Middlesex were
kept in readiness to march: double watches were posted
at the city gates, and signals of alarm appointed. The
volunteers of the city were incorporated into a regiment:
the practitioners of the law, headed by the judges, the
weavers of Spitalfields, and other communities, engaged
in association; and even the managers of the theatres
offered to raise a body of their dependents for the service
of the government. Notwithstanding these precautions
and appearances of unanimity, the trading part of the city,
and those concerned in the money corporations, were
overwhelmed with fear and dejection. They reposed
very little confidence in the courage or discipline of their
militia and volunteers: they had received intelligence
that the French were employed in making preparations
at Dunkirk and Calais for a descent upon England: they
dreaded an insurrection of the Roman Catholics, and
other friends of the house of Stuart; and they reflected
that the Highlanders, of whom by this time they had
conceived a most terrible idea, were within four days'
march of the capital. Alarmed by these considerations,
they prognosticated their own ruin in the approaching
revolution; and their countenances exhibited the plainest

marks of horror and despair. On the other hand, the Jacobites were elevated to an insolence of hope, which they were at no pains to conceal; while many people, who had no private property to lose, and thought no change would be for the worse, waited the issue of this crisis with the most calm indifference.

This state of suspense was of short duration. The young pretender found himself miserably disappointed in his expectations. He had now advanced into the middle of the kingdom, and, except a few that joined him at Manchester, not a soul appeared in his behalf; one would have imagined that all the Jacobites of England had been annihilated. The Welsh took no step to excite an insurrection in his favour; the French made no attempt towards an invasion: his court was divided into factions; the highland chiefs began to murmur, and their clans to be unruly: he saw himself with a handful of men, hemmed in between two considerable armies, in the middle of winter, and in a country disaffected to his cause. He knew he could not proceed to the metropolis without hazarding a battle, and that a defeat would be attended with the inevitable destruction of himself and all his adherents; and he had received information that his friends and officers had assembled a body of forces in the north, superior in number to those by whom he was attended. He called a council at Derby; and proposed to advance towards London: the proposal was supported by Lord Nairn with great vehemence; but, after violent disputes, the majority determined that they should retreat to Scotland with all possible expedition. Accordingly, they abandoned Derby on the sixth day of December, early in the morning, and measured back the route by which they had advanced. On the ninth their vanguard arrived at Manchester: on the twelfth they entered Preston, and continued their march northwards. The Duke of Cumberland, who was encamped at Meriden, when first apprised of their retreat, detached the horse and dragoons in pursuit of them; while General Wade began his march from Ferrybridge into Lancashire, with a view of intercepting them in their route: but at Wakefield he understood that they had already reached Wigan; he, therefore, repaired to his old post at Newcastle, after

having detached General Oglethorpe, with his horse and
dragoons, to join those who had been sent off from the
duke's army. They pursued with such alacrity, that
they overtook the rear of the rebels, with which they
skirmished, in Lancashire. The militia of Cumberland
and Westmoreland were raised and armed by the duke's
order to harass them in their march. The bridges were
broken down, the roads damaged, and the beacons lighted
to alarm the country. Nevertheless, they retreated regularly with their small train of artillery. They were
overtaken at the village of Clifton, in the neighbourhood
of Penrith, by two regiments of dragoons. These alighted,
and lined the hedges, in order to harass part of the
enemy's rear-guard, commanded by Lord John Murray,
who, at the head of the Macphersons, attacked the dragoons sword in hand, and repulsed them with some loss.
On the nineteenth day of the month, the highland army
reached Carlisle, where the majority of the English in
the service of the pretender were left, at their own desire.
Charles, having reinforced the garrison of the place,
crossed the rivers Eden and Solway into Scotland, having
thus accomplished one of the most surprising retreats
that ever was performed. But the most remarkable circumstance of this expedition was the moderation and
regularity with which those ferocious people conducted
themselves in a country abounding with plunder. No
violence was offered; no outrage committed; and they
were effectually restrained from the exercise of rapine.
Notwithstanding the excessive cold, the hunger and
fatigue to which they must have been exposed, they left
behind no sick, and lost a very few stragglers; but retired with deliberation, and carried off their cannon in
the face of their enemy. The Duke of Cumberland invested Carlisle with his whole army on the twenty-first
day of December, and on the thirtieth the garrison surrendered on a sort of capitulation made with the Duke
of Richmond. The prisoners, amounting to about four
hundred, were imprisoned in different gaols in England,
and the duke returned to London.

They invest
the castle
of Stirling.
The pretender proceeded by the way of Dumfries to
Glasgow, from which last city he exacted severe contributions, on account of its attachment to the government,

for whose service it had raised a regiment of nine hun- CHAP
dred men under the command of the Earl of Home. XIX.
Having continued several days at Glasgow, he advanced 1746.
towards Stirling, and was joined by some forces which
had been assembled in his absence by Lords Lewis
Gordon and John Drummond, brothers to the Dukes
of Gordon and Perth. This last nobleman had arrived
from France in November, with a small reinforcement
of French and Irish, and a commission as general of
these auxiliaries. He fixed his head-quarters at Perth,
where he was reinforced by the Earl of Cromartie, and
other clans, to the number of two thousand, and he was
accommodated with a small train of artillery. They
had found means to surprise a sloop of war at Montrose,
with the guns of which they fortified that harbour.
They had received a considerable sum of money from
Spain. They took possession of Dundee, Dumblaine,
Downcastle, and laid Fife under contribution. The
Earl of Loudon remained at Inverness, with about two
thousand Highlanders in the service of his majesty. He
convoyed provisions to Fort Augustus and Fort William;
he secured the person of Lord Lovat, who still temporized, and at length this cunning veteran accomplished
his escape. The Laird of Macleod, and Mr. Munro of
Culcairn, being detached from Inverness towards Aber-
deenshire, were surprised and routed by Lord Lewis
Gordon at Inverary; and that interest seemed to preponderate in the north of Scotland. Prince Charles
being joined by Lord John Drummond, invested the
castle of Stirling, in which General Blakeney commanded; but his people were so little used to enter-
prises of this kind that they made very little progress in
their operations.

By this time a considerable body of forces were as- The king's
sembled at Edinburgh, under the conduct of General troops un-
Hawley, who determined to relieve Stirling castle, and are worsted
advanced to Linlithgow on the thirteenth day of January: at Falkirk.
next day his whole army rendezvoused at Falkirk, while
the rebels were cantoned about Bannockburn. On the
seventeenth day of the month, they began their march
in two columns to attack the king's forces, and had

forded the water of Carron, within three miles of Hawley's camp, before he discovered their intention. Such was his obstinacy, self-conceit, or contempt of the enemy, that he slighted the repeated intelligence he had received of their motions and design, firmly believing they durst not hazard an engagement. At length, perceiving they had occupied the rising ground to the southward of Falkirk, he ordered his cavalry to advance, and drive them from the eminence; while his infantry formed, and were drawn up in order of battle. The Highlanders kept up their fire, and took aim so well, that the assailants were broken by the first volley: they retreated with precipitation, and fell in amongst the infantry, which were likewise discomposed by the wind and rain beating with great violence in their faces, wetting their powder, and disturbing their eyesight. Some of the dragoons rallied, and advanced again to the charge, with part of the infantry which had not been engaged; then the pretender marched up at the head of his corps de reserve, consisting of the regiment of Lord John Drummond, and the Irish piquets. These reinforcing the Camerons and the Stuarts in the front line, immediately obliged the dragoons to give way a second time; and they again disordered the foot in their retreat. They set fire to their camp, and abandoned Falkirk with their baggage and train, which last had never reached the field of battle. The rebels followed their first blow, and great part of the royal army, after one irregular discharge, turned their backs, and fled in the utmost consternation. In all probability few or none of them would have escaped, had not General Huske and Brigadier Cholmondeley rallied part of some regiments, and made a gallant stand, which favoured the retreat of the rest to Falkirk, from whence they retired in confusion to Edinburgh, leaving the field of battle, with part of their tents and artillery, to the rebels: but their loss of men did not exceed three hundred, including Sir Robert Monro, Colonel Whitney, and some other officers of distinction. It was at this period that the officers who had been taken at the battle of Preston Pans, and conveyed to Angus and Fife, finding themselves unguarded, broke their parole, and returned to Edinburgh, on pretence of their having been forcibly released by the inhabitants of those parts [h].

General Hawley, who had boasted that, with two regiments of dragoons, he would drive the rebel army from one end of the kingdom to the other, incurred abundance of censure for the disposition he made, as well as for his conduct before and after the action; but he found means to vindicate himself to the satisfaction of his sovereign. Nevertheless, it was judged necessary that the army in Scotland should be commanded by a general in whom the soldiers might have some confidence; and the Duke of Cumberland was chosen for this purpose. Over and above his being beloved by the army, it was suggested that the appearance of a prince of the blood in Scotland might have a favourable effect upon the minds of people in that kingdom; he, therefore, began to prepare for his northern expedition. Meanwhile the French minister at the Hague having represented to the States-General that the auxiliaries which they had sent into Great Britain were part of the garrisons of Tournay and Dendermonde, and restricted by the capitulation from bearing arms against France for a certain term, the states thought proper to recall them, rather than come to an open rupture with his most Christian majesty. In the room of those troops, six thousand Hessians were transported from Flanders to Leith, where they arrived in the beginning of February, under the command of their prince, Frederick of Hesse, son-in-law to his Britannic majesty. By this time the Duke of Cumberland had put himself at the head of the troops in Edinburgh, consisting of fourteen battalions of infantry, two regiments of dragoons, and twelve hundred Highlanders from Argyleshire, under the command of Colonel Campbell. On the last day of January his royal highness began his march to Linlithgow; and the enemy, who had renewed the siege of Stirling castle, not only abandoned that enterprise, but crossed the river Forth with precipitation. Their prince found great difficulty in maintaining his forces, that part of the country being quite exhausted.

CHAP. XIX.

1745. The Duke of Cumberland assumes the command of the forces in Scotland.

1746.

---

[h] Sir Peter Halket, Captain Lucy Scot, Lieutenants Farquharson and Cumming, with a few other gentlemen, adhered punctually to their parole, and their conduct was approved by his majesty.

He hoped to be reinforced in the Highlands, and to receive supplies of all kinds from France and Spain ; he,
therefore, retired by Badenoch towards Inverness, which
the Earl of Loudon abandoned at his approach.   The
fort was surrendered to him almost without opposition,
and here he fixed his head-quarters.   His next exploit
was the siege of Fort Augustus, which he in a little time
reduced.   The Duke of Cumberland having secured the
important posts of Stirling and Perth, with the Hessian
battalions, advanced with the army to Aberdeen, where
he was joined by the Duke of Gordon, the Earls of
Aberdeen and Findlater, the Laird of Grant, and other
persons of distinction.

The rebels
undertake
the siege
of Fort
William.

While he remained in this place, refreshing his troops
and preparing magazines, a party of the rebels surprised
a detachment of Kingston's horse, and about seventy
Argyleshire Highlanders, at Keith, who were either killed
or taken.   Several advanced parties of that militia met
with the same fate in different places.   Lord George
Murray invested the castle of Blair, which was defended
by Sir Andrew Agnew, until a body of Hessians marched
to its relief, and obliged the rebels to retire.   The prince
pretender ordered all his forces to assemble, in order to
begin their march for Aberdeen, to attack the Duke of
Cumberland ; but, in consequence of a remonstrance from
the clans, who declined leaving their families at the mercy
of the king's garrison in Fort William, he resolved previously to reduce that fortress, the siege of which was
undertaken by Brigadier Stapleton, an engineer in the
French service ; but the place was so vigorously maintained by Captain Scot, that in the beginning of April
they thought proper to relinquish the enterprise.   The
Earl of Loudon had retired into Sutherland, and taken
post at Dornoch, where his quarters were beaten up by
a strong detachment of the rebels, commanded by the
Duke of Perth : a major and sixty men were taken
prisoners; and the earl was obliged to take shelter in the
isle of Skye.   These little checks were counterbalanced
by some advantages which his majesty's arms obtained.
The sloop of war which the rebels had surprised at Montrose was retaken in Sutherland, with a considerable sum
of money, and a great quantity of arms on board, which

she had brought from France for the use of the pretender.
In the same county the Earl of Cromartie fell into an
ambuscade, and was taken by the militia of Sutherland,
who likewise defeated a body of the rebels at Goldspie.
This action happened on the very day which has been
rendered famous by the victory obtained at Culloden.

CHAPTER XX.

CHAP. XX. 1746. The rebels are totally defeated at Culloden.

IN the beginning of April the Duke of Cumberland began his march from Aberdeen, and on the twelfth passed the deep and rapid river Spey, without opposition from the rebels, though a detachment of them appeared on the opposite side. Why they did not dispute the passage is not easy to be conceived ; but, indeed, from this instance of neglect, and their subsequent conduct, we may conclude they were under a total infatuation. His royal highness proceed to Nairn, where he received intelligence that the enemy had advanced from Inverness to Culloden, about the distance of nine miles from the royal army, with intention to give him battle. The design of Charles was to march in the night from Culloden, and surprise the duke's army at daybreak : for this purpose the English camp had been reconnoitred ; and on the night of the fifteenth the highland army began to march in two columns. Their design was to surround the enemy, and attack them at once on all quarters ; but the length of the columns embarrassed the march, so that the army was obliged to make many halts : the men had been under arms during the whole preceding night, were faint with hunger and fatigue, and many of them overpowered with sleep. Some were unable to proceed ; others dropped off unperceived in the dark ; and the march was retarded in such a manner that it would have been impossible to reach the duke's camp before sunrise. The design being thus frustrated, the prince pretender was with great reluctance prevailed upon by his general officers to measure back his way to Culloden : at which place he had no sooner arrived, than great numbers of his followers dispersed in quest of provision ; and many, overcome with weariness and sleep, threw themselves down on the heath, and along the park walls. Their repose, however, was soon interrupted in a very disagreeable manner. Their prince, receiving intelligence that his enemies were in full march to attack him, resolved to hazard an engagement, and ordered his troops to be formed for that purpose. On the sixteenth day of April the Duke of Cumberland having made the proper dispositions, decamped from Nairn early in the morning, and after a march of nine miles perceived the Highlanders drawn up in order of battle, to the number of four thousand men, in thirteen divisions, supplied with some pieces of artillery. The royal army, which was much more numerous, the duke immediately formed into three lines, disposed in excellent order ; and about one o'clock in the afternoon the cannonading began. The artillery of the rebels was ill served, and did very little execution ; but that of the king's troops made dreadful havoc among the enemy. Impatient of this fire, their front line advanced to the attack, and about five hundred of the clans charged the duke's left wing with their usual impetuosity. One regiment was disordered by the weight of this column ; but two battalions advancing from the second line, sustained the first, and soon put a stop to their career, by a severe fire, that killed a great number. At the same time, the dragoons under Hawley, and the Argyleshire militia, pulled down a park wall that covered their right flank, and the cavalry falling in among the rebels sword in hand completed their confusion. The French piquets on their left covered the retreat of the Highlanders by a close and regular fire; and then retired to Inverness, where they surrendered themselves prisoners of war. An entire body of the rebels marched off the field in order, with their pipes playing, and the pretender's standard displayed; the rest were routed with great slaughter; and their prince was with reluctance prevailed upon to retire. In less than thirty minutes they were totally defeated, and the field covered with the slain. The road, as far as Inverness, was strewed with dead bodies; and a great number of people, who from motives of curiosity had come to see the battle, were sacrificed to the undistinguishing vengeance of the victors. Twelve hundred rebels were slain or wounded on the field, and in the pursuit. The Earl of Kilmarnock was taken; and in a few days Lord Balmerino surrendered to a country gentleman, at whose house he presented himself for this purpose. The glory of the victory was sullied by the barbarity of the soldiers. They had been provoked by their former disgraces to the most savage thirst of revenge. Not contented with the blood which was so profusely shed in the heat of action, they traversed the field after the battle, and massacred those miserable wretches who lay maimed and expiring: nay, some officers acted a part in this cruel scene of assassination, the triumph of low illiberal minds, uninspired by sentiment, untinctured by humanity. The vanquished adventurer rode off the field, accompanied by the Duke of Perth, Lord Elcho, and a few horsemen: he crossed the water of Nairn, and retired to the house of a gentleman in Stratharick, where he conferred with old Lord Lovat; then he dismissed his followers, and wandered about, a wretched and solitary fugitive, among the isles and mountains for the space of five months, during which he underwent such a series of dangers, hardships, and misery, as no other person ever outlived. Thus, in one short hour all his hope vanished, and the rebellion was entirely extinguished. One would almost imagine the conductors of this desperate enterprise had conspired their own destruction, as they certainly neglected every step that might have contributed to their safety or success. They might have opposed the Duke of Cumberland at the passage of the Spey; they might by proper conduct have afterwards attacked his camp in the night, with a good prospect of success. As they were greatly inferior to him in number, and weakened with hunger and fatigue, they might have retired to the hills and fastnesses, where they would have found plenty of live cattle for provision, recruited their regiments, and been joined by a strong reinforcement, which was actually in full march to their assistance. But they were distracted by dissensions and jealousies: they obeyed the dictates of despair, and wilfully devoted themselves to ruin and death. When the news of the battle arrived in England, the nation was transported with joy, and extolled the Duke of Cumberland as a hero and deliverer. Both Houses of Parliament congratulated his majesty on the auspicious event. They decreed, in the most solemn manner, their public thanks to his royal highness, which were transmitted to him by the speakers; and the Commons, by bill, added five-and-twenty thousand pounds per annum to his former revenue.

Immediately after the decisive action at Culloden, the duke took possession of Inverness, where six-and-thirty deserters, convicted by a court-martial, were ordered to be executed; then he detached several parties to ravage the country. One of these apprehended the Lady Mackintosh, who was sent prisoner to Inverness. They did not plunder her house, but drove away her cattle, though her husband was actually in the service of government. The castle of Lord Lovat was destroyed. The French prisoners were sent to Carlisle and Penrith: Kilmarnock, Balmerino, Cromartie, and his son, the Lord Macleod, were conveyed by sea to London; and those of an inferior rank were confined in different prisons. The Marquis of Tullibardine, together with a brother of the Earl of Dunmore, were seized and transported to the Tower of London, to which the Earl of Traquaire had been committed on suspicion: in a few

The Duke of Cumberland takes possession of Inverness, and afterwards encamps at Fort Augustus.

K k 2

months after the battle of Culloden, Murray, the pretender's secretary, was apprehended; and the eldest son
of Lord Lovat having surrendered himself, was imprisoned
in the castle of Edinburgh. In a word, all the gaols of
Great Britain, from the capital northwards, were filled
with those unfortunate captives; and great numbers of
them were crowded together in the holds of ships, where
they perished in the most deplorable manner, for want
of necessaries, air, and exercise. Some rebel chiefs
escaped in two French frigates, which had arrived on
the coast of Lochaber about the end of April, and engaged three vessels belonging to his Britannic majesty,
which they obliged to retire. Others embarked on board
of a ship on the coast of Buchan, and were conveyed to
Norway; from whence they travelled to Sweden. In
the month of May, the Duke of Cumberland advanced
with the army into the Highlands, as far as Fort Augustus, where he encamped; and sent off detachments
on all hands, to hunt down the fugitives, and lay waste
the country with fire and sword. The castles of Glengary and Lochiel were plundered and burned; every
house, hut, or habitation, met with the same fate, without distinction: all the cattle and provision were carried
off: the men were either shot upon the mountains, like
wild beasts, or put to death in cold blood, without form
of trial: the women, after having seen their husbands
and fathers murdered, were subjected to brutal violation,
and then turned out naked, with their children, to starve
on the barren heaths. One whole family was enclosed
in a barn, and consumed to ashes. Those ministers of
vengeance were so alert in the execution of their office,
that in a few days there was neither house, cottage, man,
nor beast, to be seen in the compass of fifty miles: all
was ruin, silence, and desolation.

The prince
pretender
escapes to
France.

The humane reader cannot reflect upon such a scene
without grief and horror: what then must have been the
sensation of the fugitive prince, when he beheld these
spectacles of woe, the dismal fruit of his ambition? He
was now surrounded by armed troops, that chased him
from hill to dale, from rock to cavern, and from shore
to shore. Sometimes he lurked in caves and cottages,
without attendants, or any other support but that which

the poorest peasant could supply. Sometimes he was
rowed in fisher-boats from isle to isle, among the He-
brides, and often in sight of his pursuers. For some days he appeared in woman's attire, and even passed
through the midst of his enemies unknown. But, un-
derstanding his disguise was discovered, he assumed the
habit of a travelling mountaineer, and wandered about
among the woods and heaths, with a matted beard and
squalid looks, exposed to hunger, thirst, and weariness,
and in continual danger of being apprehended. He
was obliged to trust his life to the fidelity of above fifty
individuals, and many of these were in the lowest paths
of fortune. They knew that a price of thirty thousand
pounds was set upon his head; and that, by betraying
him, they should enjoy wealth and affluence: but they
detested the thought of obtaining riches on such infamous terms, and ministered to his necessities, with the
utmost zeal and fidelity, even at the hazard of their own
destruction. In the course of these peregrinations, he
was more than once hemmed in by his pursuers, in such
a manner as seemed to preclude all possibility of escaping; yet he was never abandoned by his hope and recollection: he still found some expedient that saved him
from captivity and death; and through the whole course
of his distresses maintained the most amazing equanimity
and good humour. At length a privateer of St. Malo,
hired by the young Sheridan and some other Irish adherents, arrived in Lochnannach; and on the twentieth
day of September this unfortunate prince embarked in
the habit which he wore for disguise. His eye was
hollow, his visage wan, and his constitution greatly impaired by famine and fatigue. He was accompanied by
Cameron of Lochiel and his brother, with a few other
exiles. They set sail for France, and after having passed
unseen, by means of a thick fog, through a British squadron, commanded by Admiral Lestock, and been chased
by two English ships of war, arrived in safety at Roscau,
near Morlaix, in Bretagne. Perhaps he would have
found it still more difficult to escape, had not the vigilance and eagerness of the government been relaxed, in
consequence of a report that he had already fallen among

CHAP.
XX.

.1746.
Convulsion
in the mi-
nistry.
some persons that were slain by a volley from one of
the duke's detachments.

Having thus explained the rise, progress, and extinction of the rebellion, it will be necessary to take a retro-
spective view of the proceedings in Parliament. The
necessary steps being taken for quieting the intestine
commotions of the kingdom, the two Houses began to
convert their attention to the affairs of the continent.
On the fourteenth day of January the king repaired to
the House of Peers, and, in a speech from the throne,
gave his Parliament to understand, that the States-
General had made pressing instances for his assistance
in the present conjuncture, when they were in such
danger of being oppressed by the power of France in
the Netherlands; that he had promised to co-operate
with them towards opposing the further progress of
their enemies; and even concerted measures for that
purpose. He declared it was with regret that he asked
any further aids of his people: he exhorted them to
watch over the public credit; and expressed his entire
dependence on their zeal and unanimity. He was favoured with loyal addresses, couched in the warmest
terms of duty and affection: but the supplies were retarded by new convulsions in the ministry. The Earl
of Granville had made an effort to retrieve his influence
in the cabinet, and his sovereign favoured his pretensions.
The two brothers, who knew his aspiring genius, and
dreaded his superior talents, refused to admit such a
colleague into the administration; they even resolved
to strengthen their party, by introducing fresh auxiliaries
into the offices of state. Some of these were personally
disagreeable to his majesty, who accordingly rejected the
suit by which they were recommended. The Duke of
Newcastle and his brother, with all their adherents, immediately resigned their employments. The Earl of
Granville was appointed secretary of state, and resumed
the reins of administration; but finding himself unequal
to the accumulated opposition that preponderated against
him; foreseeing that he should not be able to secure the
supplies in Parliament; and dreading the consequences
of that confusion which his restoration had already pro-

duced, he, in three days, voluntarily quitted the helm;
and his majesty acquiesced in the measures proposed by the opposite party. The seals were re-delivered to the Duke of Newcastle and the Earl of Harrington: Mr. Pelham, and all the rest who had resigned, were re-instated in their respective employments; and offices were conferred on several individuals who had never before been in the service of the government. William Pitt, Esq., was appointed vice-treasurer of Ireland, and soon promoted to the place of paymaster-general of the forces; at the same time the king declared him a privy-counsellor. This gentleman had been originally designed for the army, in which he actually bore a commission; but fate reserved him for a more important station. In point of fortune he was barely qualified to be elected member of Parliament, when he obtained a seat in the House of Commons, where he soon outshone all his compatriots. He displayed a surprising extent and pre-cision of political knowledge, an irresistible energy of argument, and such power of elocution as struck his hearers with astonishment and admiration. It flashed like the lightning of heaven against the ministers and sons of corruption, blasting where it smote, and wither-ing the nerves of opposition: but his more substantial praise was founded upon his disinterested integrity, his incorruptible heart, his unconquerable spirit of indepen-dence, and his invariable attachment to the interest and liberty of his country.

The quiet of the ministry being re-established, the *Liberality of the* House of Commons provided for forty thousand seamen, *Commons.* nearly the same number of land forces, besides fifteen regiments raised by the nobility, on account of the re-bellion, and about twelve thousand marines. They settled funds for the maintenance of the Dutch and Hessian troops that were in England, as well as for the subsidy to the landgrave. They granted three hundred thousand pounds to the King of Sardinia; four hundred thousand pounds to the Queen of Hungary; three hundred and ten thousand pounds to defray the expense of eighteen thousand Hanoverians; about three-and-thirty thousand pounds in subsidies to the Electors of Mentz and Cologn; and five hundred thousand pounds in a vote of credit

and confidence to his majesty. The whole charge of the
current year amounted to seven millions two hundred
and fifty thousand pounds, which was raised by the land
and malt-taxes, annuities on the additional duties imposed on glass, and spirituous liquors, a lottery, a deduction from the sinking fund, and exchequer bills, chargeable on the first aids that should be granted in the next
session of Parliament.

Trial of the
rebels.
Kilmar-
nock, Bal-
merino,
Lovat, and
Mr. Rad-
cliffe are
beheaded
on Tower-
hill.

The rebellion being quelled, the legislature resolved
to make examples of those who had been concerned in
disturbing the peace of their country. In June, an act
of attainder was passed against the principal persons who
had embarked in that desperate undertaking; and courts
were opened in different parts of England for the trial
of the prisoners. Seventeen persons who had borne
arms in the rebel army were executed at Kennington-
common, in the neighbourhood of London, and suffered
with great constancy under the dreadful tortures which
their sentence prescribed: nine were put to death, in the
same manner, at Carlisle; six at Brompton, seven at
Penrith, and eleven at York; of these a considerable
number were gentlemen, and had acted as officers; about
fifty had been executed as deserters in different parts of
Scotland; eighty-one suffered the pains of the law as
traitors. A few obtained pardons, and a considerable
number were transported to the plantations. Bills of
indictment for high treason were found by the county of
Surrey against the Earls of Kilmarnock and Cromartie,
and Lord Balmerino. These noblemen were tried by
their Peers in Westminster-hall, the lord chancellor pre-
siding as lord high steward for the occasion. The two
earls confessed their crimes, and in pathetic speeches recommended themselves to his majesty's mercy. Lord
Balmerino pleaded not guilty: he denied his having
been at Carlisle at the time specified in the indictment,
but this exception was overruled: then he moved a
point of law in arrest of judgment, and was allowed to
be heard by his counsel. They might have expatiated on
the hardship of being tried by an *ex post facto* law, and
claimed the privilege of trial in the county where the
act of treason was said to have been committed. The
same hardship was imposed upon all the imprisoned

rebels: they were dragged in captivity to a strange country, far from their friends and connexions, destitute of
means to produce evidence in their favour, even if they
had been innocent of the charge. Balmerino waved this
plea, and submitted to the court, which pronounced
sentence of death upon him and his two associates.
Cromartie's life was spared; but the other two were beheaded, in the month of August, on Tower-hill. Kilmarnock was a nobleman of fine personal accomplishments: he had been educated in revolution principles,
and engaged in the rebellion, partly from the desperate
situation of his fortune, and partly from resentment to
the government, on his being deprived of a pension which
he had for some time enjoyed. He was convinced of his
having acted criminally, and died with marks of peni-
tence and contrition. Balmerino had been bred to arms,
and acted upon principle: he was gallant, brave, rough,
and resolute; he eyed the implements of death with the
most careless familiarity, and seemed to triumph in his
sufferings. In November, Mr. Radcliffe, the titular Earl
of Derwentwater, who had been taken in a ship bound
to Scotland, was arraigned on a former sentence, passed
against him in the year one thousand seven hundred and
sixteen: he refused to acknowledge the authority of the
court, and pleaded that he was a subject of France,
honoured with a commission in the service of his most
Christian majesty. The identity of his person being proved,
a rule was made for his execution; and on the eighth
day of December he suffered decapitation, with the most
perfect composure and serenity. Lord Lovat, now turned
of fourscore, was impeached by the Commons, and tried
in Westminster-hall before the lord high steward. John
Murray, secretary to the prince pretender, and some of
his own domestics, appearing against him, he was convicted of high treason, and condemned. Notwithstanding his age, infirmities, and the recollection of his conscience, which was supposed to be not altogether void of
offence, he died like an old Roman, exclaiming, " *Dulce
et decorum est pro patria mori.*" He surveyed the crowd
with attention, examined the axe, jested with the executioner, and laid his head upon the block with the utmost indifference. From this last scene of his life, one

The States-
General
alarmed at
the pro-
gress of the
French in
the Nether-
lands.

would have concluded that he had approved himself a
patriot from his youth, and never deviated from the paths
of virtue.

The flame of war on the continent did not expire at
the election of an emperor, and the re-establishment of
peace among the princes of the empire. On the contrary, it raged with double violence in consequence of
these events; for the force that was before divided
being now united in one body, exerted itself with great
vigour and rapidity. The States-General were overwhelmed with consternation. Notwithstanding the
pains they had taken to avoid a war, and the condescension with which they had soothed and supplicated
the French monarch in repeated embassies and memorials, they saw themselves stripped of their barrier, and
once more in danger of being overwhelmed by that
ambitious nation. The city of Brussels had been reduced during the winter; so that the enemy were in
possession of all the Austrian Netherlands, except a few
fortresses. Great part of the forces belonging to the
republic, were restricted from action by capitulations,
to which they had subscribed. The States were divided
in their councils between the two factions which had
long subsisted. They trembled at the prospect of seeing Zealand invaded in the spring. The Orange party
loudly called for an augmentation of their forces by sea
and land, that they might prosecute the war with vigour.
The common people, fond of novelty, dazzled by the
splendour of greatness, and fully persuaded that nothing
but a chief was wanting to their security, demanded the
Prince of Orange as their stadtholder; and even mingled
menaces with their demands. The opposite faction
dreaded alike the power of a stadtholder, the neighbourhood of a French army, and a seditious disposition
of the populace. An ambassador was sent to London
with representations of the imminent dangers which
threatened the republic, and he was ordered to solicit
in the most pressing terms the assistance of his Britannic
majesty, that the allies might have a superiority in the
Netherlands by the beginning of the campaign. The
king was very well disposed to comply with their request; but the rebellion in his kingdom, and the dis-

sensions in his cabinet, had retarded the supplies, and
embarrassed him so much, that he found it impossible
to make those early preparations that were necessary to
check the career of the enemy.

The King of France, with his general, the Count de
Saxe, took the field in the latter end of April, at the
head of one hundred and twenty thousand men, and
advanced towards the allies, who, to the number of four-
and-forty thousand, were intrenched behind the Demer,
under the conduct of the Austrian General Bathiani, who
retired before them, and took post in the neighbourhood
of Breda, the capital of Dutch Brabant. Mareschal
Saxe immediately invested Antwerp, which in a few
days was surrendered. Then he appeared before the
strong town of Mons in Hainault, with an irresistible
train of artillery, an immense quantity of bombs and warlike implements. He carried on his approaches with
such unabating impetuosity, that, notwithstanding a
very vigorous defence, the garrison was obliged to capitulate on the twenty-seventh day of June, in about eight-
and-twenty days after the place had been invested.
Sieges were not now carried on by the tedious method
of sapping. The French king found it much more expeditious and effectual to bring into the field a prodigious train of battering cannon and enormous mortars,
that kept up such a fire as no garrison could sustain, and
discharged such an incessant hail of bombs and bullets,
as in a very little time reduced to ruins the place, with
all its fortifications. St. Guisland and Charleroy met
with the fate of Mons and Antwerp; so that by the
middle of July the French king was absolute master of
Flanders, Brabant, and Hainault.

Prince Charles of Lorraine had by this time assumed
the command of the confederate army at Terheyde, which,
being reinforced by the Hessian troops from Scotland,
and a fresh body of Austrians under Count Palfi, amounted
to eighty-seven thousand men, including the Dutch forces
commanded by the Prince of Waldeck. The generals,
supposing the next storm would fall upon Namur,
marched towards that place, and took post in an advantageous situation on the eighteenth day of July, in sight
of the French army, which was encamped at Gemblours.

Here they remained till the eighth day of August, when a detachment of the enemy, commanded by Count Lowendahl, took possession of Huy, where he found a large magazine belonging to the confederates; and their communication with Maestricht was cut off. Mareschal Saxe, on the other side, took his measures so well that they were utterly deprived of all subsistence. Then Prince Charles, retiring across the Maese, abandoned Namur to the efforts of the enemy, by whom it was immediately invested. The trenches were opened on the second day of September; and the garrison, consisting of seven thousand Austrians, defended themselves with equal skill and resolution: but the cannonading and bombardment were so terrible, that in a few days the place was converted into a heap of rubbish; and on the twenty-third day of the month the French monarch took possession of this strong fortress, which had formerly sustained such dreadful attacks. Meanwhile the allied army encamped at Maestricht were joined by Sir John Ligonier, with some British and Bavarian battalions; and Prince Charles resolved to give the enemy battle. With this view he passed the Maese on the thirteenth day of September, and advanced towards Mareschal Saxe, whom he found so advantageously posted at Tongres, that he thought proper to march back to Maestricht. On the twenty-sixth day of September he crossed the Jaar in his retreat; and his rear was attacked by the enemy, who were repulsed. But Count Saxe being reinforced by a body of troops, under the Count de Clermont, determined to bring the confederates to an engagement. On the thirteenth day of the month he passed the Jaar: while he took possession of the villages of Liers, Warem, and Roucoux, they drew up their forces in order of battle, and made preparations for giving him a warm reception. On the first day of October the enemy advanced in three columns; and a terrible cannonading began about noon. At two o'clock Prince Waldeck on the left was charged with great fury; and after an obstinate defence overpowered by numbers. The villages were attacked in columns, and as one brigade was repulsed, another succeeded; so that the allies were obliged to abandon these posts, and retreat

towards Maestricht, with the loss of five thousand men,
and thirty pieces of artillery. The victory, however,
cost the French general a much greater number of
lives; and was attended with no solid advantage. Sir
John Ligonier, the Earls of Crawford [a] and Rothes,
Brigadier Douglas, and other officers of the British
troops, distinguished themselves by their gallantry and
conduct on this occasion. This action terminated the
campaign. The allies passing the Maese, took up their
winter quarters in the duchies of Limburgh and Luxem-
burgh; while the French cantoned their troops in the
places which they had newly conquered.

The campaign in Italy was altogether unfavourable to The French
the French and Spaniards. The house of Austria being and Spani-
no longer pressed on the side of Germany, was enabled compelled
to make the stronger efforts in this country; and the to abandon
Piedmont
British subsidy encouraged the King of Sardinia to act and the
with redoubled vivacity. Mareschal Maillebois occupied Milanese.
the greater part of Piedmont with about thirty thousand
men. Don Philip and the Count de Gages were at the
head of a greater number in the neighbourhood of Milan;
and the Duke of Modena, with eight thousand, secured
his own dominions. The King of Sardinia augmented
his forces to six-and-thirty thousand; and the Austrian army, under the Prince of Lichtenstein, amounted
to a much greater number; so that the enemy were
reduced to the necessity of acting on the defensive, and

[a] This nobleman, so remarkable for his courage and thirst of glory, exhibited a
very extraordinary instance of presence of mind on the morning that preceded
this battle. He and some volunteers, accompanied by his aide-du-camp, and attended by two orderly dragoons, had rode out before day to reconnoitre the situation of the enemy; and fell in upon one of their advanced guards. The sergeant
who commanded it immediately turned out his men, and their pieces were presented when the earl first perceived them. Without betraying the least mark of
disorder, he rode up to the sergeant, and, assuming the character of a French
general, told him in that language that there was no occasion for such ceremony.
Then he asked if they had perceived any of the enemy's parties ! and being
answered in the negative, " Very well, (said he,) be upon your guard ; and if you
should be attacked, I will take care that you shall be sustained." So saying, he
and his company retired before the sergeant could recover himself from the surprise occasioned by this unexpected address. In all probability he was soon sensible of his mistake ; for the incident was that very day publicly mentioned in
the French army. The Prince of Tingray, an officer in the Austrian service,
having been taken prisoner in the battle that ensued, dined with Mareschal
Count Saxe, who dismissed him on his parole, and desired he would charge himself with a facetious compliment to his old friend the Earl of Crawford. He
wished his lordship joy of being a French general, and said he could not help
being displeased with the sergeant, as he had not procured him the honour of his
lordship's company at dinner.

retired towards the Mantuan. In February, Baron Leutrum, the Piedmontese general, invested and took the
strong fortress of Aste. He afterwards relieved the
citadel of Alexandria, which the Spaniards had blocked
up in the winter, reduced Casal, recovered Valencia, and
obliged Maillebois to retire to the neighbourhood of
Genoa. On the other side, Don Philip and Count Gages
abandoned Milan, Pavia, and Parma, retreating before
the Austrians with the utmost precipitation to Placentia,
where they were joined on the third of June by the
French forces under Maillebois.

Don Philip
is worsted
at Codogno,
and after-
wards at
Porto
Freddo.

Before this junction was effected, the Spanish general
Pignatelli had passed the river Po in the night with a
strong detachment, and beaten up the quarters of seven
thousand Austrians posted at Codogno. Don Philip,
finding himself at the head of two-and-fifty thousand men
by his junction with the French general, resolved to
attack the Austrians in their camp at San Lazaro, before they should be reinforced by his Sardinian majesty.
Accordingly, on the fourth day of June, in the evening,
he marched with equal silence and expedition, and entered the Austrian trenches about eleven, when a desperate battle ensued. The Austrians were prepared for
the attack, which they sustained with great vigour till
morning. Then they quitted their intrenchments, and
charged the enemy in their turn with such fury, that
after an obstinate resistance the combined army was
broken, and retired with precipitation to Placentia, leaving on the field fifteen thousand men killed, wounded,
and taken, together with sixty colours, and ten pieces of
artillery. In a few weeks the Austrians were joined by
the Piedmontese: the King of Sardinia assumed the
chief command; and Prince Lichtenstein being indisposed, his place was supplied by the Marquis de Botta.
Don Philip retired to the other side of the Po, and
extended his conquests in the open country of the Milanese. The King of Sardinia called a council of war,
in which it was determined that he should pass the river
with a strong body of troops, in order to straiten the
enemy on one side; while the Marquis de Botta should
march up the Tydone, to cut off their communication
with Placentia. They forthwith quitted all the posts

they had occupied between the Lambro and Adda,
resolving to repass the Po, and retreat to Tortona. With
this view they threw bridges of boats over that river, and
began to pass on the ninth day of August, in the evening.
They were attacked at Rotto Freddo by a detachment of
Austrians, under General Serbelloni, who maintained the
engagement till ten in the morning, when Botta arrived :
the battle was renewed with redoubled rage, and lasted
till four in the afternoon, when the enemy retired in
great disorder to Tortona, with the loss of eight thousand
men, a good number of colours and standards, and eighteen
pieces of cannon.   This victory cost the Austrians four
thousand men killed upon the spot, including the gallant
General Bernclau.   The victors immediately summoned
Placentia to surrender; and the garrison, consisting of
nine thousand men, were made prisoners of war : Don
Philip continued his retreat, and of all his forces brought
six-and-twenty thousand only into the territories of
Genoa.

The Piedmontese and Austrians rejoining in the neigh- The Aus-
bourhood of Pavia, advanced to Tortona, of which they trians take
took possession without resistance, while the enemy of Genoa.
sheltered themselves under the cannon of Genoa. They Count
did not long continue in this situation; for on the penetrates
twenty-second day of August they were again in motion, vence.
and retired into Provence. The court of Madrid impu-
ting the bad success of this campaign to the misconduct
of Count Gages, recalled that general, and sent the Marquis de las Minas to resume the command of the forces.
In the mean time, the victorious confederates appeared before Genoa on the fourth day of December; and the senate
of that city thinking it incapable of defence, submitted
to a very mortifying capitulation, by which the gates
were delivered up to the Austrians, together with all
their arms, artillery, and ammunition; and the city was
subjected to the most cruel contributions. The Marquis
de Botta being left at Genoa with sixteen thousand
men, the King of Sardinia resolved to pass the Var, and
pursue the French and Spaniards into Provence; but,
that monarch being seized with the small-pox, the conduct of this expedition was intrusted to Count Brown,
an Austrian general of Irish extract, who had given

repeated proofs of uncommon valour and capacity. He
was on this occasion assisted by Vice-Admiral Medley,
who commanded the British squadron in the Mediterranean. The French forces had fortified the passes of the
Var, under the conduct of the Mareschal de Belleisle,
who thought proper to abandon his posts at the approach
of Count Brown; and this general, at the head of fifty
thousand men, passed the river, without opposition, on
the ninth day of November. While he advanced as far
as Draguignan, laying the open country under contribution, Baron Roth, with four-and-twenty battalions, invested Antibes, which was at the same time bombarded
on the side of the sea by the British squadron. The
trenches were opened on the twentieth day of September;
but Belleisle having assembled a numerous army, superior to that of the confederates, and the Genoese having
expelled their Austrian guests, Count Brown abandoned
the enterprise, and repassed the Var, not without some
damage from the enemy.

The Ge-
noese ex-
pel the
Austrians
from their
city.

The court of Vienna, which has always patronised
oppression, exacted such heavy contributions from the
Genoese, and its exactions were so rigorously put into
execution, that the people were reduced to despair; and
resolved to make a last effort for the recovery of their
liberty and independence. Accordingly, they took arms
in secret, seized several important posts of the city;
surprised some battalions of the Austrians; surrounded
others, and cut them in pieces; and, in a word, drove
them out with great slaughter. The Marquis de Botta
acted with caution and spirit; but being overpowered by
numbers, and apprehensive of the peasants in the country,
who were in arms, he retreated to the pass of the Bro-
chetta on the side of Lombardy, where he secured himself in an advantageous situation, until he could receive
reinforcements. The loss he had sustained at Genoa
did not hinder him from reducing Savona, a sea-port
town belonging to that republic; and he afterwards
made himself master of Gavi. The Genoese, on the
contrary, exerted themselves with wonderful industry in
fortifying their city, raising troops, and in taking other
measures for a vigorous defence, in case they should again
be insulted.

The naval transactions of this year reflected very little honour on the British nation. Commodore Peyton, who commanded six ships of war in the East Indies, shame- fully declined a decisive engagement with a French squadron of inferior force; and abandoned the important settlement of Madras, on the coast of Coromandel, which was taken without opposition in the month of September by the French commodore, De la Bourdonnais. Fort St. David, and the other British factories in India, would probably have shared the same fate, had not the enemy's naval force in that country been shattered and partly destroyed by a terrible tempest. No event of consequence happened in America, though it was a scene that seemed to promise the greatest success to the arms of England. The reduction of Cape Breton had encouraged the ministry to project the conquest of Quebec, the capital of Canada, situated upon the river St. Laurence. Commissions were sent to the governors of the British colonies in North America, empowering them to raise companies to join the armament from England; and eight thousand troops were actually raised in consequence of these directions; while a powerful squadron and transports, having six regiments on board, were prepared at Portsmouth for this expedition. But their departure was postponed by unaccountable delays, until the season was judged too far advanced to risk the great ships on the boisterous coast of North America. That the armament, however, might not be wholly useless to the nation, it was employed in making a descent upon the coast of Bretagne, on the supposition that Port L'Orient, the repository of all the stores and ships belonging to the French East India Company, might be surprised; or, that this invasion would alarm the enemy, and, by making a diversion, facilitate the operations of the Austrian general in Provence.

The naval force intended for this service consisted of sixteen great ships, and eight frigates, besides bomb-ketches and store-ships, commanded by Richard Lestock, appointed admiral of the blue division. Six battalions of land troops, with a detachment of matrosses and bombardiers, were embarked in thirty transports under the conduct of Lieutenant-General Sinclair; and the

whole fleet set sail from Plymouth on the fourteenth day
of September. On the twentieth the troops were landed
in Quimperlay bay, at the distance of ten miles from
Port L'Orient. The militia, reinforced by some detachments from different regiments, were assembled to the
number of two thousand, and seemed resolved to oppose
the disembarkation; but, seeing the British troops determined to land at all events, they thought proper to
retire. Next day General Sinclair advanced into the
country, skirmishing with the enemy in his route; and
arriving at the village of Plemure, within half a league
from Port L'Orient, summoned that place to surrender.
He was visited by a deputation from the town, which
offered to admit the British forces, on condition that
they should be restrained from pillaging the inhabitants,
and touching the magazines; and that they should pay
a just price for their provisions. These terms being rejected, the inhabitants prepared for a vigorous defence;
and the English general resolved to besiege the place
in form, though he had neither time, artillery, nor forces
sufficient for such an enterprise. This strange resolution
was owing to the declaration of the engineers, who promised to lay the place in ashes in the space of four-and-
twenty hours. All his cannon amounted to no more
than a few field pieces; and he was obliged to wait for
two iron guns, which the sailors dragged up from the
shipping. Had he given the assault on the first night
after his arrival, when the town was filled with terror
and confusion, and destitute of regular troops, in all
probability it would have been easily taken by scalade;
but the reduction of it was rendered impracticable by
his delay. The ramparts were mounted with cannon
from the ships in the harbour; new works were raised
with great industry; the garrison was reinforced by
several bodies of regular troops; and great numbers
were assembling from all parts: so that the British
forces were in danger of being surrounded in an enemy's
country. Notwithstanding these discouragements, they
opened a small battery against the town, which was set
on fire in several places by their bombs and red-hot
bullets: they likewise repulsed part of the garrison which
had made a sally to destroy their works: but their can-

non producing no effect upon the fortifications, the fire CHAP.
from the town daily increasing, the engineers owning XX.
they could not perform their promise, and Admiral Les- 1746.
tock declaring, in repeated messages, that he could no
longer expose the ships on an open coast at such a
season of the year, General Sinclair abandoned the siege.
Having caused the two iron pieces of cannon and the
mortars to be spiked, he retreated in good order to the
sea-side, where his troops were re-embarked, having sustained very inconsiderable damage since their first landing. He expected reinforcements from England, and
was resolved to wait a little longer for their arrival, in
hopes of being able to annoy the enemy more effectually.
In the beginning of October the fleet sailed to Quiberon-
bay, where they destroyed the Ardent, a French ship of
war of sixty-four guns; and a detachment of the forces
being landed, took possession of a fort on the peninsula;
while the little islands of Houat and Heydic were reduced by the sailors. In this situation the admiral and
general continued till the seventeenth day of the month,
when the forts being dismantled, and the troops re-
embarked, the fleets sailed from the French coast: the
admiral returned to England, and the transports with
the soldiers proceeded to Ireland, where they arrived in
safety.

This expedition, weak and frivolous as it may seem, Naval
was resented by the French nation as one of the greatest transac-
insults they had ever sustained; and demonstrated the the West
possibility of hurting France in her tenderest parts, by Indies.
means of an armament of this nature, well timed, and ences at
vigorously conducted. Indeed, nothing could be more Breda.
absurd or precipitate than an attempt to distress the
enemy by landing a handful of troops, without draught-
horses, tents, or artillery, from a fleet of ships lying on
an open beach, exposed to the uncertainty of weather in
the most tempestuous season of the year, so as to render
the retreat and re-embarkation altogether precarious.
The British squadrons in the West Indies performed no
exploit of consequence in the course of this year. The
commerce was but indifferently protected. Commodore
Lee, stationed off Martinico, allowed a French fleet of
merchant ships and their convoy to pass by his squadron

unmolested ; and Commodore Mitchel behaved scandalously in a rencounter with the French squadron, under
the conduct of Monsieur de Conflans, who in his return
to Europe took the Severn, an English ship of fifty guns.
The cruisers on all sides, English, French, and Spaniards,
were extremely alert; and though the English lost the
greater number of ships, this difference was more than
overbalanced by the superior value of the prizes taken
from the enemy. In the course of this year two-and-
twenty Spanish privateers, and sixty-six merchant vessels,
including ten register ships, fell into the hands of the
British cruisers : from the French they took seven ships
of war, ninety privateers, and about three hundred ships
of commerce. The new King of Spain[b] being supposed
well-affected to the British nation, an effort was made to
detach him from the interest of France, by means of the
Marquis de Tabernega, who had formerly been his favourite, and resided many years as a refugee in England.
This nobleman proceeded to Lisbon, where a negotiation
was set on foot with the court of Madrid. But his efforts
miscarried : and the influence of the queen-mother continued to predominate in the Spanish councils. The
States-General had for some years endeavoured to promote a pacification by remonstrances, and even entreaties,
at the court of Versailles : the French king at length
discovered an inclination to peace, and in September a
congress was opened at Breda, the capital of Dutch Brabant, where the plenipotentiaries of the emperor, Great
Britain, France, and Holland, were assembled; but the
French were so insolent in their demands that the conferences were soon interrupted.

Vast supplies granted by the
Commons
of England.

The Parliament of Great Britain meeting in November, the king exhorted them to concert with all possible
expedition the proper measures for pursuing the war with
vigour, that the confederate army in the Netherlands
might be seasonably augmented; he likewise gave them

[b] In the month of July, Philip King of Spain dying, in the sixty-third year of
his age, was succeeded by his eldest son Ferdinand, born of Maria-Louisa Gabriela, sister to the late King of Sardinia. He espoused Donna Maria Magdalena,
Infanta of Portugal, but had no issue. Philip was but two days survived by his
daughter, the Dauphiness of France. The same month was remarkable for the
death of Christiern VI. King of Denmark, succeeded by his son Frederick V.,
who had married the Princess Louisa, youngest daughter to the King of Great
Britain.

to understand that the funds appropriated for the support of his civil government had for some years past fallen short of the revenue intended and granted by Parliament; and said he relied on their known affection to find out some method to make good this deficiency. As all those who had conducted the opposition were now concerned in the administration, little or no objection was made to any demand or proposal of the government and its ministers. The Commons having considered the estimates, voted forty thousand seamen for the service of the ensuing year, and about sixty thousand land forces, including eleven thousand five hundred marines. They granted four hundred and thirty-three thousand pounds to the Empress Queen of Hungary; three hundred thousand pounds to the King of Sardinia; four hundred and ten thousand pounds for the maintenance of eighteen thousand Hanoverian auxiliaries; one hundred and sixty-one thousand six hundred and seven pounds for six thousand Hessians; subsidies to the Electors of Cologn, Mentz, and Bavaria; and the sum of five hundred thousand pounds to enable his majesty to prosecute the war with advantage. In a word, the supplies amounted to nine millions four hundred twenty-five thousand two hundred and fifty-four pounds; a sum almost incredible, if we consider how the kingdom had been already drained of its treasure. It was raised by the usual taxes, reinforced with new impositions on windows, carriages, and spirituous liquors, a lottery, and a loan from the sinking fund. The new taxes were mortgaged for four millions by transferable annuities, at an interest of four, and a premium of ten per centum. By reflecting on these enormous grants, one would imagine the ministry had been determined to impoverish the nation; but, from the eagerness and expedition with which the people subscribed for the money, one would conclude that the riches of the kingdom were inexhaustible. It may not be amiss to observe, that the supplies of this year exceeded, by two millions and a half, the greatest annual sum that was raised during the reign of Queen Anne, though she maintained as great a number of troops as was now in the pay of Great Britain, and her armies and fleets acquired every year fresh harvests of glory and ad-

vantage; whereas this war had proved an almost uninterrupted series of events big with disaster and dishonour.
During the last two years, the naval expense of England
had exceeded that of France above five millions sterling;
though her fleets had not obtained one signal advantage
over the enemy at sea, nor been able to protect her commerce from their depredations. She was at once a prey
to her declared adversaries and professed friends. Before
the end of summer, she numbered among her mercenaries
two empresses, five German princes, and a powerful
monarch, whom she hired to assist her in trimming the
balance of Europe, in which they themselves were immediately interested, and she had no more than a secondary concern. Had these fruitless subsidies been saved;
had the national revenue been applied with economy to
national purposes; had it been employed in liquidating
gradually the public incumbrances; in augmenting the
navy, improving manufactures, encouraging and securing
the colonies, and extending trade and navigation; corruption would have become altogether unnecessary, and
disaffection would have vanished; the people would have
been eased of their burdens, and ceased to complain:
commerce would have flourished, and produced such
affluence as must have raised Great Britain to the highest
pinnacle of maritime power, above all rivalship or competition. She would have been dreaded by her enemies;
revered by her neighbours; oppressed nations would have
crept under her wings for protection; contending potentates would have appealed to her decision; and she would
have shone the universal arbitress of Europe. How different is her present situation! her debts are enormous,
her taxes intolerable, her people discontented, and the
sinews of her government relaxed. Without conduct,
confidence, or concert, she engages in blundering negotiations; she involves herself rashly in foreign quarrels,
and lavishes her substance with the most dangerous precipitation; she is even deserted by her wonted vigour,
steadiness, and intrepidity; she grows vain, fantastical,
and pusillanimous; her arms are despised by her
enemies; and her counsels ridiculed through all Christendom.

The king, in order to exhibit a specimen of his desire

to diminish the public expense, ordered the third and CHAP.
fourth troops of his life-guards to be disbanded, and re- XX.
duced three regiments of horse to the quality of dragoons. 1746.
The House of Commons presented an address of thanks Parliament dissolved.
for this instance of economy, by which the annual sum
of seventy thousand pounds was saved to the nation.
Notwithstanding this seeming harmony between the king
and the great council of the nation, his majesty resolved,
with the advice of his council, to dissolve the present Parliament, though the term of seven years was not yet
expired since its first meeting. The ministry affected to
insinuate, that the States-General were unwilling to
concur with his majesty in vigorous measures against
France, during the existence of a Parliament which had
undergone such a vicissitude of complexion. The allies
of Great Britain, far from being suspicious of this assembly,
which had supplied them so liberally, saw with concern
that, according to law, it would soon be dismissed; and
they doubted whether another could be procured equally
agreeable to their purposes. In order to remove this
doubt, the ministry resolved to surprise the kingdom with
a new election, before the malecontents should be prepared to oppose the friends of the government. Accordingly, when the business of the session was despatched,
the king, having given the royal assent to the several
acts they had prepared, dismissed them in the month of
June with an affectionate speech, that breathed nothing
but tenderness and gratitude. The Parliament was im- 1747.
mediately dissolved by proclamation, and new writs were
issued for convoking another. Among the laws passed in
this session, was an act abolishing the heritable jurisdictions, and taking away the tenure of wardholdings in
Scotland, which were reckoned among the principal
sources of those rebellions that had been excited since
the Revolution. In the Highlands, they certainly kept
the common people in subjection to their chiefs, whom
they implicitly followed and obeyed in all their undertakings. By this act these mountaineers were legally
emancipated from slavery; but as the tenants enjoyed
no leases, and were at all times liable to be ejected from
their farms, they still depended on the pleasure of their
lords, notwithstanding this interposition of the legislature,

which granted a valuable consideration in money to every nobleman and petty baron who was thus deprived of one part of his inheritance. The forfeited estates, indeed, were divided into small farms, and let by the government on leases at an under value; so that those who had the good fortune to obtain such leases tasted the sweets of independence : but the Highlanders in general were left, in their original indigence and incapacity, at the mercy of their superiors. Had manufactures and fisheries been established in different parts of their country, they would have seen and felt the happy consequences of industry, and in a little time been effectually detached from all their slavish connexions.

The French and allies take the field in Flanders.
The operations of the campaign had been concerted in the winter at the Hague, between the Duke of Cumberland and the States-General of the United Provinces, who were by this time generally convinced of France's design to encroach upon their territories. They therefore determined to take effectual measures against that restless and ambitious neighbour. The allied powers agreed to assemble a vast army in the Netherlands ; and it was resolved that the Austrians and Piedmontese should once more penetrate into Provence. The Dutch patriots, however, were not roused into this exertion until all their remonstrances had failed at the court of Versailles ; until they had been urged by repeated memorials of the English ambassador, and stimulated by the immediate danger to which their country was exposed : for France was by this time possessed of all the Austrian Netherlands, and seemed bent upon penetrating into the territories of the United Provinces. In February, the Duke of Cumberland began to assemble the allied forces ; and in the latter end of March they took the field in three separate bodies. His royal highness, with the English, Hanoverians, and Hessians, fixed his head-quarters at the village of Tilberg : the Prince of Waldeck was posted with the Dutch troops at Breda ; and Mareschal Bathiani collected the Austrians and Bavarians in the neighbourhood of Venlo. The whole army amounted to one hundred and twenty thousand men, who lay inactive six weeks, exposed to the inclemency of the weather, and almost destitute of forage and provision.

Count Saxe, by this time created Mareschal-General of France, continued his troops within their cantonments at Bruges, Antwerp, and Brussels, declaring, that when the allied army should be weakened by sickness and mortality, he would convince the Duke of Cumberland, that the first duty of a general is to provide for the health and preservation of his troops. In April this fortunate commander took the field, at the head of one hundred and forty thousand men; and the Count de Clermont commanded a separate body of nineteen battalions and thirty squadrons. Count Lowendahl was detached on the sixteenth day of the month, with seven-and-twenty thousand men, to invade Dutch Flanders: at the same time, the French minister at the Hague presented a memorial to the states, intimating that his master was obliged to take this step by the necessity of war; but that his troops should observe the strictest discipline, without interfering with the religion, government, or commerce of the republic: he likewise declared, that the countries and places of which he might be obliged to take possession should be detained no otherwise than as a pledge, to be restored as soon as the United Provinces should give convincing proofs that they would no longer furnish the enemies of France with succours.

While the states deliberated upon this declaration, Count Lowendahl entered Dutch Brabant, and invested the town and fortress of Sluys, the garrison of which surrendered themselves prisoners of war on the nineteenth day of April. This was likewise the fate of Sas-van-Ghent; while the Marquis de Contades, with another detachment, reduced the forts Perle and Leifkenshoek, with the town of Philippine, even within hearing of the confederate army. The fort of Sanberg was vigorously defended by two English battalions; but they were overpowered, and obliged to retire to Welsthoorden; and Count Lowendahl undertook the siege of Hulst, which was shamefully surrendered by La Roque, the Dutch governor, though he knew that a reinforcement of nine battalions was on the march to his relief. Then the French general took possession of Axel and Terneuse, and began to prepare flat-bottomed boats for a descent on the island of Zealand. The Dutch people were now

CHAP. XX. 1747.

Prince of Orange elected Stadtholder, Captain-General and Admiral of the United Provinces.

struck with consternation. They saw the enemy at their doors, and owed their immediate preservation to the British squadron stationed at the Swin, under the command of Commodore Mitchel[c], who, by means of his sloops, tenders, and small craft, took such measures as defeated the intention of Lowendahl. The common people in Zealand, being reduced to despair, began to clamour loudly against their governors, as if they had not taken the proper measures for their security. The friends of the Prince of Orange did not neglect this opportunity of promoting his interest. They encouraged their discontent, and exaggerated the danger: they reminded them of the year one thousand six hundred and seventy-two, when the French king was at the gates of Amsterdam, and the republic was saved by the choice of a stadtholder: they exhorted them to turn their eyes on the descendant of those heroes who had established the liberty and independence of the United Provinces; they extolled his virtue and ability, his generosity, his justice, his unshaken love to his country. The people in several towns, inflamed by such representations to tumult and sedition, compelled their magistrates to declare the Prince of Orange stadtholder. He himself, in a letter to the states of Zealand, offered his services for the defence of the province. On the twenty-eighth day of April he was nominated Captain-General and Admiral of Zealand. Their example was followed by Rotterdam and the whole province of Holland; and on the second day of May, the Prince of Orange was, in the assembly of the States-General, invested with the power and dignity of Stadtholder, Captain-General, and Admiral of the United Provinces. The vigorous consequences of this resolution immediately appeared. All commerce and contracts with the French were prohibited: the peasants were armed and exercised: a resolution passed for making a considerable augmentation of the army: a council of war was established for inquiring into the conduct of the governors who had given up the frontier places; and orders were issued to commence hostilities against the French both by sea and land.

Meanwhile, the Duke of Cumberland took post with

[c] Not the person who commanded in the West Indies.

his whole army between the two Nethes, to cover Bergen-op-Zoom and Maestricht; and Mareschal Saxe called in his detachments, with a view to hazard a general engagement. In the latter end of May, the French king arrived at Brussels; and his general resolved to undertake the siege of Maestricht. For this purpose he advanced towards Louvain; and the confederates, perceiving his drift, began their march to take post between the town and the enemy. On the twentieth day of June, they took possession of their ground, and were drawn up in order of battle, with their right at Bilsen, and their left extending to Wirle, within a mile of Maestricht, having in the front of their left wing the village of Laffeldt, in which they posted several battalions of British infantry. The French had taken possession of the heights of Herdeeren, immediately above the allies; and both armies cannonaded each other till the evening. In the morning, the enemy's infantry marched down the hill, in a prodigious column, and attacked the village of Laffeldt, which was well fortified, and defended with amazing obstinacy. The assailants suffered terribly in their approach from the cannon of the confederates, which was served with surprising dexterity and success; and they met with such a warm reception from the British musketry as they could not withstand; but when they were broken and dispersed, fresh brigades succeeded with astonishing perseverance. The confederates were driven out of the village; yet, being sustained by three regiments, they measured back their ground, and repulsed the enemy with great slaughter. Nevertheless, Count Saxe continued pouring in other battalions, and the French regained and maintained their footing in the village after it had been three times lost and carried. The action was chiefly confined to this post, where the field exhibited a horrible scene of carnage. At noon the Duke of Cumberland ordered the whole left wing to advance against the enemy, whose infantry gave way: Prince Waldeck led up the centre: Mareschal Bathiani made a motion with the right wing towards Herdeeren, and victory seemed ready to declare for the confederates, when the fortune of the day took a sudden turn to their prejudice. Several squadrons of

CHAP.
XX.

1747.
The con-
federates
defeated at
Laffeldt.

Dutch horse, posted in the centre, gave way, and flying at full gallop, overthrew five battalions of infantry that were advancing from the body of reserve. The French cavalry charged them with great impetuosity, increasing the confusion that was already produced, and penetrating through the lines of the allied army, which was thus divided about the centre. The Duke of Cumberland, who exerted himself with equal courage and activity in attempting to remedy this disorder, was in danger of being taken; and the defeat would in all probability have been total, had not Sir John Ligonier taken the resolution of sacrificing himself and a part of the troops to the safety of the army. At the head of three British regiments of dragoons, and some squadrons of imperial horse, he charged the whole line of the French cavalry with such intrepidity and success that he overthrew all that opposed him, and made such a diversion as enabled the Duke of Cumberland to effect an orderly retreat to Maestricht. He himself was taken by a French carabineer, after his horse had been killed; but the regiments he commanded retired with deliberation. The confederates retreated to Maestricht, without having sustained much damage from the pursuit, and even brought off all their artillery, except sixteen pieces of cannon. Their loss did not exceed six thousand men killed and taken; whereas the French general purchased the victory at a much greater expense. The common cause of the confederate powers is said to have suffered from the pride and ignorance of their generals. On the eve of the battle, when the detachment of the Count de Clermont appeared on the hill of Herdeeren, Mareschal Bathiani asked permission of the commander-in-chief to attack them before they should be reinforced, declaring he would answer for the success of the enterprise. No regard was paid to this proposal; but the superior asked in his turn, where the mareschal would be in case he should be wanted? He replied, "I shall always be found at the head of my troops," and retired in disgust. The subsequent disposition has likewise been blamed, inasmuch as not above one half of the army could act, while the enemy exerted their whole force.

The confederates passed the Maese, and encamped in

the duchy of Limburgh, so as to cover Maestricht; while the French king remained with his army in the neighbourhood of Tongres. Mareschal Saxe, having amused the allies with marches and counter-marches, at length detached Count Lowendahl with six-and-thirty thousand men to besiege Bergen-op-Zoom, the strongest fortification of Dutch Brabant, the favourite work of the famous engineer Coehorn, never conquered, and generally esteemed invincible. It was secured with a garrison of three thousand men, and well provided with artillery, ammunition, and magazines. The enemy appeared before it on the twelfth day of July, and summoned the governor to surrender. The Prince of Saxe-Hilburghausen was sent to its relief, with twenty battalions and fourteen squadrons of the troops that could be most conveniently assembled: he entered the lines of Bergen-op-Zoom, where he remained in expectation of a strong reinforcement from the confederate army; and the old Baron Cronstrom, whom the stadtholder had appointed Governor of Brabant, assumed the command of the garrison. The besiegers carried on their operations with great vivacity; and the troops in the town defended it with equal vigour. The eyes of all Europe were turned upon this important siege: Count Lowendahl received divers reinforcements; and a considerable body of troops was detached from the allied army, under the command of Baron Schwartzemberg, to co-operate with the Prince of Saxe-Hildburghausen. The French general lost a great number of men by the close and continual fire of the besieged; while he, in his turn, opened such a number of batteries, and plied them so warmly, that the defences began to give way. From the sixteenth day of July to the fifteenth of September, the siege produced an unintermitting scene of horror and destruction: desperate sallies were made, and mines sprung with the most dreadful effects: the works began to be shattered; the town was laid in ashes; the trenches were filled with carnage: nothing was seen but fire and smoke; nothing heard but one continued roar of bombs and cannon. But still the damage fell chiefly on the besiegers, who were slain in heaps; while the garrison suffered very little, and could be occasionally relieved or reinforced from the lines. In a word, it was generally believed that Count Lowendahl would be baffled in his endeavours; and by this belief the governor of Bergen-op-Zoom seems to have been lulled into a blind security. At length, some inconsiderable breaches were made in one ravelin and two bastions, and these the French general resolved to storm, though Cronstrom believed they were impracticable; and on that supposition presumed that the enemy would not attempt an assault. For this very reason Count Lowendahl resolved to hazard the attack before the preparations should be made for his reception. He accordingly regulated his dispositions, and at four o'clock in the morning, on the sixteenth day of September, the signal was made for the assault. A prodigious quantity of bombs being thrown into the ravelin, his troops threw themselves into the fossé, mounted the breaches, forced open a sallyport, and entered the place almost without resistance. In a word, they had time to extend themselves along the curtains, and form in order of battle, before the garrison could be assembled. Cronstrom was asleep, and the soldiers upon duty had been surprised by the suddenness and impetuosity of the attack. Though the French had taken possession of the ramparts, they did not gain the town without opposition. Two battalions of the Scottish troops, in the pay of the States-General, were assembled in the market-place, and attacked them with such fury, that they were driven from street to street, until fresh reinforcements arriving, compelled the Scots to retreat in their turn; yet they disputed every inch of ground, and fought until two thirds of them were killed on the spot. Then they brought off the old governor, abandoning the town to the enemy: the troops that were encamped in the lines retreating with great precipitation, all the forts in the neighbourhood immediately surrendered to the victors, who now became masters of the whole navigation of the Schelde. The French king was no sooner informed of Lowendahl's success, than he promoted him to the rank of Mareschal of France, appointed Count Saxe governor of the conquered Netherlands, and returned in triumph to Versailles. In a little time after this transaction, both armies were distributed into winter-quarters, and the Duke of Cumberland embarked for England.

In Italy, the French arms did not triumph with equal success, though the Mareschal de Belleisle saw himself at the head of a powerful army in Provence. In April he passed the Var without opposition, and took possession of Nice. He met with little or no resistance in reducing Montalban, Villafranca, and Ventimiglia; while General Brown with eight-and-twenty thousand Austrians, retired towards Final and Savona. In the mean time another large body, under Count Schuylemberg, who had succeeded the Marquis de Botta, co-operated with fifteen thousand Piedmontese in an attempt to recover the city of Genoa. The French king had sent them supplies, succours, and engineers, with the Duke de Boufflers, as ambassador to the republic, who likewise acted as commander in chief of the forces employed for its defence. The Austrian general assembled his troops in the Milanese: having forced the passage of the Bochetta on the thirteenth of January, he advanced into the territories of Genoa, and the Riviera was ravaged without mercy. On the last day of March he appeared before the city, at the head of forty thousand men, and summoned the revolters to lay down their arms. The answer he received was, that the republic had fifty-four thousand men in arms, two hundred and sixty cannon, thirty-four mortars, with abundance of ammunition and provision; that they would defend their liberty with their last blood, and be buried in the ruins of their capital, rather than submit to the clemency of the court of Vienna, except by an honourable capitulation guaranteed by the Kings of Great Britain and Sardinia, the republic of Venice, and the United Provinces. In the beginning of May, Genoa was invested on all sides; a furious sally was made by the Duke de Boufflers, who drove the besiegers from their posts; but the Austrians rallying, he was repulsed in his turn with the loss of seven hundred men. General Schuylemberg carried on his operations with such skill, vigour, and intrepidity, that he made himself master of the suburbs of Bisagno; and in all probability would have reduced the city, had he not been obliged to desist, in consequence of the repeated remonstrances made by the King of Sardinia and Count Brown, who represented the necessity of his abandoning his enterprise, and drawing off his army, to cover Piedmont and Lombardy from the efforts of Mareschal de Belleisle. Accordingly, he raised the siege on the tenth day of June, and returned into the Milanese, in order to join his Sardinian majesty; while the Genoese made an irruption into the Parmesan and Placentin, where they committed terrible outrages, in revenge for the mischiefs they had undergone.

The Chevalier de Belleisle slain in the attack of Exiles.

While the Mareschal de Belleisle remained at Ventimiglia, his brother, at the head of four-and-thirty thousand French and Spaniards, attempted to penetrate into Piedmont: on the sixth day of July he arrived at the pass of Exiles, a strong fortress on the frontiers of Dauphiné, situated on the north side of the river Doria. The defence of this important post the King of Sardinia had committed to the care of the Count de Brigueras, who formed an encampment behind the lines, with fourteen battalions of Piedmontese and Austrians, while divers detachments were posted along the passes of the Alps. On the eighth day of the month the Piedmontese intrenchments were attacked by the Chevalier de Belleisle with incredible intrepidity; but the columns were repulsed with great loss in three successive attacks. Impatient of this obstinate opposition, and determined not to survive a miscarriage, this impetuous general seized a pair of colours, and advancing at the head of his troops, through a prodigious fire, pitched them with his own hand on the enemy's intrenchments. At that instant he fell dead, having received two musket balls and the thrust of a bayonet in his body. The assailants were so much dispirited by the death of their commander, that they forthwith gave way, and retreated with precipitation towards Sestrieres, having lost near five thousand men in the attack. The mareschal was no sooner informed of his brother's misfortune, than he retreated towards the Var to join the troops from Exiles, while the King of Sardinia, having assembled an army of seventy thousand men, threatened Dauphiné with an invasion; but the excessive rains prevented the execution of his design. General Leutrum was detached with twenty battalions, to drive the CHAP. XX. French from Ventimiglia; but Belleisle marching back, that scheme was likewise frustrated; and thus ended the 1747. campaign.

In this manner was the French king baffled in his A French squadron defeated and taken by the Admirals Anson and Warren. projects upon Italy; nor was he more fortunate in his naval operations. He had, in the preceding year, equipped an expensive armament, under the command of the Duke d'Anville, for the recovery of Cape Breton; but it was rendered ineffectual by storms, distempers, and the death of the commander. Not yet discouraged by these disasters, he resolved to renew his efforts against the British colonies in North America, and their settlements in the East Indies. For these purposes, two squadrons were prepared at Brest, one to be commanded by the Commodore de la Jonquiere; and the other, destined for India, by Monsieur de St. George. The ministry of Great Britain, being apprised of these measures, resolved to intercept both squadrons, which were to set sail together. For this purpose Vice-Admiral Anson and Rear-Admiral Warren took their departure from Plymouth with a formidable fleet, and steered their course to Cape Finisterre on the coast of Gallicia. On the third day of May they fell in with the French squadrons, commanded by La Jonquiere and St. George, consisting of six large ships of war, as many frigates, and four armed vessels equipped by their East India company, having under their convoy about thirty ships laden with merchandize. Those prepared for war immediately shortened sail, and formed a line of battle; while the rest, under the protection of the six frigates, proceeded on their voyage with all the sail they could carry. The British squadron was likewise drawn up in line of battle; but Mr. Warren, perceiving that the enemy began to sheer off, now their convoy was at a considerable distance, advised admiral Anson to haul in the signal for the line, and hoist another for giving chase and engaging, otherwise the French would, in all probability, escape by favour of the night. The proposal was embraced; and in a little time the engagement began with great fury about four o'clock in the afternoon. The enemy sustained the battle with equal conduct and valour, until they were overpowered by numbers, and then they struck their colours. The admiral detached three ships in pursuit of the convoy, nine sail of which were taken; but the rest were saved by the intervening darkness. About seven hundred of the French were killed and wounded in this action. The English lost about five hundred; and amongst these Captain Granville, commander of the ship Defiance. He was nephew to the Lord Viscount Cobham, a youth of the most amiable character and promising genius, animated with the noblest sentiments of honour and patriotism. Eager in the pursuit of glory, he rushed into the midst of the battle, where both his legs were cut off by a cannon ball. He submitted to his fate with the most heroic resignation, and died universally lamented and beloved. The success of the British arms in this engagement was chiefly owing to the conduct, activity, and courage of the rear-admiral. A considerable quantity of bullion was found in the prizes, which was brought to Spithead in triumph; and, the treasure being landed, was conveyed in twenty waggons to the bank of London. Admiral Anson was ennobled, and Mr. Warren honoured with the Order of the Bath.

Admiral
Hawke
obtains
another
victory
over the
French at
sea.

About the middle of June, Commodore Fox, with six ships of war, cruising in the latitude of Cape Ortegal in Gallicia, took above forty French ships, richly laden from St. Domingo, after they had been abandoned by their convoy. But the French king sustained another more important loss at sea in the month of October. Rear-Admiral Hawke sailed from Plymouth in the beginning of August, with fourteen ships of the line, to intercept a fleet of French merchant-ships bound for the West Indies. He cruised for some time on the coast of Bretagne; and at length the French fleet sailed from the isle of Aix, under convoy of nine ships of the line, besides frigates, commanded by Monsieur de Letendeur. On the fourteenth day of October the two squadrons were in sight of each other, in the latitude of Belleisle. The French commodore immediately ordered one of his great ships, and the frigates, to proceed with the trading ships, while he formed the line of battle, and waited the attack. At eleven in the forenoon Admiral Hawke displayed the signal to chase, and in half an hour both fleets were engaged. The battle lasted till night, when all the French squadron, except the Intrepide and Tonant, had struck to the English flag. These two capital ships escaped in the dark, and returned to Brest in a shattered condition. The French captains sustained the unequal fight with uncommon bravery and resolution; and did not yield until their ships were disabled. Their loss in men amounted to eight hundred: the number of English killed in this engagement did not exceed two hundred, including Captain Saumarez, a gallant officer, who had served under Lord Anson in his expedition to the Pacific Ocean. Indeed it must be owned, for the honour of that nobleman, that all the officers formed under his example, and raised by his influence, approved themselves in all respects worthy of the commands to which they were preferred. Immediately after the action, Admiral Hawke despatched a sloop to Commodore Legge, whose squadron was stationed at the Leeward Islands, with intelligence of the French fleet of merchant-ships, outward-bound, that he might take the proper measures for intercepting them in their passage to Martinique, and the other French islands. In consequence of this advice, he redoubled his vigilance, and a good number of them fell into his hands. Admiral Hawke conducted his prizes to Spithead; and in his letter to the board of Admiralty declared, that all his captains behaved like men of honour during the engagement, except Mr. Fox, whose conduct he desired might be subjected to an enquiry. That gentleman was accordingly tried by a court-martial, and suspended from his command, for having followed the advice of his officers, contrary to his own better judgment; but he was soon restored, and afterwards promoted to the rank of admiral; while Mr. Matthews, whose courage never incurred suspicion, still laboured under a suspension for that which had been successfully practised in both these late actions, namely, engaging the enemy without any regard to the line of battle.

In the Mediterranean, Vice-Admiral Medley blocked Other naval transactions. up the Spanish squadron in Carthagena; assisted the Austrian general on the coast of Villafranca; and intercepted some of the succours sent from France to the assistance of the Genoese. At his death, which happened in the beginning of August, the command of that squadron devolved upon Rear-Admiral Byng, who proceeded on the same plan of operation. In the summer, two British ships of war, having under their convoy a fleet of merchant-ships bound to North America, fell in with the Glorioso, a Spanish ship of eighty guns, in the latitude of the Western Isles. She had sailed from the Havannah, with an immense treasure on board, and must have fallen a prize to the English ships, had each captain done his duty. Captain Erskine, in the Warwick of sixty guns, attacked her with great intrepidity, and fought until his ship was entirely disabled; but being unsustained by his consort, he was obliged to haul off, and the Glorioso arrived in safety at Ferrol: there the silver was landed, and she proceeded on her voyage to Cadiz, which, however, she did not reach. She was encountered by the Dartmouth, a British frigate of forty guns, commanded by Captain Hamilton, a gallant youth, who, notwithstanding the inequality of force, engaged her without hesitation: but in the heat of the action, his ship, being set on fire by accident, was blown up, and he perished with all his crew, except a midshipman, and ten or eleven sailors, who were taken up alive by a privateer that happened to be in sight. Favourable as this accident may seem to the Glorioso, she did not escape. An English ship of eighty guns, under the commander of Captain Buckle, came up, and obliged the Spaniards to surrender, after a short but vigorous engagement. Commodore Griffin had been sent, with a reinforcement of ships, to assume the command of the squadron in the East Indies; and although his arrival secured Fort St. David's, and the other British settlements in that country, from the insults of Monsieur de la Bourdonnais, his strength was not sufficient to enable him to undertake any enterprise of importance against the enemy: the ministry of England, therefore, resolved to equip a fresh armament, that, when joined by the ships in India, should be in a condition to besiege Pondicherry, the principal settlement belonging to the French on the coast of Coromandel.

For this service a good number of independent companies was raised, and set sail, in the sequel, with a
strong squadron under the conduct of Rear-Admiral
Boscawen, an officer of unquestioned valour and capacity.
In the course of this year the British cruisers were so
alert and successful, that they took six hundred and
forty-four prizes from the French and Spaniards; whereas
the loss of Great Britain in the same time did not exceed five hundred and fifty.

All the belligerent powers were by this time heartily
tired of a war which had consumed an immensity of
treasure, had been productive of so much mischief, and
in the events of which all, in their turns, had found
themselves disappointed.   Immediately after the battle
of Laffeldt, the King of France had, in a personal conversation with Sir John Ligonier, expressed his desire
of a pacification; and afterwards his minister at the
Hague presented a declaration on the same subject to
the deputies of the States-General. The signal success of the British arms at sea confirmed him in these
sentiments, which were likewise reinforced by a variety
of other considerations.   His finances were almost exhausted, and his supplies from the Spanish West Indies
rendered so precarious by the vigilance of the British
cruisers, that he could no longer depend upon their arrival.   The trading part of his subjects had sustained
such losses, that his kingdom was filled with bankrupt-
cies: and the best part of his navy now contributed to
strengthen the fleets of his enemies.   The election of a
stadtholder had united the whole power of the States-
General against him, in taking the most resolute measures
for their own safety: his views in Germany were entirely
frustrated by the elevation of the grand duke to the imperial throne, and the re-establishment of peace between
the houses of Austria and Brandenburgh: the success of
his arms in Italy had not at all answered his expectation;
and Genoa was become an expensive ally.   He had the
mortification to see the commerce of Britain flourish in
the midst of war, while his own people were utterly impoverished. The Parliament of England granted, and
the nation paid, such incredible sums as enabled their
sovereign not only to maintain invincible navies and

formidable armies, but likewise to give subsidies to all the powers of Europe. He knew that a treaty of this kind was actually upon the anvil between his Britannic majesty and the czarina, and he began to be apprehensive of seeing an army of Russians in the Netherlands. His fears from this quarter were not without foundation. In the month of November, the Earl of Hyndford, ambassador from the King of Great Britain at the court of Russia, concluded a treaty of subsidy, by which the czarina engaged to hold in readiness thirty thousand men, and forty galleys, to be employed in the service of the confederates, on the first requisition. The States-General acceded to this agreement, and even consented to pay one-fourth of the subsidy. His most Christian Majesty, moved by these considerations, made further advances towards an accommodation, both at the Hague and in London; and the contending powers agreed to another congress, which was actually opened in March at Aix-la-Chapelle, where the Earl of Sandwich and Sir Thomas Robinson assisted as plenipotentiaries from the King of Great Britain.

The elections for the new Parliament in England had been conducted so as fully to answer the purposes of the Duke of Newcastle, and his brother Mr. Pelham, who had for some time wholly engrossed the administration. Both Houses were assembled on the tenth day of November, when Mr. Onslow was unanimously re-elected Speaker of the Commons. The session was opened, as usual, by a speech from the throne, congratulating them on the signal successes of the British navy, and the happy alteration in the government of the United Provinces. His majesty gave them to understand that a congress would be speedily opened at Aix-la-Chapelle, to concert the means for effecting a general pacification; and reminded them that nothing would more conduce to the success of this negotiation than the vigour and unanimity of their proceedings. He received such addresses as the ministers were pleased to dictate. Opposition now languished at their feet. The Duke of Bedford was become a courtier, and in a little time appointed secretary of state, in the room of the Earl of Chesterfield, who had lately executed that office, which he now resigned; and

the Earl of Sandwich no longer harangued against the
administration.   This new House of Commons, in imitation of the liberality of their predecessors, readily gratified all the requests of the government.   They voted
forty thousand seamen, forty-nine thousand land-forces,
besides eleven thousand five hundred marines ; the subsidies for the Queen of Hungary, the czarina, the King
of Sardinia, the Electors of Mentz and Bavaria, the
Hessians, and the Duke of Wolfenbuttel : the sum of two
hundred thirty-five thousand seven hundred and forty-
nine pounds was granted to the provinces of New England,
to reimburse them for the expense of reducing Cape
Breton : five hundred thousand pounds were given to his
majesty for the vigorous prosecution of the war ; and
about one hundred and fifty-two thousand pounds to the
Scottish claimants in lieu of their jurisdiction.   The
supplies for the ensuing year fell very little short of nine
millions, of which the greater part was raised on a loan
by subscription, chargeable on a new subsidy of poundage
exacted from all merchandise imported into Great Britain.
Immediately after the rebellion was suppressed, the legislature had established some regulations in Scotland,
which were thought necessary to prevent such commotions
for the future.   The Highlanders were disarmed, and an
act passed for abolishing their peculiarity of garb, which
was supposed to keep up party distinctions, to encourage
their martial disposition, and to preserve the memory of
the exploits achieved by their ancestors.   In this session
a bill was brought in to enforce the execution of that
law, and passed with another act for the more effectual
punishment of high-treason in the Highlands of Scotland.
The practice of insuring French and Spanish ships at
London being deemed the sole circumstance that prevented a total stagnation of commerce in those countries,
it was prohibited by law under severe penalties ; and this
step of the British Parliament accelerated the conclusion
of the treaty.   Several other prudent measures were
taken in the course of this session for the benefit of the
public ; and among these we may reckon an act for encouraging the manufacture of indigo in the British plantations of North America ; an article for which Great
Britain used to pay two hundred thousand pounds yearly

to the subjects of France. The session was closed on the thirteenth day of May, when the king declared to both Houses, that the preliminaries of a general peace were actually signed at Aix-la-Chapelle by the ministers of Great Britain, France, and the United Provinces; and that the basis of this accommodation was a general restitution of the conquests which had been made during the war. Immediately after the prorogation of Parliament, his majesty set out for his German dominions, after having appointed a regency to rule the realm in his absence.

Prepara-
tions for the
campaign
in the Ne-
therlands.

The articles might have been made much less unfavourable to Great Britain and her allies, had the ministry made a proper use of the treaty with the czarina; and if the confederates had acted with more vigour and expedition in the beginning of the campaign. The Russian auxiliaries might have been transported by sea to Lubeck, before the end of the preceding summer, in their own galleys, which had been lying ready for use since the month of July. Had this expedient been used, the Russian troops would have joined the confederate army before the conclusion of the last campaign. But this easy and expeditious method of conveyance was rejected for a march by land, of incredible length and difficulty, which could not be begun before the month of January, nor accomplished till midsummer. The operations of the campaign had been concerted at the Hague, in January, by the respective ministers of the allies, who resolved to bring an army of one hundred and ninety thousand men into the Netherlands, in order to compel the French to abandon the barrier which they had conquered. The towns of Holland became the scenes of tumult and insurrection. The populace plundered the farmers of the revenue, abolished the taxes, and insulted the magistrates; so that the States-General, seeing their country on the brink of anarchy and confusion, authorized the Prince of Orange to make such alterations as he should see convenient. They presented him with a diploma, by which he was constituted hereditary stadtholder and captain-general of Dutch Brabant, Flanders, and the upper quarter of Guelderland; and the East India company appointed him director and governor-general of their

commerce and settlements in the Indies. Thus invested
with authority unknown to his ancestors, he exerted himself with equal industry and discretion in new modelling,
augmenting, and assembling the troops of the republic.
The confederates knew that the Count de Saxe had a
design upon Maestricht: the Austrian general Bathiani
made repeated remonstrances to the British ministry,
entreating them to take speedy measures for the preservation of that fortress. He in the month of January
proposed that the Duke of Cumberland should cross the
sea, and confer with the Prince of Orange on this subject: he undertook, at the peril of his head, to cover
Maestricht with seventy thousand men, from all attacks
of the enemy; but his representations seemed to have
made very little impression on those to whom they were
addressed. The Duke of Cumberland did not depart
from England till towards the latter end of February;
part of March was elapsed before the transports sailed
from the Nore with the additional troops and artillery;
and the last draughts from the foot-guards were not embarked till the middle of August.

The different bodies of the confederate forces joined Siege of
each other, and encamped in the neighbourhood of Maestricht.
Cessation
Ruremond, to the number of one hundred and ten of arms.
thousand men; and the French army invested Maestricht without opposition, on the third day of April.
The garrison consisted of imperial and Dutch troops,
under the conduct of the governor, Baron d'Aylva, who
defended the place with extraordinary skill and resolution. He annoyed the besiegers in repeated sallies;
but they were determined to surmount all opposition,
and prosecuted their approaches with incredible ardour.
They assaulted the covered way, and there effected a
lodgment, after an obstinate dispute, in which they lost
two thousand of their best troops; but next day they
were entirely dislodged by the gallantry of the garrison.
These hostilities were suddenly suspended, in consequence of the preliminaries signed at Aix-la-Chapelle.
The plenipotentiaries agreed, that, for the glory of his
Christian Majesty's arms, the town of Maestricht should
be surrendered to his general, on condition that it should
be restored with all the magazines and artillery. He

accordingly took possession of it on the third day of May, when the garrison marched out with all the honours of war; and a cessation of arms immediately ensued. By this time the Russian auxiliaries to the number of thirty-seven thousand, commanded by Prince Repnin, had arrived in Moravia, where they were reviewed by their imperial majesties; then they proceeded to the confines of Franconia, where they were ordered to halt, after they had marched seven hundred miles since the beginning of the year. The French king declared, that, should they advance farther, he would demolish the fortifications of Maestricht and Bergen-op-Zoom. This dispute was referred to the plenipotentiaries, who, in the beginning of August, concluded a convention, importing, that the Russian troops should return to their own country; and that the French king should disband an equal number of his forces. The season being far advanced, the Russians were provided with winter quarters in Bohemia and Moravia, where they continued till the spring, when they marched back to Livonia. In the mean time seven-and-thirty thousand French troops were withdrawn from Flanders into Picardy, and the two armies remained quiet till the conclusion of the definitive treaty. The suspension of arms was proclaimed at London, and in all the capitals of the contracting powers: orders were sent to the respective admirals in different parts of the world to refrain from hostilities; and a communication of trade and intelligence was again opened between the nations which had been at variance. No material transaction distinguished the campaign in Italy. The French and Spanish troops who had joined the Genoese in the territories of the republic amounted to thirty thousand men, under the direction of the Duke de Richelieu, who was sent from France to assume that command on the death of the Duke de Boufflers; while Mareschal de Belleisle, at the head of fifty thousand men, covered the western Riviera, which was threatened with an invasion by forty thousand Austrians and Piedmontese, under General Leutrum. At the same time General Brown, with a more numerous army, prepared to re-enter the eastern Riviera, and recommence the siege of Genoa. But these intended operations were prevented by an armi-stice, which took place as soon as the belligerent powers had acceded to the preliminaries.

In the East Indies, Rear-Admiral Boscawen under-took the siege of Pondicherry, which, in the month of August, he blocked up by sea with his squadron, and invested by land with a small army of four thousand Europeans, and about two thousand natives of that country. He prosecuted the enterprise with great spirit, and took the fort of Area Coupan, at the distance of three miles from the town: then he made his ap-proaches to the place, against which he opened batteries, while it was bombarded and cannonaded by the shipping. But the fortifications were so strong, the garrison so numerous, and the engineers of the enemy so expert in their profession, that he made very little progress, and sustained considerable damage. At length, his army being diminished by sickness, and the rainy season ap-proaching, he ordered the artillery and stores to be re-embarked; and raising the siege on the sixth day of Oc-tober, returned to Fort St. David, after having lost about a thousand men in this expedition. In the sequel, several ships of his squadron, and above twelve hundred sailors, perished in a hurricane. The naval force of Great Britain was more successful in the West Indies. Rear-Admiral Knowles, with a squadron of eight ships, attacked Fort Louis on the south side of Hispaniola, which, after a warm action of three hours, was surrendered on capitu-lation, and dismantled. Then he made an abortive attempt upon St. Jago de Cuba, and returned to Ja-maica, extremely chagrined at his disappointment, which he imputed to the misconduct of Captain Dent, who was tried in England by a court-martial and honourably ac-quitted. On the first day of October, the same admiral, cruising in the neighbourhood of the Havannah, with eight ships of the line, encountered a Spanish squadron of nearly the same strength, under the command of the Admirals Reggio and Spinola. The engagement began between two and three o'clock in the afternoon, and con-tinued with intervals till eight in the evening, when the enemy retired to the Havannah, with the loss of two ships; one of which struck to the British admiral, and

the other was, two days after, set on fire by her own
commander, that she might not fall into the hands of
the English. Mr. Knowles taxed some of his captains
with misbehaviour, and they recriminated on his conduct. On their return to England, a court-martial was
the consequence of their mutual accusations. Those
who adhered to the commander, and the others whom
he impeached, were inflamed against each other with the
most rancorous resentment. The admiral himself did
not escape uncensured: two of his captains were reprimanded; but Captain Holmes, who had displayed uncommon courage, was honourably acquitted. Their
animosities did not end with a court-martial. A blood-
less encounter happened between the admiral and Captain Powlett: but Captain Innes and Captain Clarke
meeting by appointment in Hyde-Park with pistols,
the former was mortally wounded, and died next morning; the latter was tried, and condemned for murder,
but indulged with his majesty's pardon. No naval
transaction of any consequence happened in the Eu-
ropean seas during the course of this summer. In
January, indeed, the Magnanime, a French ship of the
line, was taken in the channel by two English cruisers,
after an obstinate engagement; and the privateers took
a considerable number of merchant-ships from the
enemy.

Conclusion
of the de-
finitive
treaty of
Aix-la-
Chapelle.

The plenipotentiaries still continued at Aix-la-Chapelle, discussing all the articles of the definitive treaty,
which was at length concluded and signed on the seventh
day of October. It was founded on former treaties, which
were now expressly confirmed, from that of Westphalia
to the last concluded at London and Vienna. The contracting parties agreed, that the prisoners on each side
should be mutually released without ransom, and all conquests restored: that the duchies of Parma, Placentia,
and Guastalla, should be ceded as a settlement to the
Infant Don Philip, and the heirs male of his body; but
in case of his ascending the throne of Spain, or of the
Two Sicilies, or his dying without male issue, that they
should revert to the house of Austria: that the King of
Great Britain should immediately after the ratification
of this treaty, send two persons of rank and distinction to

reside in France, as hostages, until restitution should be made of Cape Breton, and all the other conquests which his Britannic majesty should have achieved in the East or West Indies, before or after the preliminaries were signed: that the assiento contract, with the article of the annual ship, should be confirmed for four years, during which the enjoyment of that privilege was suspended since the commencement of the present war: that Dunkirk should remain fortified on the land side, and towards the sea continue on the footing of former treaties. All the contracting powers became guarantees to the King of Prussia for the duchy of Silesia and the county of Glatz, as he at present possessed them; and they likewise engaged to secure the Empress Queen of Hungary and Bohemia in possession of her hereditary dominions, according to the pragmatic sanction. The other articles regulated the forms and times fixed for the mutual restitution, as well as for the termination of hostilities in different parts of the world. But the right of English subjects to navigate in the American seas, without being subject to search, was not once mentioned, though this claim was the original source of the differences between Great Britain and Spain: nor were the limits of Acadia ascertained. This and all other disputes were left to the discussion of commissaries. We have already observed, that, after the troubles of the empire began, the war was no longer maintained on British principles. It became a continental contest, and was prosecuted on the side of the allies without conduct, spirit, or unanimity. In the Netherlands they were outnumbered and outwitted by the enemy. They never hazarded a battle without sustaining a defeat. Their vast armies paid by Great Britain, lay inactive, and beheld one fortress reduced after another, until the whole country was subdued; and as their generals fought, their plenipotentiaries negotiated. At a time when their affairs began to wear the most promising aspect, when the arrival of the Russian auxiliaries would have secured an undoubted superiority in the field, when the British fleets had trampled on the naval power of France and Spain, intercepted the supplies of treasure, and cut off all their resources of commerce, the British ministers seemed to treat without the least regard to the honour and advantage of their country. They left her most valuable and necessary rights of trade unowned and undecided; they subscribed to the insolent demand of sending the nobles of the realm to grace the court and adorn the triumphs of her enemy; and they tamely gave up her conquests in North America, of more consequence to her traffic than all the other dominions for which the powers at war contended: they gave up the important isle of Cape Breton, in exchange for a petty factory in the East Indies, belonging to a private company, whose existence had been deemed prejudicial to the commonwealth. What then were the fruits which Britain reaped from this long and desperate war? A dreadful expense of blood and treasure [d], disgrace upon disgrace, an additional load of grievous impositions, and the national debt accumulated to the enormous sum of eighty millions sterling.

[d] Such an expensive war could not be maintained without a very extraordinary exertion of a commercial spirit: accordingly we find that Great Britain, since the death of King William, has risen under her pressures with increased vigour and perseverance. Whether it be owing to the natural progression of trade extending itself from its origin to its *acme*, or *ne plus ultra*, or to the encouragement given by the administration to monied men of all denominations; or to necessity, impelling those who can no longer live on small incomes to risk their capitals in traffic, that they may have a chance for bettering their fortunes; or, lastly, to a concurrence of all these causes; certain it is, the national exports and imports have been sensibly increasing for these forty years: the yearly medium of woollen exports, from the year 1738 to 1743 inclusive, amounted to about three millions and a half, which was a yearly increase on the medium, of five hundred thousand pounds above the medium from 1718 to 1724. From this article, the reader will conceive the prodigious extent and importance of the British commerce.

END OF VOL. II.

GILBERT & RIVINGTON, Printers, St. John's Square, London.

Lightning Source UK Ltd.
Milton Keynes UK
UKHW021231020219
336575UK00013B/726/P